THE COMPLETE GUIDE TO AMERICAN POCKET WATCHES™ 1986

Pocket Watches From 1809—1950 Included

Catalogue — Evaluation Guide — Illustrated

By Cooksey Shugart and Tom Engle

Edited by Walter Presswood

SPECIAL CONTRIBUTORS TO THIS EDITION

Dan Crawley • Bob A. Lavoie • Peter F. Planes III
Miles F. Sandler • William L. Scolnik • David Searles • Donald J. Summar

Published and distributed to the collectors market by Overstreet Publications, Inc., 780 Hunt Cliff Dr. N.W., Cleveland, TN 37311. Distributed to the book trade by Collector Books, P. O. Box 3009, Paducah, KY 42001.

ISBN: 0-89145-323-7
ISSN: 0730-2924

OVERSTREET PUBLICATIONS, INC.
780 Hunt Cliff Dr. N. W., Cleveland, TN 37311
PH: (615) 472-4135

TABLE OF CONTENTS

ACKNOWLEDGEMENTS

The success of the fifth edition of **The Complete Guide to American Pocket Watches**$_{TM}$, published in 1985, has been indeed gratifying. It is a humbling experience for any author to see a work accepted so quickly by a market so diverse as the pocket watch field. Numbers of people have told me that the market was anxious for a book of this type, and it is my hope that this book has lived up to their expectations.

We will continue to improve this book with each edition, incorporating suggestions, ideas, and new information from people throughout the field. That we feel will result in a continually improving **Guide**.

I am especially appreciative of Bob Overstreet, author of **The Comic Book Price Guide**$_{TM}$, for his encouragement, for publishing this book, and to his family who so ably managed the production.

To Walter Presswood, who is the editor of **The Complete Guide to American Pocket Watches**$_{TM}$;

To my wife Martha, for her complete understanding and assistance in compiling this book;

To the NAWCC Museum, Hamilton Watch Co., and Bowman Techinal School, for allowing us to photograph their watches;

And to the following other people whose help was invaluable and will be long remembered: Frank Irick, John Cubbins, Harold Harris, Paul Gibson, Robert L. Ravel, M.D., William C. Heilman Jr., M.D., Thomas McEntyre, Paul Morgan, Bill Selover, Oscar Laube, Ed Kieft, Charles Wallace, Bob Walters, Jack Warren, Howard Schroeder, Edward M. McGinnis, James Gardner, Paul Zuercher, Irving E. Roth, Don Bass, Stephen Polednak, Dick Stacy, Ernest J. Lewis, Herbert McDonald, Abe Secofsky, Richard D. Walker, David Steger, Fred Favour, Ralph Warner, Estus Harris, Charles Cleves, Tom McIntyre, Ralph Ferone, Arnold C. Varey, Jeffrey Ollswang, Tom Rohr, Leon Beard, Glenn Smith, Kenneth Vergin, Thomas Rumpf, Denford Jones Photographics; and a special thanks to Peter Kushnir, Dr. J. Mauss, Robert D. Gruen, Jeff Hess, and Col. R. A. Mulholland.

Special thanks to Christie's of New York for supplying photographs of rare watches.

* * *

Send only corrections, additions, deletions and comments to Cooksey Shugart, 780 Church St. N.E., Cleveland, TN 37311. When corresponding please send a self addressed, stamped envelope.

Special pricing consultants:

Dan Crawley
(Dollar Watches)

David Searles
(Foreign Watches)

Peter Planes
(Wrist Watches)

INTRODUCTION

This book is dedicated to all pocket watch collectors who we hope will find it an enjoyable and valuable reference to carry on buying trips or to trace the lost history of that priceless family heirloom.

The origin of this book began when I was given a pocket watch which had been a part of our family for many years. After receiving the prized heirloom I wanted to know its complete history, and thus the search began. Because of the lack of a comprehensive reference on American pocket watches the venture took me through volume after volume. And over the course of ten years many hours were accumulated in running down the history of this one watch. But the research sparked my interest in the pocket watch field and pointed to the need for such a book as this one. We hope it will provide for you the answers in your searches.

— *The Author*

Pocket watches are unique collectibles. Since the beginning of civilization when man scooped up a handful of sand and created the hourglass, portable timepieces have held a fascination that demanded the attention of the wealthy and poor alike. Man has sought constantly to improve his time-measuring instruments and has made them with the finest metals and jewels. Thus, the pocket watch, in particular, became an ornamentation and a source of pride, and this accounts for its value among families for generation after generation.

The pocket watch has become precious and sentimental to so many because it was one of the true personal companions of the individual night and day. Mahatma Gandhi, the father of India and one of the rare people in the history of the world who has been able to renounce worldly possessions, was obsessed with the proper use of his time. Each minute, he held, was to be used in the service of his fellowman. And his own days were ordered by one of his few personal possessions, a sixteen-year-old, eight-shilling Ingersoll pocket watch that was always tied to his waist with a piece of string.

Another factor that has made pocket watches unique collectibles is the intricate artisanship with which they are put together. Many of the watches of yesteryear which were assembled with extreme accuracy and workmanship continue to be reliable timepieces. And they still stand out as unique because that type of watch is no longer manufactured. In today's world of mass production, the watch with individual craftsmanship containing precious jewels and metals can rarely be found—and, if it is found, it can rarely be afforded.

The pocket watch, well made, is a tribute to man's skills, artisanship and craftsmanship at their finest level. That is why the pocket watch holds a special place in the collectible field.

In America, there are about 80,000 avid pocket watch collectors. About 5 million people own two or more pocket watches. And an untold number possess at least one of these precious heirlooms.

The Complete Guide to American Pocket Watches does not attempt to establish or fix values or selling prices in the pocket watch trade market.

It does, however, *reflect* the trends of buying and selling in the collector market. Prices listed in this volume are based on data collected and analyzed from dealers and shops all over the country.

These prices should serve the collector as a guide only. The price you pay for any pocket watch will be determined by the value it has to you. The intrinsic value of any particular watch can be measured only by you, the collector, and a fair price can be derived only after mutual agreement between both the buyer and the seller.

It is our hope that this volume can help make your pocket watch collecting venture both pleasurable and profitable.

Information contained herein may not necessarily apply to every situation. Data is still being found, which may alter statements made in this book. These changes, however, will be reflected in future editions.

Hopefully, everyone interested in horology will research the American pocket watch and add to his library on the subject.

COLLECTAMANIA

Hobby — Business — Pastime — Entertainment

Just name it. More than likely someone will want to buy or sell it: books, coins, stamps, bottles, beer cans, gold, glassware, baseball cards, guns, clocks, pocket watches, comics, art, cars, and. . . . the list goes on and on.

Most Americans seem to be caught up in ***collectamania***. More and more Americans are spending hour after hour searching through antique shops, auctions, flea markets and yard sales for those rare treasures of delight that have been lying tucked away for generations just waiting to be found.

This sudden boom in the field of collecting may have been influenced by fears of inflation or disenchantment with other types of investments. But more people are coming into the field because they gain some degree of nostalgic satisfaction from these new tangible ties with yesteryear. Collecting provides great fun and excitement. The tales of collecting and the resultant "fabulous finds" could fill volumes and inspire even the non-collector to embark upon a treasure hunt.

Collecting for the primary purpose of investment may prove to have many pitfalls for the amateur. The lack of sufficient knowledge is the No. 1 cause for disappointment. The inability to spot fakes or flawed merchandise can turn excitement into disappointment. And, in many fields, high-class forgers are at work, doing good and faithful reproductions in large quantities that can sometimes fool even the experts the first time they see them.

Collecting for fun and profit can be just that if you observe a fair amount of caution. Always remember, amidst your enthusiasm, that an object may not be what it would first appear. Below are a few guidelines that may be helpful to you:

1. **Make up your mind** what you want to collect and concentrate in this area. Your field of collecting should be one that you have a genuine like for, and it helps if you can use the objects you collect. It may help to narrow your decision even further. For instance, in collecting watches, collect either only one company or one type of pocket watch.

2. **Gain all the knowledge you can** about the objects you collect. The more knowledge you have the more successful you will be in finding valuable, quality pieces. Amassing the knowledge required to be a good collector is easier if you have narrowed your scope of interest. Otherwise, it may take years to become an "expert." Don't try to learn everything there is to know about a variety of fields. This will end in frustration and disappointment. Specialize.

3. **Buy the best you can afford**, assuming the prices are fair. The advanced collector may want only mint articles; but the novice collector may be willing to accept something far less than mint condition due to caution and economics. Collectible items in better condition continue to rise in value at a steady rate.

4. **Deal with reputable dealers** whom you can trust. Talk with the dealer; get to know the seller; get a business card; know where you can contact the dealer if you have problems or if you want the dealer to help you find something else you may be looking for.

*   *   *

HOW TO USE THIS BOOK

The Complete Guide to American Pocket Watches is a simple reference, with clear and carefully selected information. The first part of the book is devoted to history, general information, and a how-to section. The second part of the guide consists mainly of a listing of pocket watch manufacturers, identification guides, and prices. This is a unique book because it is designed to be taken along as a handy pocket reference for identifying and pricing pocket watches. With the aid of this book, the collector should be able to make on-the-spot judgments as to identification, age, quality, and value. This complete guide and a pocket magnifying glass will be all you need to take on your buying trips.

* * *

Pocket watch collecting is fast growing as a hobby and business. Many people collect for the enjoyment and profit. The popularity of pocket watches continues to rise because pocket watches are a part of history. The American railroad brought about the greatest pocket watch of that time—the railroad pocket watch. And since that time America has produced some of the best quality pocket watches that money could buy. The gold-filled cases made in America have never been surpassed in quality or price in the foreign market. With the quality of movement and cases being made with *guaranteed* high standards as well as beauty, the American pocket watch became very desirable. Because they are no longer being made in the U. S. A., pocket watches continue to climb in value.

The pocket watch is collected for its beauty, quality in movement and case, and the value of metal content. Solid gold is the top of the line; platinum and silver are also very desirable. (Consider that some watches in the early 1900s sold between $700 and $1,000. This is equal to or greater than the price of a good car of the same period.)

As in the art field of limited edition prints, a pocket watch of supreme excellence is also limited and will increase in value. There is universal appeal and excitement in owning a piece of history, and your heirloom is just that. At one time pocket watches were a status symbol. Everyone competed for beauty and quality in the movement and case. Solid gold cases were adorned with elaborate engravings, diamonds, and other precious jewels. The movements were beautiful and of high quality because the manufacturers went to great lengths to provide movements that were both accurate and lovely. Fancy damaskeening on the back plates of nickel with gold lettering, 26 jewels in gold settings, and a solid gold train (gears) were features of some of the more elaborate timepieces. The jewels were red rubies, or diamond-end stones, or sapphires for the pallet stones. There were gold timing screws, and more. The faces were made by the best artisans of the day— hand-painted, jewel-studded, with fancy hands and double-sunk dials made of enamel and precious metals.

* * *

HOW TO DETERMINE MANUFACTURER

When identifying a pocket watch, look on the face or dial for the name of the company and then refer to the alphabetical list of watch companies in this book. If the face or dial does not reveal the company name you will have to seek information from the movement's back plate. The company name or the town where it was manufactured will likely be inscribed there. The name engraved on the back plate is referred to as the "signature." After locating the place of manufacture, see what companies manufactured in that town. This may require reading the histories of several companies to find the exact one. Use the process of elimination to narrow the list.

Note: Some of the hard-to-identify pocket watches are extremely collectible and valuable. Therefore, it is important to learn to identify them.

HOW TO DETERMINE AGE

After establishing the name of the manufacturer, you may be interested in the age of the watch. This information can be obtained by using the serial number inscribed on the back movement plate and referring to the production table. It is often difficult to establish the exact age, but this method will put you within a two- or three-year period of the date of the manufacture.

The case that houses the movement is not necessarily a good clue to the origin of the movement. It was a common practice for manufacturers to ship the movements to the jewelers and watchmakers uncased. The customer then married the movement and case. That explains why an expensive movement can be found in a cheaper case or vice versa.

If the "manufacturer's" name and location are no help, the inscription could possibly be that of a jeweler and his location. Thus, it becomes obvious there is no quick and easy way to identify some American-made watches. However, the following steps may be helpful. Some watches can be identified by comparing the models of each company until the correct model is found. Start by sizing the watch and then comparing the varied plate shapes and styles. The cock or bridge for the balance may also be a clue. The general arrangement of the movement as to jeweling, whether it is an open face or hunting case, and style of regulators may help to find the correct identification of the manufacturer of the movement.

Numbers on a watch case should not be considered as clues to the age of the movement because cases were both American- and foreign-made. And many of the good watches were re-cased through the years.

APPRAISING POCKET WATCHES

Pocket watch collecting is still young when compared to the fields of the standard collectibles: coins and stamps. The collectible field is growing but information is still scarce, fragmented, and sometimes unreliable. To be knowledgeable in any field, one must spend the time required to study it.

The value of any collectible is determined first by demand. Without the demand there is not a market. In the pocket watch trade, the law of supply and demand is also true. The supply of the American pocket watches has stopped and the demand among collectors continues to rise. There are many factors that make a pocket watch desired or in demand, and only time and study will tell a collector just what pocket watches are most collectible. After the collector or investor finds out what is desirable, there must be a value placed on it before it is sold. If it is priced too high, the pocket watch will not sell; but, on the other hand, if it is priced too low, it will be hard to replace at the selling price. The dealer must arrive at a fair market price that will move the watch.

There are no two pocket watches alike. This makes the appraising more difficult and oftentimes arbitrary. But there are certain guidelines one can follow to arrive at a fair market price. When pocket watches were manufactured, most companies sold the movements to a jeweler, and the buyer had a choice of dials and cases. Some high-grade movements were placed in a low-grade case and vice versa. Some had hand-painted multi-colored dials; some were plain. The list of contrasts goes on. Conditions of pocket watches will vary greatly, and this is a big factor in the value. The best movement in the best original case will bring the top price for any type of pocket watch.

Prices are constantly changing in the pocket watch field. Gold and silver markets affect the price of the cases. Scarcity and age also affect the value. These prices will fluctuate regularly.

APPRAISING GUIDELINES

Demand, supply, condition, and **value** must be the prime factors in appraising an old pocket watch.

Demand is the most important element. Demand can be determined by the number of buyers for that particular item. And a simple but true axiom is that value is determined by the price someone is willing to pay.

In order to obtain a better knowledge in appraising and judging pocket watches, the following guidelines are most useful. Consider all these factors before placing a value on the pocket watch. (There is no rank or priority to the considerations listed.)

1. Demand: Is it high or low?
2. Availability: How rare or scarce is the pocket watch? How many of the total production remain?
3. Condition of both the case and movement **(very important)**
4. Low serial numbers: The first one made would be more valuable than later models
5. Historical value
6. Age
7. Is it an early handmade pocket watch?
8. Type of Case: Beauty and eye appeal; value of metal content.
9. Is it in its original case? Very important.
10. Complications: Repeaters, for example.
11. Type of escapement
12. Size, number of jewels, type of plates (¾, full and bridge), type of balance, type of winding (key-wind, lever-set, etc.), number of adjustments, gold jeweled settings, damaskeening, gold train.
13. What grade of condition is it? Pristine, Mint, Extra Fine, Average, Fair, or Scrap?
14. Identification ability
15. Future potential as an investment
16. Quality (high or low grade), or low cost production watches (dollar watch)
17. How much will this watch scrap out for?

GRADING POCKET WATCHES,

Pricing in this book is based on the following grading system:

PRISTINE MINT (G-10): Absolutely factory new; sealed in factory box with wax paper still intact.

MINT PLUS (G-9): Still in factory box; has had paper removed for inspection only; has never been used.

MINT (G-8): Same as factory new but with very little use; no faint scratches; is original in every way—crystal, hands, dial, case, movement; used briefly and stored away; may be in box.

NEAR MINT (G-7): Completely original in every way; faint marks may be seen with a loop only; expertly repaired; movement may have been cleaned and oiled.

EXTRA FINE (G-6): May or may not be in factory box; looks as though watch was used very little; crystal may have been replaced; original case, hands, dial, and movement. If watch has been repaired, all original replacement parts have been used. Faint case scratches are evident but hard to detect with the eye. No dents and no hairline on dial are detectable.

FINE (G-5): May have new hands and new crystal, but original case, dial and movement; faint hairline in dial; no large scratches on case; slight stain on movement; movement must be sharp with only minor scratches.

AVERAGE (G-4): Original case, dial and movement; movement may have had a part replaced, but part was near to original; slight brass showing through on gold-filled case; no rust or chips in dial; may have hairlines in dial that are hard to see. All marks are hard to detect, but may be seen without a loop.

FAIR (G-3): Hairlines in dial and small chips; brass can be seen through worn spots on gold-filled case; rust marks in movement; wear in case, dial, and movement; well used; may not have original dial or case.

POOR (G-2): Watch may not run; needs new dial; case well worn; hands may be gone; replacement crystal may be needed.

SCRAP (G-1): Not running; bad dial; rusty movement; brass showing badly; may not have case; some parts not original; no crystal or hands. Good for parts.

Below is an example of how the price is affected by the different grades of the same watch:

Hamilton 992B

Grade	Price
G-10	$300
G-9	$250
G-8	$225
G-7	$190
G-6	$165
G-5	$155
G-4	$135
G-3	$65
G-2	$45
G-1	$35

The value of a watch can only be assessed after the watch has been carefully inspected and graded. It may be difficult to evaluate a watch honestly and objectively, especially in the rare or scarce models.

If the watch has any defects, such as a small scratch on it, it can not be Pristine. It is important to realize that older watches in grades of Extra Fine or above are extremely rare and may never be found.

LIMITED BUDGET COLLECTING

Most collectors are always looking for that sleeper, which *is* out there waiting to be foùnd. One story goes that the collector went into a pawn shop and asked the owner if he had any gold pocket watches for sale. The pawn broker replied, "No, but I have a 23J silver cased pocket watch at a good price." Even though the pocket watch was in a cheaper case, the collector decided to further explore the movement. When he opened the back to look at the movement, there he saw engraved on the plates 24J Bunn Special and knew right away he wanted to buy the pocket watch. The movement was running, and looked to be in first grade shape. The collector asked the price. The broker said he has been trying to get rid of the pocket watch, but had no luck and that, if he wanted it, he would sell it for $35. The collector took the pocket watch and replaced the bent-up silver case for a gold-filled J. Boss case, and sold it later for $400. He had a total of $100 invested when he sold it a month later, netting a cool $300 profit.

Most collectors want a pocket watch that is in mint or near-mint condition and original in every way. But consider the railroad pocket watches such as the Bunn Special in a cheaper case, because the railroad man was compelled to buy a watch with a quality movement, even though he may have been able to afford only a cheap case. The railroad man had to have a pocket watch that met certain standards set by the railroad company. A pocket watch should always be judged on quality and performance and not just on its appearance. The American railroad pocket watch was unsurpassed in reliability. It was durable and accurate for its time, and that accounts for its continuing value today.

If you are a limited-budget collector, you would be well advised not to go beyond your means. But pocket watch collecting can still be an interesting, adventurous, and profitable hobby. If you are to be successful in quadrupling your purchases that you believe to be sleepers, you must first be a hard worker and have perserverence and let shrewdness and skill of knowledge take the place of money. A starting place is to get a good working knowledge of how a pocket watch works. Learn the basic skills such as cleaning, mainspring and staff replacement. One does not have to be a watchmaker but should learn names of parts and what they do. If a pocket watch that you are considering buying does not work, you should know how and what it takes to get it in good running order or pass it by. Stay away from pocket watches that do not wind and set. Also avoid "odd" movements that you hope to be able to find a case for. Old pocket watches with broken or missing parts are expensive and all but impossible to have repaired. Some parts must be made by hand. The odd and low-cost production pocket watches are fun to get but hard to repair. Start out on the more common basic-jeweled lever pocket watches. The older the pocket watch, the harder it is to get parts. Buy an inexpensive pocket watch movement that runs and play with it. Get the one that is newer and for which parts can be bought; and get a book on watch repairing.

You will need to know the history and demand of a pocket watch. Know what collectors are looking for in your area. If you cannot find a buyer then, of course, someone else's stock has become yours.

1985 MARKET REPORT

After having taken some time to consolidate gains from the early 1980s, the watch market seems to have begun recovering from its recent stagnant period. Sales for many rare timepieces have begun to increase rapidly; the aspect of finding rare pocket watches whether American or European at many of the shows around the country will give truth to the supposition that many dealers and collectors have had for some time—"They just ain't out there like they were before."

It is becoming extremely difficult to locate any examples of many of the rare watches; also finding good keywinds, the more traditional Railroad watches, along with many others is like looking for a needle in a hay stack. Good watches are still around, it will just take a bit longer to find them.

Condition is becoming extremely important in all grades, but especially in the higher priced watches. A totally mint pocket watch may bring several times what it would in average or poor condition at the very least.

1985 has been a powerful year for Waltham. Early keywinds, including the 20 size, 57 models, 16 size keywind keyset, along with the 72 models and others, have really taken off. Some examples of actual sales: 20 size American Watch Co. 19 Jewel keywind $5,500; 20 size Appleton Tracy & Co. Vibrating Hairspring $4,500; C. T. Parker keywind 1857 model $3,200; J. Watson London 1857 model $1,650; 1857 model George Washington nickel keywind (for 1876 Centennial) $1,550; 1860 or 16-KW model nickel keywind 19J American Watch

Co. $4,500; 1860 or 16-KW model keywind Vibrating Hairspring AT&Co. $2,950; 1872 model 21 Jewel American Watch Co. in 18k gold hunter $2,150; Pennsylvania Special 1892 model 21 Jewel Waltham $1,675; Denver & Rio Grande 1892 model 21 Jewel Waltham $1,575; and many others in the Waltham series.

Railroad names and higher grades are becoming increasingly harder to find; as a result, many of the better grades along with RR logo dials are continuing to move on up in price. Some examples: Canadian Pacific Railroad Inspectors watch signed on case, dial, movement went for $2,450; Pennsylvania Railroad Co. B. W. Raymond Elgin keywind in original gold case went for $4,250; 24 Jewel Pennsylvania Special Illinois $3,650; 24 Jewel C&O Illinois $4,450; 24J Baltimore & Ohio Illinois $4,250; Ball up/down Indicator 19 Jewel Waltham $8,450; and many others.

Most of your unusual keywind and early American watches have begun to move up quite fast; look for Cornell (especially San Francisco), Newark, Tremont and others to continue to advance. Example: Arthur Wadsworth Keyless patent 1866 (Newark) went for $2,150; Cornell 19 Jewel Paul Cornell stemwinder $3,850; San Francisco Cornell 15 Jewel keywind $1,750; E. Howard Series II in gold hunter case $3,650; and many others.

Up/down winding Indicators are starting to move again, as are most high jewel Railroad watches; keywind are getting stronger every day, especially anything a bit out of the ordinary; watch for a major move in solid gold watches if gold moves up anything appreciable; and remember to start putting away those 12 size and 16 size common watches that are in totally mint condition—they are disappearing fast from the scene.

In 1986 the NAWCC Florida show will be held February 20-23 in Orlando. Also of interest is the National Convention to be held in Cleveland, Ohio on June 19-22, 1986. Good luck and I hope to see you at one of the shows.

CHRONOLOGY OF WATCHES

1500 First watches being made.
1505 Stackfreed came into use.
1515 French watches appear.
1525 Fuzee being used.
1530 Brass plates used for the first time.
1550 Oval or egg-shaped watches in vogue.
1570 Octagon- and hexagonal-shaped watches in vogue.

English watch produced about 1600. Note balance cock is pinned to back plate.

English watch produced about 1650. Note endless screw type regulator.

1575 Mechanism for setting up the mainspring was developed (pre-wind up).
1585 Swiss watches first appear.
1590 Chain for the fuzee first used. (Became more popular about 1650.)
1595 Rock crystal cases made.
1600 English watches first appear.
1610 Most watches were being signed.
1620 Glass used on watches to help protect dial; tabs under glass were used.
1625 "Form watches"—bizzare-shaped skulls, books, crosses, etc. produced.
1630 Tortoise shell cases first used; these lasted until 1800.
1632 Enamel was being painted in colors.
1635 White enamel dials and worm gear were used.
1640 Pair cases appear.
1650 Repousse in both gold and silver was produced.
1660 Rim used on the outer edge of the balance cock.
1675 Spiral balance spring was being used.
1677 Repeating watch with rack form of striking was produced.
1678 Four-wheel train was developed.
1680 Serial numbers began to appear as well as hallmarks.
1685 Regulator first used with balance spring.
1687 Minute hand appears.
1695 Cylinder escapement (became more popular in the 1800s).
1700 Jewels used in Swiss watches (first used in 1750 by English; initially for end stones)
1710 Dust band.
1715 Oil sink used.
1725 Rach lever used.
1750 Compensation balance introduced; all white dials made of enamel; center second hand; dumb repeaters; duplex escapements.
1760 Chronometer escapement used seconds bit at 6 o'clock position.
1765 Lever escapement developed by Mudge.
1774 Dust cap seen.
1780 Thinner watches seen, helical hair spring developed, gong wires bells began to disappear.
1790 Watches with movable figures manufactured; overcoil used by Breguet.
1800 Club foot escapement devised, single case replaces pair case, tourbillon escapement invented by Breguet.
1810 Spherical balance spring was developed.
1820 Winding by using the button on the pendant.

HISTORY

With the settlement and development of America, the American Watch came into being. The American Watch was so well made the whole world demanded and used it. Because these watches were placed on the market with reasonable prices, the common man could possess them. For the first time watches were made with interchangeable parts; each part could be taken from one watch and placed in another without altering either in any way, and both watches would still give perfect time. In America, the term "watchmaker" did not necessarily apply to one who manufactured watches, but more generally to those engaged in repairing and cleaning watches or capable of "making" and fitting any part of a watch. Today a watchmaker simply orders replacement parts due to the interchangeable parts system.

It would be hard to determine who was the first watchmaker in America. From the early 1800s, many of the movements were made in small quantities. Watches were made to order and were not carried in stock in a shop. These watches were hand-made, and the watchmaker depended upon Europe for supplies such as springs, jewels, balances, hands, etc. Therefore, watchmakers could not be regarded as total manufacturers, although the watchmaker did deliver watches of his own making for which he made some of the parts, such as the case and wheels, etc.

American watches should be divided into two periods: those made prior to 1850 (Colonial Watches) and those made after 1850 (Modern Watches). The colonial watchmakers made some of their parts and imported some parts from abroad, mainly England. To make certain parts required an investment in equipment which most watchmakers were not able or willing to make because of an insufficient number of customers that could justify the outlay of capital. Colonial watchmakers imported blanks and then finished the wheels, many times making them fit their own special designs and needs. Many of these personalized movements are signed by the watchmaker. This was not a new practice since English watchmakers had been doing it for years. Watches from the Colonial Period are certainly collectible and should be considered to be of American origin.

By 1775 Thomas Harland was very prosperous as a tradesman, as well as a watchmaker. Harland probably produced about 200 watches that were plain and of the verge type. There are no Harland watches known to be in existence, although he worked in the watch trade until about 1806 and may have trained Luther Goddard.

In 1809 Goddard (1762-1842) of Shrewbury, Mass., began to make watches of the verge type, and his company produced some 650.

Goddard could not compete with the cheaper foreign watches, but produced the greatest number of watches made in America to that date. These were hand-made and did not have interchangeable parts. A cousin to the famous clockmaker Simon Willard, Goddard served as apprentice with Simon from 1778 to 1783. His watch movements were medium size and were English in general appearance. The watch was most often placed in open-faced, silver-type cases. The plates were highly engraved and fire-gilded. The plates, wheels, barrel, fusees, cock, and some other brass parts were also made by Goddard & Company. Some of the watch parts were made by other specialists. The first watch was made in about 1812, and movements were marked as follows: L Goddard, L Goddard & Co., Luther Goddard & Son, P Goddard, L & P Goddard, D P Goddard & Co., and P & D Goddard.

Example of a **Luther Goddard** movement. His basic watch consisted of 16-18 size, pair case, open face-thick bulls-eye type, and of high quality. Total production was about 600.

In 1838 the first machine-made watch was placed on the American market by James and Henry Pitkin. These watches were ¾ plate, 16 to 18 size, and had a slow train. The machines that were used to make these watches were made by the Pitkin Brothers and were very crude. The same fate fell to the Pitkins as it did to Goddard: the cost of manufacturing was too great to compete with the foreign market. The total Pitkin production was 900 watches. A few other attempts were made but none noteworthy. Pitkin (Henry) & Brother (James F.) made watches with interchangeable parts by machines, starting about 1838. The first 50 watches were marked H & JF PITKIN. In 1841, they moved to New York City. These watches were marked Pitkin & Co., or Pitkin American Lever Watch. Some, with detached lever, were marked Pitkin & Co. (about 18's).

Jacob Custer produced 12 to 15 watches in about 1843, making all the parts except the hairspring and fusee chains.

In 1850 a small shop was built opposite Mr. Howard's Clock Co., and some English and Swiss watchmakers were put to work. A Mr. Dennison, in the spring of 1850, completed the first watch which was about 18 size, and it was designed to run eight days. It was not until 1853 that the first watch was placed on the market for sale. It was marked "Warren" and sold for about $40. The company went on to become the Waltham Company.

Aaron L. Dennison and Edward Howard both had the grand idea of mass-producing watches. In 1849, financed by Samuel Curtis, they became partners. They first started out as "Dennison, Howard and Davis" in September 1850. In 1851, they changed the name to American Horologe Co., then later that same year to the Warren Mfg. Co. In the fall of 1852 some 17 watches were made. The first watches placed on the market were made in 1853, serial numbers 18 to 120, marked "Warren." Some 800 were made after that, and they were marked "Samuel Curtis." Some others were marked "Fellows & Schell." In September 1853, the name changed once again to The Boston Watch Co., and another factory was established in Waltham, Mass., beginning operation on Oct. 5, 1854. These watches were marked C. T. Parker, Dennison & Davis P.S.B. (Nos. 1,001 to 5,000). In May 1857, the company was sold at a sheriff's auction to R. E. Robbins. The company was reorganized to form the Appleton, Tracy & Co. From the Boston Watch Co. came the E. Howard and Co. which remained at the old Boston Watch Co. factory in Rosbury, Mass. On Dec. 11, 1857, the E. Howard & Co. was formed. From the Appleton, Tracy & Co. came the Waltham Watch Company.

From this beginning all the watch factories in America sprang forth. By 1884 there were nine first-class factories making on the average of 3,650 watches a day. These American machine-made watches kept the foreign market in complete disarray until the early 1900s.

THAT GREAT AMERICAN RAILROAD POCKET WATCH

It was the late nineteenth century in America. The automobile had not yet been discovered. The personal Kodak camera still was not on the market. Women wore long dresses, and the rub board was still the most common way to wash clothes. Few homes had electricity, and certainly the radio had not yet invaded their lives. Benjamin Harrison was president. To be sure, those days of yesteryear were not quite as nostalgically simple as most reminiscing would have them be. They were slower, yes, because it took longer to get things done and longer to get from one place to another. The U. S. mail was the chief form of communication that linked this country together as America was inching toward the Twentieth Century.

Not to be underestimated is the tremendous impact of the railroad on the country during this era. Most of the progress since the 1830s had chugged along on the back of the black giant locomotives that belched steam and fire up and down the countryside. In fact the trains brought much life and hope to the people all across the country, delivering their goods and food, bringing people from one city to another, carrying the U. S. mail, and bringing the democratic process to the people by enabling candidates for the U. S. Presidency to meet and talk with people in every state.

Truly the train station held memories for most everyone and had a link with every family.

In 1891, the country had just eased into the period that historians would later term the "Gay Nineties." It was on April 19 of that year that events near Cleveland, Ohio, would occur that would clearly point out that the nation's chief form of transportation was running on timepieces that were not reliable and that the time had come for strict standards for the pocket watches used by the railroaders. From the ashes of this smouldering Ohio disaster rose the phoenix in the form of the great American railroad pocket watch, a watch unrivaled in quality and reliability.

That April morning, the fast mail train, known as No. 4, was going East. On the same track an accommodation train was going West. It was near Elyria, about 25 miles from Cleveland, Ohio, that the engineer and conductor of the accommodation train were given written orders to let the fast mail train pass them at Kipton, a small station west of Oberlin.

As the accommodation train was leaving the station at Elyria, the telegraph operator ran to the platform and verbally cautioned the engineer and conductor, "Be careful. No. 4 is on time." Replied the conductor, "Go to thunder. I know my business."

The train left Elyria on time according to the engineer's watch. What was not known was that the engineer's watch had stopped for four minutes and then started up again. Had the conductor looked at his own watch, the impending disaster could have been avoided.

The two trains met their destiny at Kipton; the accommodation train was under full brakes, but the fast mail was full speed ahead. Both engineers were killed as well as nine other people. The railroad companies (Lake Shore Railroad and Michigan Southern Railway) sustained great losses in property as did the U. S. Post Office.

Following this disaster, a commission was appointed to come up with standards for timepieces that would be accepted and adopted by all railroads. The commission learned that up to the time of the Kipton crash conductors on freight trains were depending on cheap alarm clocks. The railroading industry had grown, fast new trains were now in service, and the same lines were used by several different railways and very often, in only a short space of time, two trains would cover the same track. The industry now had to demand precision in its timekeeping.

By 1893 the General Railroad Timepiece Standards were adopted, and any watch being used in rail service—by railroaders responsible for schedules—was required to meet the following specifications:

> Be open faced, size 18 or 16, have a minimum of 17 jewels, adjusted to at least five positions, keep time accurately to within a gain or loss of only 30 seconds a week, adjusted to temperatures of 34 to 100 degrees Fahrenheit, have a double roller, steel escape wheel, lever set, micrometric regulator, winding stem at 12 o'clock, grade on back plate, use plain Arabic numbers printed bold and black on a white dial, and have bold black hands.
>
> Some also wanted a Breguet hairspring, adjusted to isochronism and 30 degrees Fahrenheit with a minimum of 19 jewels.

The railroad man was compelled to buy a timepiece more accurate than many scientific instruments of precision used in laboratories. And the American pocket watch industry was compelled to produce just such an instrument—which it did. The railroad watch was a phenomenal timekeeper and durable in long life and service. It had the most minute adjustments, no small feat because watchmaking was rendered far more difficult than clockmaking, due to the fact a clock is always in one position and watches must be accurate from several positions.

The 1893 railroad pocket watch standards were adopted by almost every railroad line. While each company had its individual standards, most all of them included the basic recommendations of the commission.

The key figure in developing the railroad watch standards was Webb C. Ball of Cleveland, Ohio, the general time inspector for over 125,000 miles of railroad in the U. S., Mexico, and Canada. Ball was authorized by the railroad officials to establish the timepiece inspection system. After Ball presented his guidelines, most American manufacturers set out to meet these standards and soon a list was available of the different manufacturers that produced watches of the grade that would pass inspection.

According to the regulations, if a watch fell behind or gained 30 seconds in 7 to 14 days, it must be sent in for adjustment or repair. Small cards were given to the engineers and conductors—the railroad timekeepers—and a complete record of the watch's performance was written in ink. All repairs and adjustments were conducted by experienced and approved watchmakers; inspections were conducted by authorized inspectors.

Because this system was adopted universally and adhered to and because American watch manufacturers produced a superior railroad watch, the traveling public was assured of increased safety and indeed the number of railroad accidents occurring as a result of the use of faulty timepieces was minimized.

Prior to the 1891 collision, some railroad companies had already initiated standards and were issuing lists of those watches approved for railroad use. Included were the Waltham 18s, 1883 model, Crescent Street Grade, and the B. W. Raymond, 18s, both in open and hunter cases with lever set or pendant set.

By the mid 1890s hunter cases were being turned down as well as pendant set. Watches meeting approval then included Waltham, 18s, 1892 model; Elgin, 7th model; and Hamilton, 17j, open face, lever set.

Hamilton Grade 992, 16 size, 21 jewels, nickel ¾ plate movement, lever set only, gold jewel settings, gold center wheel, steel escape wheel, micrometric regulator, compensating balance, adjusted to temperature, isochronism and 5 positions.

By 1900 the double roller sapphire pallets and steel escape wheels with a minimum of five positions were required.

The early Ball Watch Co. movements made by Howard used initials of railroad labor organizations such as "B. of L. E. Standard" and "B. of L. F. Standard." Ball also used the trademark "999" and "Official Railroad Standard." Some watches may turn up that are marked as "loaners." These were issued by the railroad inspectors when a watch had to be kept for repairs.

By 1920 the 18 size watch had lost popularity with the railroad men and by 1950 most railroad companies were turning them down all together.

In 1936 duties on Swiss watches were lowered by 50 percent, and by 1950 the Swiss imports had reached a level of five million a year.

In 1969 the last American railroad pocket watch was sold by Hamilton Watch Co.

RAILROAD GRADE WATCH ADJUSTMENTS

Railroad watches, as well as other fine timepieces, had to compensate for several factors in order to be reliable and accurate at all times. These compensations are called adjustments and were for heat and cold, isochronism, and five to six different positions. These adjustments were perfected only after experimentation and a great deal of careful hand labor on each individual movement.

All railroad grade watches were adjusted to a closer rate to compensate for heat and cold. The compensation balance has screws in the rim of the balance wheel which can be regulated by the watchmaker. The movement was tested in an ice box and in an oven, and if it did not keep the same time in both temperature extremes as well as under average conditions, the screw in the balance wheel was shifted or adjusted until accuracy was achieved.[1]

[1]Railroad grade watches had a compensation balance made of brass and steel. Brass was used on the outside rim and steel on the inside. Brass is softer than steel, and steel is more sensitive to temperature changes. The rim on the balance was cut to form two pieces and had two arms. Each piece was independent of the other so the rim was free to be influenced through expansion or contraction. (A small balance wheel with the same hairspring would run faster than a large balance wheel.) At a high temperature the entire balance wheel would expand in bulk and thus run slower. That is why a compensation balance was necessary. When the bulk of the balance wheel expands, the expansion of the brass on the outside of the rim is greater than that of the steel on the inside; thus it throws the loose ends of the rim toward the center. Consequently this makes the circumference smaller and therefore compensation for the increased volume is achieved.

The isochronism adjustment maintained accuracy of the watch both when the mainspring was fully wound up and when it was nearly run down. This was achieved by selecting a hairspring of exact proportions to cause the balance wheel to give the same length of arc of rotation regardless of the amount of the mainspring that had been spent.

Railroad watches were required to be adjusted to be accurate whether they were laying on their face or back, or being carried on their edges with pendants up or down, or with the three up or the nine up. These adjustments are accomplished by having the jewels in which the balance pivots rest of proper thickness in proportion to the diameter of the pivot and at the same time equal to the surface on the end of the pivot which rests on the cap jewel. To be fully adjusted for positions, the balance wheel and the pallet and escape wheel must be perfectly poised. Perfect poise is achieved when the pivots can be supported on two flat surfaces, perfectly smooth and polished, and when the wheel is placed in any position it will remain exactly as it is placed. If it is not perfectly poised, the heaviest part of the wheel will always turn to the point immediately under the lines of support.

The micrometric regulator or the patent regulator is a device used on all railroad grade and higher grade watches for the purpose of assisting in the finer manipulation of the regulator. It is arranged so that the regulator can be moved the shortest possible distance without fear of moving it too far. There is always a fine graduated index attached which makes it possible to determine just how much the regulator has been moved.

E. Howard Watch Co. Railroad Chronometer, Series 11, 16 size, 21 jewels, expressly designed for the railroad trade.

The hairspring used on the so-called ordinary and medium-grade watches is known as the flat hairspring. The Breguet hairspring was an improvement over the flat hairspring and was used on railroad and high-grade watches. The inside coil of any hairspring is attached to a collet on the balance staff and the end of the outside coil of the hairspring is attached to a stud which is held firmly by a screw in the balance wheel bridge. Two small pins with the end of each fastened to a projection in the regulator clasp the outer end of the hairspring a short distance from where it is fastened in the stud. If the regulator is moved toward the "S", these pins called curb or guard pins are moved toward the stud which lengthens the hairspring and allows the balance wheel to make a longer arc of rotation. This causes the watch to run slower because it requires a longer time for the wheel to perform the longer arc.

When the regulator is moved toward the "F" these curb pins are moved from the stud which shortens the hairspring and makes shorter arcs of the balance wheel, thus causing the movement to run faster. Sometimes, after a heavy jolt, the coil next to the outside one will catch between these curb pins and this will shorten the length of the hairspring just one round, causing a gaining rate of one hour per day. When such occurs, the hairspring can be easily released and will resume its former rate.

The Breguet hairspring which is used on railroad grade movements prevented the hairspring from catching on the curb or guard pins and protected against any lateral or side motion of the balance wheel ensuring equal expansion of the outside coil.

Railroad grade watches also used the patent or safety pinion which was developed for the purpose of protecting the train of gears from damage in the event of breakage of the mainspring.

Also used on some railroad grade watches were the non-magnetic movements achieved by the use of non-magnetic metals for the balance wheel, hairspring, roller table and pallet. Two of the metals used were iridium and paladium, both very expensive.

Rockford Grades 805-Hunting & 905-Open Face, 18 size, 21 extra fine ruby jewels in gold settings, beautifully damaskeened nickel plates, gold lettering, adjusted to temperature, isochronism and 5 positions, breguet hair spring, double roller escapement, steel escape wheel, sapphire pallets, micrometric regulator, compensating balance in recess.

RAILROAD WATCH DIALS

Railroad watch dials are distinguished by their simplicity. A true railroad watch dial contained no fancy lettering or beautiful backgrounds. The watches were designed exclusively to be functional and in order to achieve that, the dials contained bold black Arabic numbers against a white background. This facilitated ease of reading the time under even the most adverse conditions.

True railroad watches had the winding stem at the 12 o'clock position. The so-called "side winder" that winds at the 3 o'clock position was not approved for railroad use. (The side winder is a watch movement designed for a hunter case but one that has been placed in an open-faced case.)

One railroad watch dial design was patented by a Mr. Ferguson.

On this dial, the five minute numbers were much larger than the hour numbers which were on the inside. This dial never became very popular.

About 1910 the Montgomery dials began to appear. The distinguishing feature of the Montgomery dial is that each minute is numbered around the hour chapter. The five-minute divisions were in red, and the true Montgomery dial has the number "6" inside the minute register. These dials were favored by the railroad men.

The so-called Canadian dial had a 24-hour division inside the hour chapter.

The double-time hands are also found on some railroad grade watches. One hour hand was in black and the other was in red, one hour apart, to compensate for passing from one time zone to another.

Ball Watch Co. Motto: "Carry A Ball and Time Them All." This case is an example of Ball's patented Stirrup Bow. With the simple easy to read dial, this watch was a favorite among railroad men.

RAILROAD WATCH CASES

Open face cases were the only ones approved for railroad use. Railroad men sought a case that was tough and durable and one that would provide a dust-free environment for the movement. The swing-out case offered the best protection against dust, but the screw-on back and bezel were the most popular open-face cases.

The lever-set was a must for railroad-approved watches and some of the case manufacturers patented their own styles of cases, most with a heavy bow. One example is the Stirrup Bow by the Ball Watch Co. Hamilton used a bar above the crown to prevent the stem from being pulled out. And glass was most commonly used for the crystal because it was not as likely to scratch.

RAILROAD GRADE OR RAILROAD APPROVED WATCHES

Note: Not all watches listed here are railroad approved, even though all are railroad grade. See Ball Watch Co. for railroad standards.

BALL

All official R.R. standard with 19, 21, & 23J, hci5p, 18 & 16S, open face.

COLUMBUS WATCH CO.

Columbus King, 21, 23, 25J; Railway King, 17-25J; Time King, 21-25J, 18S; Ruby Model, 16S.

ELGIN

1. "Pennsylvania Railroad Co." on dial, 18S, 15J & 17J, key wind and set, first model "B. W. Raymond."
2. "No. 349," 18S, seventh model, 17-21J.
3. Veritas, B. W. Raymond, or Father Time, 18S, 21-23J.
4. Grades 270, 280, or 342 marked on back plate, 16S, 17-21J.
5. Veritas, Father Time, or Paillard Non-Magnetic, 16S, 19-23J.
6. 571, 21J or 572, 16S, 19J.
7. All wind indicator models.

HAMILTON

1. Grade 946, 23J, 18S.
2. Grades 940, 942, 21J, 18S.
3. Grade 944, 19J, 18S.
4. Grades 924, 926, 934, 936, 938, 948, 17J, 18S.
5. Grades 950, 950B, 950E, 23J, 16S.
6. Grades 992, 992B, 992E, 954, 960, 970, 994, 990, 21J, 16S.
7. Grade 996, 19J, 16S.
8. Grades 972, 968, 964, 17J, 16S.

HAMPDEN

1. Special Railway, 17J, 21J, 23J; New Railway, 23J & 17J; North Am. RR, 21J; Wm. McKinley, 21J; John Hancock, 21J & 23J; John C. Duber, 21J, 18S.
2. 105, 21J; 104, 23J; John C. Duber, 21J; Wm. McKinley, 17, 21, & 23J; New Railway, 21J; Railway, 19J; Special Railway, 23J, 16S.

E. HOWARD & CO.

1. All Howard models marked "Adjusted" or deer symbol.
2. Split plate models, 18S or N size; 16S or L size.

HOWARD WATCH CO.

All 16S with 19, 21, & 23J.

ILLINOIS

1. Bunn 15J marked "Adjusted," and Stuart, 15J marked "Adjusted," 18S.
2. Benjamin Franklin, 17-26J; Bunn 17, 19, 21, 24J; Bunn Special, 21-26J; Chesapeake & Ohio Sp., 24J; Interstate Chronometer, 23J; Lafayette, 24J; A. Lincoln, 21J; Paillard W. Co., 17-24J; Trainsmen, 23J; Pennsylvania Special 17-26J; The Railroader & Railroad King, 18S.
3. Benjamin Franklin, 17-25J; Bunn, 17-19J; Bunn Special, 21-23J; Diamond Ruby Sapphire, 21 & 23J; Interstate Chronometer, 23J; Lafayette, 23J; A. Lincoln, 21J; Paillard Non-Magnetic W. Co., 17 & 21J; Pennsylvania Special, 17, 21, & 23J; Santa Fe Special, 21J; Sangamo, 21-26J; Sangamo Special, 19-23J; Grades 161, 161A, 163, 163A, 187, and 189, 17J, 16S.

PEORIA WATCH CO.
15 & 17J with a patented regulator, 18S.

ROCKFORD
1. All 21 or more jewels, 16-18S, and wind indicators.
2. Grades 900, 905, 910, 912, 918, 945, 200, 205, 18S.
3. Winnebago, 17-21J, 505, 515, 525, 535, 545, 555, 16S.

SETH THOMAS
Maiden Lane, 21-28J; Henry Molineux, 20J; 260 Model, 18S.

SOUTH BEND
1. Studebaker 329, Grade Nos. 323, and 327, 17-21J, 18S.
2. Studebaker 229, Grade Nos. 223, 227, 293, 295, 299, 17-21J, 16S.
3. Polaris.

UNITED STATES WATCH CO., MARION
United States, 19J, gold train.

U. S. WATCH CO., WALTHAM
The President, 17J, 18S.

WALTHAM
1. 1857 KW with Pennsylvania R.R. on dial, Appleton Tracy & Co. on movement.
2. Crescent Street, 17-23J; 1883 & 1892 Models; Appleton Tracy & Co., 1892 Model; Railroader, 1892 Model; Pennsylvania Railroad; Special Railroad, Special RR King, Vanguard, 17-23J, 1892 Model; Grade 845, 18S.
3. American Watch Co., 17-21J, 1872 Models; American Watch Co., 17-23J, Bridge Models; Crescent Street, 17-21J, 1899 & 1908 Models; Premier Maximus; Railroader; Riverside Maximus, 21-23J; Vanguard, 19-23J; 645, 16S.
4. All wind indicators.

American Waltham Watch Co. Vanguard, 16 size, 19-23 jewels, winding indicator which alerts user to how far up or down the mainspring is wound. This watch was made to promote new sales in the railway industry.

Hamilton Watch Co. A favorite railroad style case by Hamilton. Note the Montgomery style dial as well as the bar above the crown.

CANADIAN PACIFIC SERVICE
RAILROAD APPROVED WATCHES
1899

WALTHAM

Vanguard, 18-16S, 19-21-23 jewels
Crescent St., 18S, 19J; 18-16S, 21J
Appleton-Tracy 17J; also No. 845, 21J
Riverside 16S, 19J; Riverside Maximus, 16S, 23J; and 16S, No. 645, 21J
C. P. R. 18-16S, 17J; also C. T. S. 18-16S, 17J

ELGIN

Veritas, 18-16S, 21-23J
B. W. R. 18-16S, 17-19-21J
Father Time 18-16S, 21J
Grade 349, 18S, 21J

HAMILTON

18S, 946, 23J; 940-942, 21J; 944, 19J; 936-938, 17J
16S, 950, 23J; 960-990-992, 21J; 952, 19J; 972, 17J

SOUTH BEND

18S, 327-329, 21J; 323, 17J
16S, 227-229, 21J; 223, 17J

BALL

All Balls 18S, 16S, 17-19-21-23J

ILLINOIS

Bunn Special, 18-16S, 21-23J; also Bunn 18-16S, 17-19J
A. Lincoln, 18-16S, 21J
Sangamo Special, 16S, 19-21-23J

SETH THOMAS

Maiden Lane, 18S, 25J; No. 260, 21J; No. 382, 17J

E. HOWARD WATCH CO.

16S Series, 0-23J, 5-19J, 2-17J, 10-21J; also No. 1, 21J

ROCKFORD

18S, Grade 918-905, 21J; Winnebago, 17J; also Grade 900, 24J
16S, Grades 545, 525, 515, 505, 21J; 655 W.I., 21J; and Grade 405, 17J

LONGINES

18S, Express Monarch, 17-19-21-23J
16S, Express Monarch, 17-19-21-23J

BRANDT-OMEGA

18S, D.D.R., 23J; C.C.C.R., 23J; C.D.R., 19J; C.C.R., 19J
16S, D.D.R., 23J; C.C.C.R., 23J; D.R., 19J; C.C.R., 19J

ZENITH
18S, Extra, 23J; Superior, 21J; Prima, 17-19J
16S, Extra, 23J

CANADIAN PACIFIC SERVICE RAILROAD APPROVED WATCHES 1928

WALTHAM
16S, Vanguard, 23J; Crescent St., 21J; Riverside, 19J

ELGIN
16S, Veritas, 23J; B. W. R., 23J; B. W. R., 21J

HAMILTON
16S, 950, 23J; 992, 21J; 996, 19J

ILLINOIS
16S, Sangamo Special, 23J; Bunn Special, 21-23J

LONGINES
16S, Express Monarch, 21-23J; Express Leader, 19J

ZENITH
16S, Extra, 23J; Superior, 21J

SOUTH BEND
16S, 227, 21J

BALL
16S, 21-23J

BRANDT
16S, D. D. R., 23J

E. HOWARD WATCH CO.
16S, Series 0, 23J; Series 10, 21J

ADJUSTMENTS

There are nine basic adjustments for watch movements. They are:

heat ... 1
cold ... 1
isochronism ... 1
positions ... 6
TOTAL ... 9

THE SIX POSITION ADJUSTMENTS ARE:

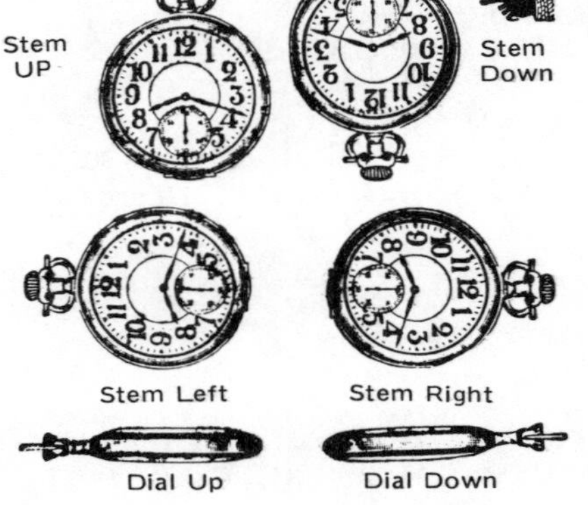

A watch with eight adjustments (the most common) will be listed in this book as: "HC15P" (heat, cold, isochronism, 5 positions).

The total number of pocket watches made for the railroad industry was small in comparison to the total pocket watches produced. Generally watches defined as "Railroad Watches" fall into five categories:

1. **Railroad Approved**—Grades and Models approved by the railway companies.[1]
2. **Railroad Grade**—Those advertised as being able to pass railroad inspection.[2]
3. **Pre-Commission Watches**—Those used by the railroads before 1893.[3]
4. **Company Watches**—Those with a railroad logo or company name on the dial.[4]
5. **Train Watches**—Those with a locomotive painted on the dial or inscribed on the case.[4]

---

[1]Not all railroad employees were required to purchase or use approved watches, just the employees that were responsible for schedules. But many employees did buy the approved watches because they were the standard in reliability.

[2]These were used primarily by those railroaders who were not required to submit their watches for inspection.

[3]There were many watches made for railroad use prior to 1893. Some of the key wind ones, especially, are good quality and highly collectible.

[4]Some manufacturers inscribed terms such as railroader, special railroad, dispatcher, etc. on the back plates of the movements.

* * *

COLONIAL WATCHMAKERS

Early American watchmakers came from Europe; little is known about them, and few of their watches exist today. Their hand-fabricated watches were made largely from imported parts. It was common practice for a watchmaker to use rough castings made by several craftsmen. These were referred to as "movements in the gray." He took these parts and finished and assembled them to make a complete watch. The watchmaker would then engrave his name on the finished timepiece.

Some of the early American watchmakers designed the cases or other parts, but most imported what they needed. The early colonial watchmakers showed little originality as designers and we can only guess how many watches were really made in America.

These early hand-made watches are almost non-existent; therefore only the name of the watchmaker will be listed. This compilation comes from old ads in newspapers and journals and other sources and is not considered to be complete.

Because of the rarity of these early watches, the owner can practically name his price.

Ephraim Clark, 18 size, non-jeweled, made between 1780-1790; a good example of a colonial watch. These early watches usually included chain driven fusees, verge type escapement, hand pierced balance cock, key wind & set; note the circular shaped regulator on the far left side of the illustrated example.

Watchmaker	City*	Approx. Date
Adams, Nathan	1	1800
Adams, William	1	1810
Aldrich, Jacob	18	1802
Allebach, Jacob	2	1825-1840
Atherton, Nathan	2	1825
Atkinson, James	1	1745
Backhouse, John	3	1725
Bagnall, Benjamin	2	1750
Bailey, John	1	1810
Bailey, William	2	1820
Baker, Benjamin	2	1825
Banks, Joseph	2	1790
Barnhill, Robert	2	1775
Barrow, Samuel	2	1771
Barry, Standish	4	1785
Basset, John F.	2	1798
Belknap, William	1	1815
Bell, William	2	1805
Benedict, S. W.	5	1835
Bigger & Clarke	4	1783
Billion, C.	2	1775-1800
Bingham & Bricerly	2	1778-1799
Birnie, Laurence	2	1774
Blundy, Charles	6	1750
Blunt & Nichols	5	1850
Bond, William	1	1800-1810
Bonnaud	2	1799
Bower, Michael	2	1790-1800
Bowman, Joseph	3	1821-1844
Boyd & Richards	2	1808
Boyter, Daniel	3	1805
Brands & Matthey	2	1799
Brandt, Aime	2	1820
Brant, Brown & Lewis	2	1795
Brazier, Amable	2	1795
Brewer, William	2	1785-1791
Brewster & Ingraham	12	1827-1839
Brown, Garven	1	1767
Brown, John	3	1840
Brownell, A. P.	21	
Burkelow, Samuel	2	1791-1799
Campbell, Charles	2	1796
Campbell, William	19	1765
Capper, Michael	2	1799
Carey, James	20	1830
Carrell, John	2	1791-1793
Carter, Jacob	2	1805
Carter, Thomas	2	1823
Carver, Jacob	2	1790
Carvill, James	5	1803
Chandlee, John	18	1795-1810
Chaudron	2	1799
Chauncey & Joseph Ives	12	1825

Watchmaker	City*	Approx. Date
Cheney, Martin	38	1800
Chick, M. M.	32	1845
Clark, Benjamin	18	1737-1750
Clark, Ephraim	2	1780-1800
Clark, John	2	1799
Clark, Thomas	1	1764
Claudon, John-		
Cook, William	1	1810
George	6	1773
Crow, George	18	1740-1770
Crow, John	18	1770-1798
Crow, Thomas	18	1770-1798
Currier & Trott	1	1800
Curtis, Solomon	2	1793-1795
Dakin, James	1	1795
Davis, Samuel	1	1820
Delaplaine, James K.	5	1786-1800
DeVacht, Joseph & Frances	7	1792
Dix, Joseph	2	1770
Downes, Anson	12	1830
Downes, Arthur	6	1765
Downes, Ephriam	12	1830
Droz, Hannah	2	1840
Droz, Humbert	2	1793-1799
Duffield, Edward W.	8	1775
Dunheim, Andrew	5	1775
Dupuy, John	2	1770
Dupuy, Odran	2	1735
Dutch, Stephen, Jr.	1	1800-1810
Eberman, George	3	1800
Eberman, John	3	1780-1820
Ellicott, Joseph	9	1763
Elsworth, David	4	1780-1800
Embree, Effingham	5	1785
Evans, David	4	1770-1773
Fales, James	21	1810-1820
Ferris, Tiba	18	1812-1850
Filder, John	3	1810-1825
Fister, Amon	2	1794
Fix, Joseph	22	1820-1840
Fowell, J & N	1	1800-1810
Frances, Basil & Alexander Vuille	4	1766
Galbraith, Patrick	2	1795
Gibbons, Thomas	2	1750
Goodfellow, William	2	1793-1795
Goodfellow & Son, William	2	1796-1799
Gooding, Henry	1	1810-1820
Green, John	2	1794
Groppengeiser, J. L.	2	1840
Grotz, Issac	23	1810-1835
Hall, Jonas	1	1848-1858
Harland, Thomas	10	1802
Harrison, James	37	1805
Hawxhurst, Nath.	5	1784
Heilig, Jacob	2	1770-1824

Watchmaker	City*	Approx. Date
Heilig, John	24	1824-1830
Hepton, Frederick	2	1785
Hodgson, William	2	1785
Hoff, John	3	1800
Hoffner, Henry	2	1791
Howard, Thomas	2	1789-1791
Howe, Jubal	37	1800
Huguenail, Charles	2	1799
Hutchins, Abel	25	1785-1818
Hyde, John E.	5	1805
Hyde & Goodrich	41	1850
Ingersoll, Daniel B.	1	1800-1810
Ingold, Pierre Frederick	5	1845-1850
Jacob, Charles & Claude	11	1775
Jackson, Joseph H.	2	1802-1810
Jeunit, Joseph	26	1763
Johnson, David	1	1690
Johnson, John	6	1763
Jones, Low & Ball	1	1830
Keith, William	37	1810
Kennedy, Patrick	2	1795-1799
Kincaid, Thomas	27	1775
Kirkwood, John	6	1761
Launy, David F.	1,5	1800
Leavenworth, Mark	39	1820
Leavenworth, Wm.	39	1810
Leslie & Co.	4	1795
Leslie & Price	2	1793-1799
Leslie, Robert	4	1788-1791
Levely, George	2	1774
Levi, Michael & Issac	4	1785
Lind, John	2	1791-1799
Lowens, David	2	1785
Ludwig, John	2	1791
Lufkins & Johnson	1	1800-1810
Lukens, Isiah	2	1825
MacDowell, Robert	2	1798
Macfarlane, John	1	1800-1810
Mahve, Matthew	2	1761
Manross, Elisha	12	1827
Martin, Patrick	2	1830
Maunroe & Whitney	25	1805-1825
Maus, Frederick	2	1785-1793
Maynard, George	5	1702-1730
McCabe, John	4	1774
McDowell, James	2	1795
McGraw, Donald	11	1767
Mends, James	2	1795
Merriman, Titus	12	1830
Merry, Charles F.	2	1799
Miller, Abraham	23	1810-1830
Mitchell, Henry	5	1787-1800
Mohler, Jacob	4	1773
Montandon, Julien	37	1812
Moollinger, Henry	2	1794
Morgan, Thomas	2,4	1774-1793

Watchmaker	City*	Approx. Date
Moris, William	28	1765-1775
Mulford, J. H.	40	1845
Mulliken, Nathaniel	1	1765
Munroe & Whitney	25	1820
Narney, Joseph	6	1753
Neiser, Augustine	2	1739-1780
Nicholls, George	5	1728-1750
Nicollette, Mary	2	1793-1799
O'Hara, Charles	2	1799
Oliver, Griffith	2	1785-1793
Ormsby, James	4	1771
Palmer, John	2	1795
Park, Seth	29	1790
Parke, Solomon	2	1791-1795
Parke, Solomon & Co.	2	1799
Parker, James	14	1790
Parker, Thomas	2	1783
Patton, Abraham	2	1799
Payne, Lawrence	5	1732-1755
Pearman, W.	33	1834
Perry, Thomas	5	1750-1775
Phillips, Joseph	5	1713-1735
Pierret, Mathew	2	1795
Pope, Joseph	1	1790
Price, Philip	2	1825
Proctor, Cardan	5	1747-1775
Proctor, William	5	1737-1760
Proud, R.	34	1775
Purse, Thomas	4	1805
Quimby, Phineas & William	15	1825
Reily, John	2	1785-1795
Rich, John	12	1800
Richardson, Francis	2	1736
Roberts, John	2	1799
Roberts, S & E	30	1830
Rode, William	2	1785
Rodger, James	5	1822-1878
Rodgers, Samuel	31	1790-1804
Russell, George	2	1840

Watchmaker	City*	Approx. Date
Saxton & Lukens	2	1828
Schriner, Martin	3	1790-1830
Schriner, M & P	3	1830-1840
Seddinger, Margaret	2	1846
Severberg, Christian	5	1755-1775
Sherman, Robert	18	1760-1770
Sibley, O. E.	5	1820
Smith, J. L.	36	1830
Smith & Goodrich	12	1827-1840
Soloman, Henry	1	1820
Souza, Sammuel	2	1820
Sprogell, John	2	1791
Spurck, Peter	2	1795-1799
Stanton, Job	5	1810
Stein, Abraham	2	1799
Stever & Bryant	16	1830
Stillas, John	2	1785-1793
Stinnett, John	2	1769
Store, Marmaduke	2	1742
Strech, Thomas	2	1782
Syderman, Philip	2	1785
Taf, John James	2	1794
Taylor, Samuel	2	1799
Tonchure, Francis	4	1805
Townsend, Charles	2	1799
Townsend, David	1	1800
Trott, Andrew	1	1800-1810
Turrell, Samuel	1	1790
Voight, Henry	2	1775-1793
Voight, Sebastian	2	1775-1799
Voight, Thomas (Henry's son)	2	1811-1835
Vuille, Alexander	4	1766
Warner, George T.	5	1795
Weller, Francis	2	1780
Wells, George & Co.	1	1825
Wells, J. S.	1	1800
Wheaton, Caleb	35	1800
Whittaker, William	5	1731-1755
Wood, John	2	1770-1793
Wright, John	5	1712-1735
Zahm, G. M.	3	1865

***Location of Watchmaker**

1. Boston, Massachusetts
2. Philadelphia, Pennsylvania
3. Lancaster, Pennsylvania
4. Baltimore, Maryland
5. New York, New York
6. Charleston, South Carolina
7. Gallipolis, Ohio
8. Whiteland, Pennsylvania
9. Buckingham, Pennsylvania
10. Norwich, Connecticut
11. Annapolis, Maryland
12. Bristol, Connecticut
13. Parktown, Pennsylvania
14. Cambridge, Ohio
15. Belfast, Maine
16. Wigville, Connecticut
17. Reading, Pennsylvania
18. Wilmington, Delaware
19. Carlisle, Pennsylvania
20. Brunswick, Maine
21. New Bedford, Massachusetts
22. Reading, Pennsylvania
23. Eastern, Pennsylvania
24. Germantown, Pennsylvania
25. Concord, Massachusetts
26. Meadville, Pennsylvania

***Location of Watchmaker**

27. Christiana Bridge, Delaware
28. Grafton, Massachusetts
29. Parktown, Pennsylvania
30. Trenton, New Jersey
31. Plymouth, Massachusetts
32. Concord, New Hampshire
33. Richmond, Virginia
34. Newport, Rhode Island
35. Providence, Rhode Island
36. Middletown, Connecticut
37. Shrewbury, Massachusetts
38. Windsor, Vermont
39. Waterbury, Connecticut
40. Albany, New York
41. New Orleans, Louisiana

Premier Maximus, 16 size, 23 diamond, ruby, sapphire jewels, gold jewel settings, gold train and winding indicator. Sold in a silver presentation box. Each watch came with a Kew certificate and solf for $620.

The Edward Howard, 16 size, 23 matched blue ruby sapphires, chronometer type balance with frosted gold bridges. Sold in a presentation box with an extra crystal and mainspring for $350.

PRESTIGE WATCHES

In 1908 Waltham's most expensive watch was a 16s, 23j, gold case (Model #1907) that was selling for about $150. That same year Waltham introduced the "Premier Maximus" which they hailed as "the finest timepiece in America." It was a 16s, 23j, gold train, diamond-end stones, 6 positions (Model #1908). The selling price was $250.

The Premier Maximus posed a challenge to the E. Howard Watch Company and, not wanting to be outdone, Howard developed the "Edward Howard" watch at a price of $350. Introduced in 1912, it was in a 18k gold case complete with matched blue sapphire jewels, free-spring balance, chronometer adjustments, gold-frost finished plates, and had an extra crystal and mainspring. The Howard ads read, "The finest watch ever produced in this or any other country." By 1914 the price of the Premier Maximus had increased to $400 with a 18k gold case and a sterling silver presentation box with a "KEW Class A Certificate."

In 1922 the Elgin Watch Company introduced their "no two alike" C. H. Hulburd presentation models at $300 to $750. At the same time the Premier Maximus was selling for $750.

In 1924 the Gruen Watch Company introduced their "50th Anniversary Watch" at $500. It was in a five-sided "Pentagon Case," about a 10s, 23j, two of the jewels were diamonds, 12k gold plates, gold-plated train.

In 1925 the 922 Masterpiece, a 12s, 23j, gold train, 5 position watch, was introduced by the Hamilton Watch Company. Hamilton ad writers labeled it, "Beauty that will always be in good taste beyond fads and passing fancies."

The marketing strategy behind the high-quality, limited production watches was to enhance the sales of their regular production line. Each company used a model that had already proved itself. Waltham's 1907 and 1908 are basically the same watch. Hamilton only added MP to the 922 model number. Marketing was intense and in 1921 Elgin and Waltham stood eye to eye in production at 24 million, but in 1922 Elgin moved ahead.

Another watch of note was the Masonic watch introduced in 1922 by the Dudley Watch Company. It was a 14s, 19j, and carried the emblem depicting the eye, compass, square, trowel, plumb, and level. In their ads, Dudley touted themselves as being "the makers of America's finest timepieces."

REPEATING WATCHES

Around 1675 a repeating mechanism was attached to a clock for the first time. The first repeating watch was made about 1677 by Thomas Tompion or Daniel Quare. Five-minute, quarter-hour and half-hour repeaters were popular by 1730. The minute repeater became common about 1830.

Repeating watch by **American Waltham Watch Co.**, 16 size, 17 jewels, hunting case, stem wind, gold train.

Fred Terstegen applied for a patent in 1882 for a repeating attachment that could be used with any American watch, key wind or stem wind. He was granted three patents: No. 311,270 on January 27, 1885, No. 3,421,844 on February 18, 1890, and No. 3,436,162 in September 1890. The Waltham Watch Co. was the only watch manufacturer to produce repeating watches in America. It is not known how many repeaters were made, but 3,500 is estimated.

OUTSTANDING, HIGH-GRADE AND SCARCE WATCHES

Note: Early American-made watches that have been recased are worth 30 to 50 percent less. The prices listed below are for watches in their original cases.

	Avg	Ex-Fn	Mint
Adams & Perry, 20S, 20J, 18K, KW	$2,200	$3,500	$5,000
Adams & Perry, 18S, 20J	1,200	1,700	2,500
J. H. Allison, 21J, Detent Chronometer	3,000	4,000	6,000
Appleton Tracy Chronodrometer, Sporting Model	2,000	2,400	3,000
Appleton Watch Co., 18S, stem attached	560	675	885
Auburndale Watch Co. (Bentley)	300	500	750
Auburndale Watch Co. (Lincoln)	300	500	600
Auburndale Watch Co. (Rotary), 20S	1,500	1,800	2,600
Ball Model with wind indicator	2,500	3,000	4,500
Ball-E. Howard & Co. VII, HC, 18K	3,500	4,000	5,500
P. S. Barlett (Pinned Plates) Model #57	300	525	775
E. F. Bowman	7,500	11,000	16,000

E. F. Bowman, 16-18 size, 17 jewels, three quarter plate, gold jewel settings, lever set, stem wind, serial number 19, c. 1880.

Grade or Name — Description	Avg	Ex-Fn	Mint
California Watch Co.	1,250	1,650	2,500
Columbus King, 25J	2,400	3,000	3,800
Columbus Railway King, 25J, OF	2,400	3,000	3,800
Columbus Railway King, 25J, HC	3,500	4,000	4,500
Columbus, 16S, 21J, Ruby Model, OF	475	600	900
Columbus, 16S, 21J, Ruby Model, HC	425	500	625

Grade or Name — Description	Avg	Ex-Fn	Mint
Cornell Watch Co. (San Francisco), 15J	1,000	1,400	2,300
Samuel Curtis Watch Co., S#s less than 200, original case	3,500	4,000	5,000
Jacob D. Custer	8,500	12,000	18,000
Dennison, Howard & Davis, S#s below 2,000, all original	1,000	1,300	1,695
Dudley No. 1, box & papers	2,600	2,800	3,200
Elgin (C. H. Hubbard), 12S	900	1,000	1,500
Lord Elgin, 23J, 16S, 14K	1,500	1,800	2,450
C. Fasoldt	8,000	10,000	14,500
Fellows and Schell, 15J	2,800	3,200	4,200
Freeport Watch Co.	4,500	5,500	7,000
Luther Goddard, with eagle bridge, S#'s 1-35	5,000	7,000	10,000
Hamilton, 7J	1,000	1,150	1,600
Hamilton, 11J, OF	1,500	1,750	2,250
Hamilton, 11J, HC	1,400	1,550	1,900
Hamilton, 21J, 16S, Model 994	700	800	1,250
Hamilton, 23J, 18S, Model 946, OF, Extra	400	450	700
Hamilton, 23J, 18S, Model 947, HC, unmarked	3,500	4,000	4,950
Hamilton, 23J, Model 947, HC, marked	4,500	5,500	6,950
Hamilton, S#s less than 400, OF	600	800	1,200
Hamilton, S#s less than 1300, HC	700	900	1,400
Hamilton, 23J, 16S, Model 951	3,000	3,500	4,500
Hamilton—Masterpiece 922, 18K, marked	550	600	800
Hampden Watch Co., 15J, 14K multi-color HC, 18S	1,150	1,450	2,200
The Howard, Davis & Dennison (S#'s 1-17)	30,000	38,000	50,000
Edward Howard in box	8,000	9,000	10,500
E. Howard & Co. (KW & KS), 15J, Series I, 18K, upright pallet	2,000	2,200	2,800
Howard & Rice, S#s 6,000-6,500	1,500	2,000	2,500
H. von der Heydt (The Self-Winding Watch Co.)	4,500	5,500	6,500
Illinois Bunn Special, 24J, 18S, HCI5P, OF	465	595	875
Illinois Bunn Special, 25J, 18S	7,000	8,000	10,000
Illinois Bunn Special, 26J, 18S	5,400	5,800	6,400
Illinois Sangamo Special, solid bow, 60 hr., marked	535	690	895
Illinois (Ben Franklin), 25J, 16S, HC	4,500	5,000	6,000
Illinois (Ben Franklin), 26J, 18S	5,000	6,000	7,500
Illinois (Ben Franklin), 21J, 18S, HCI6P	900	1,100	1,500
Illinois (Ben Franklin), 24J, 18S	2,000	2,200	3,000
Illinois (Penn Special), 25J, 18S	3,000	4,000	5,500
Illinois (Penn Special), 26J, 18S	5,000	5,800	6,500
Illinois 16S, 23J, Diamond Ruby Sapphire Model	2,500	2,800	3,600
Illinois Keywind 18S, Stuart adjusted, 5th pinion	500	600	925
Illinois Model #189, marked	325	425	675
Illinois, 18S, Southern R.R. Special, 21J, HC	1,000	1,100	1,400
Illinois Watch Co., 25J, 16S, bridge movement	4,000	4,500	5,500
Illinois Watch Co., 163A, 16S	600	725	925
Ingraham, Betty Boop, 1934	300	375	500
Mickey Mouse #1, Ingersol, 1933	250	300	400
Mozart Watch Co., 3 wheel	11,000	15,000	20,000
Nashua Watch Co., marked	18,000	22,000	28,000
Newark Watch Co., 15J, KW, KS, HC	275	350	550
New England, skeletonized	175	225	350
New York Watch Co., pendant crank type	400	550	795
N. Y. Standard W. Co., with worm gear	400	500	725

Grade or Name — Description	Avg	Ex-Fn	Mint
N. Y. Watch Co., 15J, wolf's teeth wind, all original	1,000	1,200	1,500
Otay Watch Co., California	2,000	2,200	2,400
Palmer Watch Co.	900	1,100	1,600
Palmer Watch Co. Chronometer	4,000	4,500	6,000
C. T. Parker	1,200	1,800	2,500
James & Henry Pitkin, S#'s 1-50	25,000	30,000	40,000
H & J. F. Pitkin, S#'s 50-377	18,000	21,000	25,000
A. H. Potter Chronometer	10,500	12,000	14,000
George P. Reed Chronometer	9,000	10,500	15,000
Rockford, 21J, 18S, wind indicator, No. 950	2,500	3,300	4,500
Rockford, 23J, 16S, Doll Watch Co. dial & case	1,000	1,400	2,000
Rockford, 24J, 18S, marked 'R.G.'	1,000	1,200	1,500
Rockford, 25J, 18S	3,500	5,000	6,500
Rockford, 26J, 18S	8,000	10,000	16,000
San Jose Watch Co.	800	1,800	2,400
M. S. Smith, 18S, KW	1,200	1,500	2,200
South Bend, Polaris, M#1	995	1,200	1,650
J. P. Stevens Watch Co., S#'s 1-174	3,000	4,000	5,500
Seth Thomas Maiden Lane, 21J, marked	1,200	1,400	2,000
Seth Thomas, 23J	900	1,200	1,600
Seth Thomas Maiden Lane, 24J, marked	1,500	1,750	2,500
Seth Thomas Maiden Lane, 25J, marked	2,000	2,600	3,300
Seth Thomas Maiden Lane, 28J, marked	15,000	18,000	25,000
U. S. Watch Co. (Waltham) The President, 21J	700	825	1,000
U. S. Watch Co. (Marion) (Butterfly KW & KS), 19J, SW, nickel mvt., Frederic Atherton & Co.	900	1,000	1,200
U. S. Watch Co. (Marion) 19J, SW, Pen Set, 18K, U.S.W.Co. case, HC	4,000	4,300	5,000
Waltham Crystal Watch (stone movement has transparent back plates), 4 Size	3,800	4,800	6,500
Waltham Crystal Watch (stone movement has transparent back plates), 14 Size	4,500	6,000	8,000
Waltham 5-Minute Repeater, 18K	5,000	6,000	8,000
Waltham 1-Minute Repeater, 18K, perpetual calendar	30,000	35,000	45,000
Waltham Premier Maximus with original box & papers, 18K	8,000	8,500	10,000
Watson (early Waltham), marked Boston	850	1,175	1,600
Warren Mfg. Co. (to S#29)	25,000	30,000	38,000
Washington Watch Co., 24J, LaFayette (ill.)	850	1,050	1,350

Waltham made a watch with crystal or agate (see-through) plates, a rare beauty. It was size 4, Model #1882, and size 14, Model #1874. Both were 16 jewel in gold settings, had exposed pallets and a gold train. Not many of these watches were sold because the plates did not hold up very well—they broke like glass. But it is a true collector's item. Waltham called this the "stone movement."

10 20 30 40 50 60 70 80 90 100 110

MILLIMETERS

AMERICAN MOVEMENT SIZES
LANCASHIRE GAUGE

Size	Inches	Inches	Millimeters	Size	Inches	Inches	Millimeters
18/0	18/30	.600	15.24	2	1 7/30	1.233	31.32
17/0	19/30	.633	16.08	3	1 8/30	1.266	32.16
16/0	20/30	.666	16.92	4	1 9/30	1.300	33.02
15/0	21/30	.700	17.78	5	1 10/30	1.333	33.86
14/0	22/30	.733	18.62	6	1 11/30	1.366	34.70
13/0	23/30	.766	19.46	7	1 12/30	1.400	35.56
12/0	24/30	.800	20.32	8	1 13/30	1.433	36.40
11/0	25/30	.833	21.16	9	1 14/30	1.466	37.24
10/0	26/30	.866	22.00	10	1 15/30	1.500	38.10
9/0	27/30	.900	22.86	11	1 16/30	1.533	38.94
8/0	28/30	.933	23.70	12	1 17/30	1.566	39.78
7/0	29/30	.966	24.54	13	1 18/30	1.600	40.64
6/0	1	1.000	25.40	14	1 19/30	1.633	41.48
5/0	1 1/30	1.033	26.24	15	1 20/30	1.666	42.32
4/0	1 2/30	1.066	27.08	16	1 21/30	1.700	43.18
3/0	1 3/30	1.100	27.94	17	1 22/30	1.733	44.02
2/0	1 4/30	1.133	28.78	18	1 23/30	1.766	44.86
0	1 5/30	1.166	29.62	19	1 24/30	1.800	45.72
1	1 6/30	1.200	30.48	20	1 25/30	1.833	46.56

SWISS MOVEMENT SIZES
Lignes With Their Equivalents in Millimeters and Decimal Parts of an Inch

Lignes	Inches Decimals	Millimeters
7	.622	15.79
8	.710	18.05
9	.799	20.30
10	.888	22.56
11	.977	24.81
12	1.066	27.07
13	1.154	29.32
14	1.243	31.58
15	1.332	33.84
16	1.421	36.09
17	1.510	38.35
18	1.599	40.60
19	1.687	42.86
20	1.776	45.11
21	1.865	47.37
22	1.954	49.63

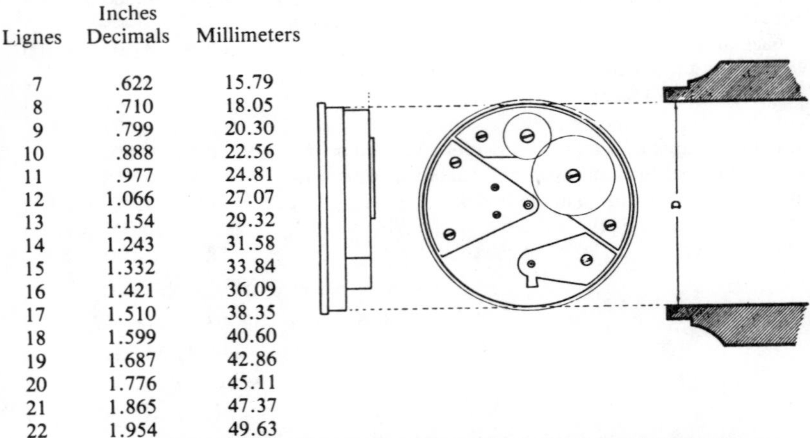

GAUGES FOR MEASURING YOUR WATCH SIZE

The size of a watch is determined by measuring the outside diameter of the dial side of the lower pillar plate. The gauges below may be placed across the face of your watch to calculate its approximate size.

AMER. MOVEMENT SIZES

SWISS MOVEMENT SIZES
LIGNES

2 4 6 8 10 12 14 16 18 20
3 5 7 9 11 13 15 17 19

WATCH CASES

One of the most appealing aspects of the pocket watch over the years must surely have been the elaborate cases in which they were housed. The very luster given off by a watch case emitted a sort of status and pride, and some folks went to great lengths to have as elaborate a case as possible.

Undoubtedly the gold cases were the standard men sought to achieve in the days when the pocket watch was most prominent. Those gold cases are eagerly sought after today by collectors.

Solid gold cases were at the top of the list in value; gold-filled was next, followed by rolled gold and gold-plated cases. Solid gold cases were of 8k, 10k, 14k, 18k, and 20k. (Pure gold is 24k.) The 20k gold was too soft and was not used often. Remember: even though a case is stamped 10k, 14k, etc., this is no guarantee that the case is solid gold.

The most common type case was the silveroid. These cases were made of 45 percent nickel, 54 percent copper, and one percent manganese. They held up extremely well, and today a silveroid case can be polished to a high gloss that will look like new with a household brass polish.

From as early as 1525 watch cases have been engraved. Tools were developed that would cut a fine "V"-shaped groove in the metal and produce a very delicate design. A turning lathe was used as early as 1780 to produce geometric patterns of intersecting and interlacing curved lines on the watch cases.

*   *   *

SOLID GOLD CASES

"Pure gold" and "solid gold" are terms often misunderstood. The terms are not interchangeable, and the differences in meaning should be noted by the collector.

Pure gold is 24 karat gold, but gold in its purest form is useless as a workable metal. Gold must be reduced to at least 22k for coinage, and is most practical at 14k to 10k for wearing.

Pure gold refers to 24k. Solid gold is anything less than 24k—but is neither gold-filled or gold-plated. Solid gold cases are made of 18k, 14k, 10k, or 8k gold throughout.

SOLID GOLD MARKS

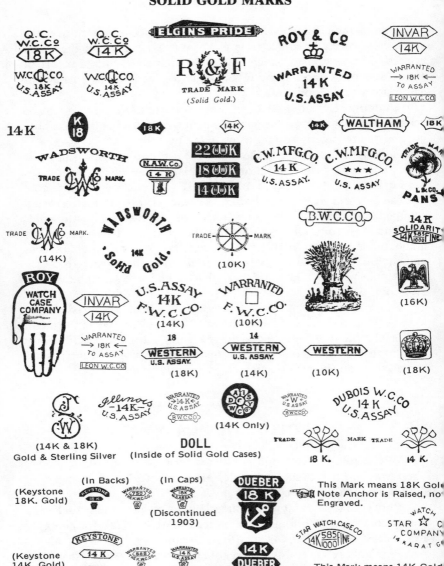

Q.C. W.C.Co 18K — W.C.Q.CO. 18K U.S. ASSAY

Q.C. W.C.Co 14K — W.C.Q.CO. 14K U.S. ASSAY

ELGIN'S PRIDE

R & F TRADE MARK (*Solid Gold.*)

ROY & Co WARRANTED 14K U.S. ASSAY

INVAR 14K — WARRANTED → 18K ← TO ASSAY — LEON W.C.CO

14K — K. 18 — 18K — 14K — 14K — WALTHAM — 18K

WADSWORTH TRADE MARK

N.A.W.Co. 14 K

22 HW K — 18 HW K — 14 HW K

C.W.MFG.CO. 14 K U.S. ASSAY.

C.W.MFG.CO. ★★★ U.S. ASSAY

TRADE MARK L&CO. PANS

B.W.C.CO.

14K SOLIDARITY 14K 585/1000 FINE

TRADE MARK. (14K)

WADSWORTH 14K Solid Gold.

TRADE MARK (10K)

ROY WATCH CASE COMPANY

INVAR 14K — WARRANTED → 18K ← TO ASSAY — LEON W.C.CO

U.S. ASSAY 14K F.W.C.CO. (14K)

WARRANTED F.W.C.CO. (10K)

(16K)

18 WESTERN U.S. ASSAY. (18K)

14 WESTERN U.S. ASSAY. (14K)

WESTERN (10K)

(18K)

(14K & 18K) Gold & Sterling Silver

Illinois -14K- U.S. ASSAY

WARRANTED → 14K ← U.S. ASSAY. BWCCO

A I S D C Y W C Co. (14K Only)

DOLL (Inside of Solid Gold Cases)

WARRANTED → W ← U.S. ASSAY BWCCO

DUBOIS W.C.CO 14 K U.S. ASSAY

TRADE MARK 18 K. — TRADE 14 K.

(Keystone 18K. Gold) — (In Backs) KEYSTONE 18 K — WARRANTED .750 THE K.W.C.CO. — (In Caps) WARRANTED 18K U.S. ASSAY (Discontinued 1903)

DUEBER 18 K — This Mark means 18K Gol Note Anchor is Raised, no Engraved.

STAR WATCH CASE CO 14K 585/1000 FINE

WATCH STAR ☆ C COMPANY 14 KARAT G

(Keystone 14K. Gold) — KEYSTONE 14 K — WARRANTED .585 THE K.W.C.CO. — WARRANTED 14 K U.S. ASSAY (Discontinued 1903)

14K DUEBER — This Mark means 14K Gold Note anchor is Raised, not Engraved.

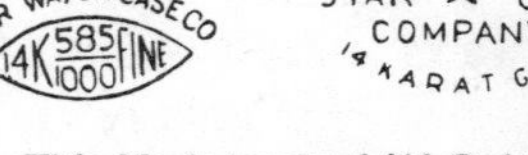

(Keystone 10K. Gold) — KEYSTONE 10 K — WARRANTED .415 THE K.W.C.CO. — WARRANTED 10 K U.S. ASSAY

FOGEL 18 K (18K. Solid Gold)

FOGEL 14 K (14K. Solid Gold)

WALTHAM — A.W.W.Co. WALTHAM MASS. U.S.A. — WALTHAM — A.W. CO. — K. 18 — $ (8K & 10K)

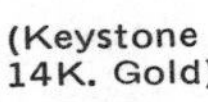

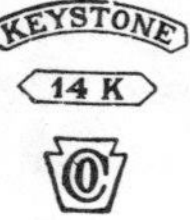

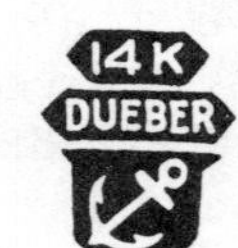

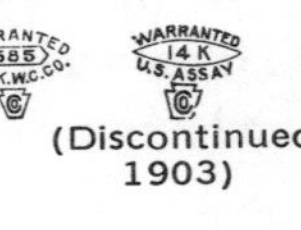

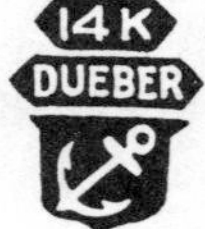

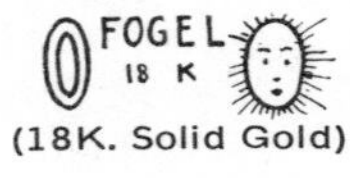

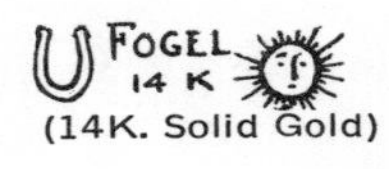

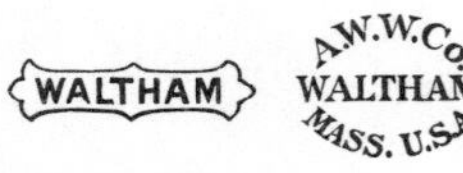

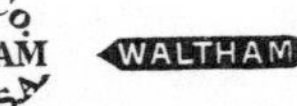

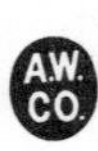

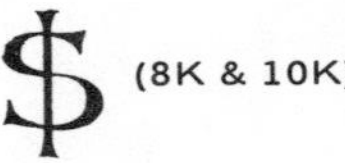

Miscellaneous Notes on Gold Cases

In 1894 solid gold cases sold for: 18 size box case $180, $200, $250; 18 size gold case $90 to $178; 6 size cases sold for $75 to $159; 0 size cases, about $45.

An 18 size movement with a full plate weighs 50 DWT; a 16 size movement with a ¾ plate weighs 35 DWT. These weights do not include the case.

Scrap gold sells for about 80 percent of the daily gold quote for 24k gold and scrap silver brings about 85 percent of the quote.

FINENESS OF GOLD KARATS

8k	.3333%
10k	.4167%
12k	.5000%
14k	.5833%
18k	.7500%
24k	1.0000% (100%)

MULTI-COLOR GOLD CASES

Multi-color gold cases in 18k and 14k first appeared around 1879. The 18k gold case did not lend itself to the multi-color process. The beauty of the colors was not as striking as in the 14k cases, and consequently did not sell as well. Because of the natural softness of 18k gold coupled with the unpopularity of the 18k multi-colored cases, the manufacturers decided to discontinue their production of them around 1882. For these reasons, 18k multi-color cases are about 100 times more scarce than the 14k cases.

The "brilliant period" for multi-color gold cases was from 1890 to 1895 which represents the peak for sales and craftsmanship. By 1910 the multi-color gold case was no longer made in the 18 and 16 sizes. However, smaller sizes continued to be produced after this date.

Determining a realistic market value for multi-color gold cases is not an easy task. The value is influenced largely by eye appeal, such as degree of height and the elaborateness of decorative design. The size and condition of the case are also prime factors. The heavier and larger the case, the more the value. Prices can range from $600 to $7,000 depending upon the size, condition and quality of the case that you have.

It might be worth noting that when gold prices decline, the value of multi-color cases seems to show little effect. On the other hand, however, when gold prices go up, the multi-color cases reflect this increase.

Included in the case value listings at the end of the case section, for your information, are estimated values of multi-color gold cases.

COMPOSITION OF MULTI-COLOR GOLD

To Achieve Multi-Color Gold	These Elements Are Added
Yellow	Silver & Copper
Red	25% Copper
Dead Leaf	30% Silver
Green	25% Silver
Water Green	40% Silver
Blue	25% Iron
Violet or Purple	Small Amount of Iron
White	Palladium, Silver, Nickel, zinc or platinum

Superior White Gold is 25 percent platinum.
14k gold-filled cases have about 5 percent gold.

GOLD FILLED CASES

Gold-filled cases are far more common than solid gold cases. Only about 5 percent of the cases were solid gold. In making the gold-filled case, the following process was used: two bars of gold, 12'' long, 2'' wide, and ½'' thick were placed on either side of a bar of base metal. The bar of base metal was ¾'' thick and the same length and width as the gold bars. These three bars were soldered together and placed under pressure and high temperature. The bars were now sent through rolling mills under tremendous pressure; this rolling was repeated until the desired thickness was reached. The new sandwich-type gold was in a sheet. Discs were punched out of the sheet and pressed in a die to form a dish-shaped cover. Finally the lip, or ridge, was added. The bezel, snap, and dust caps were added in the finishing room. Gold-filled cases are usually 10k or 14k gold. The cases were marked ten-year, fifteen-year, twenty-year, twenty-five-year, or thirty-year. The number of years indicated the duration of guarantee that the gold on the case would not wear through to the base metal. The higher the number of years indicates that more gold was used and that a higher original price was paid.

In 1924 the government prohibited any further use of the guarantee terms of 5, 10, 15, 20, 25, or 30 years. After that, manufacturers then marked their cases 10k or 14k Gold Filled and 10k Rolled Gold Plate. Anytime you see the terms ''5, 10, 15, 20, 25 and 30-year'' this immediately identifies the case as being gold-filled. The word ''guaranteed'' on the case also denotes gold-filled.

The first patent for gold-filled cases was given to J. Boss on May 3, 1859.

Rolled Gold

Rolled gold involved rolling gold into a micro thinness and, under extreme pressure, bonding it to each sheet of base metal. Rolled gold carried a five-year guarantee. The thickness of the gold sheet varied and had a direct bearing on value, as did the richness of the engraving.

Gold Gilding

Brass plates and wheels and cases are often gilded with gold. To do this, the parts are hung by a copper wire in a vessel or porous cell of a galvanic battery filled with a solution of offerro-cyanid of potassium, carbonate of soda, chloride of gold, and distilled water. An electric current deposits the gold evenly over the surface in about a six-minute period. One ounce of gold is enough for heavy gilding of six hundred watches. After gilding, the plates are polished with a soft buff using powdered rouge mixed with water and alcohol. The older method is fire-gilt which uses a gold and mercury solution. The metal is subjected to a high temperature so the mercury will evaporate and leave the gold plating. This is a very dangerous method, however, due to the harmful mercury vapor.

GOLD FILLED MARKS

The following gold-filled and rolled gold plate marks are not complete, but if you have any doubt that the case is solid gold, pay only the gold-filled price.

GOLD FILLED MARKS

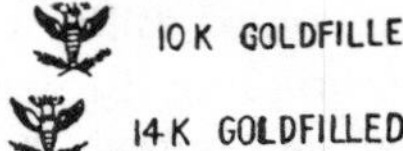

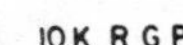

☆ 10 K ROLLED GOLD PLATE

(14K. Filled.)

(Jas. Boss 10K. Filled. 20 Years.)

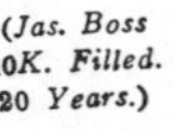

CROWN 14K. FILLED
(25 Years.)

CROWN 10K. FILLED
(20 Years.)

(Keystone Extra, Substitute for All-Gold Case.)

(Rolled Gold.)

(Jas. Boss 14K. Filled. 25 Years.)

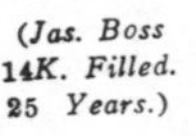

(10 Years.)

EMPRESS
(Gold Filled, 10 Years.)

FORTUNE
(Gold Filled, 20 Years.)

PREMIER
(Gold Filled, 25 Years.)

CASHIER
(Gold Filled, 25 Years.)

THE COMET
(10 Years.)

(14K. Filled.)

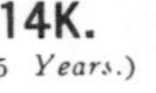

XV.
(15 Years.)

THE BELL
14K.
(25 Years.)

XX.
(20 Years.)

(25 Years.)

V.
(5 Years.)

WARRANTED
N.A.W.Co.
20 YEARS
(10K. Gold Filled.)

SILVER CASE MARKS

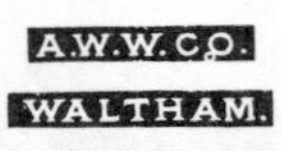

A.W.
CO.
STERLING.

KEYSTONE WATCH CASE COIN

KEYSTONE WATCH CASE STERLING

(Discontinued.)

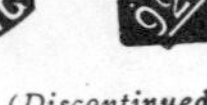

(Discontinued.)

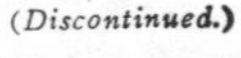

(Coin Silver with Albata Cap)
(Discontinued.)

(Coin Silver with Silver Cap)
(Discontinued.)

CHAMPION
COIN.

N.A.W.Co
STERLING
(Sterling Silver.)

(Coin Silver, with Silver Caps, Gold Joints and Crowns.)

Sterling Silver

SILVER CASE MARKS

(*Sterling Silver.*)

STERLING
SILVER
UNITED STATES
ASSAY
925/1000
FINE

ILLINOIS
W.C.CO.
ELGIN
STERLING

HUNTING CASES

A hunting case is identified by a cover over the face of the watch. The case is opened by pressing the stem of the watch. The cover was used for dress and protection and the hunter case was carried by men of status.

How To Handle A Hunting Case Watch

Hold the watch in right hand with the bow or swing ring between the index finger and thumb. Press on the stem with the right thumb to release the cover exposing the face.

When closing, don't snap the front cover. Press the crown to move the catch in, close the cover, then release the crown. This will prevent wear to the soft gold on the rim and catch.

Above: Example of a hunting case

Right: Example of a swing-out case

SWING-OUT MOVEMENTS

On some watches the movement swings out from the front. On these watches the movement can be swung out by unscrewing the crystal and pulling the stem out to release the movement. See example below.

Demi-Hunting case

Example of a 14 carat gold boxed hinged case, selling for $94 in 1890.

Below: Example of a reversible case to either hunting or open face.

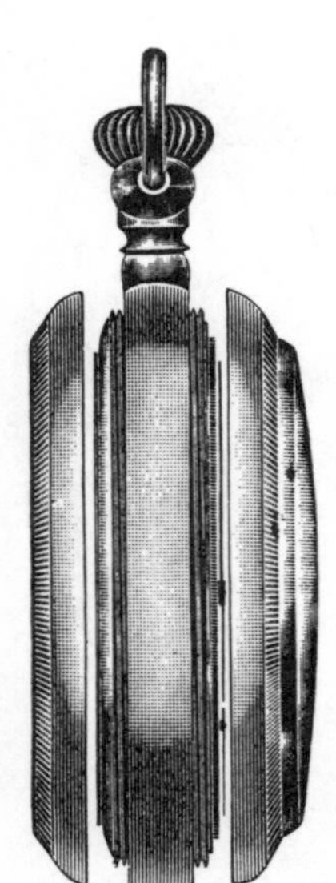

Left: Example of a screw bezel and screw back case.

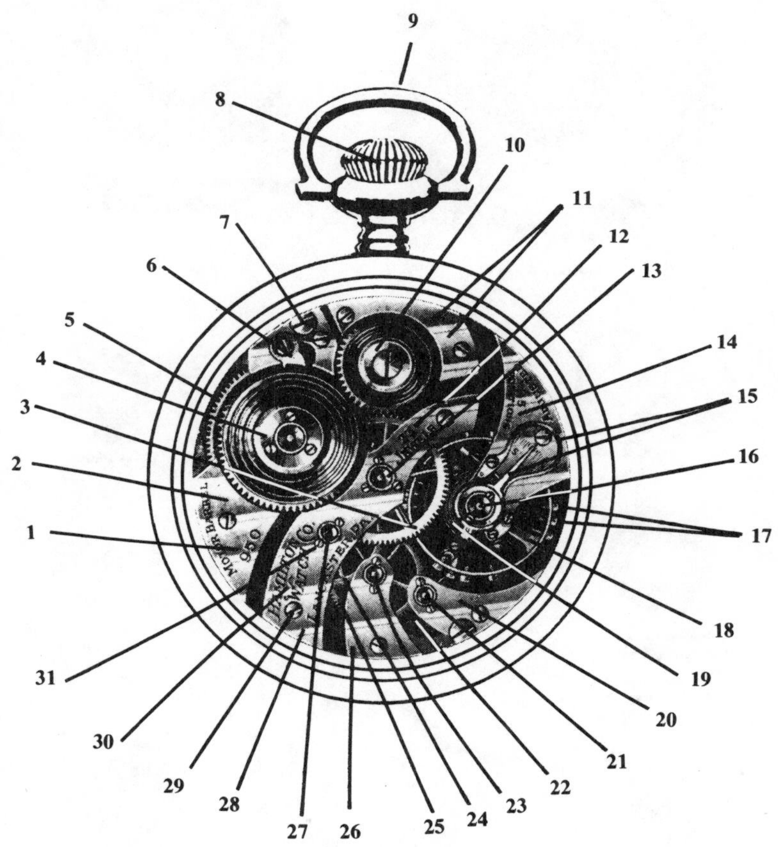

MOVEMENT IDENTIFICATION

1. Grade Number. **2.** Nickel Motor Barrel Bridge. **3.** Center Wheel (2nd Wheel). **4.** Winding Wheel with Jewel Setting. **5.** First Barrel Wheel. **6.** Winding Click. **7.** Case Screw. **8.** Pendant Crown. **9.** Pendant Bow or Swing Ring. **10.** Crown Wheel with Screw. **11** Damaskeening-horizontal pattern. **12.** Number of Jewels. **13.** Center Wheel Jewel with Setting. **14.** Adjusted to Heat, Cold, Isochronism & 5 Positions. **15.** Patented Regulator with Index & Spring. **16.** Balance End Stones (Diamonds, Rubys, & Sapphires were used). **17.** Balance Screws. **18.** Compensating Balance Wheel. **19.** Hairspring. **20.** Escapement Bridge. **21.** Escapement Wheel Jewel with Setting (Diamonds, Rubys, & Sapphires were used). **22.** Escapement Wheel. **23.** Fourth Wheel Jewel with Setting. **24.** Third Wheel. **25.** Fourth Wheel. **26.** Fourth Wheel Bridge. **27.** Third Wheel Jewel with Setting. **28.** Center & Third Wheel Bridge. **29.** Bridge Screw. **30.** Manufacturers Name & Location. **31.** Jewel Setting Screw.

WATCH PARTS

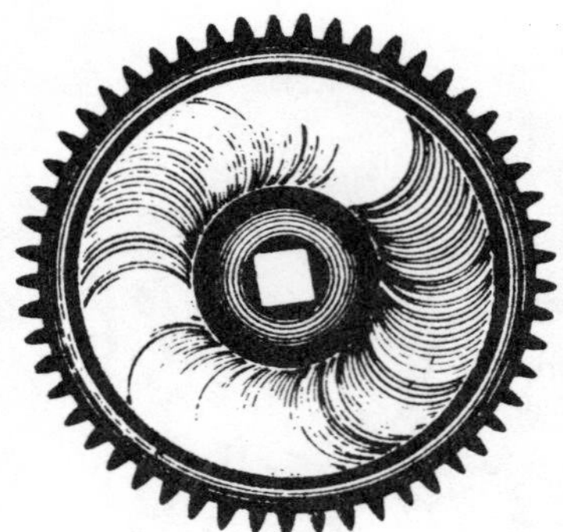

Ratchet Wheel

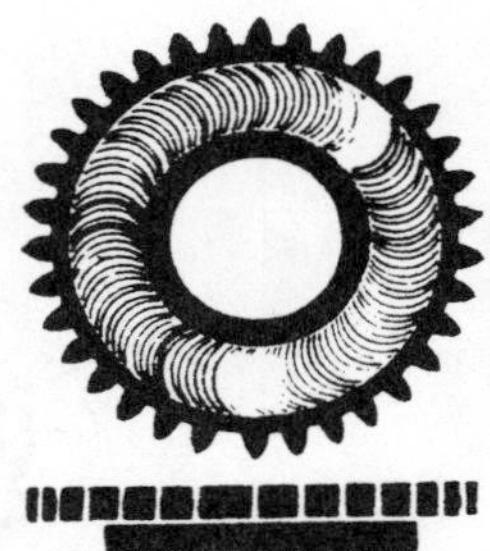

Crown or Main Wheel

Click Spring

Setting Cam

Bevel Pinion

Crown or Main Screw Washer

Winding Arbor

Winding and Setting Clutch

Setting Lever

Setting Spring

Click

Setting Spring Cam

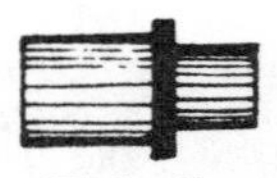

Winding Sleeve

Clutch Lever

WATCH PARTS

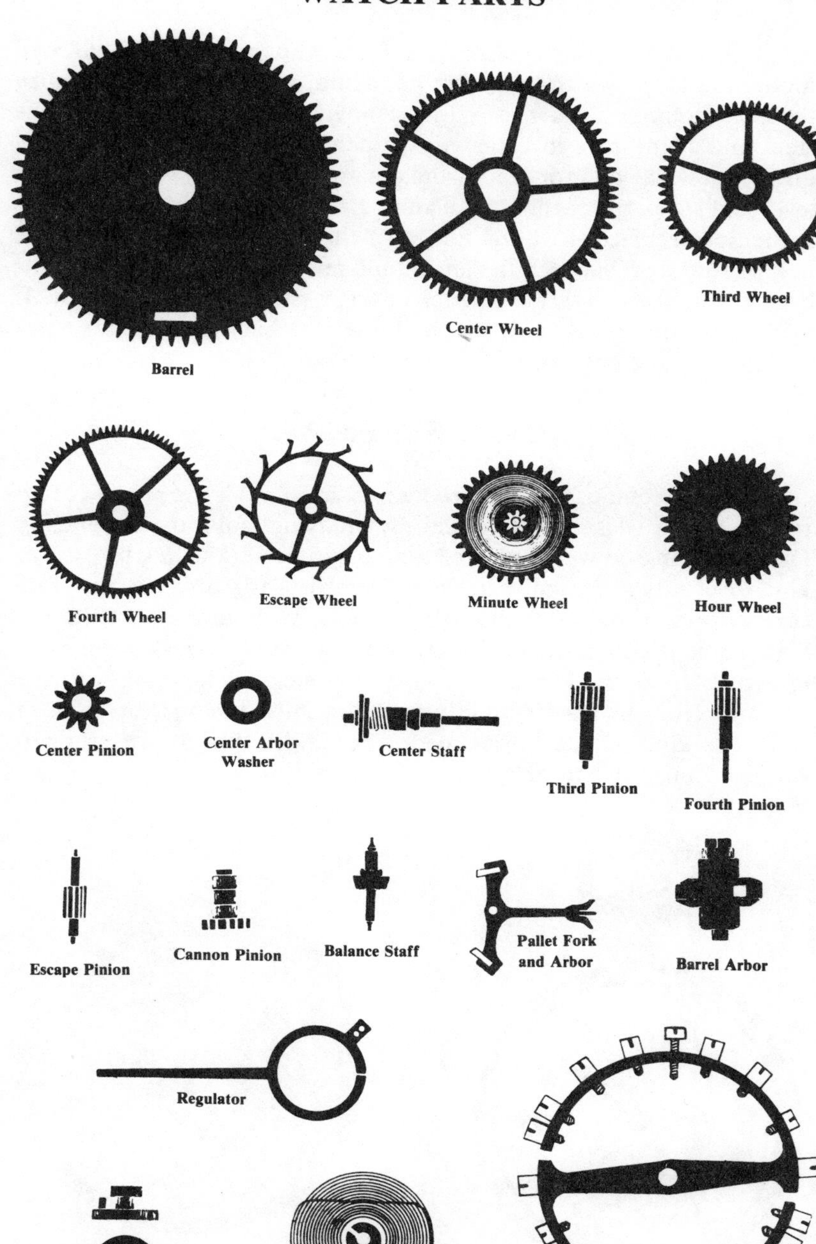
Barrel
Center Wheel
Third Wheel
Fourth Wheel
Escape Wheel
Minute Wheel
Hour Wheel
Center Pinion
Center Arbor Washer
Center Staff
Third Pinion
Fourth Pinion
Escape Pinion
Cannon Pinion
Balance Staff
Pallet Fork and Arbor
Barrel Arbor
Regulator
Combination Roller
Overcoil Hairspring
Balance Wheel

INSPECTING OPEN-FACED WATCHES

For watches with a screw-on front and back, as in railroad models, hold the watch in the left hand and, with the right hand, turn the bezel counter clockwise. While removing the bezel, hold onto the stem and swing ring in order not to drop the watch. Lay the bezel down, check the dial for cracks and crazing nicks, chips, etc. Look for lever and check to see that it will allow hands to be set. After close examination, replace the bezel and turn the watch over. Again, while holding the stem between the left thumb and index finger, remove the back cover. If it is a screw-on back cover, turn it counter clockwise. If it is a snap-on cover, look for the lip on the back and use a pocket knife to pry the back off.

DAMASKEENING

Damaskeening (pronounced dam-a-skeening) is the process of applying ornate designs on metal by inlaying gold or by etching. Damaskeening on watch plates became popular in the late 1870s. This kind of beauty and quality in the movement was a direct result of the competition in the watch industry. Illinois, Waltham, Rockford, and Seth Thomas competed fiercely for beauty. Some damaskeening was in two colors of metal such as copper and nickel. The process derives its name from Damascus, a city in Syria, most famous for its metal work. A kind of steel was made there with designs of wavy or varigated lines etched or inlaid on their swords.

Open Face Case

Example of Damaskeening

DISPLAY CASE WATCHES

Display case watches were used by salesmen and in jewelry stores to show the customer the movement. Both the front and back had a glass crystal. These are not rare, but are nice to have in a collection to show off a nice watch movement.

WATCH CASE PRODUCTION

Before the Civil War, watchmaking was being done on a very small scale, and most of the companies in business were making their own movements as well as their own cases. After the War, tradesmen set up shop specializing exclusively in cases, while other artisans were making the movements. The case factories, because of mass production, could more economically supply watch manufacturers with cases than the manufacturers could produce their own.

A patent was granted to James Boss on May 3, 1859, and the first gold-filled watch cases were made from sandwich-type sheets of metal. Boss was not the first to use gold-filled, but he did invent a new process that proved to be very successful, resulting in a more durable metal that Boss sold with a 20-year **money-back** guarantee.

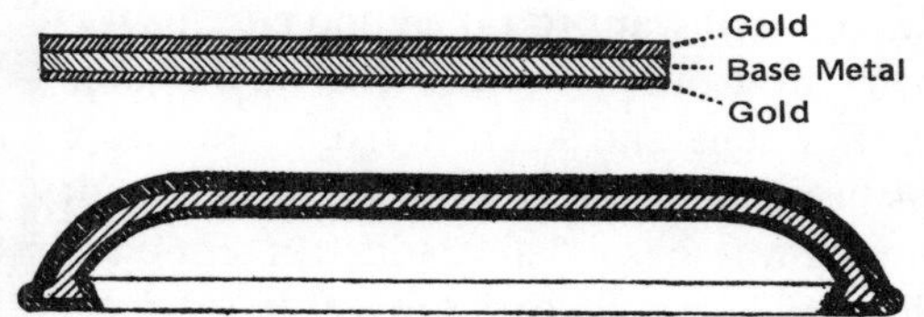

The illustration at left is a sandwiched type gold filled case.

GOLD CASE
WEIGHTS BY SIZE

Size & Style of Case	Pennyweights (DWT) Ex. Heavy	Heavy	Medium	Light	Ex. Light
18 size Hunting Case	60 to 65	50 to 55	45 to 50	40 to 45	35
16 size Hunting Case	55 to 60	45 to 50	40 to 45	35 to 40	32
18 size Open Face Case		40 to 45	38	35	
16 size Open Face Case		40	36	30	
12 size Open Face Case (Thin)					14
6 size Hunting Case	24	22	20	18	
0 size Hunting Case					14 to 16

An 18 size movement with a full plate weighs 50 DWT; a 16 size movement with a ¾ plate weighs 35 DWT. These weights do not include the case.

CARE OF WATCHES

To some people a watch is just a device that keeps time. They do not know the history of its development nor how it operates. They have no appreciation for improvements made over the years. They will seldom give it more than a fleeting thought that a watch is a true miracle of mechanical genius and skill. The average person will know it must be wound to run, that it has a mainspring and possibly a hairspring. Some even realize there are wheels and gears and, by some strange method, these work in harmony to keep time. If for some reason the watch should stop, the owner will merely take it to a watch repair shop and await the verdict on damage and cost.

To be a good collector one must have some knowledge of the components of a watch and how they work and the history of the development of the watch. To buy a watch on blind faith is indeed risky, but many collectors do it every day because they have limited knowledge.

How does a watch measure time and perform so well? Within the case one can find the fulcrum, lever, gear, bearing, axle, wheel, screw, and the spring which overcomes nature's law of gravity. All these parts harmonize to provide an accurate reading minute by minute. A good collector will be able to identify all of them.

After acquiring a watch, you will want to take good care of it. A watch should be cleaned inside and out. Dirt will wear it out much faster, and gummy oil will restrict it and keep it from running all together. After the watch has been cleaned it should be stored in a dry place. Rust is the No. 1 enemy. A watch is a delicate instrument but, if it is given proper care, it will provide many years of quality service. A pocket watch should be wound at regular intervals—about once every 24 hours, early each morning—so the mainspring has its full power to withstand the abuse of daily use. Do not carry a watch in the same pocket with articles that will scratch or tarnish the case. A fully wound watch can withstand a jar easier than a watch that has been allowed to run down. Always wind a watch and leave it running when you ship it. If you are one who enjoys carrying a watch be sure to have it cleaned at least once every two years.

EXAMINATION AND INSPECTION OF A WATCH BEFORE PURCHASING

The examination and inspection of a watch before purchasing is of paramount importance. This is by no means a simple task for there are many steps involved in a complete inspection.

The first thing you should do is to listen to a watch and see how it sounds. Many times the trained ear can pick up problems in the escapement and balance. The discriminating buyer will know that sounds cannot be relied on entirely because each watch sounds different, but the sound test is worthwhile and is comparable to the doctor putting the stethescope to a patient's heart as his first source of data.

Check the bow to see if it is fastened to the case well and look at the case to see if correction is necessary at the joints. The case should close firmly and tightly at both the back and front. (Should the case close too firmly, rub the rim with beeswax which will ease the condition and prolong the life of the rim.)

Take note of the dents, scratches, and wear and other evidences of misuse. Does the watch have a general good appearance? Check the bezel for proper fitting and the crystal to see if it is free of chips.

Remove the bezel and check the dial for chips and hairline cracks. Look for stains and discoloration and check to see if the dial is loose. It is important to note that a simple dial with only a single sunk dial is by nature a stronger unit due to the fact that a double sunk dial is constructed of three separate pieces.

If it is a stem-winder, try winding and setting. Problems in this area can be hard to correct, and parts are hard to locate and possibly may have to be handmade. If it is a lever set, pull the lever out to see if the lever sets properly into gear. Also check to see that the hands have proper clearance.

Now that the external parts have been inspected, open the case to view the movement. Check to see that the screws hold the movement in place securely. Note any repair marks and any missing screws. Make a visual check for rust and discolorations, dust, dirt and general appearance. If the movement needs cleaning and oiling, this should be deducted from the price of the watch as well as any repair that will have to be made.

Note the quality of the movement. Does it have raised gold jewel settings or a gold train (center wheel or all gears)? Are the jewels set in or pressed in? Does it have gold screws in the balance wheel? Sapphire pallets? Diamond end stones? Jeweled motor barrel? How many adjustments does it have? Does it have overall beauty and eye appeal?

Examine the balance for truth. First look directly down upon the balance to detect error truth in the roundness. Then look at it from the side to detect error in the flat swing or rotation. It should be smooth in appearance.

Examine the hairspring in the same manner to detect errors in truth. When a spring is true in the round, there will be no appearance of jumping when it is viewed from the upper side. The coils will appear to uniformly dilate and contract in perfect rhythm when the balance is in motion. Check the exposed portion of the train wheels for burred, bent, or broken teeth. Inspect pinions and pivots for wear. If a watch has complicated features such as a repeater, push the slides, plungers, and buttons to see that they are in good working order.

After the movement and case have been examined to your satisfaction and all the errors and faults are found, talk to the owner as to the history and his personal thoughts about the watch. Is the movement in the original case? Is the dial the original one? Just what has been replaced?

Has the watch been cleaned? Does it need any repairs? If so, can the seller recommend anyone to repair the watch?

Finally, see if the seller makes any type of guarantee. And get an address and phone number. It may be valuable if problems arise, or if you want to buy another watch in the future.

WATCH MOVEMENT PARTS

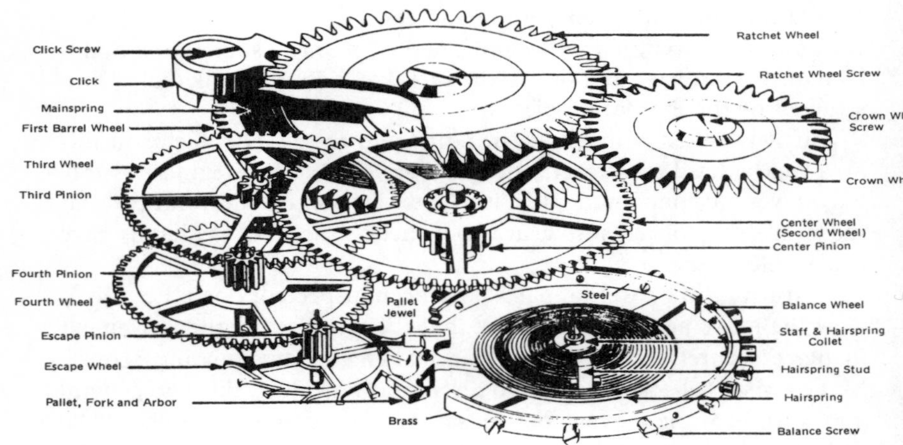

HOW A WATCH WORKS

There are five basic components of a watch:

1. The **mainspring** and its winding mechanism which provides power.
2. The **train** which consists of gears, wheels and pinions that turn the hands.
3. The **escapement** consisting of the escape wheel and balance which regulates or controls.
4. The **dial and hands** which tell the time.
5. The **housing** consisting of the case and plates which protect.

The motion of the balance serves the watch the same as a pendulum serves a clock. The balance wheel and roller oscillate in each direction moving the fork and lever by means of a ruby pin. As the lever moves back and forth it allows the escape wheel to unlock at even intervals (about 1/5 sec.) and causes the train of gears to move in one direction under the power of the mainspring. Thus, the mainspring is allowed to be let down or unwind one pulse at a time.

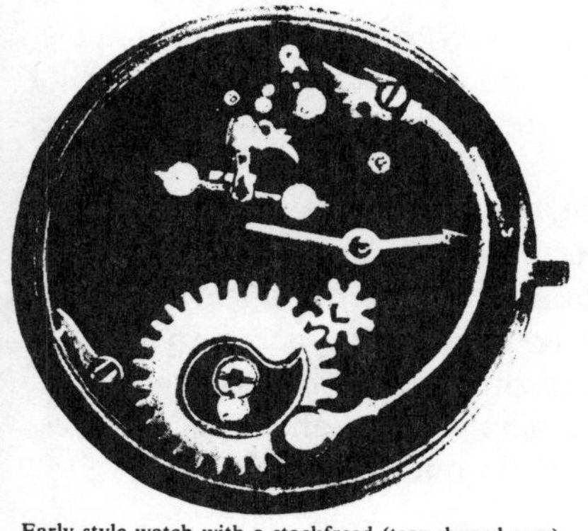

Early style watch with a stackfreed (tear shaped cam). Note the balance is dumbbell shaped.

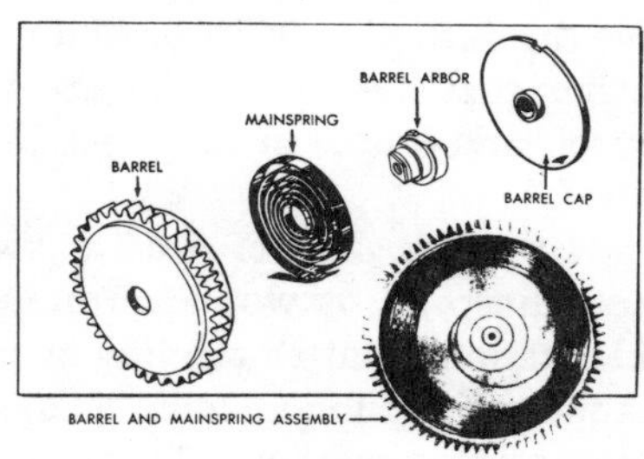

Power unit for modern watch showing the various parts.

THE MAINSPRING

Watches were developed from the early portable clocks. The coiled spring or mainspring provided the drive power. The first coiled springs were applied to clocks about 1435. For the watch, coiled springs were first used about 1510. The power from a mainspring is not consistent and this irregular power was disastrous to the first watches. The Germans' answer to irregular power was a device called a **stackfreed**. Another apparatus employed was the **fusee**. The fusee proved to be the best choice. At first catgut was used between the spring barrel and fusee. By around 1660 the catgut was replaced by a chain. Today, the fusee is still used in naval chronometers. One drawback to the fusee is the amount of space it takes up in the watch. Generally, the simplest devices are best.

The mainspring is made of a piece of hardened and tempered steel about 20 inches long and coiled in a closed barrel between the upper and lower plates of the movement. It is matched in degree of strength, width, and thickness most suitable for the watch's need or design. It is subject to differing conditions of temperature and tensions (the wound-up position having the greatest tension). The lack of uniformity in the mainspring affects the timekeeping qualities of a watch.

The power assembly in a watch consists of the mainspring, mainspring barrel, arbor, and cap. The mainspring furnishes the power to run the watch. It is coiled around the arbor and is contained in the mainspring barrel, which is cylindrical and has a gear on it which serves as the first wheel of the train. The arbor is a cylindrical shaft with a hook for the mainspring in the center of the body. The cap is a flat disk which snaps into a recess in the barrel. A hook on the inside of the mainspring barrel is for the purpose of attaching the mainspring to the barrel.

The mainspring is made of a long thin strip of steel, hardened to give the desired resiliency. Mainsprings vary in size but are similar in design; they have a hook on the outer end to attach to the mainspring barrel, and a hole in the inner end to fasten to the mainspring barrel arbor.

By turning the crown clockwise, the barrel arbor is rotated and the mainspring is wound around it. The mainspring barrel arbor is held stationary after winding by means of the ratchet wheel and click. As the mainspring uncoils, it causes the mainspring barrel to revolve. The barrel is meshed with the pinion on the center wheel, and as it revolves it sets the train wheels in motion. Pocket and wrist watches, in most cases, will run up to 36 hours on one winding.

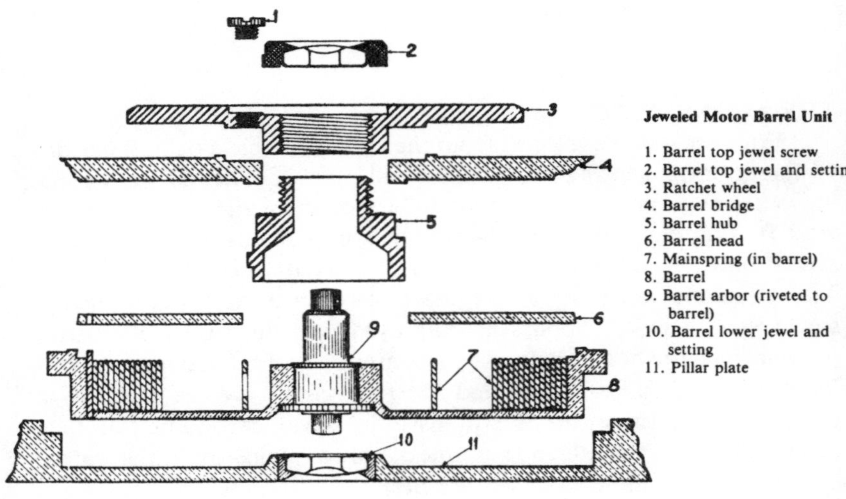

THE HAIRSPRING

The hairspring is the brain of the watch and is kept in motion by the mainspring. The hairspring is the most delicate tension spring made. It is a piece of flat wire about 12 inches long, 1/100th of an inch wide, 2½/1,000th of an inch thick, and weighs only about 1/9,000th of a pound. Thousands of these hairsprings can be made from one pound of steel. The hairspring controls the action of the balance wheel. The hairspring steel is drawn through the diamond surfaces to a third the size of a human hair. There are two kinds of hairsprings in the watches of later times, the flat one and the Breguet. The Breguet (named for its French inventor) is an overcoil given to the spring.

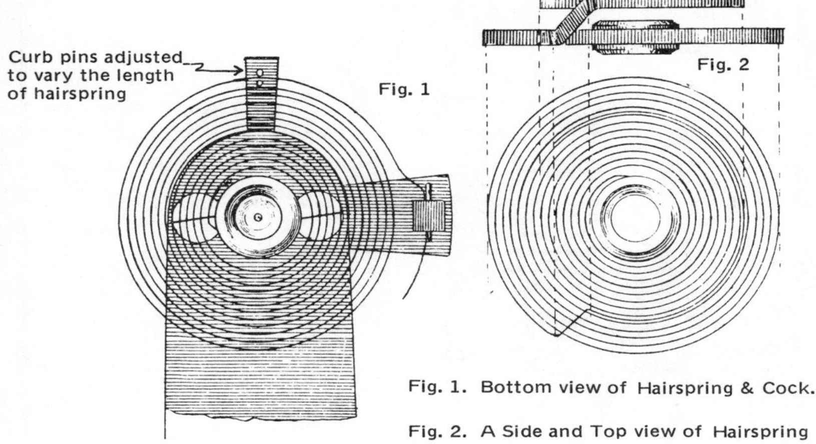

Fig. 1. Bottom view of Hairspring & Cock.

Fig. 2. A Side and Top view of Hairspring

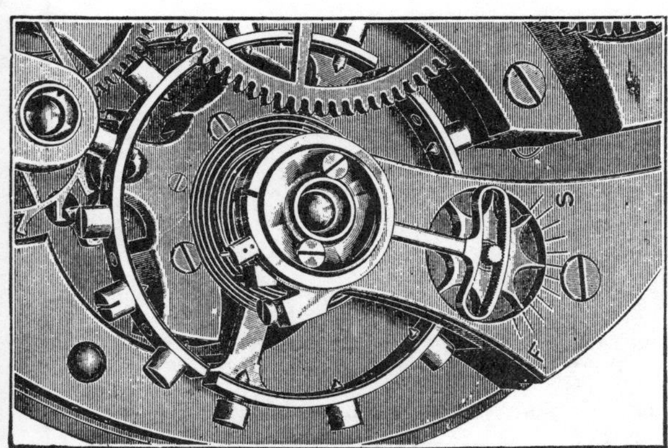

A modern style **Regulator.** Note triangular shaped hairspring stud which is located on the balance bridge between the screw and curb pin.

There are two methods for overcoil, the oldest being the way the spring is bent by hand; with the other method the overcoil is bent or completed in a form at one end and at the same time is hardened and tempered in the form. The hairspring contracts and expands 432,000 times a day.

THE TRAIN

The time train consists of the mainspring barrel, center wheel and pinion, third wheel and pinion, fourth wheel and pinion, and escape wheel which is part of the escapement. The function of the time train is to reduce the power of the mainspring and extend its time to 36 hours or more. The mainspring supplies energy in small units to the escapement, and the escapement delays the power from being spent too quickly.

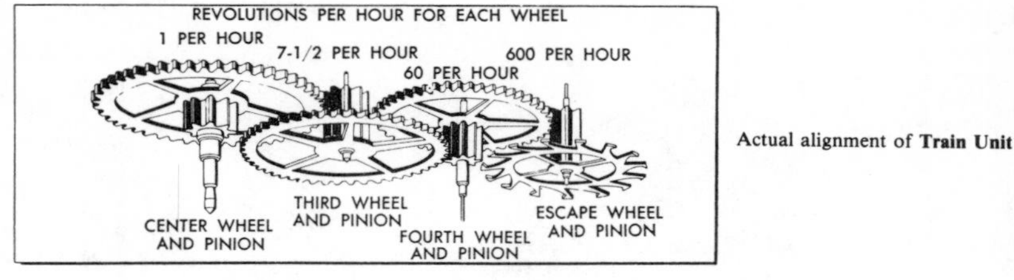

Actual alignment of **Train Unit**

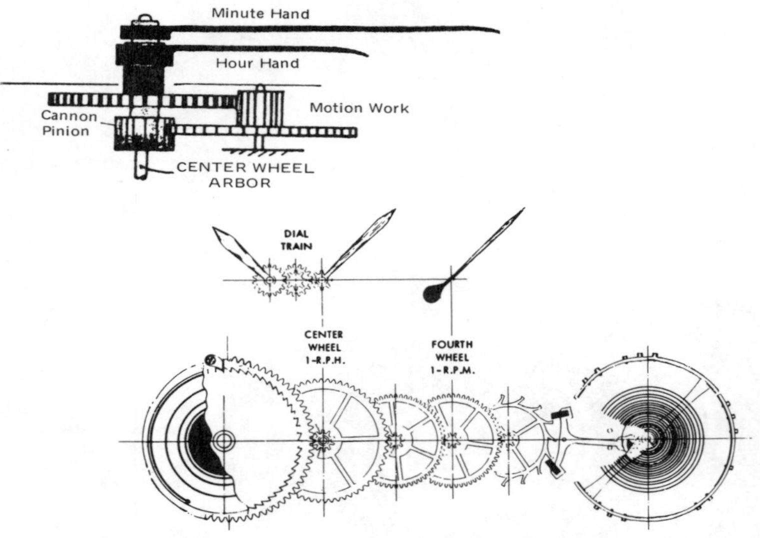

The **Train Unit** starting with the mainspring and barrel, the center wheel, the third wheel, the fourth wheel, the escape wheel, the lever, pallet and fork, and the balance wheel with hairspring.

The long center wheel arbor projects through the pillar plate and above the dial, to receive the cannon pinion and hour wheel. The cannon pinion receives the minute hand and the hour wheel the hour hand. As the mainspring drives the barrel, the center wheel is rotated once each hour.

The center wheel is in the center of the watch and turns once every hour. It is the largest wheel in the train, and the arbor or post of the center wheel carries the minute hand. The center wheel pinion is in mesh with the mainspring barrel (pinions follow and the wheel supplies the power). The center wheel is in mesh with the third wheel pinion (the third wheel makes eight turns to each turn of the center wheel). The third wheel is in mesh with the fourth wheel pinion, and the fourth wheel pinion is in mesh with the escape wheel pinion. The fourth wheel post carries the second hand and is in a 1:60 ratio to the center wheel (the center wheel turns once every hour and the fourth wheel turns 60 turns every hour). The escape wheel has 15 teeth (shaped like a flat foot) and works with two pallets on the lever. The two pallet jewels lock and unlock the escape wheel at intervals (1/5 sec.) allowing the train of gears to move in one direction under the influence of the mainspring. The lever (quick train) vibrates 18,000 times to one turn of the center wheel (every hour). The hour hand works from a motion train. The mainspring barrel makes about five turns every 36 hours.

SOLID GOLD TRAIN

Some watches have a gold train instead of brass wheels. These watches are more desirable. To identify gold wheels within the train, look at a Hamilton 992: the center wheel is made of gold and the other wheels are made of brass. (The center wheel is in the center of the watch.) Why a gold train? Gold is soft, but it has a smooth surface and it molds easily. Therefore, the wheels have less friction. These wheels do not move fast, and a smooth action is more necessary than a hard metal. Gold does not tarnish or rust and is non-magnetic. The arbors and pinions in these watches will be steel. Many watches have some gold in them, and the collector should learn to distinguish it.

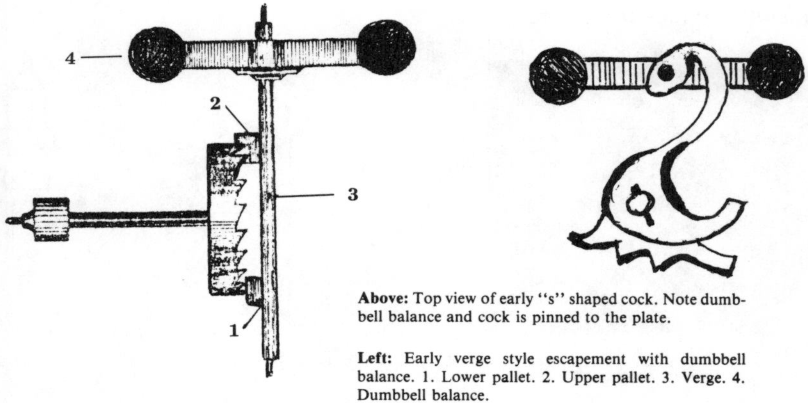

Above: Top view of early "s" shaped cock. Note dumbbell balance and cock is pinned to the plate.

Left: Early verge style escapement with dumbbell balance. 1. Lower pallet. 2. Upper pallet. 3. Verge. 4. Dumbbell balance.

TYPES OF ESCAPEMENTS

The verge escapement is the earliest form of escapement. It was first used in clocks as far back as the early 1300s. The verge escapement consists of a crown escape wheel, a verge which has two flags called pallets, and a balance. Early German watches had a balance shaped like a dumb bell; later most other watches used a balance shaped like a wheel. This German balance is called a "foliot." The crude weights of the foliot could be adjusted closer to or farther from the center of the balance for better timekeeping. Another design from that period was the circular balance. The circular balance was used by Christiaan Huygens in 1675 when he introduced the hairspring. This remarkable invention was used from that time onward.

The verge escapement was used by Luther Goddard in America as

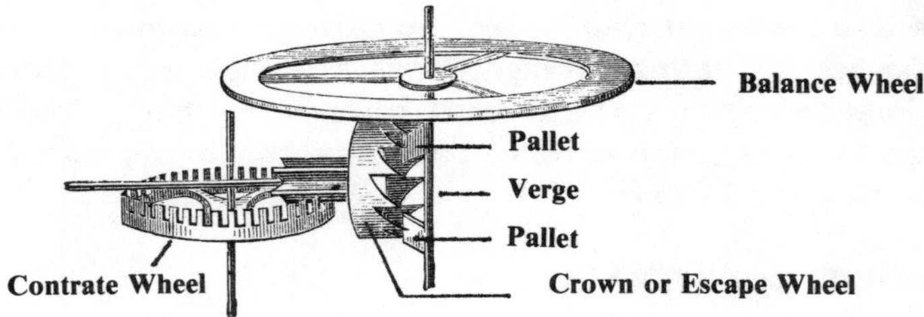

A later style **Verge Escapement** with a more common balance wheel.

well as most of the Colonial watchmakers.

About 1725 the cylinder escapement was invented by George Graham, an Englishman. His cylinder escapement was a great improvement over the verge. Even so, the cylinder escapement was not popular until Abraham Louis Breguet adopted the idea about 1765. This escapement wears out rather rapidly, unfortunately.

Note: *We have never seen a Colonial watch that used a cylinder escapement in a movement. If you have one or know where one is, please contact the author.*

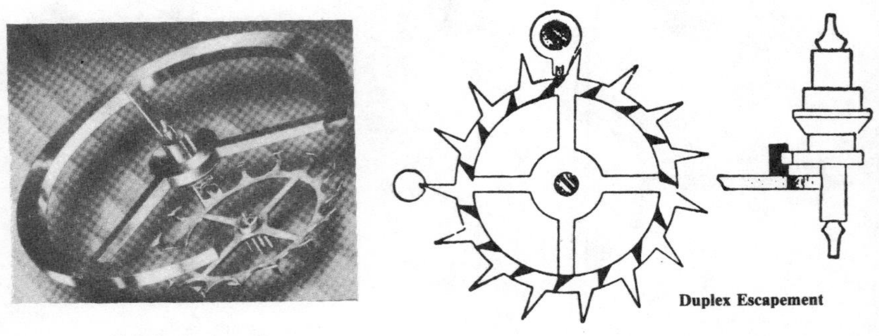

Duplex Escapement

Cylinder Escapemnet

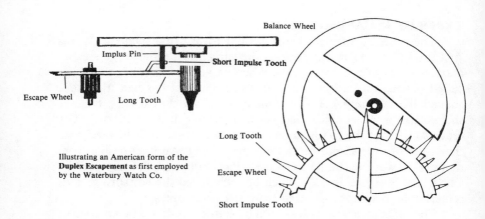

Illustrating an American form of the **Duplex Escapement** as first employed by the Waterbury Watch Co.

The duplex escapement is accredited generally to Pierre LeRoy, a Frenchman, around 1750 but was never popular in France. This type of escapement gained favor in England up to the mid 1850s. Thomas Tyrer patented it in England in 1782. The New England Watch Co. of Waterbury, Conn., used the duplex from 1898 until 1910. The Waterbury Watch Company used it from 1880 to 1898.

The roller and lever action escapement was invented by Thomas Mudge in 1750.

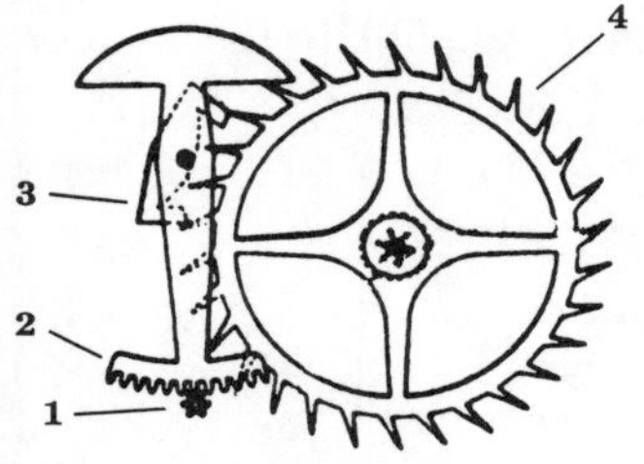

Rack and lever escapement. 1. Balance wheel pinion. 2. Rack. 3. Lever. 4. Ratchet escape wheel.

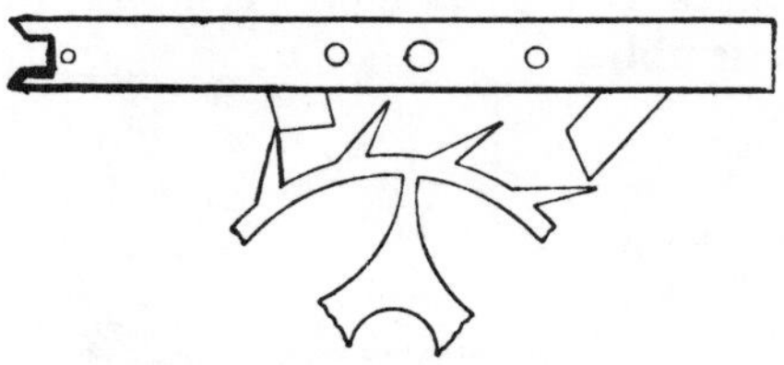
English style right angle lever which was used in earlier American made watches.

The rack lever escapement was invented by Hautefeuille in 1722. The famous Breguet used the lever early in the 1800s. By 1830 the English watchmakers had established the superiority of the lever escapement. In France and Switzerland the teeth of the lever escapement wheel were clubbed—that is to say, the point of the teeth were cut away to give a longer impulse plane. In England, pointed or ratchet teeth were preferred; also in England the right-angle lever was preferred over the straight line lever also referred to as the Swiss lever. Pitkins and Custer both used the lever escapements. The right-angle lever was used in the Warren & Samuel Curtis as well as early Elgin, Newark, Tremont, New York, early Hampden, early Illinois, and Cornell watches. The American factories settled on a Swiss style escapement (straight line lever and club tooth escape wheel) by the 1870s.

PURPOSE OF ESCAPE WHEEL

If a movement consisted only of the mainspring and a train of wheels, and the mainspring were would up, the train would run at full speed resulting in the power being spent in a few moments. For this reason, the escapement has been arranged to check it. The duty of the escapement is to allow each tooth of the escape wheel to pass at a regulated interval. The escapement is of no service alone and, therefore, must have some other arrangement to measure and regulate these intervals. This is accomplished by the balance assembly.

The escape wheel is in most cases made of steel and is staked on a pinion and arbor. It is the last wheel of the train and, therefore, connects the train with the escapement. It is constructed so that the pallet jewels move in and out between its teeth, allowing but one tooth to escape at a time. The teeth are "club-shaped" because of the addition of impulse faces to the end of the teeth.

The pallet jewels are set at an angle to make their inside corners reach over three teeth and two spaces of the escape wheel. The outside corners of the jewels will reach over two teeth and three spaces of the escape wheel with a small amount of clearance. At the opposite end of the pallet, directly under the center of the fork slot, is a steel or brass pin called the guard pin. The fork is the connecting link to the balance assembly.

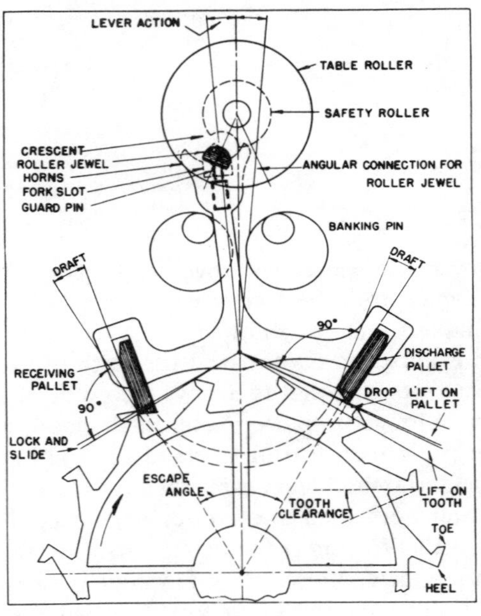

BALANCE AND HAIRSPRING

The rotation of the balance wheel is controlled by the hairspring. The inner end of the hairspring is pinned to the collet, and the collet is held friction-tight on the staff above the balance wheel. The outer end of the hairspring is pinned to a stud which is held stationary on the balance cock by the stud screw. The roller jewel is cemented in the large roller assembly, which is mounted on the staff directly under the balance wheel. Under the first roller is a smaller one which acts as a safety roller, necessary because of the crescent cut out in the roller table which allows the guard pin of the escapement assembly to pass through.

The balance wheel rotates clockwise and counterclockwise on its axis by means of the impulse it receives from the escapement. The motion of the balance wheel is constant due to the coiling and uncoiling of the hairspring. The impulse that has been transmitted to the roller jewel by the swinging of the pallet fork to the left, causes the balance to rotate in a counterclockwise direction. The position of the fork allows the roller jewel to move out of the slot of the fork freely and in the same direction. The fork continues on until it reaches the banking pin. Meanwhile the balance continues in the same direction until the tension of the hairspring overcomes the momentum of the balance wheel. When this occurs the balance returns to its original position, which causes the roller jewel to again enter the slot of the fork.

Pallet and Escape Tooth Action. The momentum that has been built up during the return of the balance, causes the roller pin to impart an impulse on the inside of the fork slot. This impulse is great enough to push the fork away from its position against the banking pin. As the fork is pushed away, it causes the pallet stone to slide on the toe of the escape wheel tooth. When the pallet stone has slid down

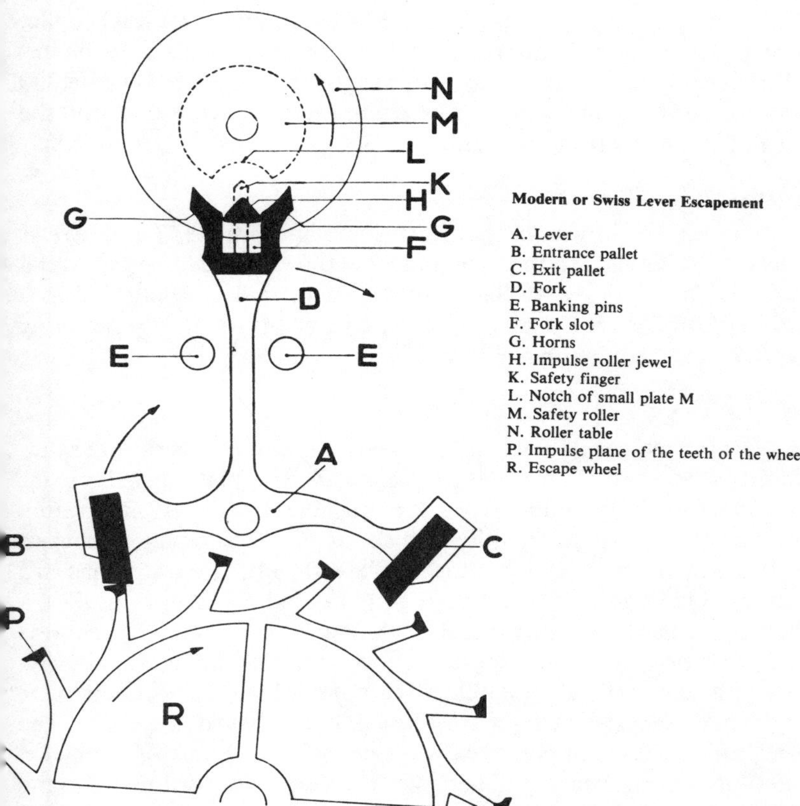

Modern or Swiss Lever Escapement

A. Lever
B. Entrance pallet
C. Exit pallet
D. Fork
E. Banking pins
F. Fork slot
G. Horns
H. Impulse roller jewel
K. Safety finger
L. Notch of small plate M
M. Safety roller
N. Roller table
P. Impulse plane of the teeth of the wheel
R. Escape wheel

to its edge, it frees the escape wheel tooth, thereby unlocking the escape wheel. The escape wheel, being impelled by the force of the mainspring, starts to rotate. As the escape wheel turns, the tooth glides along the impulse face of the pallet jewel, forcing it to move out of the way. The moving pallet carries the fork with it and imparts the impulse to the roller jewel. The right pallet stone intercepts a tooth of the escape wheel to lock it, as the fork moves toward the banking pin. Having a short "run" left to the banking pin, the pressure of the escape wheel tooth against the locking face of the pallet jewel draws the stone deeper into the escape wheel and, therefore, causes the fork to complete its run and holds it against the banking pin. Meanwhile the balance continues in a clockwise direction until the tension of the hairspring overcomes the momentum of the balance and returns it to its original position.

Rate of Escape Tooth Release. Through the motion of the escapement, the mainspring keeps the balance vibrating, and the balance regulates the train. The escape wheel has 15 teeth and is allowed to revolve 10 turns per minute. Thus, 150 teeth glide over each pallet stone in 1 minute. The gliding of the escape wheel teeth over the impulse faces of the pallet stones will cause the balance to vibrate 300 vibrations or beats per minute. These vibrations will continue until the force of the mainspring is spent.

SCREWS

Screws used in watches are very small and precise. These screws measure 254 threads to the inch and 47,000 of them can be put into a thimble. The screws were hardened and tempered and polished to a cold hard brilliance. By looking at these screws through a magnifying glass one can see the uniformity.

THE PLATES

The movement of a watch has two plates and the works are sandwiched in between. The plates are called the top plate and the pillar plate. The top plate fully covers the movement. The ¾ plate watch and the balance bridge are flush and about ¼ of a full plate is cut out to allow for the balance, thus the ¾ plate. The bridge watch has two or three fingers to hold the wheels in place and together are called a bridge, just as the balance is called the balance bridge. The metal is generally brass, but on better grade watches, nickel is used. The full plate is held apart by four pillars. In older watches the pillars were very fancy, and the plates were pinned, not screwed, together. The plates can be gilded or engraved when using brass. Some of the nickel plates have damaskeening. There are a few watches with plates made of gold. The plates are also used to hold the jewels, settings, etc. Over 30 holes are drilled in each plate for pillars, pivots, and screws.

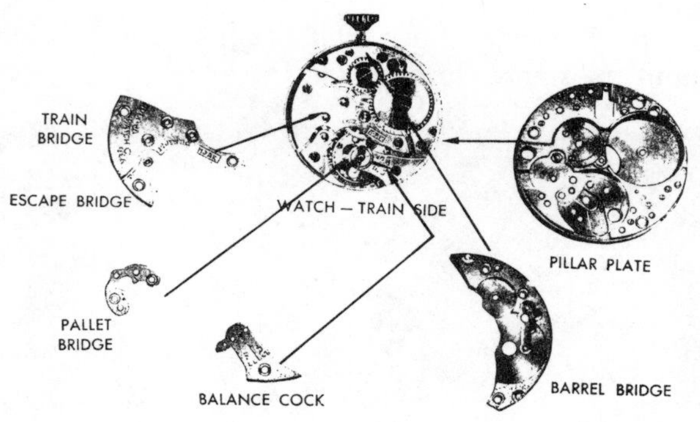

The plates and bridges which hold all the parts in proper relation to each other.

The pinion is the smaller of the two wheels that exist on the shaft or arbor. They are small steel gears and usually have six teeth called leaves. Steel is used wherever there is great strain, but where there is much friction, steel and brass are used together: one gear of brass, and a pinion of steel. After the leaves have been cut, the pinions are hardened, tempered, and polished.

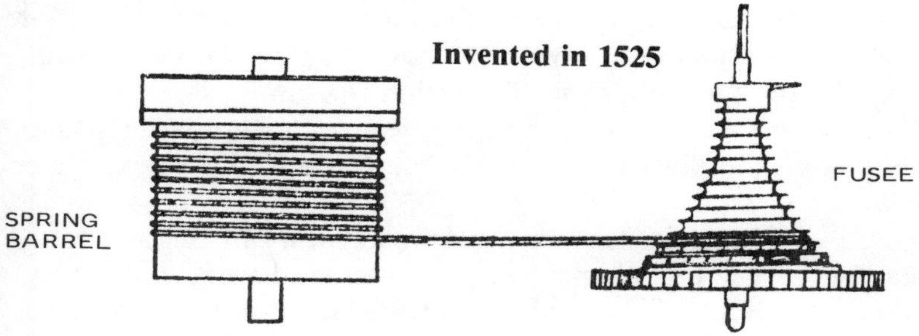

THE FUSEE

A mainspring gives less and less power as it lets down. To equalize the power a fusee was first used. Fusee leverage increases as the mainspring lets down. A fusee is smaller at the top for a full mainspring. When the chain is at the bottom, the mainspring is almost spent, and the fusee has more leverage. Leonardo da Vinci is said to have invented the fusee.

When the mainspring is fully wound, it also pulls the hardest. At that time the chain is at the small end of the fusee. As the spring grows weaker, the chain descends to the larger part of the fusee. In shifting the tension, it equalizes the power.

On the American watch, the fusee was abandoned for the most part in 1850 and an adjustment is used on the hairspring and balance wheel to equalize the power through the 24 hours. When a watch is first wound the mainspring has no more power than it does when it is nearly run down. With or without the fusee the number of parts in a watch are about the same: close to 800.

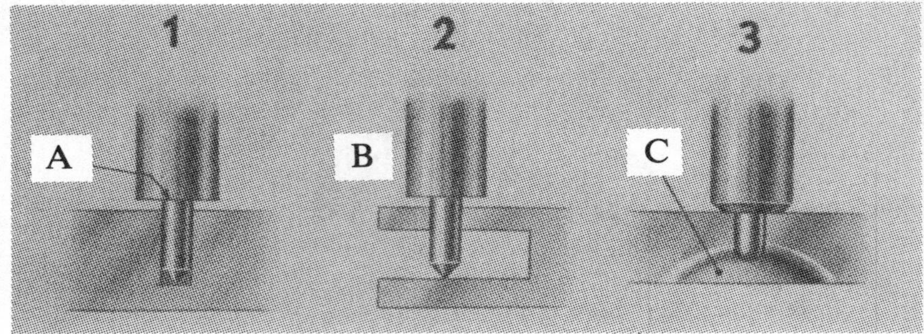

1. Illustration of pivot before 1700. 2. Pivot used in early 1700s. 3. Pivot used in late 1700s to present

JEWELS AND PIVOTS

Before 1700 holes were drilled only part way into the plates and the pivot rested directly on the bottom of the hole, as in Illustration No. 1. The shoulder of the pivot was above the plate, however, reducing part of the function, as in Illustration No. 1A.

In the early 1700s, a French watchmaker Sully improved the pivot friction as seen in Illustration No. 2B. Illustration No. 3 shows a later improvement.

N. F. de Duiller of Geneva, in conjunction with Peter and Jacob Debaufre, French immigrants living in London, developed a method of piercing jewels. This method was patented in 1704; however, it was not until around 1800 that holed jewels started to appear in watch movements and then only in high grade watches.

In the mid-1800s experiments were already being made for artificial rubies. In 1891 Fremy solved the problem and by the early 1900s the synthetic ruby was popular.

SHOCK ABSORBERS

When a watch is dropped or subjected to a hard shock, the balance and pivots usually suffer the most.

A shock-resisting device was invented by Breguet in 1789; he called it a parachute. This device was a spring steel arm supporting the endstone. The parachute gives a cushioning effect to the balance staff.

The American pocket watch industry tried to find a device to protect pocket watch pivots, but it was the Swiss who perfected the devices for wrist watches around 1930.

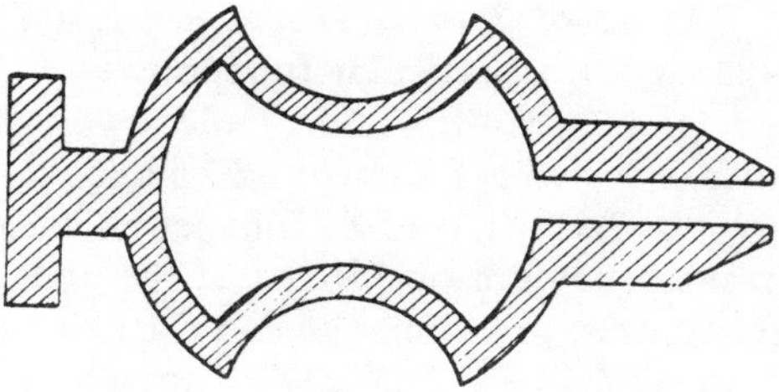

Above: Incabloc
Left: Parachute
Below: Illustrates shock absorbing system. Note end stone and spring in raised position giving a cushioning effect to the balance staff.

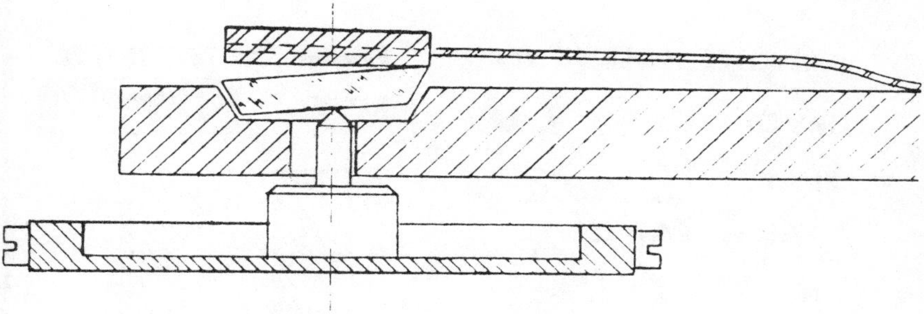

JEWEL COUNT

Jewels are used as bearings to reduce metal-to-metal contacts which produce friction and wear. They improve the performance and accuracy of the watch, and materially prolong its usefulness. The materials used for making watch jewels are diamonds, sapphires, rubies, and garnets. The diamond is the hardest but is seldom used except for cap jewels. The sapphire is the next in hardness and is the most commonly used because of its fine texture. Rubies and garnets are softer than sapphires. They add to the outward appearance of the watch but do not have the fine texture of the sapphire jewel.

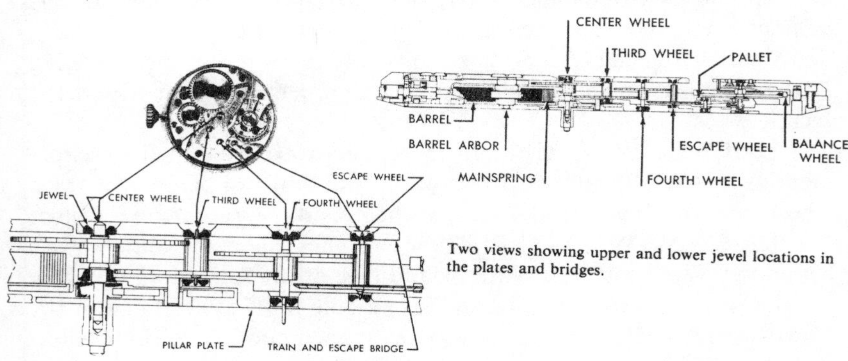

Two views showing upper and lower jewel locations in the plates and bridges.

Types of Jewels. Watch jewels are of four distinct types, each type having a particular function.

(1) HOLE JEWELS. Hole jewels are used to form the bearing surface for wheel arbors and balance staff pivots.

(2) CAP JEWELS. Cap jewels (also called end stones) are flat jewels. They are positioned at the ends of wheel staffs, outside the hole jewels, and limit the end thrust of the staff.

(3) ROLLER JEWELS. The roller jewel (pin) is positioned on the roller table to receive the impulse for the balance from the fork.

(4) PALLET JEWELS. The pallet jewels (stones) are the angular-shaped jewels positioned in the pallet to engage the teeth of the escape wheel.

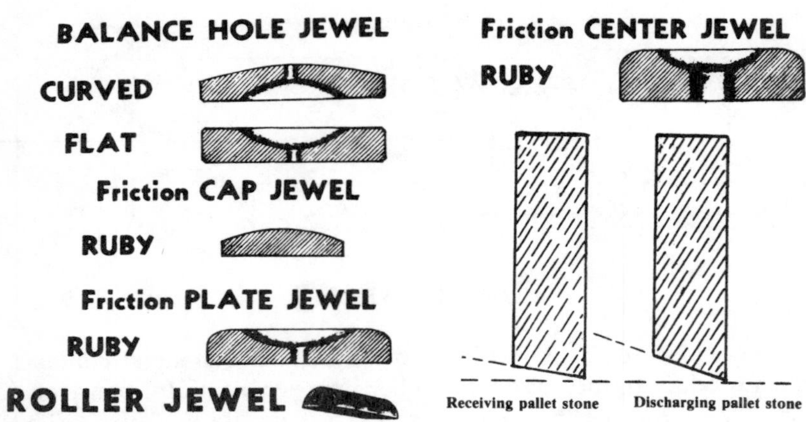

Number and Location of Jewels. Most watches have either 7, 9, 11, 15, 17, 19, 21, or 23 jewels. The location of the jewels varies somewhat in different makes and grades, but the general practice is as follows:

7-JEWEL WATCHES. Seven-jewel watches have: one hole jewel at each end of the balance staff; one cap jewel at each end of the balance staff; one roller jewel; and two pallet jewels.

9-JEWEL WATCHES. These have the seven jewels mentioned in 7-jewel watches, with the addition of a hole jewel at each end of the escape wheel.

11-JEWEL WATCHES. In these, seven are used in the escapement as in 7-jewel watches. In addition, the four top pivots (the third wheel, the fourth wheel, the escape wheel, and the pallet) are jeweled.

15-JEWEL WATCHES. These watches have the nine jewels found in 9-jewel watches, with the addition of the following: one hole jewel at each end of the pallet staff; one hole jewel at each end of the fourth-wheel staff; and one hole jewel at each end of the third-wheel staff.

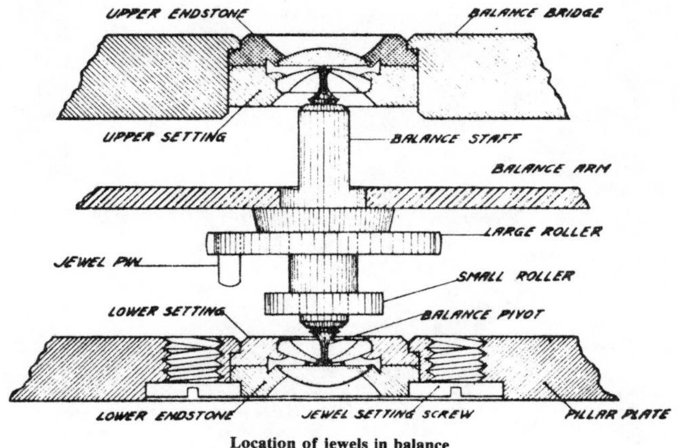

Location of jewels in balance

17-JEWEL WATCHES. The 15 jewels in 15-jewel watches are used with the addition of one hole jewel located at each end of the center wheel staff.

19-JEWEL WATCHES. In these watches, the jewels are distributed as in the 17-jewel watch, with the addition of one for each pivot of the barrel or mainspring.

21-JEWEL WATCHES. The jewels in these are distributed as in the 17-jeweled grade, with the addition of two cap jewels each for the pallet and escape wheel.

23-JEWEL WATCHES. The jewels are distributed as in the 21-jewel watch, with the addition of one for each pivot of the barrel or mainspring.

24-, 25-, and 26-JEWEL WATCHES. In all of these watches, the additional jewels were distributed as cap jewels. These were not very functional but were offered as prestige movements for the person who wanted more.

In many cases, these jewel arrangements varied according to manufacturer. All jeweled watches will not fit these descriptions.

WINDING AND SETTING

The simplest but not the most practical method for winding up the mainspring of a pocket watch was to wind the barrel staff by means of a key, but then it is necessary to open up the watch case. And the key method of winding proved unpopular, as oftentimes the key became lost.

The modern principle of the winding of the mainspring and hand-setting by pulling on the crown dates back to 1842. We owe this combination to Adrian Philippe, associate of Patek, of Geneva.

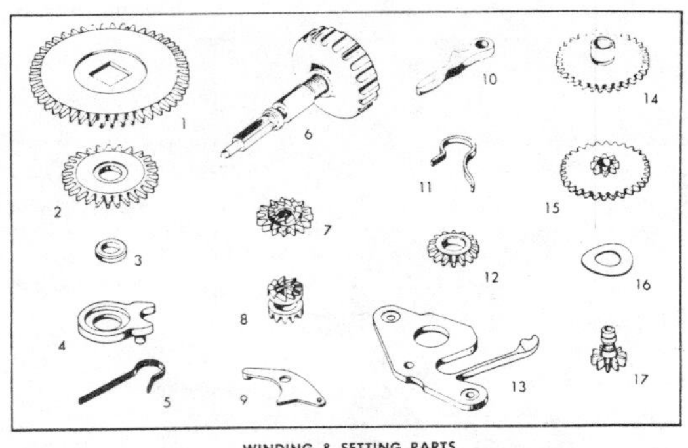

WINDING & SETTING PARTS

1. Ratchet Wheel
2. Crown Wheel
3. Crown Wheel Center
4. Click
5. Click Spring
6. Stem and Crown
7. Winding Pinion
8. Clutch Wheel
9. Setting Lever
10. Clutch Lever
11. Clutch Lever Spring
12. Setting Wheel
13. Yoke
14. Hour Wheel
15. Minute Wheel
16. Dial Washer
17. Cannon Pinion

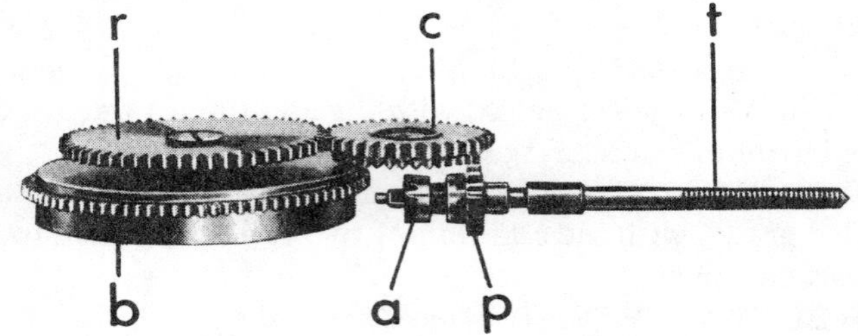

Winding Mechanism. a—Winding and setting clutch. p— Winding pinion. b—Barrel. r—Ratchet wheel. c—Crown or main wheel. t—Winding arbor.

The winding and setting mechanism consists of the stem, crown, winding pinion, clutch wheel, setting wheel, setting lever, clutch lever, clutch spring, crown wheel, and ratchet wheel. When the stem is pushed in, the clutch lever throws the clutch wheel to winding position. Then, when the stem is turned clockwise, it causes the winding pinion to turn the crown and ratchet wheels. The ratchet wheel is fitted on the square of the mainspring arbor and is held in place with a screw. When the stem and crown are turned, the ratchet wheel turns and revolves the arbor which winds the mainspring, thereby giving motive power to the train. Pulling the stem and crown outward pushes the setting lever against the clutch lever, engaging the clutch wheel with the setting wheel. The setting wheel is in constant mesh with the minute wheel; therefore, turning the stem and crown permits setting the hands to any desired time.

The dial train consists of the cannon pinion, minute, and hour wheels. The cannon pinion is a hollow steel pinion which is mounted on the center wheel arbor. A stud which is secured in the pillar plate holds the minute wheel in mesh with the cannon pinion. To the minute

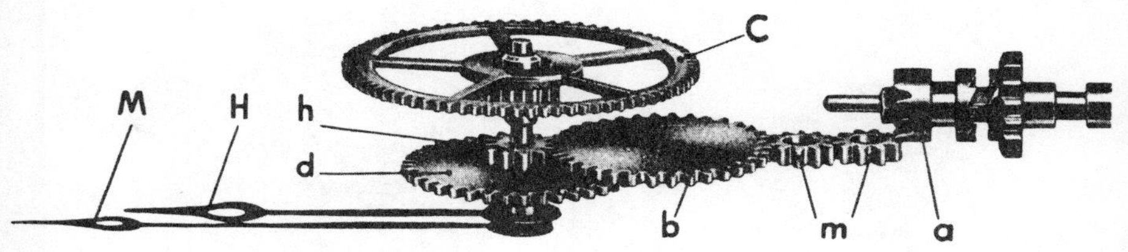

Setting Mechanism. Clutch **a** meshes with **m** and the minute works wheel **b**. The minute works wheel meshes with the canon pinion **h**. The hour canon **d** bears the hour hand **H**. **C**—Center wheel. **M**—Minute hand.

wheel is attached a small pinion which is meshed with the hour wheel.

The center arbor revolves once per hour. A hand affixed to the cannon pinion on the center arbor would travel around the dial once per hour. This hand is used to denote minutes. The minute wheel is in mesh with the cannon pinion. The hour wheel has a pipe that allows the hour wheel to set over the cannon pinion. The hour wheel meshes with the minute wheel pinion. This completes the train of the cannon pinion, minute wheel, and hour wheel. The ratio between the cannon pinion and the hour wheel is 12 to 1; therefore, the hand affixed to the hour wheel is to denote the hours. With this arrangement, time is recorded and read.

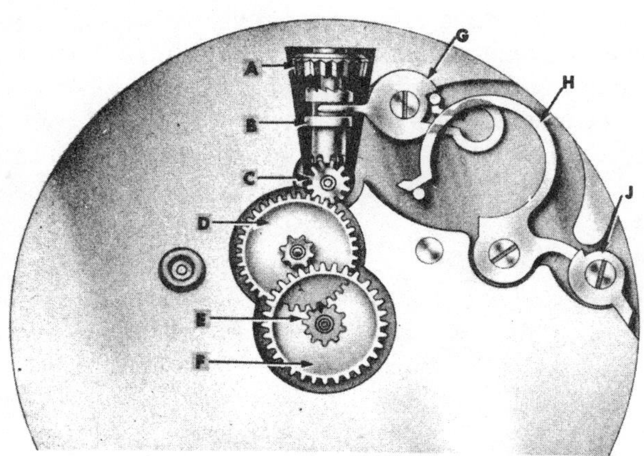

A—PINION
B—CLUTCH WHEEL
C—SETTING WHEEL
D—MINUTE WHEEL
E—CANNON PINION
F—HOUR WHEEL
G—CLUTCH LEVER
H—SETTING SPRING
J—SETTING SPRING CAM

Automatic Winding. The self-winding watch uses the movements of the body in order to wind up the mainspring slowly and nearly continuously. The first pocket self-winding watches were executed by a watchmaker from Le Locle, Abraham-Louis Perrelet, around 1770. They were improved soon after by Abraham-Louis Breguet. In the case of the pocket watch, the movements causing the winding of the watch were essentially the result of walking. This system of watches was never widely adopted. This was rather a fancy model rather than a really useful one. Herman von der Heydt was the only maker in

Early self wind pocket watch by Breguet.

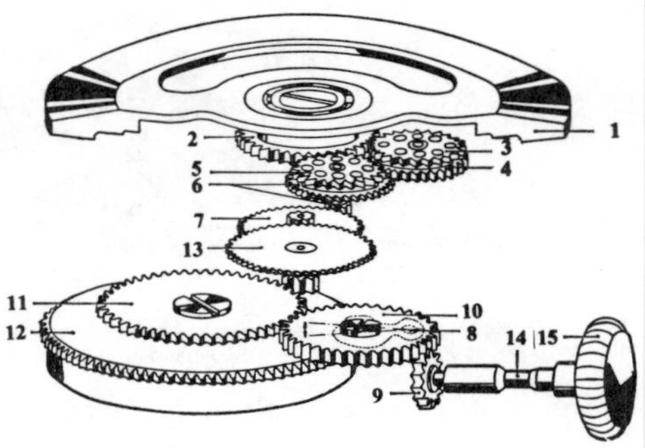

Eterna-Matic Automatic Winding Mechanism. 1—Oscillating weight. 2—Oscillating gear. 3—Upper wheel of auxiliary pawl-wheel. 4—Lower wheel of auxiliary pawl-wheel. 5—Pawl-wheel with pinion. 6—Lower wheel of pawl-wheel with pinion. 7—Transmission-wheel with pinion. 8—Crown-wheel yoke. 9—Winding-pinion. 10—Crown-wheel. 11—Ratchet-wheel. 12—Barrel. 13—Driving runner for ratchet-wheel. 14—Winding stem. 15—Winding button.

America to work with the self-winding pocket watch. However, inventors always kept in mind the idea of the self-winding watch.

In 1923, the British firm Harwood took up once again the solution of the problem of automatic winding, for wrist-watches. This was the spark which rapidly resulted in researches, in view of improving and simplifying this type of mechanism. A company to manufacture his watch was formed in London, and before long over 500 jewelers in the United Kingdom were selling his automatic watch. A second company was formed in France, and a third in the United States. The business flourished about two and one-half years. Then, in 1931, these companies liquidated.

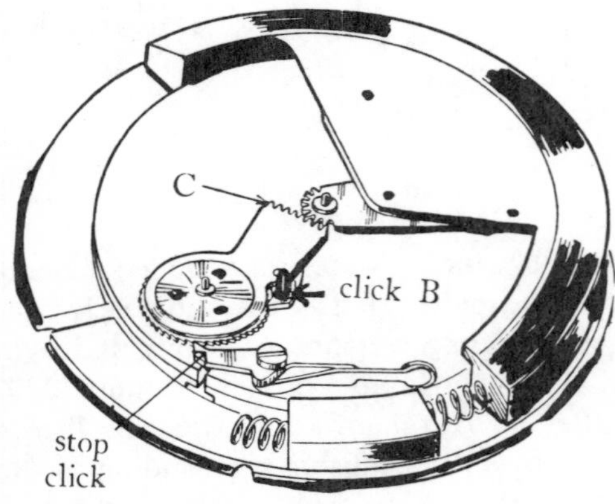

Illustration of Self Winding mechanism used by Harwood.

This 1931 wrist watch made by Perpetual Self-Winding Watch Co. Of America originally sold for $29.75

THE BALANCE ARC OF VIBRATION

If the watch is to function with any degree of satisfaction, the proper arc of motion of a balance must be no less than 225 degrees. Wind up the watch, stop the balance; upon releasing the balance, carefully observe the extent of the swing or vibration. After 30 seconds it should have reached its maximum. If it takes longer, the full power of the mainspring is not being communicated strong enough. With the watch fully wound, the balance should vibrate between 225 degrees and 315 degrees.

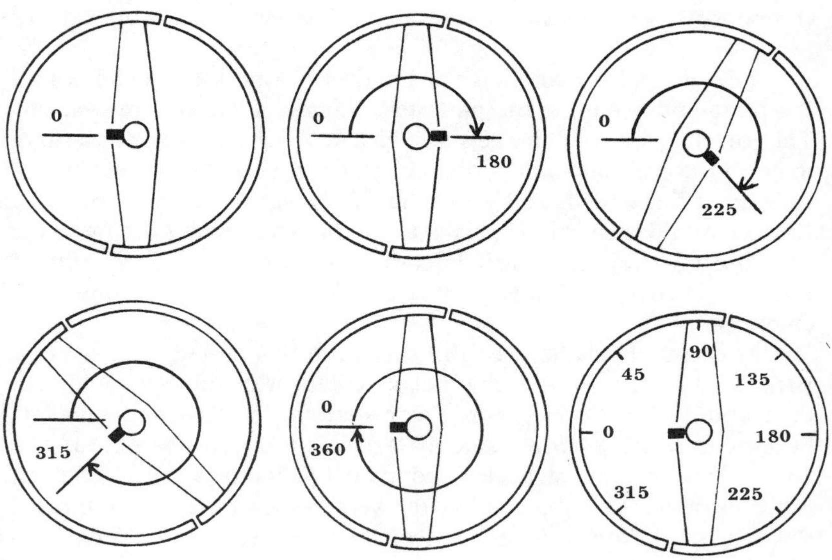

COTTAGE INDUSTRY WATCHMAKING IN COLONIAL AMERICA

The cottage industry (pre-1700s to 1800s) consisted of organized skilled craftsmen having separate divisions for the purpose of producing watches. The movements were handmade using manpowered tools. The parts generally were not given a final finish. The cottage industries were in most countries including France, England, Switzerland, Germany, and others, but not in America. Each skilled parts maker specialized in a specific part of the watch. There were fusee makers, wheel makers, plate and cock makers, spring makers, case makers and enamelers, to name a few. In the cottage industry each maker became an expert in his field, and expenses and overhead were less because fewer tools and less labor were required. Because all

components were produced separately, a larger volume of watches resulted.

The enterprising colonial watchmaker in America would order all the parts and assemble the parts to complete a finished movement. This finisher, or watchmaker, would detail the parts, such as filing them to fit, polishing and gilding the parts, fitting the movement to a case, installing a dial, and adjusting the movement to perform. The finisher would then engrave his name and town of manufacture to the movement or dial. The finisher determined the timekeeping quality of the completed watch, thus gaining a good reputation for some watchmakers.

Most watchmakers used this system in this period, even Abram Breguet to some extent. A colonial watchmaker or finisher could produce about 50 watches a year. There were few colonial watchmakers because only the wealthy could afford such a prized possession. The colonial watchmaker struggled and made repairs to exported watches. Since most of them understood the verge escapement and imported this type parts from England to produce watches, many colonial watches have the verge escapement. Few colonial watches survive today.

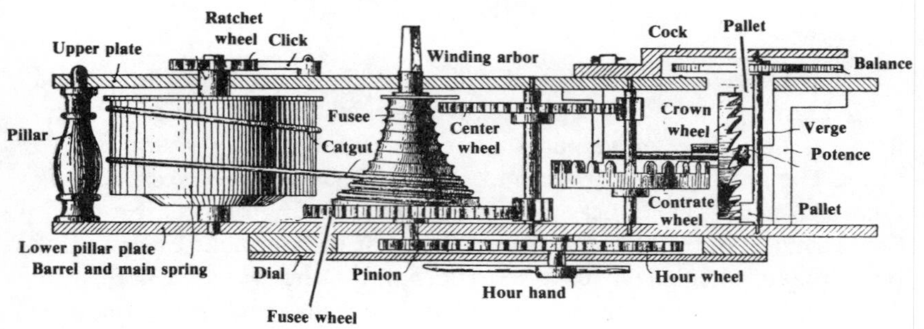

Side-view of 17th Century single-hand movement with fusee and catgut line to barrel. This three-wheel movement normally ran from 15 to 16 hours between windings. Also note the balance has no hairspring.

EBAUCHES

The stamping out of plates and bridges began with Frederic Japy of Beaucort, France, around 1770. At first, ebauches consisted of two plates with barrel and train bridges, the cock and fusee, pillars, and the clicks and assembly screws. The ebauches were stamped-out or rough movements. Japy invented machinery a common laborer could operate, including a circular saw to cut brass sheets into strips, a machine for cutting teeth in a wheel, a machine for making pillars, a press for the balance, and more. These machines were semi-automatic and were hard to keep in alignment or register. But with the aid of these new machines the principal parts of the movement could be produced in a short period of time with some precision. However, the parts of watches at this time were not interchangeable. These movements in the rough or "grey" were purchased by finishers. The finisher was responsible for fitting and polishing all parts and seeing to the freedom and depth of these working parts. He had to drill the holes to fit the dial and hands. The plates, cock and wheel, after being fitted and polished, were gilded. The finisher had to be a master watchmaker. After the parts were fitted, polished, and gilded, the movement would be reassembled, regulated for good timekeeping, and placed in a case.

Five typical Swiss Ebauches. Three with bar movements, one with a three-quarter plate, one with a half plate. Four with lever escapements, one with a cylinder escapement. The age ranges from 1860 to 1890.

In England, during the 1800s, Lancashire became the center of the movement trade. One of the better known English ebauche makers was Joseph Preston & Sons of Prescot. The movements were stamped J. P. Some Swiss ebauches would imitate or stylize the movement for the country in which they were to be sold, making it even harder to identify the origin.

As the watch industry progressed, the transformation of the ebauche to a more completed movement occurred. Automation eventually made possible the watch with interchangeable parts, standard sizing, and precision movements that did not need retouching. This automation began about 1850 with such talented mechanics as Pierre-Fredric Ingold, the Pitkins Brothers, A. L. Dennison, G. A. Leschot with Vacheron and Constantin, Patek, Phillipe, and Frederic Japy of Beaucount (still in business today as Japy Freres). The pioneers in watchmaking in the 1850s who set the standards for modern watchmaking included the Pitkin Brothers, Dennison, Howard, and Jacob Custer. By 1880 most other countries had begun to follow the lead of America in the manufacture of the complete pocket watch with interchangeable parts.

EBAUCHES S.A.

Ebauches S. A. with its main office at Neuchatel, Switzerland, consists of 17 affiliated firms:

A. Schild S. A. — Grenchen

Fabrique d'Horlogerie de Fontainemelon — Fontainemelon

Eta S. A., Fabrique d'Ebauches — Grenchen

Fabrique d'Horlogerie de Fontainemelon
Succursale du Landeron — Le Landeron

A. Michel S. A. — Grenchen

Felsa S. A. — Grenchen

Fabriques d'Ebauches Bernoises S.A.
Etablissement Aurore — Villeret

(☆)	Fabrique d'Ebauches Venus S. A.	Moutier
(TU)	Fabrique d'Ebauches Unitas S. A.	Tramelan
(FEF)	Fabrique d'Ebauches de Fleurier S. A.	Fleurier
(P)	Fabrique d'Ebauches de Peseux S. A.	Peseux
(A)	Fabriques d'Ebauches Reunies Arogno S. A.	Arogno
(EB)	Fabrique d'Ebauches de Bettlach	Bettlach
(C)	Fabrique d'Ebauches de Chezard S. A.	Chezard
(D)	Derby S. A.	La Chaux-de-Fonds
(T)	Nouvelle Fabrique S. A.	Tavannes
(R)	Valjoux S. A.	Les Bioux

WORM GEAR ESCAPEMENT

This oddity was advertised as "The Watch With a Worm in It."

Robert J. Clay of Jersey City was given a patent on October 16, 1886. Mr. Clay said, "The principal object of my invention is to provide a watch movement which is very simple and has but few parts." The worm gear or continuous screw was by no means simple. Mr. Clay and William Hanson of Brooklyn revamped the original worm gear and obtained another patent on January 18, 1887.

The first watch containing a worm gear escapement reached the market in 1887. However, the New York Standard Watch Co. soon converted to a more conventional lever escapement. About 12,000 watches with the worm gear were made, but few survived.

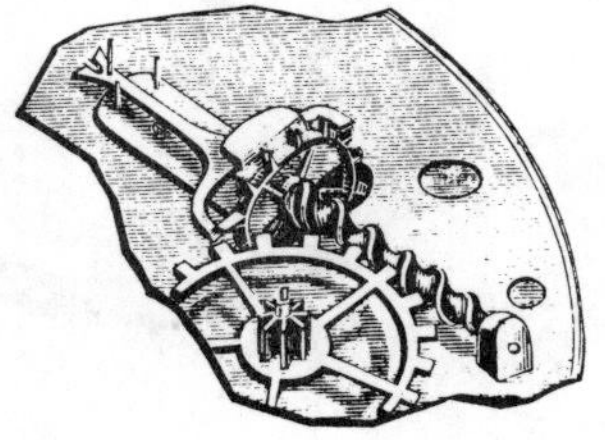

Enlarged worm gear escapement. Note endless screw was referred to by the New York Watch Co. as "a watch with a worm in it."

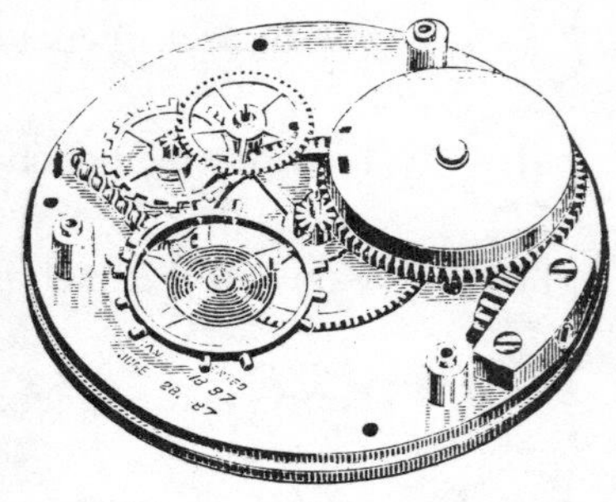

Movement with top plate removed.

DIAL MAKING

Watch dials were basically hand produced. The base is copper and the coating is generally enamel. In the process the copper plate is covered with a fine white enamel, spread with a knife to a thickness of 3/100ths of an inch. It is then allowed to dry at which time it is placed on a plate and inserted into a red hot furnace. The dial is turned frequently with a pair of long tongs. The copper would melt if it were not coated with the enamel. After the dial has been in the furnace for one minute it is removed and the resulting enamel is soft. The dial is now baked onto the copper plate or "set." The surface is rough after cooling, and it is sanded smooth with sandstone and emery. It is then bak-

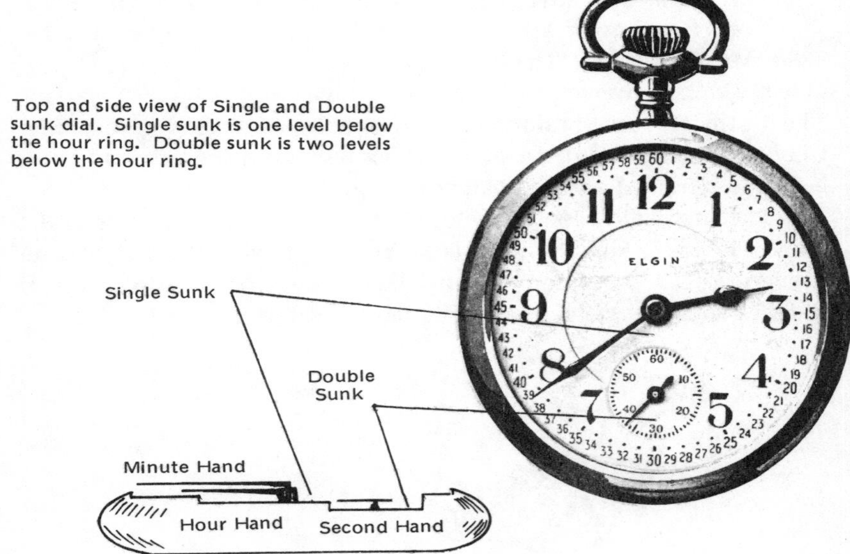

Top and side view of Single and Double sunk dial. Single sunk is one level below the hour ring. Double sunk is two levels below the hour ring.

ed again. The dial is now ready for the painter, who draws six lines across the dial using a lead pencil. Then, with a pencil of black enamel, he traces the numbers; next the numbers are finished at the ends to make them symmetrical. Then the minute marks are made. Lastly, the name of the watch company is painted onto the dial. The dial is glazed and fired again, then polished. The dial artist uses a magnifying glass and a fine camelhair brush to paint the dials and produced about one dozen per hour.

FIRST DIALS

Henri Foucy was the first man to make enamel dials in America. He came to New York from Geneva, Switzerland, in 1856 and was employed by the American Watch Factory.

CRAZING

The word "craze" means a minute crack in the glaze of the enamel. This is not a crack in the dial because the dial has a backing of copper. Crazing does little damage to structure of the enamel even though it may go all the way through to the copper.

ENAMEL

Enamel may be transparent or colored. Enamel acts as a protective surface for the metals. It is resistant to acid, corrosion, and weather. Enamel is made of feldspar, quartz, silica, borax, lead, and mineral oxides. These materials are ground into a fine powder and then fired at a temperature of about 1500 degrees Fahrenheit. The heat melts the enamel powder and unites it with the surface of the metal.

LOW COST PRODUCTION WATCHES (DOLLAR WATCHES)

Jason R. Hopkins hoped to produce a watch that would sell for no more than 50 cents as early as the 1870s. And he had a plan for which he received a patent (No. 161513) on July 20, 1875. It was a noble idea even though it was never fully realized. In 1876, Mr. Hopkins met a Mr. Fowle who bought an interest in the Hopkins watch. The movement was developed by the Auburndale Watch Co. and the Auburndale Rotary Watch was marketed in 1877. It cost $10, and 1,000 were made. The 20 size had two jewels and was open-face, pendant wind, lever set, and detent escapement. The 18 size had no jewels and was open-face.

In December, 1878, D. A. Buck introduced a new watch at a

record low price of $3.50 under the name of Benedict and Burnham Manufacturing Co. It was a rotary watch, open-face, with a skeleton dial which was covered with paper and celluloid. The movement turned around in the case, once every hour, and carried the minute hand with it. There were 58 parts and all of them were interchangeable. They had no jewels but did have a duplex style escapement. The teeth on the brass escape wheel were alternately long and short, and the short teeth were bent down to give the impulse. The main spring was about nine feet long and laid on a plate on the bed of the case. The click was also fastened to the case. The extremely long mainspring took 140 half turns of the stem to be fully wound. It came to be known as the "long wind" Waterbury and was the source of many jokes, "Here, wind my Waterbury for awhile; when you get tired, I'll finish winding it."

Above: Example of a Waterbury longwind showing the nine foot long spring.

Left: Face illustration of a Waterbury Longwind. The movement can be seen through open skeleton area around edge or face.

Right: Example of a two wheel train rather than the standard four wheel train.

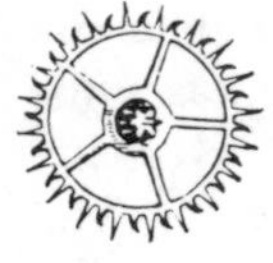

Left: Example of the escape wheel for the duplex escapement.

In 1892 R. H. Ingersoll ordered 1,000 watches produced at a cost of 85 cents each. He offered the watch for sale in his mail-order catalog for $1 each and advertised it as, "The Watch that Made the Dollar Famous." These watches were thick, sturdy and noisy and were wound from the back like a clock. The wages in 1892 were about

8 cents per hour, so it took some 13 hours of work to buy a Dollar Watch.

The E. N. Welch Manufacturing Co. was the next low cost production watch manufacturer. Then came the New York City Watch Co. In 1895, they produced a watch with a unique pendant crank to wind the movement. Next came the Western Clock Mfg. Co. in 1899 which later became the Westclox Corporation.

Also among the low cost production watches were the "comic character" watches. They have become prime collectibles in recent years.

About 70 percent of the watches sold in the U. S. were Dollar-type. These watches were characterized by the pin lever, non-jeweled for the most part, and with a face of paper or other inexpensive material. These watches were not easy to repair and the repairs cost more than the price of a new one. Thus they were thrown away, and today it is hard to find one in good condition.

DOLLAR WATCH CHARACTERISTICS:

1. Sold at a price that almost everyone could afford.
2. Used pin lever.
3. Were non-jeweled (except for a few) but rugged and practical.
4. Dial made of paper or other inexpensive material.
5. Case and Movement were sold as one unit.

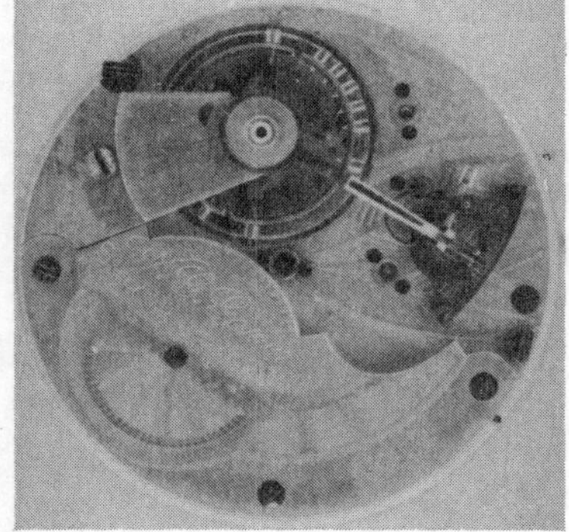

Personalized watch movement by Rockford. Engraved on movement, "W.G. Gane, Special Railway, 17j, Adj, serial No. 344551." To identify, see the Identification of Movement section of all watch companies, noting plate design & screw locations to determine that it is a **Rockford** Model No. 8.

Personalized watch movement by **Hamilton**. Engraved on movement, "Mayer, Chattanooga, Tenn., Adjusted, 21 jewels, serial No. 254507." To identify, see the Identification of Movement section of all watch companies, noting plate design & screw locations to determine that it is an 18 size, open face **Hamilton** model. Then by using the serial number, the grade can be determined.

PERSONALIZED WATCHES

It was common practice for some watch manufacturers to personalize pocket watches for jobbers, jewelry firms, and individuals. This was done either by engraving the movement or painting on the dial. Probably the Ball Watch Co. did more of this than any other jobber.

Each manufacturer used its own serial number system even though there may have been a variety of names on the movements and/or dials. Knowledge of this fact will aid the collector in identifying watches as well as determining age.

In order to establish the true manufacturer of the movement, one must study the construction, taking note of the shape of the balance, shape of the plates, location of jewels, etc. Compare each company in this volume until the manufacturer is located. The best place to start is by looking at the Hamilton and Illinois sections due to the fact that these two companies made most of the personalized watches.

After the correct manufacturer has been determined, the serial number can be used to determine the age. Taking the age, grade, size, and manufacturer into consideration, the approximate value can be derived by comparing similar watches from the parent company. If a jeweler's name and location are on the watch, this particular watch will command a higher price in that area.

For example, see the watch marked "J. R. Roche & Co. Eastport, Me." on the dial and movement with a serial number of 214407. First, it is determined that it is a size 18 watch. Then by comparing the movements to the Hamilton section and by the appearance of the patented regulator and the shape of the back plates over the winding barrel, we must learn that it was indeed made by Hamilton. By referring to the serial number, we determine that it is a grade 924. Finally, the value is determined by looking under the 924 grades. If you're selling in Eastport, Maine, the price for this particular watch may be higher there than anywhere else.

SWISS IMPORTED FAKES

Before 1871 a flood of pocket watches were made which had American-sounding names. These watches were made in foreign countries—as well as in America—and looked and sounded like high quality watches. But they were fakes of inferior quality.

These key-wind imitations of American pocket watches are a fascinating and inexpensive type watch that would make a good collection. The signatures were American-sounding and the watches closely resembled the ones they were intended to emulate. Names such as "Hampton Watch Company" might fool the casual buyer into thinking he had purchased a watch from Hampden. "Rockville Watch Co." could easily be mistaken for the American Rockford Watch Co. Initials were also used such as H. W. Co., R. W. Co., and W. W. Co., making it even harder to determine the true identity.

In 1871 Congress passed a law requiring all watches to be marked with the country of origin. The Swiss tried to get around this by printing "Swiss" on the movements so small that it was almost impossible to see. Also the word "Swiss" was printed on the top of the scroll or on a highly engraved area of the movement, making it difficult to spot.

By 1885 these Swiss imitations were of better quality and were made to resemble even more closely what was popular in America. But the Swiss fakes did not succeed and by 1900 they were no longer being sold here.

Example of a Swiss imported fake on left. Note misspelled signature P. S. Barrett and similarities to the authentic American Waltham watch 1857 Model "P. S. Bartlett," illustrated on right.

HOW TO IDENTIFY A SWISS FAKE

1. At first they were keywind and keyset; then they became stem wind, full plate, about 18 size, large jewels on the plate side, and used Roman numerals.

2. Most had American-sounding names so close to the original that it looks merely like a misspelling.

3. The material was often crudely finished with very light gilding.

4. The dial used two feet; American watches used three.

5. The balance wheel was made to look like a compensated balance, but it was not.

6. The large flat capped jewels were blue in color.

These characteristics are not present with all imported fakes. Some or none of these factors may be present. The later the date, the more closely the fake resembled the American watch.

MAIN LISTING
Pricing at Retail Level

IMPORTANT

Watches listed in this book are priced at the retail level and as having an original 14k gold-filled case and with an original white enamel single sunk dial, and with the entire original movement in good working order. Watches listed as 14k and 18k are solid gold cases. Coin or silveroid-type cases will be listed as such. Keywind and keyset watches are listed as having original coin silver cases. Dollar-type watches or low cost production watches are listed as having a base metal type case and a composition dial. Wrist watches are priced as having original gold-filled case with the movement being all original and in good working order, and the wrist watch band being made of leather except where bracelet is described.

Many of the watch manufacturers were commissioned to put jewelers' or jobbers' names on their movements in place of their own. Due to this practice, the true manufacturers of these movements are difficult to identify. These watch models are listed under the original manufacturer and can be identified by comparison with the model sections under each manufacturer. See "Personalized Watches" for more detailed information.

The prices listed were averaged from dealers' lists just prior to publication and are an indication of the retail level or what collectors will pay. Prices are provided in three categories: average condition, extra fine, and mint condition, and are shown in whole dollar amounts only. The values listed are a guide for the retail level and are provided for your information only. Dealers will not necessarily pay full retail price. Prices listed are for watches with **original** cases and dials.

Note: Descriptions and serial number ranges listed for early watches cannot be considered 100 percent accurate due to the manner in which records were kept by these companies.

WARNING: It has been reported to us that 24 Jeweled watches are being faked, especially in Illinois and Rockford watches. One method known is the altering of the number 21 on the movement to a 24. Before buying a 24 Jewel watch, compare the movement with a known 24 Jewel.

INFORMATION NEEDED—This price guide is interested in any facts and information you might have that should possibly be considered for future editions. Documented facts are needed, so please send photo or sources of information. Send to: Cooksey Shugart, 780 Church Street N.E., Cleveland, Tennessee 37311.

ABBREVIATIONS USED IN THE COMPLETE GUIDE TO AMERICAN POCKET WATCHES

★★★★—Extremely Rare; less than 20 known to exist.
★★★—Rare; less than 100 known to exist.
★★—Scarce; less than 500 known to exist.
★—Uncommon; less than 2,500 known to exist.
ADJ—Adjusted (to heat and cold)
BASE—Base metal used in cases; e.g., silveroid
BC—Box Case
BRG—Bridge plate design movement
COIN—Coin Silver
DB—Double Back
DES—Diamond End Stones
DMK—Damaskeened
DS—Double sunk dial
DR—Double roller
DWT—Penny Weight: 1/20 Troy ounce
ETP—Estimated total production
EX—Extra nice; far above average
FULL—Full plate design movement
    ¾—¾ plate design movement
    1F brg—One finger bridge design and a ¾ plate (see Illinois 16s M#5)
    2F brg—Two finger bridge design
    3F brg—Three finger bridge design
GF—Gold filled
GJS—Gold jewel settings
G#—Grade number
GT—Gold train (gold gears)
GCW—Gold center wheel
GRO—Good running order
HC—Hunter case
HCI P—Adjusted to heat, cold, isochronism, and positions; e.g., HCI5P
HL—Hairline crack
J—Jewel (as 21J)
K—Karat (as 14k solid gold—not gold filled)
KS—Key set
KW—Key wind
KW/SW—(Key Wind/Stem Wind) Transition
LS—Lever set
MCBC—Multi-Color Box Case
MCC—Multi-Color Case
MCD—Multi-Color Dial
MD—Montgomery type dial
M#—Model number
Mvt. Only—Dial and movement only; no case
NI—Nickel plates or frames
OF—Open face
P—Position (5 positions adj)

PS—Pendant set
RGP—Rolled gold plate
RR—Railroad
RRA—Railroad Approved
RRG—Railroad Grade
S—Size
SBB—Screw Back and Bezel
SRC—Swing Ring Case
SS—Single sunk dial
SW—Stem wind
S#—Serial number
TEMP—Temperature
TP—Total production
2T—Two-Tone
WGF—White gold filled
WI—Wind indicator (also as up and down indicator)
WW—Wrist watch
YGF—Yellow gold filled

ABBOTT'S STEM WIND
HENRY ABBOTT

Henry Abbott first patented his stem wind attachment on June 30, 1876. The complete Abbott's stem wind mechanism is arranged in such a way as to convert key wind to stem wind. He also made a repeater-type slide mechanism for winding. On January 18, 1881, he received a patent for an improved stem wind attachment. On the new model the watch could be wound with the crown. Abbott sold over 50,000 of these stem-wind attachments, and many of them were placed on Waltham, Elgin, and Illinois watches.

Add $100 to $250 to value of watch with this attachment.

Abbott Stem Wind Attachment. Left: Normal view of an Illinois watch movement with 'hidden' Abbott Stem Wind Attachment (pat. Jan., 18th, 1881). Right: Same watch with dial removed exposing the Abbott Stem Wind Attachment. Serial number 52045.

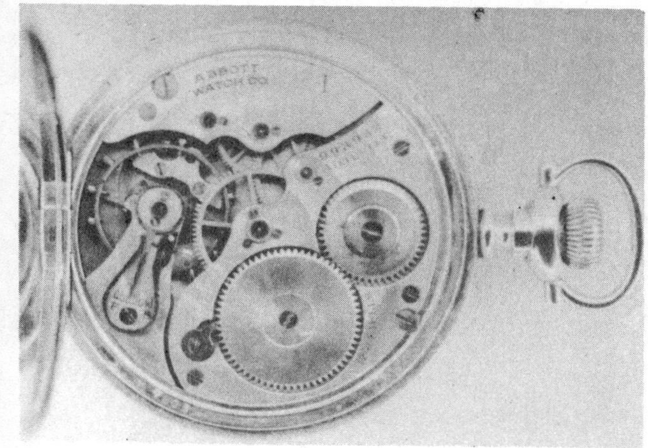

Example of **Abbott Watch Co.**, 16 size, 17 jewels, gold jeweled settings, hunting case. Note similarity to the Howard Watch Co. model 1905. Serial number 993932.

ABBOTT WATCH CO.
MADE BY HOWARD WATCH CO.
1908 — 1912

Abbott Sure Time Watches were made by the E. Howard Watch Co. (Keystone), and are similar to Howard Watch Co. 1905 model. These watches sold for $8.75 and had 17 jewels. The open face watches are actually hunting case models without the second bits register.

Description	Avg	Ex-Fn	Mint
Abbott Sure Time, 16S, 17J, ¾, OF, GF Case	$120	$195	$310
Abbott Sure Time, 16S, 17J, ¾, HC, GF Case	160	220	335
Abbott Sure Time, 16S, 17J, ¾, OF or HC, Coin	70	95	195
Abbott Sure Time, 16S, 17J, ¾, Silveroid	60	85	160

ADAMS AND PERRY WATCH MANUFACTURING COMPANY
Lancaster, Pennsylvania
1874—1877

This company, like so many others, did not have sufficient capital to stay in business for long. The first year was spent in setting up and becoming incorporated. The building was completed in mid-1875, and watches were being produced by September. The first watches were limited to three grades, and the escapement and balance were bought from other sources. By December 1875, the company was short of money and, by the spring of 1876, they had standardized their movements to 18 size. The first movement went on sale April 7, 1876. The next year the company remained idle. In August 1877 the company was sold to the Lancaster Watch Company, after making only about 800 to 1,000 watches. In 1892 Hamilton acquired the assets.

Description	Avg	Ex-Fn	Mint
20S, 20J, 18K, GJS, PS, KW, original case ★★★	$2,200	$3,500	$5,000
18S, 20J, GJS, PS ★★★	1,000	1,700	2,500
18S, 17J, GJS, PS ★★	700	900	1,450
18S, 17J, GJS, PS, Coin, Original ★★	450	500	675

Example of **Adams & Perry Watch Co.** movement. This basic model consists of 15-20 jewels, gold jeweled settings, key wind and pendant set, 18-20 size.

Example of **Adams & Perry Watch Co.** movement. This model consists of 20 jewels, gold jeweled settings, stem wind with micrometric regulator, 20 size.

J. H. ALLISON
Detroit, Michigan
1853 — 1890

The first watch J. H. Allison made was in 1853; it was a chronometer with full plate and a fusee with chain drive. The balance had time screws and sliding weights. In 1864, he made a ¾ plate chronometer with gold wheels. He also damaskeened the nickel movement. He produced only about 25 watches, of which 20 were chronometers. By 1883 he was making ¾ plate movements with a stem wind of his own design. Allison made most of his own parts and designed his own tools. He also altered some key wind watches to stem wind. Allison died in 1890.

Description		Avg	Ex-Fn	Mint
Full Plate & ¾ Plate, GT, NI, DMK	★★★	$2,500	$4,000	$5,700
Detent Chronometer Escapement, 21J, KW/KS, GJS	★★★	3,000	4,000	6,000

AMERICAN REPEATING WATCH COMPANY
Elizabeth, New Jersey
1885—1892

Around 1675, a repeating mechanism was attached to a clock for the first time. The first repeating watch was made about 1687 by Thomas Tompion or Daniel Quare. Five-minute, quarter-hour and half-hour repeaters were popular by 1730. The minute repeater became common about 1830.

Fred Terstegen applied for a patent on August 21, 1882, for a repeating attachment that would work with any American key-wind or stem-wind watch. He was granted three patents: No. 311,270 on January 27, 1885; No. 3,421,844 on February 18, 1890; and No. 3,436,162 in September 1890. Waltham was the only watch company to fabricate repeating watches in America. It is not known how many repeaters were made, but it is estimated to be from 1,300 to 3,000.

Add $1,000 to $2,000 to value of watch with this attachment.

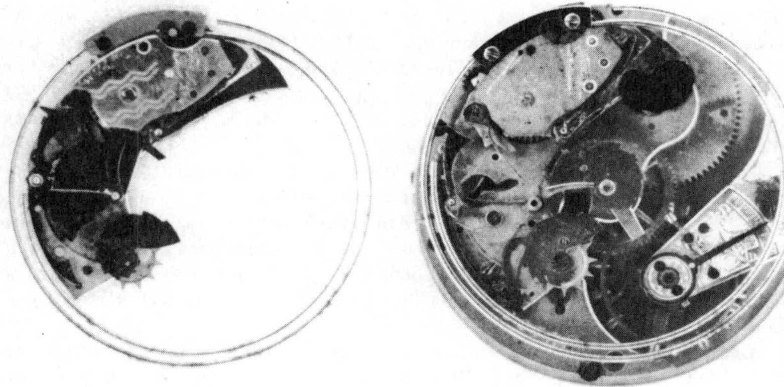

American Repeating Attachment. Illustration at left shows Terstegen's patented repeating attachment only. Illustration at right shows attachment as normally found on movement. The two outside circles on left illustration are wire gongs. The hammer can be seen at upper right.

THE AMERICAN WATCH CO.
(Waltham)
1851—1957

To trace the roots of the Waltham family one must start with the year 1850 in Roxbury, Massachusetts, No. 34 Water Street. That fall David Davis, a Mr. Dennison, and Mr. Howard together formed a watch company. Howard and Dennison had the dream of producing watches with interchangeable parts that were less expensive but did not result in less quality.

Howard served an apprenticeship to Aaron Willard Jr. in about 1829. Several years later, in 1842, Howard formed a clock and balance scale manufacturing company with Davis.

Howard and Dennison combined their ideas and, with financing provided by Samuel Curtis, the first of their watches was made in 1850. But they had problems. They were trying out all new ideas such as using jewels, making dials, and producing steel with mirror finishes. This required all new machinery and resulted in a great financial burden. They discovered, too, that although all watches were produced on the same machines and of the same style, each watch was individual with its own set of errors to be corrected. This they had not anticipated. It took months to adjust the watches to the point they were any better than any other timepieces on the market.

But Howard had perfected and patented many automatic watchmaking machines that produced precision watch parts. In 1851 the factory building was completed and the name American Horologe Company was chosen. It was not until late 1852 that the first watches were completed using the signature of "The Warren Mfg. Co.," after a famed Revolutionary War hero. The first 17 watches were not placed on the market but went to officials of the company. Watches numbered 18 through 110 were marked "Warren. . . Boston;" the next 800 were marked "Samuel Curtis;" a few were marked "Fellows & Schell" and sold for $40.

The name was changed to the Boston Watch Company in September 1853, and a factory was built in Waltham, Massachusetts, in October 1854. The movements that were produced here carried serial numbers 1,001 to 5,000 and were marked "Dennison, Howard & Davis," "C. T. Parker," and "P. S. Bartlett."

THE AMERICAN WALTHAM WATCH CO. (continued)

Boston Watch Company failed in 1857 and was sold at a sheriff's auction to Royal E. Robbins. In May 1857, it was reorganized as the Appleton, Tracy & Co., and the watches produced carried serial numbers 5,001 to 14,000, model 1857. The first movements were marked Appleton, Tracy & Co. The C. T. Parker was introduced as model 1857 and sold for $12; 399 of these models were made. Also 598 chronodrometers were produced and in January 1858 the P. S. Bartlett watch was made.

In January 1859 the Waltham Improvement Co. and the Appleton, Tracy & Co. merged to form the American Watch Company. In 1860, as Lincoln was elected president and the country was in Civil War, the American Watch Co. was faced with serious problems. The next year, business came to a standstill. There seemed to be little hope of finding a market for watches, and bankruptcy again seemed close at hand. At this point it was decided to cut expenditures to the lowest possible figure and keep the factory in operation.

American horology owes much to members of the Waltham Watch group such as Bacon, Church, Dennison, Fogg, Howard Marsh, Webster, and Woerd, who contributed much to its development and success.

In early 1861, the name "J. Watson" appeared on model 1857 (first run: Nos. 23,601 to 24,300—total production 1,200).

The next model 1857 was the "R. E. Robbins" of which 2,800 were made.

The William Ellery, marked "Wm. Ellery," (model 1857) was then introduced with the first serial number of 46,201. It was key wind and key set and had 7 to 15 jewels.

A size 10 woman's watch was marketed with first serial numbers of 44,201. It was key wind and key set, ¾ plate, 13 to 15 jewels. Some were marked "P S Bartlett" and a 15 jewel was marked "Appleton, Tracy & Co."

A special model, 10 size, serial numbers of 45,801 to 46,200, is extremely rare.

The first stem wind, beginning with serial number 410,698, was produced in 1868.

By 1880 all watches were quick train.

The last key wind was serial No. 22,577,000, about 1919, 18 size, 1883 model, 7J, sterling, produced for export.

Warren, Model 1857, 18 size, 15 jewels, hunting case, key wind & set, under sprung, serial number 58.

Samuel Curtis, Model 1857, 18 size, 15 jewels, manufactured about 1854, serial number 356.

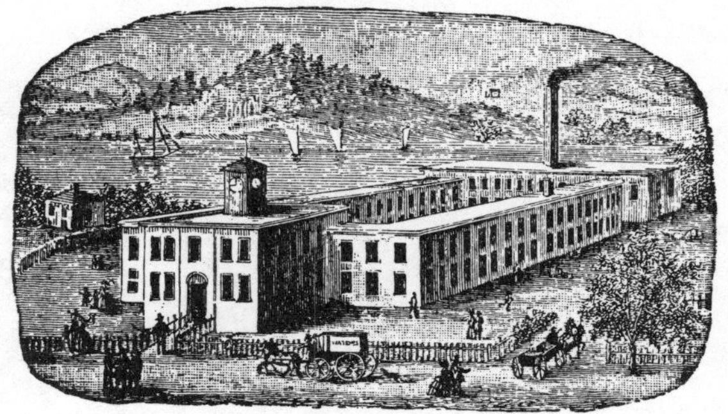

Factory of Boston Watch Co., 1857.

CHRONOLOGY OF THE DEVELOPMENT OF AMERICAN WATCH COMPANY

AMERICAN HOROLOGE CO.
Roxbury, Mass. 1851
"Howard, Davis & Dennison"
Serial No. 1-17

THE WARREN MANUFACTURING CO.
Roxbury, Mass. 1851-1853
"Warren"
Serial No. 18-110
"Samuel Curtis"
Serial No. 111-1,000

BOSTON WATCH CO.
Roxbury 1853-1854 & Waltham, Mass. 1854-1857
"C. T. Parker," "P. S. Bartlett,"
"Dennison, Howard & Davis"
Serial No. 1,001-5,000
"Fellows & Schell"
less than 100 made
(Serial No. 6,000-6,500 Howard & Rice)

TRACY, BAKER & CO.
Waltham, Mass. 1857

APPLETON, TRACY & COMPANY
Waltham, Mass. 1857-1859
"Appleton, Tracy & Co.," "C. T. Parker,"
"Chronodrometer," "P. S. Bartlett"
Serial No. 5,001-14,000

AMERICAN WATCH COMPANY
Waltham, Mass. 1859-1885

AMERICAN WALTHAM WATCH CO.
Waltham, Mass. 1885-1906

WALTHAM WATCH COMPANY
Waltham, Mass. 1906-1923

WALTHAM WATCH & CLOCK COMPANY
Waltham, Mass. 1923-1925

WALTHAM WATCH COMPANY
Waltham, Mass. 1925-1957

WALTHAM
ESTIMATED SERIAL NUMBERS AND PRODUCTION DATES

Date	Serial No.	Date	Serial No.	Date	Serial No.
1852	50	1888	3,800,000	1924	24,550,000
1853	400	1889	4,200,000	1925	24,800,000
1854	1,000	1890	4,700,000	1926	25,200,000
1855	2,500	1891	5,200,000	1927	26,100,000
1856	4,000	1892	5,800,000	1928	26,400,000
1857	6,000	1893	6,300,000	1929	26,900,000
1858	10,000	1894	6,700,000	1930	27,100,000
1859	15,000	1895	7,100,000	1931	27,300,000
1860	20,000	1896	7,450,000	1932	27,550,000
1861	25,000	1897	8,100,000	1933	27,750,000
1862	35,000	1898	8,400,000	1934	28,100,000
1863	65,000	1899	9,000,000	1935	28,600,000
1864	110,000	1900	9,500,000	1936	29,100,000
1865	180,000	1901	10,200,000	1937	29,400,000
1866	260,000	1902	11,100,000	1938	29,750,000
1867	330,000	1903	12,100,000	1939	30,050,000
1868	410,000	1904	13,500,000	1940	30,250,000
1869	460,000	1905	14,300,000	1941	30,750,000
1870	500,000	1906	14,700,000	1942	31,050,000
1871	540,000	1907	15,500,000	1943	31,400,000
1872	590,000	1908	16,400,000	1944	31,700,000
1873	680,000	1909	17,600,000	1945	32,100,000
1874	730,000	1910	17,900,000	1946	32,350,000
1875	810,000	1911	18,100,000	1947	32,750,000
1876	910,000	1912	18,200,000	1948	33,100,000
1877	1,000,000	1913	18,900,000	1949	33,500,000
1878	1,150,000	1914	19,500,000	1950	33,560,000
1879	1,350,000	1915	20,000,000	1951	33,600,000
1880	1,500,000	1916	20,500,000	1952	33,700,000
1881	1,670,000	1917	20,900,000	1953	33,800,000
1882	1,835,000	1918	21,800,000	1954	34,100,000
1883	2,000,000	1919	22,500,000	1955	34,450,000
1884	2,350,000	1920	23,400,000	1956	34,700,000
1885	2,650,000	1921	23,900,000	1957	35,000,000
1886	3,000,000	1922	24,100,000		
1887	3,400,000	1923	24,300,000		

The above list is provided for determining the approximate age of your watch. Match serial number with date.

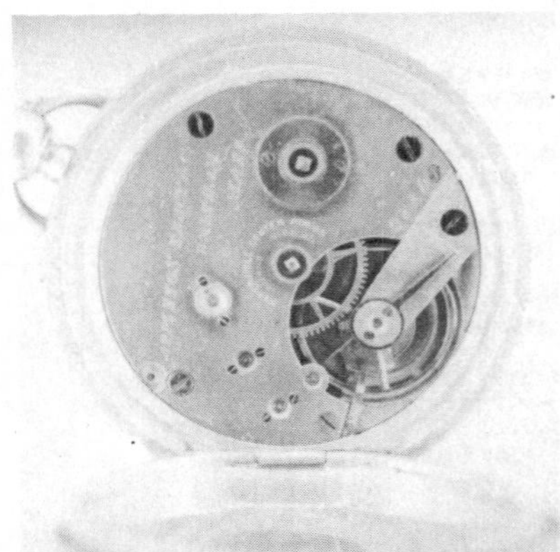

Appleton Tracy & Co., 18 size, 15 jewels, key wind & set from back, reversible center pinion pat. Nov. 30, 1858. Serial number 28800.

Model 1857, 18 size, 16 jewels, "Chronodrometer" on dial, "Appleton Tracy & Co." or "P.S. Batlett" on back plate, key wind & set.

AMERICAN WALTHAM WATCH CO.

(See American Waltham Watch Co. **Identification of Movements** section located at the end of the American Waltham price section to identify the movement, size, and model number of your watch.)

20 SIZE
MODEL 1862,-20-KW
T. P. 3,500

Grade or Name — Description		Avg	Ex-Fn	Mint
American Watch Co., 18K, HC, all original	★★	$1,800	$2,500	$3,500
American Watch Co., 15 & 17J, KW, KS, ¾, vibrating hairspring stud	★★	700	1,000	1,600
American Watch Co., 15 & 17J, KW, KS, ¾, vibrating hairspring stud, 18K HC, all original	★★	2,000	2,500	3,500
American Watch Co., 15 & 17J, ¾, KW, ADJ	★	300	500	850
American Watch Co., 19J, ¾, KW, ADJ	★★	2,400	2,800	4,000
American Watch Co., 19J, ¾, KW, ADJ, with Maltese cross stopwork, all original	★★	2,500	3,000	4,500
Amn. W. Co., 15J, ¾, KW	★	300	450	635
Amn. W. Co., 7-11J, ¾, KW	★	250	350	525
Appleton, Tracy & Co., 15J, ¾, KW, with Maltese cross stopwork, all original	★	400	550	775
Appleton, Tracy & Co., 15 & 17J, ¾, KW, ADJ, gold balance	★	450	650	1,100
Appleton, Tracy & Co., 15 & 17J, ¾, KW		250	350	595
Appleton, Tracy & Co., 15 & 17J, ¾, KW, vibrating hairspring stud	★★	1,500	2,000	3,000
Appleton, Tracy & Co., 15 & 17J, ¾, KW, vibrating hairspring stud, 18K HC	★★	1,800	2,400	3,500

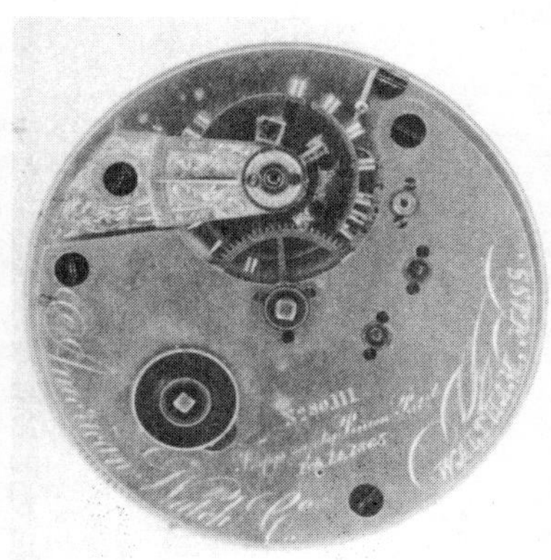

American Watch Co., Model 1862, 20 size, 17 jewels, gold balance and escape wheel, gold jeweled settings, key wind, key set from back, serial number 80111.

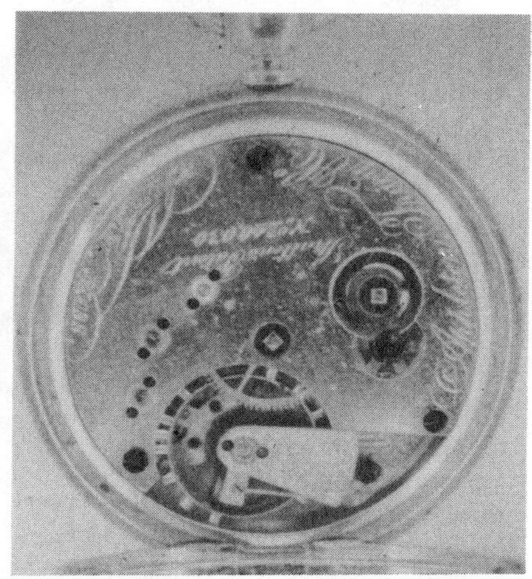

Appleton, Tracy & Co., 18 size, 15 jewels, with vibrating hair spring stud, key wind & set from back, serial number 140030.

18 SIZE
MODELS 1857, 18KW, 1862, 1870, 1877, 1879, 1883, 1892

Grade or Name — Description	Avg	Ex-Fn	Mint
American Watch Co., 17J, ¾, KW, M#18KW ★★★	$500	$750	$1,200
American Watch Co., 19J, M#18KW, ¾ ★★	1,600	2,000	2,800
American Watch Co., 19J, M#1883, HC ★★	800	1,000	1,400
American Watch Co., 17J, M#1883	65	100	175
American Watch Co., 21J, M#1883, ADJ, GJS	125	150	225
American Watch Co., 15J, M#18KW, ¾, Pat. Nov. 30, 1858, reverse pinion, original case ★★★★	1,400	2,000	3,000
American Watch Co., 15J, M#1870, KW	150	250	425
Am. Watch Co., 15J, M#1857, KW, KS	85	100	190
Am. Watch Co., 17J, M#1857, KW, KS ★	125	175	225
Am. Watch Co., 14K, HC, heavy box hinged, multi-color, (4 colors)	1,600	2,200	3,000
Am. Watch Co., 11J, thin model, KW, ¾ plate ★	185	285	400
Am. Watch Co., 15 & 17J, M#1870, KW, ADJ	150	235	325
Am. Watch Co., 11J, M#1883, SW or KW	55	75	125
Am. Watch Co., 17J, M#1892, LS	70	90	150
Am. Watch Co., 17J, M#1892, PS	60	90	140
Am. Watch Co., 21J, M#1892, LS	90	120	185
Am. Watch Co., 21J, M#1892, PS	80	120	175
Am. Watch Co., 7J, M#1883, KW	35	55	75
Am. Watch Co., 11J, M#1883, KW	50	65	85
Am. Watch Co., 15J, M#1857, SW ★	200	300	445
Appleton, Tracy & Co., 15J, M#1857, SW	100	125	185
Appleton, Tracy & Co., 7-11J, KW, M#1857 ★	110	135	200
Appleton, Tracy & Co., 15J, M#18KW, ¾, reverse pinion, Pat. Nov. 30, 1858, orig. case ★★★	800	1,200	2,000
Appleton, Tracy & Co., KW, ¾ ★	175	295	425
Appleton, Tracy & Co., 11J, thin model, KW, ¾ ★	175	285	395
Appleton, Tracy & Co., 15J, ¾, KW, with vibrating hairspring stud ★★	600	850	1,300
Appleton, Tracy & Co., Sporting,(Chronodrometer) M#1857, 16J, KW, KS, original case ★★	2,000	2,400	3,000
Appleton, Tracy & Co., 15J, M#1857, KW, 18K	600	900	1,400
Appleton, Tracy & Co., 15J, M#1857, KW	100	125	275
Appleton, Tracy & Co., 11J, M#s 1877, 1879, SW	60	75	95
Appleton, Tracy & Co., 17J, M#1892, SW, Premiere	95	125	165
Appleton, Tracy & Co., 15J, M#1892, SW	60	85	95
Appleton, Tracy & Co., 17J, M#1892, SW	55	75	115
Appleton, Tracy & Co., 19J, M#1892, SW	85	115	195
Appleton, Tracy & Co., 21J, M#1892, SW	90	125	225
Appleton, Tracy & Co., 15J, M#1883	55	65	100
Appleton, Tracy & Co., 15J, M#1877, KW	50	70	110
Appleton, Tracy & Co., 15J, M#1879, SW	50	70	110
Appleton, Tracy & Co., 17J, M#1883	60	80	120
A. W. W. Co., 7J, M#1883, SW	55	65	95
A. W. W. Co., 11J, M#1883, SW	60	70	100
A. W. W. Co., 7J, M#1883, KW	50	60	90
A. W. W. Co., 11J, M#1879	50	60	110

AMERICAN WALTHAM WATCH CO., 18 SIZE (continued)

Grade or Name — Description	Avg	Ex-Fn	Mint
A. W. W. Co., 15J, M#1879	50	60	110
A. W. W. Co., 11J, M#1883	60	70	110
A. W. W. Co., 15J, M#1883	65	75	110
A. W. W. Co., 17J, M#1892, LS, OF	80	90	135
A. W. W. Co., 17J, M#1892, PS, OF	70	80	140
A. W. W. Co., 17J, M#1892, HC	80	95	185
A. W. W. Co., 19J, M#1892	90	115	160
A. W. W. Co., 21J, M#1892	95	125	180
A. W. W. Co., 17J, "for R.R. Service" on dial	200	250	365
A. W. W. Co., 15J, OF	50	60	90
A. W. W. Co., 15J, 14K multi-color boxcase	1,200	1,600	2,400
A. W. W. Co., 11J, LS, HC	50	60	80
A. W. W. Co., 15J, HC	55	65	95

P.S. Bartlett, Model 18KW, 18 size, 11 jewels, key wind & set from back, serial number 41597.

P.S. Bartlett, Model 1857, 18 size, 11-15 jewels, serial number 945304. Note hidden key from stem.

Grade or Name — Description	Avg	Ex-Fn	Mint
P. S. Bartlett, 7J, M#1857, KW, 1st Run	250	350	500
P. S. Bartlett, 11J, M#1857, KW, 1st Run	275	375	585
P. S. Bartlett, 11J, M#1857, KW, 2nd-3rd Run	75	85	125
P. S. Bartlett, 15J, M#1857, KW, 2nd-3rd Run	100	125	165
P. S. Bartlett, 11J, LS, HC, 14K	550	650	885
P. S. Bartlett, 15J, M#1857, KW, below S#5000	200	225	325
P. S. Bartlett, 11J, M#1879, KW	55	60	80
P. S. Bartlett, 11J, M#1857, KW, Eagle inside case lid	200	250	320
P. S. Bartlett, 15J, M#1879, KW	65	75	95
P. S. Bartlett, 15J, M#1879, SW	55	65	80
P. S. Bartlett, 15J, M#1857, Sporting or Chronometer ★★★	1,800	2,400	3,200
P. S. Bartlett, 11-15J, M#1870, SW	75	85	115
P. S. Bartlett, 11-15J, M#1877, KW	85	100	135
P. S. Bartlett, 11J, M#1883, SW	50	60	90
P. S. Bartlett, 15J, M#1883, KW	55	65	95
P. S. Bartlett, 17J, M#1883, SW	85	115	125

P.S. Bartlett, 18 size, 15 jewels, Model 1857. Engraved on back "4 PR. Jewels." Serial number 13446.

Canadian Railway Time Service, Model 1892, 18 size, 17 jewels, serial number 22,017,534.

Grade or Name — Description	Avg	Ex-Fn	Mint
P. S. Bartlett, 15J, M#1883, SW	65	75	100
P. S. Bartlett, 11J, M#18KW, ¾, thin model	100	160	275
P. S. Bartlett, 11J, M#18KW, ¾, Pat. Nov. 30, 1858	500	700	1,100
P. S. Bartlett, 15J, pinned plates, KW	300	525	775
P. S. Bartlett, 15J, M#1892, SW	65	70	95
P. S. Bartlett, 17J, M#1892, SW, OF, LS	75	80	110
P. S. Bartlett, 17J, M#1892, SW, HC	80	90	120
P. S. Bartlett, 17J, M#1892, SW, OF, PS	75	80	110
P. S. Bartlett, 17J, M#1892, SW, 2-Tone	85	95	120
P. S. Bartlett, 19J, M#1892, SW	95	105	130
P. S. Bartlett, 21J, M#1892, SW	95	105	140
P. S. Bartlett, 21J, M#1892, SW, 2-Tone	100	115	150
Broadway, 7J, M#1857, KW	60	70	100
Broadway, 11J, M#1857, KW	70	80	115
Broadway, 11J, M#1877, KW, SW, NI	70	80	115
Broadway, 7J, M#1883, KW	55	60	90
Broadway, 11J, M#1883, KW	60	70	100
Broadway, 11J, M#1883, SW	60	70	95
Canadian Railway Time Service, 17J, M#1892, HCI5P	225	325	485
Central Park, 15J, M#1857, KW	75	120	150
Champion, 15J, M#1877, OF	50	65	100
Crescent Park, 15J M#1857	125	150	225
Crescent Street, 15J, M#1870, KW	150	180	225
Crescent Street, 17J, M#1870, KW ★	275	375	500
Crescent Street, 15J, M#1870, SW	125	145	195
Crescent Street, 15J, M#1883, SW, non-magnetic	100	140	200
Crescent Street, 15J, M#1883, SW, 2-Tone	110	150	210
Crescent Street, 17J, M#1883, SW	90	105	145
Crescent Street, 19J, M#1883 ★	200	260	365
Crescent Street, 17J, M#1892, SW, GJS	90	120	145
Crescent Street, 19J, M#1892, SW, HCI5P, GJS	90	115	150
Crescent Street, 21J, M#1892, SW, HCI5P, GJS	100	125	170

Crescent Street, Model 1870, 18 size, 15 jewels, series A, key wind & set from back, serial number 520,206.

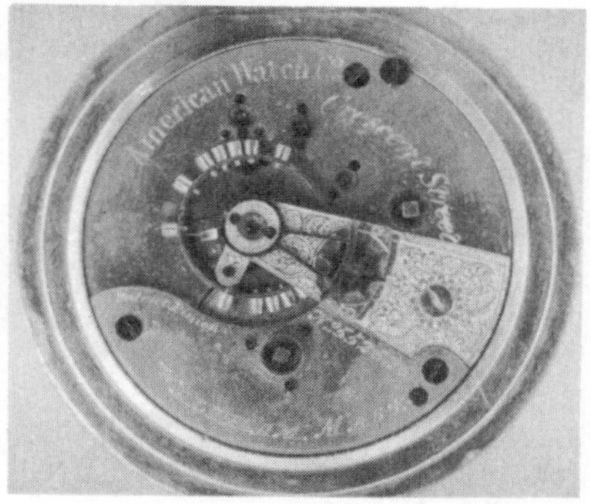

Crescent Street, Model 1870, 18 size, 15 jewels, series B, key wind & set from back, serial number 552,526.

Grade or Name — Description	Avg	Ex-Fn	Mint
Crescent Street, 21J, M#1892, WI	800	1,000	1,400
Samuel Curtis, 11-15J, M#1857, KW, S# less than 200, original silver case ★★	3,500	4,000	5,000
Samuel Curtis, 11-15J, M#1857, KW, S# less than 400, original silver case ★★	3,000	3,350	4,000
Samuel Curtis, 11-15J, M#1857, KW, S# less than 600, original silver case ★★	2,200	2,700	3,500
Samuel Curtis, 11-15J, M#1857, KW, S# less than 1,000, original silver case ★★	2,000	2,500	3,200
(Samuel Curtis not in original silver case, deduct $800 to $1,000 from value)			
Dennison, Howard, Davis, 7J, M#1857, KW ★	500	700	1,100
Dennison, Howard, Davis, 11J, M#1857, KW ★	700	1,000	1,400
Dennison, Howard, Davis, 15J, M#1857, KW ★	800	1,100	1,550
Dennison, Howard, Davis, 15J, M#1857, KW, S# less than 2,000, original case ★★	1,000	1,300	1,695
Denver & Rio Grande, 21J, M#1892, GJS, HCI3P	900	1,200	1,600
Dominion Railway, 15J, M#1883, OF, SW, train on dial	350	500	775
Wm. Ellery, 7-11J, M#1857, Boston, Mass.	65	95	125
Wm. Ellery, 7-11J, M#1857, KW	65	90	110
Wm. Ellery, 7-11J, M#KW, ¾	100	125	195

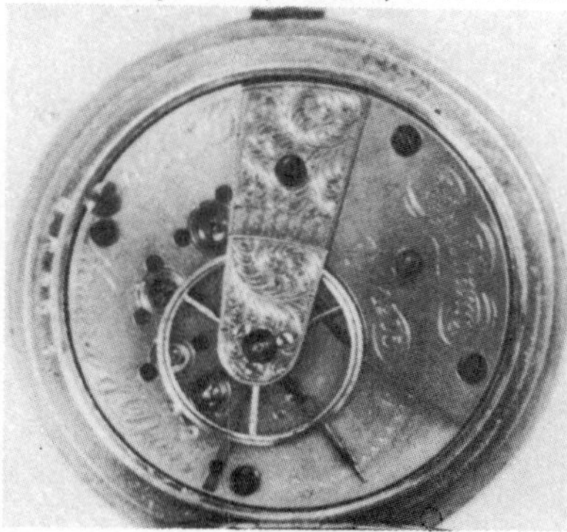

Dennison, Howard, Davis. Model 1857, 18 size, 15 jewels, under sprung, key wind, serial number 1205.

Howard & Rice, Model 1857, 18 size, 15 jewels, under sprung, serial number 6003.

AMERICAN WALTHAM WATCH CO., 18 SIZE (continued)

Grade or Name — Description	Avg	Ex-Fn	Mint
Wm. Ellery, 7-11J, M#1859, 18K, KW-KS from back, HC	1,000	1,250	1,850
Wm. Ellery, 7J, M#1857, KW, KS from back	225	375	495
Wm. Ellery, 15J, M#1857, KW	80	90	135
Wm. Ellery, 15J, M#1857, SW	100	125	150
Wm. Ellery, 7-11J, M#1877, KW, M#1879, KW	60	85	100
Wm. Ellery, 11-15J, M#1877, SW	60	85	100
Wm. Ellery, 7-11J, M#1883	55	80	95
Excelsior, M#1877, KW	80	95	140
Export, 7-11J, M#1877	65	75	95
Export, 7-11J, M#1883, KW	60	70	90
Favorite, 15J, M#1877	70	80	95
Fellows & Schell, 15J, KW, KS ★★★	2,800	3,400	4,200
Franklin, 7J, M#1877, SW	80	110	130
Home Watch Co., 7-11J, M#1857, KW	70	90	125
Home Watch Co., 7J, M#1877, KW	50	75	150
Home Watch Co., 7-11J, M#1879, SW	55	85	160
Howard, Davis & Dennison, S#1-17 ★★★★	30,000	38,000	50,000
Howard & Rice, 15J, M#1857, KW, KS (serial numbers range from 6000 to 6500) ★★	1,500	1,900	2,500
E. Howard & Co., Boston (on dial & mvt.), English style escape wheel, upright pallets, 15J, M#1857, KW, KS, S#s about 6,400 to 6,500 ★★★	2,000	2,600	3,500
Martyn Square, 7-11J, M#1857, KW, SW (exported)	125	150	185
Non-Magnetic, 15J, SW, LS, NI	85	105	135
Non-Magnetic, 17J, M#1892, SW, LS	200	225	365
C. T. Parker, 7J, M#1857, KW ★★	1,200	1,800	2,500
Pennsylvania R.R. on dial, Appleton, Tracy & Co. on Mvt., KW, KS ★★★	1,900	2,000	2,200
Pennsylvania Special, 21J, M#1892, HC ★★★	1,800	2,000	2,500
Pennsylvania Special, 21J, M#1892, OF ★★★	1,250	1,400	1,850
Pioneer, 7J, M#1883	55	65	80
Premier, 17J, M#1892, LS, OF	65	90	125
Railroad, 17J, M#1892, LS	150	185	350
Railroad, 21J, M#1892, LS	175	200	375
Railroader, 17J, M#1892, LS ★★	475	575	750

Premier, Model 1892, 18 size, 17 jewels, serial number 10539446.

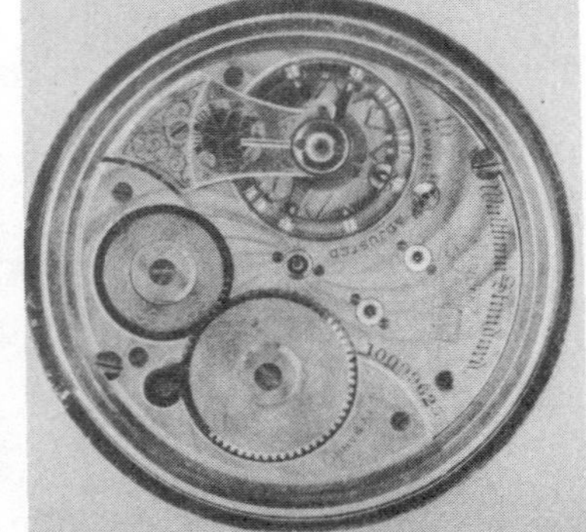

Railroad, Model 1892, 18 size, 19 jewels, HCI5P, open face, note engine & coal car engraved on movement, serial number 10,099,625.

AMERICAN WALTHAM WATCH CO., 18 SIZE (continued)

Grade or Name — Description	Avg	Ex-Fn	Mint
Railroad King, 15J, M#1883, LS	200	250	375
Railroad King, 15J, M#1883, 2-Tone	300	375	500
Railroad King, 17J, Special, M#1883, LS	350	400	525
Railroad Watches with R.R. names on dial and movement as follows:			
Canadian Pacific R.R., 17J, M#1883	175	225	295
Canadian Pacific R.R., 17J, M#1892	275	300	375
Canadian Pacific R.R., 21J, M#1892	300	350	475
Santa Fe Route, 17J, M#1883	225	280	385
Santa Fe Route, 17J, M#1892 ★	275	350	495
Riverside, 7J, M#1857	70	80	95
Riverside, 17J, M#1892 ★	200	250	395
Roadmaster, 17J, M#1892, LS ★	175	225	350
R. E. Robbins, 11J, M#1857, KW ★	375	450	675
R. E. Robbins, 15J, M#1877, KW	175	200	275
R. E. Robbins, 13J, M#1883	100	150	225
Sol, 7J, M#1883, OF	55	65	75
Sol, 17J, OF, PS	125	170	235
Special Railroad, 17J, M#1883, LS, OF	250	300	475
Special R. R. King, 15J, M#1883	240	290	465
Sterling, 7J, M#1857, KW	55	70	90
Sterling, 7-11J, M#1877, M#1879	50	60	80
Sterling, 7-11J, M#1883, KW	45	60	80
Sterling, 11J, M#1883, SW	50	65	80
Tourist, 11J, M#1877	55	70	90
Tourist, 7J, M#1877	50	60	85
Tracy, Baker & Co., 15J, original case ★★★★	5,000	7,000	10,000
Vanguard, 17J, M#1892, GJS, HC ★★★	385	440	580
Vanguard, 17J, M#1892, LS, HCI5P, DR, GJS, OF ★★	200	270	375
Vanguard, 17J, M#1892, Wind Indicator, HCI5P, DR, GJS	750	900	1,300
Vanguard, 19J, M#1892, LS, HCI5P, Diamond end stones	95	145	185
Vanguard, 19J, M#1892, LS, HCI5P, DR, GJS, OF	90	135	175

Sol, Model 1883, 18 size, 7 jewels, open face, serial number 9578232.

Vanguard, Model 1892, 18 size, 23 jewels, diamond end stone, gold jewel settings, exposed winding gears, serial number 10533465.

AMERICAN WALTHAM WATCH CO., 18 SIZE (continued)

Grade or Name — Description	Avg	Ex-Fn	Mint
Vanguard, 19J, M#1892, Wind Indicator, LS, HCI5P, DR, GJS	800	1,000	1,400
Vanguard, 19J, M#1892, HCI5P, GJS, HC ★	135	170	250
Vanguard, 21J, M#1892, Silveroid	70	85	110
Vanguard, 21J, M#1892, HC, GJS	85	110	165
Vanguard, 21J, M#1892, LS, HCI5P, DR, GJS, OF	90	120	175
Vanguard, 21J, M#1892, LS, HCI5P, Diamond end stone	100	140	185
Vanguard, 21J, M#1892, Wind Indicator, LS, HCI5P, DR, GJS ★	900	1,100	1,400
Vanguard, 23J, M#1892, LS, HCI5P, DR, GJS, OF	135	175	300
Vanguard, 23J, M#1892, LS, HCI5P, DR, GJS, HC	200	225	350
Vanguard, 23J, M#1892, LS, HCI5P, DR, GJS, Diamond end stone	175	225	325
Vanguard, 23J, M#1892, LS, HCI5P, DR, GJS, Silveroid	95	105	135
Vanguard, 23J, M#1892, Wind Indicator, LS, HCI5P, DR, GJS ★	900	1,200	1,595
Warren, 15J, M#1857, KW, KS, S#18-29, original silver case ★★★	25,000	30,000	38,000
Warren, 15J, M#1857, KW, KS, S#30-60, original silver case ★★★	15,000	18,000	24,000
Warren, 15J, M#1857, KW, KS, S#61-90, original silver case ★★★	7,000	10,000	14,000
Warren, 15J, M#1857, KW, KS, S#91-110, original silver case ★★★	5,000	6,000	8,000
(Warren not in original silver case, deduct $1,000 to $2,500)			
George Washington, M#1857, KW	250	350	600
J. Watson, 7J, M#1857, KW, KS, "Boston" ★	850	1,175	1,600
J. Watson, 7-11J, M#1857, KW, KS, "London" ★	850	1,175	1,600
45, 19J, GJS, 2-Tone, HC ★★	800	1,000	1,400
845, 21J, M#1892, OF	95	130	175
845, 21J, M#1892, HC	135	175	265
845, 21J, M#1892, Silveroid	60	70	95
820, 825, M#1883	55	75	90
836, 17J, DR, HCI4P, LS, OF	70	85	110

J. Watson, Model 1857, 18 size, 7-11 jewels, hunting case, key wind & set, serial number 28635.

845, Model 1892, 18 size, 21 jewels, railroad grade, adjusted to HCI5P, serial number 15097475.

AMERICAN WALTHAM WATCH CO., 18 SIZE (continued)

Grade or Name — Description	Avg	Ex-Fn	Mint
M#1892, 19J, Sidereal, OF ★★★	1,600	1,900	2,500
M#1892, 17J, Astronomical Sidereal ★★★	1,400	1,600	2,000

Note: Some grades are not included. Their values can be determined by comparing with similar models and grades listed.

American Watch Co., Model 16KW, 16 size, 11-15 jewels, key wind and set from back, serial number 330,635.

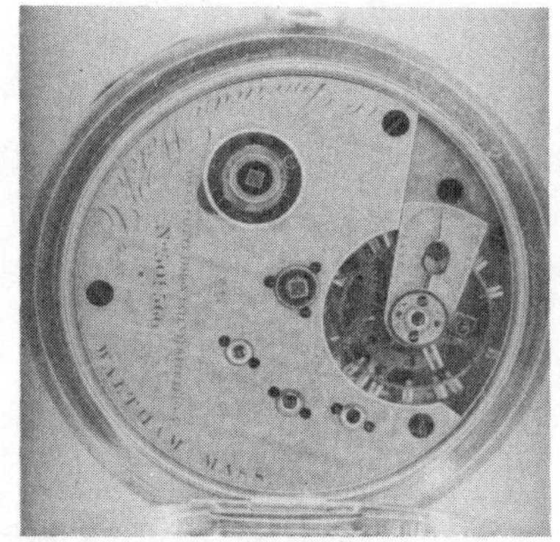

American Watch Co., Model 1868, 16 size, 19 jewels, stem wind, made by Nashua Dept., serial number 501566.

16 SIZE
MODELS 16KW, 1868, 1872, 1888, 1899, 1908, BRIDGE MODEL

Grade or Name — Description	Avg	Ex-Fn	Mint
Am. Watch Co., 11J, M#16KW, KW & KS from back original case ★★	$375	$425	$550
Am. Watch Co., 15J, M#16KW, KW & KS from back ★★	400	445	575
Am. Watch Co., 11J, M#1868, ¾, KW	175	200	240
Am. Watch Co., 15-17J, M#1868, ¾, KW	215	240	300
Am. Watch Co., 15J, M#1872, ¾, SW	100	125	195
Am. Watch Co., 16-17J, M#1872, ¾, SW	150	195	300
Am. Watch Co., 19J, M#1872, ¾, SW	300	400	635
Am. Watch Co., 7-11J, M#1888, ¾, SW	60	85	110
Am. Watch Co., 15J, M#1888, ¾, SW	75	100	130
Am. Watch Co., 17J, M#1899	75	100	145
Am. Watch Co., 7-11J, M#1899	60	80	95
Am. Watch Co., 13J, M#1899	65	85	95
Am. Watch Co. 15-16J, M#1899, HC	65	95	120
Am. Watch Co., 15J, M#1899, SW, Silveroid	50	55	70
Am. Watch Co., 15J, M#1899, SW, OF	60	85	100
American Watch Co., 19J, M#16KW, Maltese cross stopwork, all original 1860 Model ★★	1,500	2,000	3,000
American Watch Co., 17-19J, M#16KW, ¾, KW & KS from back, vibrating hairspring stud, 1860 Model ★★★	1,200	1,800	2,500
American Watch Co., 19J, M#16KW, ¾, KW & KS from back, 1860 Model, original case ★★★	1,500	2,000	3,000
American Watch Co., 15J, M#1868, ¾, KW ★★	300	350	475
American Watch Co., 17J, M#1868, ¾, KW, ADJ ★★	400	500	750

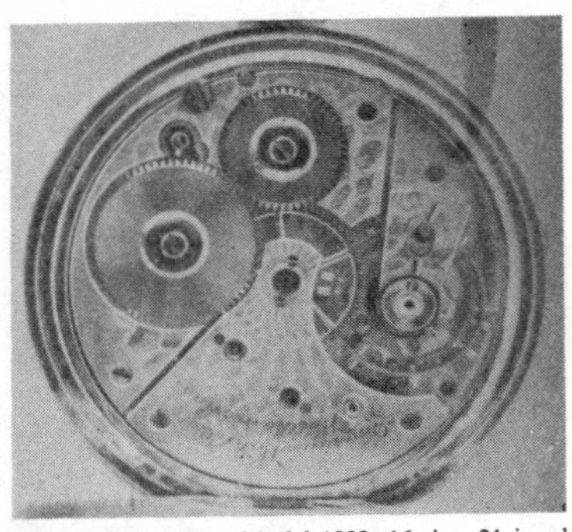

American Watch Co., Model 1888, 16 size, 21 jewels, gold train, note tadpole regulator.

American Watch Co., Bridge Model, 16 size 23 jewels, gold train, adjusted to HCI5P.

Grade or Name — Description	Avg	Ex-Fn	Mint
American Watch Co., 19J, M#1868, SW ★★★	450	550	850
American Watch Co., 17J, M#1872, ¾, SW, HC, 14K ★	995	1,100	1,250
American Watch Co., 19J, M#1872, ¾, SW ★★★	575	700	900
American Watch Co., 19J, M#1872, ¾, GJS, Woerd's Pat. sawtooth balance, all original ★★	2,000	2,500	3,200
American Watch Co., 21J, M#1872, ¾, SW ★★	800	900	1,100
American Watch Co., 21J, M#1872, ¾, SW, 18K ★★★	1,500	1,650	2,250
American Watch Co., 19J, M#1888, 14K ★★	900	1,100	1,400
American Watch Co., 19J, M#1888 ★	500	600	850
American Watch Co., 21J, M#1888, NI, ¾ ★★	750	1,000	1,350
American Watch Co., 23J, BRG, HCI5P, GT, GJS, 14K, original case ★★★	1,150	1,500	2,200
American Watch Co., 23J, BRG, HCI5P, GT, GJS, 18K, original case ★★★	1,400	1,800	2,600
American Watch Co., 23J, BRG, HCI5P, GT, GJS ★	1,000	1,400	2,000
American Watch Co., 21J, BRG, HCI5P, GT, GJS ★	450	525	775
American Watch Co., 19J, BRG, HCI5P, GT, GJS ★	350	425	675
American Watch Co., 17J, BRG, HCI5P, GT, GJS ★	325	400	635
Appleton, Tracy & Co., 15J, M#16KW, ¾, KW & KS from back, all original	325	425	625
Appleton, Tracy & Co., 15J, M#1868, ¾, KW	400	500	695
Appleton, Tracy & Co., 15J, ¾, KW, with vibrating hairspring stud, all original ★★	800	1,000	1,400
Appleton, Tracy & Co., 15J, ¾, KW, with vibrating hairspring stud, 18K, original case ★★	1,600	1,850	2,500
A. W. Co., 7J, M#1872, SW, HC ★	120	150	265
A. W. Co., 11J, M#1872, SW, HC ★	135	175	310
A. W. Co., 17J, M#1872, SW, DMK, GJS, DES, HC ★★	200	300	475
A. W. Co., 7J, M#1899, SW DMK	55	75	85
A. W. Co., 9J, SW, NI	45	60	75
A. W. Co., 11J, M#1899, SW	50	65	80
A. W. W. Co., 7J, SW, M#1888	50	65	80
A. W. W. Co., 11J, M#1888	55	70	85
A. W. W. Co., 13J, M#1888	60	75	95
A. W. W. Co., 15J, M#1899	65	80	90
A. W. W. Co., 15J, M#1888, SW, Silveroid	45	60	75

P.S. Bartlett, Model 1899, 16 size, 17 jewels, serial number 10014478.

Crescent Street, Model 1899, 16 size, 21 jewels, HCI5P, serial number 16179418.

Grade or Name — Description	Avg	Ex-Fn	Mint
A. W. W. Co., 15J, M#1888, SW	65	80	95
A. W. W. Co., 16J, M#1899, SW, DMK	70	80	95
A. W. W. Co., 17J, M#1899, SW	75	85	100
P. S. Bartlett, 17J, M#1899, OF	55	65	80
P. S. Bartlett, 17J, M#1899, HC	65	70	85
P. S. Bartlett, 17J, M#1908	65	70	85
Bond St., 7J, M#1888	50	60	75
Bond St., 11J, M#1888	55	65	80
Bond St. 15J, M#1888	55	65	80
Bond St., 7J, M#1899	45	60	75
Canadian Railway Time Service, M#1908 ★	310	350	485
Crescent St., 19J, M#1899, HCI5P, LS, OF	85	100	135
Crescent St., 19J, M#1899, HCI5P, PS, OF	80	95	125
Crescent St., 19J, M#1899, HCI5P, Silveroid	45	60	80
Crescent St., 19J, M#1899, HCI5P, PS, HC	85	110	145
Crescent St., 21J, M#1899, HCI5P, PS, OF	90	110	125
Crescent St., 21J, M#1899, HCI5P, LS, OF	90	115	125
Crescent St., 21J, M#1899, HCI5P, PS, HC	80	110	140
Crescent St., 19J, M#1908, HCI5P, LS	70	85	95
Crescent St., 19J, M#1908, HCI5P, PS	60	75	90
Crescent St., 21J, M#1908, HCI5P, LS, OF	115	125	135
Crescent St., 21J, M#1908, HCI5P, PS, OF	100	110	120
Crescent St., 21J, M#1908, HCI5P, PS, HC	120	130	150
Crescent St., 21J, M#1908, HCI5P, LS, Wind Indicator	350	390	475
Crescent St., 21J, M#1912, HCI5P, LS, Wind Indicator	350	390	475
Chronometro Superior, 21J, M#1899, LS, OF	125	150	250
Chronometro Victoria, 21J, M#1899, HC	105	120	175
Chronometro Victoria, 15J, M#1899, PS	55	65	85
Diamond Express, 17J, M#1888, PS, OF, Diamond End Stones ★	300	350	475
Electric Railway, 17J, OF, LS, HCI3P	85	125	185
Equity, 7J, M#1908, PS	45	55	65
Hillside, 7J, M#1868, ADJ	100	125	175
Hillside, 7J, M#1868, sweep sec. ★★	250	300	465
Marquis, 15J, M#1899, PS	65	75	95
Marquis, 15J, M#1908, PS	65	75	95

Premier Maximus, "Premier" on movement, "Maximus" on dial, 16 size, 23 jewels (two diamond end stones), open face, pendant set, serial number 17000014.

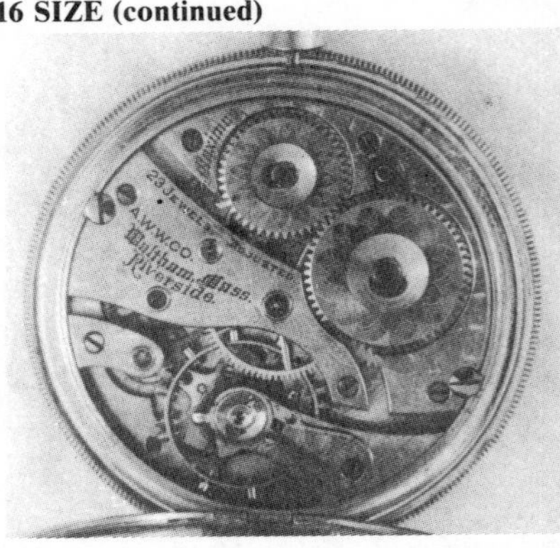

Riverside Maximus, Model 1899, 16 size, 23 jewels, gold train, gold jewel settings, diamond end stone, hunting case, serial number 12509200.

Grade or Name — Description	Avg	Ex-Fn	Mint
Non-Magnetic, 15J, NI, HC	135	155	185
Park Road, 16-17J, M#1872, PS	100	120	150
Park Road, 11-15J, M#1872, PS	90	110	135
Premier, 9J, M#1908, PS, OF	50	60	75
Premier, 11J, M#1908	60	70	85
Premier, 15J, M#1908, LS, OF	70	85	95
Premier, 17J, M#1908, PS, OF	70	90	105
Premier, 17J, M#1908, PS, OF, Silveroid	45	60	70
Premier, 21J, M#1908, Silveroid	55	75	80
Premier, 21J, M#1908, LS, OF	80	95	125
Premier Maximus, 23J, M#1908, GT, gold case, LS, GJS, HCI6P, WI, DR, 18K Maximus case ★★	7,500	8,500	10,000
Premier Maximus, 23J, M#1908, GT, gold case, LS, GJS, HCI6P, WI, DR, 18K Maximus case, sterling box and papers, extra crystal & mainspring ★★	8,500	9,500	12,000
Premier Maximus, 23J, M#1908, GT, HCI6P, YGF case ★★	2,000	2,500	3,250
Railroader, 17J, M#1888, LS, NI ★★	300	350	535
Railroad King, 17J, 2-Tone ★	195	240	375
Railroad Watches with R. R. names on dial and movement, such as Canadian Pacific RR, Santa Fe Route, etc., M#s 1888, 1899, 1908 ★	255	450	750
Repeater, 16J, M#1872, Coin, 5 min. ★★	2,500	2,700	3,500
Repeater, 16J, M#1872, 5 min., 18K ★★	3,500	4,500	6,500
Repeater, 1 min. moon phase, M#1872, Perpetual Cal., 18K case, all original ★★★	35,000	37,500	45,000
Riverside, 15J, M#1872, PS, NI	85	95	105
Riverside, 15J, M#1872, PS	65	75	85
Riverside, 16-17J, M#1888, NI, 14K	500	650	750
Riverside, 16-17J, M#1888, NI	75	85	95
Riverside, 17J, M#1888, gilded	50	60	75
Riverside, 15J, M#1888, gilded	40	50	65
Riverside, 17J, M#1899, LS, DR	75	90	115
Riverside, 17J, M#1899, LS, DR, Silveroid	60	70	85
Riverside, 19J, M#1899, LS, DR, OF	80	95	135

AMERICAN WALTHAM WATCH CO., 16 SIZE (continued)

Grade or Name — Description	Avg	Ex-Fn	Mint
Riverside, 19J, M#1899, PS, DR	85	110	135
Riverside, 21J, M#1899, LS, DR	100	125	150
Riverside, 19-21J, M#1908, HCI5P, LS, DR	85	110	135
Riverside, 19J, M#1908, HCI5P, PS, DR	75	90	125
Riverside Maximus, 21J, M#1888, LS, ADJ, GJS, GT, DR ★★	500	600	750
Riverside Maximus, 21J, M#1888, LS, ADJ, GJS, GT, DR, HC, 14K ★★	750	850	1,150
Riverside Maximus, 21J, M#1899, PS, HCI5P, GJS, GT, DR	300	400	525
Riverside Maximus, 21J, M#1899, LS, HCI5P, GJS, GT, DR	400	500	635
Riverside Maximus, 23J, M#1899, LS, HCI5P, GJS, GT, DR	450	575	685
Riverside Maximus, 23J, M#1908, PS, HCI5P, GJS, GT, DR	400	525	635
Riverside Maximus, 23J, M#1908, LS, HCI5P, GJS, GT, DR	550	650	735
Riverside Maximus, 23J, M#1908, PS, HCI5P, GJS, GT, DR, HC ★	600	700	795
Riverside Maximus, 23J, M#1908, PS, HCI5P, GJS, GT, DR, 14K, HC	995	1,300	1,850
Riverside Maximus, 21J, M#1888, LS, GT, Diamond end stones ★★	500	560	735
Riverside Maximus, 21J, M#1899, LS, GT, Diamond end stone, OF ★	395	460	600
Riverside Maximus, 21J, M#1899, LS, GT, Diamond end stone, HC ★	535	635	775
Riverside Maximus, 23J, M#1908, LS, HCI5P, Wind Indicator ★★	2,200	2,750	3,500
Roadmaster, 17J, M#1899, LS, OF GJS ★	200	250	385
Royal, 15J, M#1872, PS	50	65	75
Royal, 17J, M#1888, PS, OF	55	65	75
Royal, 17J, M#1888, PS, HC	55	65	75
Royal, 17J, M#1899, HCI5P, Silveroid	40	50	60
Royal, 17J, M#1899, LS, HCI5P	70	85	95
Royal, 17J, M#1899, PS, HCI5P	60	75	85
Royal Special, 17J, M#1888	75	85	95

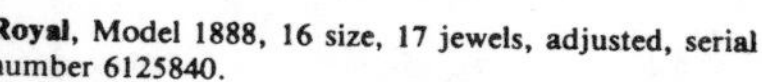

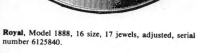

Royal, Model 1888, 16 size, 17 jewels, adjusted, serial number 6125840.

Vanguard, Model 1908, 16 size, 23 jewels, diamond end stone, gold jewel settings, exposed winding gears, serial number 11012533.

AMERICAN WALTHAM WATCH CO., 16 SIZE (continued)

Grade or Name — Description	Avg	Ex-Fn	Mint
Sol, 7J, M#1888	45	55	75
Sol, 7J, M#1908	45	55	75
Stone Movement (crystal top & bottom plates), 16J, M#1872, GJS, HCI5P ★★★	4,500	6,000	8,500
Traveler, 7J, M#1888, 1899, 1908	40	50	65
Vanguard, 19J, M#1899, PS, LS, HCI5P, GJS, DR, OF	100	125	170
Vanguard, 19J, M#1899, PS, LS, HCI5P, GJS, DR, HC	110	135	185
Vanguard, 21J, M#1899, HCI5P	100	125	170
Vanguard, 23J, M#1899, HCI5P, HC	175	225	325
Vanguard, 23J, M#1899, HCI5P, Silveroid	120	140	170
Vanguard, 23J, M#1899, LS, HCI5P, GJS, DR, OF	125	150	180
Vanguard, 23J, M#1899, PS, HCI5P, GJS, DR, OF	120	140	160
Vanguard, 23J, M#1899, PS, Wind Indicator, HCI5P, GJS, DR	325	365	435
Vanguard, 19J, M#1908, LS & PS, HCI5P, GJS, DR	90	125	160
Vanguard, 21J, M#1908, HCI5P, GJS, DR, Diamond end stone	165	180	225
Vanguard, 21J, M#1908, HCI5P, GJS, DR, PS, LS	95	105	130
Vanguard, 21J, M#1908, HCI5P, GJS, DR, PS, LS, Silveroid	85	95	115
Vanguard, 23J, M#1908, LS, HCI5P, GJS, DR	125	150	185
Vanguard, 23J, M#1908, LS, HCI5P, GJS, DR, Multi-Color Case, YGF, OF	195	210	285
Vanguard, 23J, M#1908, PS, HCI5P, GJS, DR	115	140	170
Vanguard, 23J, M#1908, HCI5P, Wind Indicator, GJS, DR	325	425	470
Vanguard, 23J, M#1908, HCI5P, GJS, Diamond end stone	165	180	230
Vanguard, 23J, M#1908, HCI5P, GJS, HC	225	260	350
Vanguard, 23J, OF, LS or PS, 14K	450	495	675
Vanguard, 23J, M#1908, HCI6P, Wind Indicator, GJS, DR	325	375	445
Vanguard, 23J, M#1908, HCI6P, Wind Indicator, Lossier, GJS, DR	335	385	445
Vanguard, 23J, M#1912, Press Jewels	100	125	170
Vanguard, 23J, M#1912, PS, military (case), Wind Indicator	300	375	500

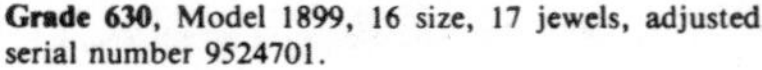

Grade 630, Model 1899, 16 size, 17 jewels, adjusted, serial number 9524701.

Grade 645, Model 1899, 16 size, 21 jewels, adjusted to HCI5P, gold center wheel.

AMERICAN WALTHAM WATCH CO., 16 SIZE (continued)

Grade or Name — Description	Avg	Ex-Fn	Mint
George Washington, 11J, M#1857	195	240	275
M#665, 19J, GJS, BRG, HC ★★	850	1,000	1,300
M#1888, G #s 650, 640	60	75	85
M#1899, G #s 610, 615, 618, 620, 625, 628, 630	60	75	85
M#1908, G #s 610, 611, 613, 614, 618, 620, 621, 623, 625, 628, 630, 635, 636, 637, 640, 641, 642	60	75	95
M#645, 21J, GCW, OF, LS	85	110	145
M#645, 19J, OF, LS	80	105	130
M#16A, 22J, HCI3P, 24 hr. dial	85	115	145
M#1621, 21J, HCI5P	85	110	140
M#1623, 23J, HCI5P	95	120	160

Note: All prices are with gold filled cases, except where otherwise noted.

Note: Some grades are not included. Their values can be determined by comparing with similar models or grades listed.

Chronograph, Model 1874 split-second, 14 size. Note two split second hands on dial.

Bond St., 14 size, 7 jewels, stem wind, open face, note pin set, serial number 2437666, c. 1884.

14 SIZE
MODELS 14KW, 1874, FULL PLATE 1884, 1895, 1897, COLONIAL-A

Grade or Name — Description	Avg	Ex-Fn	Mint
Adams Street, 7J, M#14KW, ¾, KW, Coin	$95	$125	$165
Adams Street, 11J, M#14KW, ¾, KW, Coin	115	135	175
Adams Street, 15J, M#14KW, ¾, KW	135	175	250
A. W. Co., 7J, M#14KW, ¾, KW	55	65	85
A. W. W. Co., 7J, M#1874, SW, LS, HC	50	60	75
A. W. Co., 15-16J, M#1874, ¾, SW	55	65	85
A. W. Co., 7-11J, M#s FP, 1884, & 1895	40	50	65
A. W. Co., 13J, M#1884	45	50	65
Am. Watch Co., 7-11J, KW, ¾	65	90	125
Am. Watch Co., 13J, M#1874, ¾, SW	45	60	80
Am. Watch Co., 15J, M#1874, ¾	95	140	175
Am. Watch Co., 16J, M#1874, ¾, SW	70	80	100

Chronograph, double dial, Model 1874, 14 size, 16 jewels, open face, back side of movement illustrated, serial number 1259219.

Chronograph, Model 1874-Split Second, 14 size, 15 jewels, open face, gold escape wheel, gold train, serial number 303,094.

Grade or Name —Description	Avg	Ex-Fn	Mint
Am. Watch Co., 7-11J, M#FP, KW	45	55	75
Am. Watch Co., 16J, M#1884, ¾, SW	70	80	95
Am. Watch Co., 15J, M#1897, SW	40	50	65
Bond St., 7J, M#1895, ¾, SW	40	55	75
Bond St., 9J, M#1884, ¾, KW	50	60	75
Bond St., 7J, M#1884, ¾, SW, PS	60	75	95
Beacon, 15J, M#1897, ¾, SW	40	50	65
Chronograph, 13J, M#1884, 14K, OF	600	725	995
Chronograph, 13J, M#1884, 14K, HC	700	800	1,200
Chronograph, 13J, M#1884, 18K, HC ★	950	1,050	1,500
Chronograph, 13J, M#1884	175	235	335
Chronograph, 15J, M#1884	185	250	365
Chronograph, 17J, M#1884	195	270	385
Chronograph, 17J, M#1874, split second ★	225	275	425
Chronograph, 15J, M#1874, split second, 14K ★★	1,000	1,250	1,675
Chronograph, 15J, M#1874, split second, min. register, 14K ★★	1,200	1,600	2,200
(Above in 18K case, add $250 to $400 to value)			
Chronograph, 16J, double dial, M#1874, 18K ★★	2,000	2,500	3,300
Chronometro Victoria, 15J, M#1897, ¾	65	75	95
Church St., 7J, M#1884, ¾	40	60	75
Crescent Garden, 7-11J, M#14KW, KW	60	75	100
Crescent Garden, 7J, M#FP, KW	60	70	90
Wm. Ellery, 7J, M#1874, SW	40	50	65
Gentleman, 7J, M#1884, SW	40	50	75
Hillside, 7-15J, M#1874, SW	45	55	70
Hillside, 7-11J, M#FP, SW	40	50	65
Hillside, 7-13J, M#1884, ¾, KW	40	50	65
Hillside, 11J, M#1884, ¾, KW	55	75	95
Hillside, 15J, M#1884, ¾, SW	65	75	100
Maximus, 21J, M#Colonial A	145	185	275
Maximus, 21J, M#Colonial A, 14K	300	400	575
Night Clock, 7J, M#1884, KW	65	75	95
Repeater, 16J, M#1884, SW, LS, 14K	3,000	4,000	5,850

Five Minute Repeater, Model 1884, 14 size, 13-15 jewels, hunting case, slide actuated, serial number 2809551.

Grade or Name — Description	Avg	Ex-Fn	Mint
Repeater, 16J, M#1884, SW, LS, 18K .... ★	5,000	5,500	6,850
Repeater, 16J, M#1884, SW, LS, Coin	2,000	2,200	2,700
Repeater (5 Min.), 18K, HC .... ★★	5,000	6,000	8,000
Repeater (1 Min.), perpetual calendar, moon phase, 18K .... ★★★	30,000	35,000	40,000
Riverside, 11-15J, M#s 1874, HC .... ★	100	125	200
Riverside, 15J, M#1884	55	60	80
Riverside, 19-21J, M#Colonial A .... ★★	150	185	265
Royal, 11-13J, M#s 1874, 1884	45	55	65
Seaside, 7-11J, M#1884, SW	45	55	65
Special, 7J, M#1895, HC	95	105	120
Sterling, 7J, M#1884	45	55	65
Stone Movement, M#1874, 14K .... ★★★	5,000	6,000	7,500
Waltham, Mass., 7J, Full Plate, KW	55	65	85

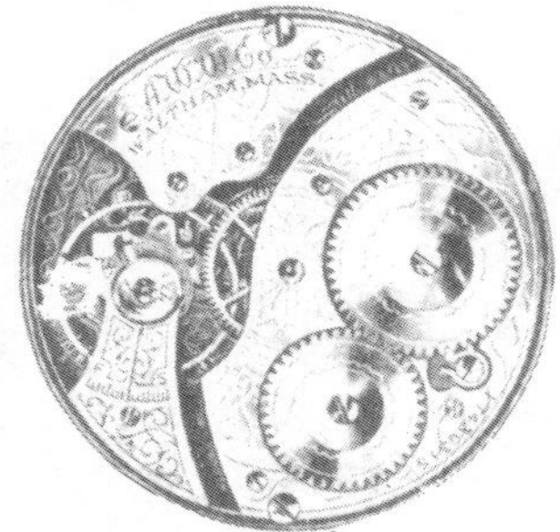

A.W.W.Co., Model 1894, 12 size, 7-11 jewels, open face or hunting.

Riverside, Colonial series, 12 size, 19 jewels, open face or hunting, adjusted to HCI5P, double roller.

12 SIZE
MODELS KW, 1894, BRIDGE, COLONIAL SERIES

Grade or Name — Description	Avg	Ex-Fn	Mint
A. W. W. Co., 7J, M#1894, 14K, OF	$190	$210	$275
A. W. W. Co., 11J, M#1894, Colonial	40	50	60
A. W. W. Co., 15J, M#1894, Colonial	55	60	65
A. W. W. Co., 15J, M#1894, Colonial, 14K, HC	200	250	385
A. W. W. Co., 17J, M#1894, Colonial	65	70	75
A. W. W. Co., 17J, M#1894, Colonial, 14K OF	200	245	325

Actual size illustration of a cushion sytle shaped watch depicting thinness with emphasis on style and beauty. This watch was popular in the 1930's.

Grade or Name — Description	Avg	Ex-Fn	Mint
P. S. Bartlett, 19J, M#1894, 14K, HC	275	325	465
P. S. Bartlett, 19J, M#1894	65	70	75
Bond St., 7J, M#1894	40	50	65
Bridge Model, 19J, GJS, HCI5P, GT	250	335	500
Bridge Model, 19J, GJS, HCI5P, GT, 18K, HC	600	700	900
Bridge Model, 21J, GJS, HCI5P, GT	300	400	600
Bridge Model, 23J, GJS, HCI5P, GT	400	500	700
Duke, 7-15J, M#1894	55	60	75
Digital Hour & Second Window, 17J	70	85	95
Elite, 17J, OF	55	65	75
Ensign, 7J, OF	40	45	55
Martyn Square, 7-11J, M#KW	175	210	275
Maximus, 21J, GJS, GT	175	225	325
Premier, 17-19J, M#1894	65	80	95
Premier, 21J, M#1894	75	80	110
Riverside, 17-19J, M#1894, Colonial	60	70	80
Riverside, 19-21J, M#1894, Colonial	70	80	90
Riverside, 19-21J, M#1894, Colonial, 14K, HC	225	260	375
Riverside Maximus, 21J, M#1894, Colonial, GT, GJS, 14K	400	465	575
Riverside Maximus, 21J, M#1894, Colonial, GT, GJS	170	225	325
Riverside Maximus, 23J, M#1894, Colonial, GT, GJS ★★	190	250	375
Riverside Maximus, 23J, M#1894, Colonial, GT, GJS, 14K	500	575	665
Royal, 17J, OF, PS	45	50	60
Royal, 19J, OF, PS	55	60	75

10 SIZE
MODEL KW, 1861, 1874

NOTE: These watches (excluding Colonial) are usually found with solid gold cases, and are therefore priced accordingly. Without cases, these watches have very little value due to the fact the cases are difficult to find. Many of the cases came in octagon, decagon, hexagon, cushion and triad shapes.

Appleton Tracy & Co., Model 10KW, 10 size, 11-15 jewels, key wind and set from back, serial number 370411.

Am. W. Co., Model 1873, 8 size, 15 jewels, serial number 691001.

Grade or Name — Description	Avg	Ex-Fn	Mint
Am. W. Co., 7-15J, M#1874, KW, 14K	$200	$235	$335
American Watch Co., 11-15J, M#1874, 14K	300	400	535
Appleton, Tracy & Co., 15J, M#1861, 14K	200	235	335
Appleton, Tracy & Co., 15J, M#1861, 18K multi-color box case	800	900	1,000
P. S. Bartlett, 11J, M#1861, KW, 14K	275	300	365
P. S. Bartlett, 13J, M#KW, gold balance, 1st S#45,801, last 46,200, 14K, Pat. Nov. 3, 1858 ★★	350	425	575
P. S. Bartlett, 13J, M#KW, gold balance, 18K	400	450	595
P. S. Bartlett, 13J, M#1861, KW, 14K	200	300	365
Crescent Garden, 7J, M#1861, KW, 14K	200	245	295
Wm. Ellery, 7,11,15J, M#1861, KW, 14K	200	245	295
Home W. Co., 7J, M#1874, KW, 14K	200	235	285
Martyn Square, 7-11J, M#1861, 14K	200	250	335
Maximus "A", 21J, 14K ★★	400	475	595
Maximus "A", 23J, 14K ★★	425	500	665
Riverside, 19J, HCI5P, GF	65	75	95
Riverside Maximus, 19-21J, HCI5P, GJS, GF	125	185	265
Riverside Maximus, 19-21J, HCI5P, GJS, 18K	450	500	685
Riverside Maximus, 23J, HCI5P, GJS, GF	195	250	375
Royal, 15J, HCI5P, GF	55	65	80

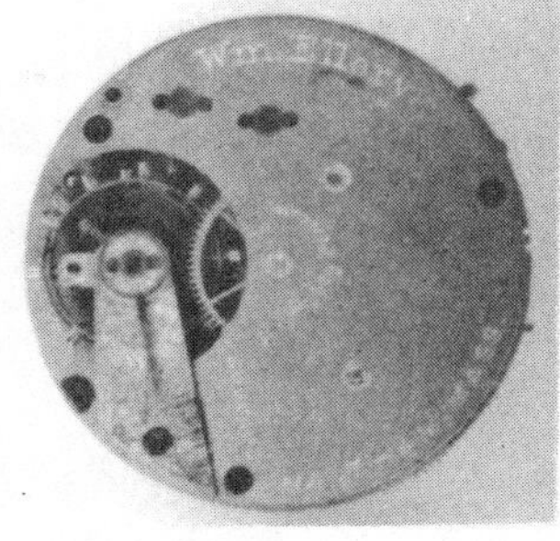

Wm. Ellery, Model 1873, 8 size, 7 jewels, ¾ plate, serial number 2679907.

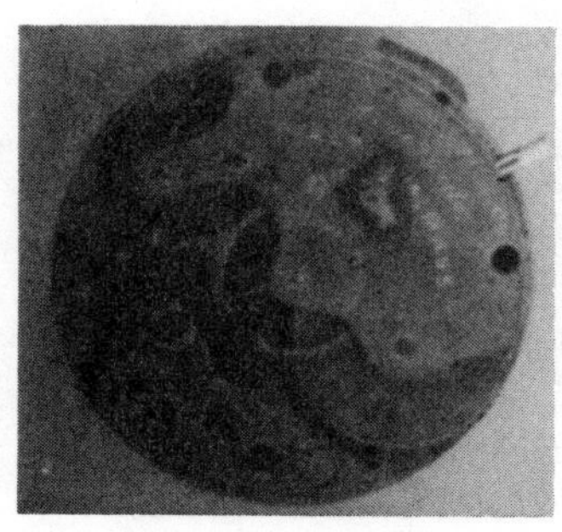

Riverside, Model 1873, 8 size, 7 jewels, serial number 931395.

8 SIZE
MODEL 1873

NOTE: Collectors usually want solid gold cases in small watches. The gold case value must be added to price listed.

Grade or Name — Description	Avg	Ex-Fn	Mint
Am. W. Co., 15J, M#1873, 14K, Multi-Color Box Hinge Case	$500	$650	$850
Am. W. Co., 15J, M#1873	65	75	85
P. S. Bartlett, 15-16J, M#1873	65	75	85
Wm. Ellery, 7-11J, M#1873	45	55	65
Wm. Ellery, 7J, 14K, HC	200	235	320
Riverside, 7-11J, M#1873, 18K, HC, 24 DWT	400	425	485
Riverside, 7-11J, M#1873	65	75	85
Royal, 7-13J, M#1873	45	55	65

6 SIZE
MODEL 1873, 1889

Grade or Name — Description	Avg	Ex-Fn	Mint
A,B,C,D,E,F,G,H,J,K	$65	$70	$85
A,B,C,D,E,F,G,H,J,K, 14K, HC	200	235	280
A. W. W. Co., 19J, 18K, HC	275	350	465
A. W. W. Co., 19J, 14K, Multi-Color gold case	500	625	795
A. W. W. Co., 7J, M#1873	65	70	80
A. W. W. Co., 15J, multi-color GF HC	175	200	245
A. W. W. Co., 11J, HC, LS	90	100	125
Am. W. Co., 7J, M#1889	55	60	75
American W. Co., 7J, KW & KS from back, 10K, HC	200	225	265
Wm. Ellery, 7J, M#1873	55	60	75
Lady Waltham, 16J, M#1873, Demi, HC, 14K	280	310	350
Lady Waltham, 16J, M#1873, 18K	375	425	525
Riverside Maximus, 21J, GT, DR	225	250	295
Riverside, 15-17J, PS	75	80	95
Seaside, 7J, M#1873	55	60	75

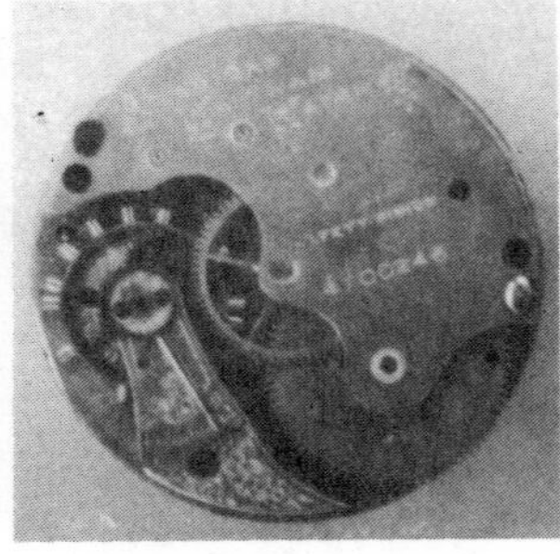

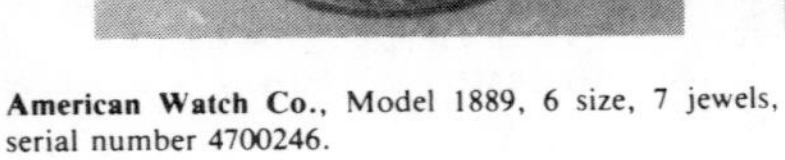
American Watch Co., Model 1889, 6 size, 7 jewels, serial number 4700246.

Stone Movement, Crystal Plate, size 4, 16 jewels, gold train, open face, serial number 28.

4 SIZE

Grade or Name — Description	Avg	Ex-Fn	Mint
Stone Movement, 4 size, crystal, 16 ruby jewels in gold settings, gold train, exposed pallets, compensation balance adjusted to temperature, isochronism, position, Breguet hairspring, and crystal top plate, 14K ... ★ ★ ★	$3,500	$4,800	$6,500

Lady Waltham, Model 1900, 0 size, 16 jewels, open face or hunting, adjusted, stem wind, pendant set, originally sold for $26.00.

A.W. Co., Model 1891, 0 size, 7 jewels, stem wind, originally sold for $13.00.

0 SIZE
MODELS 1882, 1891, 1900, 1907

Grade or Name — Description	Avg	Ex-Fn	Mint
A. W. Co., 7J, 14K, HC	$200	$245	$310
A. W. Co., 7J, SW	40	50	60
A. W. Co., 11J, ¾, SW, OF & HC	55	70	85
American Watch Co., 15J, ¾, SW, OF & HC	60	75	95
American Watch Co., 15J, ¾, SW, 14K, HC	200	250	325
P. S. Bartlett, 11J, M#1891, OF, 14K	125	140	185
P. S. Bartlett, 16J, 14K, HC	200	235	300
Lady Waltham, 15J, ¾, SW, 14K, HC	225	265	325
Lady Waltham, 15-16J, ¾, SW, OF & HC	60	70	95
Maximus, 19J, ¾, SW, OF & HC	150	175	225
Riverside, 15,16,17J, ¾, SW, OF & HC	60	70	80
Riverside, 15,16,17J, ¾, SW, OF & HC, 14K	175	230	275
Riverside Maximus, 21J, GT, multi-color gold case, 14K ★ ★	500	675	885
Riverside Maximus, 21J, ¾, GT	175	200	295
Riverside Maximus, 19J, ¾, SW, OF, HC	150	175	250
Riverside Maximus, 19J, ¾, HC, 14K ★	400	435	550
Royal, 16J, ¾, SW, OF & HC	45	50	75
Seaside, 15J, ¾, SW, HC, 14K	200	235	275
Seaside, 11J, ¾, SW, OF, multi-color dial	125	150	225
Seaside, 11J, ¾, SW, OF & HC	40	50	65
Seaside, 7J, ¾, HC	40	50	65
Seaside, 7J, ¾, HC, 14K	195	245	275
Special, 11J, M#1891, OF, 14K	160	200	225

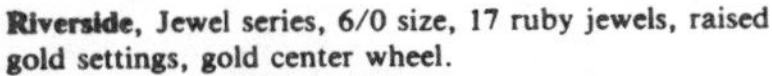

Riverside, Jewel series, 6/0 size, 17 ruby jewels, raised gold settings, gold center wheel.

Ruby, Jewel Series, 6/0 size, 15 jewels, adjusted to temperature, open face or hunting.

JEWEL SERIES 6/0

Grade or Name — Description	Avg	Ex-Fn	Mint
Riverside J Size, 17J, HC, 14K	$150	$225	$365
Ruby J Size, 15J, OF, 14K	145	220	335
Sapphire, 15J, OF, 14K	135	185	275

Round, military style, with 24 hour dial. Movement on right, 17 jewels, hack setting.

MAN'S WRIST WATCH

Style or Grade — Description	Avg	Ex-Fn	Mint
Curvex, 14K case	$75	$90	$125
Curvex, gold filled case	20	25	35
Cushion, 14K case	70	85	115
Cushion, gold filled	20	25	35
Rectangular, 14K case	75	90	125
Rectangular, gold filled	20	25	35
Tonneau, 14K case	80	95	125
Tonneau, gold filled	20	25	35
Square, 14K case	75	90	110
Square, gold filled	20	25	35
Round, gold filled case	15	20	28
Round, calendar, 14K case	95	115	165
Round, doctor's, pulsation on outer rim	40	45	55
Round, military style, stainless case	65	80	125

Square, gold filled, 6/0 size. **Tonneau**, gold filled, 6/0 size.

LADY'S WRIST WATCH

Style or Grade — Description	Avg	Ex-Fn	Mint
Locket or Wrist, convertible, 14K case	$45	$55	$75
Locket or Wrist, convertible, gold filled	15	20	28
Locket or Wrist, convertible, base metal	10	12	15
Rectangular, small, M#400, 14K	55	60	85
Rectangular, small, M#400, gold filled	15	20	28
Rectangular, small, M#400, base metal	5	8	15
Round, small, after 1940, 14K case	50	55	65
Round, small, after 1940, gold filled	10	15	25
Round, small, after 1940, base metal	5	8	15

AMERICAN WALTHAM WATCH CO.
IDENTIFICATION OF WRIST WATCH MOVEMENTS

How to Identify your Watch: Compare the movement of your watch with the illustration in this section. While comparing, note the location of the balance, jewels, screws, gears and type of back plate. Which will be clues to identifying the movement you have.

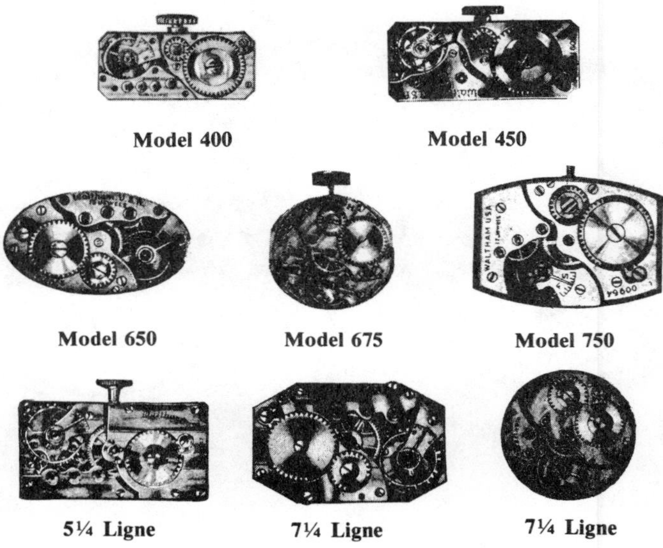

Model 400 **Model 450**

Model 650 **Model 675** **Model 750**

5¼ Ligne **7¼ Ligne** **7¼ Ligne**

AMERICAN WALTHAM WATCH CO.
IDENTIFICATION OF MOVEMENTS
BY MODEL NUMBER

How to Identify Your Watch: Compare the movement of your watch with the illustrations in this section. Upon matching the movement exactly, the model number and size can be determined. While comparing, note the location of the balance, jewels, screws, gears and type of back plate (Full, ¾, Bridge) which will be clues to identifying the movement you have. Having determined the size and model number, you can now find your watch in the main price listing by name or number (which is engraved on the movement).

20 size, 1862 or KW 20 Model. Note vibrating hairspring stud.

18 size, key wind model

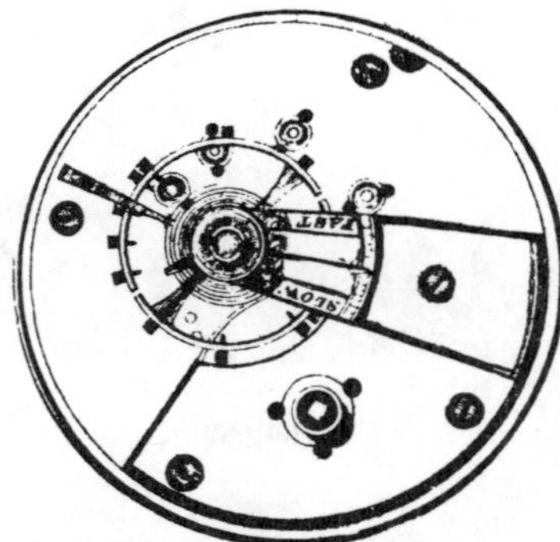

Model 1857, KW, KS

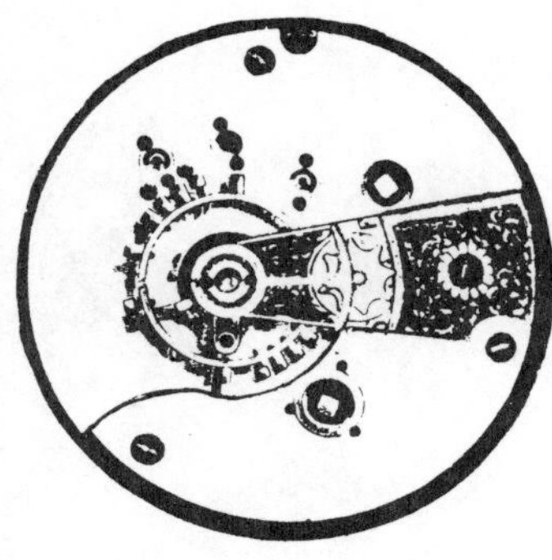

Model 1870, KW, KS from back

Model 1877, 18 size

Model 1879, 18 size

Model 1883, 18 size

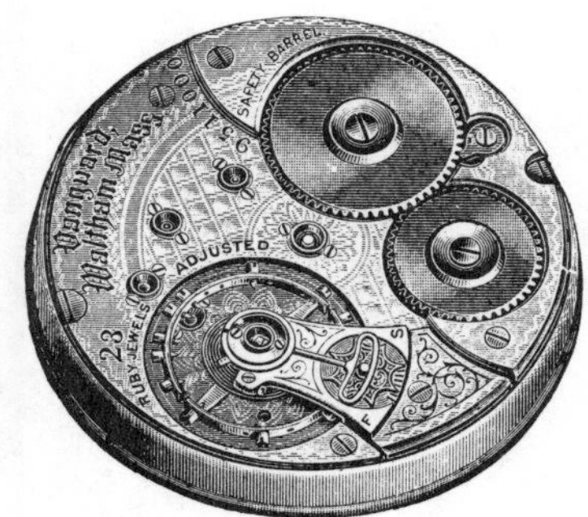

Model 1892, 18 size

Model 1868, 16 size

Model 1872, 16 size

Model 1888, 16 size
Split plate

Bridge Model, 16 size

Model 1899, 16 size

Model 1908, 16 size

Model 1874, 14 size

Model 1874 & 1884, 14 size

Model 1884, 14 size

Model 1895, 14 size

Model 1897, 14 size

Colonial Series

Colonial Series

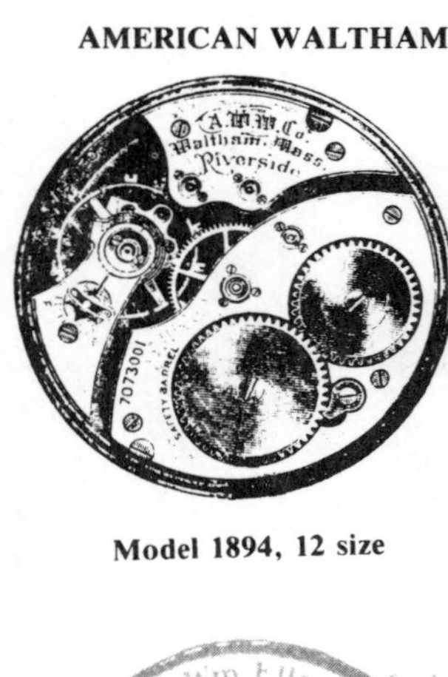

Model 1894, 12 size

Model 1894, 12 size

Model 1873, 8 size

Model 1873, 8 size

Model 1873, 6 size

Model 1889, 6 size

Model 1890, 6 size

Model 1882, 1 size

Model 1891, 0 size

Model 1900, 0 size

Model 1907, 0 size

Jewel Series

ANSONIA CLOCK COMPANY
Brooklyn, New York
Manufactured watches from
1904 — 1929

The Ansonia Watch Co. was owned by the Ansonia Clock Company in Ansonia, Connecticut. Ansonia started making clocks in about 1850 and began manufacturing watches in 1904. They produced about 10,000,000 dollar-type watches. The company was sold to a Russian investor in 1930. "Patented April 17, 1888," is on the back plate of some Ansonia watches.

Some of the watches produced by Ansonia were marketed under different labels: Ascot, Bonnie Laddie Shoes, Dispatch, Loeser, Lenox, Picadilly, Mentor, Guide, Rural, H. Rosenburg Special, Tutor, Superior, and The Sesqui-Centennial.

Description	Avg	Ex-Fn	Mint
Ansonia White Dial	$20	$25	$35
Ansonia Radium Dial	35	45	55
Ansonia in NI case, Black Dial	25	35	45
Ascot	35	50	65
Bonnie Laddie Shoes	40	80	95
Dispatch	25	40	55
Faultless	35	40	50
Guide	35	50	65
Lenox	30	35	45
Mentor	25	35	45
Tom Mix	150	185	275
Picadilly	35	45	55
Rural	25	40	60
Sesqui-Centennial	150	175	235
Superior	35	50	65
Tutor	35	50	65

Note: All grades are in good working order.

Ansonia Watch Company. Example of a basic movement, 16 size, stem wind.

Ansonia Watch Company. Example of a basic movement, 16 size, stem wind.

APPLETON, TRACY & CO.
Waltham, Massachusetts
1857 — 1859

(See The American Watch Co.)

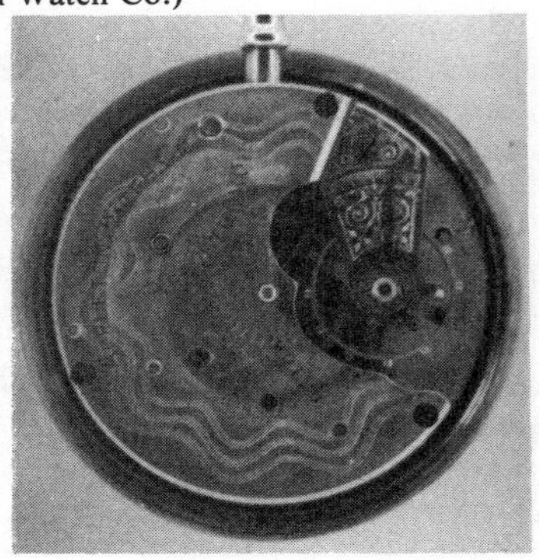

Appleton Watch Co., 18 size, 7 jewels. "The Appleton Watch Co." on dial. Engraved on movement "Appleton Watch Co., Appleton, Wis." Serial number 93106. Note that the stem is attached to movement.

APPLETON WATCH CO.
(REMINGTON WATCH CO.)
Appleton, Wisconsin
1901 — 1903

In 1901, O. E. Bell bought the machinery of the defunct Cheshire Watch Company and moved it to Appleton, Wisconsin, where he had organized the Remington Watch Company. The first watches were shipped from the factory in February 1902; production ceased in mid-1903 and the contents were sold off before the end of that year. Most movements made by this firm were modified Cheshire movements and were marked "Appleton Watch Company." Advertisements for the firm in 1903 stated that they made 16 and 18 size movements with 11, 15, or 17 jewels. Serial numbers range from 90,000 to 95,000. During the two years they were in business, the company produced about 2,000 to 3,000 watches.

Description	Avg	Ex-Fn	Mint
18S, 7J, OF, NI, ¾, DMK, SW, PS, stem attached . . . ★ ★ ★	$560	$675	$885
18S, 7J, OF, NI, ¾, DMK, SW, PS, Coin, OF . . . . . . ★ ★ ★	475	525	595
16S, 7-11J, ¾, stem attached . . . . ★ ★ ★	435	495	595

AUBURNDALE WATCH COMPANY
Auburndale, Massachusetts
1879 — 1883

This company was the first to attempt an inexpensive watch. Jason R. Hopkins was issued two patents in 1875 covering the "rotary design." The rotary design eliminated the need of adjusting to various positions, resulting in a less expensive watch. The company was formed about 1876, and the first watches were known as the "Auburndale Rotary." In 1876, equipment was purchased from the Marion Watch Co. Auburndale produced about 3,230 watches before closing in 1883.

AUBURNDALE WATCH CO. (continued)

Auburndale Timer, 18 size, 7 jewels, jump quarter and split second, winds with key, turns stem counter-clockwise to actuate watch, serial number 92.

Auburndale Rotary, 20 size, 2 jewels, lever set, stem wind, detent escapement.

Grade or Name — Description	Avg	Ex-Fn	Mint
Auburndale Rotary, 20S, 2J, LS, SW, NI case, detent ★★★	$1,550	$1,800	$2,600
Auburndale Rotary, 18S, 2J, SW, LS, NI case, lever ★★	800	1,200	1,800
Bentley, 18S, 7J, SW, LS, NI case	300	500	750
Lincoln, 18S, 7J, LS, NI case, KW	300	500	750
Auburndale Timer, 18S, 7J, SW, NI case, 10 min. timer, ¼ sec. jump, Chronograph	140	175	275
Auburndale Timer, 18S, 7J, KW, NI case, 10 min. timer, ¼ sec. jump with split seconds, Chronograph	400	500	750

AURORA WATCH CO.
Aurora, Illinois
1883 — 1890

Aurora Watch Co. was organized in mid-1883 with the goal of getting one jeweler in every town to handle Aurora watches. The first movements were 18S, full plate, and were first sold in the fall of 1884. There were several watches marked No. 1. The total production was about 215,000; over 100,000 were 18S, and some were 6S ladies' watches. For the most part Aurora produced medium to low grade and at one time made about 150 movements per day. The Hamilton Watch Co. purchased the company on June 19, 1890.

The "Guild" watch was made under special contract for the U. S. Jewelers Guild and carried the Guild trademark.

Eleven grades of hunter cases and open faces with stem wind, seven grades of key wind, and five grades with Brequet hairsprings for railroad service were made.

Description	Avg	Ex-Fn	Mint
18S, 7J, OF, KW, HC	$200	$275	$375
18S, 11J, OF, KW, HC	225	300	400
18S, 11J, 5th pinion model, OF	225	300	400
18S, 15J, OF, KW, HC	250	325	425
18S, 15 Ruby Jewels, 5th pinion, HC ★	600	700	995

(The 5th pinion model is marked 15 ruby jewels, but has 17 jewels. This was Aurora's highest grade.)

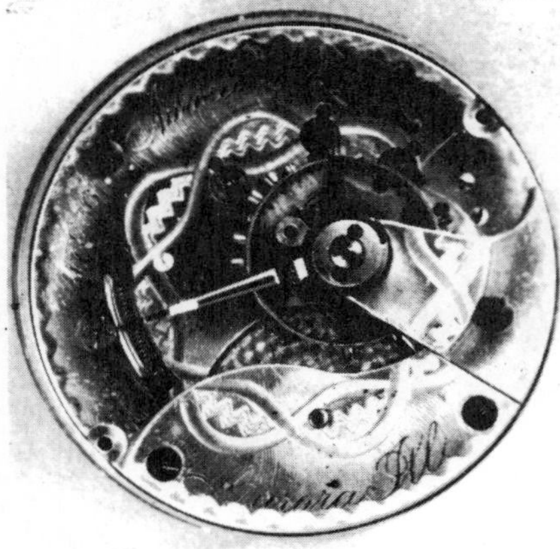

Aurora Watch Co., 18 size, 15 jewels.

Aurora Watch Co., 18 size, 11 jewels, serial number 42000. Note fifth pinion.

Description	Avg	Ex-Fn	Mint
18S, 15 Ruby Jewels, 5th pinion, OF ★★	800	1,000	1,300
18S, 11J, HC, OF, SW, Gilded, Coin	125	175	250
18S, 11J, HC, OF, SW, Gilded	125	175	250
18S, 15J, HC, OF, SW, Gilded	150	200	275
18S, 15J, Chronometer, ADJ, SW/LS, HC, NI	375	450	600
18S, made expressly for the guild	200	300	550
18S, 15J, OF, DMK, NI, GJS	225	275	375
6S, 11-15J, HC	150	200	300

Estimated Serial Nos. and Production Dates

1885 - 60,000
1886 - 110,000
1887 - 160,000
1888 - 200,000
1889 - 215,000

BALL WATCH CO.
1879 — 1969

The Ball Watch Company did not manufacture watches but did help formulate the specifications of watches used for railroad service. Webb C. Ball of Cleveland, Ohio, was the general time inspector for over 125,000 miles of railroad in the U. S., Mexico, and Canada. In 1891 there was a collision between the Lake Shore and Michigan Southern Railways trains at Kipton, Ohio. The collision was reported to have occurred because an engineer's watch had stopped for about four minutes, then started running again. The railroad officials commissioned Ball to establish the timepiece inspection system. Ball knew that the key to safe operations of the railroad was the manufacturing of sturdy, precision timepieces. He also knew they must be able to withstand hard use and still be accurate. Before this time, each railroad company had its own rules and standards. After Ball presented his guidelines, most American manufacturers set out to meet these standards and soon a list was made of different manufacturers that produced

BALL WATCH CO. (continued)

watches of the grade that would pass inspection. Each railroad employee had a card that he carried showing the record of how his watch performed on inspection. Ball was also instrumental in the formation of the Horological Institute of America.

A 1902 advertisement for Ball Watch Company read, "We do not sell movements or cases separately."

200,000 railroad watches, plus 150,000 non-railroad grade watches, were made and sold by the Ball Watch Co., totaling approximately 350,000.

BALL WATCH COMPANY
ESTIMATED SERIAL NUMBERS AND PRODUCTION DATES
FOR RAILROAD GRADE WATCHES

Hamilton

Date	Serial No.
1895	13,000
1897	20,500
1900	42,000
1902	170,000
1905	462,000
1910	600,000
1915	603,000
1920	610,000
1925	620,000
1930	637,000
1935	641,000
1938	647,000
1939	650,000
1940	651,000
1941	652,000
1942	654,000

Waltham

Date	Serial No.
1900	060,700
1905	202,000
1910	216,200
1915	250,000
1920	260,000
1925	270,000

Illinois W. Co.

Date	Serial No.
1929	800,000
1930	801,000
1931	803,000
1932	804,000

Elgin

Date	Serial No.
1904 - 1906	
S# range:	
11,853,000 - 12,282,000	

E. Howard & Co.

Date	Serial No.
1893 - 1895	
S# range:	
226,000 - 308,000	

BALL'S FIRST STANDARDS FOR R.R. USE

1. Must be 18 or 16 size.
2. Must have a minimum of 17 jewels.
3. Must be a single roller.
4. Must be lever set.
5. Must have a Breguet hairspring.
6. Must have a patent regulator.
7. Must be adjusted to isochronism and 5 positions.
8. Must be adjusted to a rate of within 30 seconds a week.
9. Must have a standard mark or number stamped on back plate.

BALL ADDED THESE LATER:

10. Must have "adjusted 5 positions" stamped on the plate.
11. Must be a double roller.
12. Must have a plain Arabic dial.
13. Must have the winding stem at 12 o'clock.
14. Must be temperature adjusted for accuracy from 30 to 95 degrees F.
15. Must have a minimum of 19 jewels.

NOTE: Ball Watches are difficult to identify at first, but if one studies the market he can soon identify most of them. The manufacturer's serial number list can be useful. Prices shown are for watches with original Ball cases, which bring top dollar and are preferred by most collectors.

BALL—AURORA
18 SIZE

Description	Avg	Ex-Fn	Mint
17J, marked Ball ★★	$1,000	$1,200	$1,500

BALL—ELGIN
18 SIZE G. F. CASES

Description	Avg	Ex-Fn	Mint
16J, G#327, HC, LS ★	$185	$250	$375
17J, G#328, HC, LS ★	185	250	375
17J, G#328, Coin, HC, LS ★	150	180	280
17J, G#329, HC, LS ★	185	250	375
21J, G#330, HC, LS ★★	350	400	550
16J, G#331, NI, OF, HCI5P, PS, Commercial Std. ★★	175	200	300
17J, G#331, NI, OF, HCI5P, PS	165	255	325
17J, G#332, OF, PS ★	165	255	325
17J, G#333, NI, OF, HCI5P, LS	175	200	310
17J, G#333, NI, HC, HCI5P, LS ★★★	1,400	1,700	2,200
21J, G#333, NI, OF, HCI5P, LS	250	325	390
21J, G#334, NI, OF, HCI5P, LS	250	325	400

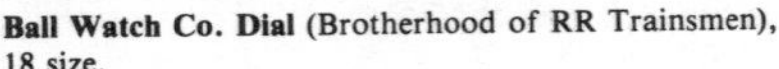
Ball Watch Co. Dial (Brotherhood of RR Trainsmen), 18 size.

Ball Watch Co. Dial (Order of Railroad Conductors), 18 size.

BALL—HAMILTON
18 SIZE G. F. CASES

Description	Avg	Ex-Fn	Mint
17J, M#999, Commercial Standard ★★	$450	$575	$750
17J, M#999, NI, OF, HCI5P, LS, Coin	150	185	275
17J, M#999, NI, OF, HCI5P, LS	180	265	350
17J, M#999, NI, OF, HCI5P, marked "Loaner" on case	185	320	400
19J, M#999, NI, OF, HCI5P, LS	195	275	400
21J, M#999, NI, OF, HCI5P, LS	235	300	425
23J, M#999, NI, OF, HCI5P, LS ★★★	2,500	3,500	5,000
Ball & Co., 17J, SR, Coin	450	600	800

Ball Watch Co., Brotherhood of RR trainmen, 18 size, 17 jewels; movement made by Hamilton, serial number 13,020.

Ball Watch Co. (Hamilton), Grade 999, 18 size, 21 jewels, sun ray damaskeening, serial number 548157, c. 1906.

Grade or Name — Description	Avg	Ex-Fn	Mint
Brotherhood of Locomotive Engineers, 17J	385	435	595
Brotherhood of Locomotive Engineers, 19J	650	750	995
Brotherhood of Locomotive Engineers, 21J	600	725	895
Brotherhood of Locomotive Firemen, 17J	385	435	595
Brotherhood of Locomotive Firemen, 19J	650	750	1,000
Brotherhood of Locomotive Firemen, 21J	600	725	895
Brotherhood of Railroad Trainsmen, 17J	385	435	595
Brotherhood of Railroad Trainsmen, 19J	650	750	995
Brotherhood of Railroad Trainsmen, 21J	600	725	895
Order of Railroad Conductors, 17J	385	435	595
Order of Railroad Conductors, 19J	650	750	995
Order of Railroad Conductors, 21J	600	725	895
Order of Railroad Telegraphers, 17J	385	435	595
Order of Railroad Telegraphers, 19J	650	750	1,000
Order of Railroad Telegraphers, 21J	600	725	895
Railroad Watch Co., 16J, OF, LS ★★	900	1,200	1,750
Railroad Watch Co., 17J, OF, LS ★★	1,000	1,300	1,895
17J, Off. Ball marked jewelers name ★	500	600	895
17J, M#999, adjusted "A"	500	600	725

BALL—DeLONG ESCAPEMENT
16 SIZE

Description	Avg	Ex-Fn	Mint
21J, 14K OF Case	$2,000	$3,000	$4,985

BALL—HAMILTON
16 SIZE G. F. CASES

Description	Avg	Ex-Fn	Mint
16J, M#976, 977, NI, OF, LS	$125	$150	$185
17J, M#974, NI, OF, LS	140	165	200
17J, M#974, NI, OF, LS, Coin	65	85	110

Top left: Ball-Hamilton, 16 size, 23 jewels. **Bottom left: Ball-Illinois**, 16 size, 23 jewels. **Above: Ball-Waltham**, 16 size, 23 jewels. These three movements are similar in appearance. To identify, note where the hair spring stud attaches to the balance bridge, which is slightly different on each movement.

Description	Avg	Ex-Fn	Mint
19J, M#999, NI, OF, LS	135	175	210
21J, M#999, NI, OF, LS	150	185	240
21J, M#999B, NI, OF, LS, HCI6P	185	225	300
21J, M#999, Coin case	95	135	170
21J, M#999 Loaner	170	200	275
23J, M#999B, NI, OF, LS, HCI6P	500	575	775
23J, M#998 Elinvar, HCI6P	600	700	1,050
23J, M#999, NI, OF, LS	500	575	675
Webb C. Ball, 21J, M#992-B, NI, OF, LS ★★★	600	750	995

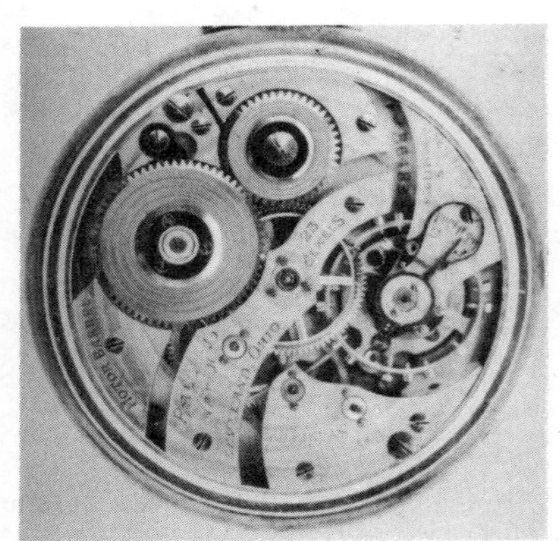

Ball-Hamilton, Model 998 Elinvar, 16 size, 23 jewels, with center bridge.

BALL—HAMPDEN
18 SIZE

Description		Avg	Ex-Fn	Mint
17J, LS, SW, OF, marked "Superior Grade"	★★★	$1,250	$1,400	$1,850
17J, LS, SW, OF, **not** marked "Superior Grade"	★★	1,000	1,200	1,600

BALL—E. HOWARD & CO.
18 SIZE

Description		Avg	Ex-Fn	Mint
17J, ¾, HC, PS, GJS, 18K, VII, HC	★★★	$3,500	$4,000	$5,500
17J, ¾, OF, PS, GJS, 14K, VIII, OF	★★	2,200	3,000	4,200

Ball & Co. (E. Howard & Co.), Series VIII, 18 size, 17 jewels, Order of Railway Conductors, serial number 307488, c. 1900.

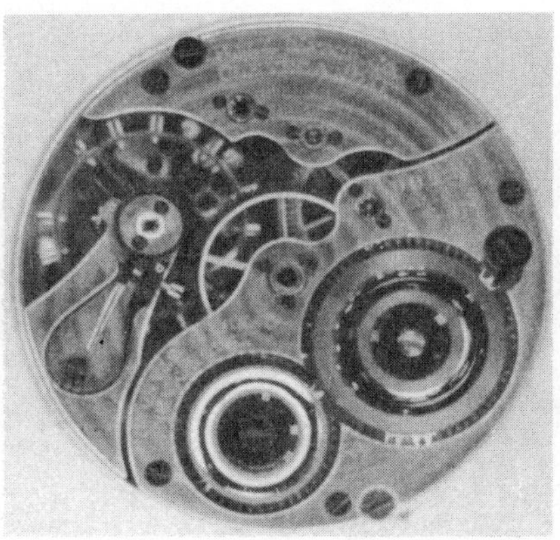

Ball-E. Howard Watch Co., 16 size, 21 jewels (Keystone). This watch believed to be one-of-a-kind prototype, serial number 982201.

BALL—E. HOWARD WATCH CO.
16 SIZE

Description	Avg	Ex-Fn	Mint
17J, OF, GJS	$2,000	$2,500	$3,500
21J, OF, GJS	2,500	3,000	4,500

FOR CANADA R.R. SERVICE

Description	Avg	Ex-Fn	Mint
16S, ¾, LS, OF, GJS	$350	$450	$575

BALL—ILLINOIS
16 SIZE

Description		Avg	Ex-Fn	Mint
23J, ¾, LS, OF, GJS	★★	$700	$875	$1,100
23J, ¾, LS, OF, GJS, 60 hr	★★	1,000	1,100	1,400

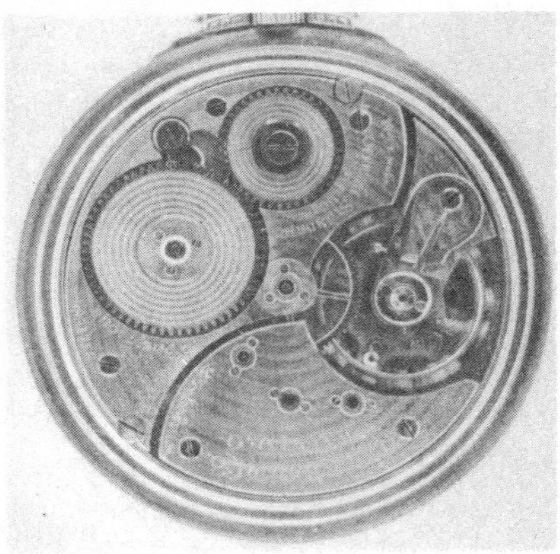

Ball Watch Co., Illinois Model, 16 size, 23 jewels. To identify, note back plates that circle around balance wheel, serial number B801758.

BALL—SETH THOMAS
18 SIZE

Description		Avg	Ex-Fn	Mint
17J, M#3, LS, OF, ¾, GJS	★★	$1,500	$2,000	$2,800

BALL—SWISS
16 SIZE

Description	Avg	Ex-Fn	Mint
21J, M#435-B, OF, LS, HCI6P	$185	$235	$285
21J, M#435-C, OF, LS, HCI6P	185	235	285
21J, M#477-B, HCI6P (BXC-Record Watch Co.)	95	135	195
17J, "Garland"	35	45	65
40mm Audemar Piguet, min. repeater, jeweled thru hammers, 18K, OF	2,000	3,000	5,000

BALL—WALTHAM
18 SIZE

Description		Avg	Ex-Fn	Mint
1892, 15J, OF, LS, SW, marked Webb C. Ball, Cleveland	★★	$800	$1,000	$1,500

BALL—WALTHAM
16 SIZE

Description		Avg	Ex-Fn	Mint
15J, HC, GCW	★★	$325	$390	$550
17J, OF, LS, ¾, HCI5P, Multi-color case, GF		250	345	400
17J, OF, LS, ¾, HCI5P		145	195	275
19J, BLF&E		495	550	700
21J, Brotherhood, marked ORC, BOFLE		495	550	700
19J, Hunting case	★★	900	1,100	1,400
19J, OF, LS, 14K		575	690	775

(BALL WATCH CO. continued)

Grade or Name — Description	Avg	Ex-Fn	Mint
19J, OF, LS, stirrup style case	175	225	275
19J, OF, LS, Coin	115	155	190
19J, OF, LS, ¾, HCI5P	175	195	250
19J, OF, LS, ¾, HCI5P, Wind Indicator ★★	2,500	3,000	4,500
21J, OF, LS, ¾, HCI5P	210	230	285
21J, LS, OF, HCI5P, marked Loaner	250	275	350
23J, LS, OF, HCI5P, NI, GJS ★	485	675	850

Ball Watch Co. (Illinois), 12 size, 19 jewels, serial number B400910.

12 SIZE
(Not Railroad Grade)

Description	Avg	Ex-Fn	Mint
19J, OF, PS	$95	$135	$170
19J, HC, PS	165	200	300

0 SIZE
(Not Railroad Grade)

Description	Avg	Ex-Fn	Mint
17-19J, OF, PS	$125	$275	$350
19J, HC, PS, "Queen" in Ball case	275	375	575

MAN'S WRIST WATCH

Style or Model — Description	Avg	Ex-Fn	Mint
Official R.R. Standard, 21J, HCI5P, 14K case	$295	$325	$400
Official R.R. Standard, 21J, HCI5P, 10K case	200	235	265
Official R.R. Standard, 21J, HCI5P, gold filled	125	140	185
Official R.R. Standard, 21J, HCI5P, stainless	80	95	120
Official R.R. Standard, 25J, HCI5P, 10K case	235	250	295
Official R.R. Standard, 25J, HCI5P, gold filled	135	150	185
Official R.R. Standard, 25J, HCI5P, stainless	85	100	135
17J, Self-wind, Wind Indicator, GF	125	145	195
M#433, 17J, gold filled	50	60	75
M#435B, 21J, gold filled	80	95	125
Vacheron & Constantin, 19J, GJS, 14K	300	350	425

NOTE: Prices for wrist watches are for stem wind and set, leather band, complete and in good working order.

BANNATYNE WATCH CO.
1905 — 1911

Mr. Bannatyne had previously worked for Ansonia, in charge of watch production. Bannatyne made non-jeweled watches that sold for about $1.50. Ingraham bought this company in 1912.

Description		Avg	Ex-Fn	Mint
18S, OF, SW, NI case	★	$250	$350	$500

ESTIMATED SERIAL NUMBERS AND PRODUCTION DATES

Date	Serial No.
1906	40,000
1908	140,000
1910	250,000

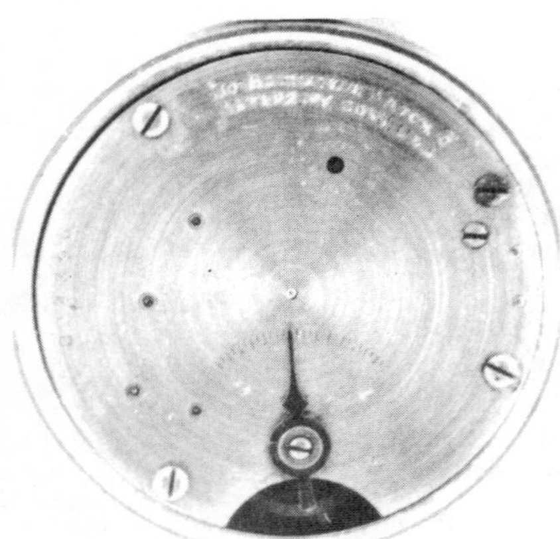
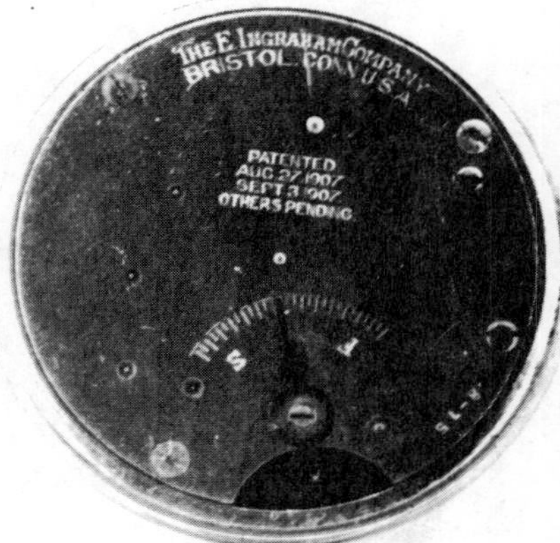

Bannatyne Watch Co. (left), **Ingraham Watch Co.** (right). Note similarity of movements. Both patented Aug. 27th, 1907 & Sept. 3rd, 1907.

BENNEDICT & BURNHAM MFG. CO.
Waterbury, Connecticut
1878 — 1880

This name will be found on the dial of the first 1,000 "long wind" Waterbury watches made in 1878. These watches had skeleton type movements with open dials that made the works visible. They contained 58 parts and were very attractive. The company was reorganized in March 1880 as the Waterbury Watch Co. and in 1868 became the New England Watch Co.

Description		Avg	Ex-Fn	Mint
18S, long wind, NI case	★★	$900	$1,000	$1,400

BOSTON WATCH CO.
(See American Watch Co.)

BOWMAN WATCH CO.
Lancaster, Pennsylvania
1877 — 1882

In March 1879, Ezra F. Bowman, a native of Lancaster, Pa., opened a retail jewelry and watch business. He employed William H. Todd to supervise his watch manufacturing. Todd had previously been employed by the Elgin and Lancaster Watch companies. Bowman made a 17S, ¾ plate, fully-jeweled movement. The escape wheel was a star-tooth design, fully capped, similar to those made by Charles Frodsham, an English watchmaker. They were stem wind with dials made by another company. Enough parts were made and bought for 300 watches, but only about 50 watches were completed and sold. Those performed very well. The company was sold to J. P. Stevens of Atlanta, Ga.

Description	Avg	Ex-Fn	Mint
17S, 21J, ¾, GJS, NI, LS, SW ★★★	$7,500	$11,000	$16,000

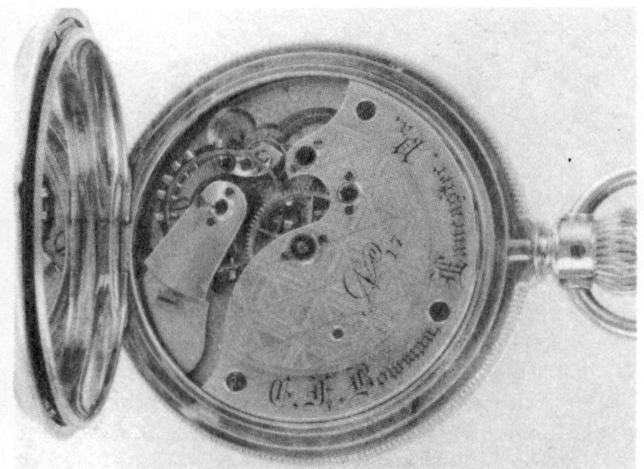

Bowman Watch Co., 16-18 size, 17 jewels, ¾ plate, gold jewel settings, lever set, stem wind. Note free sprung balance. Serial number 17, c. 1880.

ROBERT BROWN & SON
1833 — 1856
J. R. BROWN & SHARPE
1856

Providence, Rhode Island

Description	Avg	Ex-Fn	Mint
18S, KW, KS, FULL ★★★	$1,000	$1,200	$1,950

CALIFORNIA WATCH CO.
Berkeley, California
1876 — 1877

The Cornell Watch Co. was reorganized in early 1876 as the California Watch Co. The new company bought machinery to make watch cases of gold and silver. In a short while the company was in bad financial trouble and even paid its employees with wat-

CALIFORNIA WATCH CO. (continued)

ches. The business closed in the summer of 1876. Albert Troller bought the unfinished watches that were left. In about four months, he found a buyer in San Francisco. The factory was then closed and sold to the Independent Watch Co. Only about 5,000 watches were made by the California Watch Company. Serial numbers range from 25,115 to 30,174. Inscribed on the movements is "Berkeley."

Description		Avg	Ex-Fn	Mint
18S, 15J, FULL, KW, KS, "Berkeley"	★★	$1,250	$1,650	$2,500

California Watch Co., 18 size, 15 jewels, full plate.

CHESHIRE WATCH CO.
Cheshire, Connecticut
1883 — 1890

In October 1883, the Cheshire Watch Company was formed by George J. Capewell with D. A. Buck (designer of the long-wind Waterbury) as superintendent. Their first movement was 18S, ¾ gilt plate, stem wind, stem set, with the pendant attached to the movement. It fit into a nickel case which was also made at the Cheshire factory. The first watches were completed in April 1885. A new 18S nickel movement with a second hand was made to fit standard size American cases and was introduced in 1887. By that date production was at about 200 watches per day. Serial numbers range from 200 to 89,650. All Cheshire watches were sold through L. W. Sweet, general selling agent, in New York City. The factory closed in 1890, going into receivership. The receiver had 3,000 movements finished in 1892. In 1901 O. E. Bell bought the machinery and had it shipped to Appleton, Wisconsin, where he had formed the Remington Watch Company. The watches produced by Remington are marked "Appleton Watch Co." on the movements.

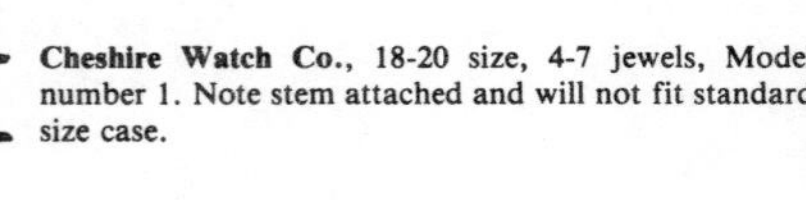

Cheshire Watch Co., 18-20 size, 4-7 jewels, Model number 1. Note stem attached and will not fit standard size case.

Cheshire Watch Co., 18 size, 4-7 jewels. This model was manufactured with stem attached and requires a special case. Model 2.

Cheshire Watch Co., 18 size, 4-7 jewels. This model fits standard 18 size cases. Model 3.

Description	Avg	Ex-Fn	Mint
20S, 4-7J, FULL, OF, SW, NI case, stem attached, 1st model ★★	$250	$350	$495
18S, 4-7J, ¾, SW, OF, NI case, stem attached, 2nd model ★	175	225	325
18S, 7J, OF, fits standard case	85	95	125
18S, 11J, OF, SW, standard case, 3rd model ★	175	195	285
18S, 15J, OF, NI, ADJ, standard case, 3rd model ★	185	200	295
18S, 21J, OF, SW, Coin, standard case, 3rd model ★★	195	225	325
6S, ¾, OF, SW, NI case ★	85	100	165

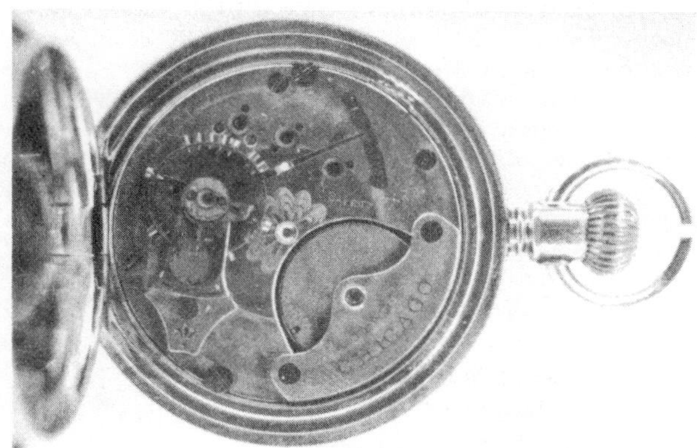

Chicago Watch Co., 18 size, 15 jewels, open face, nickel movement, serial number 209145.

CHICAGO WATCH CO.
Chicago, Illinois
1898

The Chicago Watch Company's watches were 18S, 7J, open-faced, had silveroid type cases, and were produced at low cost. They are believed to have been made by another manufacturer and sold by Chicago Watch Co.

CHICAGO WATCH CO. (continued)

Description	Avg	Ex-Fn	Mint
18S, 7J, OF	$95	$125	$185
18S, 11J, KW	325	375	450
18S, 15J, OF, SW	175	250	370
Columbus, 18S, 15J, SW, NI, HC ★★	350	425	600
Illinois, 18S, 11J, SW, NI ★★	185	225	325
Waltham, 18S, 15J ★★	185	225	300
12S, 15J	140	170	225
12S, YGF, HC	165	190	275

Columbia Watch Co., 0 size, 4 jewels, stem wind, open face and hunting, duplex escapement.

COLUMBIA WATCH CO.
Waltham, Massachusetts
c. 1896 — 1899

The Columbia Watch Company was organized in 1896 by Edward A. Locke, formerly General Manager of the Waterbury Watch Company. The firm began manufacturing an 0-size, 4-jewel gilt movement with duplex escapement in 1897. These movements were marked "Columbia Watch Co./Waltham, Mass." The firm also made movements marked "Hollers Watch Co./Brooklyn, NY," as well as nickeled movements marked "Cambridge Watch Co./New York."

Locke turned the business over to his son-in-law, Renton Whidden, in 1898, and the firm changed to an 0-size, 7-jewel nickel movement with lever escapement called the Suffolk. The firm name was not changed until early 1901.

Description	Avg	Ex-Fn	Mint
0S, 4J, SW, OF, HC, Duplex, gilded	$50	$60	$75
0S, 7J, SW, OF, lever escapement	60	75	85

COLUMBUS WATCH CO.
Columbus, Ohio
1882 — 1903

The Columbus Watch Co. grew from the Columbus Watch Mfg. Co. which was started in 1876 by D. Gruen and W. J. Savage. The company finished Swiss-imported movements in 8, 16, and 18 sizes to fit American-made cases. They continued to import movements until Nov. 18, 1882, at which time a factory was built. By Aug. 18, 1883, the first movements had been produced. There are several features that separate the Columbus from other American watches. The train is different because the barrel has 72 teeth, the center wheel 72, center pinion 11, third wheel 11 leaves. No cases were made by the company, and the mainsprings and hairsprings, as well as the jewels, were imported.

(COLUMBUS WATCH CO. continued)

The company started making its own dials in 1884. The company was producing watches at the rate of 150 a day in 1888. Serial numbers range from 20,000 to 383,000 for standard grade movements. In 1894 a block of numbers from 500,000 to 505,800 was assigned to some higher grade movements. Also in that year some movements bore the name "New Columbus Watch Co." In 1903 the Columbus Watch Co. was sold to the South Bend Watch Co.

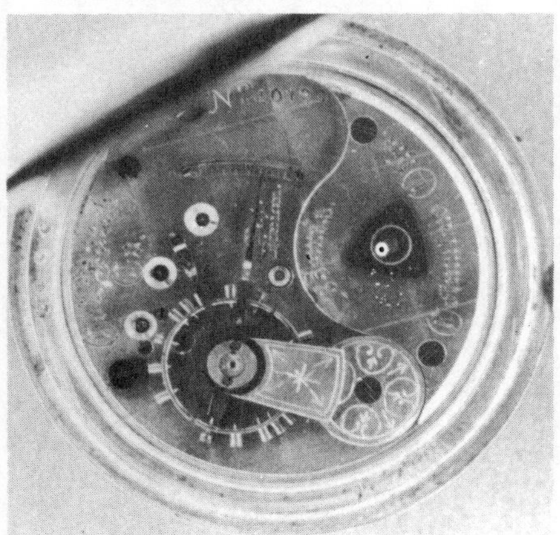

Columbus Watch Co., 18 size, 15 jewels, key wind and set, "Ohio Watch Co." on dial, "Col. Watch Co." on movement.

Columbus Watch Co., Railway King, 18 size, 23 jewels, with choo choo dial.

18 SIZE

Grade or Name — Description	Avg	Ex-Fn	Mint
Champion, 15J, NI, FULL, HC, OF	$80	$90	$150
Champion, 15J, gilt, FULL	65	75	95
Champion, 15J, gilt, FULL, Coin	55	65	80
Champion, 16J, NI, ADJ, FULL, DMK	85	95	145
Columbus W. Co., 15J, OF, LS	85	110	160
Columbus W. Co., 16J, OF, LS	95	125	175
Columbus W. Co., 17J, OF, LS	100	140	195
Columbus W. Co., 17J, OF, LS, 2-Tone	135	175	220
Columbus W. Co., 16J, KW, KS ★★★	285	400	675
Columbus W. Co., 11-15J, KW, KS	250	295	425
Columbus W. Co., 15J, KW, KS, 18K	850	950	1,300
Columbus W. Co., 15J, HC, LS, KW/SW Trans.	125	170	225
Columbus W. Co., 15J, Multi-color 14K box hinge HC	1,400	1,600	2,300
Columbus W. Co., 15J, Coin	85	90	120
Columbus W. Co., 15J, "New Columbus W. Co." on mvt.	85	90	110
Columbus W. Co., 11J, Coin	65	80	100
Columbus W. Co., 11J, HC, LS	125	150	200
Columbus W. Co., 13J, HC, LS	135	165	215
Columbus W. Co., 17J, HC, LS, Trans.	150	200	275
Columbus King, 17J	175	225	325
Columbus Watch Co., 17J, NI, 14K Multi-color box hinge HC	1,400	1,600	2,300
Columbus King, 21J	235	285	350
Columbus King, 23J	800	1,000	1,350
Columbus King, 25J ★★	2,400	3,000	3,800

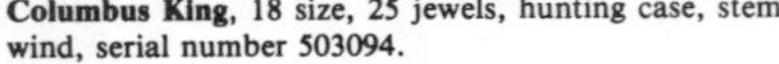

Columbus King, 18 size, 25 jewels, hunting case, stem wind, serial number 503094.

Railway King, 18 size, 23 jewels, adjusted, stem wind, open face, serial number 503315.

Grade or Name — Description	Avg	Ex-Fn	Mint
Jay Gould, 15J, OF	200	295	595
Jackson Park, 15J, NI, ADJ, OF	85	95	175
North Star, 11J, NI, FULL	80	90	110
North Star, 11J, gilt, FULL	65	70	90
North Star, 15J, gilt, FULL, Coin	75	90	120
North Star, 15J, NI, FULL	95	120	150
Ohio Watch Co., 13J, OF, KW, KS ★★	300	350	400
Railroad Monarch, 17J, ADJ	185	225	375
Railway King, 16J, ADJ, GJS, 2-Tone, Choo Choo dial	175	210	420
Railway King, 17J, ADJ, GJS, Choo Choo dial	195	235	400
Railway King, 17J, 2-Tone	175	200	300
Railway King, 19J, GJS, HCI5P, HC ★★	300	400	600
Railway King, 19J, GJS, HCI5P, OF ★★	225	285	375
Railway King, 21J, GT, HCI6P, DMK, GJS	200	275	375
Railway King, 21J, GT, HCI6P, DMK, GJS, 2-Tone	225	285	395
Railway King, 23J, HCI6P, DMK, GJS	900	1,100	1,500
Railway King, 25J, GT, HCI6P, DMK, GJS, OF ★★	2,400	3,000	3,800
Railway King, 25J, GT, HCI6P, DMK, GJS, HC ★★★	3,500	4,000	4,500
Railway King Special	135	175	275
R. W. K. Special, 17J, OF, LS, 2-Tone	195	250	295
R. W. K. Special, 19J, HC, LS, 2-Tone	295	350	425
Railway Regulator, 17J, OF	200	250	340
Railway Time Service, 17J, OF, NI	195	325	400
Time King, 17J, 2-Tone	160	190	250
Time King, 21J, GT, HCI6P, DMK, GJS, 2-Tone	225	285	340
Time King, 23J, GT, HCI6P, DMK, GJS	700	800	1,250
Time King, 25J, GT, HCI6P, DMK, GJS ★★	2,400	3,000	3,800
G#18, 16J, HC, HCI6P, GJS, DMK, NI	150	170	200
G#20-21, 7-11J, HC	70	90	125
G#28, 16J, HC, FULL, ADJ, GJS, DMK	120	135	160
G#34, 15J, HC, FULL, NI	95	115	130
G#32, 15J, HC, FULL, gilded	60	70	95
G#90, 7J, gilt, OF, FULL	50	60	80
G#90, 7J, gilt, OF, Coin	45	60	75

COLUMBUS WATCH CO., 18 SIZE (continued)

Grade or Name — Description	Avg	Ex-Fn	Mint
G#93, 15J, gilt, OF, FULL	60	75	95
G#94, 15J, NI, OF, FULL	85	95	125
G#95, 15J, NI, OF, FULL, ADJ, GJS	95	135	160
G#98, 16J, NI, OF, FULL, ADJ, GJS, DMK	110	145	170
G#99, 16J, NI, OF, FULL, HCI6P, GJS, DMK	150	190	235
G#105, 19J, GJS, 2-Tone, HC	1,000	1,200	1,500

Columbus Watch Co., 16 size, 17 jewels, gold train, serial number 228188.

Columbus Watch Co., Ruby Model, 16 size, 21 jewels, three quarter plate, gold jewel settings, gold train, adjusted to HCI6P.

16 SIZE

Grade or Name — Description	Avg	Ex-Fn	Mint
New Columbus Watch Co., 11J, ¾, OF	$75	$80	$110
New Columbus Watch Co., 15J, ¾, OF	80	90	115
New Columbus Watch Co., 16J, ¾, OF	85	95	135
New Columbus Watch Co., 17J, 14K, Multi-color HC	1,000	1,200	1,500
New Columbus Watch Co., 17J, 2-Tone	90	115	140
Ruby Model, 21J, ¾, NI, GJS, GT, OF, 2-tone ★★	475	600	900
Ruby Model, 21J, ¾, NI, GJS, HCI6P, GT, HC ★	425	500	625
G#41, HC-81, 11J, OF, gilt, ¾	50	60	80
G#43, HC-83, 11J, OF, NI, ¾	55	70	95
G#44, HC-84, 15J, OF, NI, GJS, ADJ, ¾	60	90	110
G#45, 19J, GJS, 2-Tone, HC ★★	850	1,000	1,300
G#46, HC-86, 15J, OF, NI, GJS, ADJ, ¾	95	120	155
G#47, HC-87, 16J, OF, HCI3P, GJS, ¾, NI, DMK	125	130	150
G#48, HC-88, 16J, OF, HCI6P, 14K, GJS, ¾, DMK, NI	425	460	600

6 SIZE

Grade or Name — Description	Avg	Ex-Fn	Mint
G#102-G#50, 7J, gilded	$40	$50	$65
G#101-G#51, 11J, gilded	50	60	80
G#53, 11J, NI	60	70	90
G#55, 15J, GJS, NI, 18K	395	425	575
G#55, 15J, GJS, NI	70	90	125
G#104-G#57, 16J, GJS, DMK, NI	90	130	160

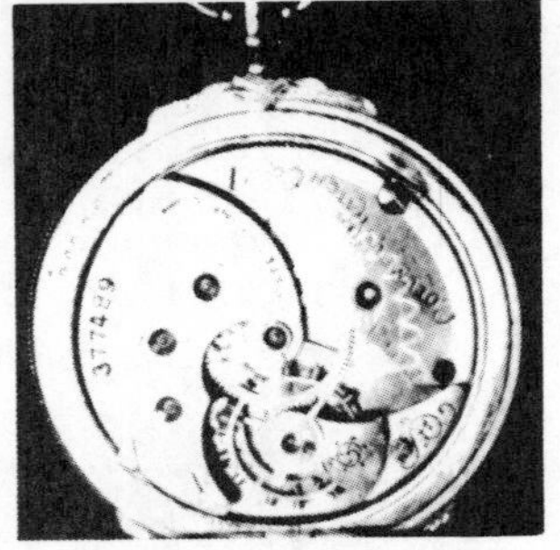

Columbus Watch Co., 6 size, 15 jewels, ¾ plate, stem wind, serial number 377,489.

New Columbus Watch Co. Example of a basic model for 6 size. Three quarter plate, 7-16 jewels, gilded and nickel.

4 SIZE

Grade or Name—Description	Avg	Ex-Fn	Mint
Columbus Watch Co., 15J, HC, gilt mvt.	$130	$145	$190
Columbus Watch Co., 15J, HC, nickel mvt.	140	155	200

COLUMBUS
ESTIMATED SERIAL NUMBERS AND PRODUCTION DATES

Date	Serial No.	Date	Serial No.
1883	23,000	1893	207,000
1884	30,000	1894	229,000
1885	40,000	1895	251,000
1886	53,000	1896	273,000
1887	75,000	1897	295,000
1888	97,000	1898	317,000
1889	119,000	1899	339,000
1890	141,000	1900	361,000
1891	163,000	1901	383,000
1892	185,000		

Special Block of Serial Nos.

Date	Serial No.
1894	500,001
1896	501,500
1898	503,000
1900	504,500
1902	505,800

CORNELL WATCH CO.
Chicago, Illinois
1870 — 1874
San Francisco, California
1875 — 1876

The Cornell Watch Co. bought the Newark Watch Co. and greatly improved on the movements being produced by Newark. In the fall of 1874, the company moved to San Francisco, Calif., with about 60 of its employees. The movements made in California were virtually the same as those made in Chicago. The company wanted to employ Chinese who would work cheaper, but the skilled employees refused to go along and went on strike. The company stayed alive until 1875 and was sold to the California Watch Co. in January 1876. But death came a few months later.

The Chronology of the Development of Cornell Watch Co.:
Newark Watch Co. 1864-1870; S#s 6901-12,000
Cornell Watch Co., Chicago, Ill. 1870-1874; S#s 12,001 to 25,000;
Cornell Watch Co., San Francisco, Calif. 1874-Jan. 1876; S#s 25,001 to 35,000;
California Watch Co., Jan. 1876-mid 1876.

CORNELL WATCH CO. (continued)

Cornell Watch Co., J.C. Adams, 18 size, 11 jewels, key wind & set, made in Chicago, Ill, serial number 13647.

Cornell Watch Co., 18 size, 11 jewels, San Francisco on movement.

18 SIZE

Grade or Name — Description		Avg	Ex-Fn	Mint
C. T. Bowen, FULL, KW	★	$350	$450	$650
C. M. Cady, 15J, SW	★	300	400	550
Paul Cornell, 19J, GJS, HCI5P, SW	★★	1,800	2,000	3,000
Cornell, 15J, KW	★	250	315	425
Cornell W. Co., 15J, KW, San Francisco on mvt.	★★★	1,000	1,400	2,300
Cornell, 11J, KW, San Francisco on mvt.	★★★	800	1,000	1,800
Cornell, 11J, KW	★	200	300	500
H. N. Hibbard, 11J, KW, ADJ	★	250	350	600
George F. Root, 15J, KW	★	255	385	650
John Evans, 15J, KW	★	200	370	550
J. C. Adams, 11J, KW	★	200	350	500
E. J. Williams, 7J, KW	★	175	250	400
George Waite, 7J, (Hyde Park), KW	★	275	395	600
Ladies Stemwind	★	150	200	275

JACOB D. CUSTER
Norristown, Pennsylvania
1840 — 1845

At the age of 19, Jacob Custer repaired his father's watch. He was then asked to repair all the watches within his community. Custer was basically self-taught and had very little formal education and little training in clocks and watches. He made all the parts except the hairspring and fusee chains. The watches were about 14 size, and only 12 to 15 watches were made. The 14S fusee watches had lever escapement, ¾ plate and were sold in his own gold cases. He made a few chronometers, one with a helical spring.

Description		Avg	Ex-Fn	Mint
14S, OF, engraved on mvt. "J. D. Custer, Patented Feb. 4, 1843, #2,939"	★★★	$8,500	$12,000	$18,000

DUDLEY WATCH CO.
Lancaster, Pennsylvania
1920 — 1925

William Wallace Dudley became interested in watches and horology at the age of 13 and became an apprentice making ship chronometers in Canada. When he moved to America, he worked for the South Bend and Illinois Watch companies and the Trenton Watch Co. before going to Hamilton Watch Co. in Lancaster. He left Hamilton at age 69 to start his own watch company. In 1922 his first watches were produced; they were 14S, 19J, and were labeled Models 1894 and 1897. Watch parts, dials and hands were Swiss made. The winding mechanism was made at the Dudley factory. The cases came from Wadsworth Keystone and the Star Watch Case Co. Dudley also made a 12S, 19J watch. By 1924, the company was heavily in debt, and on February 20, 1925, a petition for bankruptcy was filed. The Masonic Watch was his most unusual.

Dudley Watches				**Total Production**
Dudley Watch Co.	1920-1925	Model No. 1	S# 500-1,900	1,400
P. W. Baker Co.	1925-1935	Model No. 2	S# 2,001-4,800	1,600
XL Watch Co., N.Y.	1935-1976	Model No. 3	S# 4,801-6,500	1,000
			Total	4,000

Model No. 1, 14S, 19J, OF, can be distinguished by the "Holy Bible" engraved on the winding arbor plate.

Model No. 2, 12S, 19J, used the 910 and 912 Hamilton wheels and escapement, has a flat silver-colored Bible.

Model No. 3, 12S, can be distinguished by the silver Bible which was riveted in place and was more three-dimensional.

The earliest Model 1 serial number is 507. The earliest Model 2 serial number is 2,015. The XL Watch Co. serial numbers ran from 4,801 to 6,500. The highest serial number was on a Model 2: 6,404.

The distinguishing thing about the Masonic watch is that the movement is constructed by using the symbols of the Masons: trowel, plumb, level, square and compass. The square and compass support the mainspring barrel and the trowel supports the balance.

Dudley Watch Co., Model 1, 14 size, 19 jewels, open face, flip back, serial number 1232.

DUDLEY WATCH CO. (continued)

Dudley Watch Co., Model 1, 14 size, 19 jewels, open face, flip back, serial number 1232.

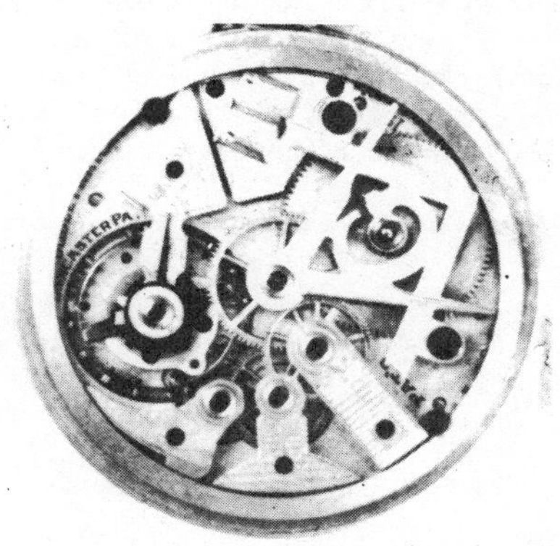

Dudley Watch Co., Model 2, 12 size, 19 jewels, open face, serial number 2410.

12 SIZE—14 SIZE
"MASONS" MODEL

Grade or Name—Description	Avg	Ex-Fn	Mint
14S, Dudley, 19J, 14K, flip open back, S#1 ★★★	$5,000	$7,000	$10,000
14S, M#1, 19J, OF, 14K, flip open back ★	2,400	2,600	3,000
12S, M#1, 19J, OF, 14K, flip open back, w/box & papers ★	2,600	2,800	3,200
12S, M#2, 19J, OF, flip open back, GF ★	1,600	1,700	1,975
12S, M#2, 19J, OF, 14K, flip open back case ★	1,850	2,000	2,400
12S, M#3, 19J, OF, display case, GF ★	1,400	1,500	1,800
12S, M#3, 19J, OF, 14K flip open case ★	1,700	1,900	2,200

DUEBER WATCH CO.
(See Hampden Watch Co.)

ELGIN WATCH CO.
(NATIONAL WATCH CO.)
Elgin, Illinois
1864 — 1964

This was the largest watch company in terms of production; in fact, Elgin produced half of the total number of pocket watches (Dollar-type not included). Some of the organizers came from Waltham Watch Co., including P. S. Bartlett, D. G. Currier, Otis Hoyt, Charles H. Mason and others. The idea of beginning a large watch company for the mid-West was discussed by J. C. Adams, Bartlett and Blake. After a trip to Waltham, Adams went back to Chicago and approached Benjamin W. Raymond, a former mayor of Chicago, to put up the necessary capital to get the company started. Adams and Raymond succeeded in getting others to pledge their financial support also. The National Watch Co. (Elgin) was formed in August 1864. A factory site in Elgin, Illinois, where the city had donated 35 acres of land, was selected. The factory was completed in 1866, and the first movement was a B. W. Raymond, 18S, full plate design.

ELGIN WATCH CO. (continued)

The first watches were put on the market in 1867, selling for about $115, and all were quick train. The first stem wind model was an H. L. Culver with serial No. 155,001, lever set and quick train. In 1874 the name was changed to the Elgin National Watch Co. which produced watches into the 1950s.

Some Serial Nos. have the first two numbers replaced by a letter; i.e., 39,482,000 would be X482,000.

X—39	V—46
C,E,T&Y—42	H—47
L—43	N—48
U—44	F—49
J—45	S—50

ELGIN ESTIMATED SERIAL NUMBERS AND PRODUCTION DATES

Date	Serial #	Date	Serial #	Date	Serial #
1867	10,000	1897	7,100,000	1926	29,100,000
1868	35,000	1898	7,550,000	1927	30,050,000
1869	65,000	1899	8,200,000	1928	31,500,000
1870	95,000	1900	9,000,000	1929	32,000,000
1871	120,000	1901	9,250,000	1930	32,500,000
1872	155,000	1902	9,700,000	1931	33,000,000
1873	170,000	1903	10,100,000	1932	33,800,000
1874	210,000	1904	10,900,000	1933	35,100,000
1875	320,000	1905	11,900,000	1934	35,000,000
1876	390,000	1906	12,600,000	1935	35,750,000
1877	475,000	1907	12,900,000	1936	36,200,000
1878	500,000	1908	13,550,000	1937	37,100,000
1879	580,000	1909	14,000,000	1938	37,900,000
1880	750,000	1910	14,900,000	1939	38,200,000
1881	900,000	1911	15,900,000	1940	39,100,000
1882	1,000,000	1912	16,500,000	1941	40,200,000
1883	1,300,000	1913	17,200,000	1942	41,100,000
1884	1,500,000	1914	17,900,000	1943	42,200,000
1885	1,700,000	1915	18,400,000	1944	42,600,000
1886	2,000,000	1916	19,500,000	1945	43,200,000
1887	2,400,000	1917	20,100,000	1946	43,800,000
1888	2,900,000	1918	21,000,000	1947	44,200,000
1889	3,400,000	1919	22,000,000	1948	45,100,000
1890	3,900,000	1920	23,000,000	1949	46,000,000
1891	4,500,000	1921	24,050,000	1950	47,000,000
1892	4,800,000	1922	25,100,000	1951	48,000,000
1893	4,900,000	1923	26,050,000	1952	49,000,000
1894	5,550,000	1924	27,000,000	1953	50,000,000
1895	5,900,000	1925	28,050,000	1956	55,000,000
1896	6,550,000				

Elgin Movements

	1st App.	1st S#		1st App.	1st S#
18S B. W. Raymond	April 1867	101	10S Lady Elgin	Jan. 1869	40,001
18S H. L. Culver	July 1867	1,001	10S Frances Rubie	Aug. 1870	50,001
18S J. T. Ryerson	Oct. 1867	5,001	10S Gail Borden	Sept. 1871	185,001
18S H. H. Taylor	Nov. 1867	25,001	10S Dexter Street	Dec. 1871	201,001
18S G. M. Wheeler	Nov. 1867	6,001	First Stem Wind	June 1873	
18S Matt Laflin	Jan. 1868	9,001	1st Nickel Movement	Aug.15, 1879	
18S Father Time	No date	2,300,001	Convertible	Fall 1878	
18S Veritas	No date	8,400,001			

Some collectors seek out low serial numbers and will usually pay a premium for them. The lower the number, the more desirable the watch. The table shown below lists the first serial number of each size watch made by Elgin.

Size	1st Serial Nos.	Size	1st Serial Nos.
18	101	10	40,001
17	356,001	6	570,001
16	600,001	0	2,889,001
14	351,001		

ELGIN

(See **Elgin Identification of Movements** section located at the end of the Elgin price section to identify the movement, size and model number of your watch.)

(Prices are with gold filled cases except where noted.)

California Watch, 18 size, 15 jewels, gilded, key wind & set, serial number 200,700.

Convertible, 18 size, 21 jewels, converts to either hunting or open face.

18 SIZE

Grade or Name — Description	Avg	Ex-Fn	Mint
Advance, 11J, gilded, KW, HC, FULL	$50	$75	$115
Age, 7J, gilded, KW, FULL, HC	80	115	145
Atlas Watch Co., 7J, HC, LS, FULL	40	60	80
California Watch, 15J, gilded, HC, KW, KS, FULL	95	115	145
Chief, 7J, gilded, KW, FULL, HC	80	95	125
Convertible, 7J, G#98	80	95	125
H. L. Culver, 15J, gilded, KW, KS, FULL, HC, ADJ, low S#	175	250	325
H. L. Culver, 15J, gilded, KW, KS, FULL, HC, ADJ	125	150	190
H. L. Culver, 15J, KW, KS, 14K, HC	525	575	800
H. L. Culver, 15J, gilded, KW, KS, FULL, HC	80	100	145
H. L. Culver, 15J, gilded, SW, FULL, HC	85	95	110
H. L. Culver, 15J, gilded, KW, FULL, LS, HC	95	110	150
Elgin W. Co., 7J, OF, SW	40	50	75
Elgin W. Co., 7J, KW, gilded	45	50	75
Elgin W. Co., 11J, KW, LS	60	70	90
Elgin W. Co., 11J, LS, HC, 9K-10K	325	350	425
Elgin W. Co., 11J, LS, HC, Silveroid	40	50	65
Elgin W. Co., 11J, LS, OF	40	50	60
Elgin W. Co., 13J, SW, PS/LS, Silveroid	40	50	65
Elgin W. Co., 13J, SW, PS/LS	60	70	95
Elgin W. Co., 15J, KW, LS	60	70	95
Elgin W. Co., 15J, SW, LS, OF	60	70	95
Elgin W. Co., 15J, SW, LS, YGF, Multi-color box	250	300	495
Elgin W. Co., 15J, SW, LS, Silveroid	50	60	70
Elgin W. Co., 15J, SW, LS, HC	60	85	95
Elgin W. Co., 15J, KW, hidden key	125	145	175
Elgin W. Co., 17J, SW, LS, Silveroid	60	70	80
Elgin W. Co., 17J, SW, LS	85	95	125
Elgin W. Co., 17J, SW, Multi-color, 14K, HC	1,400	1,600	2,200

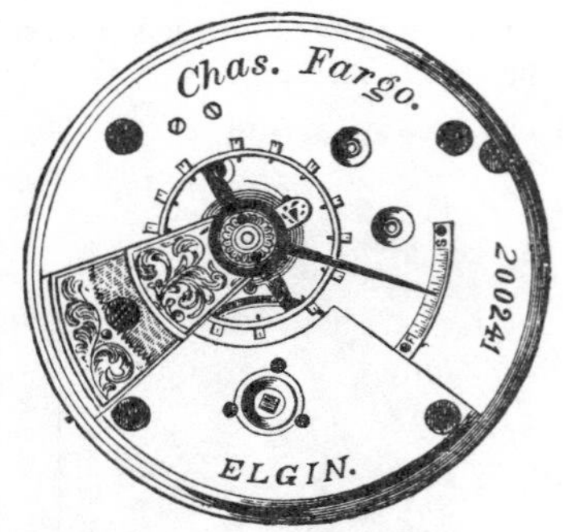

Charles Fargo, 18 size, 7 jewels, gilded, key wind & set, hunting case.

Elgin W. Co., Grade 297, 18 size, 15 jewels.

Grade or Name — Description	Avg	Ex-Fn	Mint
Elgin W. Co., 21J, SW, LS, OF	75	95	135
Elgin W. Co., 21J, SW, LS, box case	140	200	285
Elgin W. Co., 21J, LS, HC, 14K	525	600	800
Elgin W. Co., 21J, SW, LS, Silveroid	70	80	90
Elgin W. Co., 21J, SW, LS, HC	80	90	135
Elgin W. Co., 21J, Wind Indicator	600	800	1,000
Elgin W. Co., 21J, Wind Indicator, free sprung	600	800	1,200
Charles Fargo, 7J, gilded, KW, HC	150	185	250
J. V. Farwell, 11J, gilded, KW, HC	250	300	450
Father Time, 17J, NI, KW, FULL, HC, DMK ★	195	300	575
Father Time, 17J, NI, FULL, OF, DMK	55	70	95
Father Time, 17J, SW, OF, Silveroid	45	60	80
Father Time, 17J, SW, HC	60	85	110
Father Time, 20J, NI, SW, FULL, HC, DMK ★	175	200	325
Father Time, 21J, NI, SW, FULL, OF, GJS, DMK	70	95	135
Father Time, 21J, NI, SW, ¾, OF, GJS, DMK	90	115	185
Father Time, 21J, GJT, HCI5P, Diamond end stone	100	125	195
Father Time, 21J, NI, SW, ¾, OF, GJS, Wind Indicator, DMK	750	850	1,350
Father Time, 21J, SW, ¾, GJS, wind indicator, HC	900	1,100	1,550
Father Time, G#367, 36S, 21J, NI, SW, ¾, OF, GJS, Wind Indicator, free sprung	750	850	1,350
W. H. Ferry, 15J, gilded, KW, HC	75	95	135
W. H. Ferry, 11J, gilded, KW, HC	60	80	95
Mat Laflin, 7J, gilded, KW, HC	55	70	135
National W. Co., 7J, KW, KS	50	60	90
National W. Co., 11J, KW, KS	60	70	100
National W. Co., 15J, KW, KS	80	95	115
National W. Co., 15J, KW, KS, Silveroid	40	55	65
National W. Co., 15J, SW	80	90	110
M. G. Ogden, 15J, KW, HC	80	100	125
M. G. Ogden, 11J, gilded, KW, HC	80	95	140
Overland, 17J, NI, KW, HC, DMK	65	80	105
Overland, 17J, NI, SW, HC, DMK	65	80	105
Pennsylvania Railroad Co. on dial, B. W. Raymond on mvt., 15J, KW, KS ★★★	1,800	2,000	2,600

Pennsylvania Railroad Co. on dial, **B.W. Raymond** on movement. One of the first railroad watches commissioned by Penn. RR Co., 18 size, 15 jewels, key wind and set, serial number 123245, ca. 1874.

Grade or Name — Description	Avg	Ex-Fn	Mint
B. W. Raymond, 15-17J, KW, low S# under 500	400	575	750
B. W. Raymond, 15J, gilded, KW, FULL	60	80	95
B. W. Raymond, 17J, gilded, KW, FULL	60	85	100
B. W. Raymond, 15J, SW	60	85	100
B. W. Raymond, 17J, NI, FULL, OF	70	90	125
B. W. Raymond, 17J, Silveroid	40	60	80
B. W. Raymond, 17J, NI, FULL, HC	75	95	135
B. W. Raymond, 15J, box case, 14K	675	875	1,150
B. W. Raymond, 15J, 18K, 46 DWT	875	1,000	1,250
B. W. Raymond, 17J, gilded, NI, SW, FULL, ADJ	60	70	90
B. W. Raymond, 19J, NI, ¾, SW, OF, GJS, DMK, GT	85	100	145
B. W. Raymond, 19J, NI, ¾, SW, OF, GJS, Wind Indicator, DMK	500	600	950
B. W. Raymond, 19J, ¾, GJS, GT, Diamond end stone	100	125	155
B. W. Raymond, 21J, ¾, GJS, GT, Diamond end stone, OF	130	150	175
B. W. Raymond, 21J, SW, Silveroid	65	70	85
B. W. Raymond, 21J, SW, GJS, GT, DES, HC	135	155	200
B. W. Raymond, 21J, NI, ¾, SW, GJS, DMK, GT	100	120	150
B. W. Raymond, 21J, NI, ¾, SW, GJS, Wind Indicator, DMK	650	750	1,100
J. T. Ryerson, 7J, gilded, FULL, KW, HC	85	100	140
Solar W. Co., 15J, Multi-color dial	95	115	150
Standard, 17J, OF, LS	100	120	150
Sundial, 7J, SW, PS	45	60	75
H. H. Taylor, 15J, gilded, FULL, KW, HC	85	90	135
H. H. Taylor, 15J, NI, FULL, KW, HC, DMK	95	120	135
H. H. Taylor, 15J, NI, FULL, SW, HC, DMK, quick train	95	130	155
H. H. Taylor, 15J, SW, Silveroid	45	50	65
H. H. Taylor, 15J, SW, slow train	60	70	95
Veritas, 21J, SW, Silveroid	60	75	120
Veritas, 21J, SW, GJS, GT, HC	110	125	175
Veritas, 21J, ¾, NI, GJS, OF, DMK, GT	110	135	175
Veritas, 21J, ¾, GJS, GT, Diamond end stones	120	145	185
Veritas, 21J, ¾, GJS, GT, Diamond end stones, HC	150	185	250
Veritas, 21J, ¾, NI, GJS, OF, Wind Indicator, DMK	1,000	1,100	1,400
Veritas, 21J, ¾, NI, GJS, HC, Wind Indicator, DMK	1,100	1,200	1,600

B.W. Raymond, 18 size, 23 jewels, wind indicator, note small winding indicator gear next to crown wheel.

H.H. Taylor, 18 size, 15 jewels, key wind & set, serial number 288797.

Grade or Name — Description	Avg	Ex-Fn	Mint
Veritas, 23J, ¾, NI, GJS, OF, DMK, GT	160	200	295
Veritas, 23J, ¾, GJS, HC, GT	200	225	375
Veritas, 23J, ¾, NI, GJS, OF, DMK, GT, Diamond end stone	235	260	340
Veritas, 23J, ¾, Wind Indicator, GJS, OF, DMK, GT, 14K	1,400	1,750	2,100
Veritas, 23J, ¾, NI, GJS, OF, Wind Indicator, DMK	1,000	1,200	1,600
Veritas, 23J, SW, Silveroid	110	120	160
Veritas, 23J, SW, NI, GJS, GT, LS, HC	195	220	325
Veritas, 23J, SW, OF, 14K	475	575	775
G. M. Wheeler, 11J, gilded, KW	60	70	85
G. M. Wheeler, 13-15J, gilded, FULL, KW	70	80	95
G. M. Wheeler, 15J, NI, FULL, KW, DMK	80	90	115
G. M. Wheeler, 15J, SW, NI, FULL, DMK	80	90	125
G. M. Wheeler, 17J, KW, NI, FULL, DMK	80	90	130
G. M. Wheeler, 17J, SW, NI, FULL, DMK	70	90	115

MOVEMENTS WITH NO NAME

Grade or Name — Description	Avg	Ex-Fn	Mint
No. 5 & No. 17, 7J, gilded, FULL, OF, HC	40	50	60
No. 23 & No. 18, 11J, gilded, FULL, OF, HC	45	50	65
No. 69, 15J, M#1, KW, quick train	85	90	120
No. 316 & No. 317, 15J, NI, FULL, OF, HC, DMK	60	70	90
No. 316 & No. 317, 15J, NI, FULL, ADJ, OF, HC, DMK	70	80	95
No. 316 & No. 317, 15J, Silveroid	40	50	65
No. 326 & No. 327, 15J	60	70	80
No. 335 & No. 336, 17J, Silveroid	60	70	80
No. 335 & No. 336, 17J, NI, FULL, HC, OF, DMK	70	90	120
No. 378 & No. 379, 19J, NI, FULL, HC, OF, DMK	75	100	135
No. 348 & No. 349, 21J, NI, FULL, HC, OF, GJS, DMK	75	90	125
No. 345, 19J, GJS, 2-Tone, HC	1,000	1,200	1,500

17 SIZE

Grade or Name — Description	Avg	Ex-Fn	Mint
Avery, 7J, gilded, KW, FULL, HC	$60	$80	$110

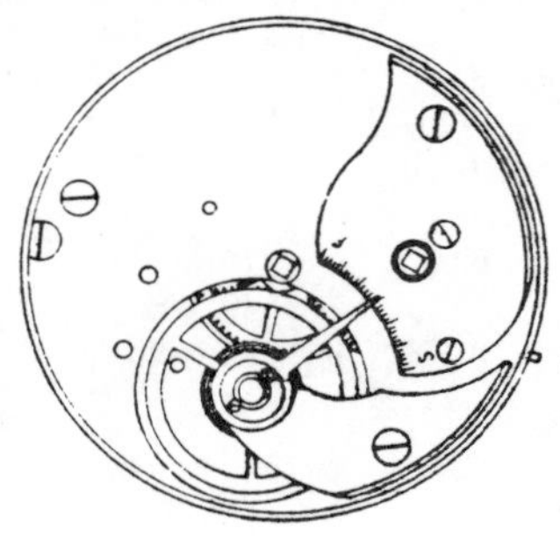

Elgin Watch Co., Model 1, 17 size, full plate, hunting, key wind and set.

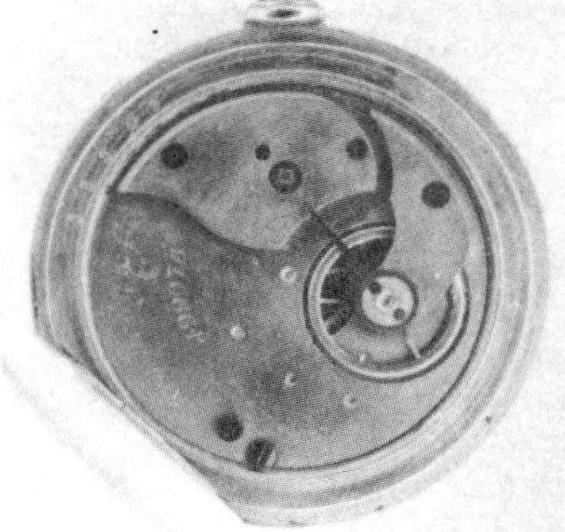

Elgin Watch Co., 17 size, 7 jewels, key wind & set, serial number 199076. Made for Kennedy & Co.

Grade or Name — Description	Avg	Ex-Fn	Mint
Leader, 7J, gilded, KW, FULL, HC	60	80	110
Leader, 7J, gilded, KW, FULL, HC, early movement	70	90	120
Sunshine, 15J, KW, KS from back	80	90	130
M#11, 14, 15, 51, 59: 7J, gilded, KW, FULL, HC	70	90	135
17 Size, KW, Silveroid	50	60	70

16 SIZE

Grade or Name — Description	Avg	Ex-Fn	Mint
Blind Man's Watch, 17J	$100	$110	$150
Convertible Model, 13J, BRG	70	90	120
Convertible Model, 15J, BRG, ADJ, 14K, HC	495	540	700
Convertible Model, 15J, ADJ, DMK, 3F BRG, HC	100	140	175
Convertible Model, 15J, ¾, ADJ, DMK, GJS	80	110	145
Convertible Model, 15J, Silveroid	50	70	95
Convertible Model, 15J, 3F BRG, OF	100	140	170
Convertible Model, 21J, 3F BRG	900	1,100	1,450
Convertible Model, 21J, ¾, ADJ, DMK, GJS	400	500	750

Doctors Watch, 16 size, 15 jewels, fourth model, gold jewel settings, gold train, sweep second hand, serial number 926458.

ELGIN WATCH CO., 16 SIZE (continued)

Grade or Name — Description	Avg	Ex-Fn	Mint
Convertible Model, 21J, 3F BRG, 14K	1,400	1,700	2,000
Doctors Watch, 15J, 4th Model, NI, GT, sweep second hand ★	150	185	275
Doctors Watch, 15J, 4th Model, gilded, sweep second hand, coin silver case ★	125	150	195
Doctors Watch, 15J, 4th Model, sweep second hand, 14K	475	500	650
Elgin W. Co., 7J, OF or HC	40	50	70
Elgin W. Co., 9J, OF	45	55	75
Elgin W. Co., 11J, OF or HC	55	75	100
Elgin W. Co., 13J, OF	60	80	110
Elgin W. Co., 13J, OF or HC, Silveroid	40	50	70
Elgin W. Co., 13J, HC	60	70	100
Elgin W. Co., 15J, HC	75	80	110
Elgin W. Co., 15J, OF, Silveroid	40	50	60
Elgin W. Co., 15J, OF	75	85	110
Elgin W. Co., 15J, HC, 14K	475	485	600
Elgin W. Co., 17J, OF	75	95	105
Elgin W. Co., 17J, 14K, HC	475	495	600
Elgin W. Co., 17J, Silveroid	45	55	65
Elgin W. Co., 17J, HC	80	95	110
Elgin W. Co., 19J, OF, LS	80	110	135
Elgin W. Co., 21J, HC	85	115	140
Elgin W. Co., 21J, OF, Silveroid	55	65	75
Elgin W. Co., 21J, OF	100	125	145
Elgin W. Co., 17J, LS, multi-color HC, GF	225	275	375
Elgin W. Co., 17J, multi-color HC, 14K	700	950	1,300

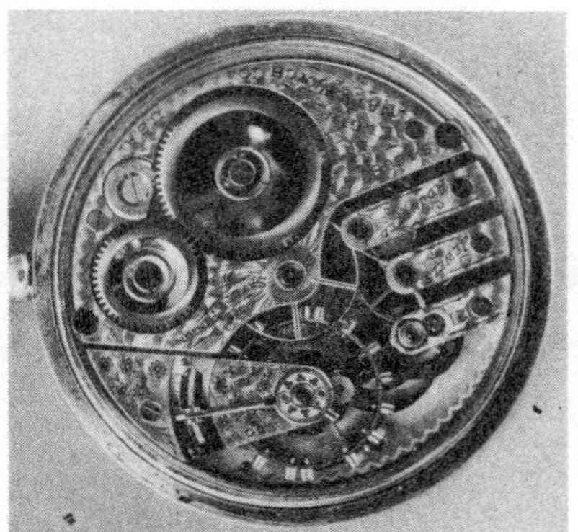

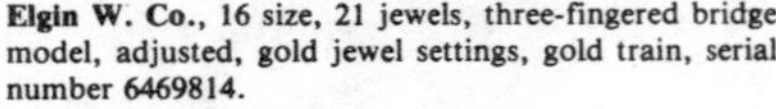

Elgin W. Co., 16 size, 21 jewels, three-fingered bridge model, adjusted, gold jewel settings, gold train, serial number 6469814.

Elgin Watch Co., 16 size, 21 jewels, converts to open face or hunting case, serial number 607061.

Grade or Name — Description	Avg	Ex-Fn	Mint
3F Bridge Model, 15J, NI, DMK	60	70	100
3F Bridge Model, 17J, HCI3P, NI, DMK, GJS	70	80	110
3F Bridge Model, 17J, HCI5P, NI, DMK, GJS, GT	80	90	125
3F Bridge Model, 21J, HCI5P, NI, DMK, GJS, GT	135	150	225
Father Time, 17J, ¾, NI, OF, GJS, DR, DMK	60	85	115
Father Time, 21J, ¾, NI, HC, GJS, DR, DMK	90	100	145
Father Time, 21J, ¾, NI, OF, GJS, DR, Wind Indicator	375	400	550

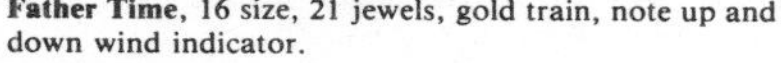

Father Time, 16 size, 21 jewels, gold train, note up and down wind indicator.

Father Time, 16 size, 21 jewels, gold train, note up and down wind indicator, serial number 18,106,465.

Grade or Name — Description	Avg	Ex-Fn	Mint
Father Time, 21J, Silveroid	60	70	80
Father Time, 21J, NI, GJS, DR, OF	90	100	150
Lord Elgin, 21J, GJS, DR, HCI5P, 3F BRG, 14K ★★	1,500	1,800	2,450
Lord Elgin, 23J, GJS, DR, HCI5P, ¾, 14K ★★	1,500	1,800	2,450
B. W. Raymond, 17J, ¾, GJS, 14K	475	525	650
B. W. Raymond, 17J, ¾, GJS, SW, HC	125	150	185
B. W. Raymond, 17J, 3F BRG ★★	200	240	325
B. W. Raymond, 17J, Silveroid	100	125	155
B. W. Raymond, 17J, GJS, SW, OF	125	150	185
B. W. Raymond, 17J, ¾, GJS, DR, HCI5P, DMK	150	175	250
B. W. Raymond, 19J, ¾, GJS, DR, HCI5P, DMK, OF	90	100	130
B. W. Raymond, 19J, OF, 14K, 30 DWT	450	510	575
B. W. Raymond, 19J, ¾, GJS, DR, HCI5P, DMK, Wind Indicator	300	350	425
B. W. Raymond, 19J, Silveroid	50	60	75
B. W. Raymond, 19J, GJS, HCI5P, HC	95	115	160
B. W. Raymond, 21J, 14K, OF	480	500	575
B. W. Raymond, 21J, Silveroid	60	70	85
B. W. Raymond, 21J, ¾, GJS, DR, HCI5P, HC	95	120	185
B. W. Raymond, 21J, ¾, GJS, DR, HCI5P, DMK, OF	90	110	150
B. W. Raymond, 21J, ¾, GJS, DR, HCI5P, DMK, Wind Indicator	300	345	475
B. W. Raymond, 22J, WWII Model, sweep second hand	90	100	135
B. W. Raymond, 23J, ¾, GJS, DR, HCI5P, DMK	175	225	275
B. W. Raymond, 23J, ¾, GJS, DR, HCI5P, DMK, Wind Indicator	425	540	675
B. W. Raymond, 23J, ¾, GJS, DR, HCI5P, DMK, Wind Indicator, military style	400	450	600
Repeater, Terstegen, 5 min., 21J, 2 gongs ★★	2,000	3,000	4,500
Veritas, 21J, 3F brg, GJS ★	195	250	325
Veritas, 21J, GJS, DR, HCI5P, DMK, ¾, HC	195	250	325
Veritas, 21J, GJS, DR, HCI5P, DMK, ¾, Wind Indicator	575	675	850
Veritas, 21J, GJS, SW ,Grade 360 ★	360	420	495
Veritas, 21J, GJS, SW, HCI5P, OF ,Grade 270	125	150	200
Veritas, 23J, GJS, HCI5P, 14K, OF	575	695	850
Veritas, 23J, GJS, HCI5P, HC	280	355	475

Veritas, 16 size, 23 jewels, solid gold train, gold jewel settings, adjusted to HCI5P, serial number 16678681.

Grade 241, 18 size, 17 jewels, hunting case, three-fingered bridge.

Grade or Name — Description	Avg	Ex-Fn	Mint
Veritas, 23J, GJS, DR, HCI5P, DMK, ¾, OF ,Grade 376	250	295	395
Veritas, 23J, GJS, DR, HCI5P, DMK, ¾, Diamond end stone ,Grade 350 ★	450	525	695
Veritas, 23J, GJS, DR, HCI5P, DMK, ¾, Wind Indicator	675	775	950
G. M. Wheeler, 17J, DR, HCI3P, DMK, ¾	60	85	110
G. M. Wheeler, 17J, 3F BRG	70	95	135
G. M. Wheeler, 17J, HC, 14K	400	500	625
WWII Model, 17J	70	90	120
WWII Model, 21J	90	115	150
M#13, 9J	45	50	75
M#48, 13J	45	60	85

MODELS WITH NO NAMES

Grade or Name — Description	Avg	Ex-Fn	Mint
Grade #270, 21J, 3F BRG, GJS, marked mvt.	$135	$175	$225
Grade #280, 17J, marked on mvt.	120	150	200
Grade #290 & #291, 7J, OF, ¾, NI, DMK	35	45	65
Grade #291, 7J, ¾, HC, 14K	450	500	600
Grade #312 & #313, 15J, ¾, NI, DR, DMK	45	55	75
Grade #381 & #382, 17J, ¾, NI, DR, DMK	65	70	90
Grade #145, 19J, GJS, BRG, HC ★★	850	1,000	1,300
Grade #156, 21J, ¾, NI, DR, DMK, GT, GJS	175	250	335
Grade #156, 21J, ¾, NI, DR, DMK, GT, GJS, HC, 14K	475	500	590
Grade #162, 21J, SW, PS, NI, GJS, GT	225	270	385
Grade #72-91, 21J, 3F BRG ★★	325	450	625
Grade #571, 21J, HCI5P, OF	95	125	165

14 SIZE

Grade or Name — Description	Avg	Ex-Fn	Mint
Lord Elgin, 17J, SS, ¾, OF	$200	$225	$275
7J, ¾, M#1, gilded, KW, 14K, HC	340	395	465
7J, ¾, M#1, gilded, KW, YGF	40	50	65
11J, ¾, M#1, gilded, KW, YGF, HC	45	55	70
11J, ¾, M#1, gilded, KW, YGF, OF	40	50	60

ELGIN WATCH CO., 14 SIZE (continued)

Grade or Name — Description	Avg	Ex-Fn	Mint
13J, ¾, M#1, gilded, KW	40	60	75
15J, ¾, M#1, gilded, KW	55	65	80
7J, ¾, M#2, SW, OF	40	45	60
15J, ¾, M#2, SW, OF	55	60	75
15J, ¾, M#2, SW, 14K, HC	325	385	475

Example of a 12 size 17 jewel Elgin with a personalized logo on dial.

Lord Elgin, 12 size, 21 jewels, gold train, gold jewel settings, serial number 24999947.

12 SIZE

Grade or Name — Description	Avg	Ex-Fn	Mint
Elgin W. Co. #30, 7J, ¾, gilded, KW	$45	$55	$75
Elgin W. Co. #189, 19J, HC, ¾, NI	90	110	140
Elgin W. Co. #190-194, 23J, HC, OF, GJS, ¾, HCI5P, NI, DMK, GT	125	145	185
Elgin W. Co. #236 & #237, 21J, HC, OF, GJS, ¾, HCI5P, NI, DMK, GT	75	90	125
Elgin W. Co. #301 & #302, 7J, ¾, HC, OF, NI	40	50	65
Elgin W. Co. #314 & #315, 15J, ¾, HC, OF, NI	50	60	75
Elgin W. Co. #383 & #384, 17J, ¾, HC, OF, NI	55	65	80
Elgin W. Co., 15J, 14K, Multi-color	575	675	835
Elgin W. Co., 15J, Silveroid	30	35	50
Elgin W. Co., 15J, HC, 14K	340	370	425
Elgin W. Co., 17J, OF, 14K	350	390	450
Elgin W. Co., 19J, HC, 14K	360	400	465
Elgin W. Co., 19J, 14K, OF	185	225	270
C. H. Hubbard, 19J, thin BRG model, 14K case ★	900	1,100	1,500
Lord Elgin, 23J, HC, GJS, DR, HCI5P, DMK, NI	175	225	385
Lord Elgin, 17J, HC	75	100	130
Lord Elgin, 19J, HC	110	130	195
Lord Elgin, 21J, 14K, OF	350	400	495
Lord Elgin, 21J, HC	110	135	195
B. W. Raymond, 19J, HC, OF, ¾, GJS, HCI5P, DR, DMK, NI	60	75	110
G. M. Wheeler, 17J, ¾, DR, HCI5P, DMK, NI, OF	55	60	75
G. M. Wheeler, 17J, ¾, DR, HCI5P, DMK, NI, HC	65	75	95

Lord Elgin, 12 size, 23 jewels, gold jewel settings, adjusted to HCI5P, originally sold for $110.00.

G. M. Wheeler, 12 size, 17 jewels, adjusted to HCI3P, originally sold for $27.00.

10 SIZE
(HC)

Grade or Name — Description	Avg	Ex-Fn	Mint
Dexter St., 7J, KW, HC, 14K	$200	$275	$295
Dexter St., 7J, ¾, gilded, KW, HC, gold filled	75	85	110
Frances Rubie, 7J, ¾, gilded, KW, HC, 14K	550	600	695
Gail Borden, 11J, ¾, gilded, KW, HC, 14K	295	335	420
Gail Borden, 11J, ¾, KW, HC, gold filled	70	90	125
Lady Elgin, 15J, ¾, gilded, KW, HC, 14K	295	340	420
21 or 28, 7J, ¾, gilded, KW, HC, gold filled	75	80	95
Elgin, multi-color case, gold filled, HC	165	200	300
Elgin, 15J, Silveroid, HC	30	40	50
Elgin, 15J, YGF, HC	40	60	95

Frances Rubie, Grade 23, 10 size, 15 jewels, key wind & set.

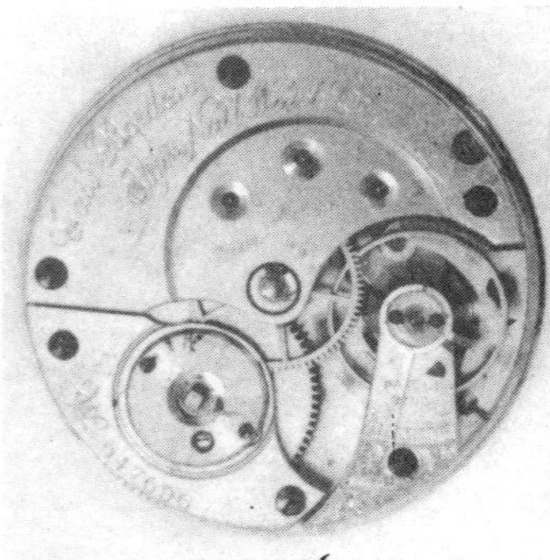

Gail Borden, Grade 22, 10 size, 11 jewels, key wind & set, serial number 947696.

6 SIZE
(HC Only)

Grade or Name — Description	Avg	Ex-Fn	Mint
Atlas, 7J, HC	$25	$30	$65
Elgin W. Co. #286, 7J, HC, ¾, DMK, NI	45	55	80
Elgin W. Co. #295, 15J, HC, ¾, DMK, NI	50	60	95
Elgin W. Co., 7J, HC, 10K	150	170	210

ELGIN WATCH CO., 6 SIZE (continued)

Elgin W. Co., Grade 121, 6 size, 15 jewels, hunting, serial number 4500445.

Elgin W. Co., Grade 67, 6 size, 11 jewels, serial number 1149615.

Grade or Name — Description	Avg	Ex-Fn	Mint
Elgin W. Co., 7J, HC, ¾, 14K	200	260	325
Elgin W. Co., 15J, SW, HC, Enamel case, 18K	700	1,000	1,400
Elgin W. Co., 15J, YGF	50	60	85
Elgin W. Co., 15J, HC, ¾, 14K	175	200	300
Elgin W. Co., 15J, HC, ¾, 10K	175	200	265
Elgin W. Co., 15J, HC, ¾, 18K	275	300	450
Elgin W. Co., 15J, HC, GF multi-color case	175	225	275
Elgin W. Co., 11J, HC, 14K	175	250	320
Elgin W. Co., 15J, demi-HC	75	100	150
Elgin W. Co., 15J, 14K, Multi-color HC	450	500	775

Elgin W. Co., 6 size, 15 jewels.

Elgin W. Co., Grade 201-HC, 205-OF, 0 size, 19 jewels, gold train.

Elgin W. Co., Grade 200-HC, 204-OF, 0 size, 17 jewels, gold jewel settings.

0 SIZE

Grade or Name — Description	Avg	Ex-Fn	Mint
Atlas W. Co., 7J, HC	$30	$35	$50
Elgin W. Co., 7J, NI, ¾, DR, DMK	35	40	60
Elgin W. Co:, 15J, NI, ¾, DR, DMK, OF	40	45	65
Elgin W. Co., 15J, NI, ¾, DR, DMK, HC	45	55	75
Elgin W. Co., 17J, NI, ¾, DR, DMK, ADJ	50	60	80
Elgin W. Co., 19J, NI, ¾, DR, DMK, GJS, ADJ	55	65	90
Elgin W. Co., 15J, HC, 14K	175	200	325
Elgin W. Co., 15J, HC, multi-color GF	135	175	270

ELGIN WATCH CO., 0 SIZE (continued)

Grade or Name — Description	Avg	Ex-Fn	Mint
Elgin W. Co., 15J, OF, multi-color dial	100	135	195
Elgin W. Co., 11J, HC, 14K	175	200	325
Elgin W. Co., 7J, HC, 10K	155	175	240
Elgin W. Co., 15J, 14K, Multi-color	475	550	650
Elgin W. Co., 15J, 14K, Multi-color + diamond	500	575	725
Frances Rubie, 19J, HC ★	150	200	295

3-0 and 5-0 SIZE

Grade or Name—Description	Avg	Ex-Fn	Mint
Lady Elgin, 15J, PS	$65	$80	$115
Lady Elgin, 15J, 14K, HC	175	200	295
Lady Raymond, 15J, PS	65	80	115
Elgin W. Co., 7J, HC	50	55	70

Lady Elgin, 5/0 size, 17 jewels, gold jewel settings, originally sold for $42.50.

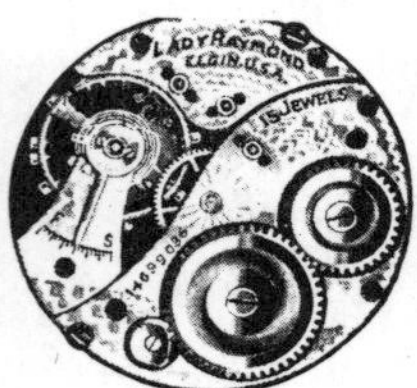

Lady Raymond, 5/0 size, 15 jewels, originally sold for $24.20.

MAN'S WRIST WATCH

Style or Model — Description	Avg	Ex-Fn	Mint
B. W. Raymond, R.R. approved, 23J, 14K case	$125	$165	$195
B. W. Raymond, R.R. approved, 23J, gold filled	95	115	145
B. W. Raymond, R.R. approved, 23J, stainless	70	80	95
Lord Elgin, 21J, rectangular case, 14K	95	115	135
Lord Elgin, 17J, rectangular case, 14K	80	90	110
Lord Elgin, 17J, rectangular gold filled case	30	35	45
Lord Elgin, 21J, round 14K case	75	85	110
Lord Elgin, 21J, round gold filled case	30	35	45
Lord Elgin, 21J, round case 14K, diamond on dial (12)	165	175	245
Official Boy Scout on case, c. 1934	100	135	185
Doctor's Model, "duo dial," rectangular gold filled case	100	125	155
Rectangular, 14K case, diamond dial	165	175	245
Rectangular, gold filled case	40	55	65
Tonneau, gold filled case	45	50	60
Round, gold filled case	20	25	35
Round, stainless steel case	10	15	25
Square, gold filled case	25	30	40
Curvex, gold filled case	25	30	45

LADY'S WRIST WATCH

Style or Model — Description	Avg	Ex-Fn	Mint
Lady Elgin, small, 14K case, after 1940	$50	$60	$75
Lady Elgin, small, gold filled case, after 1940	12	15	25
Rectangular, small, 14K case, after 1940	40	45	60
Rectangular, gold filled case, after 1940	20	25	45
Rectangular, 14K case w/small diamond	125	150	195

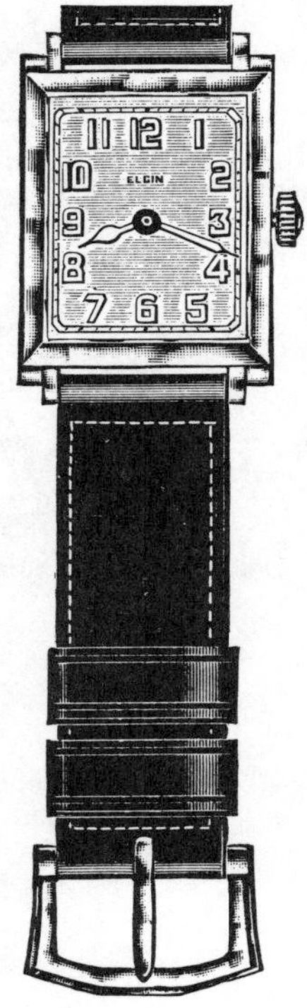

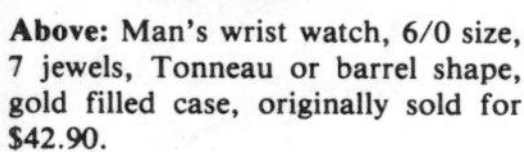

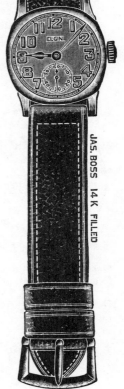

Above: Man's wrist watch, 6/0 size, 7 jewels, Tonneau or barrel shape, gold filled case, originally sold for $42.90.

Center: Man's wrist watch, 10/0 size, 15 jewels, solid gold case, rectangular shape, originally sold for $83.80. **Right:** Man's wrist watch, 6/0 size, 7 jewels, round shape, gold filled case, originally sold for $40.20.

ELGIN NATIONAL WATCH CO. IDENTIFICATION OF MOVEMENTS BY MODEL NUMBER

How to Identify Your Watch: Compare the movement of your watch with the illustrations in this section. Upon matching the movement exactly, the model number and size can be determined. While comparing, note the location of the balance, jewels, screws, gears and type of back plate (Full, ¾, Bridge) which will be clues in identifying the movement you have. Having determined the size and model number, you can now find your watch in the main price listing by name or number (which is engraved on the movement).

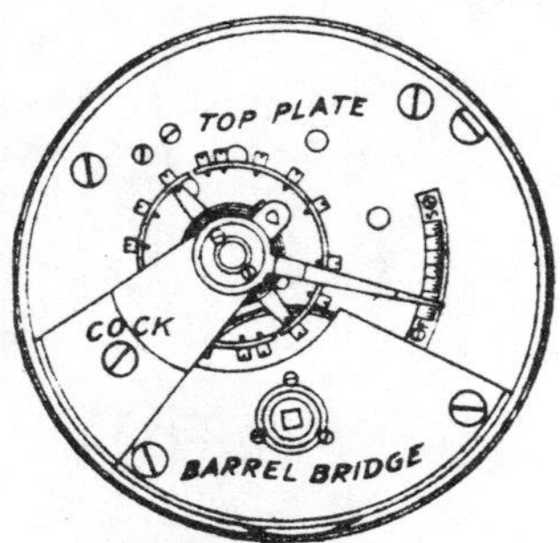

Model 1, 18 size, full plate, hunting, key wind & set, first serial number 101, Apr, 1867.

Model 2-4, 18 size, full plate, hunting, lever set, first serial number 155,001, June, 1873.

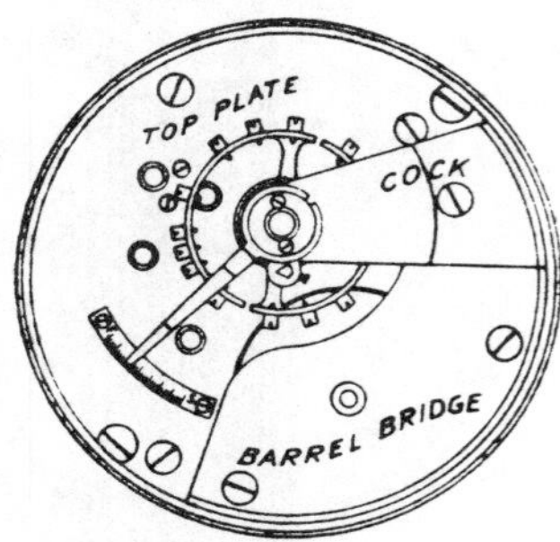

Model 5, 18 size, full plate, open face, pendant set, first serial number 2,110,001, Grade 43, Dec., 1885.

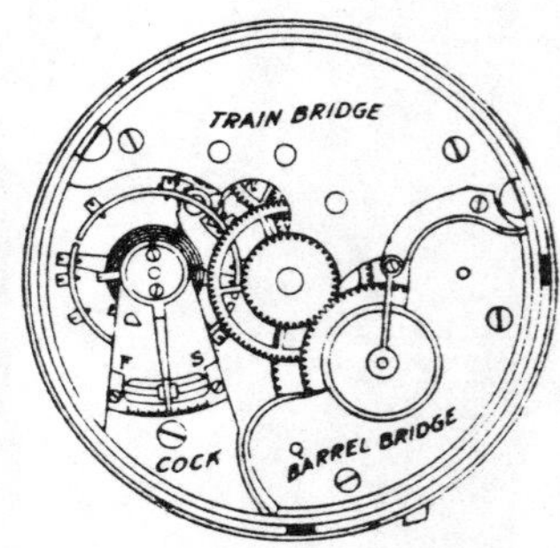

Model 6, 18 size, three-quarter plate, hunting, open face, pendant set.

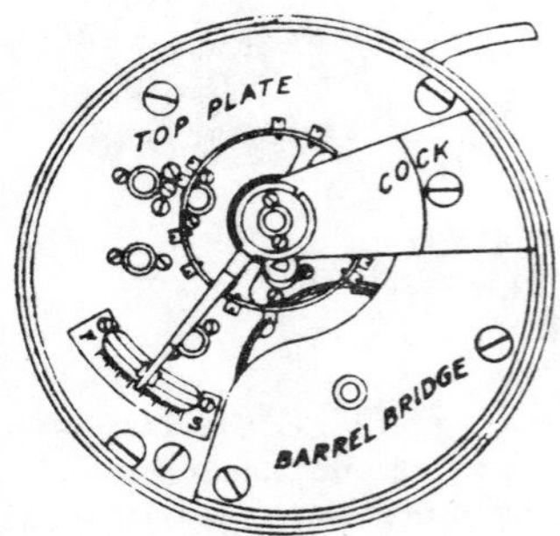

Model 7, 18 size, full plate, open face, lever set, first serial number 6,563,821, Grade 265, Apr., 1897.

Model 8, 18 size, three-quarter plate, open face, lever set, first serial number 8,400,001, Grade 214, Dec., 1900.

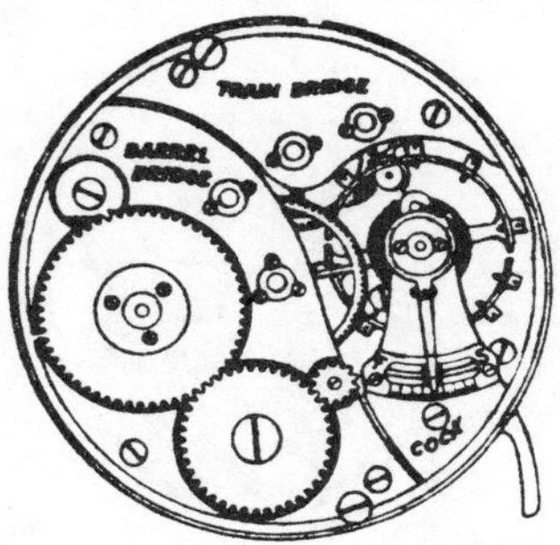

Model 8, 18 size, three-quarter plate, open face, lever set with winding indicator.

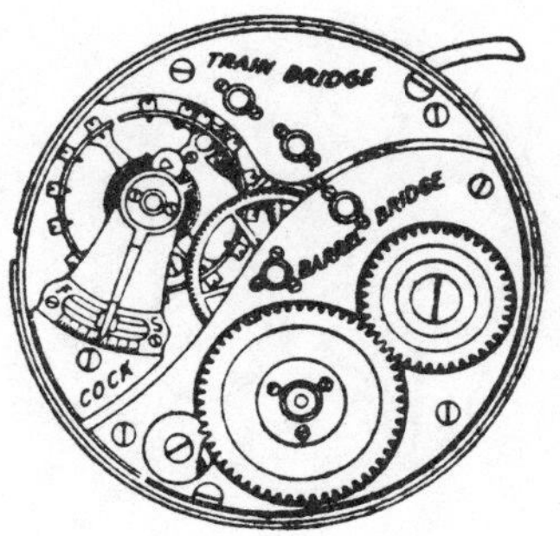

Model 9, 18 size, three-quarter plate, hunting, lever set, first serial number 9,625,001, Grade 274, May, 1904.

Model 9, 18 size, three-quarter plate, hunting, lever set with winding indicator.

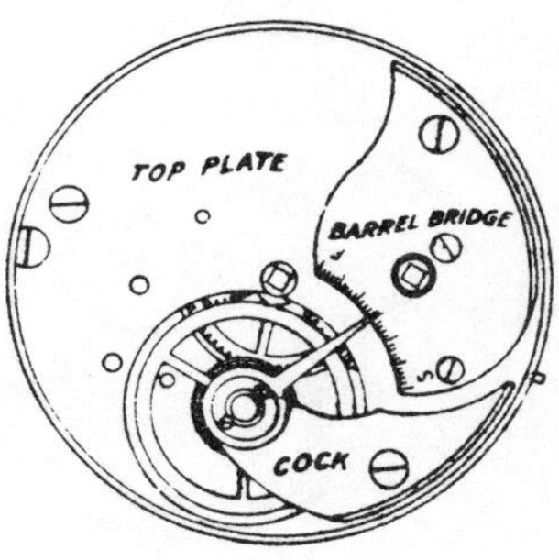

Model 1, 17 size, full plate, hunting, key wind and set.

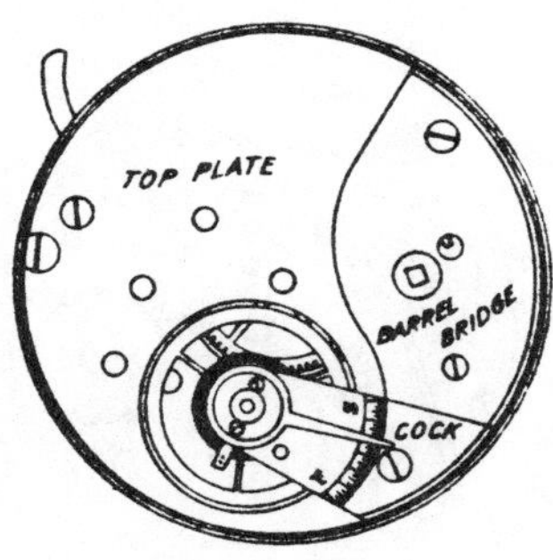

Model 2, 17 size, full plate, hunting, lever set.

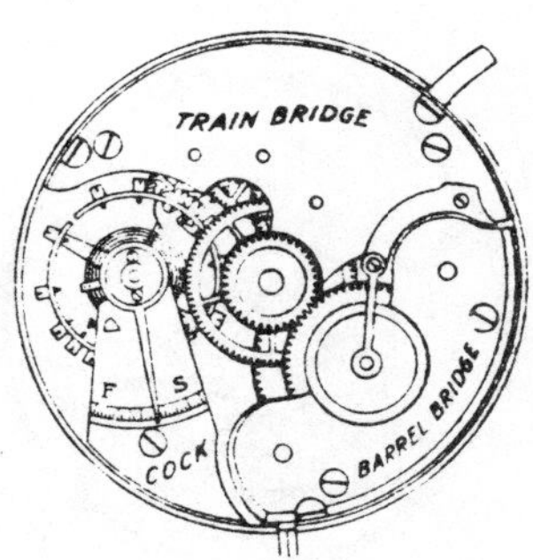

Model 1, 16 size, three-quarter plate, hunting & open face, lever set.

ELGIN WATCH CO. (continued)

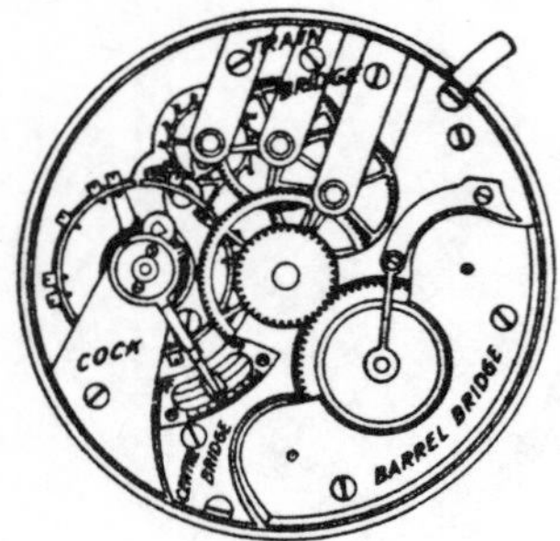

Model 2, 16 size, three-quarter plate, bridge, hunting & open face, lever set.

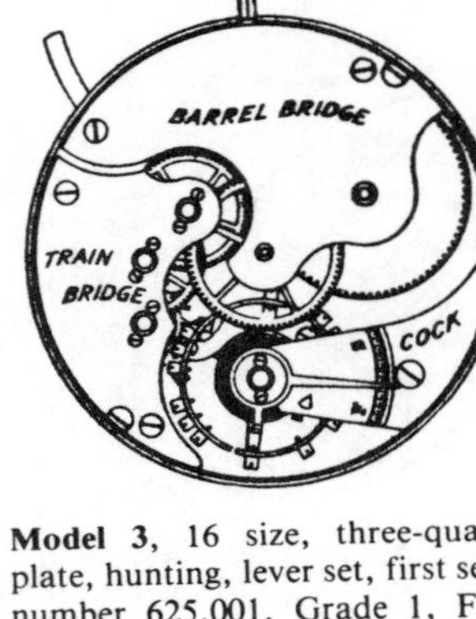

Model 3, 16 size, three-quarter plate, hunting, lever set, first serial number 625,001, Grade 1, Feb., 1879.

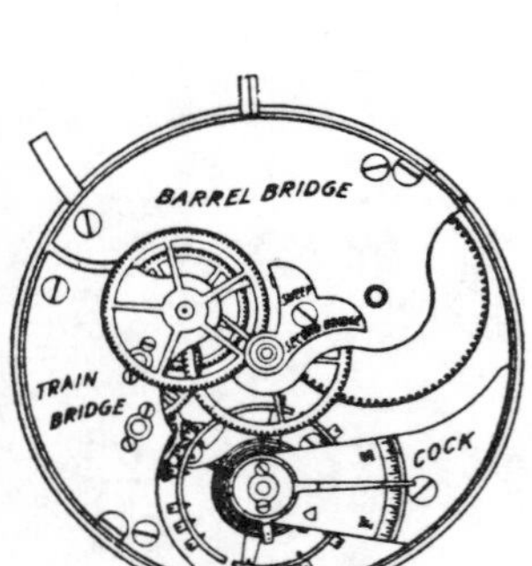

Model 4, 16 size, three-quarter plate, sweep second, hunting & open face, lever set.

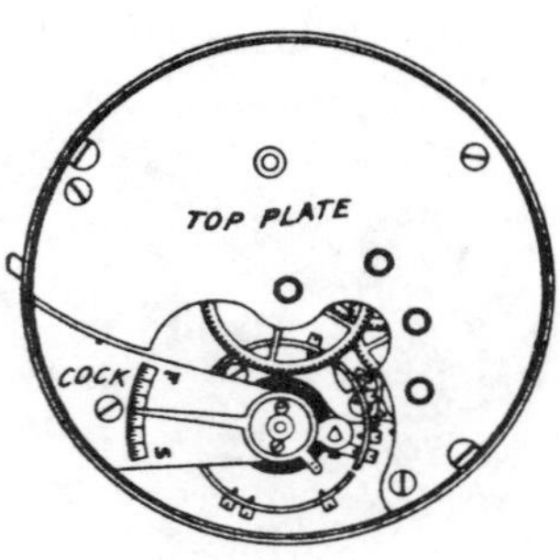

Model 5, 16 size, three-quarter plate, open face, pendant set.

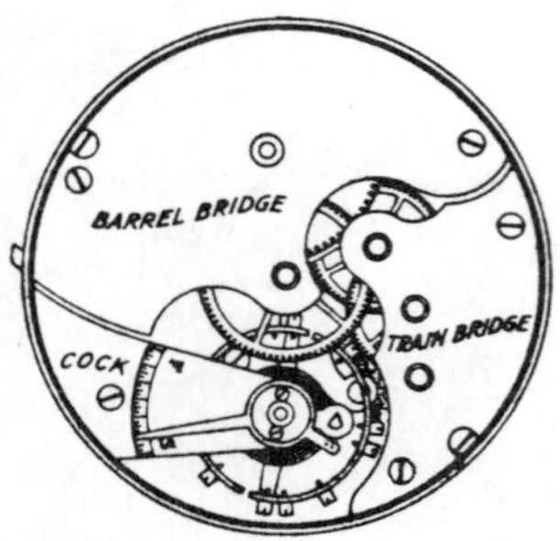

Model 5, 16 size, three-quarter plate, open face, pendant set, first serial number 2,811,001, Grade 105, Oct., 1887.

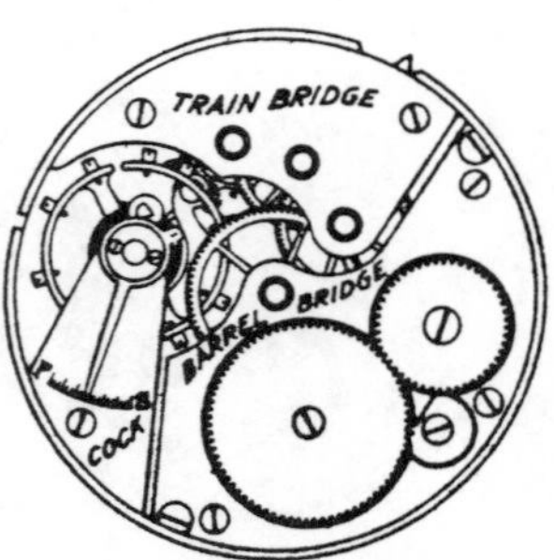

Model 6, 16 size, three-quarter plate, hunting, pendant set, first serial number 6,458,001, Grade 151, Aug., 1895.

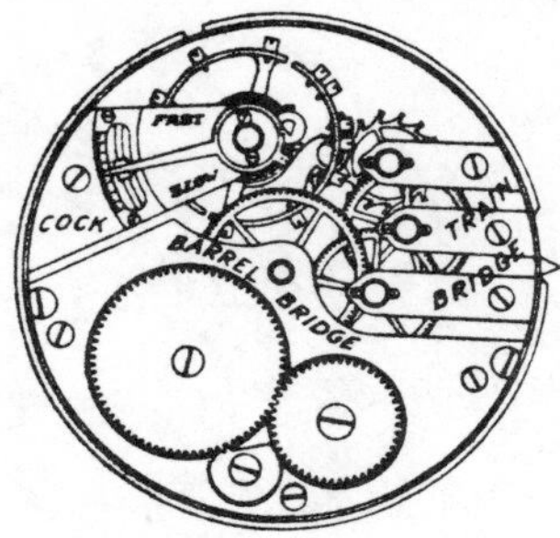

Model 6, 16 size, three-quarter plate, bridge, hunting, pendant set, first serial number 6,463,001, Grade 156, May, 1896.

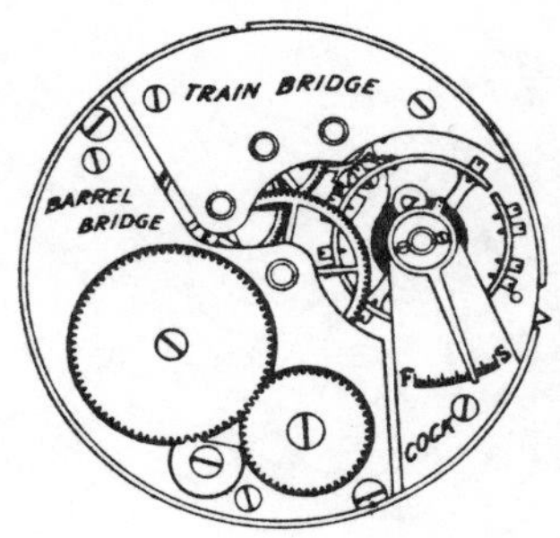

Model 7, 16 size, three-quarter plate, open face, pendant set, first serial number 6,464,001, Grade 157, Sept., 1895.

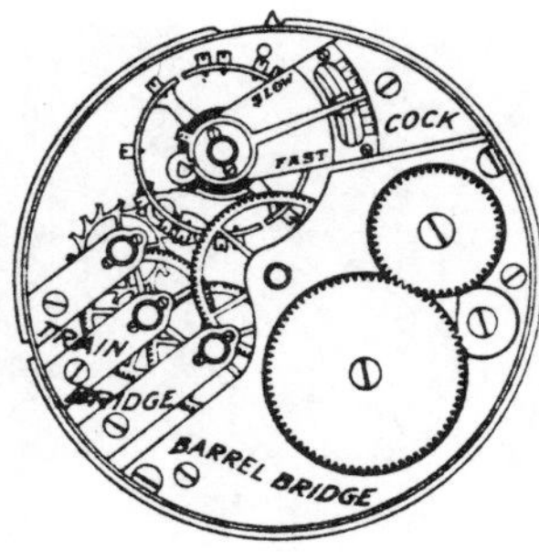

Model 7, 16 size, three-quarter plate, bridge, open face, pendant set, first serial number 6,469,001, Grade 162, Apr., 1896.

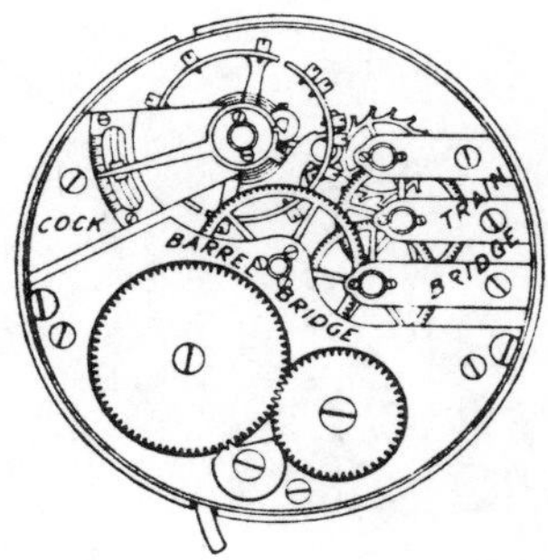

Model 8, 16 size, three-quarter plate, bridge, hunting, lever set, serial number 12,283,001, Grade 341, Jan., 1907.

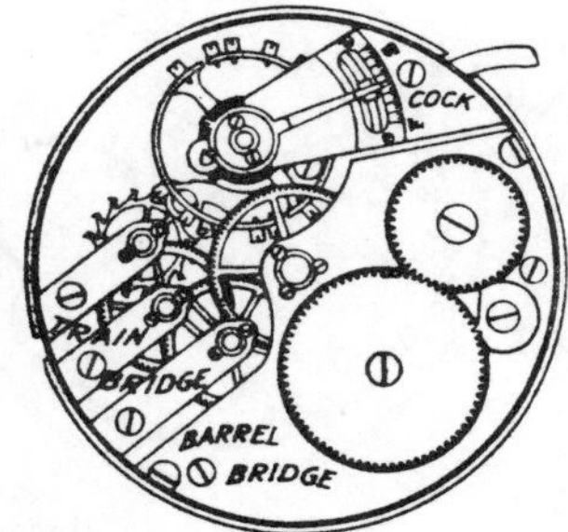

Model 9, 16 size, three-quarter plate, bridge, open face, lever set, first serial number 9,250,001, Grade 270, July, 1902.

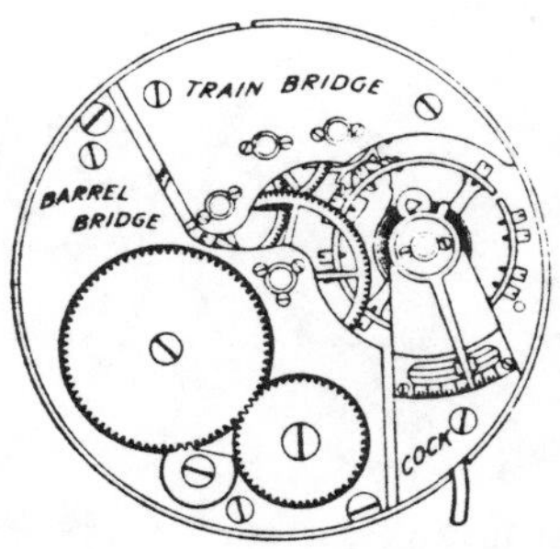

Model 13, 16 size, three-quarter plate, open face, lever set, first serial number 12,717,001, Grade 350, June, 1908.

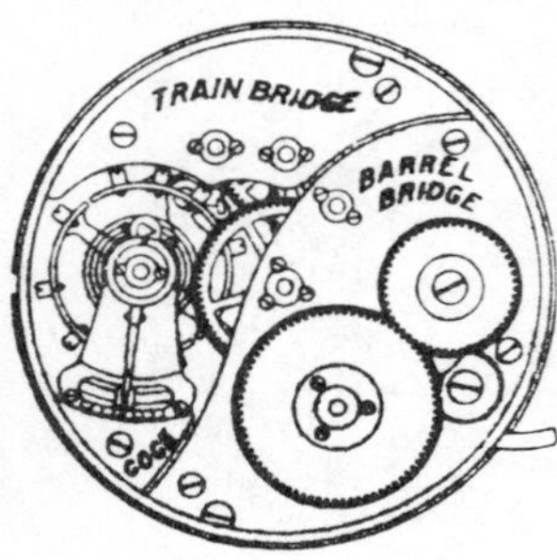

Model 14, 16 size, three-quarter plate, hunting, lever set.

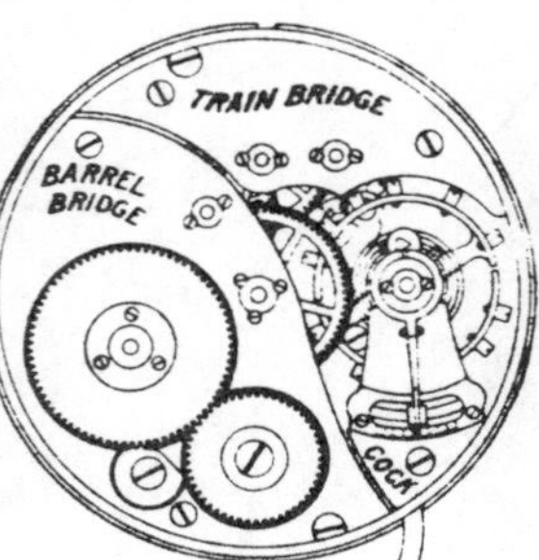

Model 15, 16 size, three-quarter plate, open face, lever set.

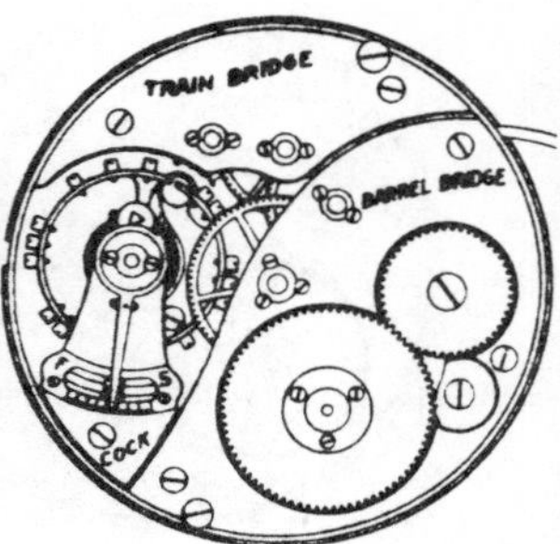

Model 17, 16 size, three-quarter plate, hunting, lever set.

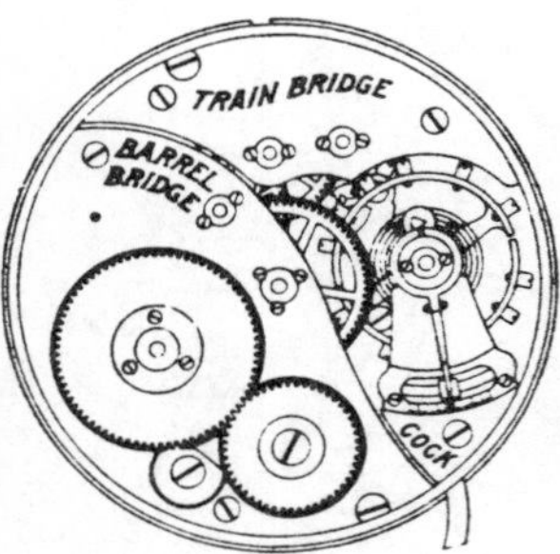

Model 19, 16 size, three-quarter plate, open face, lever set with winding indicator.

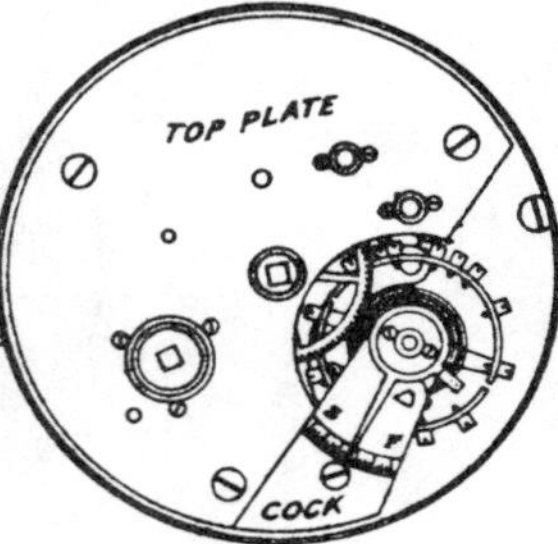

Model 1, 14 size, three-quarter plate, hunting, key wind and set.

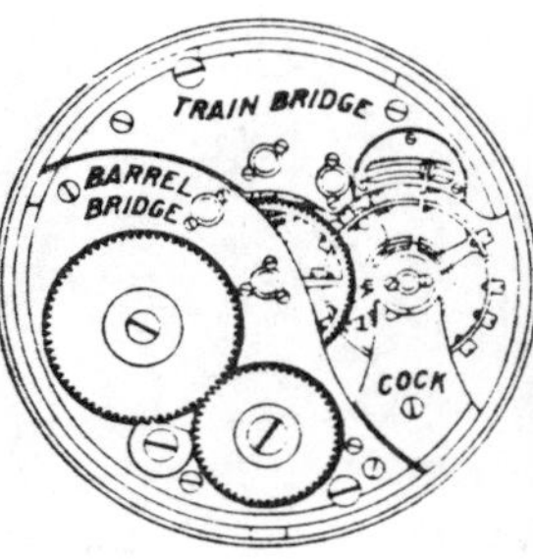

Model 2, 14 size, three-quarter plate, open face, pendant set.

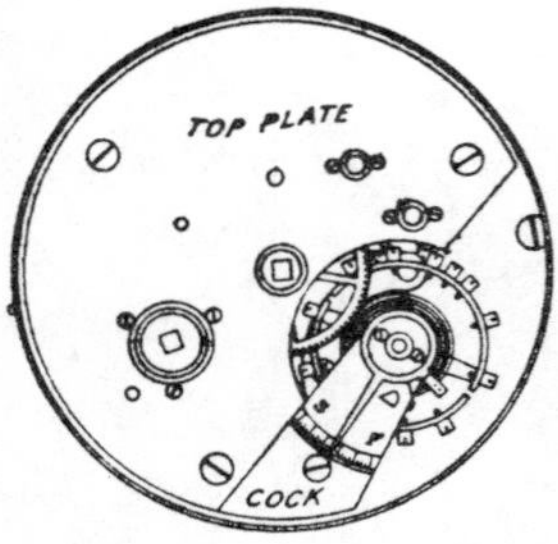

Model 1, 12 size, three-quarter plate, hunting, key wind and set.

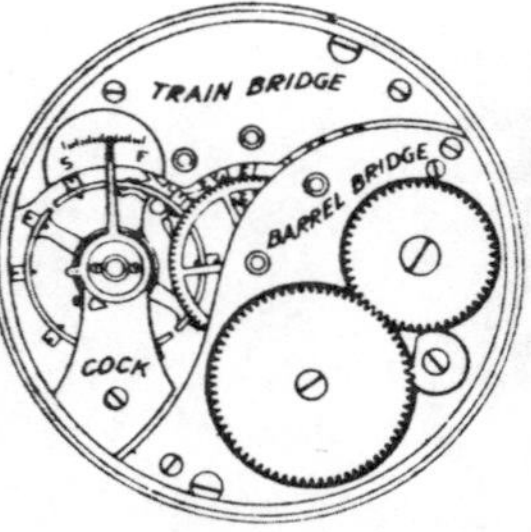

Model 2, 12 size, three-quarter plate, hunting, pendant set, first serial number 7,410,001, Grade 188, Dec., 1897.

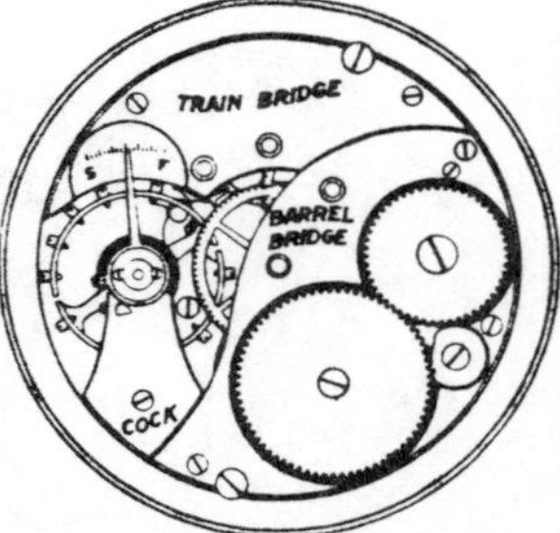

Model 2, 12 size, three-quarter plate, spread to 16 size, hunting, pendant set.

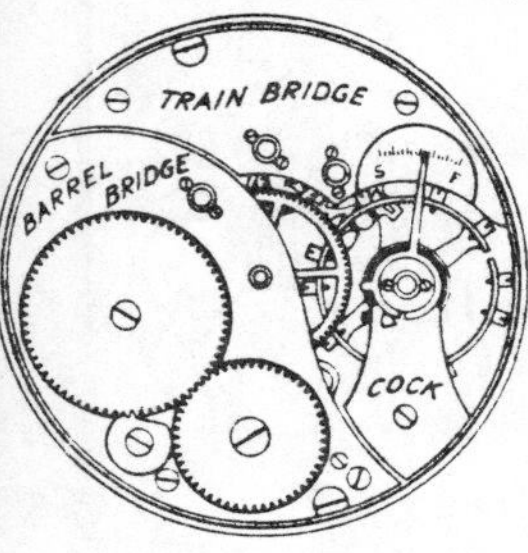

Model 3, 12 size, three-quarter plate, open face, pendant set, serial number 7,423,001, Grade 192, May 1898.

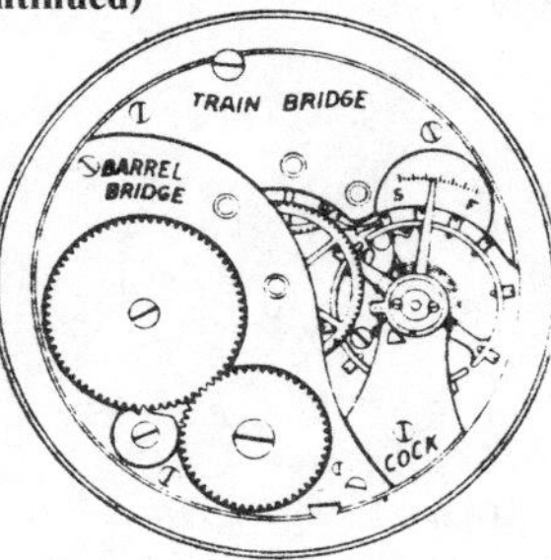

Model 3, 12 size, three-quarter plate, spread to 16 size, open face, pendant set.

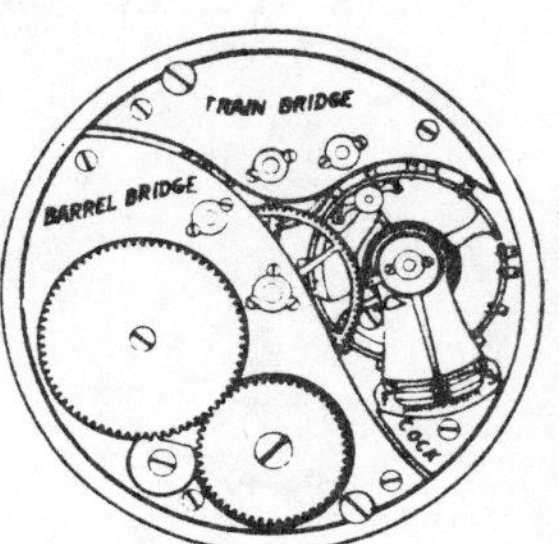

Model 4, 12 size, three-quarter plate, open face, pendant set, serial number 16,311,001, Grade 392, July, 1912.

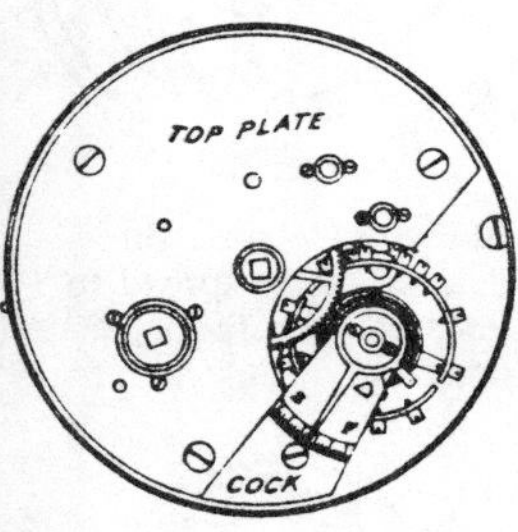

Model 1, 10 size, three-quarter plate, style 1, hunting, key wind and set.

Model 1, 10 size, three-quarter plate, style 2, hunting, key wind and set.

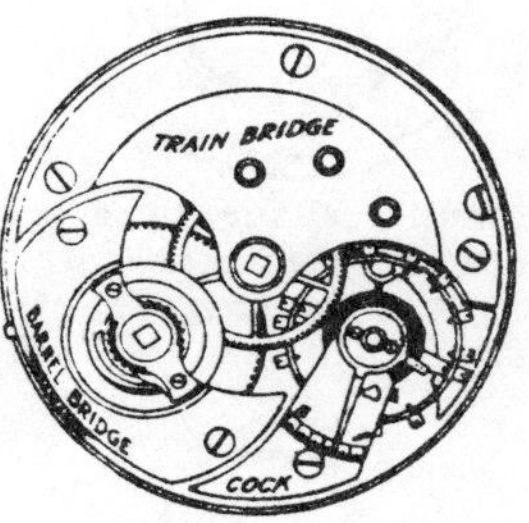

Model 1, 10 size, three-quarter plate, style 3, hunting, key wind and set.

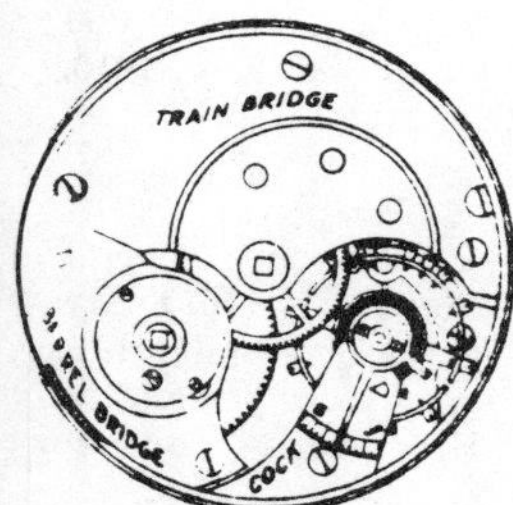

Model 1, 10 size, three-quarter plate, style 4, hunting, key wind and set.

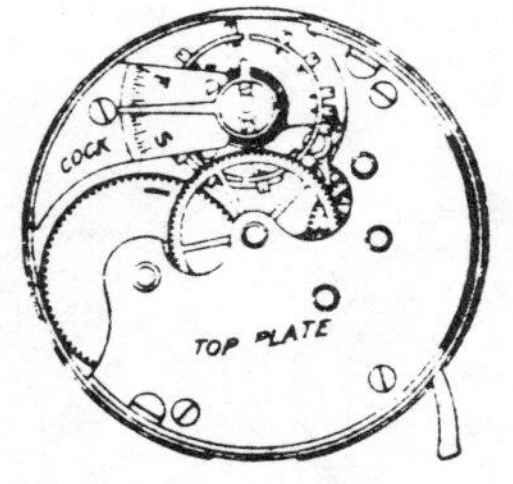

Model 1, 6 size, three-quarter plate, hunting, lever set.

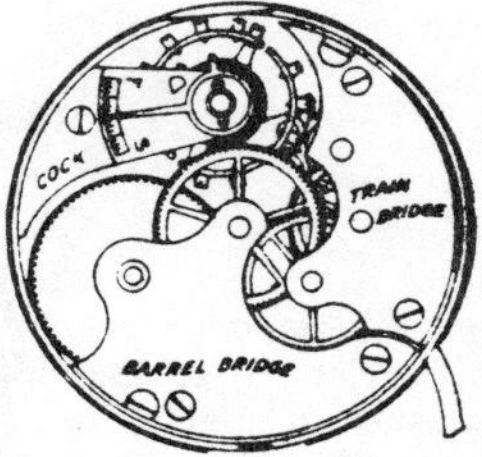

Model 1, 6 size, three-quarter plate, hunting, lever set.

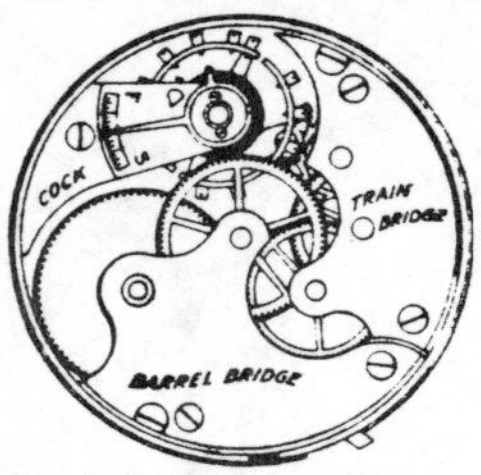

Model 2, 6 size, three-quarter plate, hunting, pendant set, first serial number 4,449,001, Grade 117, March, 1891.

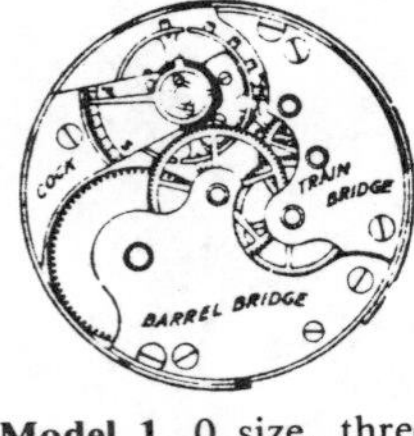

Model 1, 0 size, three-quarter plate, hunting, pendant set, first serial number 2,889,001, Grade 113, Aug., 1885.

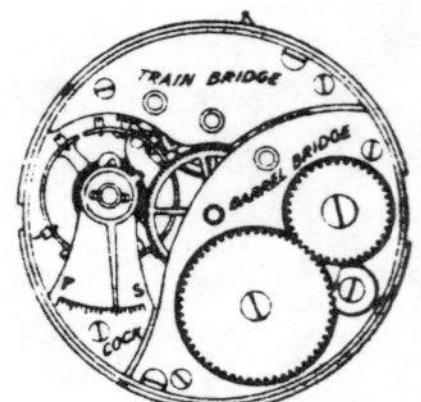

Model 2, 0 size, three-quarter plate, hunting, pendant set, first serial number 7,868,001, Grade 198, Dec., 1898.

Model 2, 0 size, three-quarter plate, spread to 12 size, hunting, pendant set.

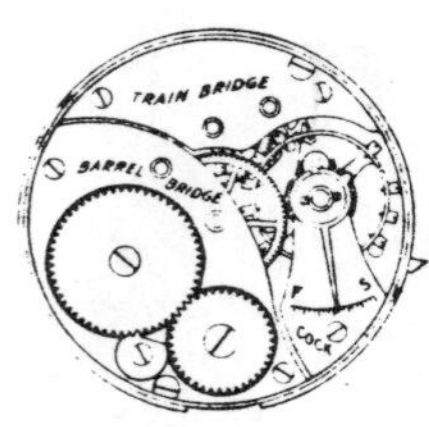

Model 3, 0 size, three-quarter plate, open face, pendant set.

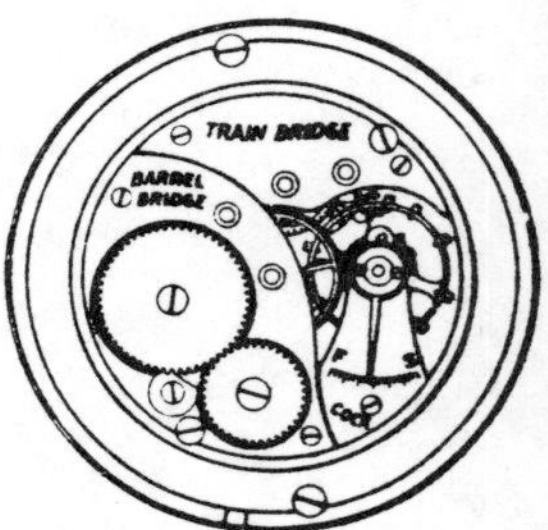

Model 3, 0 size, three-quarter plate, spread to 12 size, open face, pendant set.

Model 2, 3-0 size, three-quarter plate, hunting, pendant set, first serial number 18,149,001, Grade 413, Feb., 1915.

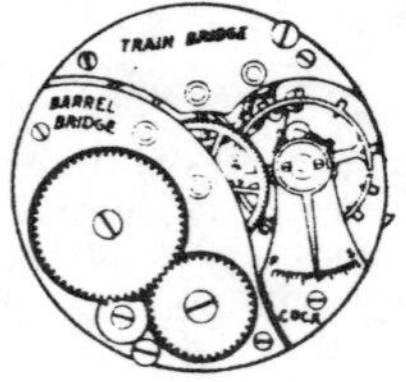

Model 3, 3-0 size, three-quarter plate, open face, pendant set, first serial number 18,179,001, Grade 414, March, 1915.

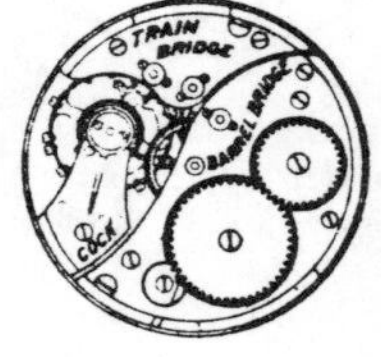

Model 1, 5-0 size, three-quarter plate, hunting, pendant set, first serial number 14,699,001, Grade 380, Feb., 1910.

Model 2, 5-0 size, three-quarter plate, open face, pendant set, first serial number 17,890,001, Grade 399, Feb., 1914.

Model 1, 10-0 size, three-quarter plate, open face, pendant set, first serial number 8,752,001, Grade 255, Apr., 1902.

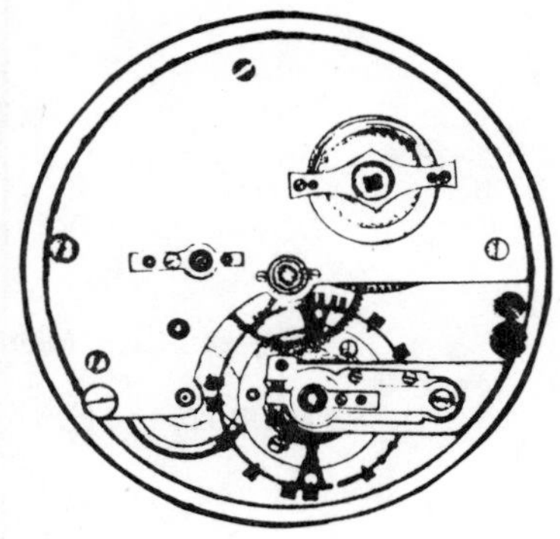

Charles Fasoldt, 18-20 size, 16 jewels, gold jewel settings, key wind & set, half plate, series I.

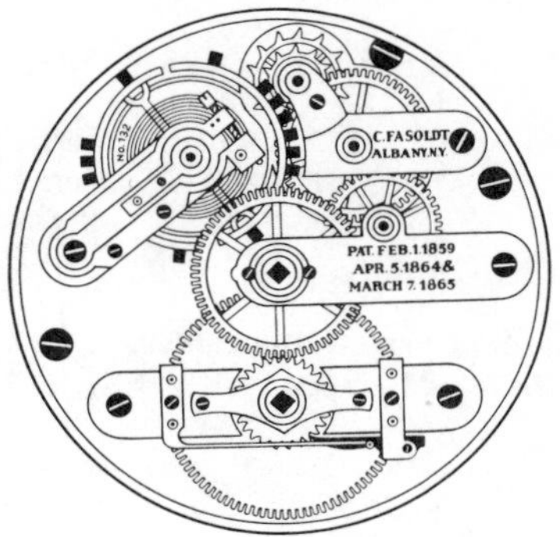

Charles Fasoldt, 18-20 size, 16 jewels, key wind & set, bar movement; note patented regulator, series II.

CHARLES FASOLDT WATCH CO.
Rome, New York
1849 — 1861

Albany, New York
1861 — 1878

Charles Fasoldt came to the United States in 1848. One of his first watches, Serial No. 27, was for a General Armstrong and was an eight-day movement. About the same time, he made several large regulators and a few pocket chronometers. He displayed some of his work at fairs in Utica and Syracuse and received four First-Class Premiums and two diplomas. In 1850, he patented a micrometric regulator (generally called the Howard Regulator because Howard bought the patent). He also patented a chronometer escapement in 1855-1865, a watch regulator in 1864, and a hairspring stud in 1877. He was also known for his tower clocks, receiving many awards and medals. He made about 500 watches in Albany and about 50 watches in Rome.

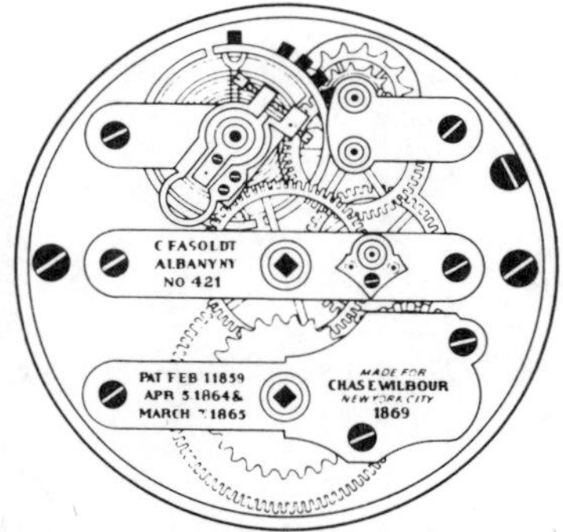

Charles Fasoldt, 18-20 size, 16 jewels, stem wind, key set, bar movement, series III.

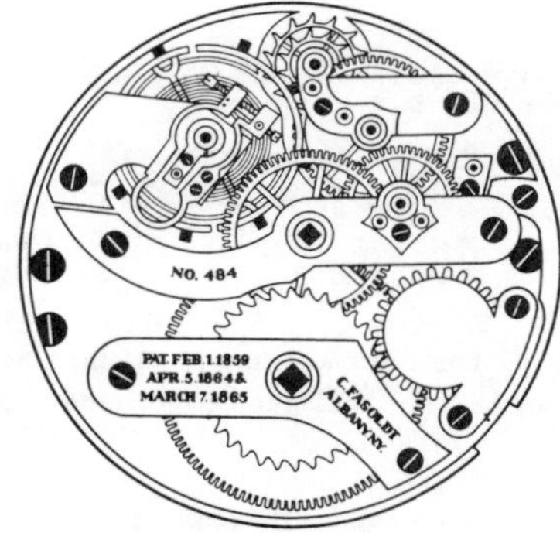

Charles Fasoldt, 18-20 size, 16 jewels, stem wind, key set, bar movement, series III.

CHARLES FASOLDT WATCH CO. (continued)

Year	Model	Style	Serial Range
1855 - 1864	Series I	KW, ½ plate	5- 59
1865 - 1868	Series II	KW, Bar	61-161
1868 - 1878	Series III	SW, Bar	335-540

Grade or Name — Description	Avg	Ex-Fn	Mint
18—20 SIZE, 16J, GJS, KW, KS . . . . ★★★	$8,000	$10,000	$14,500

FITCHBURG WATCH CO.
Fitchburg, Massachusetts
1875 — 1878

In 1875 S. Sawyer decided to manufacture watches. He hired personnel from the U. S. Watch Company to build the machinery, but by 1878 the company had failed. It is not known how many, if any, watches were made. The equipment was sold to Cornell and other watch companies.

E.H. Flint dial and movement, 18 size, 4-7 jewels, open face, key wind & set, "Lancaster Pa." on dial, "Patented Sept. 18th, 1877" on movement.

E. H. FLINT
Cincinnati, Ohio
1877 — 1879

The Flint watch was patented September 18, 1877, and about 50 watches were made. The serial number is found under the dial.

Grade orName — Description	Avg	Ex-Fn	Mint
18 Size, 4-7J, KW, Full Plate, OF, Silveroid case . . . . . ★★★	$3,000	$3,500	$5,000

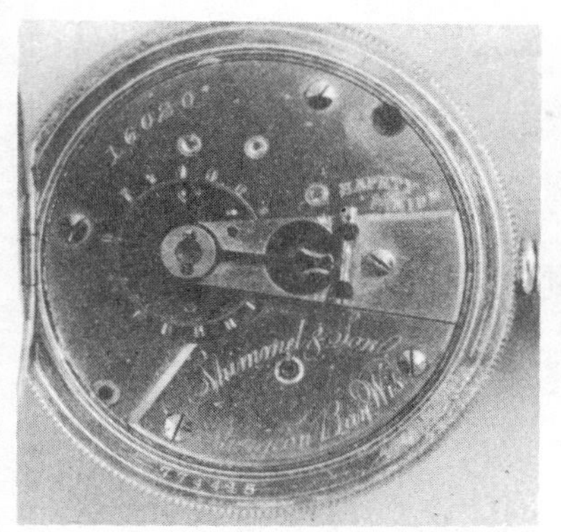

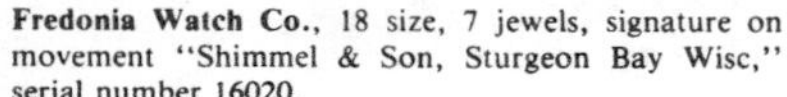

Fredonia Watch Co., 18 size, 7 jewels, signature on movement "Shimmel & Son, Sturgeon Bay Wisc," serial number 16020.

Fredonia Watch Co., 18 size, 7 jewels, serial number 6595.

FREDONIA WATCH CO.
Fredonia, New York
1883 — 1885

This company sold the finished movements acquired from the Independent Watch Co. These movements had been made by other companies. The Fredonia Watch Company was sold to the Peoria Watch Co. in 1885, after having produced approximately 20,000 watches.

Chronology of the Development of Fredonia:

Independent Watch Co.	1880-1883
Fredonia Watch Co.	1883-1885
Peoria Watch Co.	1885-1895

Grade or Name — Description	Avg	Ex-Fn	Mint
18S, 11J, KW, KS, HC, Coin	$200	$250	$550
18S, 15J, SW, Multi-color, 14K, HC	1,200	1,500	2,200
18S, KW, Reversible case	275	350	625
18S, 15J, SW, LS, Gilt	195	240	475
18S, 15J, straight line escapement, NI	300	350	595
18S, 15J, HC, low serial number	345	395	625
18S, 15J, personalized mvt.	195	235	475
18S, 15J, KW, HC, marked Lakeshore W. Co.	195	235	475

Fredonia Watch Co. with a reversible case; changes to either hunting or open face.

Freeport Watch Co. Example of a basic movement, 18 size, 15 jewels, key wind & set, serial number 2.

FREEPORT WATCH CO.
Freeport, Illinois
1874 — 1875

Probably less than 20 watches made by Freeport have survived. Their machinery was purchased from Mozart Co. A Mr. Hoyt was engaged as superintendent. A building was erected but was destroyed by fire on Oct. 21, 1875. A safe taken from the ruins contained 300 completed movements which were said to be ruined.

Grade or Name — Description		Avg	Ex-Fn	Mint
18S, KW, KS	★★★	$4,500	$5,500	$7,000

LUTHER GODDARD
Shrewsbury, Massachusetts
1809 — 1825

The first significant attempt to produce watches in America was by Luther Goddard. William H. Keith, who became president of Waltham Watch Co. (1861-1866) and was once apprenticed to Goddard, said that the hands, dials, round and dove-tail brass, steel wire, mainsprings and hairsprings, balance verge, chains, and pinions were all imported. The plates, wheels, and brass parts were cast at the Goddard shop, however. He also made the cases for his movements which were of the usual style—open faced, dou-

D. Goddard, 18-20 size, 15 jewels, "Worcester, Mass." on movement, key wind & set, solid balance, under sprung, serial number 8.

L. Goddard & Co., 16-18 size, pair case, open face-thick bulls-eye type, and of high quality for the time.

LUTHER GODDARD (continued)

ble case—and somewhat in advance of the prevalent style of thick bull's eye watches of the day. About 600 watches were made which were of high quality and more expensive than the imported type. The first watch was produced about 1812 and was sold to the father of ex-governor Lincoln of Worcester, Massachusetts. In 1820 his watches sold for about $60.

About 1870 Goddard built a shop one story high with a hip roof about 18' square; it had a lean-to at the back for casting. The building was for making clocks, but a need for watches developed and Goddard made watches there. He earned the distinction of establishing the first watch factory in America.

His movements were marked as follows: L. Goddard, L. Goddard & Co., Luther Goddard & Son, P. Goddard, L & P Goddard, D. P. Goddard & Co., P. & D. Goddard. Frank A. Knowlton purchased the company and operated it until 1933.

Chronology of the Development of Luther Goddard:

Luther Goddard, "L Goddard," Luther Goddard & Son	1809-1825	D. Goddard & Son	1842-1850
L Goddard & Co.	1817-1825	Luther D. Goddard	1850-1857
P & D Goddard	1825-1842	Goddard & Co.	1857-1860
		D. Goddard & Co. (also Benjamen Goddard)	1860-1872

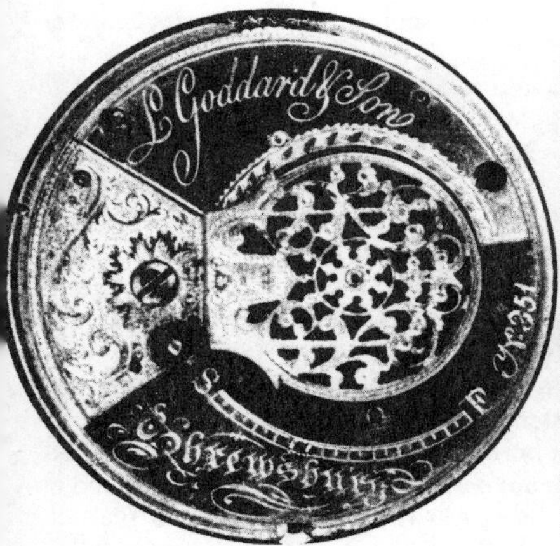

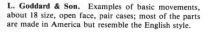

L. Goddard & Son. Examples of basic movements, about 18 size, open face, pair cases; most of the parts are made in America but resemble the English style.

P. Goddard, about 18 size, pair case, verge escapement, chain driven fusse, c. 1815-17, made in shrewsbury, Mass., serial number 600.

Grade or Name — Description		Avg	Ex-Fn	Mint
Luther Goddard, S#1-35 with eagle on balance bridge	★★★	$5,000	$7,000	$10,000
Luther Goddard, without eagle on cock	★	3,500	4,000	6,500
Luther Goddard, L. Goddard, Luther Goddard & Son,	★★	2,800	3,200	4,200
L. Goddard & Co., P & D Goddard, D. Goddard & Son	★	1,800	2,300	3,000
Benjamin Goddard, Luther D. Goddard, Goddard & Co., D. Goddard & Co.	★	1,600	2,000	2,800
P. Goddard, with eagle on cock	★	2,000	2,400	3,200

HAMILTON WATCH CO.
Lancaster, Pennsylvania
December 14, 1892 — Present

Hamilton's roots go back to the Adams & Perry Watch Manufacturing Co. On Sept. 26, 1874, E. F. Bowman made a model watch, and the first movement was produced on April 7, 1876. It was larger than an 18S, or about a 19S. The movement had a snap-on dial and the patented stem-setting arrangement. They decided to start making the watches to a more standard size of 18, and no more than 1,000 of the large-size watches were made. Work had commenced on Sept. 1, 1877, at the Lancaster Watch Co. The watches were designed to sell at a cheaper price than normal. It had a one-piece top ¾ plate and a pillar plate that was fully ruby-jeweled (4½ pairs). It had a gilt or nickel movement and a new stem-wind device designed by Mosely & Todd. By mid-1878, the Lancaster Watch Co. had made 150 movements. Four grades of watches were produced: Keystone, Fulton, Franklin, and Melrose. In September 1879 the company had manufactured 334 movements. In 1880 some 1,250 movements had been made. In mid-1882, about 17,000 movements had been assembled. All totaled, about 20,000 movements were made.

The first Hamilton movement to be sold was No. 15 to W. C. Davis on January 31, 1893. The No. 1 movement was finished on April 25, 1896, and it was never sold. The No. 2 was finished on April 25, 1893, and was shipped to Smythe & Ashe of Rochester, N. Y. Nos. 1 & 2 are at the N.A.W.C.C. museum.

The Hamilton Watch Co. today maintains a complete record of watch serial numbers and purchasers, and owners can write to the company to obtain data concerning specific watches.

Chronology of the Development of Hamilton:

Adams & Perry Watch Co.	Sept. 1874-May 1876
Lancaster, Pa., Watch Co.	Aug. 1877-Oct. 1887
Lancaster, Pa., Watch Co.	Nov. 1877-May 1879
Lancaster Watch Co.	May 1883-1886
Keystone Standard Watch Co.	1886-1890
Hamilton Watch Co.	Dec. 14, 1892-1969

In 1893 the first watch was produced with the Hamilton label. The watches became very popular with the railroad men and by 1923 some 53 percent of Hamilton's production was railroad watches. Most Hamilton movements were fitted with a 42-hour mainspring. The Elinvar hairspring was patented in 1931 and used in all movements thereafter. On October 15, 1940, Hamilton introduced the 992B which were all fitted with the Elinvar hairspring. Although the Hamilton Watch Co. is still in business today making modern type watches, they last produced American-made watches in 1969.

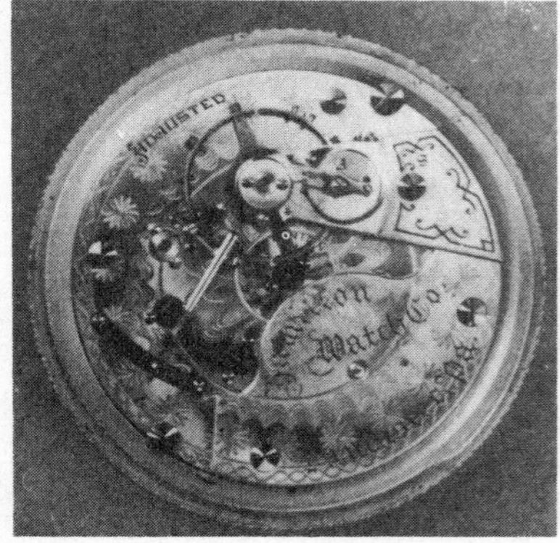

Grade 936, 18 size, 17 jewels, serial number 1, c. 1893.

Grade 936, 18 size, 17 jewels, serial number 2, c. 1893.

Grade 937, 18 size, 17 jewels, hunting case. Note serial number 1047. Hunting case models began with 1001.

Hamilton Watch Co., 18 size, 7 jewels, serial number 2934.

HAMILTON ESTIMATED SERIAL NUMBERS AND PRODUCTION DATES

Date	Serial No.	Date	Serial No.	Date	Serial No.	Date	Serial No.
1893	1-2,000	1906	590,000	1919	1,700,000	1931	2,450,000
1894	5,000	1907	756,000	1920	1,790,000	1932	2,500,000
1895	10,000	1908	921,000	1921	1,860,000	1933	2,600,000
1896	14,000	1909	1,087,000	1922	1,900,000	1934	2,700,000
1897	20,000	1910	1,050,500	1923	1,950,000	1935	2,800,000
1898	30,000	1911	1,290,500	1924	2,000,000	1936	2,900,000
1899	40,000	1912	1,331,000	1925	2,100,000	1937	3,000,000
1900	50,000	1913	1,370,000	1926	2,200,000	1938	3,200,000
1901	90,000	1914	1,410,500	1927	2,250,000	1939	3,400,000
1902	150,000	1915	1,450,500	1928	2,300,000	1940	3,600,000
1903	260,000	1916	1,517,000	1929	2,350,000	1941	3,800,000
1904	340,000	1917	1,580,000	1930	2,400,000	1942	4,025,000
1905	425,000	1918	1,650,000				

NOTE: The serial numbers and dates listed above are only close approximations. The actual date of your watch could vary 2 to 3 years from the listed date.

The Hamilton Masterpiece

The adjoining illustration shows the Masterpiece in a platinum case. The dial is sterling silver with raised gold numbers and solid gold hands. This watch sold for $685.00 in 1930. All 922 MP Models included the following: 23 jewels, were adjusted to heat, cold, isochronism, and five positions, with a motor barrel, solid gold train, steel escape wheel, double roller, sapphire pallets and a micrometric regulator.

HAMILTON SERIAL NUMBERS AND GRADES

To help determine the size and grade of your watch, the following serial number list is provided. Serial numbers 30,001 through 32,000, which are omitted from the list, were not listed by Hamilton. To identify your watch, simply look up its serial number which will identify the grade. After determining the grade, your watch can be easily located in the pricing section.

No.	Grade
1-20	936
21-30	932
31-60	936
61-400	932
401-1000	936
1001-20	937
1021-30	933
1031-60	937
1061-1100	933
1101-300	937
1301-600	933
1601-2000	937
2001-3000	7J
3001-100	931
3101-500	935
3501-600	931
3601-900	935
3901-4000	931
4001-300	930
4301-5100	934
5101-400	926
5401-600	934
5601-6000	930
6001-600	936
6601-700	938
6701-800	936
6801-7000	932
7001-10	17J
7011-600	937
7601-700	939
7701-800	937
7801-8000	933
8001-700	936
8701-800	938
8801-9000	936
9001-300	937
9301-600	939
9601-800	937
9801-900	933
9901-10000	939
10001-200	938
10201-400	936
10401-50	932
10451-500	936
10501-700	938
10701-900	936
10901-11000	938
11001-12000	936
12001-200	939
12201-13000	937
13001-400	999
13401-14000	938
14001-15000	999
15001-300	939
15301-15401	21J
15302-700	937
15701-16000	939
16001-100	931
16101-200	930
16201-300	927
16301-400	931
16401-600	927
16601-17000	931
17001-500	929
17501-18000	931
18001-200	928
18201-300	926
18301-500	928
18501-19500	930
19501-700	926
19701-20000	930
20001-300	934
20301-500	926
20501-21000	999
21001-300	935
21301-500	927
21501-800	935
21801-22500	927
22501-800	931
22801-23000	935
23001-200	928
23201-500	7J
24001-500	926
24501-25000	934
25001-100	11J
25101-400	927
25401-800	931
25801-26000	935
26001-500	930
26501-27000	928
27001-28000	929
28001-29000	999
29001-800	927
29801-30000	935
32001-300	926
32301-700	930
32701-33000	934
33001-500	931
33501-800	927
33801-34000	935
34001-500	928
34501-700	930
34701-800	926
34801-35000	934
35001-800	931
35801-36000	935
36001-37000	928
37001-38000	929
38001-500	926
38501-600	930
38601-900	934
38901-39000	926
39001-200	931
39201-500	935
39501-700	927
39701-900	935
39901-40000	931
40001-200	930
40201-500	934
40501-41000	926
41001-500	929
41501-42000	927
42001-43000	999
43001-300	941
43301-500	943
43501-700	937
43701-900	941
43901-44000	943
44001-02	21J
44003-400	938
44401-500	942
44501-45000	936
45001-46000	929
46001-500	926
46501-800	934
46801-47000	930
47001-500	927
47501-700	935
47701-48000	931
48001-05	942
48006-300	940
48301-500	942
48501-900	940
48901-49000	942
49001-400	927
49401-900	925
49901-50	11J
50071-500	962
50501-750	960
50751-50850	964
50851-51000	960
51001-51300	16s
51301-400	963
51401-650	961
51651-750	965
51751-52000	961
52001-300	16s
52301-500	976
52501-700	974
52701-800	966
52801-53000	976
53001-53070	16s
53071-53500	977
53501-900	975
53901-54000	967
54001-200	972
54201-300	974
54301-500	976
54501-700	974
54701-800	968
54801-55000	976
55001-300	973
55301-600	977
55601-700	969
55701-800	977
55801-56000	975
56001-300	974
56301-500	976
56501-600	966
56601-800	972
56801-900	974
56901-57000	976
57001-300	977
57301-500	975
57501-600	973
57601-800	975
57801-58000	977
58001-100	972
58101-200	974
58201-300	972
58301-400	966
58401-500	976
58501-600	972
58601-800	974
58801-59000	976
59001-300	973
59301-500	967
59501-700	975
59701-60000	977
60001-500	976
60501-700	974
60701-61000	976
61001-200	975
61201-500	977
61501-600	973
61601-800	975
61801-62000	977
62001-100	972
62101-300	974
62301-500	976
62501-700	974
62701-900	972
62901-63000	974
63001-500	977
63501-600	975
63601-800	977
63801-900	975
63901-64000	973
64001-100	976
64101-200	972
64201-300	974
64301-600	972
64601-700	976
64701-900	974
64901-65000	976
65001-200	973
65201-300	977
65301-400	975
65401-500	973
65501-700	977
65701-900	975
65901-66000	977
66001-200	976
66201-300	974
66301-500	972
66501-600	976
66601-700	974

HAMILTON WATCH CO. (continued)

No.	Grade
66701-800	972
66801-67000	974
67001-100	977
67101-300	975
67301-600	973
67601-800	975
67801-68000	977
68001-800	960
68801-69000	964
69001-100	977
69101-200	975
69201-400	973
69401-600	975
69601-70000	977
70001-200	976
70201-400	970
70401-600	968
70601-900	972
70901-71000	974
71001-200	975
71201-500	971
71501-700	975
71701-90	973
71791-800	969
71801-900	977
71901-72000	975
72001-100	974
72101-300	976
72301-600	974
72601-700	968
72701-900	976
72901-73000	972
73001-200	975
73201-300	973
73301-74000	977
74001-400	974
74401-600	972
74601-75000	976
75001-76799	HWW*
76002-76800	HWW*
77001-100	969
77101-300	973
77301-500	975
77501-600	971
77601-700	973
77701-900	975
77901-78000	977
78001-500	970
78501-700	972
78701-900	974
78901-79000	976
79001-100	973
79101-300	975
79301-700	977
79701-900	975
79901-80000	973
80001-200	972
80201-400	974
80401-600	970
80601-700	972
80701-900	974
80901-81000	976
81001-300	961
81301-500	965
81501-82000	961
82001-300	972
82301-500	974
82501-600	970
82601-700	972
82701-800	974
82801-900	968
82901-83000	976
83001-400	977
83401-500	971
83501-700	975
83701-800	973
83801-900	975
83901-84000	969
84001-400	974
84401-500	970
84501-700	972
84701-800	968
84801-85000	976
85001-200	937
85201-900	941
85901-86000	943
86001-87000	928
87001-88000	929
88001-500	926
88501-89000	930

No.	Grade
89001-500	941
89501-90000	937
90001-100	926
90101-950	999
91001-92000	925
92001-200	940
92201-93000	936
93001-94000	927
94001-003	934
94004-95000	928
95001-96000	923
96001-100	942
96101-700	940
96701-97000	936
97001-900	929
97901-98000	927
98001-99000	924
99001-100000	925
100001-101000	924
101001-102000	925
102001-103000	922
103001-104000	927
104001-105000	940
105001-500	925
105501-106000	927
106001-107000	940
107001-400	941
107401-500	943
107501-800	941
107801-108000	943
108001-200	928
108201-109000	926
109001-500	927
109501-110000	925
110001-900	940
110901-111000	942
111001-500	937
111501-112000	941
112001-200	928
112201-113000	926
113001-114000	925
114001-003	940
114004-115000	936
115001-116000	927
116001-117000	940
117001-118000	925
118001-119000	999
119001-120000	925
120001-121000	924
121001-500	941
121501-122000	943
122001-300	940
122301-400	942
122401-123000	940
123001-124000	941
124001-100	942
124101-800	940
124801-125000	942
125001-126000	927
126001-127000	924
127001-128000	941
128001-129000	936
129001-130000	925
130001-500	924
130501-131000	926
131001-132000	925
132001-100	926
132101-200	934
132201-500	926
132501-133000	924
133001-134000	937
134001-135000	924
135001-136000	925
136001-137000	926
137001-100	11J
137101-138000	927
138001-139000	940
139001-140000	937
140001-300	938
140301-141000	942
141001-142000	941
142001-143000	940
143001-100	927
143101-144000	925
144001-145000	924
145001-146000	925
146001-400	934
146401-147000	924
147001-148000	927
148001-149000	940

No.	Grade
149001-150000	925
150001-151000	924
151001-400	927
151401-500	935
151501-152000	927
152001-153000	936
153001-154000	941
154001-155000	936
155001-156000	927
156001-157000	940
157001-158000	925
158001-159000	940
159001-160000	941
160001-161000	940
161001-162000	941
162001-163000	926
163001-164000	943
164001-165000	940
165001-166000	925
166001-167000	924
167001-168000	927
168001-169000	940
169001-400	935
169401-170000	927
170001-171000	999
171001-172000	925
172001-100	934
172101-173000	926
173001-174000	925
174001-175000	924
175002-176000	HWW*
175001-699	HWW*
176001-177000	940
177001-178000	927
178001-179000	942
179001-500	935
179501-180000	927
180001-181000	940
181001-182000	941
182001-300	926
182301-400	934
182401-183000	926
183001-184000	941
184001-185000	940
185001-186000	925
186001-187000	942
187001-188000	927
188001-189000	924
189001-190000	925
190001-191000	926
191001-192000	927
192001-193000	924
193001-194000	925
194001-195000	926
195001-500	935
195501-196000	927
196001-197000	926
197001-198000	937
198001-199000	936
199001-200000	925
200001-201000	926
201001-202000	925
202001-500	926
202501-203000	934
203001-204000	927
204001-100	934
204101-500	926
204501-205000	934
205001-206000	941
206001-207000	940
207001-208000	927
208001-900	999
208901-209000	940
209001-210000	925
210001-211000	940
211001-212000	927
212001-213000	940
213001-500	941
213501-600	937
213601-214000	925
214001-215000	924
215001-216000	927
216001-217000	940
217001-218000	927
218001-219000	940
219001-220000	925
220001-221000	924
221001-222000	927
222001-223000	926
223001-02	927

HAMILTON WATCH CO. (continued)

No.	Grade
223003-04	941
223005	937
223006-224000	927
224001-225000	924
225001-226000	927
226001-227000	940
227001-228000	925
228001-229000	924
229001-230000	925
230001-500	926
230501-231000	924
231001-565	937
231566-232000	927
232001-233000	940
233001-234000	941
234001-235000	940
235001-236000	941
236001-237000	936
237001-238000	941
238001-239000	926
239001-500	943
239501-240000	941
240001-241000	940
241001-242000	941
242001-243000	940
243001-244000	927
244001-245000	936
245001-246000	925
246001-247000	940
247001-248000	927
248001-249000	940
249001-250000	927
250001-251000	926
251001-252000	927
252001-253000	924
253001-254000	925
254001-255000	940
255001-256000	925
256001-257000	926
257001-258000	941
258001-259000	924
259001-260000	941
260001-261000	940
261001-262000	927
262001-263000	926
263001-264000	925
264001-265000	940
265001-266000	927
266001-267000	940
267001-268000	925
268001-269000	940
269001-270000	927
270001-271000	940
271001-272000	925
272001-273000	926
273001-274000	941
274001-275000	924
275002-100	HWW*
275102-200	HWW*
275202-460	HWW*
275462-500	HWW*
276001-277000	940
277001-278000	941
278001-279000	940
279001-280000	925
280001-281000	936
281001-282000	927
282001-283000	926
283001-284000	925
284001-500	934
284501-900	924
284901-285000	999
285001-286000	925
286001-287000	940
287001-288000	927
288001-289000	940
289001-290000	927
290001-800	936
290801-291000	938
291001-292000	925
292001-500	940
292501-293000	942
293001-294000	925
294001-295000	926
295001-296000	927
296001-297000	940
297001-298000	927
298001-299000	940
299001-300000	925
300001-300	972
300301-500	970

No.	Grade
300501-900	974
300901-301000	968
301001-400	975
301401-500	971
301501-302000	973
302001-100	990
302101-200	992
302201-300	990
302301-900	992
302901-303000	990
303001-100	973
303101-300	971
303301-800	975
303801-304000	973
304001-100	970
304101-400	972
304401-305000	974
305001-100	973
305101-200	971
305201-300	969
305301-900	975
305901-306000	973
306001-400	972
306401-307000	974
307001-100	975
307101-300	971
307301-400	975
307401-500	973
307501-600	975
307601-700	971
307701-900	975
307901-308000	969
308001-700	990
308701-309000	992
309001-100	971
309101-400	973
309401-310000	975
310001-400	970
310401-311000	974
311001-700	975
311701-312000	973
312001-200	970
312201-500	972
312501-600	968
312601-313000	974
313001-100	973
313101-400	971
313401-600	969
313601-314000	975
314001-600	974
314601-900	972
314901-315000	970
315001-100	971
315101-400	973
315401-316000	975
316001-200	992
316201-300	972
316301-500	992
316501-317000	972
317001-600	975
317601-700	969
317701-318000	973
318001-100	972
318101-900	974
318901-319000	970
319001-100	971
319101-320000	975
320001-300	972
320301-400	968
320401-321000	974
321001-200	973
321201-322000	975
322001-323000	974
323001-700	975
323701-324000	973
324001-325000	960
325001-100	965
325101-326000	961
326001-327000	974
327001-300	971
327301-500	973
327501-328000	975
328001-300	992
328301-500	990
328501-329000	992
329001-330000	975
330001-100	992
330101-500	990
330501-331000	992
331001-200	973

No.	Grade
331201-400	975
331401-500	969
331501-700	971
331701-800	973
331801-332000	975
332001-200	992
332201-800	972
332801-333000	974
333001-500	975
333501-700	971
333701-900	973
333901-334000	975
334001-200	972
334201-800	992
334801-335000	990
335001-600	975
335601-800	971
335801-900	973
335901-336000	975
336001-200	972
336201-337000	974
337001-338000	975
338001-200	974
338201-900	992
338901-339000	990
339001-300	971
339301-500	973
339501-340000	975
340001-200	974
340201-300	972
340301-600	970
340601-341000	974
341001-200	973
341201-342000	975
342001-300	990
342301-343000	992
343001-344000	975
344001-200	970
344201-400	972
344401-345000	974
345001-346000	975
346001-300	992
346301-347000	974
347001-180	993
347181-200	991
347201-300	975
347301-400	973
347401-700	993
347701-900	991
347901-348000	973
348001-200	970
348201-800	974
348801-349000	972
349001-350000	975
350001-300	990
350301-400	974
350401-600	990
350601-351000	992
351001-352000	975
352001-100	968
352101-353000	974
353001-354000	975
354001-400	992
354401-355000	974
355001-800	975
355801-900	973
355901-356000	993
356001-500	990
356501-357000	974
357001-358000	975
358001-359000	974
359001-360000	975
360001-550	960
360801-361000	960
361001-100	993
361101-300	991
361301-400	993
361401-700	975
361701-20	973
361721-362000	975
362001-900	974
362901-363000	990
363001-364000	975
364001-365000	974
365001-100	975
365101-300	973
365301-366000	975
366001-367000	974
367001-500	975
367501-368000	993
368001-369000	974

HAMILTON WATCH CO. (continued)

No.	Grade
369001-370000	992
370001-100	990
370101-400	992
370401-500	974
370501-800	990
370801-371400	992
371401-500	972
371501-373500	974
373501-700	990
373701-374000	992
374001-200	974
374201-700	990
374701-375000	974
375001-100	993
375101-500	991
375501-376000	975
376001-200	972
376201-500	974
376501-377000	992
377001-200	973
377201-378000	975
378001-379000	974
379001-380800	992
380801-381000	990
381001-382000	992
382001-100	990
382101-383000	974
383001-300	992
383301-700	990
383701-384000	972
384001-700	974
384701-900	972
384901-385000	974
385001-600	972
385601-800	974
385801-386000	990
386001-800	974
386801-900	992
386901-387000	972
387001-100	990
387101-900	992
387901-388000	972
388001-400	990
388401-389000	992
389001-391000	974
391001-300	972
391301-392000	974
392001-800	992
392801-393000	990
393001-400	975
393401-600	973
393601-394000	993
394001-200	972
394201-395000	974
395001-100	993
395101-900	991
395901-396000	993
396001-397000	992
397001-200	990
397201-398000	992
398001-200	972
398201-399000	992
399001-600	993
399601-400000	975
400001-401000	924
401001-402000	940
402001-404000	924
404001-405000	926
405001-406000	924
406001-407000	940
407001-408000	926
408001-416000	940
416001-417000	926
417001-418000	940
418001-419000	926
419001-420000	941
420001-421000	940
421001-422000	926
422001-423000	924
423001-425000	926
425001-426000	924
426001-500	936
426501-427000	944
427001-428000	924
428001-429000	926
429001-430000	925
430001-431000	924
431001-432000	925
432001-433000	940
433001-434000	924
434001-500	946

No.	Grade
434501-600	942
434601-435000	946
435001-436000	924
436001-438500	940
438501-800	946
438801-900	942
438901-440000	946
440001-441000	924
441001-442000	940
442001-400	946
442401-500	942
442501-443000	946
443001-444000	926
444001-445000	924
445001-446000	927
446001-447000	924
447001-448000	925
448001-449000	926
449001-450000	924
450001-451000	926
451001-452000	925
452001-453000	940
453001-454000	924
454001-456000	940
456001-457000	999
457001-458000	940
458001-459000	999
459001-110	946
459111-118	942
459119-200	946
459201-700	942
459701-460000	946
460001-461900	940
461901-462000	940
462001-463000	999
463001-500	940
463501-464000	940
464001-466000	926
466001-467000	924
467001-468000	926
468001-469000	940
469001-470000	924
470001-471000	926
471001-472000	946
472001-473000	924
473001-474000	940
474001-475000	924
475001-476000	940
476001-477000	924
477001-478000	940
478001-479000	926
479001-480000	944
480001-481000	926
481001-482000	927
482001-483000	924
483001-484000	926
484001-485000	940
485001-486000	925
486001-487000	999
487001-488000	924
488001-489000	999
489001-492000	924
492001-493000	940
493001-494000	946
494001-495000	944
495001-496000	940
496001-497000	925
497001-498000	999
498001-499000	936
499001-501000	940
501001-900	926
501901-502000	934
502001-503000	926
503001-504000	999
504001-507000	940
507001-508000	999
508001-509900	940
509901-510000	942
510001-511500	940
511501-700	942
511701-517000	940
517001-519000	924
519001-521000	925
521001-523000	944
523001-524000	946
524001-531000	940
531001-532000	926
532001-10	934
532011-533000	926
533001-535500	999
535501-536000	940

No.	Grade
536001-537000	936
537001-538000	924
538001-543000	940
543001-544000	927
544001-200	934
544201-545000	926
545001-546000	925
546001-547000	924
547001-548000	926
548001-549000	999
549001-551000	946
551001-553000	944
553001-555000	940
555001-556000	936
556001-558000	924
558001-560000	925
560001-561000	999
561001-562000	926
562001-564000	924
564001-565000	926
565001-568000	940
568001-569000	936
569001-571000	924
571001-576000	940
576001-200	942
576201-578000	940
578001-580000	924
580001-582000	926
582001-584000	925
584001-585000	927
585001-587000	999
587001-592000	940
592001-593000	926
593001-594000	924
594001-601000	940
B600001-601000	999 Ball
601001-601800	926
B601001-601800	999 Ball
601801-602000	934
B601801-602000	999 Ball
602001-603000	926
B602001-603000	999 Ball
603001-604000	926
B603001-604000	999 Ball
604001-605000	926
B604001-605000	999 Ball
605001-606000	925
B605001-606000	999 Ball
606001-607000	925
B606001-607000	999 Ball
607001-608000	925
B607001-608000	999 Ball
608001-613000	924
B608001-613000	999 Ball
613001-614000	925
B613001-614000	999 Ball
614001-616500	924
B614001-616500	999 Ball
616501-617000	934
B616501-617000	999 Ball
617001-619000	926
B617001-619000	999 Ball
619001-620000	927
B619001-620000	999 Ball
620001-622700	940
B620001-622700	999 Ball
622701-623000	942
B622701-623000	999 Ball
623001-624000	941
B623001-624000	999 Ball
624001-625000	936
B624001-625000	999 Ball
625001-626000	925
B625001-626000	999 Ball
626001-627000	926
B626001-627000	999 Ball
627001-628000	924
B627001-628000	999 Ball
628001-630800	925
B628001-630800	999 Ball
631001-636000	940
B631001-636000	999 Ball
636001-637000	941
B636001-637000	999 Ball
637001-638000	936
B637001-638000	999 Ball
638001-639000	926
B638001-639000	999 Ball
639001-640000	925
B639001-640000	999 Ball

HAMILTON WATCH CO. (continued)

No.	Grade
640001-642000	924
B640001-644400	999 Ball
644401-645000	940
645001-645500	927
B645001-645500	999 Ball
645501-646000	925
B645501-646000	999 Ball
646001-647000	926
B646001-647000	999 Ball
647001-648000	940
B647001-648000	999 Ball
648001-649000	940
B648001-649000	998 Ball
B649001-650000	998 Ball
B650001-651000	999 Ball
651001-652000	940
B651001-652000	998 Ball
652001-652700	924
B652001-652700	998 Ball
652701-652800	924
652801-652900	927
652901-653000	937
653001-655000	940
B653001-655000	999 Ball
655001-655200	924
B655001-655200	999 Ball
655201-656000	924
656001-657000	926
657001-659000	927
659001-660000	925
660001-661000	927
661001-662000	924
662001-664000	940
664001-666000	924
666001-667000	940
667001-668000	941
668001-669000	926
669001-670000	999
670001-100	937
670501-673000	925
673001-675000	926
675001-677000	940
677001-678000	924
678001-679200	927
679201-680000	926
680001-685000	924
685001-687000	940
687001-688000	925
688001-689000	946
689001-694000	940
694001-696000	924
696001-697000	941
697001-700000	924
700001-702000	974
702001-703800	992
703801-704000	990
704001-400	992
704401-705000	990
705001-700	972
705701-706000	974
706001-707000	990
707001-800	972
707801-708000	990
708001-709500	975
709501-710000	973
710001-800	993
710801-711000	991
711001-300	973
711301-712000	975
712001-600	993
712601-713000	991
713001-714900	975
714901-715000	991
715001-716000	993
716001-100	972
716101-717000	974
717001-200	991
717201-718000	975L
718001-721500	974
721501-722000	992
722001-724000	974
724001-725000	972
725001-726000	974
726001-727000	992
727001-728000	974
728001-729000	992
729001-730000	975
730001-731000	992
731001-732000	975
732001-734000	992
734001-735000	975
735001-736000	974

No.	Grade
736001-738000	975
738001-739000	974
739001-740000	975
740001-100	974
740101-200	972
740201-900	974
740901-741000	975
741001-742000	992
742001-743000	974
743001-300	975
743301-400	993
743401-744000	975
744001-500	974
744501-745000	992
745001-747000	975
747001-700	974
747701-748000	972
748001-749500	992
749501-750000	974
750001-100	961
750101-200	961
750201-700	950
750701-751000	952
751001-752000	960
752001-500	952
752501-753000	950
753001-500	952
753501-754000	950
754001-100	960
754101-500	952
754501-755000	960
755001-400	992
755401-500	974
755501-700	972
755701-900	974
755901-756000	972
756001-757000	974
757001-300	975
757301-500	993
757501-758000	975
758001-100	972
758101-759000	992
759001-760000	975
760001-400	992
760401-600	972
760601-800	974
760801-761000	992
761001-400	975
761401-600	993
761601-762000	975
762001-200	992
762201-300	972
762301-763000	974
763001-300	993
763301-600	973
763601-764000	975
764001-300	992
764301-400	972
764401-765000	974
765001-300	992
765301-767000	974
767001-600	992
767601-800	972
767801-768000	974
768001-769000	975
769001-700	992
769701-770000	972
770001-100	974
770101-771200	992
771201-400	972
771401-772000	974
772001-773000	975
773001-800	992
773801-774000	972
774001-775000	975
775001-500	952
775501-776000	950
776001-300	973
776301-700	993
776701-777000	975
777001-300	972
777301-778300	974
778301-800	992
778801-900	972
778901-779300	974
779301-780100	992
780101-300	972
780301-781300	992
781301-400	972
781401-500	974
781501-782000	992
782001-783000	975

No.	Grade
783001-600	992
783601-784000	974
784001-785000	992
785001-500	952
785501-786000	950
786001-787000	992
787001-400	974
787401-788000	972
788001-791300	992
791301-792600	974
792601-900	972
792901-793700	992
793701-900	990
793901-794000	992
794001-200	972
794201-795000	974
795001-796400	992
796401-800	972
796801-797200	974
797201-500	954
797501-798000	974
798001-500	990
798501-800	972
798801-799000	974
799001-200	954
799201-600	992
799601-800000	954
800001-802000	974
802001-200	954
802201-2	972
802203-300	954
802301-500	972
802501-803700	974
803701-804200	954
804201-806000	974
806001-807000	975
807001-500	993
807501-808800	975
808801-809000	993
809001-500	974
809501-600	972
809601-810000	974
810001-300	990
810301-812000	974
812001-700	992
812701-813000	974
813001-814000	974P
814001-800	974L
814801-815900	992
815901-816000	974L
816001-817000	974P
817001-819000	974L
819001-820000	974P
820001-821500	974L
821501-822000	990L
822001-700	992L
822701-823000	974L
823001-824000	974P
824001-826000	975P
826001-500	975L
826501-827000	993
827001-828000	975P
828001-829000	974L
829001-830000	974P
830001-500	990L
830501-831000	992L
831001-100	954P
831101-200	972P
831201-500	954P
831501-832000	974P
832001-400	974L
832401-833000	992L
833001-834000	990L
834001-600	974P
834601-800	974L
834801-835000	974P
835001-600	992L
835601-800	990L
835801-836000	974L
836001-500	974P
836501-900	954P
836901-837000	974P
837001-838000	975P
838001-839000	975L
839001-400	974L
839401-700	992L
839701-840000	990L
840001-400	952L
840401-900	950L
840901-841000	952L
841001-842000	975P

HAMILTON WATCH CO. (continued)

No.	Grade
842001-843000	974L
843001-844000	974P
844001-200	993
844201-845000	975
845001-200	992
845201-400	972
845401-700	954
845701-846000	972
846001-500	952
846501-847000	950
847001-200	972
847201-849000	974
849001-850000	975
850001-300	992
850301-800	990
850801-851000	972
851001-400	993
851401-852000	975
852001-853000	992
853001-854000	974
854001-600	950
854601-900	952
854901-855100	960L
855101-856000	950L
856001-857840	975
857841-858000	975L
858001-500	974
858501-859000	972
859001-860000	974
860001-862300	992
862301-400	954
862401-500	972
862501-600	954
862601-800	972
862801-863000	974
863001-864000	992
864001-865000	975
865001-866000	992
866001-600	974
866601-700	954
866701-867000	972
867001-868000	975
868001-869000	992
869001-870000	975
870001-872000	992
872001-200	993
872201-874000	975
874001-800	974
874801-875000	975
875001-300	952
875301-876000	975
876001-600	993
876601-877000	975
877001-400	992
877401-700	975
877701-878000	993
878001-879400	975
880001-600	992
880601-882400	974
882401-883400	992
883401-884100	974
884101-885300	992
885301-886000	974
886001-887000	992
887001-300	974
887301-890300	992
890301-891000	974
891001-600	992
891601-892200	978
892201-896200	992
896201-897800	974
897801-898000	972
898001-899100	992
899101-500	978
899501-900000	974
900001-902000	940
902001-904000	926
904001-906000	924
906001-914000	940
914001-916000	926
916001-917000	927
917001-919000	925
919001-921000	940
921001-923000	924
923001-500	999
923501-924000	925
924001-926000	940
926001-100	927
927001-929000	926
929001-933000	924
933001-935000	925
935001-937000	926

No.	Grade
937001-939000	940
939001-941000	924
941001-944000	940
944001-949000	926
949001-952000	925
952001-958000	924
958001-960000	926
960001-968000	940
968001-970000	926
970001-971700	924
971701-972000	948
972001-973000	924
973001-974000	936
974001-975400	924
975401-25 Spec.	926
975426-976000	924
976001-979000	940
979001-100	942
979101-981000	940
981001-982000	948
982001-984000	924
984001-986000	940
986001-987000	946
987001-988000	936
988001-992000	940
992001-996000	924
996001-999998	940
999999-1000000	947
1000001-1000300	972
1000301-1003000	992
1003001-1004000	974
1004001-900	992
1004901-1007100	974
1007101-1008300	992
1008301-1009500	974
1009501-1010700	992
1010701-1011200	972
1011201-1012700	974
1012701-1013000	992
1013001-1015000	978
1015001-300	974
1015301-1016000	992
1016001-300	975
1016301-600	973
1016601-1018000	993
1018001-1020000	992
1020001-1022600	950
1022601-1023000	952
1023001-700	992
1023701-1024500	974
1024501-600	974
1024601-1025000	972
1025001-1027000	975
1027001-400	993
1027401-1029600	975
1029601-1030000	973
1030001-1032000	992
1032001-1033000	974
1033001-200	972
1033201-800	954
1033801-1035300	974
1035301-600	972
1035601-1036000	974
1036001-300	972
1036301-800	954
1036801-1037000	992L
1037001-1038000	974
1038001-1039000	992
1039001-200	972
1039201-500	978
1039501-1040300	974
1040301-1041000	992
1041001-1042000	974
1042001-700	992
1042701-1043000	972
1043001-700	978
1043701-1044000	992
1044001-1045000	974
1045001-1046000	992
1046001-1047000	975
1047001-1048000	974L
1048001-1049000	992
1049001-500	990
1049501-1051000	992
1051001-200	975
1051201-1052000	993
1052001-500	972P
1052501-900	954
1052901-1053000	974
1053001-1054000	992
1054001-1056000	974
1056001-1057000	975

No.	Grade
1057001-1061300	992
1061301-1062300	972
1062301-1066000	992
1066001-1068000	974
1068001-1069000	975
1069001-1070000	974
1070001-1071000	992L
1071001-1073000	975P
1073001-1075000	992
1075001-1076200	974L
1076201-700	972L
1076701-1077000	978L
1077001-1079000	974P
1079001-1080000	992L
1080001-100	952L
1080101-200	960L
1080201-400	994L
1080401-1081000	950L
1081001-1082000	978L
1082001-400	993L
1082401-1083000	973L
1083001-1084000	990L
1084001-1085000	992L
1085001-1086000	992L
1086001-1088000	974P
1088001-1091000	992L
1091001-200	978L
1091201-1092000	974L
1092001-1093000	992L
1093001-1095000	974P
1095001-1096000	992P
1096001-400	974L
1096401-1097000	974P
1097001-1098000	992L
1098001-400	975P
1098401-1099000	975L
1099001-600	993L
1099601-1100000	975P
1100001-1104000	992L
1104001-1105000	974P
1105001-1106000	992L
1106001-500	978L
1106501-1107000	972L
1107001-1109000	992L
1109001-1111000	972L
1111001-1112000	974L
1112001-1113000	974P
1113001-1116000	992L
1116001-900	974P
1116901-1117000	974L
1117001-1119000	992L
1119001-1120000	978L
1120001-1122000	992L
1122001-1123000	974P
1123001-500	972P
1123501-1125000	974P
1125001-1127000	992L
1127001-1128000	972L
1128001-1129000	974L
1129001-1130500	974P
1130501-1131000	956P
1131001-1132000	992L
1132001-1133000	990L
1133001-1134000	978L
1134001-1135000	972L
1135001-1137000	992L
1137001-1138000	956P
1138001-1139000	956P
1139001-1140000	978L
1140001-1141000	972L
1141001-1142000	956P
1142001-500	974P
1142501-1145000	974L
1145001-1146000	975P
1146001-500	956P
1146501-1149000	974P
1149001-1150000	974L
1150001-600	950L
1150601-1151800	952L
1151801-1152000	952P
1152001-900	950P
1152901-1153200	952P
1153201-300	
1153301-500	994P
1153501-800	994L
1153801-1154000	960L
1154001-500	950L
1154501-1155000	950P
1155001-200	994P
1155201-500	994L
1156001-1158000	996L
1158001-1160000	974P

HAMILTON WATCH CO. (continued)

No.	Grade
1160001-1162000	992L
1162001-500	993L
1162501-1164000	992L
1164001-1166000	974P
1166001-1167000	974L
1167001-1168000	956P
1168001-1169000	975P
1169001-1170000	974P
1170001-1174000	956P
1174001-1176000	974P
1176001-1177000	992L
1177001-1178000	956P
1178001-1179000	974P
1179001-1181000	996L
1181001-1182000	992L
1182001-1183000	996L
1183001-1184400	974P
1184401-1185400	956P
1185401-1186000	974P
1186001-1187000	992L
1187001-1188000	996L
1188001-1189000	992L
1189001-1190000	974P
1190001-1192000	996L
1192001-1193000	975P
1193001-1194000	974P
1194001-1195000	956P
1195001-1196000	974P
1196001-1199000	992L
1199001-1201000	974P
1201001-1202000	975P
1202001-1203000	992L
1203001-1204000	974P
1204001-500	956P
1204501-1206000	974P
1206001-1207000	992L
1207001-1210000	974P
1210001-1212000	992L
1212001-1213000	974P
1213001-500	996L
1213501-1214000	992L
1214001-1214600	993L
1214601-1215000	975P
1215001-1216000	974L
1216001-1219000	992L
1219001-1220000	974P
1220001-1221000	992L
1221001-1223500	974P
1223501-1224000	956P
1224001-1227000	992L
1227001-1228000	972L
1228001-700	992L
1228701-1229000	990L
1229001-500	956P
1229501-1230000	974P
1230001-1231000	974L
1231001-1232000	992L
1232001-1233000	974P
1233001-1236000	992L
1236001-500	974P
1236501-1237000	956P
1237001-500	996L
1237501-1238000	992L
1238001-1239000	956P
1239001-1241000	992L
1241001-1242000	975P
1242001-400	974L
1242401-1243000	972L
1243001-500	996L
1243501-1244000	992L
1244001-1245000	974P
1245001-1246000	992L
1246001-300	974P
1246301-800	956P
1246801-1247000	974L
1247001-1248000	992L
1248001-1249700	974P
1249701-1250000	956P
1250001-1252000	983
1252001-1253000	985
1253001-1257000	983
1257001-900	985
1260001-970	Chro.*
1260971-1265000	
1265001-1266000	956P
1266001-1267000	974P
1267001-1268200	978L
1268201-1269000	978L
1269001-600	992L
1269601-1270000	992L
1270001-1271700	956P

No.	Grade
1271701-1272000	974P
1272001-1274000	996L
1274001-500	993L
1274501-700	992L
1274701-1275000	992L
1275001-1276000	972L
1276001-1277000	974L
1277001-1278000	992L
1278001-1279000	975P
1279001-1280000	974P
1280001-1281000	992L
1281001-800	974P
1281801-1282000	956P
1282001-1284000	996L
1284001-1285000	992L
1285001-1286000	956P
1286001-1288000	978L
1288001-500	993L
1288501-1289100	992L
1289101-700	990L
1289701-1290000	992L
1290001-1291500	974P
1291501-1292000	992P
1292001-1297000	992L
1297001-1298000	974P
1298001-1299000	992L
1299001-1300000	975P
1300001-1301000	974P
1301001-1302000	974L
1302001-500	992L
1302501-1303000	990L
1303001-500	972L
1303501-1304000	972P
1304001-1305000	978L
1305001-1306000	956P
1306001-1307000	974P
1307001-1308500	992L
1308501-1309000	993L
1309001-1310000	974L
1310001-1311000	972L
1311001-1312000	992L
1312001-800	974P
1312801-1313000	956P
1313001-1317000	992L
1317001-1318000	956P
1318001-1321000	992L
1321001-300	990L
1321301-1322000	992L
1322001-700	974L
1322701-1323000	972L
1323001-1324000	992L
1324001-1325000	996L
1325001-1326500	975P
1326501-1327000	993L
1327001-300	956P
1327301-1329000	974P
1329001-1330000	992L
1330001-1331300	974L
1331301-800	972L
1331801-1332000	978L
1332001-1334000	992L
1334001-400	974P
1334401-1335000	956P
1335001-300	978L
1335301-1336000	972L
1336001-1337000	992L
1337001-1338200	996L
1338201-1339000	996L
1339001-1340000	956P
1340001-1341000	992L
1341001-300	972L
1341301-500	974L
1341501-1342000	978L
1342001-1343000	992L
1343001-400	956P
1343401-1344000	974P
1344001-1345000	992L
1345001-600	974L
1345601-1346000	972L
1346001-1348000	975P
1348001-1349000	974P
1349001-1350000	992L
1350001-600	972L
1350601-1351000	974L
1351001-1352000	993L
1352001-1352300	974L
1352301-800	978L
1352801-1353000	974L
1353001-500	972P
1353501-1354200	956P
1354201-700	992P

No.	Grade
1354701-1355000	974P
1355001-1356000	992L
1356001-1357000	974P
1357001-1359800	992L
1359801-1361000	996L
1361001-1362000	992L
1362001-600	974P
1362601-1363000	956P
1363001-1364000	992L
1364001-1365000	975P
1365001-800	956P
1365801-1367000	974P
1367001-1369400	992L
1369401-1370000	996L
1370001-1371000	974L
1371001-600	996L
1371601-1373000	992L
1373001-1374000	975P
1374001-1375000	992L
1375001-1376000	950L
1376001-1377000	992L
1377001-1378300	974P
1378301-1379000	956P
1379001-1380200	972L
1380201-1381000	978L
1381001-500	956P
1381501-1383000	974P
1383001-1384000	992L
1384001-1386100	974P
1386101-1387000	956P
1387001-1388000	992L
1388001-400	978L
1388401-1389000	978L
1389001-300	956P
1389301-1390000	956P
1390001-1391000	992L
1391001-500	956P
1391501-1392000	974P
1392001-1393000	992L
1393001-1394000	974P
1394001-1396000	992L
1396001-500	972L
1396501-1398000	974L
1398001-400	974P
1398401-1399000	956P
1399001-1400000	992L
1400001-1401000	936
1401001-1403000	924
1403001-1409000	940
1409001-500	946
1409501-1410000	940
1410001-1414000	924
1414001-300	941
1414501-1415000	925
1415001-1417000	924
1417001-1419000	940
1419001-1420000	924
1420001-1421000	940
1421001-1422000	924
1422001-1424000	940
1424001-1428000	924
1428001-1430000	940
1430001-200	924
1430201-400	948
1430401-1431000	924
1431001-1433000	940
1433001-1438000	924
1438001-500	926
1438501-1439500	924
1439501-1440000	926
1440001-1441000	940
1441001-1442000	924
1442001-500	926
1442501-1444000	924
1444001-1445000	940
1445001-1447000	924
1447001-1448200	940
1449001-1450500	924
1500001-600	974P
1500601-1501200	956P
1501201-1502000	974P
1502001-1503000	993L
1503001-1504000	996L
1504001-500	974L
1504501-1505200	972L
1505201-700	978L
1505701-1506000	974L
1506001-1507000	975P
1507001-1508000	992L
1508001-400	974P
1508401-1509000	956P

HAMILTON WATCH CO. (continued)

No.	Grade
1509001-1510000	992L
1510001-1511000	974L
1511001-1512000	975P
1512001-1513200	992L
1513201-600	992P
1513601-1514000	992L
1514001-200	956P
1514201-1515000	974P
1515001-1516000	992L
1516001-1517000	974P
1517001-1520000	992L
1520001-1521200	974L
1521201-1522000	978L
1522001-600	974P
1522601-1525000	956P
1525001-1527000	996L
1527001-1528000	992L
1528001-1531000	974P
1531001-1533000	992L
1533001-600	974P
1533601-1534000	956P
1534001-100	975P
1535101-200	975P
1535201-600	975P
1535601-1536000	993L
1536001-1537000	972L
1537001-1538000	992L
1538001-800	956P
1538801-1539000	974P
1539001-1540000	992L
1540001-500	992P
1540501-1541000	992L
1541001-1542200	974P
1542201-800	956P
1542801-1543000	974P
1543001-1544000	996L
1544001-1545000	992L
1545001-400	978L
1545401-1546000	974L
1546001-1548000	992L
1548001-600	974L
1548601-1549000	972L
1549001-1550000	974P
1550001-500	972P
1550501-1552000	974P
1552001-1555000	992L
1555001-1557000	993P
1557001-800	972L
1557801-1558000	974L
1558001-500	956
1558501-1559700	956P
1559701-1560000	974P
1560001-1561000	975P
1561001-1563000	992L
1563001-1565000	978L
1565001-1567000	992L
1567001-1568000	974L
1568001-1569000	992L
1569001-1571000	972L
1571001-1572000	974P
1572001-1573000	975P
1573001-1575000	974P
1575001-400	950L
1575401-1576000	950P
1576001-1577000	950L
1577001-1578000	975P
1578001-1580000	992L
1580001-1581200	974L
1581201-1582000	956P
1582001-1583000	974P
1583001-1584000	992L
1584001-1585000	978L
1585001-1586000	972L
1586001-1587000	992L
1587001-500	992P
1587501-1589000	992L
1589001-500	956P
1589501-1590000	974P
1590001-1591000	974L
1591001-1592000	992L
1592001-1593000	974P
1593001-1595000	992L
1595001-200	974P
1595201-900	956P
1595901-1596000	974P
1596001-1611000	992L
1611001-1612100	974P
1612101-1613000	956P
1613001-600	996L
1614001-900	956P
1614901-1615000	974P

No.	Grade
1615001-1625000	992L
1625001-200	950L
1625201-1626000	952L
1626001-1627000	974P
1627001-1633000	992L
1633001-1635000	950L
1635001-1636000	992L
1636001-1637000	956P
1637001-1638000	974P
1638001-1642800	992L
1642801-1643000	992P
1643001-1644000	992L
1644001-1646000	974L
1646001-1648000	972L
1648001-1649000	992L
1649001-1652000	974P
1652001-1653000	950L
1653001-1654000	956P
1654001-1657000	974P
1657001-1660000	992L
1660001-1661000	978L
1661001-1663000	974P
1663001-1664000	974L
1664001-1665000	950L
1665001-1666000	974P
1666001-1667000	956P
1667001-1669000	974P
1669001-1670000	978L
1670001-1671000	974P
1671001-300	992L
1671301-900	992P
1671901-1672000	992L
1672001-1676000	974P
1676001-1678000	992L
1678001-1679000	974P
1679001-1681000	974L
1681001-1682000	974P
1682001-1683000	956P
1683001-1685000	974P
1685001-1686000	992L
1686001-1688000	974P
1688001-500	978L
1689001-600	975P
1690001-1691000	956
1691001-1693000	992L
1693001-1696000	956P
1696001-1699000	992L
1699001-1703000	974P
1703001-1704000	992L
1704001-1705000	956P
1705001-1706000	974P
1706001-1707100	992L
1708001-1714000	992L
1714001-1715000	974P
1715001-1717000	992L
1717001-800	956
1718001-1750000	992L
1750001-1761000	900
1761001-1765000	914
1765001-1767000	920
1767001-1768000	914
1768001-1769000	900
1769001-1770000	920
1770001-1778200	914
1778201-1779000	910
1779001-1780000	920
1780001-1782000	910
1782001-500	920
1782501-1783000	900
1783001-1808000	910
1808001-1810000	914
1810001-1811000	910
1811001-1813000	900
1813001-1818000	910
1818001-1819000	914
1819001-1821000	910
1821001-1822000	914
1822001-1827000	910
1827001-600	914
1827601-1829100	910
1829101-500	914
1829501-1830000	910
1830001-1831000	900
1831001-1832000	920
1832001-700	910
1832701-1833300	914
1833301-1834500	910
1834501-1835400	914
1835401-1836900	910
1836901-1837400	914
1837401-1839000	910

No.	Grade
1839001-500	914
1839501-1844700	910
1844701-1845700	914
1845701-1848300	910
1848301-1849500	914
1849501-1851900	910
1851901-1853100	914
1853101-1856800	910
1856801-1857900	914
1857901-1860300	910
1860301-1861000	914
1861001-1863000	900
1863001-700	920
1863701-1864300	900
1864301-1865000	920
1865001-500	914
1865501-1870300	910
1870301-1871500	914
1871501-1875100	910
1875101-600	914
1875601-1876500	910
1876501-1877500	914
1877501-1878700	910
1878701-1880000	914
1880001-300	920
1880301-1881500	900
1881501-700	920
1881701-900	900
1881901-1882900	920
1882901-1885000	900
1885001-1887400	910
1887401-1888600	914
1888601-1891000	910
1891001-1892200	914
1892201-1894600	910
1894601-1895800	914
1895801-1899000	910
1899001-300	900
1899301-1900000	920
1900001-400	910
1900401-1902100	914
1902101-1907000	910
1907001-1909000	914
1909001-1910000	910
1910001-500	920
1910501-1911000	900
1911001-1913000	920
1913001-1914000	900
1914001-1920000	910
1920001-1922000	920
1922001-1924000	910
1924001-1925000	900
1925001-1936000	910
1936001-1937000	920
1937001-900	900
1940001-1941000	914
1941001-1949000	910
1949001-1950000	914
1950001-1962000	910
1962001-1963000	914
1963001-1975000	910
1975001-1976000	914
1976001-1980000	910
1980001-1981000	914
1981001-1988500	910
1989001-400	914
2000001-2001700	988
2001701-2002400	986
2002401-800	988
2002801-2003100	986
2004001-2035000	986
2035001-2037200	981
2040001-2064900	986
2100001-2191300	986A
2200001-2248000	987
2248001-2300000	987F
2300001-2311000	992L
2311001-2312000	974L
2312001-2321700	992L
2321701-2323000	974L
2323001-2326000	992L
2326001-2327000	974P
2327001-2333000	992L
2333001-2336000	974P
2336001-2338000	992L
2338001-2339000	974P
2339001-2340000	974L
2340001-2341000	974P
2341001-2346000	992L
2346001-2347000	974P
2347001-2356000	992L

HAMILTON WATCH CO. (continued)

No.	Grade
2356001-2358000	974P
2358001-2364000	992L
2364001-2365000	974P
2365001-2374000	992L
2374001-2375000	974P
2375001-2378000	992L
2378001-2380000	974L
2380001-2383000	992L
2383001-2384000	950L
2384001-2385000	992L
2385001-2396000	974P
2386001-2390000	992L
2390001-2391000	974P
2391001-2393000	992L
2393001-2395000	974P
2395001-2397000	992L
2397001-2398000	974L
2398001-2401000	992L
2401001-2402000	974P
2402001-2407000	992L
2407001-2409000	974P
2409001-2413000	992L
2413001-2414000	974P
2414001-2415000	974L
2415001-2418000	992L
2418001-2420000	974P
2420001-2422000	992L
2422001-2423000	974P
2423001-2432000	992L
2432001-2433000	974P
2433001-2434000	992L
2434001-2435000	974P
2435001-2437000	992L
2437001-2438000	974P
2438001-2442000	992L
2442001-2445000	974P
2445001-2451000	992L
2451001-2453000	974P
2453001-2455000	992L
2455001-2456000	974P
2456001-2457000	992L
2457001-2458000	950L
2458001-2459000	974L
2459001-2461000	992L
2461001-2462000	974L
2462001-2464000	992L
2464001-2466000	974P
2466001-2468000	992L
2468001-2469000	974P
2469001-2472000	992L
2472001-2473000	974P
2473001-2474000	992L
2474001-2475000	974P
2475001-2476000	992L
2476001-2477000	974P
2477001-2490000	992L
2490001-2492000	974L
2492001-2504000	992L
2504001-2505000	950L
2505001-300	950L
2506001-2526000	992L

No.	Grade
2526001-2528000	974P
2528001-2533000	992L
2533001-2534000	974P
2534001-2535000	992L
2535001-2536000	974P
2536001-2537000	974L
2537001-2538000	974P
2538001-2539000	974L
2539001-2542000	974P
2542001-2543000	992L
2543001-2545000	974P
2545001-2547000	992L
2547001-2548400	974P
2548401-2548600	974L
2548601-2548700	974P
2548701-2550000	974L
2550001-2551000	992L
2551001-2552000	974L
2552001-2555000	992L
2555001-2555600	974L
2555701-2557000	974L
2558001-2560000	992L
2560001-2561000	974L
2561001-2563000	992L
2563001-2564000	974L
2564001-2566000	992L
2566001-2566800	974L
2567001-2581000	992L
2581001-2583900	992E
2583901-2584300	992L
2584301-2596000	992E
2596001-2597000	974L
2597001-2608000	992E
2608001-2608800	974L
2609001-2611000	992E
2611001-2611400	950L
2611401-2613000	950E
2613001-2618000	992E
2618001-2619000	950E
2619001-2631000	992E
2631001-2631600	950E
2631801-2632000	950E
2632001-2639000	992E
2639001-2641000	950E
2641001-2649000	992E
2649001-2650600	950E
2651001-2655300	992E
2900001-2911500	979
2911601-2931900	979F
3000001-3002300	922
3002301-3002500	922M.P.
3002501-3003800	922
3003801-3004000	922M.P.
3004001-3006100	922
3006101-3006300	922M.P.
3006301-3008000	922
3008001-3008600	922M.P.
3008601-3010000	922
3010001-3010500	922
3010501-3010700	922M.P.
3010701-3011900	922

No.	Grade
3011901-3012500	922M.P.
3012501-3013100	922
3013101-3013700	922M.P.
3013701-3015700	922
3050001-3054800	902
3054801-3056000	922
3056001-3060800	902
3061001-3065100	904
3100001-3133800	916
3135001-3152700	918
3200001-3460900	912
4000001-4447201	987F
4447301-4523000	987E
A-001 to A-8450	980B
1B-001 to 1B-4000	999B
2B-001 to 2B-700	999B
2B-701 to 2B-800	950B
C-001 to C-169000	992B
E-001 to E-114000	989
E-114001 to E-140400	989E
F-101 to F-57600	995
F-57601 to F-59850	995A
F-59851 to F-62000	995
F-62001 to F-63000	995A
F-63001 to F-63800	995
F- 63801 to F-286200	995A
G-001 to G-13600	980
G-13601 to G-14600	980 & 980A
G-14601 to G-44500	980
G-44501 to G-45000	980A
G-45001 to G-47400	980
G-47401 to G-48400	980A
G-48401 to G-58200	980
G-58201 to G-58700	980A
G-58701 to G-61600	980
G-61601 to G-62500	980A
G-62501 to G-67500	980
G-67501 to G-68600	980A
G-68601- to G-486000	980
H-001 to H-1000	921
H-1001 to H-1800	400 & 921
H-1801 to H-2000	921
H-2001 to H-2800	400 & 921
H-2801 to H-3500	400
H-3501 to H-30000	921
H-50001 to H-57500	401
J-001 to J-320000	982
M-001 to M-58000	982M
N-001 to N-223000	721
O-1 to 0408000	987A
R-001 to R-1400	923
S-001 to S-3400	950B
SS-001 to SS-71500	987S
T-001 to T-312000	911
V-001 to V-38000	911M
X-001 to X-125000	917

*Hamilton 36 size chronometer watch

*Haydn W. Wheeler model

NOTE: The above serial number and grade listing is an actual Hamilton factory list and is accurate in most cases. However, it has been brought to our attention that in rare cases the serial number and grade number do not match the list. One example is the Hayden W. Wheeler model.

(See Hamilton Watch Co. **Serial Numbers and Grades** section located at the end of the Hamilton Watch price section to identify the movement, size and grade of your watch.)

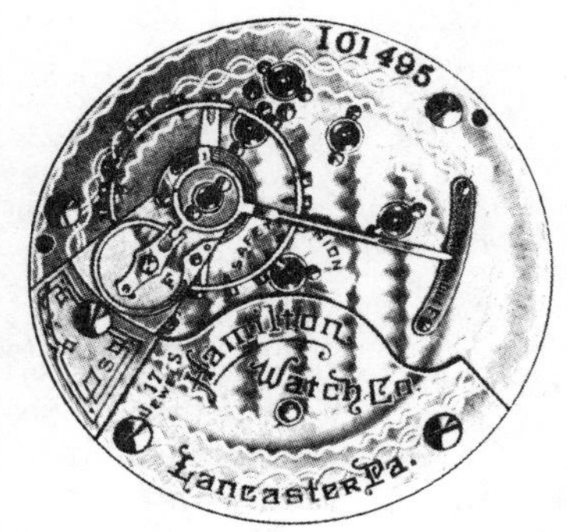

Grade 925, 18 size, 17 jewels, hunting case, serial number 101495.

Grade 932, 18 size, 16 jewels, open face, serial number 6,888.

HAMILTON
18 SIZE

Grade or Name — Description	Avg	Ex-Fn	Mint
7J, OF, LS, FULL ★★	$1,000	$1,150	$1,600
11J, HC, LS, FULL ★★★	1,400	1,550	1,900
11J, OF, LS, FULL ★★★	1,500	1,750	2,250
922, 15J, OF ★	450	600	800
923, 15J, HC ★	550	675	1,000
924, 17J, NI, OF, DMK	50	60	80
925, 17J, NI, HC, DMK	75	85	135
926, 17J, NI, OF, DMK, ADJ	60	80	100
927, 17J, NI, HC, DMK, ADJ	65	85	125
928, 15J, NI, OF	100	150	195
929, 15J, NI, HC, 14K	700	795	900
929, 15J, NI, HC	200	250	325
930, 16J, NI, OF, Silveroid	80	100	120
930, 16J, NI, OF	125	160	225
931, 16J, NI, HC	250	300	425
932, 16J, NI, OF ★★	400	500	725
932 *(S#s less than 400 up to $1,200)*			
933, 16J, NI, HC ★★	500	600	825
933 *(S#s less than 1,300 up to $1,400)*			
934, 17J, NI, OF, DMK, DR, HCI5P	100	120	170
934, 17J, NI, OF, HCI5P, Silveroid	75	90	105
934, 17J, NI, OF, HCI5P, Coin	85	100	130
935, 17J, NI, HC, DMK, DR, HCI5P ★	100	125	195
936, 17J, NI, OF, DMK, DR	85	100	140
936 *(Early S#s less than 400 up to $1,200)*			
937, 17J, NI, HC, DMK, DR	125	150	200
937 *(S#s less than 1,300 up to $1,200)*			
938, 17J, NI, OF, DMK, DR ★★	500	600	775
939, 17J, NI, HC, DMK, DR ★★	550	650	875
940, 21J, NI, OF, DMK, DR, HCI5P, GJS	75	95	150
940, 21J, NI, OF, 2-Tone	100	120	175

HAMILTON WATCH CO., 18 SIZE (continued)

Grade or Name — Description	Avg	Ex-Fn	Mint
940, 21J, NI, OF, Extra	125	145	245
940, 21J, NI, OF, Coin	65	80	100
940, 21J, NI, OF, Special	150	225	325
941, 21J, NI, HC, GJS, Marked	145	175	250
941, 21J, NI, HC, GJS, Special	275	350	495
941, 21J, NI, HC, DMK, DR, HCI5P, GJS	175	200	350
942, 21J, NI, OF, DMK, DR, HCI5P, GJS	160	185	265
943, 21J, NI, HCI5P, GJS, Silveroid ★	95	105	175
943, 21J, NI, HC, DMK, DR, HCI5P, GJS ★	200	275	375
943, Burlington Special, 21J	550	650	900
944, 19J, NI, OF, DMK, DR, HCI5P, GJS	150	180	300
945, 19J, GJS, 2-Tone, HC ★★	1,000	1,200	1,500
946, Anderson (jobber name on movement), 14K	900	1,000	1,300
946, 23J, Extra, OF, GJS	400	450	775
946, 23J, "Loaner" on case	425	475	625
946, 23J, NI, OF, DMK, DR, HCI5P, GJS	400	475	600
947, 23J, NI, HC, DMK, DR, HCI5P, GJS, not marked "947" ★	3,500	4,000	4,950
947, 23J, NI, HC, HCI5P, GJS, marked "947" ★★	4,500	5,500	6,950
947, 23J, Extra, NI, GJS, marked 947, 14K, HC ★★★	5,000	6,000	8,000
948, 17J, NI, OF, DMK, DR, HCI5P, GJS ★	250	300	425
948, 17J, NI, DMK, DR, HCI5P, GJS, OF, Coin ★	200	245	350
The Banner, 17J, M#927, HC, ADJ	110	135	195
Burlington Special, 21J, HCI5P	175	200	295
Inspectors Standard, 21J	200	295	450
The Union, 17J	100	120	175
The Union, 17J, Silveroid	65	75	135
The Union, 17J, G#925, HC	175	200	350

Note: Some movements are marked with grade numbers, some are not. Add $25 to $75 for a marked movement. The first *hunting case* was a Model #937 which begins with Serial #1001.

Note: All prices are with gold filled cases, except where otherwise noted.

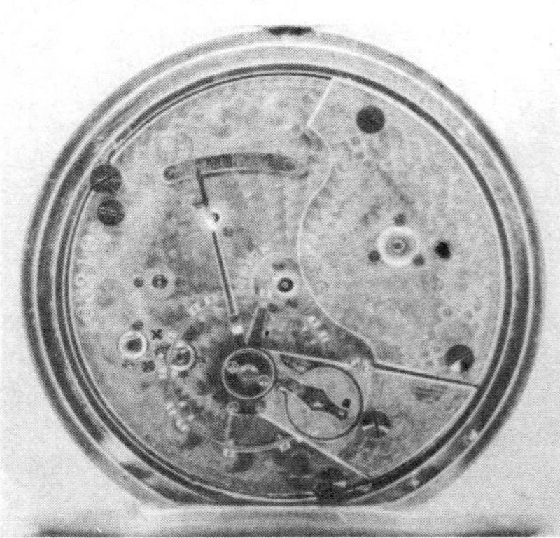

Grade 947 (marked), 18 size, 23 jewels, gold jewel settings, hunting case, adjusted to HCI5P, serial number 163,219.

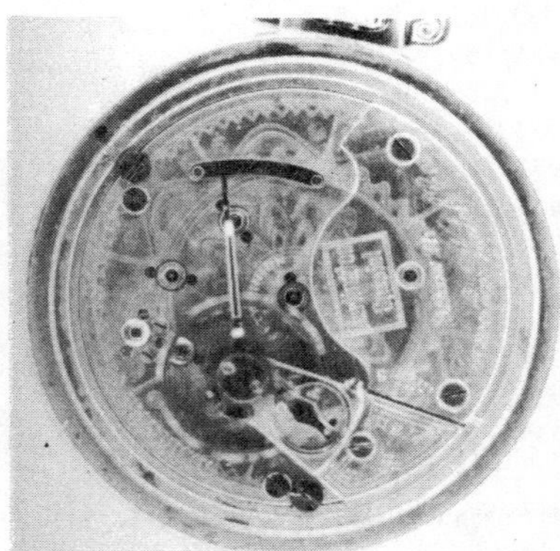

Burlington Special, 18 size, 21 jewels, Grade 943, open face, serial number 121614.

Grade 950, 16 size, 23 jewels, pendant set, gold train, gold jewel settings, serial number 1020650.

Grade 961, 16 size, 21 jewels, gold train, gold jewel settings, serial number 81,848.

16 SIZE

Grade or Name — Description		Avg	Ex-Fn	Mint
950, 23J, LS, DR, GT, 14K		$600	$700	$850
950, 23J, LS, DR, OF, BRG, GJS, HCI5P, NI, GT		300	350	475
950, 23J, PS, DR, OF, GJS, BRG, HCI5P, NI, GT		315	350	495
950B, 23J, LS, OF, HCI5P, NI, DR, BRG		325	350	475
950E, 23J, LS, OF, HCI5P, NI, DR, BRG		350	385	525
951, 23J, PS, HC, HCI5P, NI, GT, GJS, DR	★★	3,000	3,500	4,500
951, 23J, PS, HC, HCI5P, NI, GT, GJS, DR, 14K	★★	3,400	3,900	5,000
952, 19J, LS or PS, OF, BRG, HCI5P, NI, GJS, DR		150	175	300
952, 19J, LS or PS, HCI5P, OF, 14K		450	545	650
953, 19J, LS or PS, HC, GJS, GT	★★	1,800	2,100	3,500
954, 17J, LS or PS, OF, ¾, DR, HCI5P		65	80	110
954, 17J, OF, HCI5P, Silveroid		40	50	65
956, 17J, PS, OF, ¾, DR, HCI5P		70	85	125
960, 21J, PS, OF, BRG, GJS, GT, DR, HCI5P	★	300	325	535
960, 21J, LS, OF, BRG, GJS, GT, DR, HCI5P	★	325	350	475
961, 21J, PS & LS, HC, BRG, GJS, GT, DR, HCI5P	★	395	450	585
962, 17J, PS, OF, BRG	★★	500	600	825
963, 17J, PS, HC, BRG	★★	550	650	875
964, 17J, PS, OF, BRG	★★	650	695	925
965, 17J, PS, HC, BRG	★★	500	595	850
966, 17J, PS, OF, ¾	★★	600	670	900
967, 17J, PS, HC, ¾	★★	625	675	925
968, 17J, PS, OF, ¾	★	375	495	675
969, 17J, PS, HC, ¾	★	425	525	685
970, 21J, PS, OF, ¾		150	195	250
971, 21J, PS, HC, ¾		175	225	275
972, 17J, PS & LS, OF, ¾, NI, GJS, DR, HCI5P, DMK		65	85	145
973, 17J, PS & LS, HC, ¾, NI, DR, HCI5P		80	110	175
974, 17J, PS & LS, OF, ¾, NI, HCI3P		45	50	75
974, 17J, OF, PS, HCI3P		60	70	100
974, 17J, OF, 2-tone		75	95	150
2974B, 17J, OF, HCI3P		70	85	125
975, 17J, PS & LS, HC, ¾, NI, HCI3P		55	60	85

Grade 992B, 16 size, 21 jewels, adjusted to HCI5P.

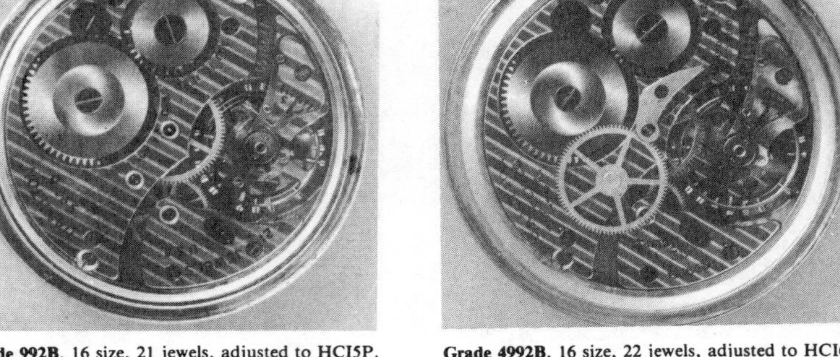

Grade 4992B, 16 size, 22 jewels, adjusted to HCI6P.

Grade or Name — Description	Avg	Ex-Fn	Mint
976, 16J, PS, OF, ¾	145	180	235
977, 16J, PS, HC, ¾	150	185	240
978, 17J, LS, OF, ¾, NI, DMK	60	70	95
990, 21J, LS, OF, GJS, DR, HCI5P, DMK, NI, ¾, GT	135	150	270
991, 21J, LS, HC, ¾, GJS, HCI5P, DMK, NI, GT	175	200	295
992, 21J, OF, ¾, LS, GJS, HCI5P, DR, NI, DMK	95	110	175
992, 21J, OF, ¾, PS & LS, GJS, HCI5P, DR, NI, DMK, 2-Tone	150	185	295
992, 21J, Extra, OF, ¾, PS & LS, GJS, HCI5P, DR, NI, DMK	135	155	300
992, 21J, ¾, PS, GJS, HCI5P, OF	95	135	190
992, 21J, Elinvar, ¾, GJS, HCI5P	135	160	200
992, 21J, Special, OF, ¾, PS & LS, GJS, HCI5P, DR, NI, DMK, 'Adj. for RR Service' on dial	200	275	395
992B, 21J, 2-Tone	145	175	250
992B, 21J, LS, OF, ¾	135	165	225
992B, 21J, OF, ¾, silver case	95	115	145
3992B, 22J, HCI6P ★	120	175	265
4992B, 22J, LS, OF, ¾, HCI6P, 24-hour dial	85	95	160

Grade 996, 16 size, 19 jewels, open face, gold jewel settings, serial number 152060.

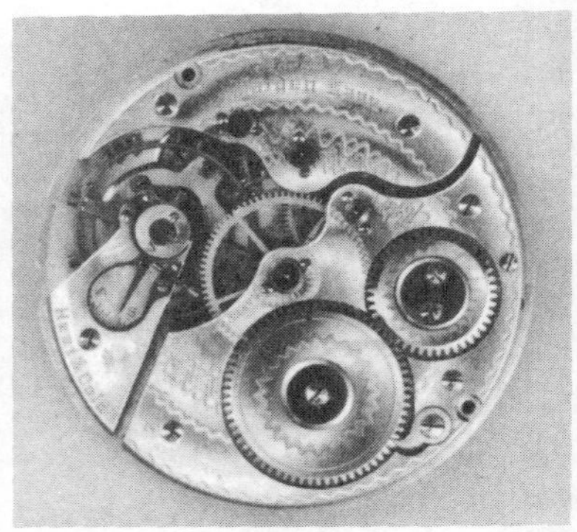

Hayden W. Wheeler, 16 size, 17 jewels, adjusted to heat & cold, serial number 56029.

HAMILTON WATCH CO., 16 SIZE (continued)

Grade or Name — Description	Avg	Ex-Fn	Mint
993, 21J, PS, HC, GJS, HCI5P, DR, NI, DMK	135	195	285
993, 21J, LS, HC, GJS, HCI5P, DMK, DR, NI	140	195	275
993, 21J, LS, HC, GJS, HCI5P, DMK, DR, NI, 14K	550	600	700
993, 21J, LS, HC, GJS, HCI5P, DMK, DR, NI, GF multi-color case	275	325	425
994, 21J, PS, BRG, LS, OF, GJS, GT, DR, HCI5P, DMK ★	700	800	1,350
995, 19J, GJS, BRG, HC ★★	1,200	1,300	1,650
996, 19J, LS, OF, ¾, GJS, DR, HCI5P, DMK	100	120	195
DeLong Escapement, 21J ★★★	2,500	3,000	5,000
Official Standard, 17J, OF	275	300	450
Union Special, 17J	110	125	150
Hayden W. Wheeler, 17J, OF ★	400	500	750
Hayden W. Wheeler, 17J, HC ★	450	550	850
Hayden W. Wheeler, 21J ★	600	700	975
Hayden W. Wheeler, 21J, 14K H.W.W. case	1,000	1,100	1,400

Grade 918, 12 size, 19 jewels, adjusted to HCI3P, serial number 3136257.

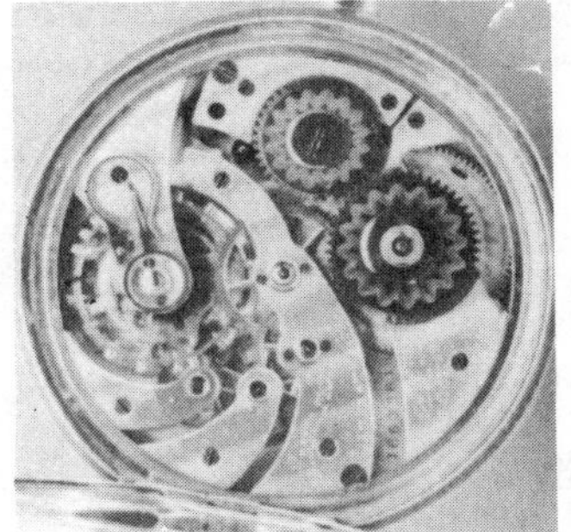

Grade 920, 12 size, 23 jewels, gold train, gold jewel settings, serial number 1863381.

12 SIZE

(Some cases were octagon, decagon, cushion, etc.)

Grade or Name — Description	Avg	Ex-Fn	Mint
900, 19J, BRG, DR, HCI5P, GJS, OF, 14K	$280	$295	$395
900, 19J, BRG, DR, HCI5P, GJS, OF	80	95	155
902, 19J, BRG, DR, HCI5P, GJS	85	100	185
902, 19J, BRG, DR, HCI5P, GJS, 14K	285	300	395
904, 21J, BRG, DR, HCI5P, GJS, GT	90	100	175
910, 17J, ¾, DR, ADJ	40	50	70
912, 17J, ¾, DR, ADJ	40	50	70
914, 17J, ¾, DR, HCI3P, GJS	40	50	70
914, 17J, ¾, DR, HCI3P, GJS, 14K	240	250	285
916, 17J, ¾, DR, HCI3P	40	50	70
916, 17J, HCI3P, silver case	35	40	50
918, 19J, HCI3P, WGF	65	85	150
918, 19J, ¾, DR, HCI3P, GJS, OF	85	100	195
920, 23J, BRG, DR, HCI5P, GJS, GT, OF	165	180	260
920, 23J, BRG, DR, HCI5P, GJS, GT, 14K	365	385	450
922, 23J, BRG, DR, HCI5P, GJS, GT, 14K	365	385	450
922, 23J, BRG, DR, HCI5P, GJS, GT, OF	165	185	250

HAMILTON WATCH CO., 12 SIZE (continued)

Grade or Name — Description	Avg	Ex-Fn	Mint
922 MP, 18K case	600	650	800
922 MP, GF	275	350	475
400, 21J, ¾, ADJ ★	150	225	350

Grade 922MP, 12 size, 23 jewels, serial number 3013390, c. 1930.

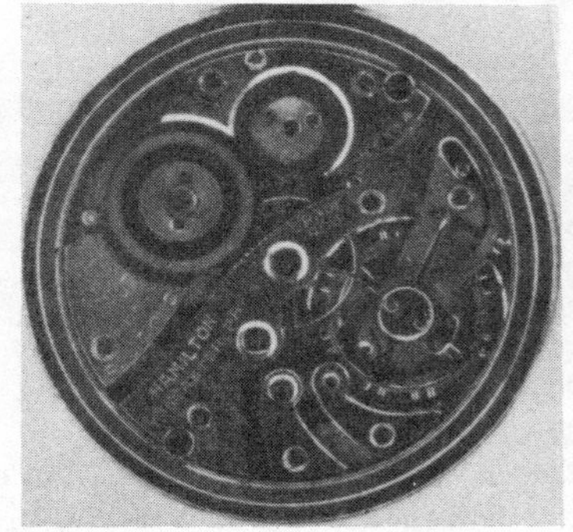

Grade 400, 12 size, 21 jewels. Note five tooth click on motor barrel.

10 SIZE

Grade or Name — Description	Avg	Ex-Fn	Mint
917, 17J, ¾, DR, HCI3P	$40	$50	$75
917, 17J, ¾, DR, HCI3P, 14K	195	210	295
921, 21J, BRG, DR, HCI5P	60	70	90
923, 23J, BRG, DR, HCI5P	125	150	225
923, 23J, M.P.G.F.	275	300	450
923, 23J, M.P., 18K	550	600	800
945, 23J, HCI5P	90	100	165

0 SIZE

Grade or Name — Description	Avg	Ex-Fn	Mint
981, 17J, ¾, HCI3P, DR, 18K, HC	$210	$250	$325
983, 17J, HCI3P, DR, GJS, 18K, HC	210	250	325
985, 19J, BRG, HCI3P, DR, GJS, GT, 18K, HC	300	310	375
Lady Hamilton, 14K case, OF	175	200	275

Example of Hamilton's thin model, 12-10 size, in a decagon case, 14K gold filled, originally sold for $52.00.

Above: **Grade 983HC, 982OF**, 0 size, 17 jewels, gold jewel settings. Right: Example of a Chronometer, 35 size, 21 jewels, mounted in gimbles with a wind indicator.

HAMILTON WATCH CO. (continued)

Top: **Pocket Chronometer**, 36 size, 21 jewels, gold jewel settings, HCI5P, serial number 1260382.

Right: **Chronometer** in gimbles and box, 35 size, wind indicator.

CHRONOMETER

Grade or Name — Description	Avg	Ex-Fn	Mint
35S, M#22, 21J, Wind Indicator, HCI6P, in gimbles and box, lever	$300	$375	$475
36S, M#36, 21J, Wind Indicator, in gimbles and box	800	950	1,300
36S, M#36, 21J, Wind Indicator, in Hamilton sterling pocket watch case with bow	1,000	1,350	1,850
35S, M#22, 21J, Wind Indicator, HCI6P, in a large base metal OF case	250	295	495
85S, M#21, 14J, Fusee, Detent Escapement	900	1,000	1,400

CHRONOGRAPH
GRADE 23

Grade or Name — Description	Avg	Ex-Fn	Mint
16S, 19J	$150	$175	$275

MAN'S WRIST WATCH

(Prices for wrist watches are for stem wind and set, leather band, complete and in good working order.)

Style or Model — Description	Avg	Ex-Fn	Mint
Doctor's Model, "duo dial," 17J, gold filled	$135	$155	$195
Flintridge, 19J, 14K case, pop up cover, M#987	500	595	750
Flintridge, 17J, 14K case, pop up cover, M#989	400	500	650
M#982, 19J, GJS, Hamilton 18K gold case	150	175	235
M#982, 19J, GJS, Hamilton 14K gold case	100	135	180
M#982, 19J, GJS, Hamilton GF case	40	45	55
M#979, 19J, GJS, 14K Hamilton case	120	150	200
M#979, 19J, GJS, gold filled Hamilton case	40	45	55

HAMILTON WATCH CO. (continued)

Style or Model — Description	Avg	Ex-Fn	Mint
M#987, 17J, gold filled Hamilton case	45	50	75
Round or Square case, 22J, 14K	100	120	145
Round, selfwind, 23J, gold filled	45	50	60
Round, selfwind, 25J, gold filled case	85	95	125
Round, selfwind, 17J, 14K case	95	110	135
Time Zone Dial (P.M.C.E.), Round 14K case	125	140	175
Electric Model 500, 14K case	95	115	140
Electric Model 500, gold filled	40	50	75
Electric Model 500, 12 diamond on dial	225	255	295
Tonneau case, 17J, 14K case	165	185	225
Tonneau case, 17J, gold filled case	45	50	75
Rectangular Curvex, 19J, 14K case	155	195	225
Cushion, 14K case, 17J	95	125	145
Cushion, 17J, gold filled case	35	40	55
Round, 17J, small diamonds on bezel & dial, 14K	295	325	375
Round, 17J, small diamonds on dial, 14K	155	175	195
Round, 17J, 14K case	95	125	135
Round, 17J, gold filled case	40	45	75
Round, 17J, stainless steel	15	20	35
Square, 17J, 14K, diamond on dial	165	175	195
Square, 17J, 14K case	95	115	135
Square, 17J, gold filled case	40	45	65

Flint Ridge, man's wrist watch, sports model with a protective spring cover, Grade 987, solid gold case, originally sold for $125.00. (Grade 979 sold for $150.00).

LADY'S WRIST WATCH

Style or Model — Description	Avg	Ex-Fn	Mint
Locket or Wrist, convertible watch, 14K case	$65	$70	$85
Locket or Wrist, convertible watch, gold filled	50	55	75
Tonneau, 14K case	65	75	85
Tonneau, gold filled	20	25	35
Cushion, 14K case	60	70	80
Cushion, gold filled	20	25	35
Cushion, stainless steel	10	15	22
Rectangular or Square, 14K case	50	60	80
Rectangular or Square, gold filled	20	25	35
Rectangular or Square, stainless steel	15	20	28
Small case with small diamonds on bezel	100	115	135
Small case with small diamonds on case & bezel	135	145	185
Small case with small diamonds on case & bezel & bracelet	495	525	695
Large case, large diamonds on bezel	195	225	295
Large case, large diamonds on bezel & case & bracelet	350	425	595
Large diamonds on bezel & case, cover over dial, diamond bracelet	1,000	2,000	4,000

HAMILTON WATCH COMPANY IDENTIFICATION OF MOVEMENT BY MODEL NUMBER

How to Identify Your Watch: Compare the movement with the illustrations in this section. While comparing, note the location of the balance, jewels, screws, gears and back plate (Full, ¾, Bridge) which will be clues in identifying the movement you have. Having determined the size, the Grade can also be found by looking up the serial number of your watch in the Hamilton Serial Number And Grades list.

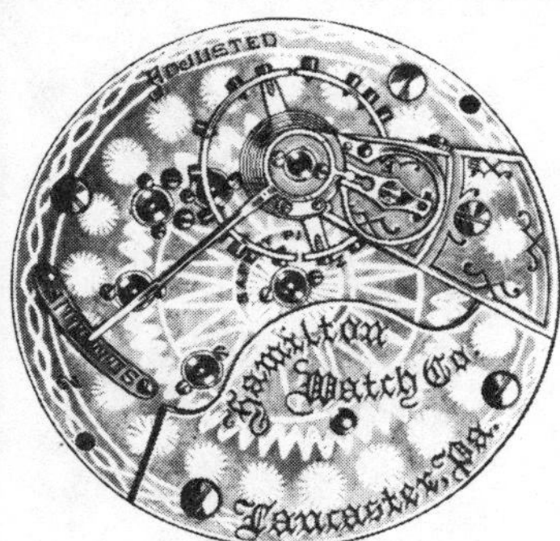

Grade 936, 18 size
Open face, 17 jewels, single roller before No. 426001, double roller after No. 426000

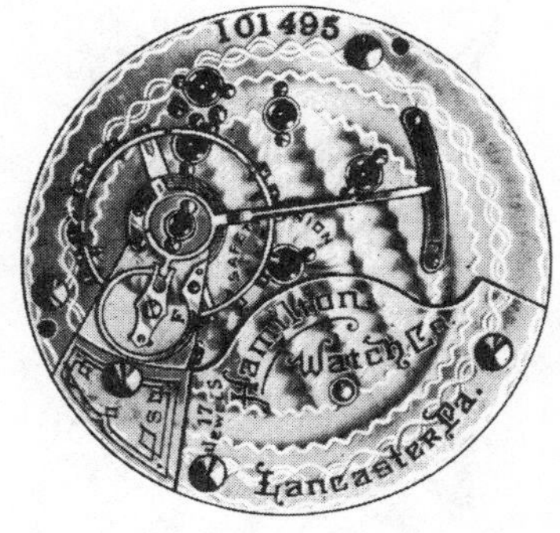

Grade 925, 18 size
Hunting, 17 jewels, single roller

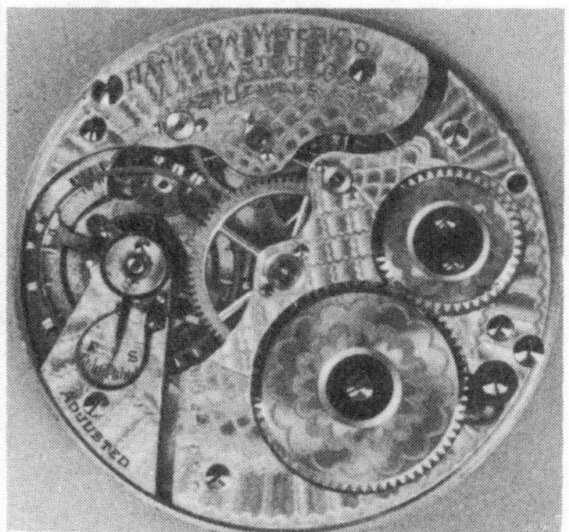

Grade 971, 16 size
Hunting, 21 jewels, ¾ plate movt.

Grade 992, 16 size
Open face, ¾ plate movt., 21 jewels, single roller before No. 377001, double roller after No. 379000

Grade 992B, 16 size
Open face, ¾ plate movt., 21 jewels, double roller

Grade 950, 16 size
Open face, bridge movt., 23 jewels, double roller

Grade 950B, 16 size
Open face, bridge movt., 23 jewels, double roller

Grade 902, 12 size
Open face, bridge movt., 19 jewels, double roller

Grade 912, 12 size
Open face, ¾ plate movt., 17 jewels, double roller

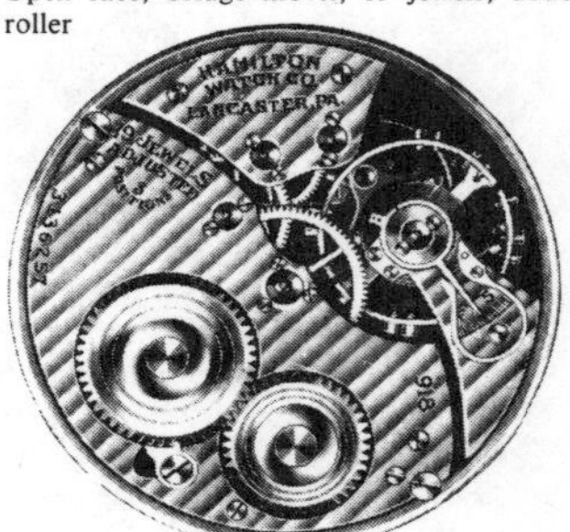

Grade 918, 12 size
Open face, ¾ plate movt., 19 jewels, double roller

Grade 922, 12 size
Open face, bridge movt., 23 jewels, double roller

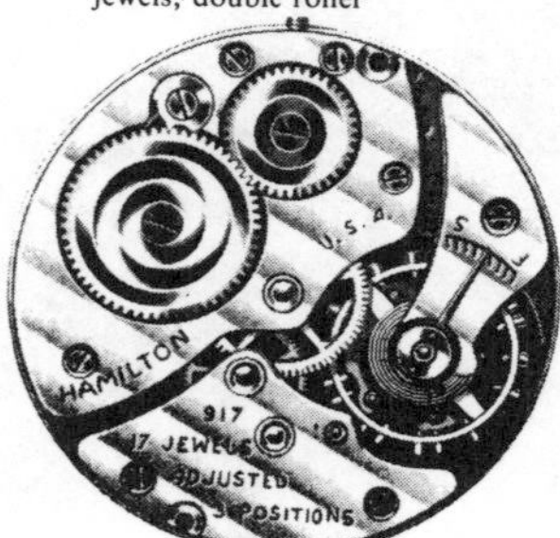

Grade 917, 10 size
Open face, ¾ plate movt., 17 jewels, double roller

Grade 921, 10 size
Open face, bridge movt., 21 jewels, double roller

Grade 923, 10 size
Open face, bridge movt., 23 jewels, double roller

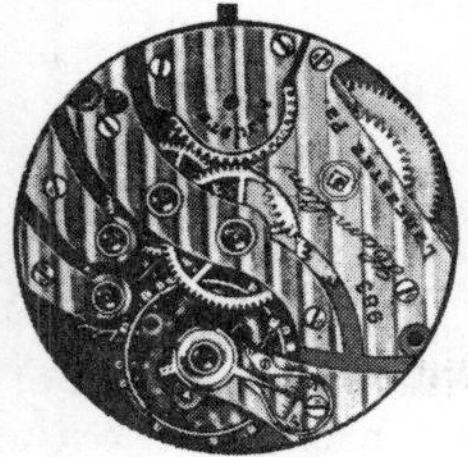

Grade 983, 0 size
Hunting, bridge movt., 17 jewels, double roller

Grade 979, 6/0 size
Hunting, ¾ plate movt., 19 jewels, double roller

Grade 986, 6/0 size
Open face, ¾ plate movt., 17 jewels, double roller

Grade 986A, 6/0 size
Open face, ¾ plate movt., 17 jewels, double roller

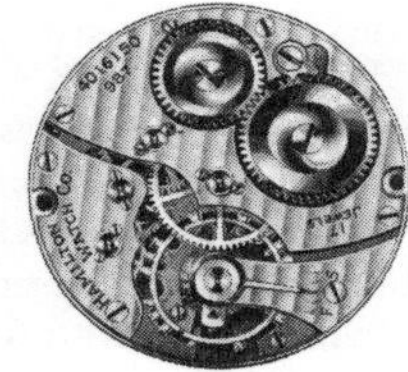

Grade 987, 6/0 size
Hunting, ¾ plate movt., 17 jewels, double roller

Grade 987A, 6/0 size
Open face, ¾ plate movt., 17 jewels, double roller

Grade 987S, 6/0 size
Hunting, ¾ plate movt., 17 jewels, double roller

Grade 747, 8/0 size
Open face, ¾ plate movt., 17 jewels, double roller

Grade 980, 14/0 size
Open face, ¾ plate movt., 17 jewels, double roller

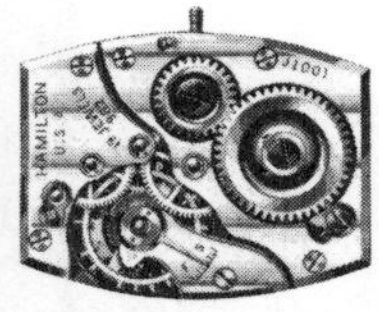

Grade 982, 14/0 size
Open face, ¾ plate movt., 19 jewels, double roller

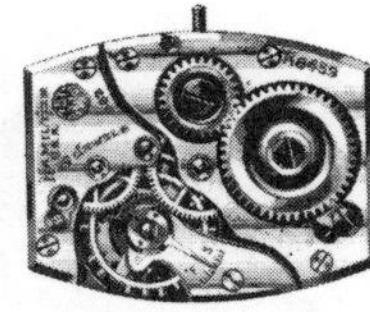

Grade 982M, 14/0 size
Open face, ¾ plate movt., 19 jewels, double roller

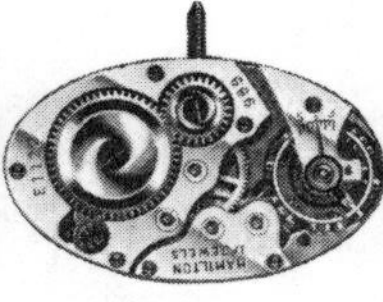

Grade 989, 18/0 size
Open face, ¾ plate movt., 17 jewels, double roller

Grade 997, 20/0 size
Open face, ¾ plate movt., 17 jewels, double roller

Grade 721, 21/0 size
Open face, ¾ plate movt., 17 jewels, double roller

Grade 995, 21/0 size
Open face, ¾ plate movt., 17 jewels, double roller

Grade 911, 22/0 size
Open face, ¾ plate movt., 17 jewels, double roller

Grade 911M, 22/0 size
Open face, ¾ plate movt., 17 jewels, double roller

HAMPDEN WATCH CO.
(DUEBER WATCH CO.)
Springfield, Massachusetts
Canton, Ohio
1876 — 1930

The New York Watch Co. preceded Hampden, and before that Don J. Mozart (1864) produced his three-wheel watch. Mozart was assisted by George Samuel Rice of New York and, as a result of their joint efforts, the New York Watch Co. was formed in 1866 in Providence, Rhode Island. It was moved in 1867 to Springfield, Massachusetts. Two grades of watches were decided on, and the company started with a 18S, ¾ plate engraved "Springfield." They were sold for $60 to $75. The 18S, ¾ plate were standard production, and the highest grade was a "George Walker" that sold for about $200 and a 16S, ¾ plate "State Street" which had steel parts and exposed balance and escape wheel that were gold plated.

John C. Dueber started manufacturing watch cases in about 1864 and bought a controlling interest in a company in 1886. About this time a disagreement arose between Elgin, Waltham, and the Illinois Watch companies. Also at this time an anti-trust law was passed, and the watch case manufacturers formed a boycott against Dueber. Dueber was faced with a major decision as to whether to stay in business or surrender to the watch case companies or buy a watch company. He decided to buy the Hampden Watch Co. of Springfield, Mass. By 1889 the operation had moved to Canton, Ohio. By the end of the year the company was turning out 600 watches a day. The first 16 size watch was produced in 1890. In 1894 Hampden introduced the first 23J movement made in America.

Chronology of the Development of Hampden Watch Co.:
The Mozart Watch Co., Providence, R. I. — 1864-1866
New York Watch Co., Providence, R. I. — 1866-1867
New York Watch Co., Springfield, Mass. — 1867-1875
New York Watch Mfg. Co., Springfield, Mass. — 1875-1876
Hampden Watch Co., Springfield, Mass. — 1877-1886
Hampden-Dueber Watch Co., Springfield, Mass. — 1886-1888
Hampden Watch Co., Canton, Ohio — 1888-1923
Dueber Watch Co., Canton, Ohio — 1888-1923
Dueber-Hampden Watch Co., Canton, Ohio — 1923-1931
Amtorg, U.S.S.R. — 1930-

HAMPDEN ESTIMATED SERIAL NUMBER AND PRODUCTION DATES

Date	Serial No.	Date	Serial No.	Date	Serial No.
1877	60,000	1893	775,000	1909	2,536,000
1878	91,000	1894	833,000	1910	2,664,000
1879	122,000	1895	888,500	1911	2,792,000
1880	153,000	1896	944,000	1912	2,920,000
1881	184,000	1897	1,000,000	1913	3,048,000
1882	215,000	1898	1,128,000	1914	3,176,000
1883	250,000	1899	1,256,000	1915	3,304,000
1884	300,000	1900	1,384,000	1916	3,432,000
1885	350,000	1901	1,512,000	1917	3,560,000
1886	400,000	1902	1,642,000	1918	3,680,000
1887	450,000	1903	1,768,000	1919	3,816,000
1888	500,000	1904	1,896,000	1920	3,944,000
1889	555,500	1905	2,024,000	1921	4,072,000
1890	611,000	1906	2,152,000	1922	4,200,000
1891	666,500	1907	2,280,000	1923	4,400,000
1892	722,000	1908	2,408,000	1924	4,600,000

Dueber Watch Co., 18 size, 15 jewels, nickel movement, Model 3, hunting case.

Dueber Grand, 18 size, 17 jewels, open face, originally sold for $20.00.

HAMPDEN
18 SIZE

Grade or Name — Description	Avg	Ex-Fn	Mint
Anchor, 17J, ADJ, GJS, DMK	$65	$70	$95
"3" Ball, 17J, ADJ, NI, DMK	60	70	95
Champion, 7J, ADJ, FULL, gilded, NI	50	60	75
Correct Time, 15J, HC	95	125	195
Dueber, 16J, gilded, DMK	70	80	95
Dueber, 17J, gilded, DMK	75	85	125
John C. Dueber, 15J, gilded, DMK	75	85	110
John C. Dueber, 17J, gilded, ADJ, DMK	80	90	130
John C. Dueber, Sp., 17J, gilded, ADJ, DMK	85	95	140
John C. Dueber, 17J, Silveroid	40	50	65
Dueber Grand, 17J, Silveroid	40	50	65
Dueber Grand, 17J, ADJ, HC	125	150	185
Dueber Grand, 21J, ADJ, DMK, NI, HC	135	155	195
Dueber W. Co., 11J	60	70	85
Dueber W. Co., 15J, DMK	75	85	110
Dueber W. Co., 16J	80	95	125
Dueber W. Co., 17J, DMK, ADJ, OF	70	80	115
Dueber W. Co., 17J, Silveroid	40	50	70
Dueber W. Co., 17J, DMK, ADJ, HC	95	125	165
Dueber W. Co., 19J, ADJ, GJS, HC ★	300	475	575
Dueber W. Co., 21J, HCI5P, GJS, OF	80	100	125
Dueber W. Co., 21J, GJS, HCI5P, HC	90	110	150
Homer Foot, gilded, KW, (Early)	150	185	235
Gladiator, KW	65	80	110
Gladiator, 11J, NI, DMK	50	60	80
Gulf Stream Sp., 21J, OF, LS	95	135	175
Hampden W. Co., 7J, KW, KS	65	75	95
Hampden W. Co., 7J, SW, OF	45	50	65
Hampden W. Co., 11J, OF, HC, KW	50	60	85
Hampden W. Co., 11J, OF, HC, SW	50	60	90
Hampden W. Co., 15J, OF, HC, KW	90	105	135
Hampden W. Co., 15J, HC, SW	55	65	85
Hampden W. Co., 15J, SW, Silveroid	30	40	55

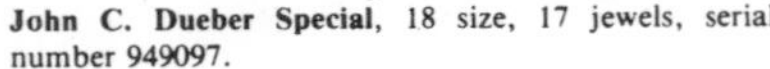

John C. Dueber Special, 18 size, 17 jewels, serial number 949097.

Hampden Watch Co., 18 size, 7 jewels, key wind & set, Model 1.

Grade or Name — Description	Avg	Ex-Fn	Mint
Hampden W. Co., 15J, SW, OF	55	60	85
Hampden W. Co., 15J, Multi-color, 14K, HC	1,150	1,450	2,200
Hampden W. Co., 16J, OF	80	95	110
Hampden W. Co., 17J, SW, Silveroid	35	45	60
Hampden W. Co., 17J, SW, OF	55	70	95
Hampden W. Co., 17J, HC, SW	60	85	125
Hampden W. Co., 17J, LS, HC, 14K	490	550	750
Hampden W. Co., 17J, LS, HC, 10K	300	380	550
Hampden W. Co., 21J, OF, HC, SW	85	95	135
Hampden W. Co., 25J, GJS, HCI5P, 2-Tone, HC	1,500	1,800	2,300
John Hancock, 17J, GJS, HCI3P	75	85	95
John Hancock, 21J, GJS, HCI3P	95	105	135
John Hancock, 23J, GJS, HCI5P	125	145	225
Hayward, 15J, KW	125	145	175
Hayward, 11J, SW	50	60	80
Lafayette, 11J, NI	80	90	120
Lafayette, 15J, NI, KW	100	125	165
Lafayette, 15J, NI	75	85	125
Lakeside, 15J, NI, SW	80	90	135

Menlo Park, 18 size, 17 jewels, serial number 1184116.

New Railway, 18 size, 23 jewels, open face only, gold jewel settings, originally sold for $50.00, Model 2.

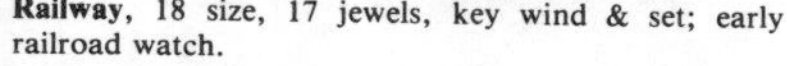

Railway, 18 size, 17 jewels, key wind & set; early railroad watch.

Special Railway, 18 size, 23 jewels, HCI5P, serial number 3357284.

Grade or Name — Description	Avg	Ex-Fn	Mint
M. J. & Co. Railroad Watch Co., 15J, HC	250	335	495
Menlo Park, 17J, NI, ADJ	85	120	175
Mermod, Jaccard & Co., 15J, KW, HC	120	145	200
Metropolis, 15J, NI, SW	75	85	120
Wm. McKinley, 17J, HCI3P	70	80	110
Wm. McKinley, 21J, GJS, HCI5P	80	110	135
New Railway, 17J, GJS, HCI5P	75	85	110
New Railway, 19J, GJS, HCI5P	165	195	245
New Railway, 21J, Silveroid	55	65	85
New Railway, 21J, GJS, HCI5P, HC	135	165	250
New Railway, 21J, GJS, HCI5P, OF	80	100	135
New Railway, 23J, GJS, HCI5P	175	225	295
New Railway, 23J, GJS, HCI5P, 14K, OF	450	500	675
North Am. RR, 21J, GJS, HCI5P, OF, LS	95	135	175
North Am. RR, 21J, GJS, HCI3P, HC, PS	125	145	195
Pennsylvania Special, 17J, GJS, HCI5P, DR, NI ★★	700	800	975
J. C. Perry, 15J, KW, gilded	100	120	160
J. C. Perry, 15J, NI, SW	70	80	95
J. C. Perry, 15J, gilded, SW	60	65	80
Railway, 15J, gilded	60	65	80
Railway, 17J, NI	70	85	125
Railway, 15J, KW, marked on mvt. ★★	650	800	995
Railroad with R.R. names on dial and movement:			
Canadian Pacific RR, 17J ★	275	300	385
Canadian Pacific RR, 21J ★	625	650	785
Special Railway, 17J, GJS, HCI5P, NI, DR	65	80	110
Special Railway, 21J, GJS, HCI5P, NI, DR, 2-Tone	80	95	145
Special Railway, 23J, GJS, HCI5P, NI, DR, 2-Tone	195	235	375
Special Railway, 23J, Silveroid	125	180	265
Special Railway, 23J, 14K, HC	600	690	775
Springfield, 7-11J, KW, gilded	60	70	95
Springfield, 7-11J, SW, NI	50	60	80
Standard, 15J, gilded	55	65	85
State Street, 15J, NI, LS, (Early KW)	125	150	235
Theo. Studley, 15J, KW, KS, HC	140	160	195

HAMPDEN WATCH CO., 18 SIZE (continued)

Grade or Name — Description	Avg	Ex-Fn	Mint
Tramway Special, 17J, NI	100	120	175
Woolworth, 11J, KW	90	110	140
Grade 45 HC & 65 OF, 11J	55	60	70
Grade 60, 15J, LS	60	65	80
Grade 80 & 81, 17J, ADJ	65	75	90
Grade 85, 19J, GJS, 2-Tone, HC ★★	1,000	1,200	1,500
Grade 125, 21J, HCI3P, OF	65	75	90

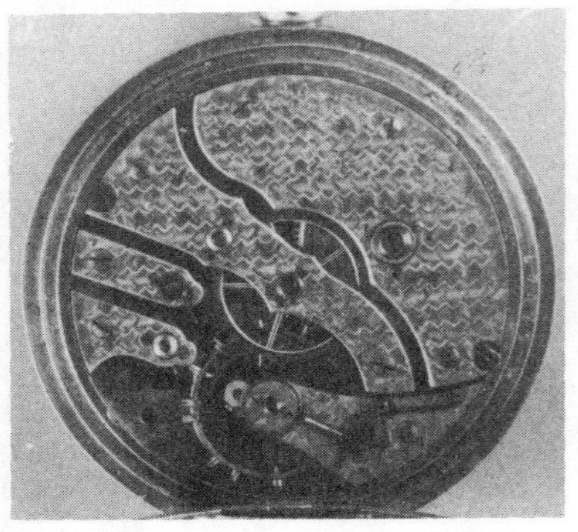

Hampden W. Co., Bridge Model, 16 size; 23 jewels, 2-tone movement, serial number 1899430.

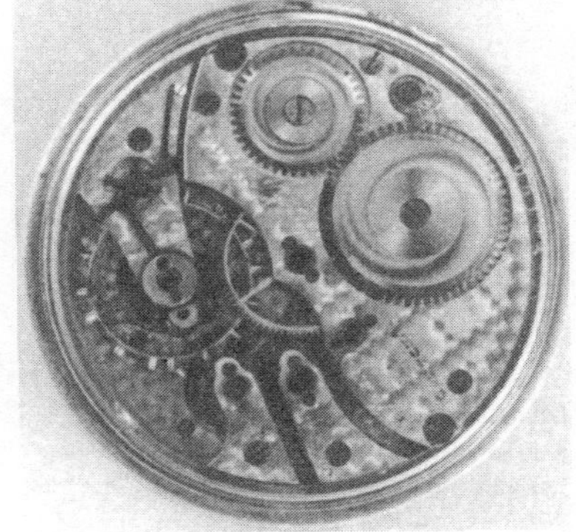

Hampden W. Co., 16 size, 17 jewels, gold jewel settings, serial number 3075235.

16 SIZE

Grade or Name — Description	Avg	Ex-Fn	Mint
Champion, 7J, NI, ¾, gilded, coin, OF & HC	$40	$50	$65
Champion, 7J, NI, ¾, gilded, OF & HC	45	60	80
Chronometer, 21J, NI, HCI3P, GJS	100	130	185
John C. Dueber, 17J, GJS, NI, HCI5P, ¾	65	80	125
John C. Dueber, 21J, GJS, NI, HCI5P, ¾	80	90	150
John C. Dueber, 21J, GJS, NI, HCI5P, DR, BRG	115	140	185
Dueber Watch Co., 17J, ADJ, ¾	65	70	95
Hampden W. Co., 7J, SW, OF, HC	45	50	65

Wm. McKinley, or Grade 105, 16 size, 21 jewels, gold jewel settings, adjusted to HCI5P.

Railway, 16 size, 17 jewels, adjusted to HCI5P, serial number 2271866.

HAMPDEN WATCH CO., 16 SIZE (continued)

Grade 104, 16 size, 23 jewels, gold jewel settings, gold train, adjusted to HCI5P, serial number 2801184.

Grade 108, 16 size, 17 jewels, open face and hunting, serial number 1042051.

Grade or Name — Description	Avg	Ex-Fn	Mint
Hampden W. Co., 11J, SW, OF, HC	55	60	70
Hampden W. Co., 15J, SW, OF, HC	60	70	90
Hampden W. Co., 17J, SW, OF	65	75	95
Hampden W. Co., 17J, 14K, Multi-color, HC	800	1,100	1,500
Hampden W. Co., 17J, Silveroid	40	50	60
Hampden W. Co., 17J, SW, HC	70	80	125
Hampden W. Co., 21J, SW, Silveroid	65	70	85
Hampden W. Co., 21J, SW, OF, HC	90	105	175
Hampden W. Co., 23J, HCI5P, GJS, ¾	180	205	265
Hampden W. Co., 23J, Series 2, HC "Freesprung", GJS, GT	275	350	535
Masonic Dial, 23J, GJS, 2-Tone porcelain dial	310	350	425
Wm. McKinley, 17J, GJS, HCI5P, NI, DR, ¾	60	70	95
Wm. McKinley, 21J, GJS, HCI5P, NI, DR, ¾	85	100	135
Wm. McKinley, 21J, GJS, HCI5P, NI, DR, ¾, Coin	70	80	95
Wm. McKinley, 21J, GJS, HCI5P, NI, DR, BRG	100	120	160
New Railway, 21J, GJS, HCI5P	85	100	135
New Railway, 23J, GJS, HCI5P, LS, HC	200	285	425
Ohioan, 21J, HCI3P, GJS, ¾	125	160	235
Railway, 19J, GJS, HCI5P, BRG, DR	150	165	225
Special Railway, 23J, HCI5P, NI, BRG, DR	175	225	340
Gen'l Stark, 15J, DMK, BRG	60	70	85
Gen'l Stark, 17J, DMK, BRG	75	80	95
95, 21J, marked "95", GJS	100	145	225
97 HC, 98 HC, & 108 OF, 17J, HCI3P, NI, ¾, DMK	65	70	85
99, 15J, ¾, HC	50	60	70
103, 21J, GJS, HCI5P, NI, BRG, DR	90	110	130
104, 23J, GJS, HCI5P, NI, BRG, DR, DMK	175	210	275
105, 21J, GJS, HCI5P, NI, ¾, DR, DMK	90	110	130
106, 107 OF, & 108, 17J, SW, NI	60	70	85
109, 15J, ¾, OF	45	50	60
110, 11J, ¾	50	55	65
115-120, 21J, SW, NI, OF	90	115	140
340, 17J, SW, NI	60	70	85
440, 15J, 2-tone	55	65	85

HAMPDEN WATCH CO., 16 SIZE (continued)

Grade or Name — Description	Avg	Ex-Fn	Mint
555, 21J, GT, GJS, Chronometer on dial	100	130	195
600, 17J, SW, NI	60	70	85

Dueber Grand, 12 size, 17 jewels, gold jewel settings, hunting case, serial number 1737354.

Dueber Grand, 12 size, 17 jewels, gold jewel settings, open face, pin set, serial number 1732255.

12 SIZE

Grade or Name — Description	Avg	Ex-Fn	Mint
Champion, 7J, SW	$35	$40	$60
Dueber Grand, 17J, BRG	45	50	70
Hampden W. Co., 7J, SW, OF	30	40	50
John Hancock, 21J, BRG	55	65	85
Gen'l Stark, 15J, BRG	40	50	70
Gen'l Stark, 15J, pin set	30	40	50
207-300 HC & 302 OF, 7J, ¾	30	40	60
304 HC & 306 OF, 15J, ¾	30	40	60
305-308 HC & 310 OF, 17J, ¾	65	85	110
307, 17J	65	85	110
312 HC & 314 OF, 21J, ¾, HCI5P	80	95	135
Hampden W. Co., 17J, 14K, Multi-color, HC	475	600	875
31 OF, 17J, SW, 14K	275	325	475

Paul Revere. Example of Hampden Watch Co.'s extra thin series showing face and movement, 12 size, 17-19 jewels, adjusted to HCI5P.

HAMPDEN WATCH CO. (continued)

12 SIZE (THIN MODEL)

Grade or Name — Description	Avg	Ex-Fn	Mint
Aviator, 17J, HCI4P	$40	$50	$70
Aviator, 19J, HCI4P	45	50	80
Beacon, 17J	35	40	55
Nathan Hale, 15J	40	50	60
Minuteman, 17J	50	60	80
Paul Revere, 17J, 14K, OF	295	350	450
Paul Revere, 17J	55	60	75
Paul Revere, 19J	60	70	85

Note: Some 12 Sizes came in cases of octagon, decagon, hexagon, triad, and cushion shapes.

6 SIZE

Grade or Name — Description	Avg	Ex-Fn	Mint
200, 7J	$45	$60	$80
206, 11J	50	60	90
213, 15J	60	75	95
220, 17J	75	85	110
Hampden W. Co., 15J, multi-color GF, HC	150	175	265
Hampden W. Co., 15J, Multi-color, 14K, HC	475	575	795

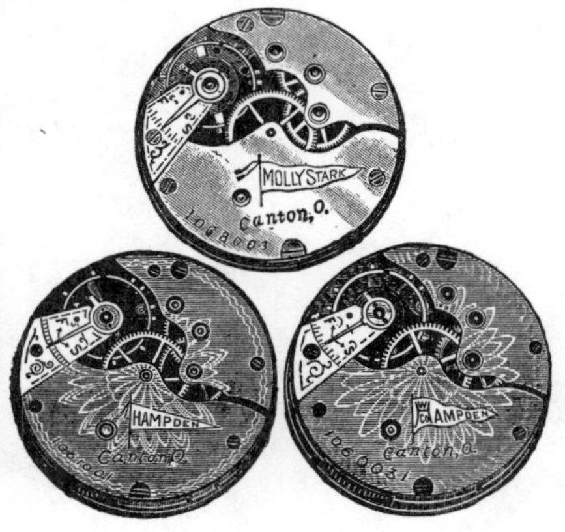

Top left: **Molly Stark**, 000 size, 7 jewels, hunting or open face, originally sold for $12.00.

Bottom left: **Four Hundred Series**, 000 sizes, 11, 15 & 16 jewels, gold jewel settings, originally sold for from $20-25.

000 SIZE

Grade or Name — Description	Avg	Ex-Fn	Mint
Diadem, 15J, 14K, OF Case	$135	$155	$160
Diadem, 15J, HC, 14K	185	240	295
Diadem, 15J	80	110	145
Molly Stark, 7J	85	120	135
Molly Stark, 7J, 14K, HC	175	230	295
Molly Stark, 7J, Pin Set	90	130	155
Four Hundred, 11, 15, 16, & 17J	80	90	110
14K Multi-color, HC	400	450	625

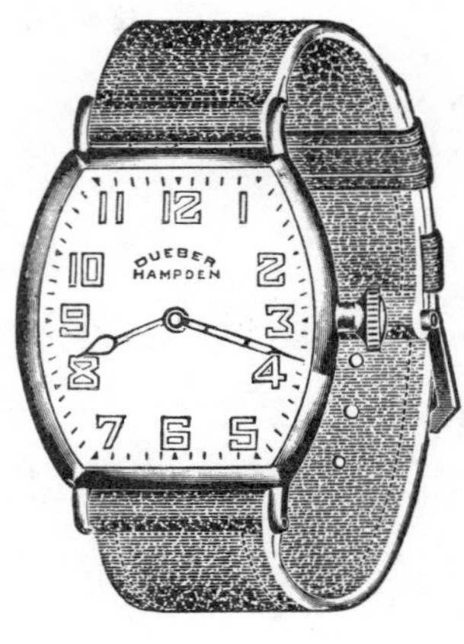

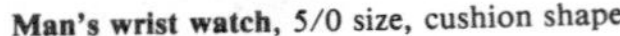

Man's wrist watch, 5/0 size, cushion shape

Man's wrist watch, 5/0 size, Tonneau or barrel shape

MAN'S WRIST WATCH

Style or Grade — Description	Avg	Ex-Fn	Mint
Tonneau, 14K case	$80	$90	$115
Tonneau, gold filled	30	35	45
Cushion, 14K case	55	65	95
Cushion, gold filled	30	35	45
Rectangular, 14K case	55	65	95
Rectangular, gold filled	30	35	45
Rectangular, stainless steel	10	15	25
Round, 14K case	50	60	80
Round, gold filled	30	35	45
Round, stainless steel	10	15	25

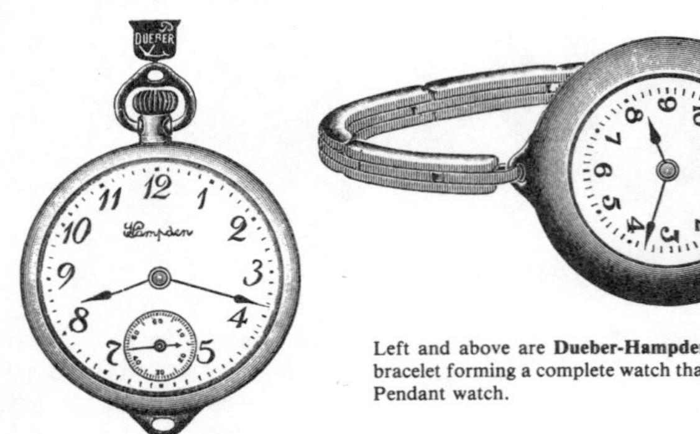

Left and above are **Dueber-Hampden Bracelet Watches** with detachable bracelet forming a complete watch that can also be worn as a Chatelaine or Pendant watch.

LADY'S WRIST WATCH

Style or Grade — Description	Avg	Ex-Fn	Mint
Moley Stark Model or Diadem Model, gold filled	$20	$25	$35

HAMPDEN WATCH CO.
IDENTIFICATION OF MOVEMENTS

How to Identify Your Watch: Compare the movement of your watch with the illustration in this section. While comparing, note the location of the balance, jewels, screws, gears and type of back plate (Full, ¾, Bridge) which will be clues in identifying the movement you have.

Series I, 18 size
Hunting or open face, key wind & set

Series II, 18 size
Hunting, stem wind, pendant or lever set

Series III, 18 size
Hunting, stem wind, pendant or lever set

Series IV, 18 size
Open face, stem wind, lever set

Series I, 16 size
Open face, stem wind, pendant or lever set

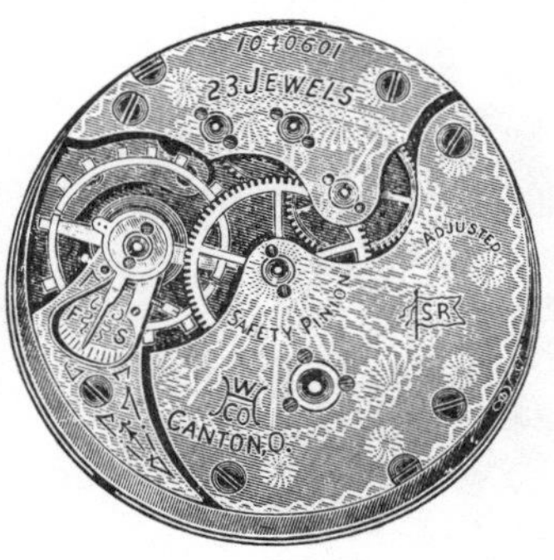

Series II, 16 size
Hunting, stem wind, pendant or lever set

Series III, 16 size
Open face, stem wind, pendant set

Series IV, 16 size
Hunting, stem wind, pendant or lever set

Series V, 16 size
Open face, stem wind, pendant or lever set

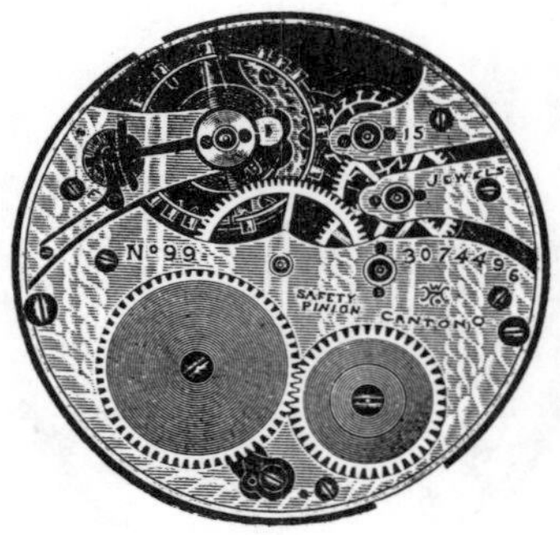

Series VI, 16 size
Hunting, stem wind, pendant set

Series VII, 16 size
Open face, stem wind, pendant set

Series III, 12 size
Open face, stem wind, pendant set

Series I, 12 size
Hunting, stem wind, lever set

Series II, 12 size
Open face, stem wind, lever set

Series IV, 12 size
Open face, stem wind, pendant set

Series V, 12 size
Open face, stem wind, pendant set

Series I, 6 size
Open face, stem wind

Series I, 3/0 size
Hunting, stem wind

Series II, 3/0 size
Open face, stem wind, pendant set

Series III, 3/0 size
Hunting, lever or pendant set

Series IV, 3/0 size
Hunting, stem wind, pendant or lever set

HERMAN VON DER HEYDT
Chicago, Illinois
1883

Herman von der Heydt patented a self-winding watch on Feb. 19, 1884. A total of 35 watches were hand-made by von der Heydt. The watches were 18S, full plate, lever escapement and fully-jeweled. The wind mechanism was a gravity type made of heavy steel and shaped like a crescent. The body motion let the heavy crescent move which was connected to a ratchet on the winding arbor, resulting in self-winding. Five movements were nickel and sold for about $90; the gilded model sold for about $75.

HERMAN VON DER HEYDT (continued)

Grade or Name — Description		Avg	Ex-Fn	Mint
18S, 19J, FULL, NI	★★★	$4,500	$5,000	$6,500
18S, 19J, FULL, gilded	★★★	3,000	3,500	4,000

Example of **Herman Von Der Heydt** patented self winding watch, 18 size, 19 jewels, crescent shaped winding weight.

E. HOWARD & CO.
Boston (Roxbury), Massachusetts
December 11, 1858 — 1903

After the failure of the Boston Watch Company (1853-57), Edward Howard decided to personally attempt the successful production of watches on the interchangeable machine-made parts system. He and Charles Rice, his financial backer, being unable to buy out the defunct watch company in Waltham, did remove (per a prior claim) the watches in progress, the tools and machinery to Howard and Davis' Roxbury factory (first watch factory in America) in late 1857. During their first year, the machinery was retooled for the production of a revolutionary new watch of Howard's design. Also, the remaining Boston Watch Co. movements were completed (E. Howard & Co. dials, Howard & Rice on the movement). By the summer of 1858, Edward Howard had produced his first watch. On December 11, 1858 the firm of E. Howard & Co. was formed for the manufacture of high-grade watches. Howard's first model was entirely different from any watch previously made. It introduced the more accurate "quick beat" train to American watchmaking. The top plate was in two sections and had six pillars instead of the usual four in a full plate. The balance was gold or steel at first, then later it was a compensation balance loaded with gold screws. Reed's patented barrel was used for the first time. The size, based on the Dennison system, was a little larger than the regular 18 size. In 1861, a ¾ plate model was put on the market. By now, most movements were being stamped with "N" to designate Howard's 18 size. On February 4, 1868 Howard patented a new steel motor barrel which was to supersede the Reed's, but not before some 28,000 had been produced. Also, in 1868 Howard introduced the stemwinding movement and was probably the first company to market such a watch in the U. S. By 1869, Howard was producing their "L" or 16 size as well as their first nickel movements. In 1870, G. P. Reed's micrometer regulator was patented for use by E. Howard & Co. The Reed style "whiplash" regulator has been employed in more pocket watches, worldwide, than any other type. In 1878, the manufacturing of keywind movements was discontinued. Mr. Howard retired in 1882, but the company continued to produce watch movements in the grade and style set by him until 1903. This company was the first to adjust to all six positions. Their dials were always a hard enamel and always bore the name "E. Howard & Co., Boston." In 1903, the company transferred

E. HOWARD & CO. (continued)
all rights to use the name "Edward Howard" in conjunction with the production of watches to the Keystone Watch Case Co. which stamped most of its models "Howard" on the dial and "E. Howard Watch Co., Boston. U.S.A." on the movement. Edward Howard's company never produced its own watch cases, the great majority of which were solid gold or silver. Keystone, however, produced complete watches, many of which are in gold filled.

Chronological Development of E. Howard & Co.:
Howard, Davis & Dennison, Roxbury, Mass., 1850
American Horologue Company, Roxbury, Mass., 1851
Warren Manufacturing Company, Roxbury, Mass., 1851-53
Boston Watch Co., Roxbury, Mass. — 1853-1854/Waltham, Mass., 1854-57
Howard & Rice, Roxbury, Mass., 1857-58 (E. Howard & Co. on dials)
E. Howard & Co., Roxbury, Mass. — 1858-1903

Keystone Watch Case Co. (Howard line), Jersey City, N. J., 1903-30

E. HOWARD & CO.
15 JEWELS
APPROXIMATE DATES, SERIAL NOS., AND TOTAL PRODUCTION

Serial Number	Date	Series	Total Prod.
-2,000	-1860	I (18S)	2,000
2,001-3,000	1860-1861	II (18S)	1,000
3,001-3,500	1861	i(10S) & K(14S)	200
3,501-28,000	1861-1871	III (18S)	24,500
30,001-50,000	1868-1882	IV (18S)	20,000
50,001-71,000	1869-1899	V (16S)	21,000
100,001-105,500	1869-1899	VI (6S)	5,500
200,001-227,000	1880-1899	VII (18S)	27,000
*228,001-231,000	1895	VII (18S)	3,000
300,001-309,000	1884-1899	VIII (18S)	9,000
*309,001-310,000	1895	VIII (18S)	1,000
400,001-405,000	1890-1895	IX (18S)	5,000
500,001-501,500	1890-1899	X (12S)	1,500
*600,001-601,500	1896	XI (16S)	1,500
*700,001-701,500	1896	XII (16S)	1,500
Approx. Total Production			**123,700**

** ¾ Split Plates with 17 Jewels*

Deer

Adjusted to HCI6P

Horse

Adjusted to HCI - No positions

Hound

Unadjusted

The above symbols appear on some E. Howard & Co. models and refer to the grade and adjustments. On some of the earlier movements, "adjusted," and "heat and cold" appear on the balance bridge rather than the above symbols. "Adjusted" refers to isochronism, heat and cold, and positions. "Heat and cold" refers to adjustment to temperature and isochronism. The plain movement with no symbols or wording on the bridge are adjusted only to isochronism.

E. Howard & Co. (continued)

E. HOWARD & CO. WATCH SIZES

Letter	Inches	Approx. Size
N	1 13/16	18
L	1 11/16	16
K	1 10/16	14
J	1 9/16	12
I	1 8/16	10

Letter	Inches	Approx. Size
H	1 7/16	8
G	1 6/16	6
F	1 5/16	4
E	1 4/16	2
D	1 3/16	0

Series I, 18 size, 15 jewels, upright pallets, note Maltese cross winding stop work, serial number 201.

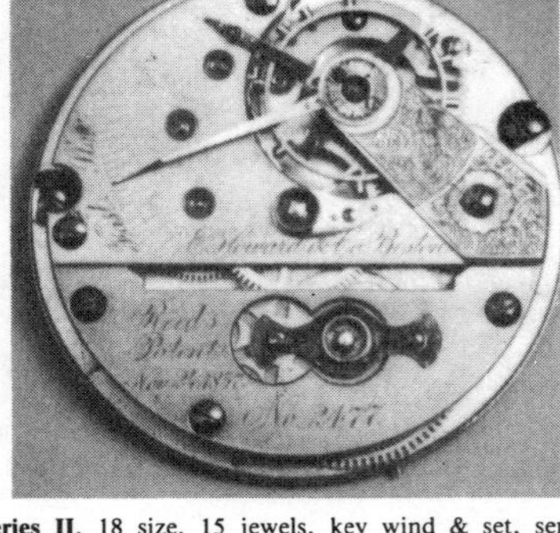

Series II, 18 size, 15 jewels, key wind & set, serial number 2,477.

E. HOWARD & CO.
N SIZE (18)

Series or Name — Description		Avg	Ex-Fn	Mint
E. Howard & Co. on dial and movement, 1857 Model, upright pallets, English style escape wheel, KW & KS, silver case	★★	$1,500	$2,000	$2,500
I, 15J, gilded, KW, 18K, HC or OF, upright pallets	★★	2,200	2,800	3,800
I, 15J, gilded, KW, 18K, HC or OF, horizontal pallets	★	2,100	2,700	3,700
I, 15J, gilded, KW, silver HC	★	1,400	1,700	2,200
I, 15J (movement only)	★	700	1,000	1,500
II, 15J, gilded, KW, 18K, HC or OF	★	1,800	2,300	3,200
II, 15J, gilded, KW, silver HC	★	1,200	1,450	2,000

Series III, 18 size, 15 jewels, note center wheel rack regulator, serial number 22,693.

Series IV, 18 size, 15 jewels, key wind and set, serial number 37893.

Series VII, 18 size, 15 jewels, nickel movement, note running deer on movement, "adjusted" on bridge, serial number 219304.

Series VII, 18 size, 17 jewels, ¾ split plate, serial number 228,055.

Series or Name — Description	Avg	Ex-Fn	Mint
II, 15J (movement only) ★	600	800	1,200
III, 15J, gilded, KW, 18K, HC	1,100	1,400	2,000
III, 15J, gilded, KW, silver case	500	700	900
III, 15J, nickel, KW, silver case	650	900	1,300
III, 15J, gilded, KW, 18K, Mershon's Patent	1,200	1,500	2,100
III, 15J, gilded, KW, 18K, Coles Escapement	1,400	1,650	2,300
III, 15J (movement only)	175	225	350
IV, 15J, gilded or nickel, KW, 18K, HC	900	1,300	1,700
IV, 15J, gilded or nickel, SW, 18K, HC	800	1,200	1,600
IV, 15J (movement only)	150	200	300
VII, 15J, gilded or nickel, SW, 14K, HC	750	1,000	1,500
VII, 17J, nickel, split plate, SW, 14K, HC ★	1,000	1,350	1,900
VII, 17J, nickel, split plate, SW, GF, HC ★	375	525	650
VII, 19J, nickel, split plate, SW, 14K HC ★★★	2,500	3,000	4,300
VII, 15J (movement only)	110	150	225
VIII, 15J, gilded or nickel, SW, 14K, OF	700	900	1,400
VIII, 17J, nickel, split plate, SW, 14K, OF ★	1,000	1,350	1,900
VIII, 17J, nickel, split plate, SW, GF, OF ★	425	525	750

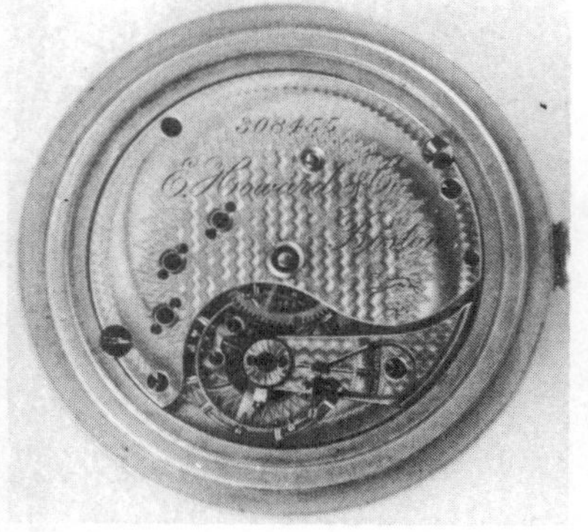

Series VIII, 18 size, 15 jewels, serial number 308455.

Series VIII, 18 size, 17 jewels, split plate model, gold jewel settings, serial number 309904.

E. HOWARD & CO., N (18) SIZE (continued)

Series or Name — Description	Avg	Ex-Fn	Mint
VIII, 15J (movement only)	110	150	225
IX, 15J, gilded, SW, 14K, HC	700	950	1,400
IX, 15J, gilded, SW, GF, HC	300	375	475
IX, 15J (movement only)	100	140	200
VII, Ball, 17J, nickel, SW, 14K, HC ★★★	3,500	4,000	5,500
VII, Ball, 17J, nickel, SW, GF, HC ★★★	2,200	2,800	3,800
VIII, Ball, 17J, nickel, SW, 14K, OF ★★	2,200	3,000	4,200
VIII, Ball, 17J, nickel, SW, GF, OF ★★	1,500	2,000	2,750
I, Isochronism, 15J, gilded, KW, helical hairspring ★★★	3,500	5,000	7,000

Prices are for complete watches with specially made Howard cases and dials. **NOTE:** E. Howard & Co. movements will not fit standard cases properly.

Series IX, 18 size, 15 jewels, hunting. This series is guilded only and hound grade exclusively, serial number 402,873.

Series V, 16 or L size, Prescott Model, 15 jewels, hunting, serial number 50434.

L SIZE (16)

Series or Name — Description	Avg.	Ex-Fn	Mint
V, 15J, gilded, KW, 18K, HC	$1,000	$1,400	$1,800
V, 15J, gilded, KW, 18K, Coles Escapement ★	1,300	1,600	2,000

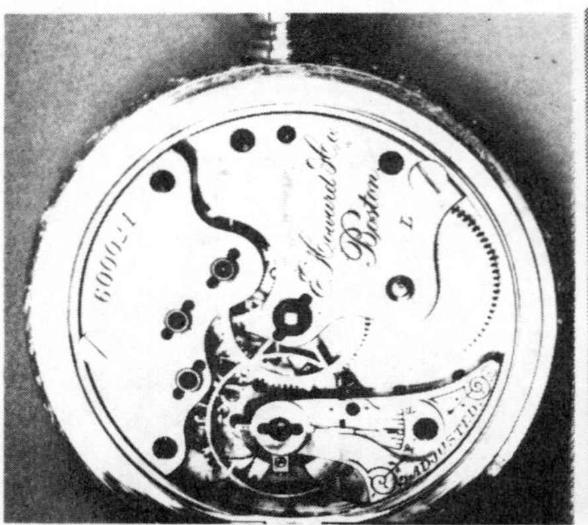

Series XI, 16 size, 17 jewels, split plate model, niekel movement, gold jewel settings, serial number 600,021.

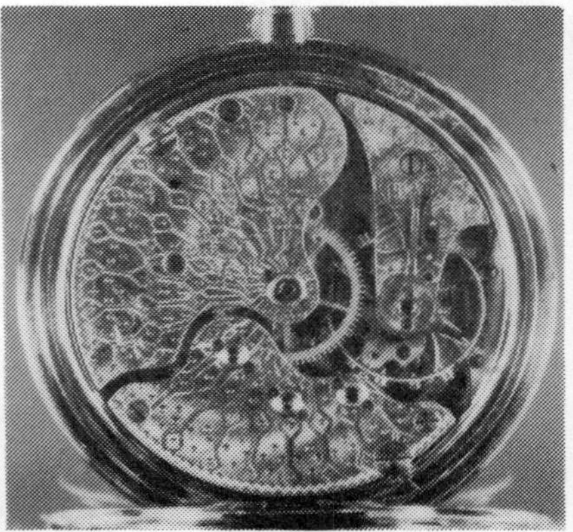

Series XII, L-16 size, 21 jewels, split plate model, nickel movement, gold lettering, gold jewel settings, serial number 700899.

E. HOWARD & CO., L (16) SIZE (continued)

Series or Name — Description	Avg	Ex-Fn	Mint
V, 15J, gilded or nickel, SW, 14K, HC	700	900	1,400
V, 15J, gilded, SW, 14K, Coles Escapement ★	1,200	1,500	1,900
V, 15J (movement only)	100	140	200
XI, 17J, nickel, split plate, SW, 14K, HC ★	1,100	1,450	2,000
XI, 17J, nickel, split plate, SW, GF, HC ★	400	500	675
XI, 17J (movement only)	200	300	475
XII, 17J, nickel, split plate, SW, 14K, OF ★	1,000	1,300	1,900
XII, 17J, nickel, split plate, SW, GF, OF ★	375	475	650
XII, 17J (movement only)	175	275	450
XII, 21J, nickel, split plate, SW, 14K OF ★★★	2,500	3,500	5,000

K SIZE (14)

Series or Name — Description	Avg	Ex-Fn	Mint
15J, gilded, KW (movement only) ★★★	$2,200	$2,700	$3,500
15J, gilded, KW, 18K, HC ★★★	3,500	6,000	8,000

Series K, 14 or K size, 15 jewels, key wind & set, serial number 3,005.

Series X, 12 or J size, 15 jewels, note deer on movement, serial number 501361.

J SIZE (12)

Series or Name — Description	Avg	Ex-Fn	Mint
X, 15J, nickel, hound, SW, 14K, OF ★	$900	$1,250	$1,650
X, 15J, nickel, horse, SW, 14K, OF ★	1,000	1,300	1,750
X, 15J, nickel, deer, SW, 14K, OF ★	1,100	1,400	1,850
X, 15J, hound (movement only) ★	250	400	575

I SIZE (10)

Series or Name — Description	Avg.	Ex-Fn	Mint
15J, gilded, KW, 18K HC	$3,500	$6,000	$8,000
15J, gilded, KW (movement only) ★★★	2,200	2,700	3,500

E. HOWARD & CO. (continued)

I size (10 size), 15 jewels, guilded, key wind, serial number 3,404.

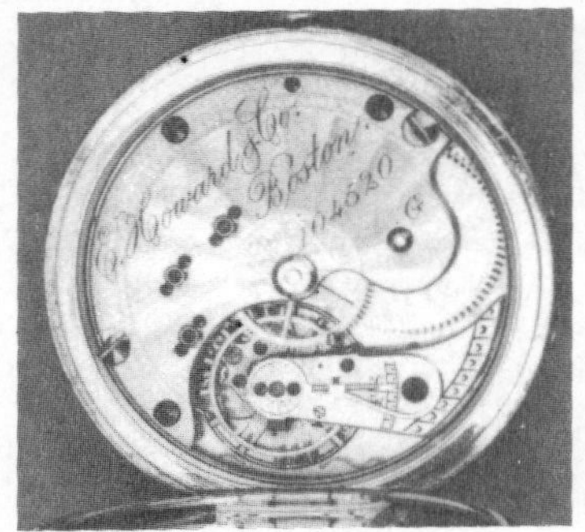

Series VI, 6 or G size, 15 jewels, stem wind, serial number 104,520.

G SIZE (6)

Series or Name — Description	Avg	Ex-Fn	Mint
VI, 15J, gilded, KW, 18K, HC	$1,400	$1,800	$2,400
VI, 15J, gilded or nickel, SW, 18K, HC	1,000	1,400	1,900
VI, 15J, gilded or nickel, SW, 14K, HC	800	1,100	1,600
VI, 15J (movement only)	175	225	350

E. HOWARD WATCH CO.
Waltham, Massachusetts
1903 — 1930

The Howard name was purchased by the Keystone Watch Case Co. in 1902. The watches are marked "E. Howard Watch Co. Boston, U. S. A." There were no patent rights transferred, just the Howard name. The "Edward Howard" chronometer was the highest grade, 16 size, and was introduced in 1912 for $350.

ESTIMATED SERIAL NUMBERS AND PRODUCTION DATES

Date	Serial No.
1903	900,000
1909	980,000
1912	1,100,000
1915	1,285,000
1917	1,340,000
1921	1,400,000
1930	1,500,000

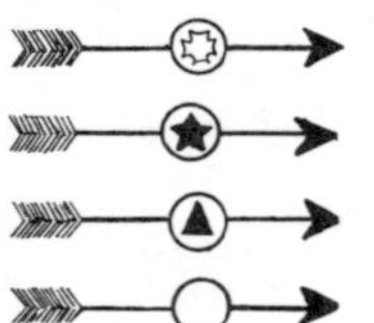

The opposite arrows denote number of jewels and adjustments in each grade.
Cross—23 jewel, 5 positions

Star—21 jewel, 5 positions

Triangle—19 jewel, 5 positions

Circle—17 jewel, 3 positions

E. HOWARD WATCH CO.
(KEYSTONE)
16 SIZE

Series or Name — Description	Avg	Ex-Fn	Mint
Series 0, 23J, BRG, HCI5P, DR, Ruby banking pins	$425	$500	$650
Series 0, 23J, BRG, HCI5P, DR, jeweled barrel	475	550	695
Series 0, 23J, BRG, HCI5P, DR, OF, 14K	800	895	995

E. Howard Watch Co., Series 0, 16 size, 23 jewels, in original E. Howard Watch Co. swing-out movement Keystone Extra gold filled case.

Series or Name — Description	Avg	Ex-Fn	Mint
No. 1, 21J, BRG, HCI5P, DR ★★★	300	345	450
Series 1, 21J, BRG, HCI5P, DR	235	260	325
Series 2, 17J, BRG, HCI5P, DR, HC	175	200	250
Series 2, 17J, BRG, HCI5P, DR, OF	120	135	175
Series 3, 17J, ¾, HCI3P, DR, Model 1905	90	100	135
Series 3, 17J, OF, 14K	375	450	525
No. 5, 19J, GJS, BRG, HC ★	400	550	850
Series 5, 19J, BRG, HCI5P, DR, 14K	475	550	695
Series 5, 19J, BRG, HCI5P, DR, 1907 Model	185	220	275
Series 9, 17J, ¾, HCI5P, DR	175	220	285
Series 9, 17J, ¾, HCI5P, DR, 14K	450	500	595
Series 10, 21J, BRG, HCI5P, DR	235	260	375
No. 10, 21J, BRG, HCI5P, DR	245	275	395
Series 11, 21J, R.R. Chrono.,HCI5P, DR	235	260	375
"Edward Howard," 23 blue sapphire J, HCI6P, GJS, GT, DR — Serial numbers below 300, without box ★★	6,000	7,000	9,000

Series 11, Railroad Chronometer, 16 size, 21 jewels, adjusted to HCI5P, serial number 1317534.

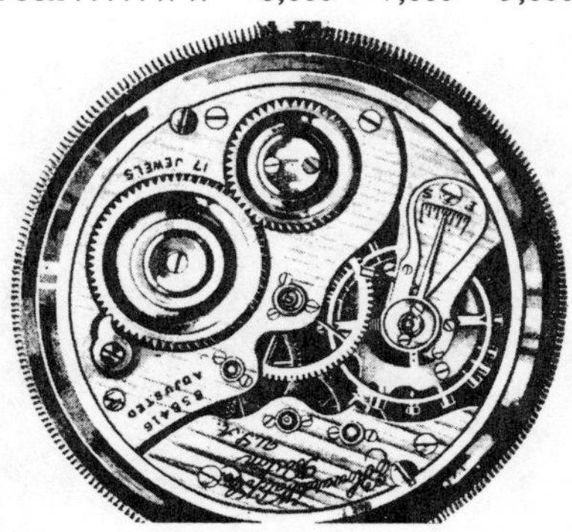

Edward Howard Model, 16 size, 23 blue sapphire jewels, frosted gold bridge, serial number 77, c. 1914.

Series 11, Railroad Chronometer, 16 size, 21 jewels, adjusted to HCI5P, serial number 1317534.

Edward Howard Model, 16 size, 23 blue sapphire jewels, frosted gold bridge, serial number 77, c. 1914.

Series or Name — Description	Avg	Ex-Fn	Mint
"Edward Howard," 23 blue sapphire J, HCI6P, GJS, GT, DR — Serial numbers below 300, with original box and papers ★★	8,000	9,000	11,000
23J, E. Howard W. Co. S# on movement and Waltham S# under dial (mfg. by Waltham), 14K ★★	1,200	1,400	1,600
17J Hamilton Model, ¾	225	275	295

12 SIZE

Series or Name — Description	Avg	Ex-Fn	Mint
Series 6, 19J, BRG, DR, HCI5P, 1908 Model, 14K, HC	$350	$375	$425
Series 6, 19J, BRG, DR, HCI5P, 14K, OF	195	235	295
Series 6, 19J, BRG, DR, HCI5P	75	100	125
Series 7, 17J, BRG, DR, HCI3P, 14K, OF	325	360	390
Series 7, 17J, BRG, DR, HCI3P	100	110	135
Series 8, 21J, BRG, DR, HCI5P	135	140	165
Series 8, 23J, BRG, DR, HCI5P, 14K, OF	400	475	575
Series 8, 23J, BRG, DR, HCI5P	165	190	275
Series 8, 23J, BRG, DR, HCI5P, 14K, HC	450	525	625

Series 8, 12 size, 23 jewels, adjusted to HCI5P, serial number 1105787.

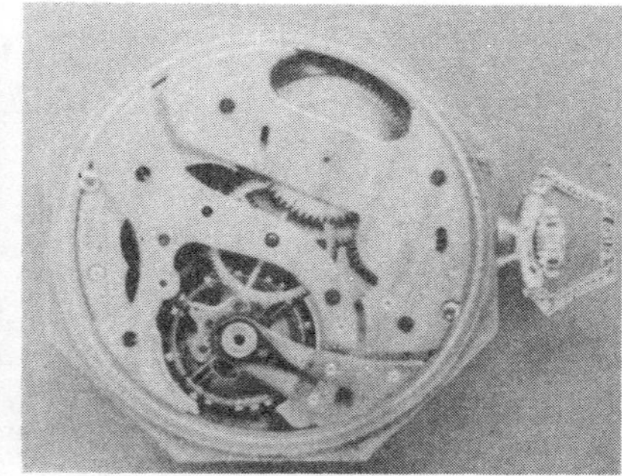

E. Howard Watch Co., 10 size, 17 jewels, HCI3P, serial number 61230.

10 SIZE

Series or Name — Description	Avg	Ex-Fn	Mint
Thin Model, 21J, ADJ, 14K case	$190	$220	$275
Thin Model, 19J, ADJ, 14K case	160	190	250
Thin Model, 17J, ADJ, 14K case	135	180	240

Note: Found with octagon, decagon, hexagon, triad, and cushion shaped cases.

ILLINOIS SPRINGFIELD WATCH CO.
Springfield, Illinois
1869 — 1927

The Illinois Springfield Watch Company was organized mainly through the efforts of J. C. Adams. The first directors were J. T. Stuart, W. B. Miller, John Williams, John W. Bunn, George Black and George Passfield. In 1879 the company changed all its watches to a quick train movement by changing the number of teeth in the fourth wheel. The first mainspring made by the company was used in 1882. The next year soft enamel dials were used.

The Illinois Watch Co. used more names on its movements than any other watch manufacturer. To identify all of them requires extensive knowledge by the collector plus a good working knowledge of watch mechanics. Engraved on some early movements, for example, are "S. W. Co." or "I. W. Co., Springfield, Ill." To the novice these abbreviations might be hard to understand, thus making Illinois watches difficult to identify. But one saving clue is that the location "Springfield, Illinois" appears on most of these watches. It is important to learn how to identify these type watches because some of them are extremely collectible. Examples of some of the more valuable of these are: the Benjamin Franklin (size 18 or 16, 25 or 26 jewels), Paillard's Non-Magnetic, Pennsylvania Special, C & O, and B & O railroad models.

The earliest movements made by the Illinois Watch Co. are listed below. They made the first watch in early 1872, but the company really didn't get off the ground until 1875. Going by the serial number, the first watch made was the Stuart. Next was the Mason, followed by the Bunn, the Miller, and finally the Currier. The first stem-wind was made in 1875.

The Illinois Watch Company was sold to Hamilton Watch Co. in 1927. The Illinois factory continued to produce Illinois watches under the new management until 1932. After 1933 Hamilton produced watches bearing the Illinois name in their own factory until 1939.

Illinois made watches for other companies which are listed below. These watches, for the most part, did not contain the Illinois name. But most all contain the Illinois serial numbers (Exceptions: Ball, Paillard, & J. P. Stevens). Their age can be determined by simply looking up the serial numbers on the Illinois Serial Numbers List, and the model can be compared to the Illinois model diagrams for identification purposes.

(See **Illinois Identification of Movements** section located at the end of the Illinois price section to identify the movement, size and model number of your watch.)

(Prices are with gold filled cases except where noted.)

ILLINOIS ESTIMATED SERIAL NUMBERS AND PRODUCTION DATES

Date	Serial No.	Date	Serial No.	Date	Serial No.
1872	5,000	1893	1,120,000	1914	2,600,000
1873	20,000	1894	1,160,000	1915	2,700,000
1874	50,000	1895	1,220,000	1916	2,800,000
1875	75,000	1896	1,250,000	1917	3,000,000
1876	100,000	1897	1,290,000	1918	3,200,000
1877	145,000	1898	1,330,000	1919	3,400,000
1878	210,000	1899	1,370,000	1920	3,600,000
1879	250,000	1900	1,410,000	1921	3,750,000
1880	300,000	1901	1,450,000	1922	3,900,000
1881	350,000	1902	1,500,000	1923	4,000,000
1882	400,000	1903	1,650,000	1924	4,500,000
1883	450,000	1904	1,700,000	1925	4,700,000
1884	500,000	1905	1,800,000	1926	4,800,000
1885	550,000	1906	1,840,000	1927	5,000,000
1886	600,000	1907	1,900,000	(Sold to Hamilton)	
1887	700,000	1908	2,100,000	1928	5,200,000
1888	800,000	1909	2,150,000	1929	5,350,000
1889	900,000	1910	2,200,000	1930	5,400,000
1890	1,000,000	1911	2,300,000	1931	5,500,000
1891	1,040,000	1912	2,400,000	1932	5,600,000
1892	1,080,000	1913	2,500,000		

(See **Illinois Identification of Movements** section located at the end of the Illinois price section to identify the movement, size and model number of your watch.)

(Prices are with gold filled cases except where noted.)

Illinois Watch Co., Bates Model, 18 size, 7 jewels, key wind & set, serial number 43876, c. 1874.

Bunn, 18 size, 16 jewels, hunting case, serial number 1,185,809.

ILLINOIS
18 SIZE

Grade or Name — Description	Avg	Ex-Fn	Mint
Alleghany, 11J, KW, Silveroid	$65	$75	$120
Alleghany, 11J, M#1, NI, KWM#	80	95	140
Alleghany, 11J, M#2, NI, Transition	75	85	100
America, 7J, M#3, Silveroid	65	75	90
America, 7J, M#1-2, KW, FULL	85	100	135
America Special, 7J, M#1-2, KW, FULL	95	115	155
Army & Navy, 19J, GJS, HCI5P, FULL	240	275	385
Army & Navy, 21J, GJS, HCI5P, FULL	265	300	435

ILLINOIS WATCH CO., 18 SIZE (continued)

Grade or Name — Description	Avg	Ex-Fn	Mint
B & O R.R. Special, 17J, GJS, ADJ	250	285	475
B & O R.R. Special, 21J, GJS, NI, ADJ	800	1,100	1,600
B & R Standard, 24J, GJS, ADJ	1,300	1,500	2,200
Bates, 7J, M#1-2, KW, FULL	120	130	160
Benjamin Franklin U.S.A., 17J, ADJ, NI	500	600	835
Benjamin Franklin U.S.A., 21J, GJS, HCI6P, NI ★	900	1,100	1,500
Benjamin Franklin U.S.A., 21J, GJS, HCI5P, NI ★	800	1,000	1,400
Benjamin Franklin U.S.A., 24J, GJS, HCI6P, FULL, NI, DMK ★	2,000	2,200	3,000
Benjamin Franklin U.S.A., 25J, GJS, HCI6P, FULL, NI, DMK ★★★★	6,000	6,500	8,500
Benjamin Franklin U.S.A., 26J, GJS, HCI6P, FULL, DR, NI, DMK ★★★	5,000	6,000	7,500
Bunn, 15J, M#1, KW, KS, FULL, OF	675	775	975
Bunn, 15J, M#1, KW, KS, ADJ, FULL	700	825	1,050
Bunn, 15J, KW/SW transition	375	400	565
Bunn, 15J, KW, Coin	450	480	535
Bunn, 15J, KW, M#1, HC	600	700	950
Bunn, 16J, KW, OF	500	650	825
Bunn, 17J, SW, M#1, HC ★	275	300	485
Bunn, 17J, SW, NI, Coin	125	140	185
Bunn, 17J, SW, M#3, 5th pinion, gilded	550	600	750
Bunn, 17J, SW, NI, FULL	125	145	195
Bunn, 19J, SW, NI, FULL, OF, LS, GJS	230	270	395
Bunn, 19J, SW, OF, Coin	200	225	350
Bunn, 19J, SW, GJS, FULL, HC ★	295	350	575
Bunn, 21J, SW, OF, Coin ★	150	195	375
Bunn, 21J, SW, GJS, FULL, HC ★	350	375	495
Bunn, 21J, M#5&6, OF, LS, NI, FULL, GJS ★	185	250	375
Bunn, 24J, SW, NI, FULL, LS, GJS ★	525	650	1,000
Bunn, 24J, SW, NI, FULL, LS, GJS, HC ★	700	900	1,350
Bunn Special, 17J, GJS, ADJ, DR, OF	125	155	225
Bunn Special, 17J, GJS, ADJ, DR, 2-Tone ★	145	160	285
Bunn Special, 17J, SW, Silveroid ★	95	115	150

Bunn Special, 18 size 24 jewels, adjusted, serial number 1413435.

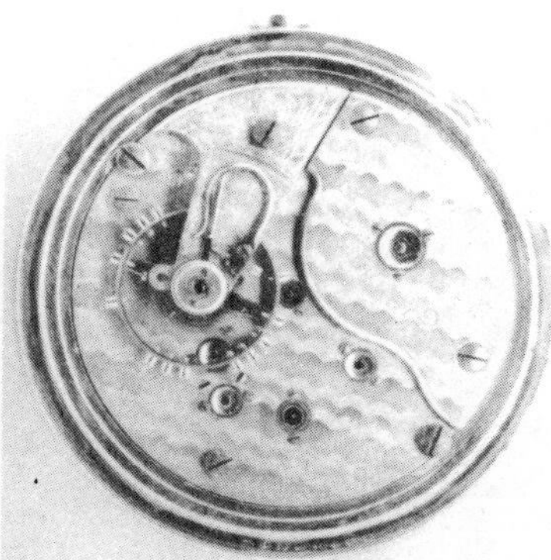

Bunn Special, 18 size, 26 Ruby jewels, "J. Home & Co." on dial, adjusted to six positions, gold jewel settings, serial number 2019415

ILLINOIS WATCH CO., 18 SIZE (continued)

Grade or Name — Description	Avg	Ex-Fn	Mint
Bunn Special, 17J, SW, GJS, ADJ, HC ★	250	300	400
Bunn Special, 19J, GJS, ADJ, DR	200	250	375
Bunn Special, 21J, SW, Coin	125	140	175
Bunn Special, 21J, GJS, ADJ, HC	225	290	375
Bunn Special, 21J, GJS, ADJ, DR, OF	140	165	250
Bunn Special, 21J, GJS, HCI5P, HC, 14K	825	875	1,000
Bunn Special, 21J, GJS, ADJ, 2-Tone	160	195	250
Bunn Special, 21J, GJS, HCI5P, DR	160	195	290
Bunn Special, 21J, Extra, GJS	185	225	365
Bunn Special, 23J, GJS, ADJ, DR, OF	300	350	425
Bunn Special, 23J, GJS, HCI6P, DR, OF	325	375	475
Bunn Special, 23J, GJS, HCI6P, DR, 2-Tone, OF	325	365	475
Bunn Special, 23J, GJS, ADJ, DR, HC ★	1,800	2,200	2,400
Bunn Special, 24J, GJS, HCI5P, DR, HC	700	750	975
Bunn Special, 24J, GJS, HCI5P, DR, 14K, HC	1,300	1,400	1,600
Bunn Special, 24J, GJS, HCI5P, DR, OF	465	595	850
Bunn Special, 24J, GJS, HCI6P, DR, OF	575	650	900
Bunn Special, 25J, GJS, HCI6P, DR ★★★	7,000	8,000	10,000
Bunn Special, 26J, GJS, HCI6P, DR ★★	5,400	5,800	6,400
Central Truck Railroad, 15J, KW, KS	200	275	400
Chesapeake & Ohio Special, 21J, GJS, 2-Tone ★	900	1,100	1,600
Chesapeake & Ohio Special, 24J, NI, ADJ, GJS ★	1,600	1,900	2,250
Columbia, 11J, M#3, 5th Pinion	100	120	150
Columbia, 11J, M#1 & 2, FULL, KW	70	80	120
Columbia, 11J, M#1 & 2, Silveroid	45	50	65
Columbia Special, 11J, M#1-2-3, FULL, KW	65	90	125
Columbia Special, 11J, M#1-2-3, FULL, KW, transition	75	80	95
Comet, 11J, M#3, OF, LS, SW	65	70	85
Commodore, 17J, HC	150	185	275
Currier, 11J, KW, FULL, OF	85	120	160
Currier, 11J, KW, FULL, Coin	85	120	150
Currier, 11J, KW, HC	100	120	160
Currier, 11J, KW/SW, HC	85	120	160
Currier, 11J, transition, OF	75	85	100
Currier, 11J, M#3, OF	75	85	95

Diurnal, 18 size, 7 jewels, key wind & set, only one run, total production 2,000, serial number 86757.

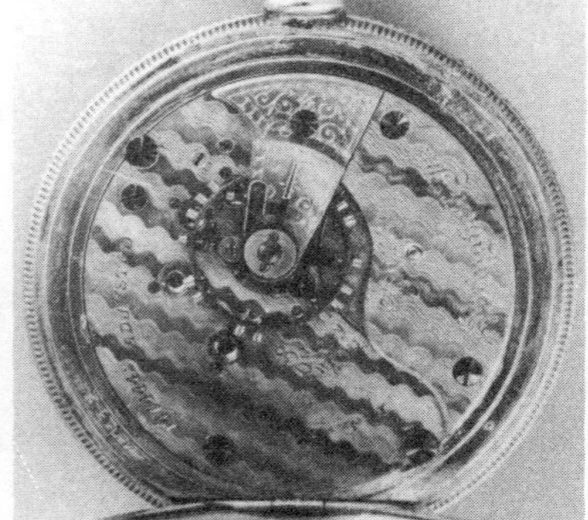

Ill. W. Co., 18 size, 17 jewels, adjusted, 2-tone movement, serial number 1404442.

ILLINOIS WATCH CO., 18 SIZE (continued)

Grade or Name — Description	Avg	Ex-Fn	Mint
Currier, 13J, M#3, OF	80	90	110
Dauntless, 11J	70	80	100
Dean, 15J, M#1, KW, FULL, HC	150	175	225
Diurnal, 7J, KW, KS, HC, Coin ★	75	95	125
Eastlake, 11J, SW, KW, Transition	75	90	120
Enterprise, M#2, ADJ	75	90	120
Eureka, 11J	75	90	110
Forest City, 11J, HC	85	95	135
General Grant or General Lee, 11J, M#1, KW	195	220	295
Hoyt, 9-11J, M#1-2, KW, FULL	85	100	135
Illinois Watch Co., 11J, M#1-2, KW, FULL	60	70	95
Illinois Watch Co., 11J, M#3	65	80	95
Illinois Watch Co., 13J, M#1-2, KW, FULL	80	95	120
Illinois Watch Co., 15J, M#1-2, KW, FULL	85	100	125
Illinois Watch Co., 15J, G#106, KW, ADJ, FULL, NI	100	125	175
Illinois Watch Co., 17J, M#3, 5th Pinion	200	225	275
Illinois Watch Co., 15J, SW, ADJ, DMK, NI	75	80	95
Illinois Watch Co., 15J, transition	65	70	85
Illinois Watch Co., 15J, SW, Silveroid	50	60	70
Illinois Watch Co., 15J, SW, 9K, HC	300	400	575
Illinois Watch Co., 17J, SW, Silveroid	55	60	75
Illinois Watch Co., 17J, SW, ADJ	80	90	105
Illinois Watch Co., 17J, transition	90	100	125
Interior, 7J, KW, FULL	80	110	125
Interior, 7J, M#3	70	85	110
Interstate Chronometer, 17J, HC	350	475	625
Interstate Chronometer, 17J, OF	300	350	525
Interstate Chronometer, 23J, HCI5P, GJS, NI, OF	950	1,050	1,300
Interstate Chronometer, 23J, HCI5P, GJS, NI, HC	1,050	1,100	1,450
Iowa W. Co., 7J, M#1-2, KW, FULL	125	175	250
King of the Road, 16&17J, NI, OF & HC, LS, FULL, ADJ ★	350	425	625
Lafayette, 24J, GJS, HCI6P, NI, SW, OF	900	1,050	1,400
Lakeshore, 17J, OF, LS, NI, FULL, SW	70	80	135
Landis W. Co., 7-11J	85	90	145
Liberty Bell, 17J, NI, SW, FULL	70	80	110
Liberty Bell, 17J, Silveroid	45	55	65

Miller, 18 size, 17 jewels, 5th pinion model which changes hunting case to open face.

Pennsylvania Special, 18 size, 26 jewels, adjusted to HCI6P, 2-tone movement, serial number 1742913.

ILLINOIS WATCH CO., 18 SIZE (continued)

Grade or Name — Description	Avg	Ex-Fn	Mint
A. Lincoln, 21J, Silveroid	65	75	125
A. Lincoln, 21J, HCI5P, NI, GJS, HC	135	150	250
A. Lincoln, 21J, HCI5P, NI, FULL, DR, OF, GJS	125	145	185
Maiden Lane, 17J, 5th Pinion	395	450	595
Manhatten, 11J, HC, NI, FULL, KW, LS	75	95	135
Mason, 7J, KW, KS, HC, FULL	85	125	195
Miller, 15J, Silveroid	75	85	120
Miller, 15J, M#1, HC, KW, FULL	100	125	175
Miller, 15J, M#1, HC, KW, FULL, ADJ	175	200	280
Miller, 15J, KW, FULL, OF	100	120	150
Miller, 17J, 5th Pinion, ADJ	275	300	375
Monarch W. Co., 17J, NI, ADJ, SW, FULL	100	125	190
Montgomery Ward, 17J, OF, GJS	95	120	165
Montgomery Ward, 21J	125	150	195
Montgomery Ward Timer, 21J, Silveroid	95	110	135
Montgomery Ward, 24J, OF	995	1,200	1,500
Montgomery Ward, 24J, HC ★	1,500	1,700	2,000
Muscatine W. Co., 15J, LS, NI, HC	120	135	195
Non-Magnetic W. Co., 21J, OF	225	275	375
Paillard Non-Magnetic W. Co., 15J, NI	60	75	95
Paillard Non-Magnetic W. Co., 17J, GJS, NI, HCI5P	75	80	120
Paillard Non-Magnetic W. Co., 21J, GJS, NI, HCI5P	195	225	295
Paillard Non-Magnetic W. Co., 23J, GJS, NI, HCI5P	600	800	1,000
Paillard Non-Magnetic W. Co., 24J, GJS, NI, HCI5P	1,200	1,400	1,700
Pennsylvania Special, 17J, GJS, HCI3P ★	600	700	850
Pennsylvania Special, 21J, DR, HCI5P ★	850	1,000	1,500
Pennsylvania Special, 24J, DR, GJS, ADJ ★	1,600	2,000	3,000
Pennsylvania Special, 25J, DR, GJS, ADJ, NI ★★	5,000	5,800	6,500
Pennsylvania Special, 26J, DR, GJS, ADJ, NI ★★	5,000	5,800	6,500
Plymouth W. Co., 17J, SW, FULL	85	100	135
Potomac, 17J, OF, FULL, ADJ, NI	125	135	155
The President, 17J, DMK, FULL, 10K gold case	700	800	1,000
The Railroader, 15J, OF, FULL, ADJ, NI	160	195	325
Railroad King, 15-17J, FULL, NI, ADJ	350	400	575
Railway Engineer, 15J	160	175	250
Railway Regulator, 15J, KW, KS, gilt	375	500	675

The President, 18 size, 17 jewels, chalmer patented regulator, serial number 1,240,909.

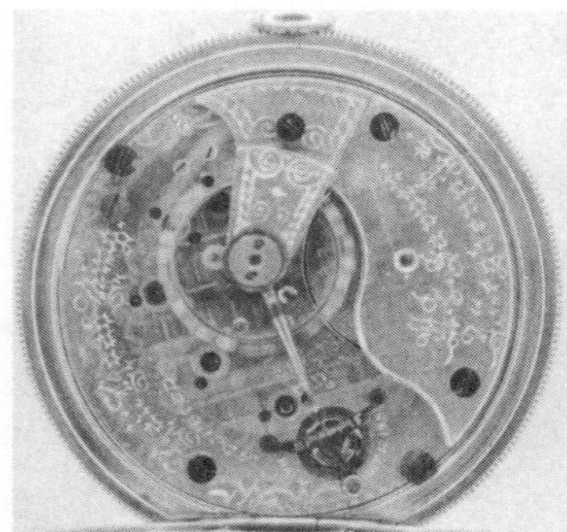

Railroad King, 18 size, 17 jewels, Fifth Pinion Model, adjusted, note Chalmer patented regulator, serial number 1160836

Sears & Roebuck Special, 18 size, 17 jewels, serial number 1,481,879.

Washington Watch Co., Lafayette model, 18 size, 24 Ruby jewels, gold jewel settings, adjusted, serial number 3392897

Grade or Name — Description	Avg	Ex-Fn	Mint
S. W. Co., 15J, M#1, KW, HC	85	95	140
Sears & Roebuck Special, 17J, GJS, NI, DMK, ADJ	95	120	165
Senate, 17J, NI, DMK, FULL	95	110	175
Southern R.R. Special, 21J, LS, ADJ, OF ★	800	900	1,250
Southern R.R. Special, 21J, M#5, LS, ADJ, HC ★	1,000	1,100	1,400
J. P. Stevens, 17J, SW. FULL, NI	650	700	950
Stuart, 15J, M#1, KW, KS	500	625	850
Stuart, 15J, M#1, KW, KS, transition ★	375	400	550
Stuart, 15J, M#1, KW, KS, marked ADJ ★★	700	800	950
Stuart, ADJ, KW, Abbotts Conversion, 18K, HC ★★	1,500	1,700	1,950
Stuart, 15J, M#1, KW, KS, Coin ★★	400	525	850
Stuart, 17J, M#3, 5th Pinion ★★	375	450	875
Stuart, 17J, M#3, 5th Pinion, ADJ ★★	500	600	925
Transition Models, 17J, OF	120	130	150
Time King, 17J, OF, LS, FULL, NI	100	125	185
Time King, 21J, OF, LS, FULL	135	185	275
Vault Time Lock for Mosler, 15J, 72 hr.	65	75	95

Vault Time Lock for Mosler Lock Co., Covington, Ky. Movement is 18 size, 15 jewels, open face, Model number 6, serial number 4576540. Note 72 hour dial.

ILLINOIS WATCH CO., 18 SIZE (continued)

Grade or Name — Description	Avg	Ex-Fn	Mint
Washington W. Co. (See Army & Navy, Liberty Bell, Lafayette, Senate)			
65, 15J, HC, LS, M#2	75	90	125
101, 11J, FULL, SW, KW, OF	60	80	120
101, 11J, SW, KW, Silveroid	50	70	95
101, 11J, SW, KW, HC	75	95	150
102, 13J, SW, KW, Silveroid	50	70	125
102, 13J, SW, KW, OF	70	80	125
102, 13J, FULL, SW, KW, HC	75	85	140
104, 15J, M#2, HC ★★	250	300	585
104, 17J, M#3, OF ★★★	275	325	650
105, 17J, M#3, OF ★★★	375	475	725
105, 15J, M#2, GJS, ADJ, FULL, KW, KS, HC ★★	275	350	650
106, 15J, ADJ, FULL, KW, KS	115	130	160
444, 17J, OF, NI, ADJ, FULL	70	80	125
445, 19J, GJS, 2-Tone, HC ★★	1,000	1,200	1,500
1905 Special, 21J, OF, NI, HCI5P	300	400	600

ILLINOIS
16 SIZE

Grade or Name — Description	Avg	Ex-Fn	Mint
Adams Street, 17J, ¾, SW, NI, DMK, HC	$185	$225	$350
Adams Street, 21J, 3F brg, NI, DMK	250	375	450
Ak-Sar-Ben (Nebraska backward), 17J, OF, GCW	110	125	165
Ariston, 21J, GJS, HCI6P, OF	395	475	695
Ariston, 23J, GJS, HCI6P, OF	600	800	1,100
Ariston, 23J, GJS, HCI6P, HC	700	900	1,200
Arlington Special, 17J, OF	70	80	125
Arlington Special, 17J, OF, Silveroid	45	50	65
Army & Navy, 19J, GJS, HCI5P, NI, 1F brg	125	150	175
Army & Navy, 21J, GJS, HCI5P, 1F brg	135	155	185

Ben Franklin, 16 size, 25 jewels, gold jewel settings, gold train, serial number 2242138.

Bunn Special, Model 163, 16 size, 23 jewels, gold jewel settings, gold train, 60 hour movement, serial number 5421504.

ILLINOIS WATCH CO., 16 SIZE (continued)

Grade or Name — Description	Avg	Ex-Fn	Mint
B & M Special, 17J, BRG, HCI4P	135	150	225
B & O Standard, 21J	250	375	475
Benjamin Franklin, 17J, ADJ, DMK, ¾	200	325	475
Benjamin Franklin, 21J, GJS, HCI5P, DR, GT, ¾	500	650	850
Benjamin Franklin, 25J, GJS, HCI6P, DR, GT, ¾, OF ★	3,500	4,000	4,700
Benjamin Franklin, 25J, GJS, HCI6P, DR, GT, ¾, HC ★★	4,500	5,000	6,000
Bunn, 17J, LS, OF, NI, ¾, GJS, HCI5P	95	110	150
Bunn, 19J, LS, OF, NI, ¾, GJS, HCI5P	100	115	165
Bunn, 19J, LS, OF, NI, ¾, GJS, HCI5P, 60 hour	275	325	500
Bunn, 19J, marked Jewel Barrel	160	200	300
Bunn Special, 19J, LS, OF, NI, ¾, HCI6P, GT	175	225	290
Bunn Special, 19J, LS, OF, NI, ¾, HCI6P, GT, Silveroid	140	160	200
Bunn Special, 19J, LS, OF, NI, ¾, HCI6P, GT, 60 hour	300	350	465
Bunn Special, 21J, LS, OF, NI, GJS, Silveroid	80	90	120
Bunn Special, 21J, LS, OF, NI, GJS, HC ★★★	650	900	1,200
Bunn Special, 21J, LS, OF, NI, ¾, GJS, HCI6P, GT	125	150	190
Bunn Special, 21J, LS, OF, NI, ¾, GJS, HCI6P, GT, 60 hour	185	225	275
Bunn Special, 21J, LS, OF, NI, ¾, GJS, HCI6P, GT, 60 hr. Elinvar	225	275	375
Bunn Special, 21J, 60 hr., 14K, OF	485	570	675
Bunn Special, 23J, LS, OF, NI, ¾, GJS, HCI6P, GT	275	325	375
Bunn Special, 23J, LS, OF, NI, ¾, GJS, HCI6P, GT, 60 hour	350	450	585
Bunn Special, 23J, LS, OF, NI, ¾, GJS, HCI6P, GT, with 23J 60-hour on dial	450	550	675
Burlington W. Co., 19J, ¾, NI, HCI3P	70	85	125
Burlington W. Co., 19J, BRG, NI, HCI3P	75	90	135
Burlington W. Co., 19J, ¾, NI, HCI3P, Silveroid	40	55	95
Burlington W. Co., 19J, ¾, HC	85	100	195
Burlington W. Co., 19J, 3F brg, NI, HCI3P	75	95	125
Burlington W. Co., 21J, ¾, NI, HCI3P	95	115	150
Burlington W. Co., 21J, HCI6P, GJS ★★	500	600	795
Burlington, Bull Dog, 21J, SW, LS, GJS, GT	175	250	375
Capitol, 19J, OF, ¾, NI, HCI5P	95	125	175
C & O Special, 21J, ¾, NI, ADJ	600	700	900

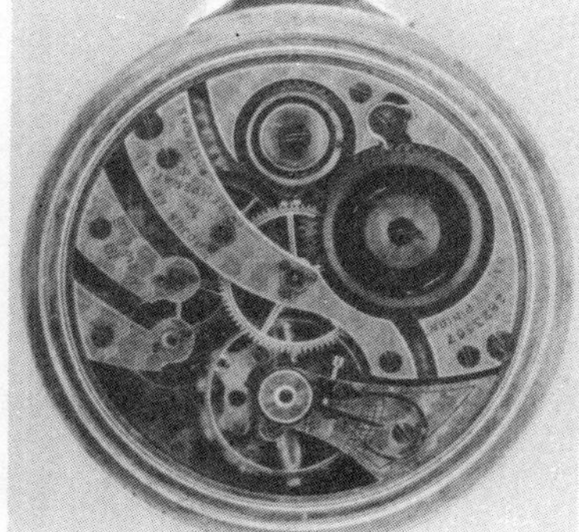

Burlington, 16 size, 19 jewels, gold center wheel, serial number 2823667

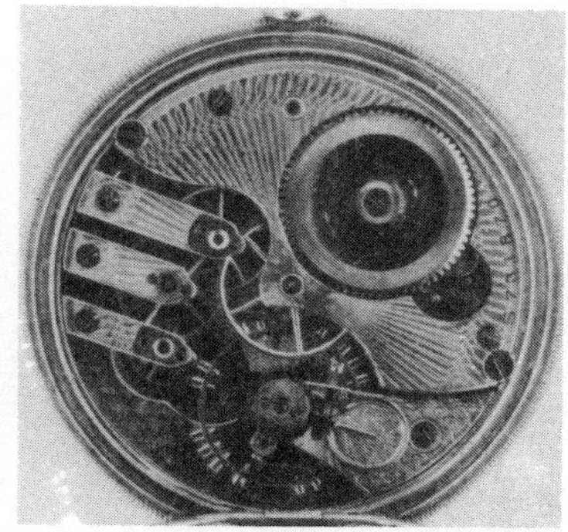

Illinois Watch Co., 16 size, 25 jewels, three-fingered bridge, gold train, hunting. Note serial number S731870.

ILLINOIS WATCH CO., 16 SIZE (continued)

Grade or Name — Description	Avg	Ex-Fn	Mint
DeLong Escapement, 21J, GJS, HCI6P, 14K OF	2,000	3,000	4,985
Diamond, Ruby, Sapphire, 21J, GJS, GT, HCI6P, NI, BRG, DR ★	1,100	1,200	1,500
Diamond, Ruby, Sapphire, 23J, GJS, GT, HCI6P, NI, BRG, DR ★★	2,500	2,800	3,600
Dispatcher, 19J, HCI3P	65	75	135
Forest City, 17J, KW/SW, gilted, FULL	150	175	225
Franklin Street, 15J, ¾, NI, ADJ	65	70	95
Getty Model, 21J	145	180	250
Getty Model, 17J	75	85	120
Great Northern Special, 17J, BRG, ADJ	225	275	375
Great Northern Special, 19J, BRG, ADJ	275	300	465
Great Northern Special, 21J, BRG, ADJ, HCI3P	300	325	535
Illinois Central, 17J, 2-Tone, GT	75	95	120
Illinois Watch Co., 7J, M#1-2-3	60	70	95
Illinois Watch Co., 11J, M#1-2-3	65	75	85
Illinois Watch Co., 11J, ¾, OF	70	80	90
Illinois Watch Co., 11J, ¾, Silveroid	40	50	60
Illinois Watch Co., 11J, ¾, HC	80	90	120
Illinois Watch Co., 15J, M#1-2-3, Silveroid	45	50	65
Illinois Watch Co., 15J, M#1-2-3, HC	75	85	135
Illinois Watch Co., 15J, M#1-2-3, OF	70	90	100
Illinois Watch Co., 15J, ¾, ADJ	85	95	115
Illinois Watch Co., 15J, 3F brg, GJS	80	100	130
Illinois Watch Co., 17J, 14K, HC	500	525	650
Illinois Watch Co., 17J, SW, Silveroid	50	60	70
Illinois Watch Co., 17J, SW, HC	80	90	140
Illinois Watch Co., 17J, M#1-2-3	75	80	95
Illinois Watch Co., 17J, ¾, ADJ	100	120	150
Illinois Watch Co., 17J, 3F brg, GJS, HCI5P	125	150	190
Illinois Watch Co., 19J, M#1, ¾, GJS, HCI5P	150	170	265
Illinois Watch Co., 19J, ¾, BRG, HCI3P	80	90	100
Illinois Watch Co., 21J, Silveroid	65	70	95
Illinois Watch Co., 21J, GJS, HC	120	135	170
Illinois Watch Co., 21J, ¾, GJS, HCI5P	115	130	165

Interstate Chronometer, 16 size, 23 jewels, one-fingered bridge, serial number 2,327,614.

A. Lincoln, 16 size, 21 jewels, gold jewel settings, gold train, adjusted to HCI5P, serial number 2237406.

ILLINOIS WATCH CO., 16 SIZE (continued)

Grade or Name — Description	Avg	Ex-Fn	Mint
Illinois Watch Co., 21J, 3F brg, GJS, HCI5P	150	175	235
Illinois Watch Co., 23J, GJS	185	235	335
Illinois Watch Co., 25J, 3F brg, GJS, HCI5P ★★★★	4,000	4,500	5,500
Interstate Chronometer, 17J, GCW, HCI5P, HC	275	300	450
Interstate Chronometer, 17J, GCW, HCI5P, OF	250	285	400
Interstate Chronometer, 23J, 1F brg, ADJ, OF	900	1,000	1,200
Interstate Chronometer, 23J, 1F brg, ADJ, HC	1,000	1,100	1,350
Lafayette, 23J, 1F brg, GJS, HCI5P, GT	750	850	1,000
Lakeshore, 17J, OF	70	80	100
Lakeshore, 17J, HC	75	90	125
Landis W. Co., 15J	55	65	95
Liberty Bell, 17J	80	95	135
A. Lincoln, 21J, ¾, GJS, HCI5P	95	115	195
Marine Special, 21J, ¾, HCI3P	95	120	175
Monroe, 17J, NI, ¾, OF (Washington W. Co.)	85	110	150
Monroe, 15J, ¾, OF (Washington W. Co.)	75	85	120
Our No. 1, 15J, HC, M#1	145	195	295
Paillard Non-Magnetic Watch Co., 11J, ¾	65	80	100
Paillard Non-Magnetic Watch Co., 15J, ¾	70	85	110
Paillard Non-Magnetic Watch Co., 17J, ¾, HCI5P, DMK	75	90	120
Paillard Non-Magnetic Watch Co., 21J, ¾, GJS, HCI5P, DMK	295	385	550
Pennsylvania Special, 23J, ¾, GJS, HCI5P	995	1,250	1,800
Plymouth W. Co., 17J, HC & OF	80	95	135
Precise, 21J, OF, LS, HCI3P	120	145	190
Quincy Street, 17J, ¾, NI, DMK, ADJ	70	80	100
Railroad Dispatcher, 11J, HC	150	175	250
Railroad Official, 23J, 3F brg	500	600	750
Railway King, 17J, OF	150	195	275
Sangamo, 21J, GJS, HC	250	295	375
Sangamo, 21J, GJS, HCI5P, Silveroid	75	85	110
Sangamo, 21J, ¾, GJS, DR, HCI6P	125	150	190
Sangamo, 23J, ¾, GJS, DR, HCI6P	140	180	275
Sangamo, 25J, M#5, ¾, GJS, DR, HCI6P ★★★	5,500	6,000	7,500

Sangamo, 16 size, 23 jewels, adjusted to HCI6P, gold jewel settings, gold train, serial number 2222797.

Sangamo Special, 16 size, 19 jewels, 60 hour movement, adjusted to HCI6P, gold jewel settings, gold train, serial number 4720522.

ILLINOIS WATCH CO., 16 SIZE (continued)

Grade or Name — Description	Avg	Ex-Fn	Mint
Sangamo, 26J, M#5, ¾, GJS, DR, HCI6P	6,500	7,500	8,500
Sangamo Extra, 21J, ¾, GJS, DR, HCI6P	350	400	600
Sangamo Special, 19J, BRG, GJS, GT, HCI6P	350	375	475
Sangamo Special, 19J, BRG, GJS, GT, HCI6P, 60 hour	400	525	700
Sangamo Special, 19J, BRG, GJS, GT, HCI6P, HC	725	835	1,000
Sangamo Special, 21J, Silveroid	140	180	275
Sangamo Special, 21J, HC	700	800	1,000
Sangamo Special, 21J, BRG, GJS, GT, HCI6P	400	450	600
Sangamo Special, 21J, BRG, GJS, GT, Diamond end cap	400	475	625
Sangamo Special, 23J, BRG, GJS, GT, HCI6P	325	375	450
Sangamo Special, 23J, BRG, GJS, GT, HCI6P, Diamond end stone	360	385	475
Sangamo Special, 23J, BRG, GJS, GT, HCI6P, marked 60 hour, rigid bow	535	690	895
Sangamo Special, 23J, BRG, GJS, GT, HCI6P, **not** marked 60 hour, rigid bow	425	500	600
Sangamo Special, 23J, BRG, GJS, GT, HCI6P, HC	800	925	1,200
Santa Fe Special, 17J, BRG, HCI3P	140	170	225
Santa Fe Special, 21J, ¾, HCI5P, OF	175	250	375
Santa Fe Special, 21J, ¾, HCI5P, HC	275	325	400
Sears, Roebuck & Co. Special, 17J, ADJ	85	100	140
Senate, 17J, OF, NI, ¾	85	100	135
Standard, 15J	55	60	75
Stewart, 17J	65	70	90
Stewart Special, 17J	75	85	110
Time King, 17J, OF	65	75	110
Victor, 21J, ¾, HCI5P	75	85	120
161 Bunn Special, 21J, ¾, HCI6P, 60 hour	175	200	275
161A Bunn Special, 21J, ¾, HCI6P, 60 hour	350	400	475
161A Elinvar Bunn Special, 21J, ¾, HCI6P, 60 hour	350	400	485
161B, Bunn Special, 60 hour, pressed jewels ★★★	1,500	2,000	2,800
163 Bunn Special, 23J, GJS, HCI6P, ¾, 60 hour	350	400	575
163 Elinvar Bunn Special, 23J, GJS, HCI6P, 60 hour ★	675	800	1,000
163A Bunn Special, 23J, GJS, HCI6P, ¾, 60 hour	600	725	925
163A Elinvar Bunn Special, 23J, GJS, HCI6P, ¾, 60 hour	600	725	925

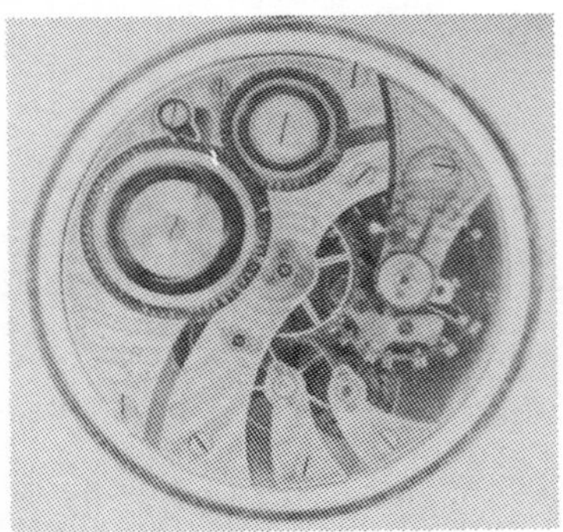

Time King, 16 size, 19 jewels, three positions, tu-tone, serial number 3830534.

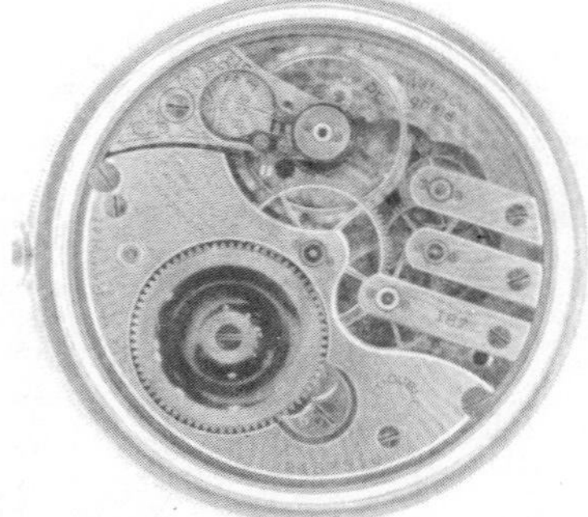

Grade 187, 16 size, 17 Ruby jewels, three-fingered bridge model, gold jewel settings, gold train, HCI5P, serial number 2487510

ILLINOIS WATCH CO., 16 SIZE (continued)

Grade or Name — Description	Avg	Ex-Fn	Mint
163A Elinvar Bunn Special, 23J, GJS, HCI6P, ¾, 60 hour, #206 case, marked 60 hr. on dial ★★	750	850	1,000
167L, 17J, marked	125	150	175
167, 17J	50	60	85
169, 19J, HCI3P	75	80	95
175, 19J, GJS, BRG, HC ★	850	1,000	1,350
177, 19J, SW, LS, 60 hour, HCI5P, OS	400	525	650
179, 21J, HC, 3F brg, marked Ruby Jewels	300	400	585
187, 17J, 3F brg, HCI5P, GJS, GT	200	235	395
189, 21J, 3F brg, HCI6P, GJS, GT, DR, marked Ruby Jewels	325	425	675
333, 15J, HC	85	95	130
555, 17J, ¾, ADJ	90	100	125
777, 17J, ¾, ADJ	90	100	125
900, 19J, LS, HCI3P, Silveroid	65	70	85

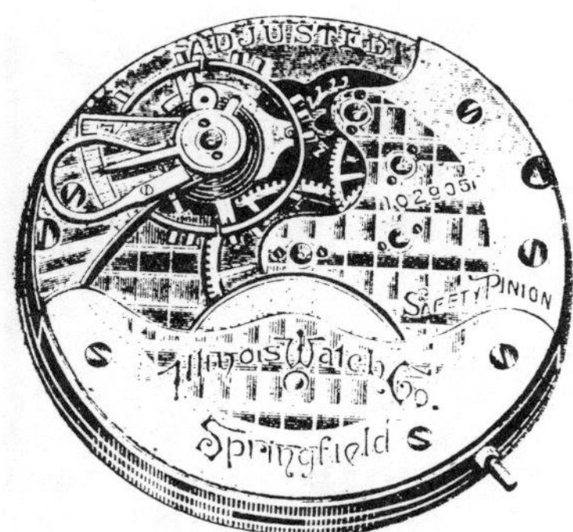

Illnois Watch Co., 14 size, 16 jewels, adjusted to HCI5P:

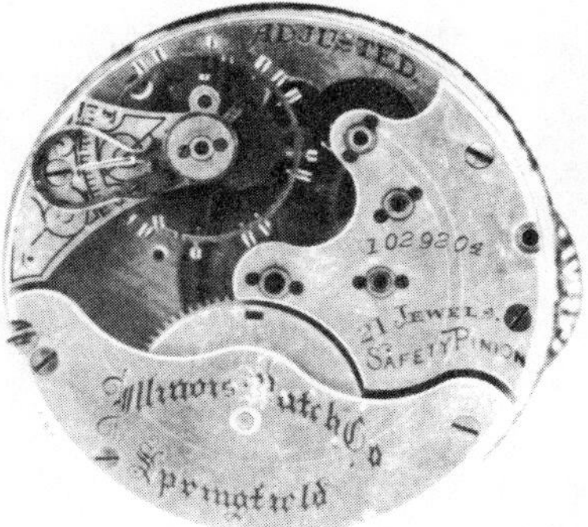

Illinois Watch Co., 14 size, 21 jewels, adjusted, nickel movement, gold jewel settings, serial number 1029204

ILLINOIS
14 SIZE

Grade or Name — Description	Avg	Ex-Fn	Mint
Illinois Watch Co., 7J, M#1-2-3, SW	$40	$50	$65
Illinois Watch Co., 11J, M#1-2-3, SW	50	60	75
Illinois Watch Co., 15J, M#1-2-3, SW	60	70	90
Illinois Watch Co., 16J, M#1-2-3, SW	75	80	115
Illinois Watch Co., 21J, M#1-2-3, SW	90	110	135
Illinois Watch Co., 21J, Silveroid	60	70	90

THE MARQUIS—AUTOCRAT
12 SIZE — THIN MODEL
17 Jewels, Adjusted 3 Positions

Example of Illinois Thin Model, 12 size, 17 jewels, adjusted to 3 positions.

ILLINOIS
12 SIZE and 13 SIZE

Grade or Name — Description	Avg	Ex-Fn	Mint
Aristocrat, 19J, OF	$40	$55	$70
Ariston, 23J, OF	160	175	235
Autocrat, 17J, HCI3P, ¾	60	70	85
Autocrat, 19J, HCI3P, ¾	75	85	120
Benjamin Franklin, 17J, OF	175	250	375
Burlington W. Co., 21J, OF	60	70	80
Central, 17J, OF, 2-Tone	45	50	65
Diamond Ruby Sapphire, 21J, HCI5P, GJS	275	325	435
Elite, 19J, OF	60	70	80
Illini, 21J, HCI5P, 14K, HC	275	300	375
Illini, 21J, HCI5P, BRG, GJS	75	100	145
Illini, 23J, HCI5P, BRG, GJS	135	165	245
Illinois Watch Co., 15J, OF	40	50	65
Illinois Watch Co., 17J, OF, 14K	200	225	290
Illinois Watch Co., 17J, HC, GF	55	65	85
Illinois Watch Co., 19J, OF	65	70	85
Illinois Watch Co., 21J, OF	60	70	95
Illinois Watch Co., 21J, HC	80	90	120
Interstate Chronometer, 21J, GJS, OF	150	175	235
Interstate Chronometer, 21J, GJS, HC	175	200	285
A. Lincoln, 19J, HCI5P, GJS, DR	65	75	95

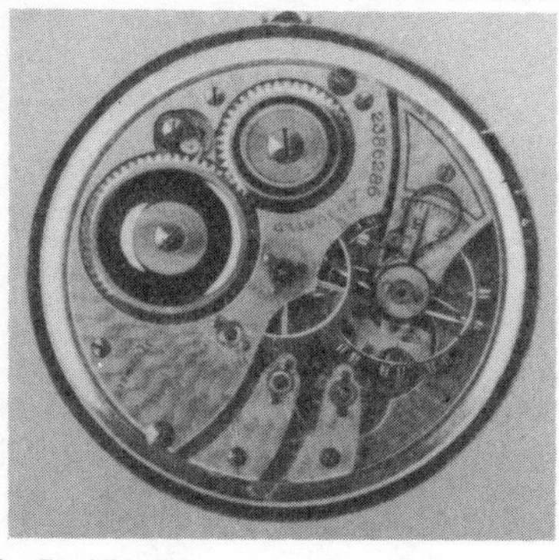

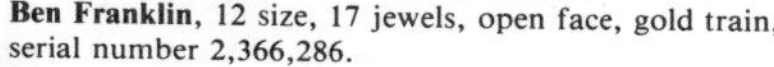

Ben Franklin, 12 size, 17 jewels, open face, gold train, serial number 2,366,286.

Illini, 12 size, 21 jewels, bridge model, serial number 3,650,129. Note five tooth click.

Grade or Name — Description	Avg	Ex-Fn	Mint
A. Lincoln, 21J, HCI5P, DR, GJS	75	85	120
Maiden America, 17J, ADJ	60	70	90
Marquis, 17J, OF	50	60	70
Railroad Dispatch Special, 17J, SW, GT	75	80	95
Santa Fe Special, 21J	95	105	165
Sterling, 17J, OF	35	40	55
Stewart Special, 17J, SW, HCI3P	50	55	60
Stewart Special, 19J, SW, OF, GT	55	60	65
Time King, 19J, SW, HCI3P	60	65	85
Time King, 21J, SW, HCI3P	70	75	110
Transit, 19J, OF, PS	60	65	70
Washington W. Co., 11J, HC	80	110	150
Washington W. Co., Army & Navy, 19J	90	130	165
121, 21J, HCI3P	65	75	95
127, 17J	35	40	55
129, 19J, HCI3P	55	60	65
219, 11J, M#1	30	40	50
403, 15J, BRG	40	45	55
405, 17J, BRG, ADJ	55	65	75
409, 21J, BRG, Diamond, Ruby, Sapphire, HCI5P, GJS	275	325	395

Maiden America, 12 size, 17 jewels, serial number 2820499.

Santa Fe Special, 12 size, 21 jewels, three-quarter plate, serial number 3414422.

ILLINOIS WATCH CO., 12 & 13 SIZE (continued)

Grade or Name — Description	Avg	Ex-Fn	Mint
410, 23J, BRG, GJS, HCI6P, DR	150	170	225
410, 23J, BRG, GJS, HCI6P, DR, 14K, OF	350	375	400

ILLINOIS
8 SIZE

Grade or Name — Description		Avg	Ex-Fn	Mint
Arlington, 7J, ¾	★	$95	$105	$175
Rose LeLand, 13J, ¾	★★	150	175	240
Stanley, 7J, ¾	★★★	185	200	285
Mary Stuart, 15J, ¾	★★	175	200	265
Sunnyside, 11J, ¾	★	95	125	175
151, 7J, ¾		45	50	65
152, 11J, ¾		55	60	70
155, 11J, ¾		65	70	80
155, 11J, ¾, Coin		30	40	55

Illinois Watch Co., 8 size, 7 jewels.

Grade 144, 6 size, 15 jewels, serial number 590290.

ILLINOIS
6 SIZE

Grade or Name — Description	Avg	Ex-Fn	Mint
Illinois W. Co., 7J, LS, HC, 14K	$190	$225	$300
Illinois W. Co., 7J, OF, HC	50	60	85
Illinois W. Co., 7J, OF, Coin	40	45	50
Illinois W. Co., 11J, OF, HC	55	75	100
Illinois W. Co., 15J, OF, HC, 14K	260	285	325
Illinois W. Co., 17J, OF, HC	65	80	120
Illinois W. Co., 19J, OF, HC	75	95	140
Washington W. Co., 15J, HC, Liberty Bell	125	165	250

ILLINOIS
4 SIZE

Grade or Name — Description	Avg	Ex-Fn	Mint
Illinois W. Co., 7J, LS, HC	$50	$55	$95
Illinois W. Co., 11J, LS, HC	60	65	100
Illinois W. Co., 15J, LS, HC	70	75	110

ILLINOIS
0 SIZE

Grade or Name — Description	Avg	Ex-Fn	Mint
Illinois W. Co., 7J, LS, HC, 10K	$150	$190	$250
201, 11J, BRG, NI	75	90	125
203, 15J, BRG, NI	85	110	135
204, 17J, BRG, NI	100	120	150
Interstate Chronometer, 15J, HC, SW	175	200	275
Interstate Chronometer, 17J, HC, SW	185	210	285
Washington W. Co., Liberty Bell, 15J, ADJ	150	175	250
Washington W. Co., Mt. Vernon, 17J, ADJ	160	185	275

Grade 201, 0 size, 11 jewels, originally sold for $8.10.

Grade 203, 0 size, 15 jewels, originally sold for $10.40.

Grade 204, 0 size, 17 jewels, originally sold for $12.83.

MAN'S WRIST WATCH

Style or Grade — Description	Avg	Ex-Fn	Mint
Tonneau, 14K case	$125	$150	$200
Tonneau, gold filled	50	55	70
Tonneau, stainless	25	30	40
Tonneau, sec. bits at 9 o'clock, 14K case	130	155	225
Tonneau, sec. bits at 9 o'clock, gold filled	55	60	75
Tonneau, sec. bits at 9 o'clock, stainless	25	30	45
Square, 14K case	95	125	175
Square, gold filled	35	40	50
Square, stainless	25	30	40

ILLINOIS WATCH CO. (continued)

Grade or Name — Description	Avg	Ex-Fn	Mint
Rectangular, 14K case	95	115	165
Rectangular, gold filled	45	50	60
Rectangular, stainless	25	30	35
Illinois dial, Hamilton mvt., rectangular case	20	25	30
Illinois dial, Hamilton mvt., round case	10	15	22
Military style, with black dial, gold filled	40	45	55
White dial, luminus hand & numbers	40	45	55

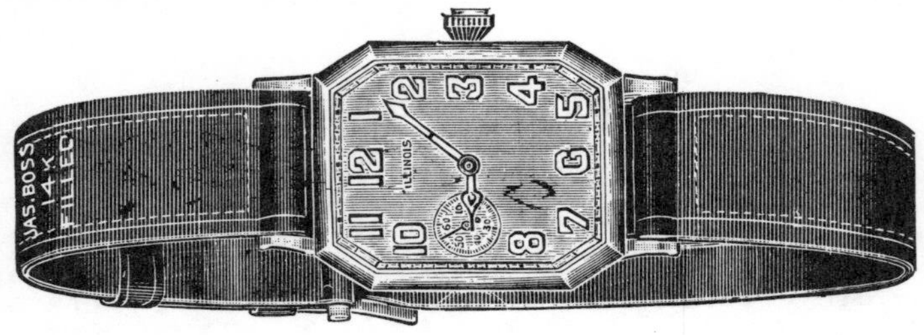

Rectangular, 6/0 size, 15 jewels, gold filled case, originally sold for $49.20.

Rectangular, Grade 207, 12/0 size, 17 jewels.

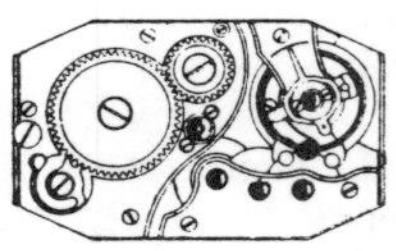

Rectangular, 18/0 size, first, second & third model.

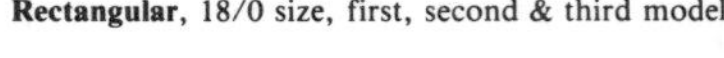

Tonneau, 3/0 size, 17 jewels.

Rectangular, 18/0 size, 17 jewels.

LADY'S WRIST WATCH

Style of Grade — Description	Avg	Ex-Fn	Mint
Locket or Wrist Watch, convertible, 14K case	$55	$65	$85
Locket or Wrist Watch, convertible, gold filled	20	25	35
Locket or Wrist Watch, convertible, stainless	10	15	22
Rectangular, 14K case	50	55	65
Rectangular, gold filled	30	35	45
Square, gold filled	25	30	40
Square, stainless	15	20	32
Oval dial, gold filled	25	30	40
Oval dial, stainless	15	20	30
Purse style watch, with leather cover	40	45	55
Round, Illinois dial, Hamilton mvt., gold filled	15	20	30
Round, Illinois dial, Hamilton mvt., stainless	10	12	20

ILLINOIS SPRINGFIELD WATCH CO.
IDENTIFICATION OF MOVEMENTS
BY MODEL NUMBER

How to Identify Your Watch: Compare the movement of your watch with the illustrations in this section. Upon matching the movement exactly, the model number and size can be determined. While comparing, note the location of the balance, jewels, screws, gears and type of back plate (Full, ¾, Bridge) which will be clues in identifying the movement you have. Having determined the size and model number, you can now find your watch in the main price listing by name or number (which is engraved on the movement).

THE ILLINOIS WATCH COMPANY GRADE AND MODEL CHART

Size	Model	Plate Design	Setting	Hunting or Open Face	Type Barrel	Started w/ Serial No.	Remarks
18	1	Full	Key	Htg	Reg	1	Course train
	2	Full	Lever	Htg	Reg	38,901	Course train
	3	Full	Lever	OF	Reg	46,201	Course train, 5th pinion
	4	Full	Pendant	OF	Reg	1,050,001	Fast train
	5	Full	Lever	Htg	Reg	1,256,101	Fast train, RR Grade
	6	Full	Lever	OF	Reg	1,144,401	Fast train, RR Grade
16	1	Full	Lever	Htg	Reg	1,030,001	Thick model
	2	Full	Pendant	OF	Reg	1,037,001	Thick model
	3	Full	Lever	OF	Reg	1,038,001	Thick model
	4	¾ & brg	Lever	Htg	Reg	1,300,001	Getty model
	5	¾ & brg	Lever	OF	Reg	1,300,601	Getty model
	6	¾ & brg	Pendant	Htg	Reg	2,160,111	DR&Improved RR model
	7	¾ & brg	Pendant	OF	Reg	2,160,011	DR&Improved RR model
	8	¾ & brg	Lever	Htg	Reg	2,523,101	DR&Improved RR model
	9	¾ & brg	Lever	OF	Reg	2,522,001	DR & Improved model
	10	Cent brg	Lever	OF	Motor	3,178,901	Also 17s Ex Thin RR Gr 48 hr
	11	¾	Lever & Pen	OF	Motor	4,001,001	RR grade 48 hr
	12	¾	Lever & Pen	Htg	Motor	4,002,001	RR grade 48 hr
	13	Cent brg	Lever	OF	Motor	4,166,801	Also 17s RR grade 60 hr
	14	¾	Lever	OF	Motor	4,492,501	RR grade 60 hr
	15	¾	Lever	OF	Motor	5,488,301	RR grade 60 hr Elinvar
13	1	brg	Pendant	OF	Motor		Ex Thin gr 538 & 539
14	1	Full	Lever	Htg	Reg	1,009,501	Thick model
	2	Full	Pendant	OF	Reg	1,000,001	Thick model
	3	Full	Lever	OF	Reg	1,001,001	Thick model
12	1	¾	Pendant	OF	Reg	1,685,001	
Thin	2	¾	Pendant	Htg	Reg	1,748,751	
	3	Cent brg	Pendant	OF	Reg	2,337,011	Center bridge
	4	Cent brg	Pendant	Htg	Reg	2,337,001	Center bridge
	5	Cent brg	Pendant	OF	Motor	3,742,201	Center bridge
	6	Cent brg	Pendant	Htg	Motor	4,395,301	Center bridge
12T	1	True Ctr brg	Pendant	OF	Motor	3,700,001	1 tooth click, Also 13s
	2	True Ctr brg	Pendant	OF	Motor	3,869,301	5 tooth click
	3	¾	Pendant	OF	Motor	3,869,201	2 tooth click
8	1	Full	Key or lever	Htg	Reg	100,001	Plate not recessed
	2	Full	Lever	Htg	Reg	100,101	Plate is recessed
6	1	¾	Lever	Htg	Reg	552,001	
4	1	¾	Lever	Htg	Reg	551,501	
0	1	¾	Pendant	OF	Reg	1,815,901	
	2	¾	Pendant	Htg	Reg	1,749,801	
	3	Cent brg	Pendant	OF	Reg	2,644,001	
	4	Cent brg	Pendant	Htg	Reg	2,637,001	

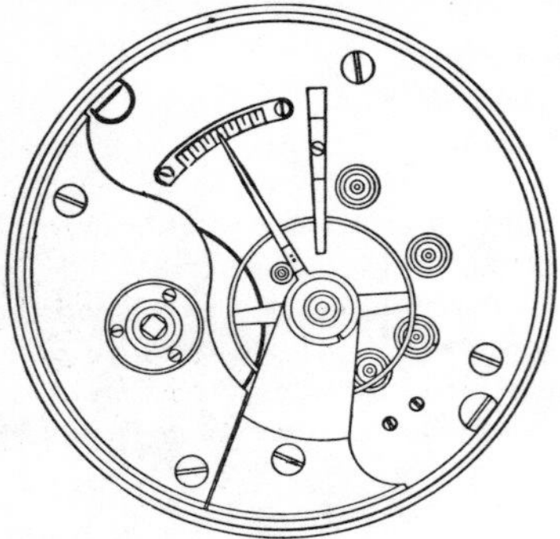

Model 1, 18 size, hunting, key wind & set.

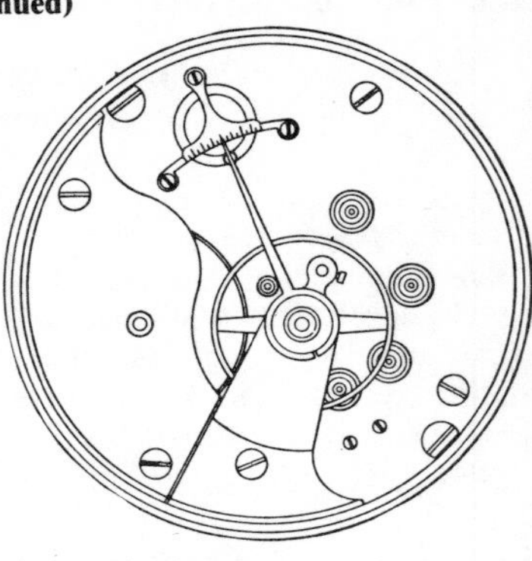

Model 2, 18 size, hunting, lever set, coarse train.

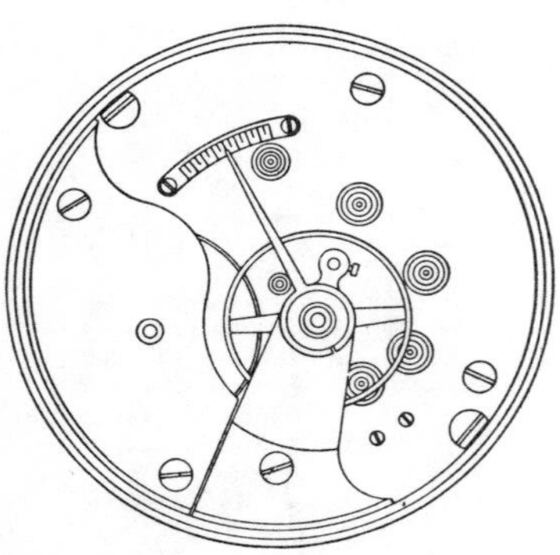

Model 3, 18 size, open face, lever set, coarse train, with fifth pinion.

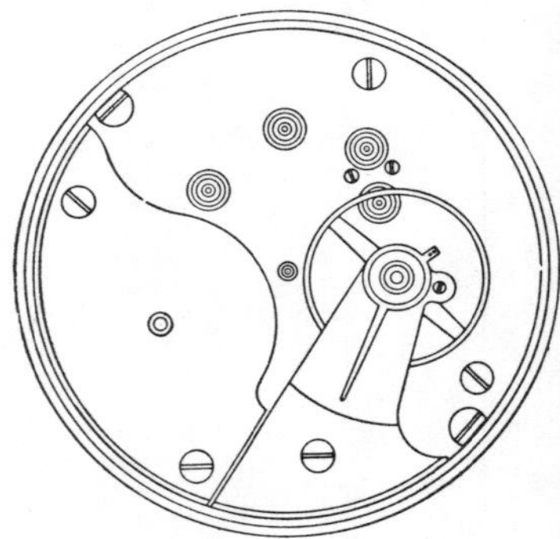

Model 4, 18 size, open face, pendant set, fine train.

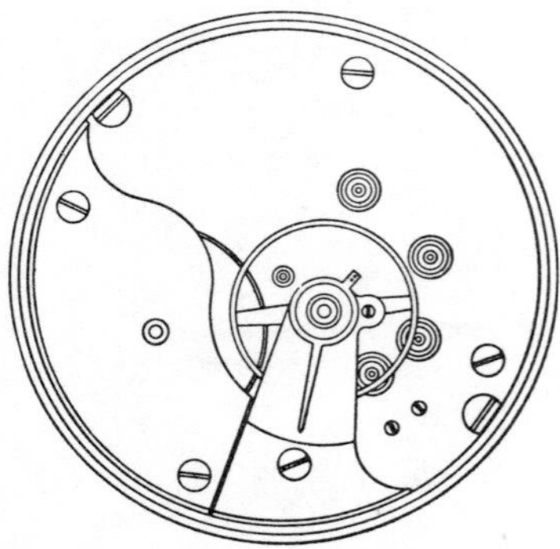

Model 5, 18 size, hunting, lever set, fine train.

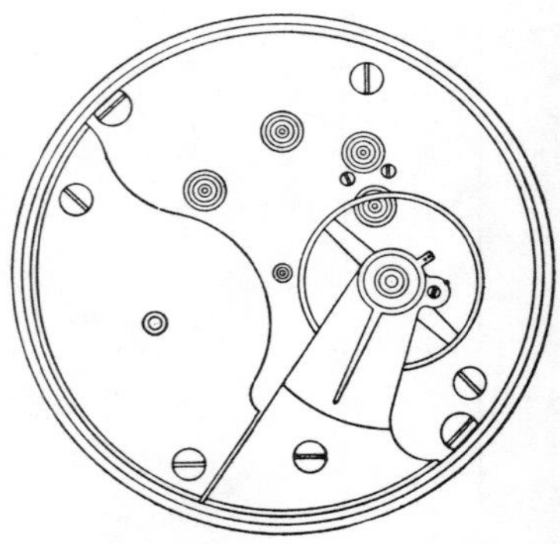

Model 6, 18 size, open face, lever set, fine train.

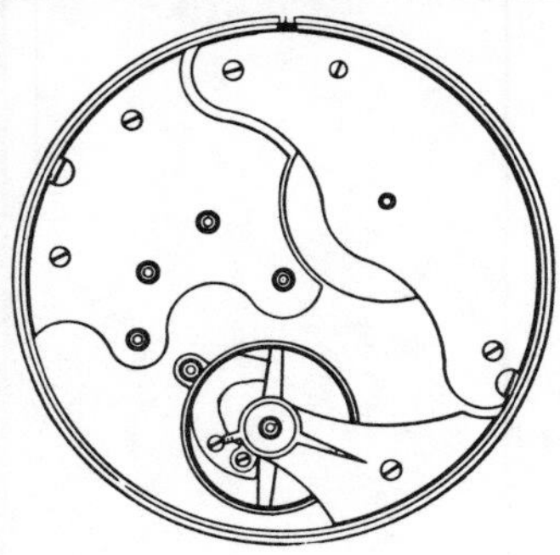

Model 1, 16 size, hunting, lever set.

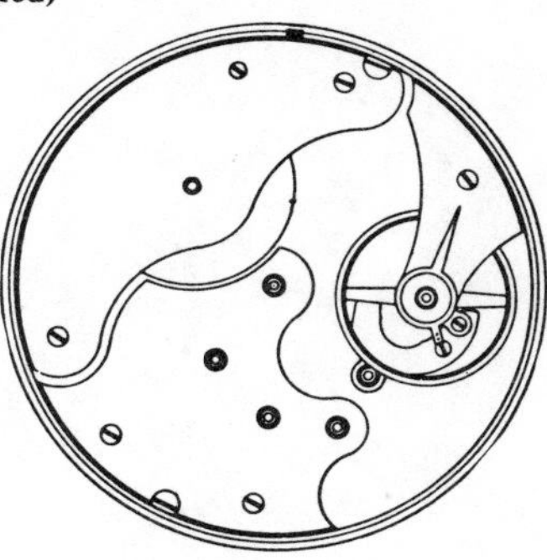

Model 2, 16 size, open face, pendant set.

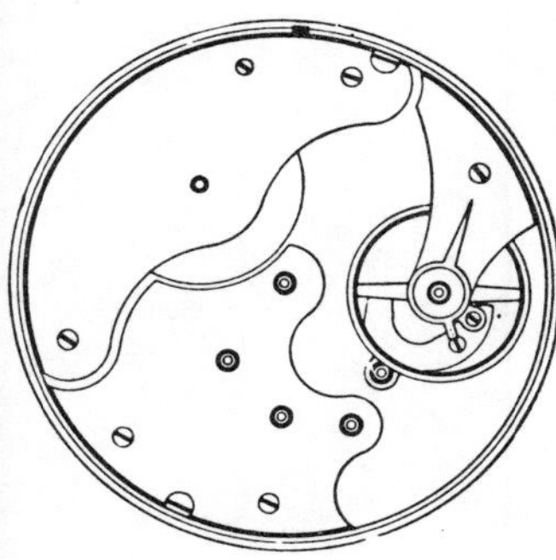

Model 3, 16 size, open face, lever set.

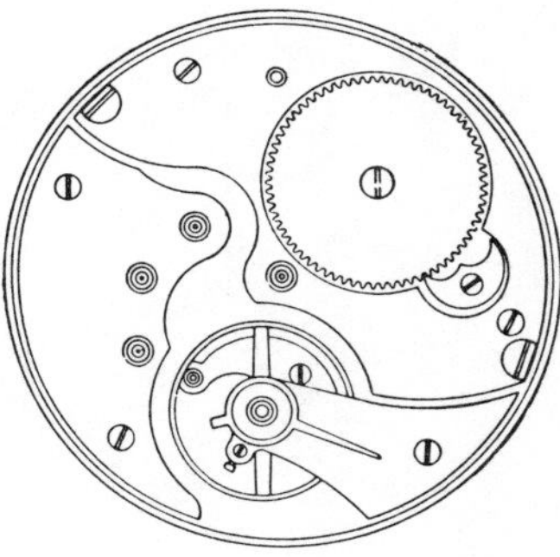

Model 4, 16 size, three-quarter plate, hunting, lever set.

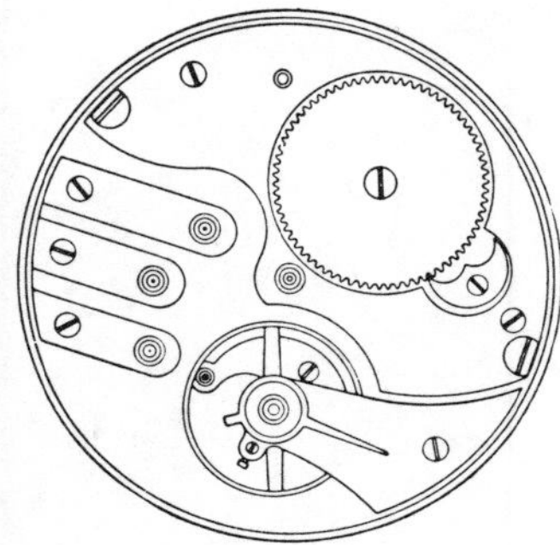

Model 4, 16 size, three-quarter plate, bridge, hunting, lever set.

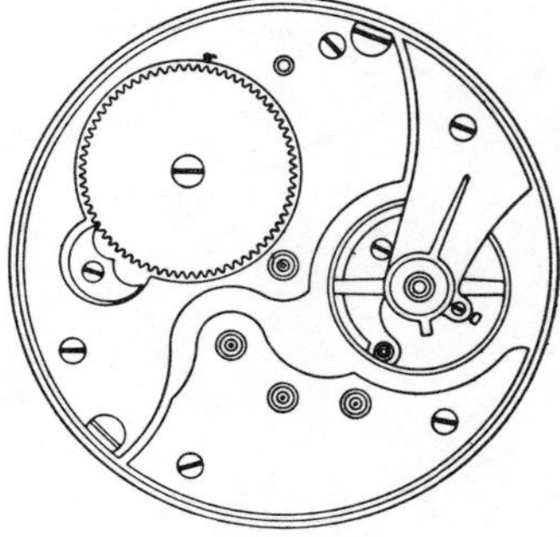

Model 5, 16 size, three-quarter plate, open face, lever set.

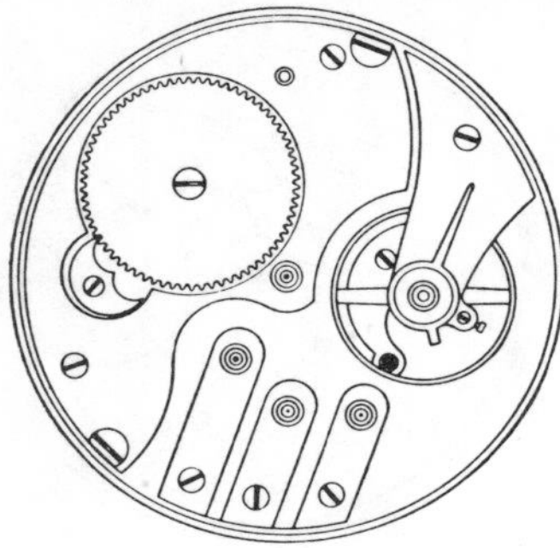

Model 5, 16 size, three-quarter plate, bridge, open face, lever set.

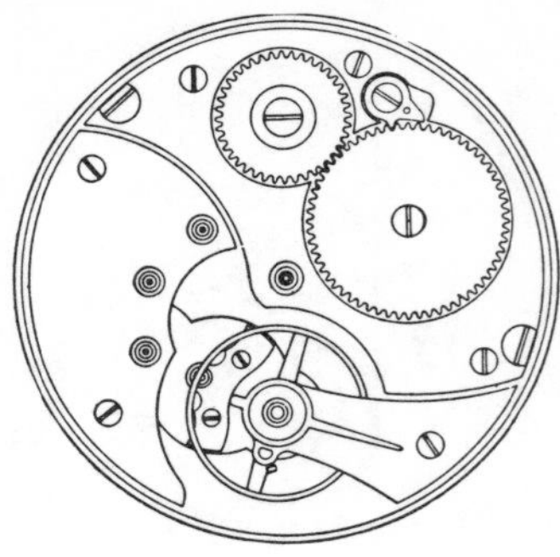

Model 6, 16 size—Pendant set
Model 8, 16 size—Lever set
hunting, three-quarter plate

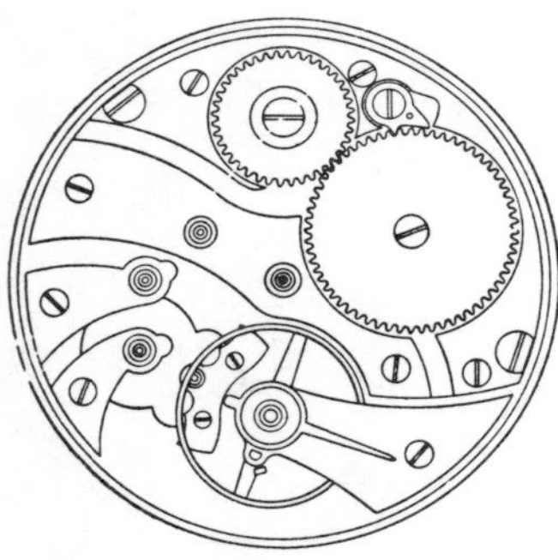

Model 6, 16 size—Pendant set
Model 8, 16 size—Lever set
hunting, bridge model

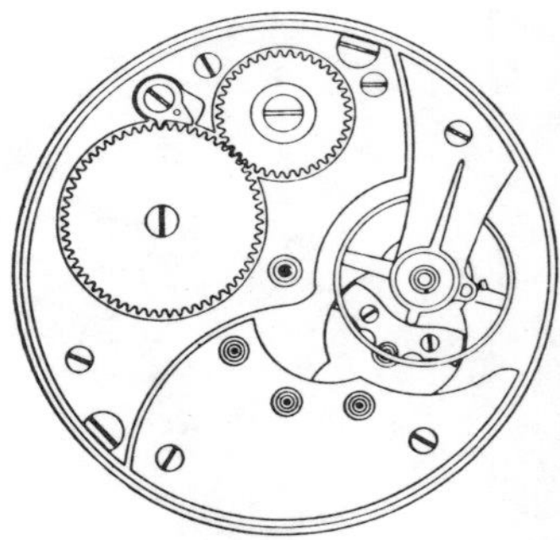

Model 7, 16 size—Pendant set
Model 9, 16 size—Lever set
open face, three-quarter plate

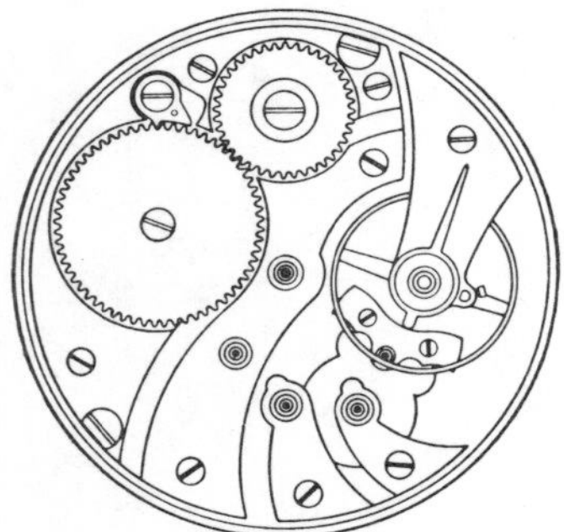

Model 7, 16 size—Pendant set
Model 9, 16 size—Lever set
open face, bridge model

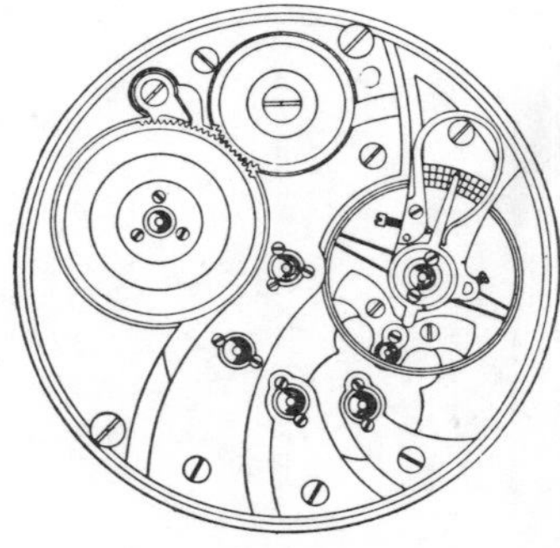

Model 10, 16 size, bridge, extra thin, open face, lever set, motor barrel.

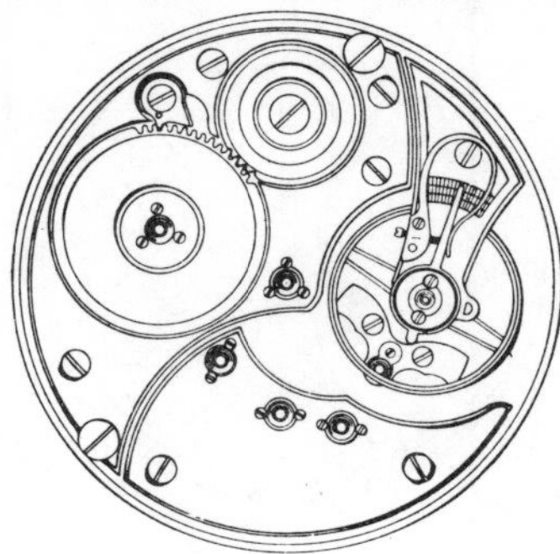

Model 11, 16 size, three-quarter plate, open face, pendant set, motor barrel.

Model 12, 16 size, three-quarter plate, hunting, pendant set, motor barrel.

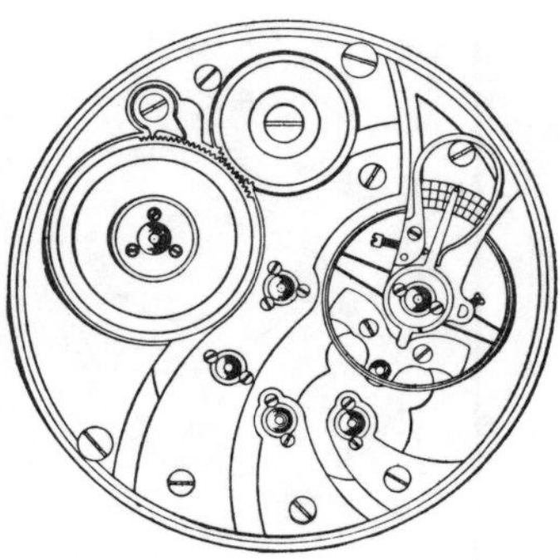

Model 13, 16 size, bridge, open face, lever set, motor barrel.

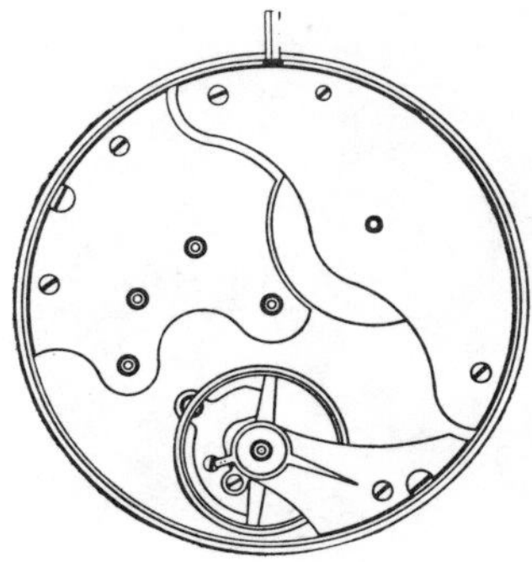

Model 1, 14 size, hunting, lever set.

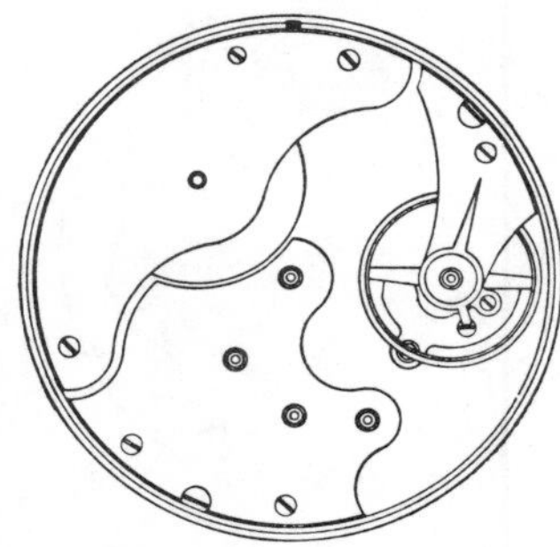

Model 2, 14 size, open face, pendant set.

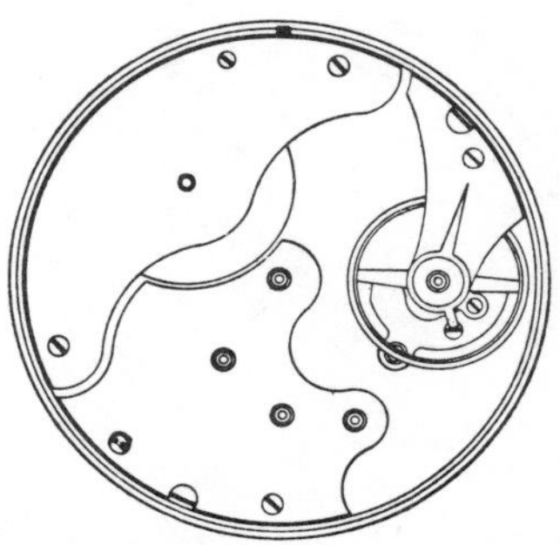

Model 3, 14 size, open face, lever set.

Model 1, 13 size, bridge, extra thin, open face, pendant set, motor barrel.

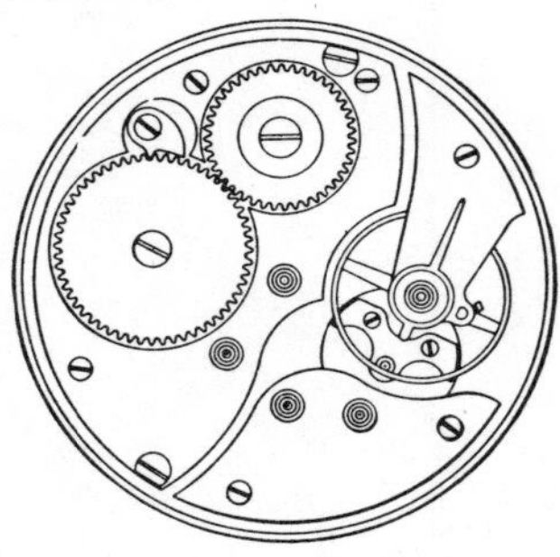

Model 1, 12 size, three-quarter plate, open face, pendant set.

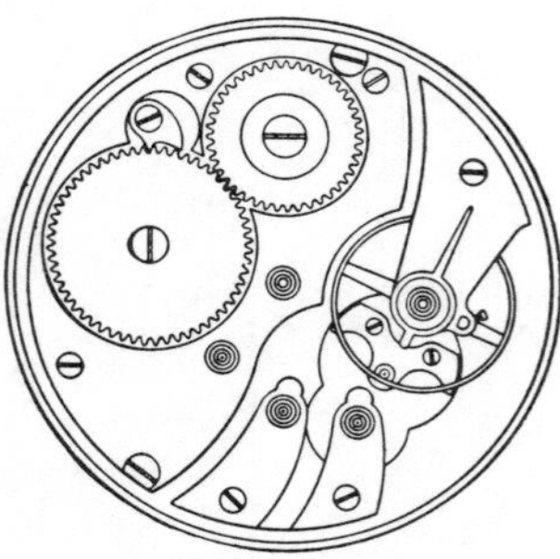

Model 1, 12 size, three-quarter plate, bridge, open face, pendant set.

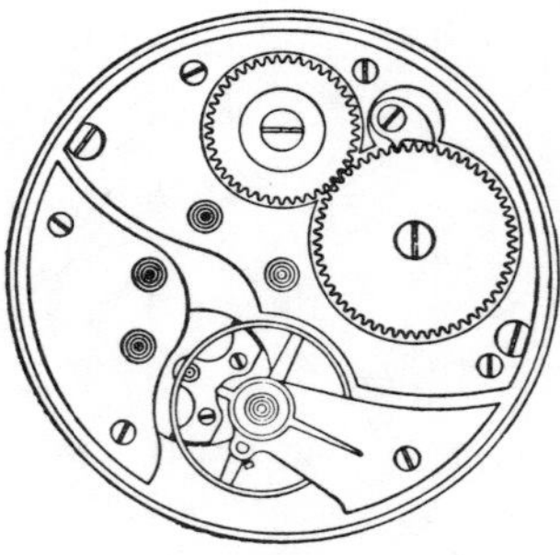

Model 2, 12 size, three-quarter plate, hunting, pendant set.

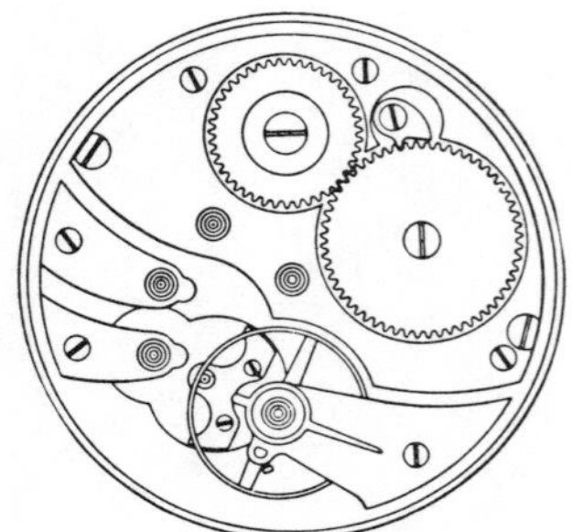

Model 2, 12 size, three-quarter plate, bridge, hunting, pendant set.

Model 3, 12 size, **Model 4**, 12 & 14 size, bridge, open face, pendant set.

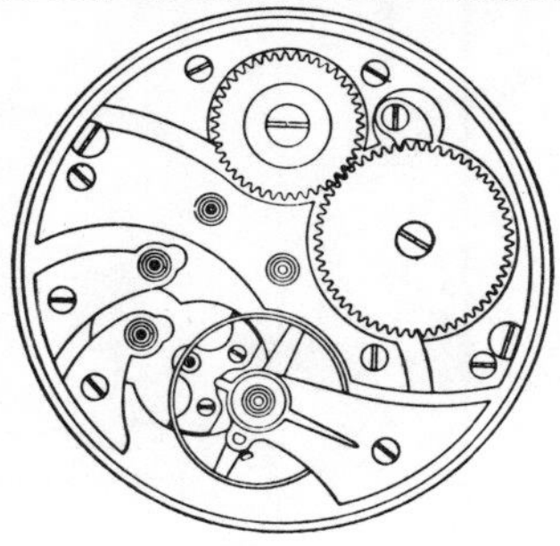

Model 4, 12 size, bridge, hunting, pendant set.

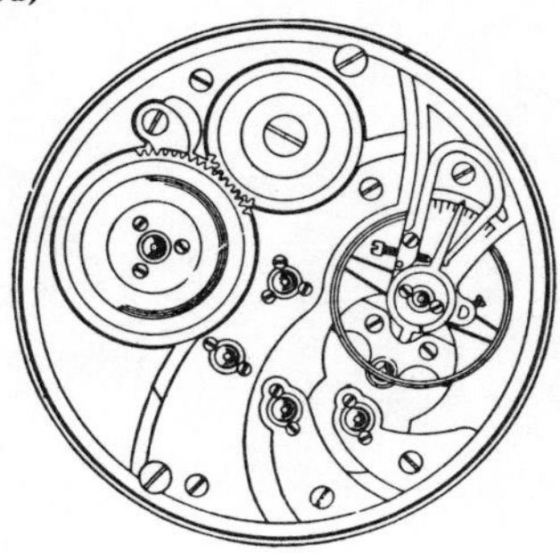

Model 5, 12 size, bridge, open face, pendant set, motor barrel.

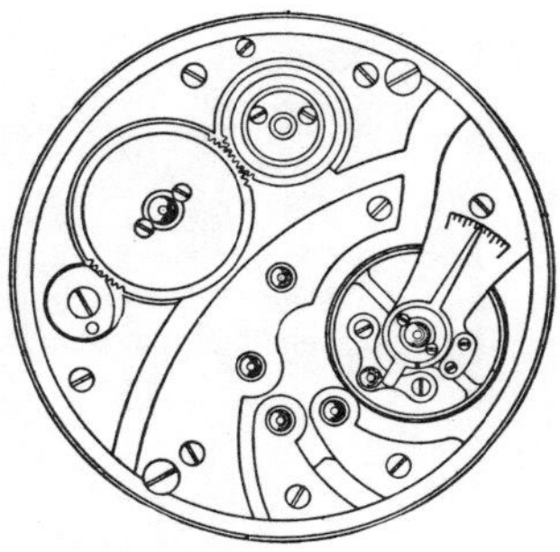

Model 1, 12 size, extra thin, bridge, open face, pendant set, motor barrel.

Model 2, 12 size, extra thin, bridge, open face, pendant set, motor barrel.

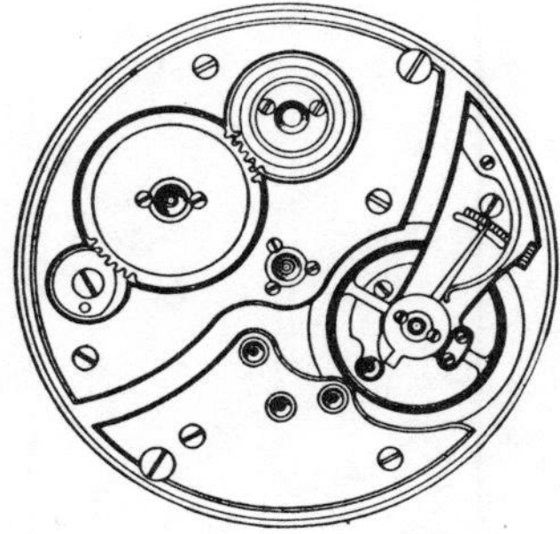

Model 3, 12 size, extra thin, three-quarter plate, open face, pendant set, motor barrel.

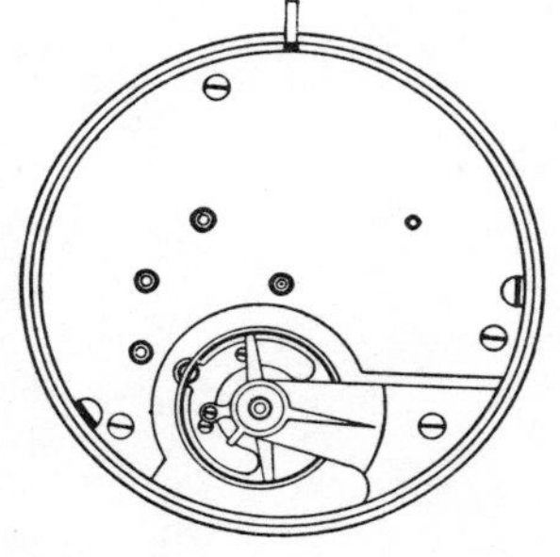

Model 1, 8 size, hunting, key or lever set.

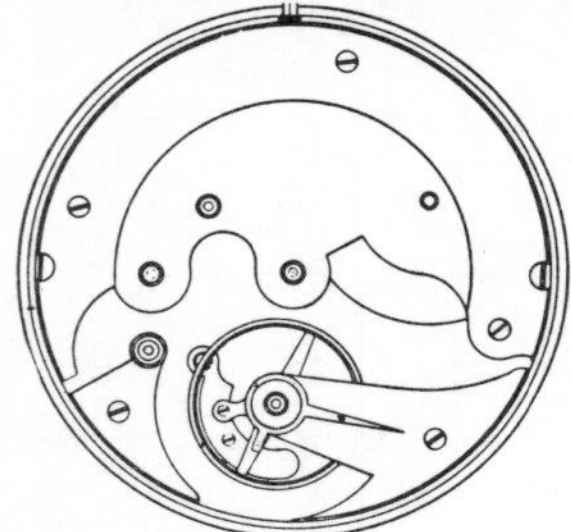

Model 2, 8 size, hunting, lever set.

Model 1, 6 size, hunting, lever set.

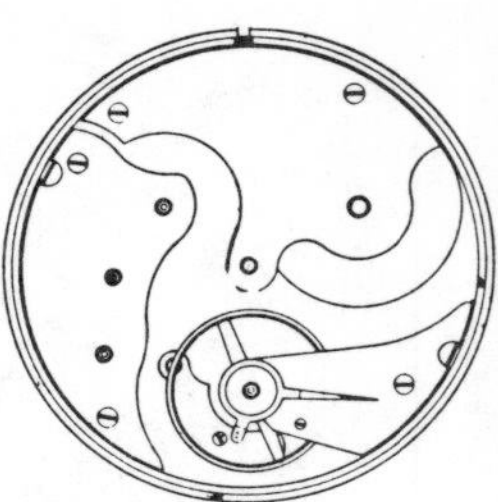

Model 1, 4 size, hunting, lever set.

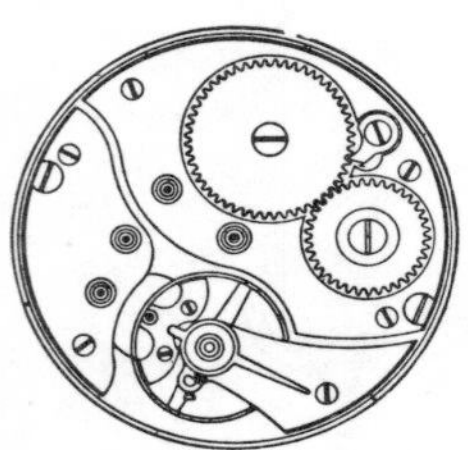

Model 1, 0 size, three-quarter plate, open face, pendant set.

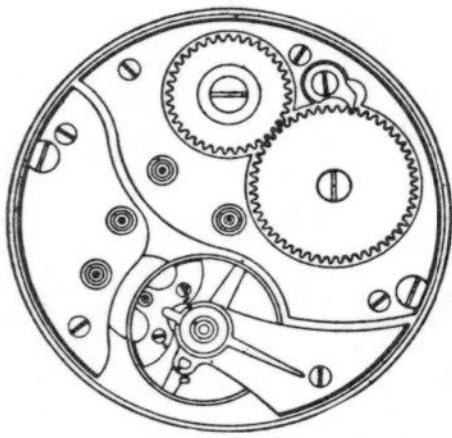

Model 2, 0 size, three-quarter plate, hunting, pendant set.

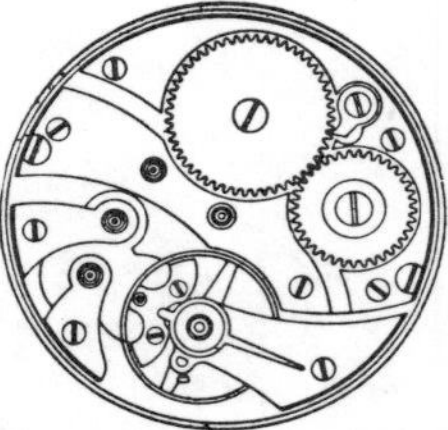

Model 3, 0 size, bridge, open face, pendant set.

Model 4, 0 size, bridge, hunting, pendant set.

Model 3, 3/0 size, bridge, open face, pendant set.

Model 4, 3/0 size, bridge, hunting, pendant set.

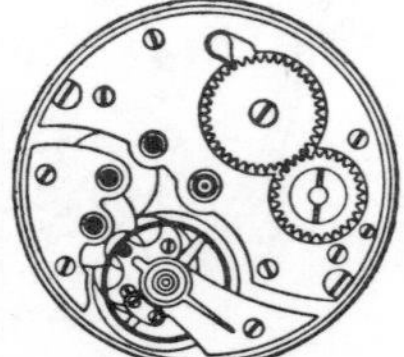

Model 1, 6/0 size, three-quarter plate, open face, pendant set.

Model 2, 6/0 size, bridge, open face, pendant set.

INDEPENDENT WATCH CO.
Fredonia, New York
1880 — 1885

The California Watch Company was idle for two years before it was purchased by brothers E. W. Howard and C. M. Howard. They had been selling watches by mail for sometime and started engraving their own names and using American-made watches. Their chief supply came from Hampden Watch Co., Illinois, U. S. Watch Co. of Marion, and Cornell Watch Co. They formed the Independent Watch Co. in 1880, but were not a watch factory in the true sense. They had other manufacturers engrave their name on the top plates and on the dials of their watches. These watches were sold by mail order and sent to the buyer C. O. D. The names used on the movements were "Mark Twain," "Howard Bros.," "Independent Watch Co.," "Fredonia Watch Co.," and "Lakeshore Watch Co., Fredonia, N. Y."

The company later decided to manufacture watches and used the name Fredonia Watch Co. But they found that selling watches two different ways was no good. The business survived until 1885 at which time the owners decided to move the plant to a new location at Peoria, Illinois. Approximately 350,000 watches were made that sold for $16.

Chronology of the Development of Independent Watch Co.:

Independent Watch Co.	1880-1883
Fredonia Watch Co.	1883-1885
Peoria Watch Co.	1885-1895

Grade or Name — Description	Avg	Ex-Fn	Mint
18S, 7J, KW, KS, OF, by U.S. W. Co. Marion, with butterfly cutout ★	$325	$425	$650
18S, 11J, KW, KS, by Hampden	160	175	250
18S, 11J, KW, KS, Coin	140	160	220
18S, 11J, KW, KS	150	175	230
18S, 15J, KW, KS	160	185	235
18S, Howard Bros., 11J, KW, KS	200	225	325
18S, Independent W. Co., 11J	150	175	220
18S, Lakeshore W. Co., 15J, KW, HC, by N.Y. W. Co.	145	195	275
18S, Mark Twain, 11J, KW, KS	250	300	495

Independent Watch Co., 18 size, 11 jewels, key wind & set, made by Hampden Watch Co. (Model Number 1), serial number 170,844.

Independent Watch Co., 18 size, 15 jewels, key wind, made by U.S. Marion Watch Co., note butterfly cut-out, serial number 192,661.

ROBERT H. INGERSOLL & BROS.
New York, New York
Made Watches 1892 — 1922

In 1892 this company published a catalog for the mail order trade. It contained men's watch chains and a "silverine" watch for $3.95. It was not a true Ingersoll but a "Universal," introduced that same year to the dealers. The first $1 watches were jeweled; "Reliance" had seven jewels. In 1916, Ingersoll's production was 16,000 a day. The slogan was "The Watch that Made the Dollar Famous." The first 1,000 watches were made by Waterbury Clock Co. By 1922 the Ingersoll line was completely taken over by Waterbury. U. S. Time Corp. acquired Waterbury in 1944, and continued to use the Ingersoll name on certain watches.

ESTIMATED SERIAL NUMBERS AND PRODUCTION DATES

Date	Serial No.	Date	Serial No.	Date	Serial No.
1892	150,000	1905	10,000,000	1918	47,500,000
1893	310,000	1906	12,500,000	1919	50,000,000
1894	650,000	1907	15,000,000	1920	55,000,000
1895	1,000,000	1908	17,500,000	1921	58,000,000
1896	2,000,000	1909	20,000,000	1922	60,500,000
1897	2,900,000	1910	25,000,000	1923	62,000,000
1898	3,500,000	1911	30,000,000	1924	65,000,000
1899	3,750,000	1912	38,500,000	1925	67,500,000
1900	6,000,000	1913	40,000,000	1926	69,000,000
1901	6,700,000	1914	41,500,000	1927	70,500,000
1902	7,200,000	1915	42,500,000	1928	71,500,000
1903	7,900,000	1916	45,500,000	1929	73,500,000
1904	8,100,000	1917	47,000,000	1930	75,000,000

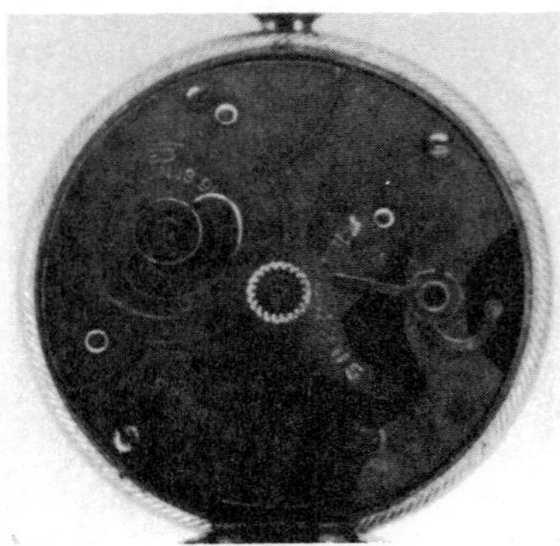

Ingersoll Back Wind & Set, patent date Dec. 23, 1890 and Jan. 13, 1891, c. late 1890s.

Ingersoll Blind Man's Watch.

INGERSOLL
DOLLAR TYPE

NOTE: In some specialty markets, the comic character watches may bring higher prices in top condition.

Grade or Name — Description	Avg	Ex-Fn	Mint
Ingersoll Back Wind ★	$60	$75	$125
American Pride	75	80	90

INGERSOLL DOLLAR TYPE (continued)

Big Bad Wolf, Three Pigs, blinking eyes.

Example of an Ingersoll **Dizzy Dean** watch, c. 1935.

Grade or Name — Description	Avg	Ex-Fn	Mint
Are U My Neighbor	15	20	30
B. B. H. Special, Backwind	50	60	75
Big Bad Wolf, Three Pigs, die-debossed back	125	175	275
Blind Man Pocket Watch	30	40	50
Buck	15	20	25
Buster Brown (two models), 1904	100	150	250
Champion (many models)	35	70	150
Chancery	50	60	75
Chicago Expo. 1933	125	150	295
Climax	35	40	60
Cloverine	50	60	75
Coca Cola (beware of fakes)	135	150	185
Colby	15	20	25
Columbus	35	50	70
Columbus (3 ships on back of case)	150	200	300
Connecticut W. Co.	25	35	45
Cord	10	25	30
Crown	15	20	25
Dan Dee	10	15	20
Defiance	20	35	45
Delaware W. Co.	15	20	25
Devon Mfg. Co.	10	15	20
Dizzy Dean	75	95	175

Donald Duck, with **Mickey** on back.

INGERSOLL DOLLAR TYPE (continued)

Grade or Name — Description	Avg	Ex-Fn	Mint
Donald Duck, with Mickey on back	95	135	235
Eclipse (many models)	15	20	40
Eclipse Radiolite	20	30	35
Ensign	15	20	25
Escort	20	25	35
Freedom	25	30	35
Flash Gordon, 1939	125	165	225
Gotham	10	20	30
Graceline	35	40	50
Gregg	10	20	30
Junior (several models)	10	20	30
Junior Radiolite	30	35	40
Kelton	5	10	15
Lapel Watches	20	35	40
Leeds	10	15	20
Liberty U.S.A., backwind	70	85	125
Liberty Watch Co.	20	25	30
Major	5	10	15
Maple Leaf	20	25	35
Master Craft	5	10	15

Mickey Mouse, Model 1.

Mickey Mouse, Model 2, note the earliest model has the tallest stem as in Model 1.

Grade or Name — Description	Avg	Ex-Fn	Mint
Mickey Mouse, M#1, die-debossed back, 1933 ★★	250	300	400
Mickey Mouse, M#2	200	250	300
Mickey Mouse, M#3	150	175	250
Mickey Mouse, M#4	100	125	150
Mickey Mouse Lapel Watch	125	150	200
Mickey Mouse Wrist Watch	45	50	75
Midget (several models)	20	35	50
Monarch	15	20	25
Moon Mullins	150	200	225
New West	20	25	35
New York World's Fair, 1939	150	200	295

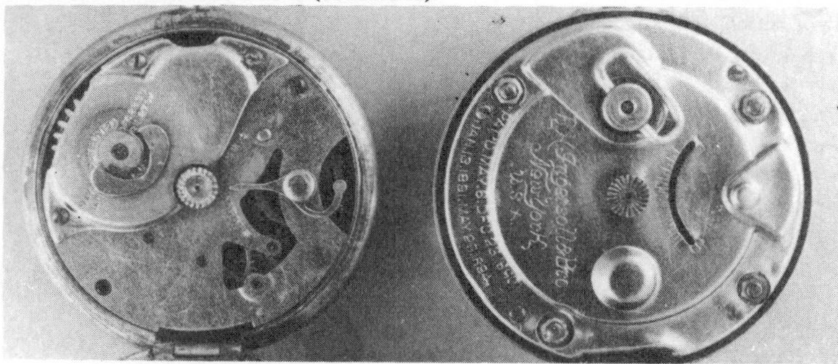

Ingersoll Back Wind, c. 1895. Yankee Back Wind, c. 1893.

Grade or Name — Description	Avg	Ex-Fn	Mint
Overland	35	40	50
Pan American Expo., Buffalo	125	150	295
Paris World Expo.	200	250	300
Patrol	25	30	45
Perfection	25	35	45
Pilgram	30	35	40
Premium Back Wind and Set	40	50	75
Progress, 1933 World's Fair Chicago	150	175	295
Puritan	20	35	40
Quaker	35	40	45
Radiolite	25	30	35
Reliance, 7J	20	25	30
Remington W. Co. USA	45	50	75
Royal	5	10	20
St. Louis World Fair (two models)	150	200	350
The Saturday Post	125	150	200
Scout "Be Prepared"	125	150	250
Senator	35	40	50
Senior	20	25	35
Sir Leeds	20	25	30
Solar	20	30	40
Souvenir Special	30	40	50
Sterling	35	40	50
Ten Hune	50	60	75
Three Little Pigs, Big Bad Wolf	150	200	275
Tom Mix, die-debossed back	200	250	300
Traveler with Bed Side Stand	25	35	50
Triumph	50	65	75
Triumph Penset	125	150	200
True Test	20	25	30
Trump	25	30	35
USA (two models)	50	75	150
Universal, 1st model	150	200	300
Uncle Sam	30	40	50
George Washington	100	125	150
Waterbury (several models)	25	30	35
Winner	15	20	25
Winner with S.B.B.	35	40	50

INGERSOLL DOLLAR TYPE (continued)

Grade or Name — Description	Avg	Ex-Fn	Mint
Yankee Backwind	60	70	120
Yankee Radiolite	25	30	35
Yankee Radiolite with S.B.B.	35	40	50
Yankee Bicycle Watch	75	125	200
Yankee Special (many models)	40	75	200
Yankee, Perpetual calendar on back of case	20	35	50

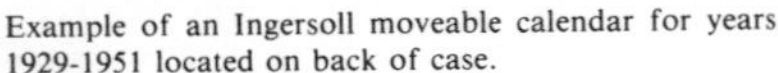

Example of an Ingersoll moveable calendar for years 1929-1951 located on back of case.

Example of an Ingersoll watch made in Great Britain.

INGERSOLL LTD.
(GREAT BRITAIN)

Grade or Name — Description	Avg	Ex-Fn	Mint
Ingersoll Ltd. (many models)	$50	$75	$100
Dan Dare, 1953 (similar to Buck Rogers)	120	140	160

INGERSOLL TRENTON

Grade or Name — Description	Avg	Ex-Fn	Mint
16S, 7J, 3F Brg	$45	$50	$60
16S, 15J, 3F Brg	50	60	65
16S, 17J, 3F Brg, ADJ	60	80	95
16S, 19J, 3F Brg, HCI5P	125	135	195
12S, 4J	30	35	50

WRIST WATCHES

Style or Grade — Description	Avg	Ex-Fn	Mint
Alice in Wonderland	$35	$40	$50
Cinderella	30	35	45
Daisy Duck	25	30	40
Donald Duck #1, Mickey on band	100	135	195
Donald Duck, with round case	50	55	65
Donald Duck, birthday model	80	95	125
Flash Gordon	85	95	125
Mickey Mouse #1 (1933), metal link bracelet	135	170	235
Mickey Mouse #1 (1933), metal link bracelet, with box	185	235	345
Mickey Mouse (1935), with charm bracelet, Tonneau case	125	155	185
Mickey Mouse, Mickey on leather band, round case	115	125	165
Mickey Mouse, round case, plain leather band	50	65	85
Mickey Mouse, Tonneau case, leather band, sec. hand	55	65	85
Mickey Mouse, Tonneau case, leather band, no sec. hand	40	50	70
Pinocchio	25	30	35
Pluto	25	30	35
3 Little Pigs	35	40	50
Man's wrist watch, Tonneau case	10	12	18
Man's wrist watch, rectangular case	8	9	12
Man's wrist watch, square case	5	7	10
Man's wrist watch, round case	4	5	8
Man's or Lady's Radiolite	20	22	27
Lady's wrist watch	5	7	10
Midget for lady	15	22	27

Ingersoll, 0 Size, radiolite dial.

Ingersoll, 6/0 Size, radiolite dial.

Example of a **Buck Rogers**, c. 1938.

New York to Paris, airplane model commemorating Lindbergh's famous flight.

E. INGRAHAM CO.
Bristol, Connecticut
1912 — 1968

The E. Ingraham Co. purchased the Bannatyne Co. in 1912. They produced their first American pocket watch in 1913. A total of about 65 million American-made pocket watches were produced before they started to import watches in 1968.

NOTE: In some specialty markets the comic character watches may bring higher prices in top condition.

Grade or Name — Description	Avg	Ex-Fn	Mint
Ingraham W. Co. (many models)	$15	$25	$35
Aristocrat Railroad Sp.	15	25	30
Autocrat	10	15	20
Beacon	10	15	20
Biltmore	5	10	15
Biltmore Radium	10	15	20
Betty Boop (1934), die-debossed back ★★★	300	375	500
Bristol	10	15	20
Buck Rogers, die-debossed back	150	200	295
Captain Marvel	200	250	300
Captain Midnight	200	250	300
Clipper	10	15	20
Comet	10	15	18
Companion, sweep second hand	10	15	25
Cub	10	12	16
Dixie	5	10	14
Dot	8	15	18
Endura	10	15	20
Everbrite (all models)	15	20	25

E. INGRAHAM CO. (continued)

Grade or Name — Description	Avg	Ex-Fn	Mint
Ingraham USA	5	10	12
Jockey	10	12	15
Laddie	20	25	30
Laddie Athlete	25	30	50
Lady's Purse Watch, with fancy bezel	30	35	40
Lendix Extra	20	25	35
Master	5	12	15
Miss Ingraham	20	25	35
New York to Paris	125	175	295
Overland	25	30	35
The Pal	10	20	25
Pastor, stop watch	35	40	55
Pathfinder, compass on pendant	50	60	75
Patriot	85	125	200
Peerless	20	25	30
Peter Pan, pin set	20	25	35
Pilot	20	24	32
Pocket Pal	10	15	20
Pony	15	20	25
Pride	15	20	25
Princess	15	20	25
Pup	20	30	35
Reliance	35	40	50
Rex	10	15	20
Rite Time	25	30	35
Roy Rogers (1951)	85	125	185
St. Regis	10	15	20
Secometer	15	20	30
Sentinel	10	15	20
Sentinel Click	10	15	20
Sentinel Fold Up Travel	35	40	50
Sentry	20	25	30
Silver Star	10	20	25
Sterling	15	25	30
Sterling W. Co. Stop Watch, fly back to zero	35	40	55

Example of **Path Finder** showing compass in crown.

Example of a Roy Rogers & Trigger with sweep second hand.

E. INGRAHAM CO. (continued)

Grade or Name — Description	Avg	Ex-Fn	Mint
Sturdy	5	12	15
Target	5	10	15
Time Ball	20	25	35
Time & Time	20	30	40
Top Flight	10	15	20
Top Notch	30	35	40
Tower	10	15	20
Trail Blazer	75	125	200
Unbreakable Crystal	25	30	35
Uncle Sam (all models)	35	40	45
Uncle Sam Backwind & Set	50	60	70
Viceroy	15	20	25
Victory	15	20	25
Zep	95	135	295

WRIST WATCHES

Style or Grade — Description	Avg	Ex-Fn	Mint
Dale Evans, Tonneau	$45	$55	$70
Porky Pig	60	70	85
Roy Rogers, Tonneau, white dial	55	60	85
Roy Rogers, Tonneau, green dial	45	55	75
Wrist-O-Crat	15	20	27
Rectangular	5	7	10
Round	5	7	10
Tonneau	8	10	15

Left: Example of a basic **International Watch Co.** movement with patent dates of Aug. 19, 1902, Jan. 27, 1903 & Aug. 11, 1903. Right: Example of a **Highland**.

INTERNATIONAL WATCH CO.
Newark City, New Jersey
1902 — 1907

This company produced only non-jeweled or low-cost production type watches that were inexpensive and nickel plated. Names on their watches include: Berkshire, Madison, and Mascot.

INTERNATIONAL WATCH CO. (continued)

Grade or Name — Description	Avg	Ex-Fn	Mint
Berkshire, OF ★	$50	$75	$135
Highland ★	35	55	95
Madison, 18S, OF ★	40	65	110
Mascot, OF ★	30	50	85

KANKAKEE WATCH CO.
Kankakee, Illinois
1900

This company reportedly became the McIntyre Watch Co. Little other information is available.

Grade or Name — Description	Avg	Ex-Fn	Mint
16S, BRG, NI ★★★	$3,500	$4,000	$5,000

Example of a basic **Keystone** movement, about 16-18 size, 7-11 jewels, stem wind, serial number 420843, c. 1888.

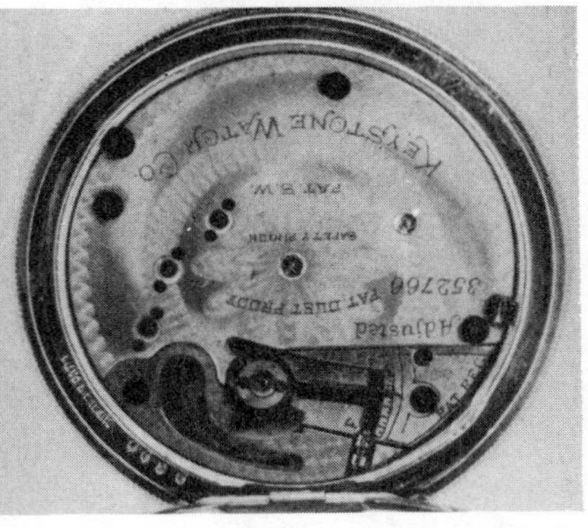

Keystone Watch Co., dust proof model, 18 size, 15 jewels, serial number 352,766.

KEYSTONE STANDARD WATCH CO.
Lancaster, Pennsylvania
1886 — 1890

Abram Bitner agreed to buy a large number of stockholders' shares of the Lancaster Watch Co. at 10 cents on the dollar; he ended up with 5,625 shares out of the 8,000 that were available. Some 8,900 movements had been completed but not sold at the time of the shares purchase. The company Bitner formed assumed the name of Keystone Standard Watch Co. as the trademark but in reality existed as the Lancaster Watch Co. The business was sold to Hamilton Watch Co. in 1891. Total production was 48,000.

Grade or Name — Description	Avg	Ex-Fn	Mint
18S, 20J, ¾, LS, HC ★★	$400	$550	$750
18S, 7-15J, OF, KW	70	80	115

KEYSTONE STANDARD WATCH CO. (continued)

Grade or Name — Description	Avg	Ex-Fn	Mint
18S, 15J, dust proof, ADJ	125	150	195
18S, 15J, dust proof, OF	65	75	150
18S, 15J, dust proof, HC	95	135	200
18S, West End, 15J, HC	75	125	175
18S, 11J, dust proof	60	70	85
18S, 7-15J, OF, SW, ¾, LS	40	50	80
6S, 7-10J, HC	40	50	85

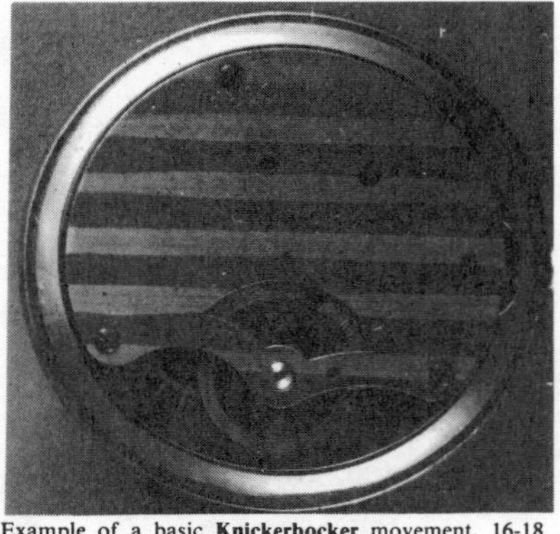

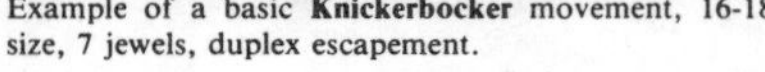

Example of a basic **Knickerbocker** movement, 16-18 size, 7 jewels, duplex escapement.

Example of a basic **Knickerbocker** movement with a duplex escapement, 16-18 size.

KNICKERBOCKER WATCH CO.
New York, New York
1890 — 1930

This company imported and sold Swiss and low-cost production American watches.

Grade or Name — Description	Avg	Ex-Fn	Mint
6S, Duplex	$40	$50	$65
10S, Barkley "8 Day"	25	35	55
12S, 7J, OF	45	55	85
18S, 7J, OF, PS, NI, duplex escapement	50	60	80
16S, 7J	45	50	75

LANCASTER WATCH CO.
Lancaster, Pennsylvania
1877 — 1886

Work commenced on Sept. 1, 1877, at the Lancaster Watch Co. The watches produced there were designed to sell at a cheaper price than normal. They had a solid top, ¾ plate, and a pillar plate that was fully ruby-jeweled (4½ pairs). They had a gilt and nickel movement and a new stem-wind device, modeled by Mosly & Todd. By mid-1878 the Lancaster Watch Co. had produced 150 movements. Four grades of watches were made: Keystone, Fulton, Franklin, and Melrose. In September 1879 the company had made 334 movements. In 1880 the total was up to 1,250 movements. And by mid-1882 about 17,000 movements had been produced. All totaled, about 20,000 watch movements were made.

LANCASTER WATCH CO. (continued)

About 75 8-Size Ladies' watches were also made.

Chronology of the Development of Lancaster Watch Co.:

Adams and Perry Watch Mfg. Co. — 1874-1876
Lancaster Watch Co. — 1877-1878
Lancaster Pa. Watch Co. — 1878-1879
Lancaster Watch Co. — 1879-1886
Keystone Standard Co. — 1886-1890
Hamilton Watch Co. — 1892-1958

LANCASTER
18 SIZE
(All ¾ Plate)

Grade or Name — Description	Avg	Ex-Fn	Mint
Chester, 7J, KW, gilded	$75	$95	$135
Comet, 7J, NI	85	110	140
Delaware, 20J, ADJ, SW, gilded	150	225	325
Denver, 7J, gilded	60	90	125
Denver, 7J, gilded, Silveroid	40	50	65
Elberon, 7J, dust proof	60	70	95
Ben Franklin, 7J, KW, gilded	175	225	295
Ben Franklin, 11J, KW, gilded	190	245	325
Fulton, 7J, ADJ, KW, gilded	125	150	185
Fulton, 11J, ADJ, KW, gilded	135	160	195
Girard, 15J, ADJ, gilded	100	120	165
Hoosac, 11J, OF	135	170	225
Keystone, 15J, ADJ, gilded, GJS	95	110	125
Keystone, 15J, ADJ, gilded, GJS, Silveroid	60	70	85
Lancaster, 7J, SW	55	60	70
Lancaster, 15J, SW, Silveroid	60	70	75
Lancaster, 15J, OF	100	120	150
Lancaster Pa., 20J, ADJ, NI ★	400	500	650
Lancaster Watch, 20J, DR, ADJ, NI, GJS, 14K HC ★	700	800	1,025
Malvern, 7J, gilded	65	70	95
Melrose, 15J, NI, ADJ, GJS	95	120	150

Lancaster Watch Co., 18 size, 20 jewels, gold jeweled settings, stem wind & pendant set, serial number 1747.

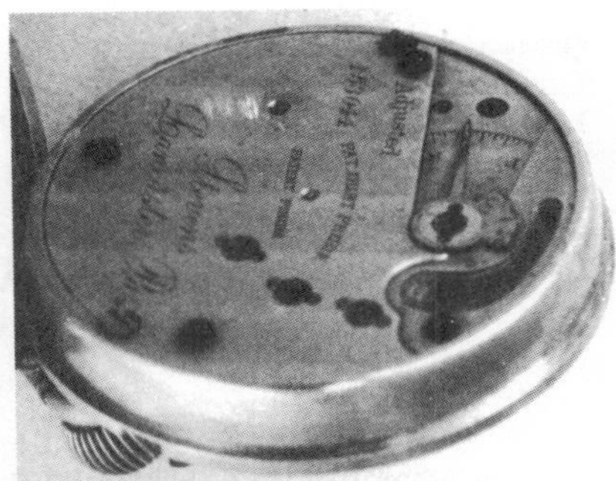

Stevens Model, 18 size, 15 jewels, adjusted, dust proof model, swing-out movement, c. 1886.

LANCASTER WATCH CO. (continued)

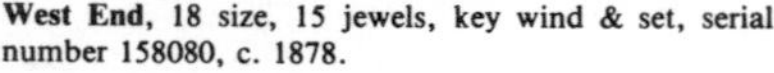

West End, 18 size, 15 jewels, key wind & set, serial number 158080, c. 1878.

Example of a basic **Lancaster** movement, 8-10 size, 15 jewels, serial number 317812.

Grade or Name — Description	Avg	Ex-Fn	Mint
Nation Standard American Watch Co., 7J, HC	200	225	275
New Era, 7J, gilded, KW	75	100	145
New Era, 7J, gilded, KW, Silveroid	40	60	90
Paoli, 7J, NI	50	60	85
Wm. Penn, 20J, ADJ, NI, dust proof	200	325	525
Radnor, 7J, gilded	65	75	85
Record, 7J, Silveroid	40	50	60
Record, 15J, NI	75	100	125
Ruby, 16J, NI	275	310	375
Sidney, 15J, NI	100	125	175
Stevens, 15J, ADJ, NI	150	175	225
West End, 19J, HC, KW, gilded ★★	300	375	475
West End, 15J, HC, KW, KS	175	200	275
West End, 15J, SW	50	65	85
West End, 15J, SW, Silveroid	40	50	65

8 SIZE

Grade or Name — Description	Avg	Ex-Fn	Mint
Flora, gilded	$70	$80	$125
Lady Penn, 20J, GJS, ADJ, NI	200	300	425
Lancaster W. Co., 7J	70	80	125

MANHATTAN WATCH CO.
New York, New York
1883 — 1891

The Manhattan Watch Co. made low cost production watches mainly. A complete and full line of watches was made, and most were cased and styled to be sold as a complete watch. The watches were generally 16S with full plate movements. The patented

MANHATTAN WATCH CO. (continued)
winding mechanism was different. These watches were in both the hunter and open-face cases and later had a sweep second hand. Total production was 160,000 or more watches.

16 SIZE

Grade or Name — Description		Avg	Ex-Fn	Mint
OF, with back wind	★	$150	$175	$225
OF, stop watch	★	125	150	185
7J, OF	★	50	60	85
7J, HC	★	95	110	135
Stallcup, 7J, OF	★	100	125	175

12 SIZE

Grade or Name — Description		Avg	Ex-Fn	Mint
12S	★	$75	$95	$135

Manhattan Watch Co., Chronograph, 18-16 size, note two buttons on top; one sets hands, the other stops and starts watch, serial number 117480.

Manhattan Watch Co., 18 size, chronograph. Note two buttons on top; one sets hands, the other starts and stops watch.

MANISTEE WATCH CO.
Manistee, Michigan
1908 — 1912

The Manistee watches, first marketed in 1909, were designed to compete with the low-cost production watches. Dials, jewels, and hairsprings were not produced at the factory. The first movement was 18S, 7J, and sold for about $5. Manistee also made 5J, 15J, 17J, and 21J watches in cheap cases in sizes 16 and 12. Estimated total production was 60,000. Most were sold by Star Watch Case Co.

Example of a basic **Manistee** movement, 16-18 size, 17 jewels, open face, three-quarter plate.

18 TO 12 SIZE

Grade or Name — Description		Avg	Ex-Fn	Mint
18S, 7J, HC or OF	★	$225	$300	$575
16S, 7J, HC	★	145	200	375
16S, 15J, Silveroid	★	85	125	175
16S, 7J, OF	★	125	140	195
16S, 15-17J, OF	★	175	250	385
16S, 19J, HC	★	185	275	425
16S, 21J, OF	★	200	295	450
12S, 15J	★	135	150	195

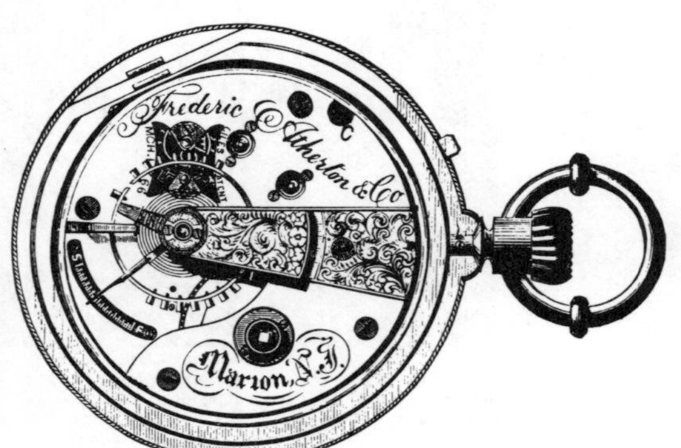

Example of a ***Frederick Atherton & Co.*** movement, 18 size, 19 jewels, pin set. Note butterfly cut-out.

MARION WATCH CO.
Marion, New Jersey
1873 — 1875

The Marion Watch Co. continued with most of the staff of the United States Watch Co., and many of the same movements were made. About 4,000 watches were produced during the two-year history of the company. Serial numbers begin at about 170,000.

(Also see United States Watch Co., Marion, New Jersey.)

MARION
18 SIZE

Grade or Name — Description	Avg	Ex-Fn	Mint
Wm. Alexander, 15J, KW/SW, HC	$275	$350	$425
Wm. Alexander, 15J, NI, KW	200	275	350
Wm. Alexander, 15J, NI, SW	225	300	375
Frederick Atherton & Co., 19J, NI, KW, GJS, HCIP ★	700	800	1,000
Frederick Atherton & Co., 19J, NI, SW, GJS, HCIP ★	900	1,000	1,200

Asa Fuller, 18 size, 11 jewels, gilded, stem or key wind.

United States Watch Co. on movement, **Marion Watch Co.** on dial, 18 size, 19 jewels, gold jewel settings, key wind and set.

Grade or Name — Description	Avg	Ex-Fn	Mint
Frederick Atherton & Co., 19J, gilded, KW, GJS, HCIP ★	500	675	850
Frederick Atherton & Co., 19J, gilded, SW, GJS, HCIP, HC ★	650	750	980
Frederick Atherton & Co., 19J, gilded, SW, GJS, HCIP OF ★	500	600	725
S. M. Beard, 15J, KW	250	300	395
S. M. Beard, 15J, NI, SW	250	300	395
George Channing, 15J, gilded, KW	250	320	425
J. W. Deacon, 11J, gilded, SW or KW	185	230	395
Empire City Watch Co., 15J, NI, SW	300	340	475
Asa Fuller, 11J, gilded, SW or KW	200	260	340
Asa Fuller, 11J, gilded, SW or KW, Coin OF	200	260	340
Asa Fuller, 11J, gilded, SW or KW, Coin HC	225	275	365
John W. Lewis, 15J, NI, SW or KW	275	340	495
Marion Watch Co., 15J, gilded, KW, ADJ	350	395	475
Marion Watch Co., 15J, gilded, SW, ADJ	400	425	525
Henry Randel, 15J, NI, KW, ADJ	250	325	425
Henry Randel, 15J, NI, SW, ADJ, OF	250	325	425
Henry Randel, 15J, NI, SW, ADJ, Coin	275	350	475
Henry Randel, 15J, NI, SW, HC	225	300	400
G. A. Read, 7J, Coin	200	250	325

MARION WATCH CO. (continued)

Grade or Name — Description	Avg	Ex-Fn	Mint
G. A. Read, 7J, gilded, SW	175	200	320
G. A. Read, 7J, gilded, KW	165	185	300
Edwin Rollo, 15J, gilded, KW	200	275	325
Rural New Yorker, 15J, KW, KS	275	325	450
Rural New Yorker, 15J, KW, KS, Coin	275	325	450
Fayette Stratton, 15J, Coin	250	300	400
Fayette Stratton, 15J, gilded, KW	250	300	400
Fayette Stratton, 15J, gilded, SW	275	325	400
United States Watch Co., 19J, NI, GJS, HCIP, KW ★★	750	900	1,200
United States Watch Co., 19J, NI, GJS, HCIP, SW ★★★	900	1,100	1,600
United States Watch Co., 19J, NI, GJS, HCIP, SW, 18K, HC, U.S. W. Co. case ★★★	4,000	4,300	5,000
A. H. Wallis, 17J, NI, HCIP, KW	325	375	500
A. H. Wallis, 17J, NI, HCIP, SW	350	400	550
A. H. Wallis, 17J, NI, HCI5P, Coin	325	375	500
I. H. Wright, 11J, gilded, KW, SW	200	250	350
Young America, 7J, gilded, KW or SW	250	300	425
Young America, 7J, gilded, KW or SW, Coin	250	300	425

14 OR 16 SIZE

Grade or Name — Description	Avg	Ex-Fn	Mint
United States Watch Co., 19J, NI, HCIP, GJS ★	$1,000	$1,100	$1,375

10 SIZE

Grade or Name — Description	Avg	Ex-Fn	Mint
Chas. G. Knapp, 15J, Coin	$100	$130	$175
Chas. G. Knapp, 15J, gilded	110	135	185
R. F. Pratt, 15J, gilded	110	135	185
United States Watch Co., 19J, GJS, KW, NI ★	350	450	675
United States Watch Co., 19J, GJS, SW, NI ★	425	535	725

McINTYRE WATCH CO.
Kankakee, Illinois
1905 — 1911

This company probably bought the factory from Kankakee Watch Co. In 1908 Charles DeLong was made master watchmaker, and he designed and improved the railroad watches. Only a few watches were made, estimated total production being about ten watches.

Grade or Name — Description	Avg	Ex-Fn	Mint
16S, 21J, BRG, NI, WI ★★★	$2,500	$3,000	$4,000
16S, 23J, BRG, NI, WI ★★★	3,000	3,400	5,000
12S, 19J, BRG ★★★	650	800	1,000

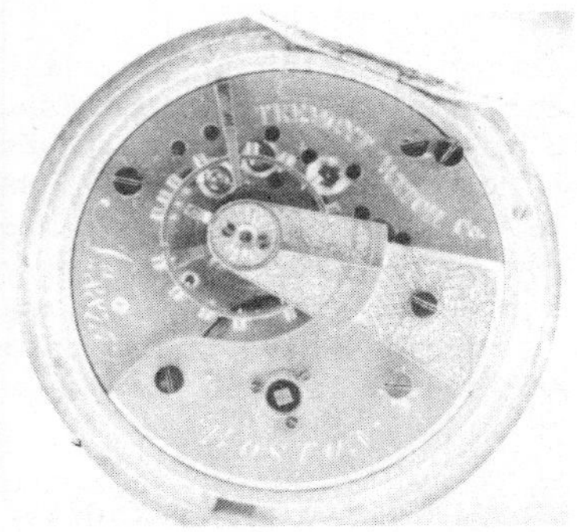

Example of a basic **Melrose Watch Co.** movement, 18 size, 15 jewels, key wind & set.

MELROSE WATCH CO.
Melrose, Massachusetts
1866 — 1868

Melrose Watch Co. began as Tremont Watch Co. and imported the expansion balances and escapements. Dials were made first by Mr. Gold and Mr. Spear, then later by Mr. Hull and Mr. Carpenter. Tremont had hoped to produce 600 sets of trains per month. They were 18S, key wind, fully jeweled movements and were engraved "Tremont Watch Co." In 1866 the company moved, changed its name to Melrose Watch Co., and started making complete watch movements, including a new style 18S movement engraved "Melrose Watch Co." About 3,000 were produced. Some watches are found with "Melrose" on the dial and "Tremont" on the movement. Serial numbers start at about 30,000.

Grade or Name — Description		Avg	Ex-Fn	Mint
18S, 7J, KW, KS	★★	$250	$285	$450
18S, 11J, KW, KS, OF	★★	300	335	500
18S, 15J, KW, KS	★★	375	400	575
18S, 15J, KW, KS, Silveroid	★★	250	285	450

MOZART WATCH CO.
Providence, Rhode Island
Ann Arbor, Michigan
1864 — 1870

In 1864 Don J. Mozart started out to produce a less expensive three-wheel watch in Providence, R. I. Despite his best efforts, the venture was declared a failure by 1866. Mozart left Providence and moved to Ann Arbor, Mich. There, again, he started on a three-wheel watch and succeeded in producing thirty. The three-wheel watch was not a new idea except to American manufacturers. Three-wheel watches were made many decades before Mozart's first effort, but credit for the first American-made three-wheel watch must go to him. The size was about 18 and could be called a ¾ or full plate movement. The balance bridge was screwed on the top plate, as was customary. The round bridge partially covered the opening in the top plate and was just large enough for the balance to oscillate. The balance was compensated and somewhat smaller than the usual

MOZART WATCH CO. (continued)

diameter. Mozart called it a chronolever, and it was to function so perfectly it would be free from friction. That sounded good but was in no way true. The watch was of the usual thickness of the American watches of 18S. The train had a main wheel with the usual number of teeth and a ten-leaf center pinion, but it had a large center wheel of 108 teeth and a third wheel of 90 teeth, with a six-leaf third (escape) pinion. The escape wheel had 30 teeth and received its impulse directly from the roller on the staff, while the escape tooth locked on the intermediate lever pallet. The escape pinion had a long pivot that carried the second hand, which made a circuit of the dial, once in 12 seconds: The total number of Mozart watches produced was 165, and about 30 of these were the three-wheel type.

Grade or Name — Description		Avg	Ex-Fn	Mint
18S, ¾, KW, KS, 3-wheel	★★★	$11,000	$15,000	$20,000
18S, ¾, KW, KS	★★	4,500	6,000	7,500

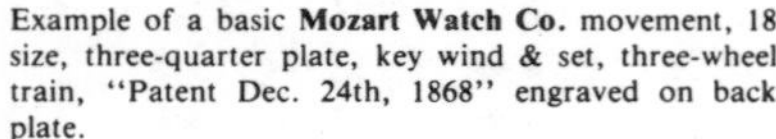
Example of a basic **Mozart Watch Co.** movement, 18 size, three-quarter plate, key wind & set, three-wheel train, "Patent Dec. 24th, 1868" engraved on back plate.

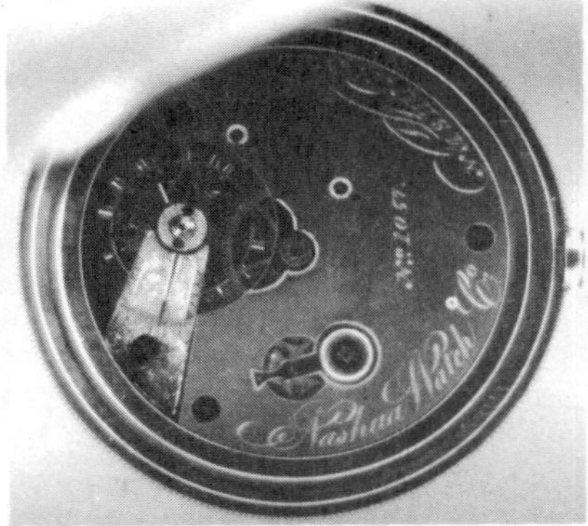

Nashua Watch Co. (marked), 20 size, 19 jewels, key wind & set from back, serial number 1,057.

NASHUA WATCH CO.
Nashua, New Hampshire
1859 — 1862

One of the most important contributions to the American Watch industry was made by the Nashua Watch Co. of Nashua, New Hampshire. Founded in 1859 by B. D. Bingham, the company hired some of the most innovative and creative watchmakers in America and produced an extremely high grade American pocket watch.

His company included N. P. Stratton, C. V. Woerd, Charles Moseley, James H. Gerry, and James Gooding, among others. Most of the persons connected with the Nashua Watch Company became famous for various advances in the production of watch manufacture at one time or another. Many had extremely important American patents on various inventions that came to be regarded as a benchmark of the best America was capable of making in watches at the time.

The Nashua Watch Co. is important for many reasons: it was the first American company to produce a truly superior high grade movement; the ¾ plate design used by Nashua became the standard for over 40 years in the American marketplace; perhaps most importantly, the watches designed by the Nashua Watch Co., and later by the Nashua division of the American Watch Co., became the leaders in the production of the highest quality watches made in America and forced the entire Swiss watch industry to change their technology to compete with the Nashua designs.

Nashua continually won awards for their various models of watches both here and in Europe. By virtue of their sheer technical superiority and classical elegance, Nashua became known universally as the innovator and most inventive producer of watches America ever knew.

The original Nashua company produced material for about 1,000 movements but, except for a handful, almost the entire production was finished by the American Watch Company at Waltham, Mass., after R. E. Robbins took over Nashua in 1862 when the company was in grave financial difficulties. Robbins was very happy about the arrangement since he got back almost all the watchmaking geniuses who had left him in 1859 to join Nashua. Robbins incorporated the Nashua Division into the American Watch Company as its high grade experimental division.

Over the years, many of the major advances were made by the Nashua division of Waltham, including the 1860 model 16-size keywind keyset, the 1862 model 20-size keywind keyset, the 1870 model 18-size keywind keyset, pin set, and lever set (which became the first American advertised Railroad watch), the 1868 model 16-size stemwind, and the 1872 model 17-size stemwind. The Nashua division also influenced greatly the 1888 model and the 1892 model by Waltham.

Since almost all the production material made by Nashua from 1859 until its incorporation into the American Watch Company in 1862 was unfinished by Nashua, only about four examples of the 20-size keywind keyset from the back signed Nashua Watch Co. are known to exist.

Grade or Name — Description		Avg	Ex-Fn	Mint
Nashua (marked), 19J, KW, KS, ¾, 18K	★★★	$18,000	$22,000	$28,000
Nashua (unmarked), 15J, KW, KS, ¾, silver case	★★	10,000	13,000	17,000

NEWARK WATCH CO.
Newark, New Jersey
1864 — 1870

Arthur Wadsworth, one of the designers for Newark Watch Co., patented an 18 Size full plate movement. The first movements reached the market in 1867. This company produced only about 4,000 watches before it was sold to the Cornell Watch Co.

The Chronology of the Development of Newark Watch Co.:
Newark Watch Co. 1864-1870; S#s 6,901 to 12,000;
Cornell Watch Co., Chicago, Ill. 1870-1874; S#s 12,001 to 25,000;
Cornell Watch Co., San Francisco, Calif. 1874-Jan. 1876; S#s 25,001 to 35,000;
California Watch Co., Jan. 1876-mid 1876.

Grade or Name — Description		Avg	Ex-Fn	Mint
18S, 15J, KW, KS, HC	★★	$275	$350	$550
18S, 15J, KW, KS, OF	★★	250	325	500
18S, 7J, KW, KS	★★	200	285	475
J. C. Adams, 11J, KW, KS	★★	275	350	450

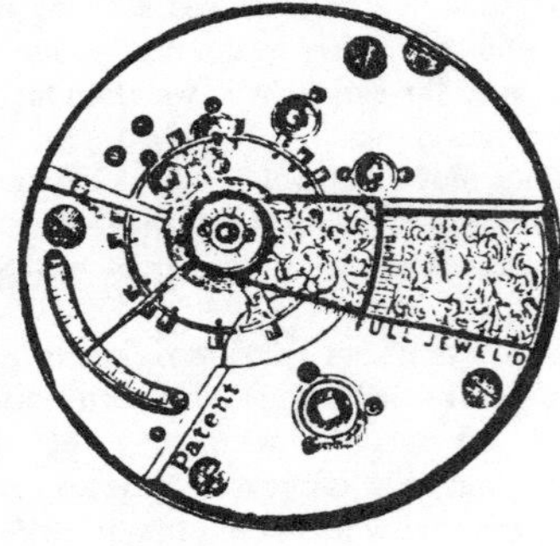

Example of a basic **Newark Watch Co.** movement, 18 size, 7-15 jewels, key wind & set.

Grade or Name — Description		Avg	Ex-Fn	Mint
J. C. Adams, 11J, KW, KS, Coin	★★	250	325	400
Edward Biven, 15J, KW, KS	★★	275	350	500
Robert Fellow, KW, KS	★★	350	450	625
Newark Watch Co., 7-15J, KW, KS	★★	275	350	425
Arthur Wadsworth, SW	★★	275	320	450
Arthur Wadsworth, 18S, 15J, 18K, HC ("Arthur Wadsworth, New York" on dial; "Keyless Watch, Patent #3655, June 19, 1866" engraved on movement)	★★	1,800	2,000	2,500

Front and back view of a skeletonized **New England Watch Co.** movement. This watch is fitted with a glass back and front, making the entire movement and wheels visible, 4 jewels, silver hands, black numbers, originally sold for $10-13.

NEW ENGLAND WATCH CO.
Waterbury, Connecticut
1898 — 1914

The New England Watch Co., formerly the Waterbury Watch Co., made a watch with a duplex escapement, gilt, 16S, open faced. Watches with the skeletonized movement are very desirable. The company later became Timex Watch Co.

NEW ENGLAND WATCH CO. (continued)

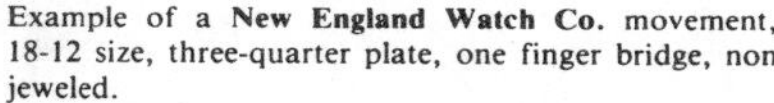
Example of a **New England Watch Co.** movement, 18-12 size, three-quarter plate, one finger bridge, non jeweled.

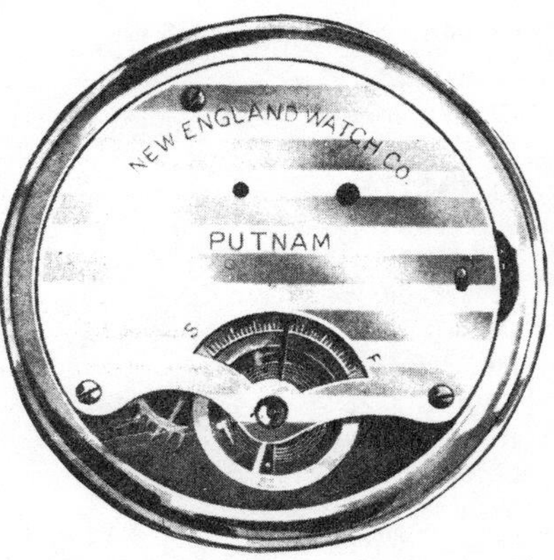

Example of a **New England Watch Co.** movement, 18 size, open face. Note the duplex escapement.

Grade or Name — Description	Avg	Ex-Fn	Mint
16S, OF, duplex, skeleton, good running order ★★	$175	$225	$350
12S, 16S, 18S, OF, pictures on dial: ladies, dogs, horses, trains, flags, ships, cards, etc.	100	120	150
12S, 16S, 18S, OF, duplex escapement, good running order	30	40	60
12S, 16S, 18S, OF, pin lever escapement, good running order	15	25	45
6S, duplex	35	40	55
Addison	35	40	55
Alden	35	40	55
Americus, duplex	20	25	30
Avour, duplex escapement	35	40	55
Cadish, duplex escapement	35	40	55
Cavour	45	60	85

New England Watch Co., multi-colored dials, showing an assorted selection.

NEW ENGLAND WATCH CO. (continued)

Grade or Name — Description	Avg	Ex-Fn	Mint
Columbian	15	20	30
Cruiser, duplex	45	50	69
Dan Patch, 7J ★★	200	240	300
Excelsor, 7J	65	70	95
Gabour	65	70	85
Hale, 7J	25	30	45
Jockey, duplex	55	60	75
Oxford	15	20	30
Padishah, duplex	45	50	65
Putnam	65	70	85
Rugby, stop watch	65	70	85
Scout	40	45	55
Senator, duplex escapement	40	45	55
Trump, duplex	15	20	30
Tuxedo	15	20	35

WRIST WATCHES

Style or Grade — Description	Avg	Ex-Fn	Mint
Alden	8	10	15
Hale	8	10	15
New England model	5	7	10
Waterbury	15	18	25

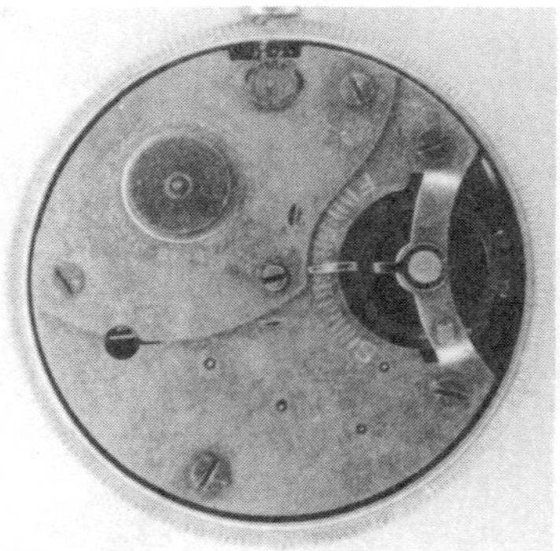

Example of a **New Haven** movement, stem wind.

Example of a **New Haven** movement, stem wind, patented Sept., 25th, 1899; Jan., 23rd, 1900.

NEW HAVEN CLOCK AND WATCH CO.
New Haven, Connecticut
1853 — 1956

The company started making watches in early 1880 in New Haven and produced the regular 16S, lever watch. These sold for $3.75. The company soon reached a production of about 200 watches per day, making a total of some 40 million watches.

Example of **Kaiser Wilhelm.**

Example of Lone Ranger.

Grade or Name — Description	Avg	Ex-Fn	Mint
Always Right	$30	$35	$40
Beardsley—Radiant	35	40	45
Buddy	30	35	40
Bull Dog	30	35	40
Buster Brown	40	50	60
Captain Scout	30	35	48
Chronometer	30	35	40
Elite	20	25	30
Football Timer	35	45	50
Ford Special	50	60	75
Hamilton	30	35	40
Handy Andy	35	40	45
Jerome USA	30	35	40
Kaiser Wilhelm ★★	100	150	225
Kermit	35	40	45
Laddie	20	25	35
Leonard Watch Co.	15	20	35
Leonard	20	25	30
Lone Ranger (1939)	85	100	175
Mastercraft Rayolite	30	35	40
Miracle	20	25	30
Nehi	35	40	65
New Haven, pin lever, SW	25	30	40
New Haven, back wind	45	50	60
Panama Official Souvenir, 1915	150	195	300
Pastor Stop Watch	50	60	75
Peter Pan	35	40	50
Popeye & Wimpy ★★	150	175	250
Sports Timer	50	60	75
Surity	10	15	20
Tip Top	10	15	25
Tip Top Jr.	10	15	25
Tommy Ticker	25	30	35
Traveler, with travel case	30	40	50
True Time Teller Tip Top	35	40	50
USA	25	30	35

Example of **Popeye & Wimpy**, about 16 size, non-jeweled, c. 1935.

New Haven Clock Co., Tip Top.

WRIST WATCHES

Style or Grade — Description	Avg	Ex-Fn	Mint
Boy Scout, Tonneau case	75	85	100
Dick Tracy, Tonneau case	95	115	150
Dick Tracy, round case	40	50	65
Gene Autry	65	75	95
Joe Palooka	55	60	85
Li'l Abner	40	45	55
Lone Ranger	55	65	85
Orphan Annie, Tonneau case	85	95	125
Popeye	95	110	135
Smitty	55	60	75
Tip Top	8	10	15
New Haven model, Tonneau case	12	15	20
New Haven model, rectangular	8	10	15
New Haven model, round case	5	7	10

NEW HAVEN WATCH CO.
New Haven, Connecticut
1883 — 1887

This company was organized October 16, 1883 with the intention of producing W. E. Doolittle's patented watch; however, this plan was soon abandoned. They did produce a "Model A" watch, the first reaching the market in the spring of 1884. Batch or lot numbers were used instead of serial numbers, and watches can be found bearing the same batch number. Estimated total production was 2,000 to 3,000. The original capital became absorbed by Trenton Watch Company.

Grade or Name — Description	Avg	Ex-Fn	Mint
"A" Model, about 18S, pat. Dec. 27, '81 ★★★	$200	$275	$475
Alpha Model, pat. Dec. 27, '81	200	275	475

Example of a basic **New Haven Watch Co.** movement with batch or lot number 65. Note this is not a serial number.

NEW YORK WATCH CO.
&
NEW YORK CITY WATCH CO.
New York, New York
1890 — 1897

This company manufactured the Dollar-type watches, which had the pendant-type crank. The patent number 526,871, dated October 1894, was held by S. Schisgall.

Grade or Name — Description	Avg	Ex-Fn	Mint
20S, no jewels, good running order ....★★★	$400	$550	$795

New York City Watch Co., 20 size, "Lever Winder" on dial. This watch is wound by cranking the pendant, pin lever escapement, patent number 526871.

NEW YORK CHRONOGRAPH WATCH CO.
New York, New York
1883 — ?

This company sold about 18,000 watches marked "New York Chronograph Watch Co," manufactured by Manhattan Watch Co. They used a sweep second hand.

Grade or Name — Description	Avg	Ex-Fn	Mint
18S, 7J, HC	$60	$85	$250
18S, 7J, OF ★	50	75	225
16S, 7J, SW, OF ★	60	80	150
16S, 9J, SW, OF ★	75	90	160
16S, 9J, SW, OF, Silveroid	55	60	75

NEW YORK STANDARD WATCH CO.
Jersey City, New Jersey
1885 — 1929

The first watch reached the market in early 1888 and was a 18S. The most interesting feature was the escapement which was a straight line lever with a "worm gear escapement." This was patented by R. J. Clay. All watches were quick train and open-faced. The company also made its own cases and sold a complete watch. A prefix number was added to the serial number after the first 10,000 watches were made. Estimated total production was 7,000,000.

N. Y. STANDARD
16 AND 18 SIZE

Grade or Name — Description	Avg	Ex-Fn	Mint
18S, 7J, N. Y. Standard, KW, KS	$175	$250	$475
18S, 7J, N. Y. Standard, SW	45	60	75
18S, 15J, N. Y. Standard, SW, LS, HC	75	90	120
Chronograph, 7J, ¾, NI, DMK, SW, second hand stop, and fly back	125	150	185
Chronograph, 13J, sweep sec., stop & fly back	135	165	195
Chronograph, 15J, ¾, NI, DMK, SW, second hand stop, and fly back	150	175	215
Columbus, 7J	45	60	75

Chronograph, 16-18 size, 7 jewels, stem wind, second hand stop and fly back, three-quarter plate, serial number 5334322.

Example of a basic **New York Standard** movement, 18 size, 7 jewels, stem wind, serial number 296893.

Remington W. Co. (marked on movement & case), 16 size, 11 jewels, 2-tone damaskeening, serial number CC021331.

New York Standard, with worm gear (located under cut-out star), 18 size, 7 jewels, serial number 31138.

Grade or Name — Description	Avg	Ex-Fn	Mint
Crown W. Co., 7J, OF or HC	35	50	65
Crown W. Co., 15J, OF or HC	40	55	75
Dan Patch, 7J, stop watch ★	200	260	375
Dan Patch, 17J, stop watch ★★	300	380	550
Edgemere, 7J, OF & HC	35	40	60
Excelsior, 7J, OF or HC	35	40	55
Hi Grade	25	30	45
Ideal	25	30	45
New Era, 7J, OF or HC, (Poor Man's Dudley)	35	50	65
New York Standard W. Co., 11J, ¾	45	50	65
New York Standard, 7J, ¾	35	40	45
New York Standard, 15J, BRG	45	55	65
New York Standard, with worm gear ★	400	500	725
Pan American, 7J, OF	35	40	60
Perfection, 7J, OF or HC	35	40	55
Perfection, 15J, OF or HC, NI	55	60	75
Remington W. Co., 11J, marked mvt. & case	75	90	115
Solar W. Co., 7J	45	50	65
18S Tribune USA, 23J, HC or OF, Pat. Reg. Adj.	80	90	135
Wilmington	25	30	45

Note: For watches with O'Hara Multi-Color Dials, add $75 to value in mint condition.

12 SIZE

Grade or Name — Description	Avg	Ex-Fn	Mint
N. Y. Standard, 7J, OF	$25	$30	$45
N. Y. Standard, 7J, HC, Multi-Color dial	100	125	185

6 SIZE AND 0 SIZE

Grade or Name — Description	Avg	Ex-Fn	Mint
Empire State W. Co., 7J	$45	$50	$75
Standard USA, 7J	35	40	55
6S, Columbia, 7J, HC	60	70	80
6S N. Y. Standard, 7J, HC	55	75	95

NEW YORK STANDARD WATCH CO. (continued)

Grade or Name — Description	Avg	Ex-Fn	Mint
6S, Orient, SW	35	40	60
6S, Progress, 7J, YGF	40	60	75
0S, Ideal, 7J, HC	50	60	85
0S, N. Y. Standard, 7J, HC	65	75	95

WRIST WATCHES

Style or Grade — Description	Avg	Ex-Fn	Mint
Round case, gold filled	$10	$15	$25
Round case, base metal	5	7	12

18 size, 5th Model, hunting

18 size, 6th Model, open face

18 size, No. 80

18 size, No. 64

18 size, No. 360

18 size, No. 60

18 size, No. 165

18 size, 4th Model

16 size, No. 94

16 size, No. 91

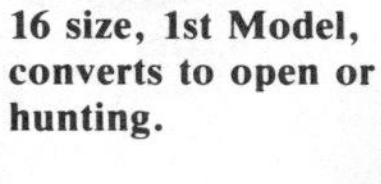

16 size, 1st Model, converts to open or hunting.

16 size, No. 1516

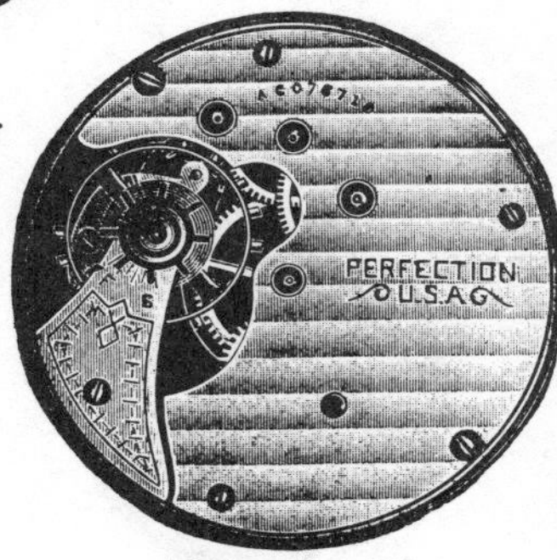

16 size, No. 390

12 size, No. 170

12 size, No. 1570

12 size, hunting

12 size, No. 1512

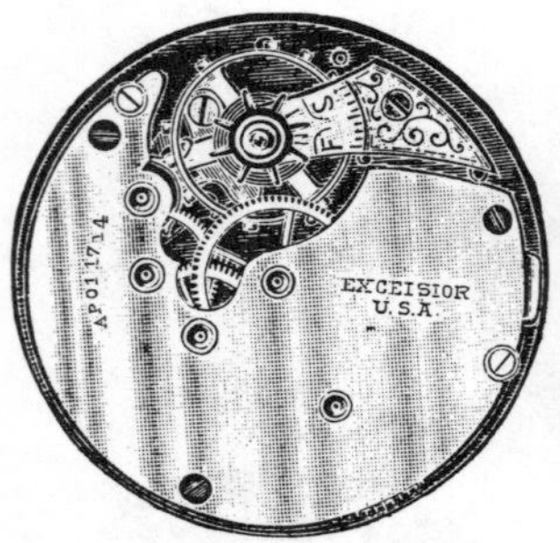

12 size, No. 370

6 size, No. 146

6 size, No. 44

0 size, No. 300

3/0 size, No. 730

10/0 size, No. 1015

NEW YORK WATCH CO.
Springfield, Massachusetts
1866 — 1876

The New York Watch Co. had a rather difficult time getting started in business. The name of the company was changed from the Mozart Watch Co. to the New York Watch Co., and it was located in Rhode Island. Before any watches had been produced, the factory was moved to Springfield, Mass., in 1867. A factory was built there, but before any watches were made a fire occurred on April 23, 1870. About 100 watches were produced during that year. Shortly after the fire, in 1870, a newly-designed watch was introduced. The first movements reached the market in 1871, and the first grade was a fully-jeweled adjusted movement called "Frederick Billings." The standard 18S and the Swiss Ligne systems were both used in gauging the size of these watches. The New York Watch Co. used full signatures on its movements. The doors closed in the summer of 1876.

In January 1877, the Hampden Watch Co. was organized and commenced active operation in June 1877.

Chronology of the Development of New York Watch Co.:
The Mozart Watch Co., Providence, R. I. — 1864-1866
New York Watch Co., Providence, R. I. — 1866-1867
New York Watch Co., Springfield, Mass. — 1867-1875
New York Watch Mfg. Co., Springfield, Mass. — 1875-1876
Hampden Watch Co., Springfield, Mass. — 1877-1886
Hampden-Dueber Watch Co., Springfield, Mass. — 1886-1888
Hampden Watch Co., Canton, Ohio — 1888-1923
Dueber Watch Co., Canton, Ohio — 1888-1923
Dueber-Hampden Watch Co., Canton, Ohio — 1923-1931
Amtorg, U.S.S.R. — 1930-

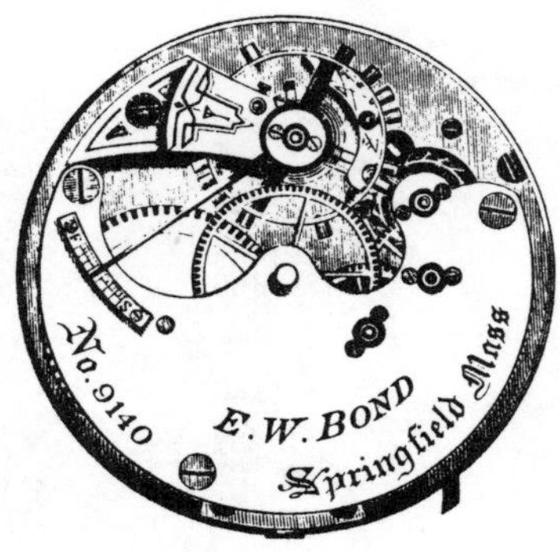

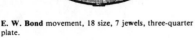

E. W. Bond movement, 18 size, 7 jewels, three-quarter plate.

Chas. E. Hayward, 18 size, 15 jewels, key wind & set, serial number 18733.

N. Y. W. SPRINGFIELD
18 TO 20 SIZE

Grade or Name — Description	Avg	Ex-Fn	Mint
Aaron Bragg, 7J, KW, KS ★	$200	$250	$325

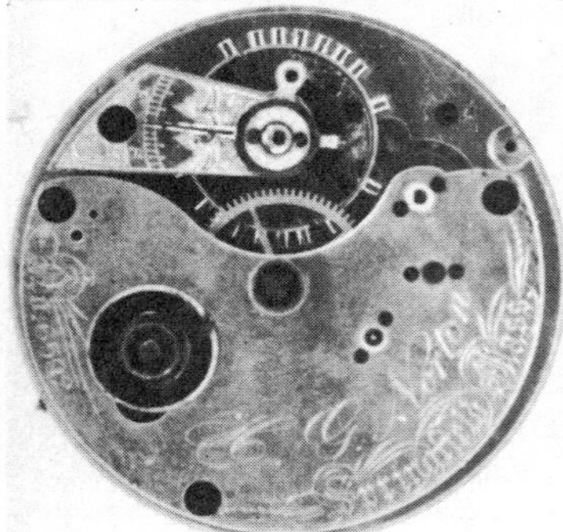

H.G. Norton, 18 size, 15 jewels, three-quarter plate, gold escape wheel, serial number 6592.

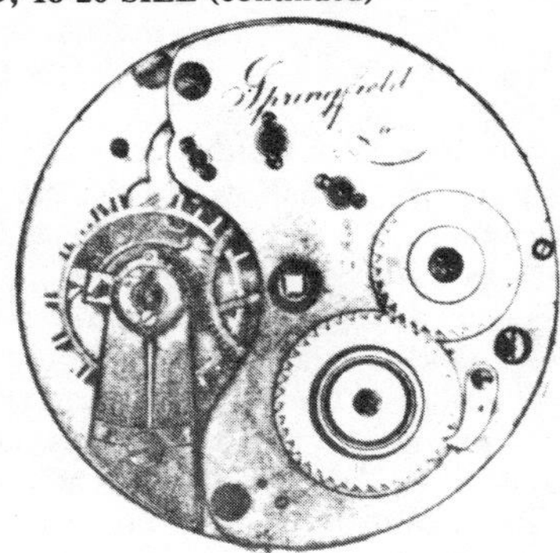

New York Watch Co., 18 size, 15 jewels, ¾ plate, key wind & set, note wolf teeth winding.

Grade or Name — Description	Avg	Ex-Fn	Mint
Frederick Billings, 15J, KW, KS ★★	175	200	235
E. W. Bond, 15J, ¾ ★★	575	675	795
J. A. Briggs, 11J, KW, KS, from back ★★★	225	300	425
Albert Clark, 15J, KW, KS, from back, ¾ ★★	225	265	335
Homer Foot, 15J, KW, KS, from back, ¾ ★★	225	265	300
Herman Gerz, 11J, KW, KS ★	95	160	250
John Hancock, 7J, KW, KS	85	120	195
John Hancock, 7J, KW, KS, Silveroid	75	100	145
John Hancock, 7J, KW, KS, Coin	85	120	185
Chas. E. Hayward, 15J, KW, KS	225	250	295
Chas. E. Hayward, 15J, KW, KS, Coin	200	225	270
John L. King, 15J, KW, KS, from back, ¾ ★★	265	300	425
New York Watch Co., 7J, KW, KS ★	150	170	195
New York Watch Co., 15J, KW, KS, (Serial Nos. below 75)	1,300	1,500	2,000
New York Watch Co., 15J, KW, KS, Wolf's Teeth winding, all original ★★★	1,000	1,200	1,500
New York Watch Co., 11J, KW, KS ★★	145	200	325
H. G. Norton, 15J, KW, KS, from back, ¾ ★★	225	250	350
J. C. Perry, 15J ★	150	185	225
J. C. Perry, 15J, Silveroid ★	140	175	215

State Street movement, 18 size, 11 jewels, three-quarter plate.

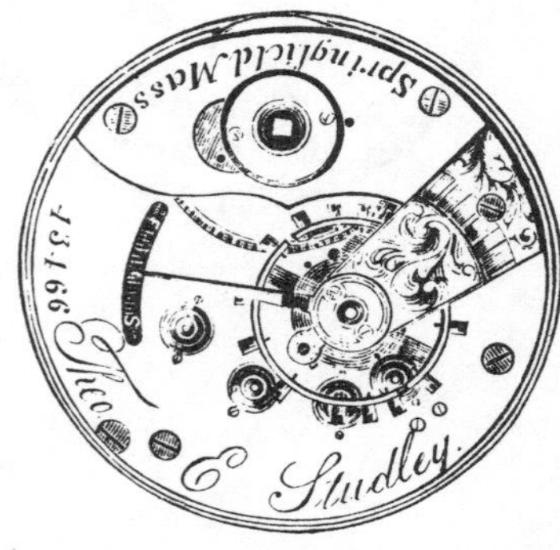

Theo E. Studley movement, 18 size, 15 jewels, key wind & set, full plate.

NEW YORK WATCH CO., SPRINGFIELD, 18-20 SIZE (continued)

Grade or Name — Description	Avg	Ex-Fn	Mint
Railway, 15J, KW, FULL, Coin ★	375	425	600
Railway, 15J, KW, KS, FULL ★	375	425	600
Geo. Sam Rice, 7J, KW, KS ★	175	195	235
Springfield, 19J, KW, KS, from back, ADJ, Wolfsteeth wind ★★★	1,300	1,400	2,000
State Street, 11J, ¾, SW ★	245	275	375
State Street, 11J, ¾, SW, Silveroid ★	195	225	295
Theo E. Studley, 15J, KW, Coin	140	165	215
Theo E. Studley, 15J, KW, KS	150	170	225
George Walker, 17J, KW, ¾, ADJ	275	300	400
Chester Woolworth, 15J, KW, KS	175	190	235
Chester Woolworth, 11J, KW, KS	160	180	220
Chester Woolworth, 11J, KW, KS, Silveroid	150	160	200
Chester Woolworth, 11J, KW, KS, ADJ	175	195	250
#4, 15J, ADJ, KW, KS	110	130	150
#5, 15J, KW, KS	95	110	125
#6, 11J, KW, KS	75	80	95
#6, 11J, KW, KS, Silveroid	65	70	85

NOTE: Some KW, KS watches made by the New York Watch Co. have a hidden key. If you unscrew the crown, and the crown comes out as a key, add $100 to the listed value.

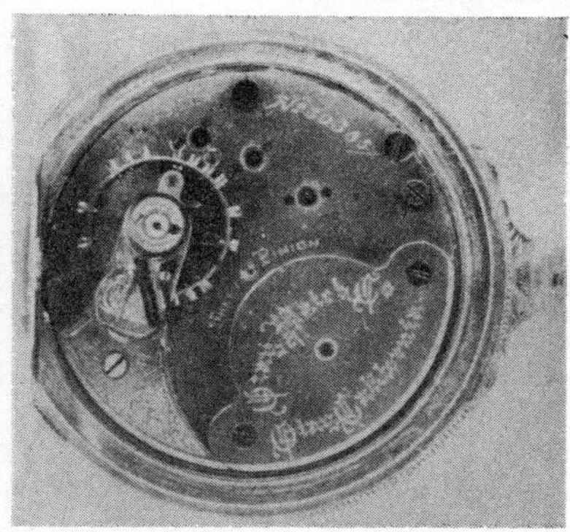

Otay Watch Co., Otay, Calif., 18 size, 15 jewels, open face, adjusted, serial number 30385.

OTAY WATCH CO.
Otay, California
1889 — 1894

This company produced about 1,000 watches with a serial number range of 1,000 to 1,500 and 30,000 to 31,000. The company was purchased by a Japanese manufacturer in 1894. Names on Otay movements include: Golden Gate, F. A. Kimball, Native Sun, Overland Mail, R. D. Perry, and P. H. Wheeler.

18 SIZE

Grade or Name — Description	Avg	Ex-Fn	Mint
California, 15J, LS, HC, NI ★★★	$2,000	$2,200	$2,500

OTAY WATCH CO., 18 SIZE (continued)

Grade or Name — Description		Avg	Ex-Fn	Mint
Golden Gate, 15J, LS, HC, OF, NI	★★★	1,500	1,800	2,500
F. A. Kimball, 15J, LS, HC, Gilt	★★	1,200	1,400	1,700
Native Son, 15J, LS, HC, NI	★★	1,600	1,800	2,500
Overland Rail, 15J, LS, HC, NI	★★	1,800	2,000	2,700
R. D. Perry, 15J, LS, HC, Gilt	★★	850	950	1,250
P. H. Wheeler, 15J, LS, HC, Gilt	★★	750	850	1,150

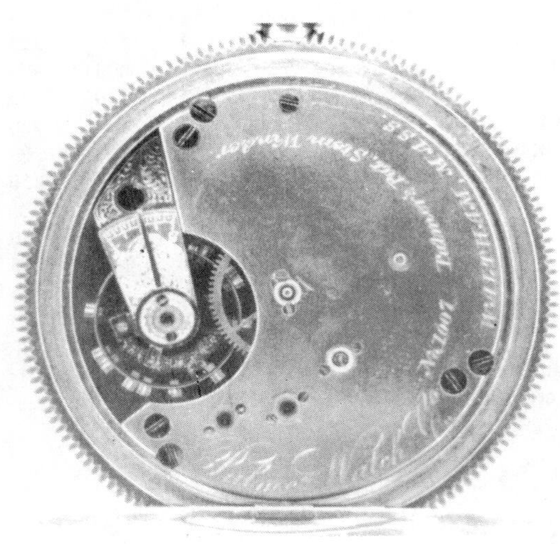

D.D. Palmer Watch Co., 18 size, 15 jewels, "Palmer's Pat. Stem Winder" on movement, serial number 1007.

D. D. PALMER WATCH CO.
Waltham, Massachusetts
1864 — 1875

In 1858, at age 20, Mr. Palmer opened a small jewelry store in Waltham, Mass. Here he became interested in pocket chronometers. At first he bought the balance and jewels from Swiss manufacturers. In 1864 he took a position with the American Watch Co. and made the chronometers in his spare time (only about 25 produced). They were 18S, ¾ plate, gilded, key wind, and some were nickel. At first they were fusee driven, but he mainly used going barrels. About 1870, Palmer started making lever watches and by 1875 he left the American Watch Co. and started making a 10S keywind, gilded-movement, and a 16S, ¾ plate, gilt and nickel, and a stem wind of his own invention (a vibrating crown wheel). In all he made about 1,500 watches. The signature appearing on the watches was "Palmer W. Co. Wal., Mass."

He basically had three grades of watches: Fine—Solid Nickel; Medium—Nickel Plated; and Medium—Gold Gilt. They were made in open-face and hunter cases.

Grade or Name — Description		Avg	Ex-Fn	Mint
18S, 15-17J, ¾ Plate, KW, Chronometer	★★★	$4,000	$4,500	$6,000
16S, 17J, NI, OF	★★	900	1,100	1,600

PEORIA WATCH CO.
Peoria, Illinois
1885 — 1895

The roots of this company began with the Independent Watch Co. (1880-1883). These watches marked "Marion" and "Mark Twain" were made by the Fredonia Watch Co. (1883-1885). Peoria Watch Co. opened Dec. 19, 1885, and made one model of railroad watch in 1887. They were 18S, quick train, 15 jewel, and all stem wind. These watches are hard to find, as only about 3,000 were made. Peoria also made railroad watches for A. C. Smith's Non-Magnetic Watch Co. of America from 1884-1888. The 18S watches were full plate, adjusted, and had whiplash regulator.

The Peoria Watch Co. closed in 1889, having produced about 47,000 watches.

Peoria Watch Co., 18 size, 15 jewels, lever set, "Made for Railway Service" on movement, serial number 17548.

Grade or Name — Description	Avg	Ex-Fn	Mint
18S, 15J, SW, personalized name	$160	$200	$285
18S, Peoria W. Co., 15J, SW, OF	165	200	275
18S, Peoria W. Co., 15J, SW, HC	170	210	285
18S, Peoria W. Co., 15J, SW, low S#	265	325	475
18S, Anti-Magnetic, 15J, SW	185	220	350
18S, Non-Magnetic Watch Co. of America, 15J, NI, SW, GJS, HCI5P, OF	275	325	475
18S, Non-Magnetic Watch Co. of America, NI, SW, GJS, HCI5P, HC	280	335	485
18S, Made for Railway Service, 15J, NI, GJS, HCI5P, OF	265	295	425
18S, Made for Railway Service, NI, GJS, HCI5P, HC	295	325	475

PHILADELPHIA WATCH CO.
Philadelphia, Pennsylvania
1874 — 1886

Eugene Paulus organized the Philadelphia Watch Co. about 1874. Most all the parts were made in Switzerland, and finished and cased in this country. Estimated total production of the company is 12,000 watches.

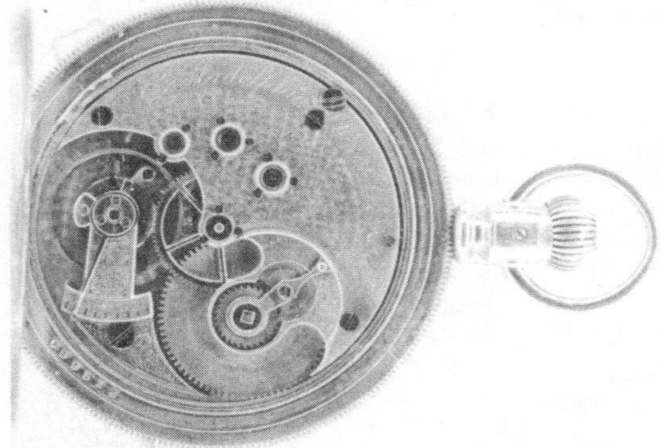

Philadelphia Watch Co., 16 size, 15 jewels, gold jeweled settings, hunting case model, "Paulus Patents 1868, Aug. 25th, Nov. 3rd" on movement, serial number 5751.

Grade or Name — Description		Avg	Ex-Fn	Mint
18S, 15J, KW, KS	★	$275	$325	$450
18S, 15J, SW, OF	★	325	400	570
18S, HC, KW, KS, 18K case	★	1,200	1,400	1,800
18S, HC, KW, KS, Silveroid	★	145	165	225
16S, 15J, KW, KS	★	155	185	250
16S, 19J, KW, KS, GJS	★	375	475	625
8S-6S, 11J, HC	★	150	175	225
8S-6S, 15J, HC	★	160	180	240
8S-6S, Paulus, 19J, KW, KS	★	225	300	425
000S, 7J, HC, PS	★	125	150	225

JAMES & HENRY PITKIN
Hartford, Connecticut
New York, New York
1838 — 1852

Henry Pitkin was the first to attempt the manufacture of watches by machinery. The machines were of Pitkin's original design and very crude, but he had some brilliant ideas. His first four workers were paid $30 a year plus their board. After much hardship, the first watches were produced in the fall of 1838. The watches had going barrels, not the fusee and chain, and the American flag was engraved on the plates to denote they were American made and to exemplify the true spirit of American independence in watchmaking.

The first 50 watches were stamped with the name "Henry Pitkin." Others bore the firm name "H & J F Pitkin." The movements were about 16S and ¾ plate. The plates were rolled brass and stamped out with dies. The pinions were lantern style with tight leaves. The movement had a slow train of 14,400 beats per hour. Pitkin's first plan was to make the ends of the pinions conical and let them run in the ends of hardened steel screws, similar to the Marine clock balances. A large brass setting was put in the plates and extended above the surface. Three screws with small jewels set in their ends were inserted so that they closed about the pivot with very small end shake. This proved to be too expensive and was used in only a few movements. Next, he tried to make standard

JAMES & HENRY PITKIN (continued)

type movements extend above the plates with the end shake controlled by means of a screw running down into the end of the pivots, reducing friction. This "capped jewel train" was used for a while before he adopted the standard ways of jeweling. The escape wheels were the star type, English style. The balance was made of gold and steel. These movements were fire gilded and not interchangeable. The dials, hands, mainsprings and hairsprings were imported. The rounded pallets were manufactured by Pitkin, and the cases for his watches were made on the premises. As many as 900 watches could have been made by Pitkin.

Example of a basic **Henry Pitkin** movement, 16 size, key wind & set.

Grade or Name — Description		Avg	Ex-Fn	Mint
Henry Pitkin S#1-50	★★★★	$25,000	$30,000	$40,000
H. & J. F. Pitkin & Co., S#50-377	★★★	18,000	21,000	25,000
Pitkin & Co., New York, S#378-up	★★★	14,000	16,000	18,000
W. Pitkin, Hartford, Conn., S# approx. 40,000, fusee lever, KW, Coin	★★	450	500	600

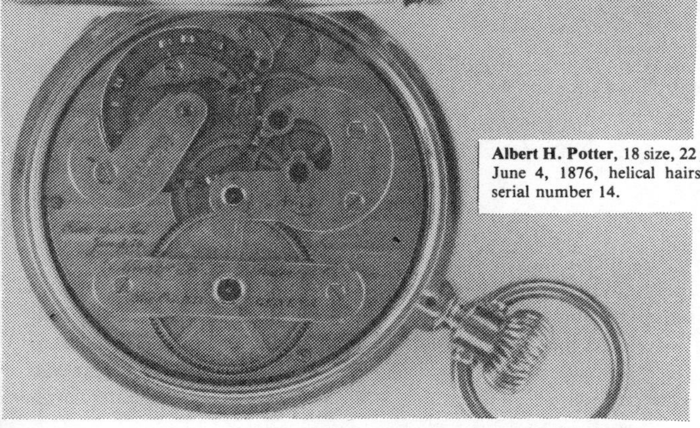

Albert H. Potter, 18 size, 22 jewels, pat. Oct. 11, 1875 & June 4, 1876, helical hairspring, detent escapement, serial number 14.

ALBERT H. POTTER WATCH CO.
New York, New York
1855 — 1875

Albert Potter started his apprenticeship in 1852. After this he moved to New York to take up watchmaking on his own. He made about 35 watches in all that sold for $225

ALBERT H. POTTER WATCH CO. (continued)

to $350. Some were chronometers, some were lever escapements, key wind, gilded movements, some were fusee driven, both bridge and ¾ plate. Potter was a contemporary of Charles Fasoldt and John Mulford, both horological inventors from Albany, N. Y. Potter moved to Cuba in 1861 but came back to New York in 1868. In 1872 he worked in Chicago and formed the Potter Brothers Company with his brother William. He moved to Geneva about 1876. His company produced a total of about 600 watches, but only about 40 of those were made in the U. S.

Grade or Name — Description	Avg	Ex-Fn	Mint
18S, 29J, 18K HC, 1 min. repeater, Geneva	$5,500	$6,500	$8,000
18S, BRG lever, Chronometer, signed A. H. Potter, New York ★★★★	10,500	12,000	14,000
18S, BRG lever with wind indicator ★★★	5,000	6,500	7,500
18S-20S, Tourbillion, signed A. H. Potter, Boston, gilded ★★★★	15,000	17,000	20,000
16S-18S, 22J, helical spring, detent escapement, Geneva	2,500	3,500	4,300
4S, 21J, ¼ hour repeater, 18K HC, Geneva	2,800	3,500	4,200

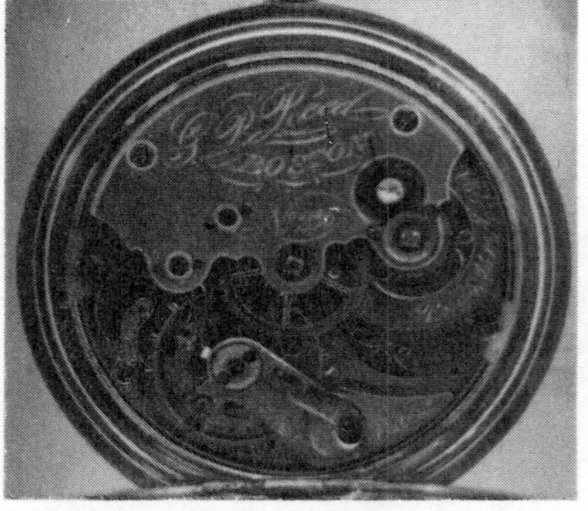

George P. Reed, 18 size, 15 jewels, key & stem wind, key & lever set, lever escapement, 48 hour up and down wind indicator, serial number 235.

George P. Reed, 18 size, 15 jewels, key & stem wind, key & lever set, lever escapement, 48 hour up and down wind indicator, serial number 5.

GEORGE P. REED
Boston, Massachusetts
1865 — 1885

In 1854, George P. Reed entered the employment of Dennison, Howard and Davis, in Roxbury, Mass., and moved with the company to Waltham, Mass. Here he was placed in charge of the pinion finishing room. While there he invented and received a patent for the mainspring barrel and main timing power combination. This patent was dated February 18, 1857. Reed returned to Roxbury with Howard who purchased his patented barrel. He stayed with the Howard factory until 1865 as foreman and adjuster, after which time he left for Boston to start his own account.

He obtained a patent on April 7, 1868, for an improved chronometer escapement which featured simplified construction. He made about 100 chronometers with his improved escapement, to which he added a stem-wind device. His company turned out about 100 watches the first three years. Most, if not all, of his watches run for two days and have up and down indicators on the dial. They are both 18S and 16S, ¾ plate, nickel, and are artistically designed. Reed experimented with various combinations of

GEORGE P. REED (continued)

lever and chronometer escapements. One such watch was a rotary watch he made in 1862 and called the "Monitor." It was the first rotary watch made in America. In all, Reed made a total of about 550 watches, and these are valuable to collectors.

Grade or Name — Description	Avg	Ex-Fn	Mint
18S, 15J, LS, OF or HC, Wind Indicator, chronometer escapement .... ★★★★	$9,000	$10,500	$15,000
16S, 15J, LS, OF or HC, **not** chronometer .... ★★★	6,500	7,000	9,000
16S, 15J, LS, OF, 31 day calendar .... ★★★	6,500	7,000	9,000

ROCKFORD WATCH CO.
Rockford, Illinois
1873 — 1915

The Rockford Watch Company's equipment was bought from the Cornell Watch Co. Also two of Cornell's employees came to work for Rockford: C. W. Parker and P. H. Wheeler. The factory was located 93 miles from Chicago on the Rock River. The first watch was placed on the market on May 1, 1876. They were key wind, 18S, full plate expansion balance. By 1877 the company was making ¾ plate nickel movements that fit standard size cases. Three railroads came through Rockford, and the company always advertised to the railroad men—and were very popular with them. The company had some problems in 1896, and the name changed to Rockford Watch Co. Ltd. It closed in 1915.

ROCKFORD ESTIMATED SERIAL NUMBERS AND PRODUCTION DATES

Date	Serial No.	Date	Serial No.	Date	Serial No.	Date	Serial No.
1876	5,000	1886	110,000	1896	290,000	1906	620,000
1877	15,000	1887	125,000	1897	320,000	1907	650,000
1878	25,000	1888	140,000	1898	350,000	1908	690,000
1879	35,000	1889	150,000	1899	385,000	1909	730,000
1880	50,000	1890	165,000	1900	415,000	1910	765,000
1881	60,000	1891	175,000	1901	450,000	1911	820,000
1882	70,000	1892	195,000	1902	480,000	1912	850,000
1883	80,000	1893	200,000	1903	515,000	1913	880,000
1884	90,000	1894	230,000	1904	550,000	1914	930,000
1885	100,000	1895	260,000	1905	580,000	1915	1,000,000

(See Rockford Watch Co. **Identification of Movements** section located at the end of the Rockford price section to identify the movement, size, and model number of your watch.)

(Prices are with gold filled cases except where noted.)

NOTE: Some grades are not included. Their values can be determined by comparing with similar models or grades listed.

ROCKFORD
18 SIZE

Grade or Name — Description	Avg	Ex-Fn	Mint
Belmont USA, 21J, LS, OF, NI, M#7	$185	$250	$375
Chronometer, 17J, ADJ, OF, G925	175	230	360

ROCKFORD WATCH CO., 18 SIZE (continued)

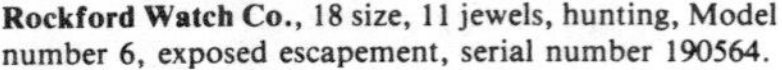

Rockford Watch Co., 18 size, 11 jewels, hunting, Model number 6, exposed escapement, serial number 190564.

Special Railway, 18 size, 17 jewels, hunting, Model number 8, serial number 344551.

Grade or Name — Description	Avg	Ex-Fn	Mint
Dome Model, 9J, brass plates ★	75	110	150
King Edward, Plymouth W. Co., 21J, 14K	700	800	975
King Edward (Sears), 21J, GJS, ADJ, NI	300	375	535
King Edward (Sears), 21J, GJS, ADJ, NI, Silveroid	245	295	375
Pennsylvania Special, 25J, LS, HCI6P, OF ★★★	3,000	4,000	6,000
Railway King, 21J, OF	325	400	650
The Ramsey Watch, 11J, NI, KW or SW	100	120	150
The Ramsey Watch, 15J, NI, KW or SW	115	140	165
The Ramsey Watch, M#7, 21J, OF, NI, ADJ	275	350	475
Rockford Early KW-KS, M#1-2, with low Serial Nos. less than 500 ★	400	600	900
Rockford Early KW-KS, M#1-2, with low Serial Nos. less than 500, Coin ★	350	550	895
Rockford Early KW-KS, M#1-2, with reversible case	175	200	395
Rockford Early KW-KS, M#1-2, S#s less than 100 ★★	1,000	1,400	2,000
Rockford, 7J, SW, FULL	40	50	70
Rockford, 7J, KW, FULL	60	75	95
Rockford, 7J, KW, FULL, Silveroid	50	60	75
Rockford, 9J, SW, FULL	45	55	75
Rockford, M#1, 9J, KW, FULL	75	90	145
Rockford, 11J, SW, FULL	55	65	95
Rockford, M#1-2, 11J, KW, FULL	85	100	145
Rockford, M#1-2, 11J, transition, FULL	100	125	160
Rockford, 11J, KW, Coin	75	90	140
Rockford, 11-15J, KW, HC, M#5, ¾ Plate, Coin ★	200	350	550
Rockford, 13J	50	60	85
Rockford, 15J, SW, FULL	60	75	95
Rockford, 15J, KW, FULL, multi-color dial	175	225	325
Rockford, 15J, SW, 2-Tone movement	95	110	150
Rockford, 15J, KW, FULL, ADJ	195	220	275
Rockford, 15J, KW/SW	75	85	125
Rockford, 15J, KW/SW, Silveroid	60	70	95
Rockford, 15J, M#6, exposed escapement wheel, FULL, HC, LS ★	275	350	450

Rockford movement, 18 size, 15 jewels, model 10, hunting, lever set, note recessed balance wheel.

Grade 900, 18 size, 24 jewels, HCI5P. **Warning:** 24 jewel fakes have been made from 21 jewel movements. The fakes are missing the eliptical jewel setting on the barrel bridge.

Grade or Name — Description	Avg	Ex-Fn	Mint
Rockford, 15J, M#6, exposed wheel, Coin ★	225	300	400
Rockford, M#1, 15J, KW, FULL	100	125	175
Rockford, 16J, GJS, NI, DMK, SW	70	80	120
Rockford, 16J, GJS, NI, DMK, SW, Silveroid	50	60	85
Rockford, 16J, GJS, NI, DMK, SW, Coin	60	70	95
Rockford, 17J, NI, DMK, SW	75	85	125
Rockford, 17J, GJS, NI, DMK, SW, HCI5P	100	125	175
Rockford, 17J, GJS, NI, SW, 2-Tone	120	135	185
Rockford, M#1-2, 19J, KW, FULL, GJS, ADJ	850	1,200	1,800
Rockford, 19J, transition, HC, GJS	400	500	700
Rockford, 21J, SW, Silveroid	75	95	140
Rockford, 21J, GJS, OF, HCI5P, wind indicator ★★	2,500	3,000	4,000
Rockford, 21J, SW, DMK, ADJ, HC	145	180	325
Rockford, 21J, NI, DMK, ADJ, OF	135	175	275
Rockford, 21J, GJS, NI, DMK, HCI5P, marked "RG"	175	225	295
Rockford, 24J, GJS, SW, LS, HCI5P, NI, DMK, marked "RG"	1,000	1,200	1,500
Rockford, 24J, GJS, SW, LS, HCI5P, marked "RG," HC ★	1,200	1,400	1,800
Rockford, 25J, GJS, SW, LS, HCI5P, NI, DMK ★★	3,500	5,000	6,500
Rockford, 26J, GJS, SW, LS, HCI5P, NI, DMK ★★★	8,000	10,000	16,000
The Syndicate Watch Co., M#7, 15J, LS, NI, HC	100	135	195
Winnebago, 17J, LS, GJS, HCI5P, DR, NI, DMK	135	175	275
Winnebago, 17J, LS, GJS, HCI5P, DR, NI, DMK, Silveroid	120	145	240
40, 15J, M#3, HC ★★	175	250	350
43, 15J, M#3, HC, 2-Tone	70	80	125
66, 11J, M#7, OF	60	70	90
66, 11J, M#7, OF, Silveroid	35	40	60
66, 11J, M#7, HC	65	80	95
81, 9J, M#3, HC, Gilt ★	165	200	295
82, Special, 21J, SW ★★	275	350	425
83, 15J, M#8, HC, 2-Tone	120	150	225
86, 15J, M#7, OF, NI	60	70	90

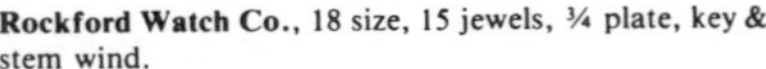

Rockford Watch Co., 18 size, 15 jewels, ¾ plate, key & stem wind.

Grade 918, 18 size, 21 jewels, double roller, gold jewel settings, adjusted to HCI5P, serial number 769276.

Grade or Name — Description	Avg	Ex-Fn	Mint
93, 9J, M#8, HC, Gilt	90	125	175
94, 9J, M#7, OF	40	50	70
200-205, 17J, M#9, OF, NI, LS	75	85	120
245, 19J, HC, GJS, 2-Tone ★	1,000	1,200	1,600
800, 24J, GJS, DR, HCI5P, DMK, HC ★	1,400	1,600	2,000
805, 21J, GJS, HCI5P, NI, DMK, HC, marked "RG"	195	275	425
810, 21J, NI, DMK, ADJ, HC	250	350	550
820, 17J, HC, SW ★★	175	250	325
825, 17J, HC, FULL	100	150	190
830, 17J, HC, FULL	90	130	165
835, 17J, HC, FULL	85	120	155
835, 17J, HC, FULL, Silveroid	50	60	80
845, 21J, HC, GJS, FULL ★	375	450	650
870, 7J, HC, FULL	85	95	145
900, 24J, GJS, DR, HCI5P, OF, NI, DMK ★★	1,200	1,400	2,000
900, 24J, GJS, DR, HCI5P, 14K, OF case ★★	1,400	1,600	2,400
905, 21J, GJS, DR, HCI5P, OF, NI, DMK	250	275	435
910, 21J, NI, DMK, 1 ADJ, OF	200	225	300
912, 21J, OF ★★	375	475	600
915, 17J, M#9, OF, SW ★★★	295	375	550
918, 21J, OF, NI, GJS, HCI5P, DR	150	175	225
918, 21J, OF, NI, GJS, HCI5P, DR, Silveroid	95	115	160
918, 21J, OF, NI, GJS, HCI5P, DR, Coin	115	135	185
930, 17J, OF	90	120	145
935, 17J, OF	75	90	125
945, 21J, M#9, OF, SW	145	165	295
950, 21J, OF, NI, GJS, HCI5P, DR, Wind Indicator ★★	2,500	3,300	4,500
970, 7J, OF	55	60	70
970, 7J, OF, Silveroid	40	45	55

16 SIZE

Grade or Name — Description	Avg	Ex-Fn	Mint
Commodore Perry, 21J, OF, GJS, GT, marked "RG"	$350	$450	$600

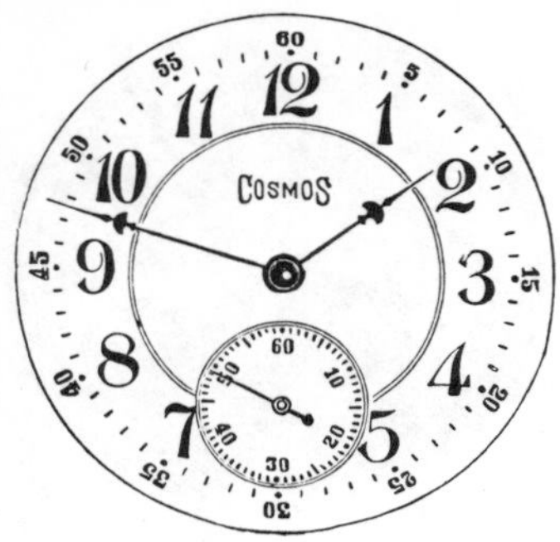

Examples of a **Cosmos** face and movement, 16 size, 17 jewels, open face, gold jewel settings.

Grade or Name — Description	Avg	Ex-Fn	Mint
Cosmos, 17J, OF, GJS, LS, DMK	225	275	500
Doll Watch Co., 23J, marked dial & mvt. ★★★	1,000	1,400	2,000
Dome Model, 15J	55	70	100
Dome Model, 17J	65	80	135
Dome Model, 17J, 2-tone, HC	130	155	225
Iroquois, 17J, DR, 14K, HC	525	575	700
Iroquois, 17J, DR	110	135	195
Peerless, 17J, OF, NI, LS, DMK	85	100	125
Pocahontas, 17-21J, GJS, HCI5P, DR	195	250	425
Prince of Wales (Sears), 21J	195	225	385
Prince of Wales (Sears), 21J, 14K	550	675	795
Rockford, 7J, ¾	55	60	75
Rockford, 9J, ¾, SW, OF	60	70	80
Rockford, 9J, SW, Silveroid	45	55	65
Rockford, 9J, SW, HC	65	75	120
Rockford, 11J, SW, Silveroid	50	60	70
Rockford, 11J, ¾	70	80	100
Rockford, 15J, ¾, ADJ, OF	75	90	110
Rockford, 15J, ¾, ADJ, Silveroid	60	70	80
Rockford, 15J, ¾, ADJ, HC	80	95	150
Rockford, 16J, ¾, SW, Silveroid	65	75	85
Rockford, 16J, ¾, ADJ, NI, DMK	125	160	195
Rockford, 17J, ¾	85	105	135
Rockford, 17J, ¾, 2-Tone, marked "RG"	155	195	275
Rockford, 17J, BRG, HCI3P, DR	150	175	250
Rockford, 17J, GJS, HCI5P, DR, Wind Indicator	485	575	795
Rockford, 17J, BRG, Silveroid	65	70	85
Rockford, 17J, ¾, Silveroid	60	70	80
Rockford, 21J, ¾, SW, Silveroid	70	80	90
Rockford, 21J, BRG, SW, Silveroid	75	85	100
Rockford, 21J, ¾, GJS, HCI5P	125	150	185
Rockford, 21J, BRG, GJS, HCI5P, GT, DR	175	225	290
Rockford, 21J, GJS, HCI5P, DR, Wind Indicator	595	700	995
Winnebago, 17J, BRG, GJS, HCI5P, NI	150	180	275
Winnebago, 21J, BRG, GJS, HCI5P, NI	210	240	325
100, 16J, M#1, HC, ¾, 2-Tone	200	250	325
100S, 21J, Special, HC, ¾, LS	225	280	375

ROCKFORD WATCH CO., 16 SIZE (continued)

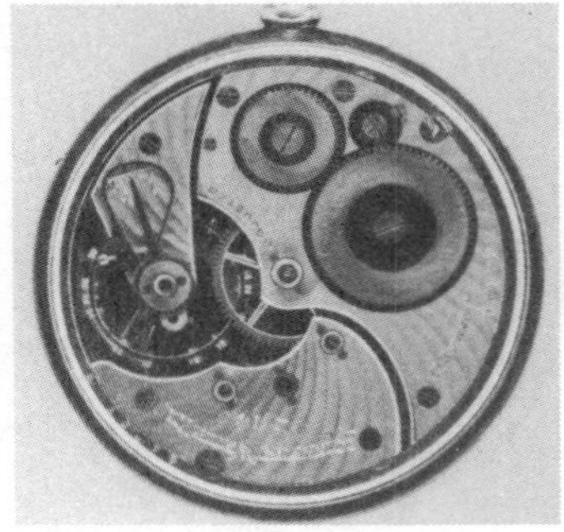

Example of a **Rockford** movement, 16 size, 21 jewels, three-quarter plate, serial number 842520.

Grade 500-HC, 505-OF, 16 size, 21 jewels, gold jewel settings, gold train, adjusted to HCI6p, marked "RG," originally sold for $100.00

Grade or Name — Description	Avg	Ex-Fn	Mint
102, 15J, HC, M#1 ★	195	250	350
103, 15J, HC, M#1	125	150	195
115-125, 17J, Special, HC ★★★	395	500	675
120-130, 17J, HC ★★★	335	450	625
400 & 405, 17J, NI, HCI5P, GJS, DR, BRG	100	125	175
445, 19J, HC, GJS, BRG ★★	850	1,000	1,400
500, 21J, BRG, NI, GJS, HCI5P, GT, HC ★★	400	500	700
501, 21J, GJS, HC ★★★	800	900	1,100
505, 21J, BRG, NI, GJS, HCI5P, GT, OF ★★	400	500	700
510, 21J, BRG, NI, GJS, HCI5P, GT, HC ★	350	400	500
515 & 525, 21J, OF, ¾	140	160	225
520, 21J, HC, ¾	160	185	245
520, 21J, BRG, NI, GJS, HCI5P, HC ★	300	375	500
530, 21J, HC, GJS, HCI5P ★	195	250	335
535, 21J, OF, ¾ ★	195	250	325
537, 21J, OF, GJS, HCI5P ★★	385	435	650
545, 21J, OF	135	150	195
561, 17J, BRG	125	150	180
566, 17J, BRG	125	150	180
572, 17J, BRG, NI, GJS, HCI5P	70	80	95
573, 17J, BRG, NI	70	80	95

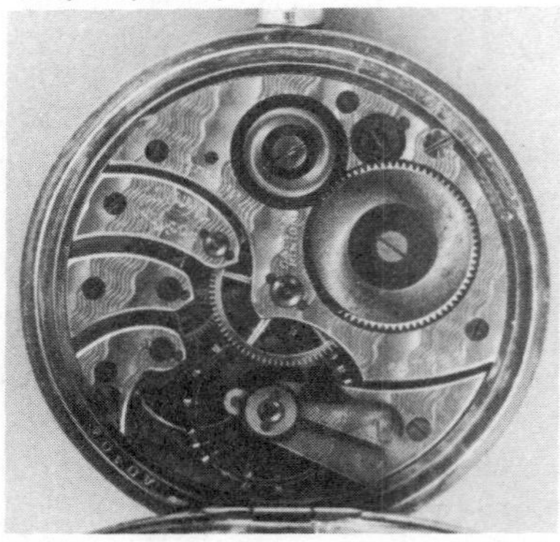

Rockford movement, 16 size, 17 jewels, bridge model, hunting case, serial number 881,125.

Rockford Watch Co., 16 size, 17 jewels, wind indicator, note extra wind indicator gear, serial number 916,203.

ROCKFORD WATCH CO., 12 SIZE (continued)

Grade or Name — Description		Avg	Ex-Fn	Mint
578-579, 17J, PS, GJS	★★	200	250	475
584 & 585, 15J, ¾, NI		65	70	85
620-625, 21J, HC, ¾	★	185	200	575
655, 21J, OF, Wind Indicator, marked 655	★	700	800	1,100

12 SIZE

Grade or Name — Description		Avg	Ex-Fn	Mint
Iroquois, 17J, BRG, DR, ADJ		$60	$80	$100
Pocahontas, 21J, GJS, HCI5P, BRG, DR		100	120	165
Rockford, 15J, BRG		35	40	55
Rockford, 17J, BRG, NI, DR, ADJ		50	60	70
Rockford, 21J, BRG, NI, DR, ADJ		60	80	110
Rockford, 21J, BRG, NI, DR, ADJ, Silveroid		40	50	90
300, 23J, ¾, HC, GJS, HCI5P	★★★	285	350	475
305, 23J, BRG, NI, GJS, HCI5P, GT, OF	★★★	285	350	475
310-315, 21J, BRG, NI, GJS, HCI5P		100	110	130
320-325, 17J, BRG, NI, ADJ, DR		45	60	80
330, 17J, BRG, NI, DR		40	50	65
335, 17J, BRG, NI, DR, OF		40	50	70
340-345, 21J, M#1	★	195	225	295

8 SIZE

Grade or Name — Description	Avg	Ex-Fn	Mint
15J, ¾, HC, LS, 14K, 40 DWT	$475	$550	$675
15J, ¾, HC, LS	125	175	225

Rockford movement, 6 size, 17 jewels, quick train, straight line escapement, compensating balance, adjusted to temperature, micrometric regulator, three-quarter damaskeened plates.

6 SIZE

Grade or Name — Description	Avg	Ex-Fn	Mint
9J, HC, NI	$65	$80	$110
15J, ¾, NI	45	60	75
16J, ¾, NI	70	85	100
17J, ¾, ADJ, NI	80	100	130

ROCKFORD WATCH CO. (continued)

0 SIZE

Grade or Name — Description	Avg	Ex-Fn	Mint
Plymouth Watch Co., 15J, HC	$175	$200	$275
7J, BRG	150	175	250
11J, BRG, NI, DR	160	185	260
15J, BRG, NI, DR	170	195	270
17J, BRG, NI, DR	180	205	280
17J, BRG, NI, DR, in marked Rockford HC in dust cover ring	325	400	575

WRIST WATCHES

Wrist Watch - Iroquois, 17J, Chrome case	95	120	165

ROCKFORD WATCH CO. IDENTIFICATION OF MOVEMENTS BY MODEL NUMBER

How to Identify Your Watch: Compare the movement of your watch with the illustrations in this section. Upon matching the movement exactly, the model number and size can be determined. While comparing, note the location of the balance, jewels, screws, gears and type of back plate (Full, ¾, Bridge) which will be clues in identifying the movement you have. Having determined the size and model number, you can now find your watch in the main price listing by name or number (which is engraved on the movement).

Model 1, 18 size, full plate, hunting, key wind & set.

Model 2, 18 size, full plate, hunting, lever set.

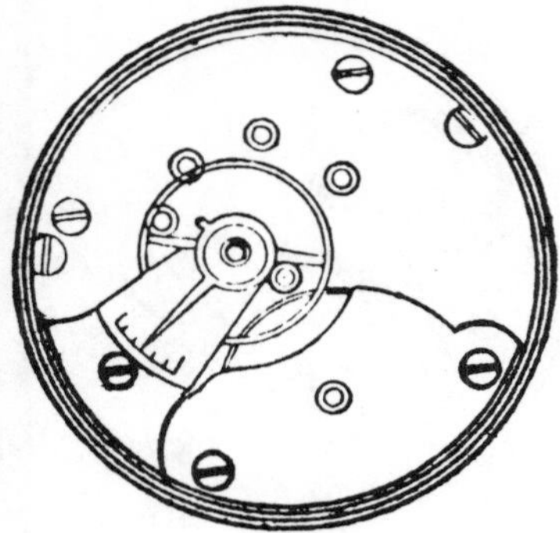

Model 3, 18 size, full plate, hunting, lever set.

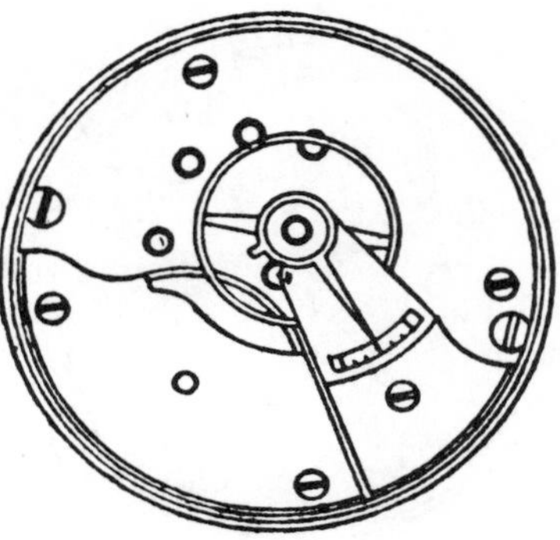

Model 4, 18 size, full plate, open face, lever set.

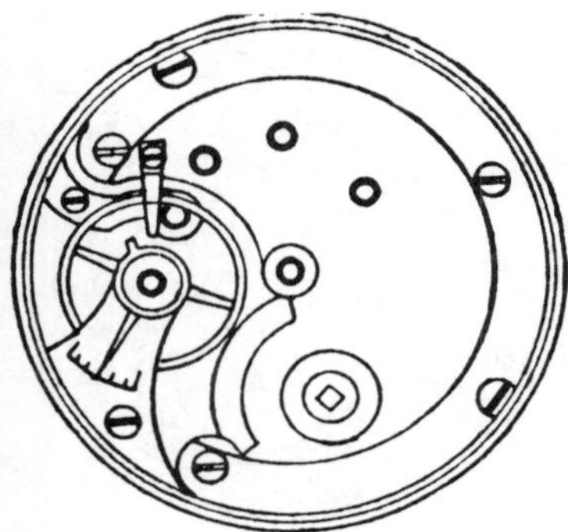

Model 5, 18 size, three-quarter plate, hunting, lever set.

Model 6, 18 size, full plate, hunting, lever set, exposed escapement.

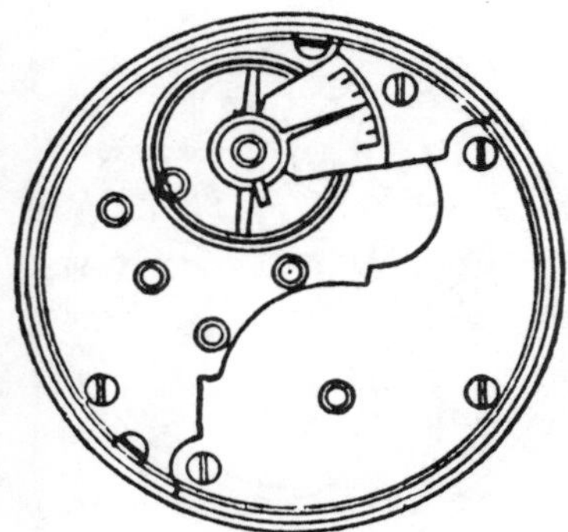

Model 7, 18 size, full plate, open face, lever set.

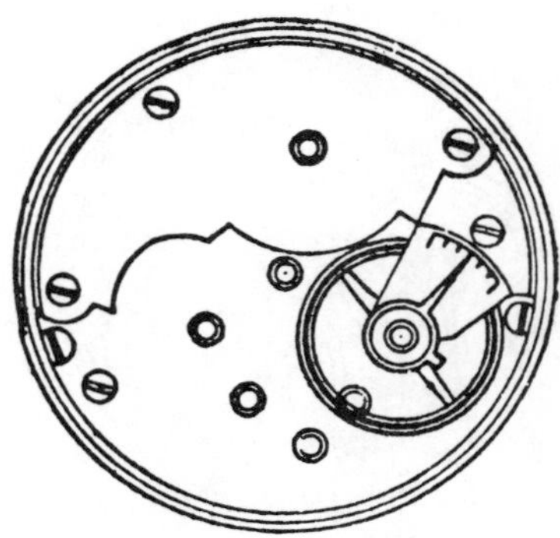

Model 8, 18 size, full plate, hunting, lever set.

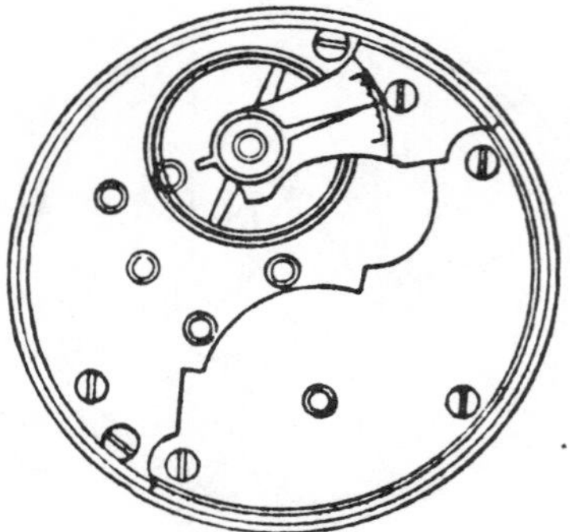

Model 9, 18 size, full plate, open face, lever set.

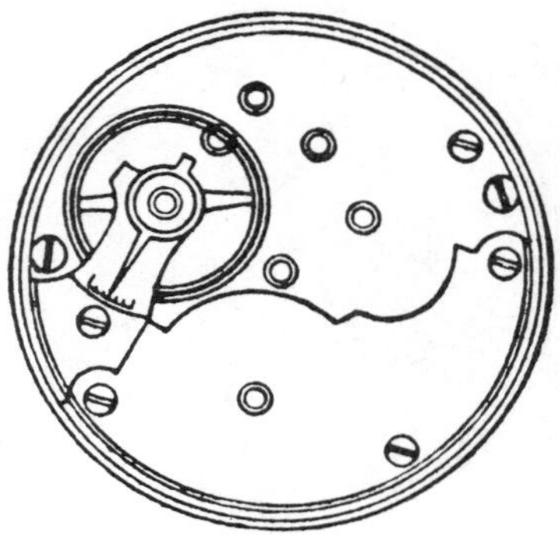

Model 10, 18 size, full plate, hunting, lever set.

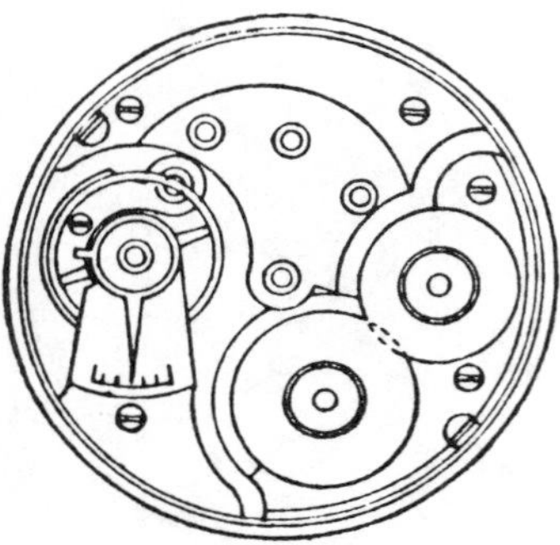

Model 1, 16 size, three-quarter plate, hunting, lever set.

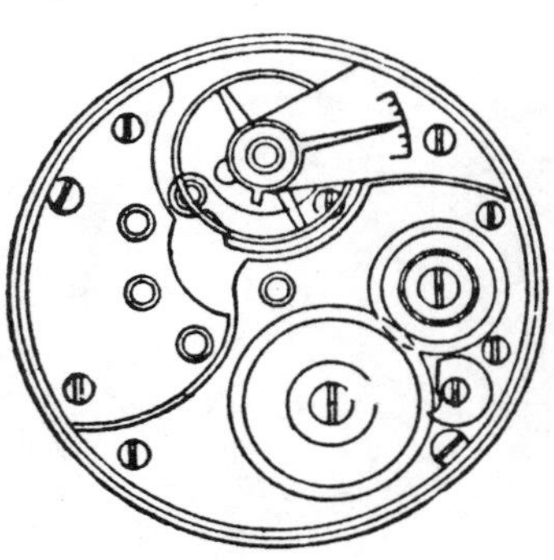

Model 2, 16 size, three-quarter plate, open face, pendant & lever set.

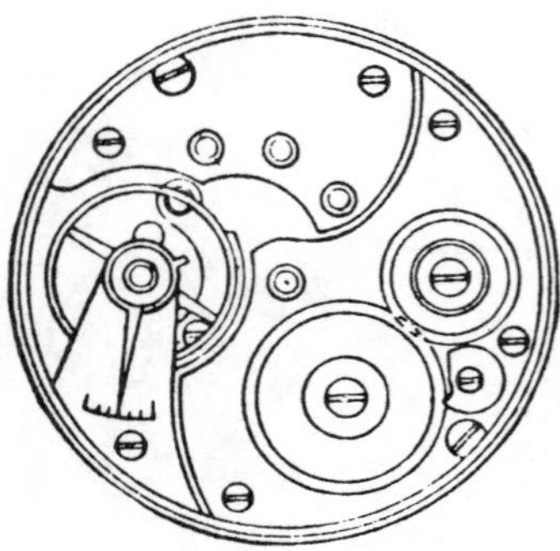

Model 3, 16 size, three-quarter plate, hunting, pendant & lever set.

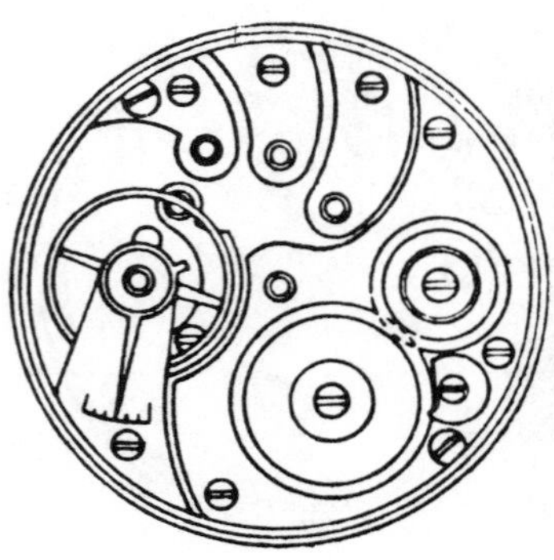

Model 4, 16 size, three-quarter plate, bridge, hunting, pendant & lever set.

ROCKFORD WATCH CO. (continued)

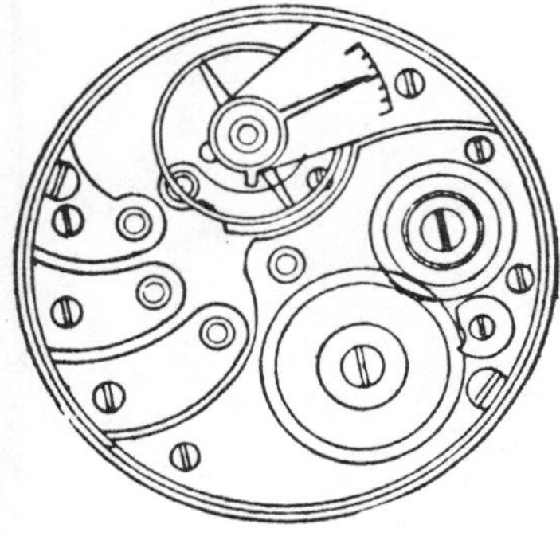

Model 5, 16 size, three-quarter plate, bridge, open face, pendant & lever set.

Model 1, 6 & 8 size, three-quarter plate, hunting, lever set.

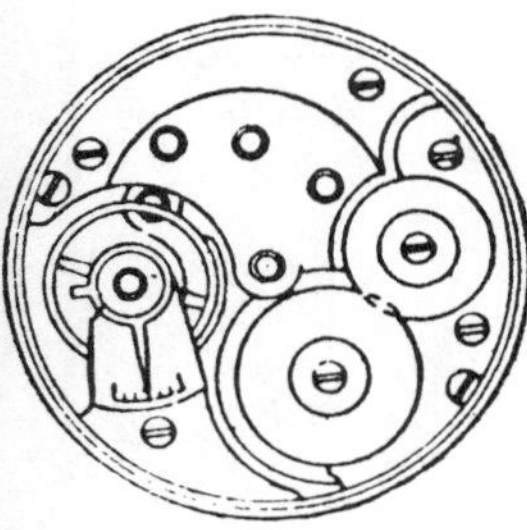

Model 2, 6 size, three-quarter plate, hunting, lever set.

Model 1, 0 size, three-quarter plate, bridge, hunting, pendant set.

Model 2, 0 size, three-quarter plate, bridge, open face, pendant set.

SAN JOSE WATCH CO.
San Jose, California
1891

Very few watches were made by the San Jose Watch Co., and very little is known about them.

Grade or Name — Description		Avg	Ex-Fn	Mint
16S, SW	★★★	$800	$1,500	$2,400

THE SELF-WINDING WATCH CO.
Chicago, Illinois

(See **Herman von der Heydt**)

Example of a basic **M. S. Smith & Co.** movement, 18 size, 15 jewels, three-quarter plate, key wind & set.

M. S. SMITH & CO.
Detroit, Michigan
1870 — 1874

Eber B. Ward purchased the M. S. Smith & Co. which was a large jewelry firm. These watches carried the Smith name on them. A Mr. Hoyt was engaged to produce these watches and about 100 watches were produced before the Freeport Watch Co. purchased the small firm.

Grade or Name — Description		Avg	Ex-Fn	Mint
18S, 15J, ¾, KW, KS	★★★	$1,200	$1,700	$2,200
6S, 15J, SW	★★	400	525	675

SOUTH BEND WATCH CO.
South Bend, Indiana
March 1903 — December 1929

Three brothers George, Clement and J. M. Studebaker purchased the successful Columbus Watch Co. The first South Bend watches were full plate and similar to the Columbus watches. The serial numbers started at 380,501 whereas the Columbus serial numbers stopped at about 500,000. The highest grade watch was a "Polaris," a 16S, ¾ plate, 21 jewels, and had an open face. This watch sold for about $100. The 227 and 229 were also high grade. The company identified its movements by model numbers 1, 2, and 3, and had grades from 100 to 431. The even numbers were hunting cases, and the odd numbers were open-faced cases. The lowest grade was a 203, 7J, that sold for about $6.75. The company closed on Dec. 31, 1929.

SOUTH BEND ESTIMATED SERIAL NUMBERS AND PRODUCTION DATES

Date	Serial No.	Date	Serial No.	Date	Serial No.	Date	Serial No.
1903	380,501	1910	620,000	1917	865,000	1924	1,110,000
1904	410,000	1911	655,000	1918	900,000	1925	1,145,000
1905	445,000	1912	690,000	1919	935,000	1926	1,180,000
1906	480,000	1913	725,000	1920	970,000	1927	1,215,000
1907	515,000	1914	760,000	1921	1,005,000	1928	1,250,000
1908	550,000	1915	795,000	1922	1,040,000	1929	1,275,000
1909	585,000	1916	825,000	1923	1,075,000		

SOUTH BEND WATCH CO. (continued)

South Bend movement, 18 size, 17 jewels, stem wind, hunting, serial number 426726.

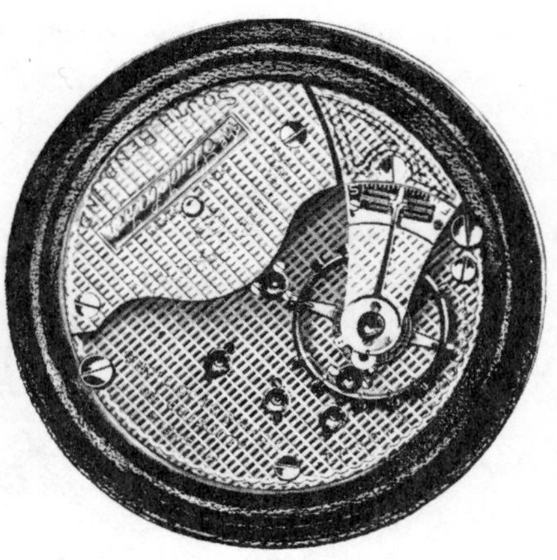

Studebaker, 18 size, 17 jewels, gold jewel settings, stem wind.

SOUTH BEND
18 SIZE

Grade or Name — Description	Avg	Ex-Fn	Mint
South Bend, 15J, OF, HC, Silveroid	$50	$55	$90
South Bend, 15J, OF, HC	75	100	140
South Bend, 17J, OF, HC	90	125	175
South Bend, 21J, OF	125	170	225
South Bend, 21J, HC, 14K	650	700	750
South Bend, 21J, OF, HC, Silveroid	75	85	135
South Bend, 21J, SW, HC	125	150	195
The Studebaker, G#323, 17J, OF, GJS, NI, HCI5P	200	250	350
The Studebaker, G#328, 21J, HC, GJS, NI, FULL, HCI5P	235	295	450
The Studebaker, G#329, 21J, OF, GJS, NI, FULL, HCI5P	225	275	400
304, 15J, HC	95	120	160
305, 15J, OF	60	75	110
305, 15J, OF, Silveroid	35	45	70
309, 17J, OF	65	80	115
312, 17J, HC, NI, ADJ	70	90	125
313, 17J, OF, NI, ADJ, marked 313 ★	135	150	195
327, 21J, OF, HCI5P	120	150	185
327, 21J, OF, HCI5P, Silveroid	75	90	115
330 HC & 331 OF, 15J, M#1, LS	60	75	95
332, 15J, HC	100	125	175
333, 15J, OF	60	75	95
337, 17J, OF	65	80	95
340 HC & 341 OF, 17J, M#1, ADJ, NI, HCI3P	75	95	135
342 HC & 343 OF, 17J, M#1, LS	70	90	110
344, 17J, HC, NI, HCI3P	125	150	190
345, 17J, OF, NI, HCI3P	75	95	135
346, 17J, HC, NI	110	135	175
347, 17J, OF, NI	70	80	110
355, 19J, GJS, 2-Tone, HC ★★	1,000	1,200	1,500

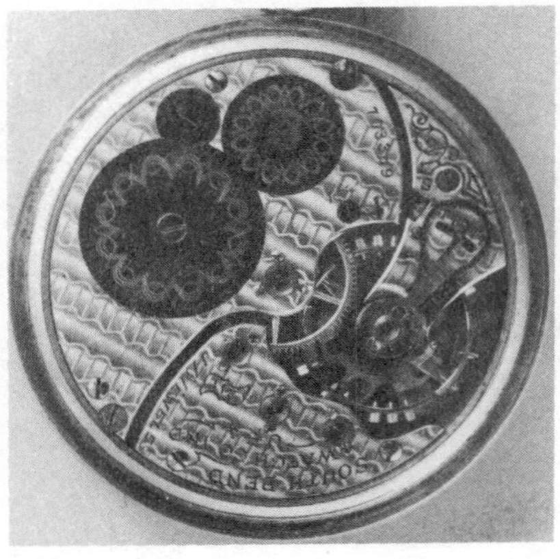

Grade 211, 16 size, 17 jewels, three-quarter plate, serial number 703389.

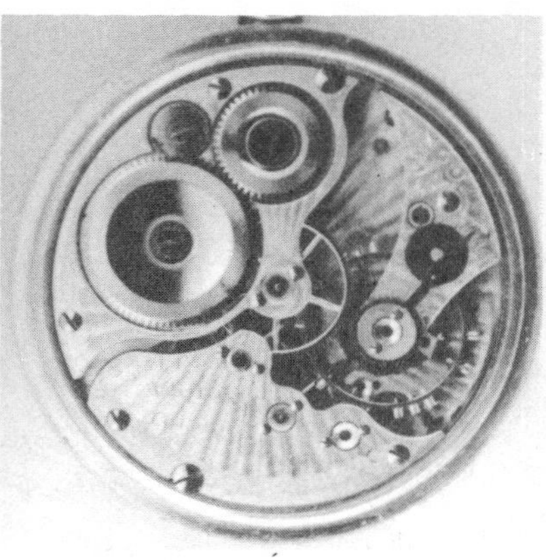

Grade 295, 16 size, 21 jewels, first model, gold jewel settings, gold train, open face, serial number 518,022.

16 SIZE

Grade or Name — Description	Avg	Ex-Fn	Mint
Polaris, 21J, M#1, HCI5P, ¾, NI, DR, GJS, GT . . . . . . ★★	$995	$1,200	$1,650
South Bend, 7J, HC or OF	65	85	130
South Bend, 9J, HC or OF	70	90	135
South Bend, 15J, HC or OF	75	95	150
South Bend, 15J, OF, Silveroid	40	50	60
South Bend, 17J, HC or OF	90	100	160
South Bend, 17J, HC, 14K	465	565	665
South Bend, 21J, HC or OF	100	135	190
The Studebaker "223," M#2, 17J, HCI5P, BRG, GJS, DR, GT	195	250	325
The Studebaker 229, 21J, M#2, HCI5P, BRG, GJS, DR, GT	225	275	375

Grade 219, 16 size, 19 jewels, adjusted to HCI4P, serial number 879850.

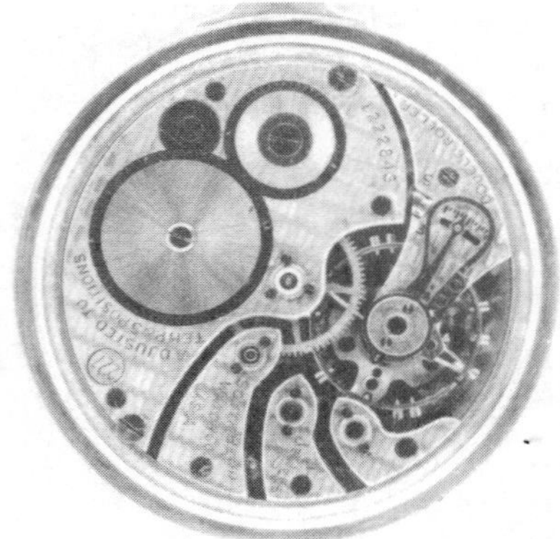

Grade 227, 16 size, 21 jewels, gold jewel settings, adjusted to HCI5P, serial number 1222843.

SOUTH BEND WATCH CO., 16 SIZE (continued)

Grade or Name — Description	Avg	Ex-Fn	Mint
203, 7J, ¾, NI, OF	40	50	70
204, 15J, ¾, NI, HC	40	60	80
207, 15J, OF, PS	40	65	80
209, 9J, M#2, OF, PS	45	55	70
211, 17J, M#2, ¾, NI, OF	65	75	90
212, 17J, M#2, HC, LS, heat & cold	70	80	100
215, 17J, M#2, OF, LS, heat & cold	70	80	90
215, 17J, M#2, OF, Silveroid	45	55	70
217, 17J, M#2, OF, BRG, NI, DR, HCI3P	75	85	110
219, 19J, M#2, OF, NI, DR, HCI4P	80	90	125
223, 17J, M#2, OF, LS, HCI5P	195	250	325
227, 21J, M#2, BRG, NI, LS, OF, DR, HCI5P	110	120	155
245, 19J, GJS, BRG, HC ★★	850	1,000	1,300
260 OF & 261 HC, 7J, M#1, HCI3P	40	50	70
280, 15J, M#1, BRG, HCI3P	50	60	80
281, 15J, M#1, OF	50	60	80
290, 17J, M#1, LS, HCI3P, HC	95	125	175
291, 17J, M#1, OF, HCI3P	90	120	160
292, 19J, M#1, HC, ¾, GJS, NI, DR, HCI5P ★	150	170	220
293, 19J, M#1, OF, ¾, GJS, NI, DR, HCI5P ★	125	145	195
294, 21J, M#1, HCI5P, GJS, GT, HC, marked 294 ★★	225	275	395
295, 21J, M#1, OF, LS, HCI5P, GJS, GT, marked 295 ★	195	235	300
298, 17J, M#1, HC, HCI3P	95	125	165
299, 17J, M#1, OF, HCI3P	90	120	160

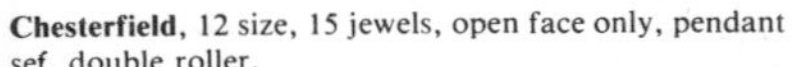

Chesterfield, 12 size, 15 jewels, open face only, pendant sef, double roller.

Chesterfield, 12 size, 21 jewels, open face only, bridge, gold jewel settings, pendant set, double roller, adjusted to HCI5P.

12 SIZE
(OF Only)

Grade or Name — Description	Avg	Ex-Fn	Mint
Chesterfield, 15J, BRG, NI, DR	$40	$50	$85
Chesterfield, 17J, BRG, NI, GJS, DR, HCI3P	50	60	95
Chesterfield, 21J, BRG, NI, GJS, DR, HCI5P	65	85	125
Digital, 17J	125	145	175
South Bend, 15J	35	40	55

SOUTH BEND WATCH CO., 12 SIZE (continued)

Grade or Name — Description	Avg	Ex-Fn	Mint
South Bend, 17J	40	50	65
South Bend, 17J, Silveroid	30	40	50
South Bend, 19J	60	70	80
South Bend, 21J	70	80	95
Studebaker, 21J, ¾, NI, HCI5P	95	135	195
407, 15J, Silveroid	30	35	50
407, 15J	35	45	60
411, 17J, DR	40	50	70
415, 17J, ADJ to temp.	45	55	75
419, 17J, HCI3P	55	65	80
429, 19J, HCI4P, GT, GJS	65	75	95
431, 21J, HCI5P, DR	70	85	110
431, 21J, HCI5P, Silveroid	40	50	75

6 SIZE

Grade or Name — Description	Avg	Ex-Fn	Mint
South Bend, 11J, G#180, HC	$85	$100	$140
South Bend, 15J, G#170, HC	90	110	150
South Bend, 17J, G#160, HC	95	115	160

South Bend, 6 size, 15 jewels.

Grade 120-HC, 121-OF, 0 size, 17 jewels, bridge, nickel, double roller, pendant set.

0 SIZE

Grade or Name — Description	Avg	Ex-Fn	Mint
South Bend, 15J, OF, PS	$35	$40	$60
Grade 100 HC & 101 OF, 7J, PS	35	40	55
Grade 110 HC & 111 OF, 15J, 3F Brg, DR	50	60	75
Grade 120 HC & 121 OF, 17J, BRG, NI, DR, PS	50	60	75

SOUTH BEND WATCH CO.
IDENTIFICATION OF MOVEMENTS
BY MODEL NUMBER

How to Identify Your Watch: Compare the movement of your watch with the illustrations in this section. Upon matching the movement exactly, the model number and size can be determined. While comparing, note the location of the balance, jewels, screws, gears and type of back plate (Full, ¾, Bridge) which will be clues in identifying the movement you have. Having determined the size and model number, you can now find your watch in the main price listing by name or number (which is engraved on the movement).

18 SIZE—MODEL 1

Open Face and Hunting. Lever Set

Grade Numbers and Description of Movements

No. 341—Open Face, 17 Jewels, Lever Set, Adjusted to Temperature & 3 Positions.
No. 340—Hunting, 17 Jewels, Lever Set, Adjusted to Temperature and 3 Positions.
No. 343—Open Face, 17 Jewels, Lever Set.
No. 342—Hunting, 17 Jewels, Lever Set.
No. 331—Open Face, 15 Jewels, Lever Set.
No. 330—Hunting, 15 Jewels, Lever Set.

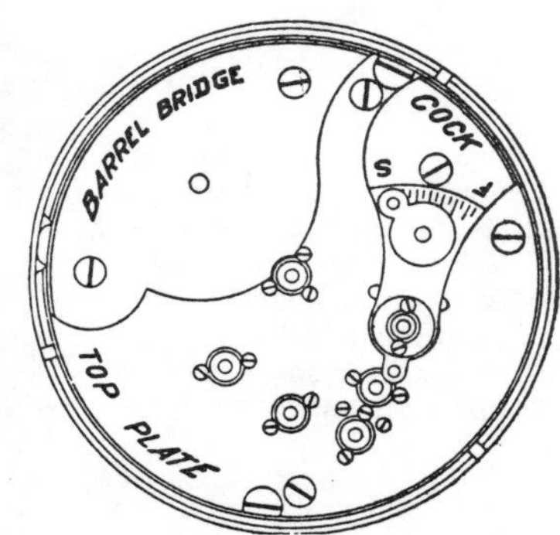

Full Plate, Open Face.

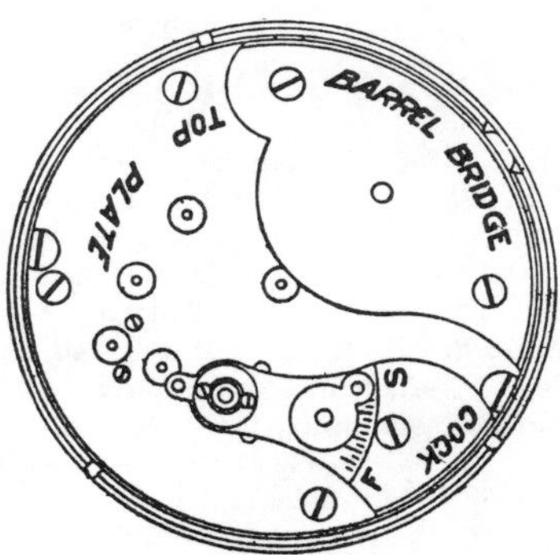

Full Plate, Hunting.

18 SIZE—MODEL 2

Open Face and Hunting. Lever Set

Grade Numbers and Description of Movements

No. 329—21J, Open Face, "Studebaker," Adjusted to Temperature and 5 Positions.
No. 328—21J, Hunting, Adjusted to Temperature and 5 Positions.
No. 327—21J, Open Face, Adjusted to Temperature and 5 Positions.
No. 323—17J, Open Face, "Studebaker," Adjusted to Temperature and 5 Positions.
No. 345—17J, Open Face, Adjusted to Temperature and 3 Positions.
No. 344—17J, Hunting, Adjusted to Temperature and 3 Positions.
No. 313—17J, Open Face, Adjusted to Temperature.
No. 312—17J, Hunting, Adjusted to Temperature.
Nos. 309, 337, 347—17J, Open Face.
No. 346—17J, Hunting.
Nos. 333, 305—15J, Open Face.
Nos. 332, 304—15J, Hunting.

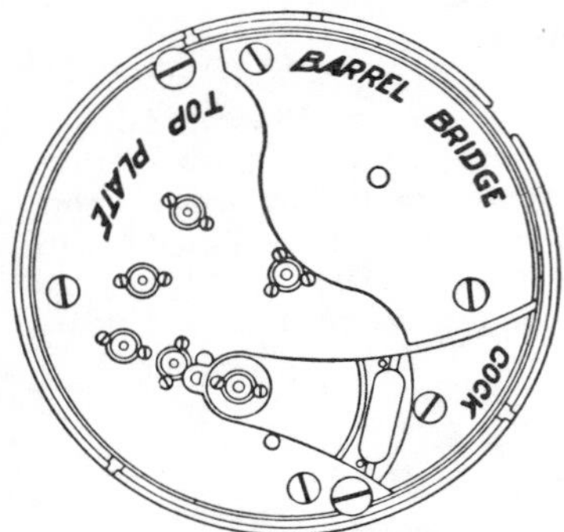

Full Plate, Open Face.

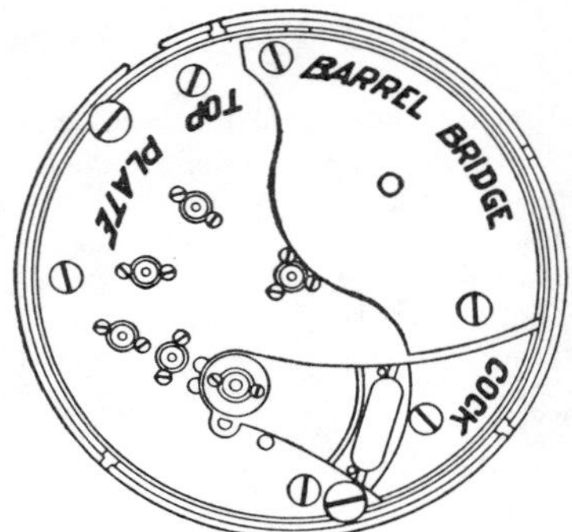

Full Plate, Hunting.

16 SIZE—MODEL 1

Open Face and Hunting. Lever Set
Grade Numbers and Description of Movements

No. 295—Open Face, 21 Jewels, Adjusted to Temperature and 5 Positions.
No. 204—Hunting, 21 Jewels, Adjusted to Temperature and 5 Positions.
No. 293—Open Face, 19 Jewels, Adjusted to Temperature and 5 Positions.
No. 292—Hunting, 19 Jewels, Adjusted to Temperature and 5 Positions.
No. 299—Open Face, 17 Jewels, Adjusted to Temperature and 3 Positions.
No. 298—Hunting, 17 Jewels, Adjusted to Temperature and 3 Positions.
No. 291—Open Face, 17 Jewels, Adjusted to Temperature and 3 Positions.
No. 290—Hunting, 17 Jewels, Adjusted to Temperature and 3 Positions.
No. 281—Open Face, 15 Jewels.
No. 280—Hunting, 15 Jewels.
No. 261—Open Face, 7 Jewels.
No. 260—Hunting, 7 Jewels.

Three Quarter Plate
Open Face

Three Quarter Plate
Hunting

16 SIZE—MODEL 2

Open Face and Hunting. Pendant and Lever Set

Grade Numbers and Description of Movements

No. 229—21J, Open Face, Lever Set, "Studebaker," Adjust. to Temp. and 5 Positions.
No. 227—21J, Open Face, Lever Set, Adjusted to Temperature and 5 Positions.
No. 219—19J, Open Face, Pendant Set, Adjusted to Temperature and 4 Positions.
No. 223—17J, Open Face, Lever Set, "Studebaker," Adjust. to Temp. and 5 Positions.
No. 217—17J, Open Face, Lever Set, Adjusted to Temperature and 3 Positions.
No. 215—17J, Open Face, Pendant Set, Adjusted to Temperature.
No. 212—17J, Hunting, Lever Set, Adjusted to Temperature.
No. 211—17J, Open Face, Pendant Set.
No. 207—15J, Open Face, Pendant Set.
No. 204—15J, Hunting, Lever Set.
No. 209— 9J, Open Face, Pendant Set.
No. 203— 7J, Open Face, Pendant Set.

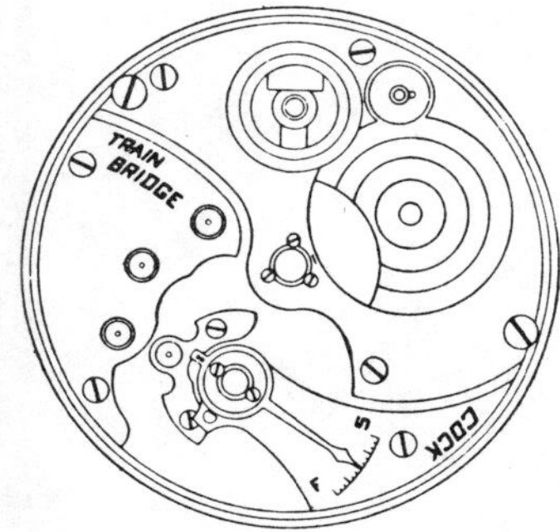

Three-Quarter Plate
Hunting

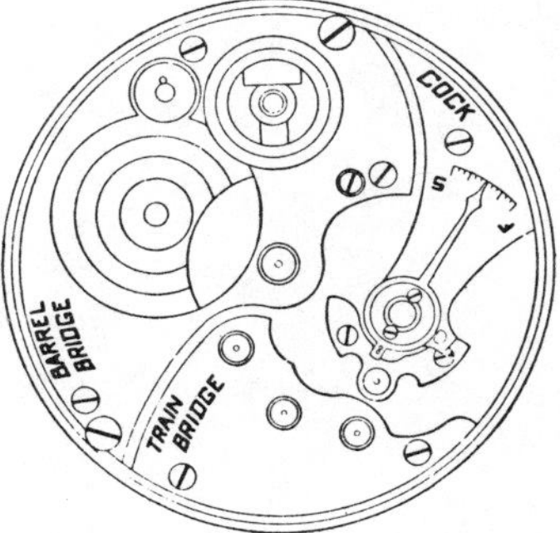

Three-Quarter Plate
Open Face

Bridges, Open Face.

12 SIZE — MODEL 1

Chesterfield Series and Grade 429 Special

Made in Pendant Set
Open Face Only

Grade Numbers and Description of Movements

No. 431—21J, Adjusted to Temperature and 5 Positions.
No. 429—19J, Adjusted to Temperature and 4 Positions.
No. 419—17J, Adjusted to Temperature and 3 Positions.
No. 415—17J, Adjusted to Temperature.
No. 411—17J.
No. 407—15J.

Bridges

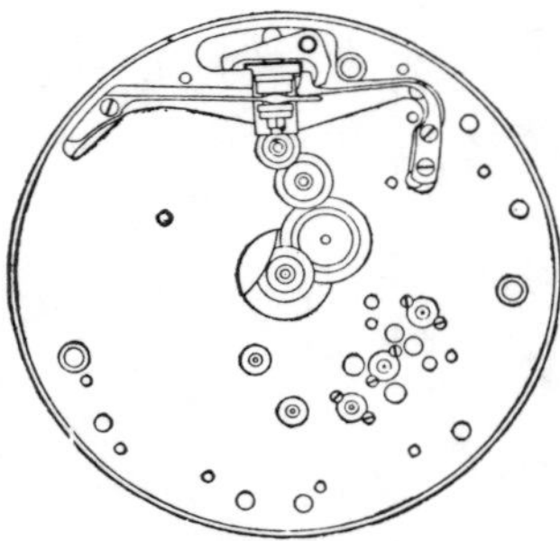
Lower Plate
Dial Side

6 SIZE—MODEL 1

Hunting

Grade No. 180, 17 Jewels
Grade No. 170, 15 Jewels
Grade No. 160, 11 Jewels

Serial Number Range
380,501 to 389,900

Three Quarter Plate

0 SIZE—MODEL 1

Open Face, No second hand, Hunting has second hand

Open

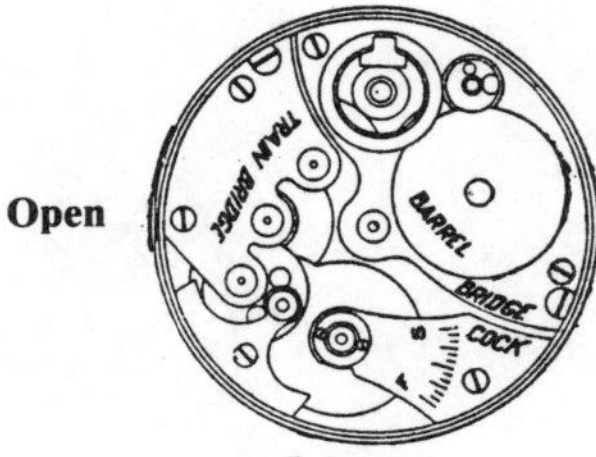

7 Jewels
Three Quarter Plate

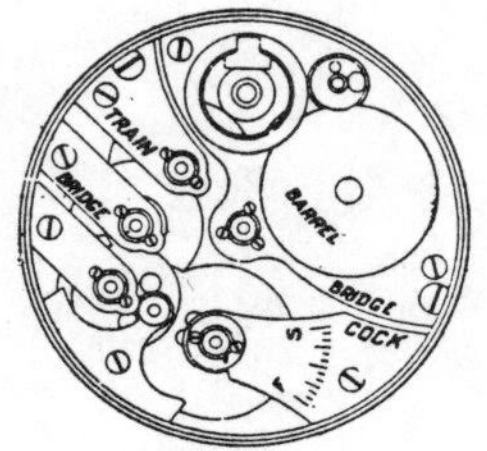

15 and 17 Jewels
Bridges

Hunting

Model numbers 1 & 2 serial numbers under 659,700. All open face and hunting parts for this model except dial and fourth pinion are interchangeable.

0 SIZE—MODEL 2

Open Face, No second hand, Hunting has second hand

Open Face
Grade
101—7 Jewels
111—15 Jewels
121—17 Jewels

7 Jewels
Three Quarter Plate

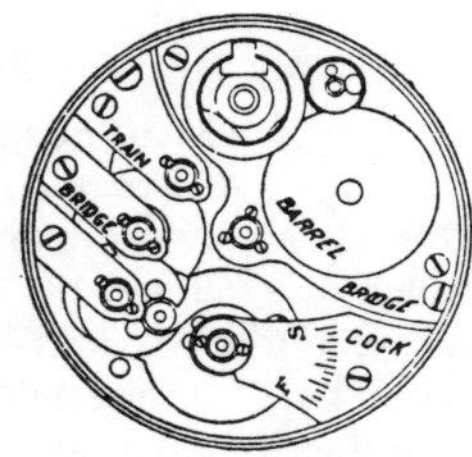

15 and 17 Jewels,
Bridges

Hunting
Grade
100—7 Jewels
110—15 Jewels
120—17 Jewels

0 SIZE — MODEL 3

Both Open Face and Hunting have second hand

Grade Numbers and Description of Movements

No. 151—21J, Open Face, Bridge Model.
No. 150—21J, Hunting, Bridge Model.
No. 121—17J, Open Face, Bridge Model.
No. 120—17J, Hunting, Bridge Model.

Open Face Bridges
Grade 151, 21J
Grade 121, 17J

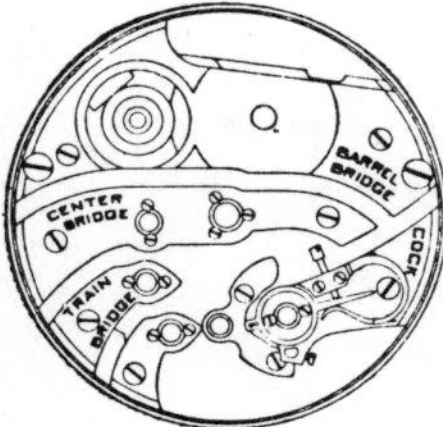

Hunting Bridges
Grade 150, 21J
Grade 120, 17J

Example of a basic original J. P. Stevens movement, 18 size, 15 jewels, note patented eccentric style regulator, serial number 65.

J.P. Stevens Watch Co. movement by Waltham, 18 size, 11 jewels, serial number 1240058.

J. P. STEVENS WATCH CO.
Atlanta, Georgia
1882 — 1887

In mid-1881 J. P. Stevens bought part of the Springfield Watch Co. of Massachusetts and some watch components from E. F. Bowman. He set up his watchmaking firm over his jewelry store in Atlanta, Ga., and started to produce the unfinished watch which was 16S and 18S and to which was added the "Stevens Patent Regulator." This regulator is best described as a simple disc attached to the plate which has an eccentric groove cut for the arm of the regulator to move in. This regulator is a prominent feature of the J. P. Stevens, and only the top is jeweled. These watches were 16S, ¾ plate, stem wind and had a nickel plate with damaskeening. About 50 of these watches were made. A line of gilt movements was added. The pallet and fork are made of one piece aluminum. The aluminum was combined with 1/10 copper and formed an exceedingly tough metal which will not rust or become magnetized. The lever of this watch is only one-third the weight of a steel lever. The aluminum lever affords the least possible resistance for overcoming inertia in transmitting power from the escape wheel to the balance. In 1884, the company was turning out about ten watches a day at a price of $20 to $100 each. In the spring of 1887 the company failed. Only 174 true Stevens watches were made, but other watches carried the J. P. Stevens name.

16 TO 18 SIZE

Grade or Name — Description	Avg	Ex-Fn	Mint
Original Model, Serial Nos. 1 to 174 ★★★	$3,000	$4,000	$5,500
Aurora, 17J ★	350	400	650
Columbus W. Co., 17J ★	400	425	675
Elgin, 17J ★	275	350	550
Hamilton, 17J ★	375	425	650

J. P. STEVENS WATCH CO., 16-18 SIZE (continued)

Grade or Name — Description	Avg	Ex-Fn	Mint
Hampden, 17J . . . . ★	225	295	425
Illinois, 17J . . . . ★	650	700	900
N. Y. W. Co., 17J, Full Plate, S#s range in 500s	695	750	995
N. Y. W. Co. "Bond" Model, S#s range in 500s . . . . ★★	850	995	1,200
16S Swiss, 17J, Longines . . . . ★	175	200	275
Waltham, 17J . . . . ★	400	450	550

J. P. Stevens movement made by **Hampden**, 18 size, 17 jewels, note eccentric style regulator, serial number 1695.

J.P. Stevens Watch Co., 6 size, 11 jewels, exposed winding gears.

6 SIZE

Grade or Name — Description	Avg	Ex-Fn	Mint
Ladies Model, 15J, LS, HC, 14K	$500	$575	$650
Ladies Model, 15J, LS, GF cases	195	250	395
Ladies Model, 15J, LS, GF cases, Swiss made	165	225	325

Suffolk Watch Co., 0 Size, 7 jewels, serial number 216, 841.

SUFFOLK WATCH CO.
Waltham, Massachusetts
c. 1899 — 1901

The Suffolk Watch Company officially succeeded the Columbia Watch Company in March 1901. However, the Suffolk 0-size, 7-jewel nickel movement with lever escape-

SUFFOLK WATCH CO. (continued)

ment was being manufactured in the Columbia factory before the end of 1899. More than 25,000 movements were made. The factory was closed after it was purchased by the Keystone Watch Case Company on May 17, 1901. The machinery was moved to the nearby factory of the United States Watch Company (purchased by Keystone in April 1901), where it was used to make the United States Watch Company's 0-size movement, introduced in April 1902.

Both the Columbia Watch Company and the Suffolk Watch Company made 0-size movements only.

Grade or Name — Description	Avg	Ex-Fn	Mint
OS, 7J, NI, HC	$45	$65	$95

SETH THOMAS WATCH CO.
Thomaston, Connecticut
1883 — 1915

Seth Thomas is a very prominent clock manufacturer, but in early 1883, the company made a decision to manufacture watches. The watches were first placed on the market in 1885. They were 18S, open face, stem wind, ¾ plate, and the escapement was between the plates. The compensating balance was set well below the normal. They were 11J, 16,000 bpm train, but soon went to 18,000 or quick train. In 1886, the company started to make higher grade watches and produced four grades: 7J, 11J, 15J, and 17J. That year the output was 100 watches a day.

SETH THOMAS ESTIMATED SERIAL NUMBERS AND PRODUCTION DATES

Date	Serial No.	Date	Serial No.	Date	Serial No.
1885	5,000	1895	690,000	1905	1,700,000
1886	20,000	1896	780,000	1906	1,900,000
1887	40,000	1897	870,000	1907	2,100,000
1888	80,000	1898	960,000	1908	2,300,000
1889	150,000	1899	1,050,000	1909	2,500,000
1890	235,000	1900	1,140,000	1910	2,725,000
1891	330,000	1901	1,230,000	1911	2,950,000
1892	420,000	1902	1,320,000	1912	3,175,000
1893	510,000	1903	1,410,000	1913	3,490,000
1894	600,000	1904	1,500,000	1914	3,600,000

20th Century (Wards), 18 size, 11 jewels.

Edgemere, 18 size, 17 jewels, serial number 786773.

Liberty, 18 size, 7 jewels, hunting or open face, eagle on movement.

Maiden Lane, 18 size, 28 jewels, gold jewel settings, HCI5P, dated 8,1.99. No serial number.

SETH THOMAS
18 SIZE

Grade or Name — Description	Avg	Ex-Fn	Mint
Century, 7J, OF or HC	$40	$60	$85
Century, 15J, OF or HC	50	65	95
Chautauqua, 15J, GJS, M#5	125	160	225
Eagle Series, 7J, No. 36 OF, No. 37 HC	70	80	110
Eagle Series, 11J, No. 106 OF, No. 107 HC	75	85	120
Eagle Series, 15J, No. 206 OF, No. 207 HC	80	95	135
Eagle Series, 17J, No. 210 OF, No. 211 HC	85	100	145
Eagle Series, 17J, NI, ¾	90	115	160
Edgemere, 11J	70	80	110
Edgemere, 17J	75	85	125
Keywind M#4, 7J, 11J, & 15J, ¾	225	300	450
Lakeshore, 17J, GJS, ADJ, NI	195	245	295
Liberty, 7J, ¾, eagle on back plate	65	85	125
Maiden Lane, 17J, GJS, DR, HCI6P, NI, marked ★★	900	1,100	1,500
Maiden Lane, 19J, GJS, DR, HCI6P, NI, marked ★★★	1,000	1,300	1,800

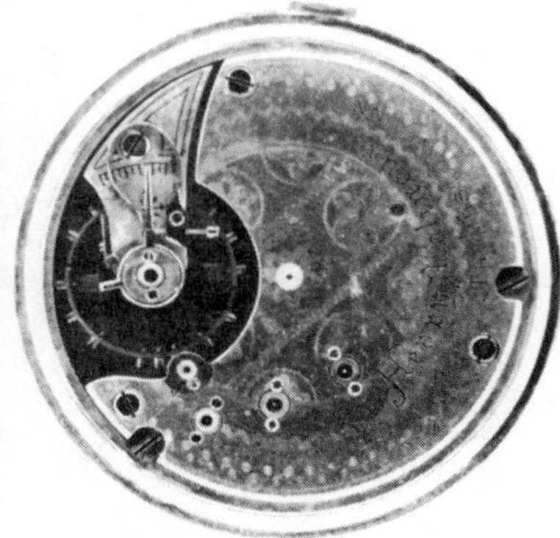

Henry Molineux, 18 size, 17 jewels, "Corona W. Co. USA" on dial, open face, serial number 54951.

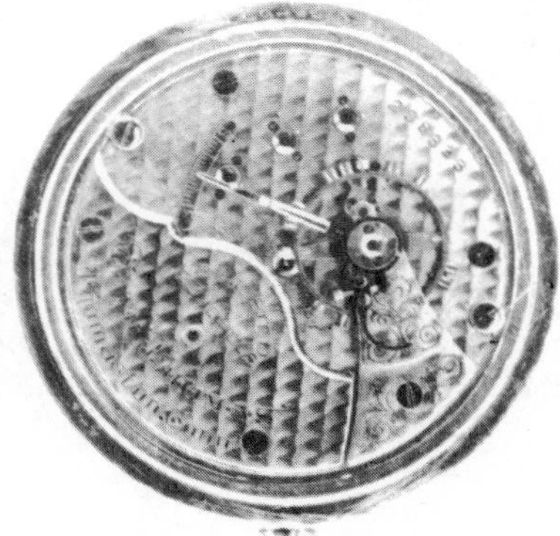

Seth Thomas, 18 size, 23 jewels, gold jewel settings, adjusted, serial number 298333.

SETH THOMAS WATCH CO., 18 SIZE (continued)

Grade or Name — Description	Avg	Ex-Fn	Mint
Maiden Lane, 21J, GJS, DR, HCI6P, NI, marked .... ★	1,200	1,400	2,000
Maiden Lane, 24J, GJS, DR, HCI6P, marked .... ★★★	1,500	1,750	2,500
Maiden Lane, 25J, GJS, DR, HCI6P, NI, marked ..... ★★	2,000	2,500	3,300
Maiden Lane, 28J, GJS, DR, HCI5P, NI, marked . ★★★★	15,000	18,000	25,000
Henry Molineux, M#3, 17J, ¾, GJS, ADJ .... ★★	400	450	550
Henry Molineux, M#2, 17J, GJS, ADJ .... ★★	400	450	550
Henry Molineux, M#2, 20J, GJS, ADJ .... ★★★	1,000	1,400	1,900
Monarch Watch Co., 7-15J, 2-tone	50	60	75
Republic USA, 7J, OF	50	55	65
S. Thomas, 7J, ¾, multi-color dial	135	155	225
S. Thomas, 7J, ¾	40	50	75
S. Thomas, 11J, ¾	50	60	85
S. Thomas, 11J, ¾, Silveroid	35	45	60
S. Thomas, 15J, ¾, HC	95	125	180
S. Thomas, 15J, ¾, Silveroid	40	50	65
S. Thomas, 15J, ¾, OF	60	70	110
S. Thomas, 16J, ¾	65	85	125
S. Thomas, 17J, ¾, OF	80	90	115
S. Thomas, 17J, ¾, 2-Tone	135	160	250
S. Thomas, 17J, ¾, Silveroid	50	60	75
S. Thomas, 17J, ¾, HC	100	135	195
S. Thomas, 21J, GJS, DR, HCI5P	250	295	395
S. Thomas, 23J, GJS, DR, HCI5P .... ★★	900	1,200	1,600
20th Century (Wards), 11J	70	80	110
20th Century (Wards), 11J, 2-Tone	75	85	120
Wyoming Watch Co., 7J, OF	125	140	195
33, 7J, ¾, gilded	40	50	70
37, 7J, ¾, NI	50	60	75
44, 11J, ¾, gilded	50	60	80
47, 7J, gilded, FULL	55	65	85
48, 7J, NI, FULL	60	70	80
70, 15J, ¾, gilded	60	70	90
80, 17J, ¾, gilded, ADJ	70	80	110
101, 15J, ¾, gilded, ADJ	65	75	105
149, 15J, gilded, FULL	50	60	90
159, 15J, NI, FULL	55	65	95
169, 17J, NI, FULL	70	80	100
170, 15J, ¾, NI	50	60	85
179, 17J, ¾, NI, ADJ	60	75	100
180, 17J, ¾, NI	60	70	90
182, 17J, DR, NI, FULL	125	140	175
201, 15J, ¾, NI, ADJ	65	80	110
245, 19J, GJS, 2-Tone, HC	1,000	1,200	1,500
260, 21J, DR, HCI6P, NI, FULL	225	275	365
281-282, 17J, OF, LS, FULL, DR, HCI3P	160	180	275
382, 17J, OF, LS, FULL, DR, HCI5P	160	180	275

16 SIZE

Grade or Name — Description	Avg	Ex-Fn	Mint
Centennial, 7J, ¾, NI	$45	$50	$85

Centennial, 16 size, 7 jewels, three-quarter nickel plate.

Grade 36, 16 size, 7 jewels, open face, three-quarter nickel plate.

Grade or Name — Description	Avg	Ex-Fn	Mint
Locust, 7J, NI, ¾	45	50	85
Locust, 17J, NI, ADJ, ¾	55	60	90
Republic USA, 7J	45	50	80
25, 7J, OF, BRG	40	50	80
26, 15J, OF, BRG, GJS	60	75	90
27, 17J, OF, BRG, GJS	70	80	95
28, 17J, OF, BRG, HCI3P, GJS	75	80	110
326, 7J, OF, ¾, NI	40	50	80
328, 15J, OF, ¾, NI	60	75	95
332, 7J, ¾, NI	50	60	80
334, 15J, NI, ADJ, ¾, DMK	80	95	150
336, 17J, ADJ, ¾, DMK	155	175	210

Seth Thomas, 12 size, 7 jewels, open face.

Seth Thomas, 12 size, 17 jewels, gold jewel settings, gold center wheel, open face, HCI3P.

SETH THOMAS WATCH CO. (continued)

12 SIZE

Grade or Name — Description	Avg	Ex-Fn	Mint
Republic USA, 7J	$40	$50	$60
25, 7J, OF, BRG	40	50	65
26, 15J, OF, BRG, GJS	60	70	80
27, 17J, OF, BRG, GJS	70	80	90
28, 17J, OF, BRG, HCI3P, GJS	75	80	95
326, 7J, OF, ¾, NI	40	50	65
328, 15J, OF, ¾, NI	60	70	80

Example of a basic **Seth Thomas** movement, 6 size, 7 jewels, serial number 441839. Sometimes appears in a 12 size case.

Grade 45, 6 size, 7 jewels, open face, three-quarter nickel plate.

6 SIZE
(Some 6 Size were used to fit 12 Size cases)

Grade or Name — Description	Avg	Ex-Fn	Mint
Century, 7J, NI, ¾	$45	$50	$65
Eagle Series, 7J, ¾, NI, DMK, 205 HC, 45 OF	55	60	75
Eagle Series, 15J, ¾, NI, DMK, 245 HC, 35 OF	65	70	85
Republic USA, 7J	45	50	65
Seth Thomas, 7J, ¾, HC, 14K, 26 DWT	295	340	395
Seth Thomas, 11J, ¾	70	80	100
35, 7J, HC, NI, DMK, ¾	45	60	75
119, 16J, HC, GJS, NI, DMK, ¾	75	90	120
205, 15J, HC	55	60	70
320, 7J, OF, NI, DMK, ¾	60	80	140
322, 15J, OF	55	60	70

0 SIZE

Grade or Name — Description	Avg	Ex-Fn	Mint
Seth Thomas, 7J, OF, HC, No. 1	$70	$85	$165
Seth Thomas, 15J, OF, HC, GJS, No. 3	80	95	175
Seth Thomas, 17J, OF, HC, GJS, PS, No. 9	90	115	185

WRIST WATCHES

Style or Grade — Description	Avg	Ex-Fn	Mint
Round, made in U.S.A., gold filled	$25	$30	$45
Round, Swiss-made	5	7	10

SETH THOMAS WATCH CO.
IDENTIFICATION OF MOVEMENTS
BY MODEL NUMBER

How to Identify Your Watch: Compare the movement of your watch with the illustrations in this section. Upon matching the movement exactly, the model number and size can be determined. While comparing, note the location of the balance, jewels, screws, gears and type of back plate (Full, ¾, Bridge) which will be clues in identifying the movement you have. Having determined the size and model number, you can now find your watch in the main price listing by name or number (which is engraved on the movement).

Model 1, 18 size, Open Face

Model 2, 18 size, Hunting

Model 3, 18 size, Open Face

Model 4, 18 size, Key Wind

SETH THOMAS WATCH CO. (continued)

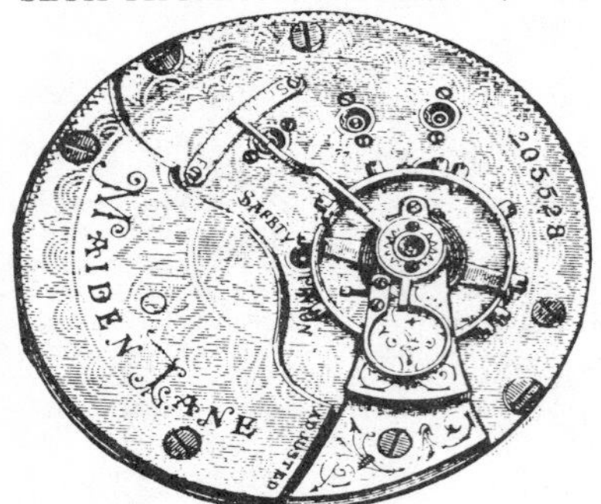

Model 5, 18 size, Maidgn Lane Series, Open Face.

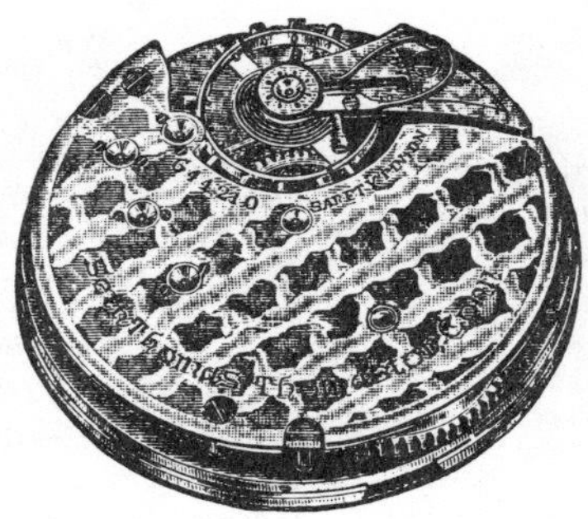

Model 6, 18 size, Open Face

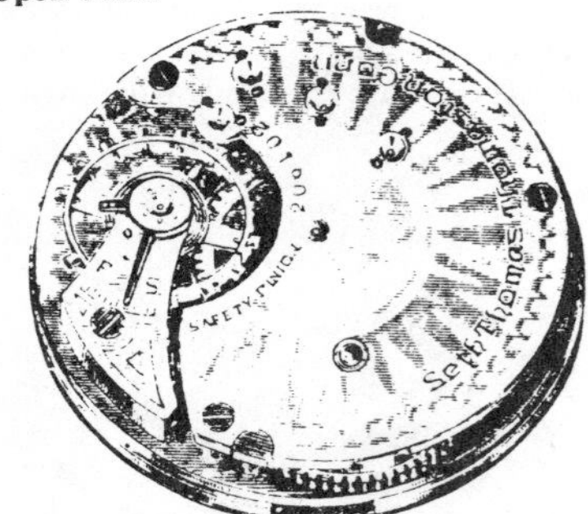

Model 7 & 9, 18 size

Model 8, 18 size

Model 10, 18 size, Open Face

Model 11, 18 size, Hunting

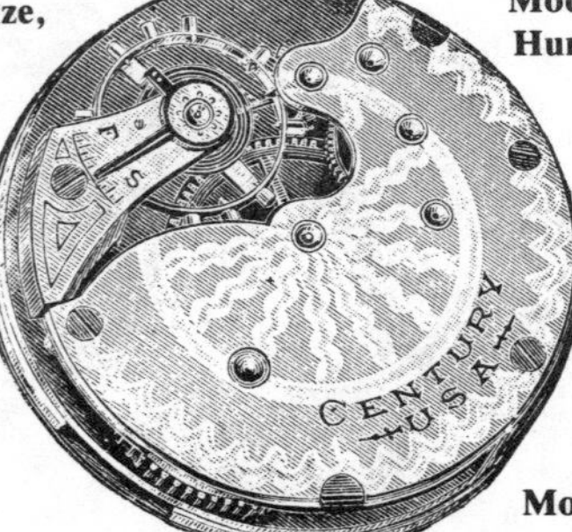

Model 13, 18 size, Hunting

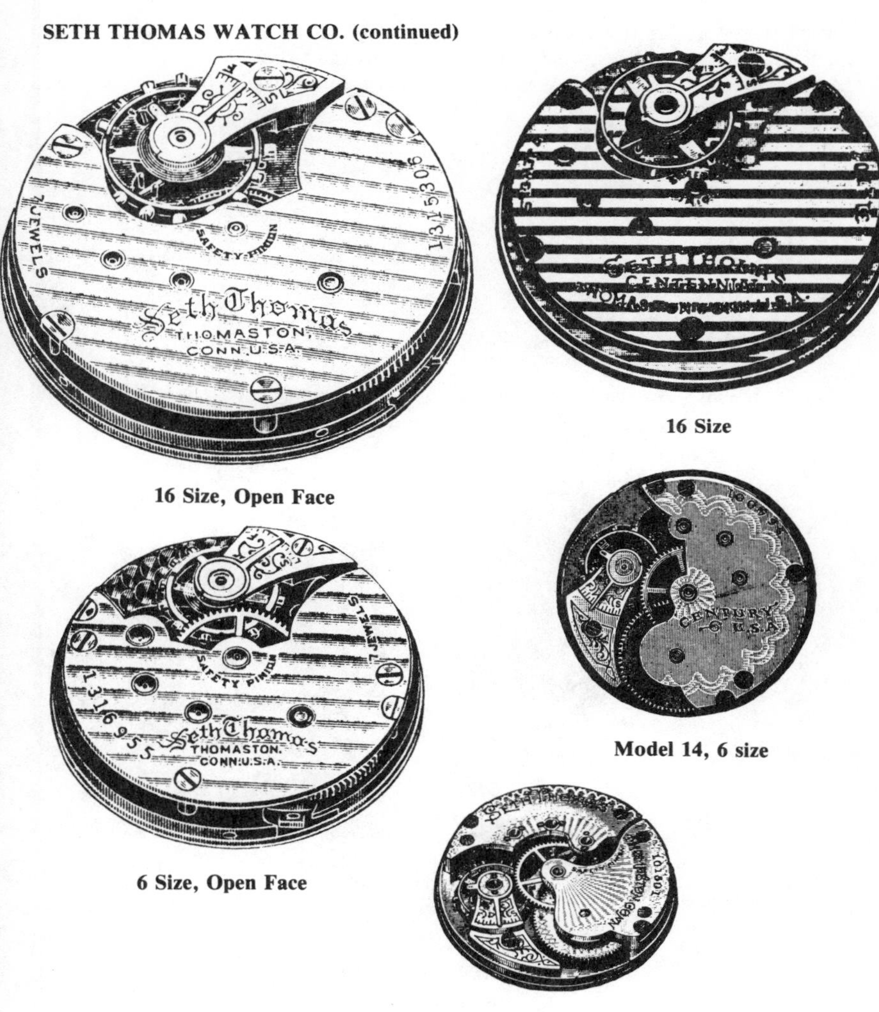

16 Size, Open Face

16 Size

6 Size, Open Face

Model 14, 6 size

Model 16 & 17, 6 size

TREMONT WATCH CO.
Boston, Massachusetts
1864 — 1866

In 1864 A. L. Dennison thought if he could succeed in producing a good movement at a more reasonable price there would be a ready market. Dennison went to Switzerland to find a supplier of cheap parts as arbors were too high in America. He found a source of parts, mainly the train and escapement and the balance. About 600 sets were to be furnished. In 1865, the first movements were ready for the market. They were 18S, key wind, fully jeweled, and were engraved "Tremont Watch Co." In 1886, the company moved from Boston to Melrose. Another 18S was made, and the company

TREMONT WATCH CO. (continued)
made its own train and escapement. The watches were engraved "Melrose Watch Co., Melrose, Mass." The Tremont Watch Co. produced about 5,000 watches before being sold to the English Watch Co.

Grade or Name — Description		Avg	Ex-Fn	Mint
18S, 7J, KW, KS	★★	$200	$265	$375
18S, 11J, KW, KS	★★	200	265	375
18S, 15J, KW, KS, Silveroid, recased	★	145	195	295
18S, 15J, KW, KS, gilded	★	200	265	400
18S, 15J, KW, KS, HC, 14K	★	625	700	900
18S, 15J, KW, KS, gilded, Washington Street	★★	350	375	600
18S, 17J, KW, KS, gilded	★	300	350	550
18S, 15J, KW, KS from back, ¾ plate	★★★	1,800	1,900	2,200

Tremont Watch Co. with *Washington Street Boston* engraved on movement, 18 size, 15 jewels, key wind and set, serial number 5264.

Tremont Watch Co., 18 size, 7 jewels, key wind & set, serial number 1849.

TRENTON WATCH CO.
Trenton, New Jersey
1885 — 1908

Trenton watches were marketed under the following labels: Trenton, Ingersoll, Fortuna, Illinois Watch Case Company, Calumet U.S.A., Locomotives Special, Marvel Watch Co., and Reliance Watch Co.

Serial numbers started at 2,001 and ended at 4,100,000. Total production was about 1,934,000.

Chronology of the Development of Trenton Watch Co.:
New Haven Watch Co., New Haven, Conn. — 1883-1887
Trenton Watch Co., Trenton, N. J. — 1887-1908
Sold to Ingersoll — 1908-1922

TRENTON WATCH CO. (continued)

TRENTON MODELS AND GRADES
With Years of Manufacture and Serial Numbers

Date	Numbers	Size	Model	Date	Numbers	Size	Model
1887-1889	2,001- 61,000	18	1	1900-1903	2,000,001-2,075,000	6	2
1889-1891	64,001- 135,000	18	2	1902-1905	2,075,001-2,160,000	6	3 LS
1891-1898	135,001- 201,000 *[1]	18	3			12	2 LS
1899-1904	201,001- 300,000	18	6	1905-1907	2,160,001-2,250,000	6	3 PS
1891-1900	300,001- 500,000	18	4			12	2 PS
1892-1897	500,001- 600,000	6	1	1899-1902	2,500,001-2,600,000	3/0	1
1894-1899	650,001- 700,000	16	1	ca. 1906	2,800,001-2,850,000	6	3 PS
1898-1900	700,001- 750,000	6	2			12	2 PS
1900-1904	750,001- 800,000 *[2]	18	4	1900-1904	3,000,001-3,139,000	16	2
1896-1900	850,001- 900,000	12	1	1903-1907	3,139,001-3,238,000	16	3 OF
1898-1903	900,001-1,100,000	18	5	1903-1907	3,500,001-3,600,000	16	3 HC
1902-1907	1,300,001-1,400,000	18	6	1905-1907	4,000,001-4,100,000	0	1

[1] *7 jewel grades made only during 1891; 9 jewel chronograph made 1891-1898.*
[2] *A few examples are KWKS for export to England.*

Trenton movement, 18 size, 4 jewels, serial number 4744.

Trenton movement, 18 size, 7 jewels, 4th model, serial number 788313.

TRENTON
18 SIZE

Grade or Name — Description	Avg	Ex-Fn	Mint
M#1-2, gilded, OF or HC ★	$150	$175	$300
M#3, 7J, ¾	65	70	95
M#3, 9J, ¾	75	85	105
M#4, 7J, FULL	60	70	95
M#4, 11J, FULL	60	70	95
M#4, 15J, FULL	70	80	110
M#4-5, FULL, OF or HC, NI	60	75	110
New Haven Watch Co. style, M#1, 4J	75	100	135
Trenton, 7J, KW, KS ★	225	275	375

16 SIZE

Grade or Name — Description	Avg	Ex-Fn	Mint
M#1-2, 7J, ¾, NI, HC or OF	$75	$100	$175
M#3, 7J, 3F BRG	45	60	85

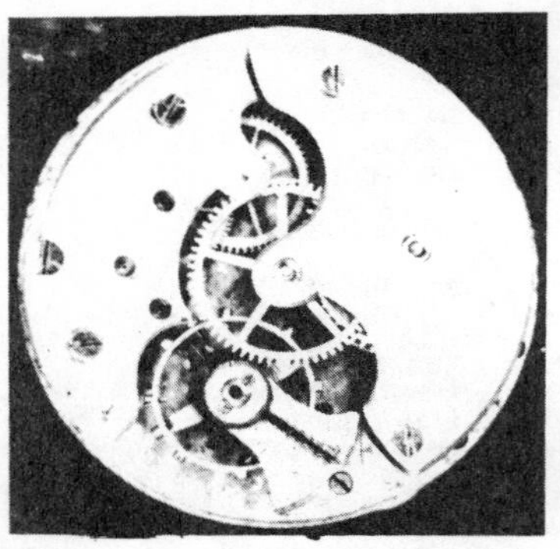

Trenton movement, 18 size, 7 jewels, serial number 148945.

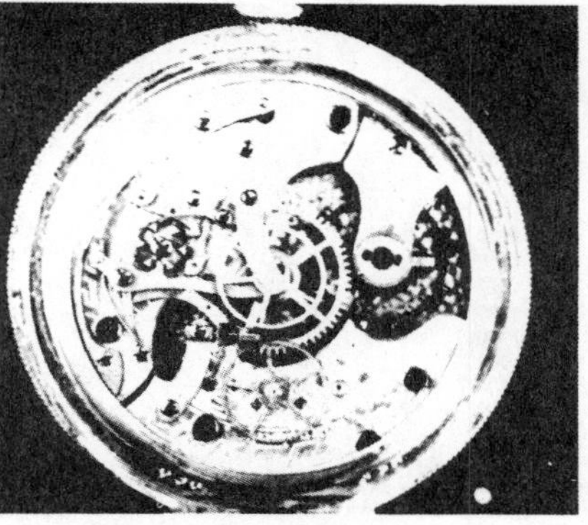

Chronograph, 16 size, 9 jewels, third model; start, stop & fly back, sweep second hand.

Grade or Name — Description	Avg	Ex-Fn	Mint
M#3, 11J, 3F BRG	50	65	95
M#3, 15J, 3F BRG	55	70	95
7,11,15J, 3F BRG, NI	60	80	115
Chronograph, 9J, start, stop, & fly back	125	150	225
Convertible Model, 7J, HC or OF	75	95	135
Grade #30 & 31, 7J	30	40	65
Grade #35, 36 & 38, 11J	40	50	75
Grade #45, 16J	40	50	75
Grade #125, 12J	40	60	95
Ingersoll Trenton, 7J, 3F BRG	45	50	65
Ingersoll Trenton, 15J, 3F BRG, NI, ADJ	50	60	65
Ingersoll Trenton, 17J, 3F BRG, NI, ADJ	60	80	95
Ingersoll Trenton, 19J, 3F BRG, NI, HCI5P	125	135	195
Peerless, 7J, SW, LS	45	55	75
Reliance, 7J	45	55	75

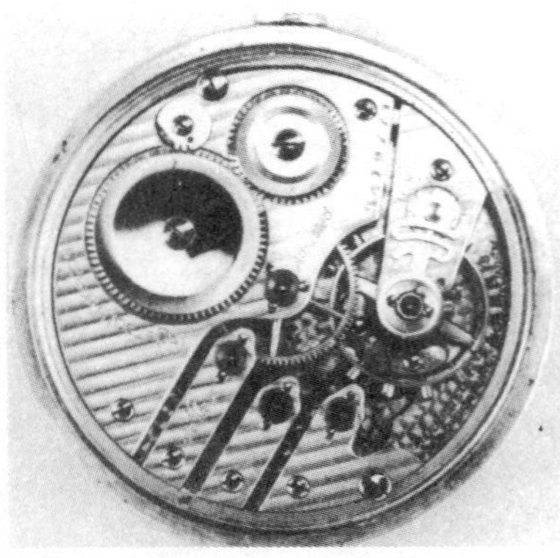

Ingersoll Trenton movement, 16 size, 19 jewels, three-fingered bridge, adjusted, serial number 3419771.

Ingersoll Trenton movement, 16 size, 12 jewels; *Edgemere* engraved on movement.

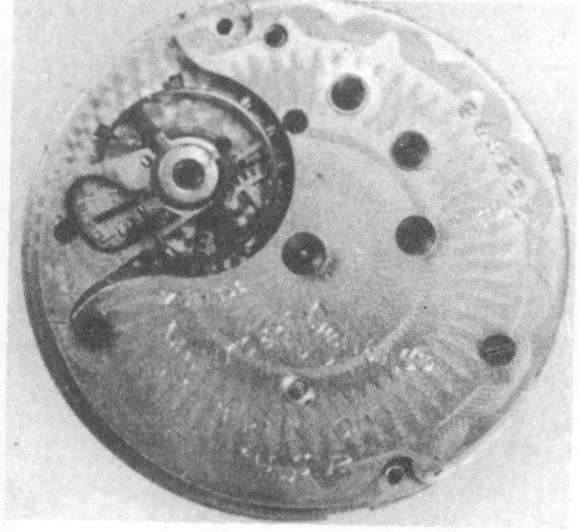

Reliance, 16 size, 7 jewels, serial number 241265.

Trenton movement, convertible model, 16 size, 7 jewels.

12 SIZE

Grade or Name — Description	Avg	Ex-Fn	Mint
"Fortuna," 7J, BRG	$40	$50	$60
M#1, 7J, ¾	40	50	60
Monogram, 7J, SW	40	50	60

Example of a basic **Trenton Watch Co.** movement, 6 size, 7 jewels, open face & hunting, nickel damaskeened.

6 SIZE

Grade or Name — Description	Avg	Ex-Fn	Mint
7J, ¾, NI	$35	$40	$60
7J, 3F BRG	40	50	65
15J, 3F BRG	45	60	75

0 SIZE

Grade or Name — Description	Avg	Ex-Fn	Mint
7J, 3F BRG	$65	$80	$110
15J, 3F BRG	70	95	125

UNITED STATES WATCH CO.
Marion, New Jersey
1864 — 1872

The United States Watch Co. was conceived in 1863, and the building which was started in August 1864 was completed in the summer of 1865. The first watch was not put on the market until late summer 1867 and was called the "Frederic Atherton." It was 18S, full plate, gilt movement, exposed pallet and expansion balance. A distinctive feature of the company's movements was the patented opening in the plates. The opening was shaped like a butterfly and allowed the escapement to be inspected. In 1868 the Edwin Rollo model was released, in 1869 the S. M. Beard, A. H. Wallis and John Lewis models were produced, and in 1870 the G. A. Read, J. W. Deacon and Chas. Knapp models appeared on the market. By 1869, the production level had reached 100 movements a day. That same year the company came out with a high grade watch called the "United States;" it was a ¾ plate, nickel, 16S, gold train movement. There were 19 ruby jewels, three pairs of conical pivots, a Breguet hairspring, compensation balance, adjusted to heat, cold, isochronism and positions. It was finely damaskeened and frost-finished. This watch was priced at $475, the highest price for a watch of that type in America.

In 1872, the name was changed to Marion Watch Co. on paper only. At this time the prices were lowered to much less on most of the grades, but this proved to be a mistake. The company failed in 1874, and the machinery was sold to the Fredonia Watch Co. and the Fitchburg Watch Co. Some may have been sold to the Auburndale Watch Co. also. The company produced some 286,000 watches in the ten years it was in business.

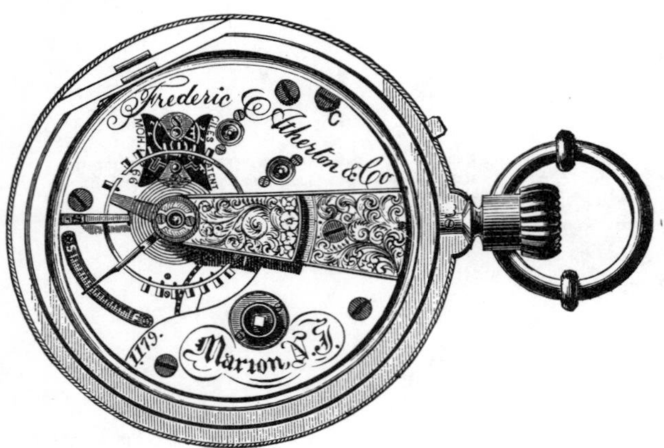

Example of a **Frederick Atherton & Co.** movement, 18 size, 19 jewels, gold jewel settings, key wind & pin set. Note butterfly cut-out.

UNITED STATES WATCH CO., MARION, N. J.
18 SIZE

Grade or Name — Description	Avg	Ex-Fn	Mint
Wm. Alexander, 15J, Coin	$275	$350	$425
Wm. Alexander, 15J, NI, KW	195	225	350
Wm. Alexander, 15J, NI, SW	235	300	375
Frederic Atherton & Co., 19J, NI, KW, GJS, HCIP	700	800	1,000
Frederic Atherton & Co., 19J, NI, SW, GJS, HCIP	900	1,000	1,200

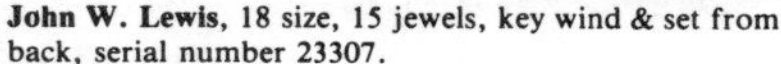

John W. Lewis, 18 size, 15 jewels, key wind & set from back, serial number 23307.

Edwin Rollo, 18 size, 15 jewels, gilded, key wind & set, note butterfly cut-out, serial number 110214.

Grade or Name — Description	Avg	Ex-Fn	Mint
Frederic Atherton & Co., 19J, gilded, KW, GJS, HCIP, OF	500	600	725
Frederic Atherton & Co., 19J, gilded, SW, GJS, HCIP, HC ★	650	750	980
S. M. Beard, 15J, NI, KW	250	300	395
S. M. Beard, 15J, SW	250	300	395
S. M. Beard, 15J, KW, Coin	250	300	395
George Channing, 15J, KW, Coin	250	320	425
George Channing, 15J, gilded, KW	250	320	425
J. W. Deacon, 11J, gilded, SW	195	230	395
J. W. Deacon, 11J, gilded, KW	185	210	395
Empire City Watch Co., 15J, NI, SW	300	340	475
Benjamin Franklin, 15J, KW	450	600	775
Asa Fuller, 11J, gilded, KW or SW	195	260	340
Asa Fuller, 11J, gilded, SW, OF	195	260	340
Asa Fuller, 11J, gilded, SW, HC	225	275	365
John W. Lewis, 15J, SW	225	340	495
John W. Lewis, 15J, NI, KW	225	340	495
Marion Watch Co., 15J, gilded, KW, ADJ	350	395	475
Marion Watch Co., 15J, gilded, SW, ADJ	400	425	525
Pennsylvania R.R., 15J, KW, w/butterfly cut-out	1,000	1,200	1,800
Henry Randel, 15J, NI, KW, ADJ	250	325	425
Henry Randel, 15J, NI, KW, ADJ, Coin	230	315	375
Henry Randel, 15J, NI, SW, ADJ	275	350	475
G. A. Read, 7J, gilded, SW or KW	200	275	325
Edwin Rollo, 15J, gilded, KW	200	250	325
Royal Gold, Am. W., N. Y., 15J, KW	375	460	695
Rural New York, 15J, gilded, KW, KS	275	325	450
Rural New York, 15J, gilded, KW, KS, Coin	275	325	450
Fayette Stratton, 15J, Coin	250	300	400
Fayette Stratton, 15J, gilded, KW	275	300	425
Fayette Stratton, 15J, gilded, SW	300	350	475
United States Watch Co., 19J, NI, GJS, HCIP, KW ★★★	750	950	1,200
United States Watch Co., 19J, NI, GJS, HCIP, SW ★★★	995	1,200	1,600
United States Watch Co., 19J, GJS, HCI5P, 18K, HC, dial movement and case all marked, pin set ★★★	4,000	4,300	5,000

Edwin Rollo, 18 size, 15 jewels, key wind & set from back, serial number 289025.

United States Watch Co., 18 size, 19 jewels, gold jewel settings, key wind & pin set, serial number 24054.

Grade or Name — Description	Avg	Ex-Fn	Mint
A. H. Wallis, 17J, NI, HCIP, KW	325	375	500
A. H. Wallis, 17J, NI, HCIP, SW	350	400	550
I. H. Wright, 11J, gilded, KW, SW	200	250	350
Young America, 7J, gilded, KW or SW	250	300	425
Any personalized movement w/butterfly cut-out	*225*	*275*	*450*

Note: 18S, ¾ plate are scarce.

14 SIZE

Grade or Name — Description	Avg	Ex-Fn	Mint
Royal Gold American Watch, N. Y., 15J, ¾, KW	$275	$360	$575

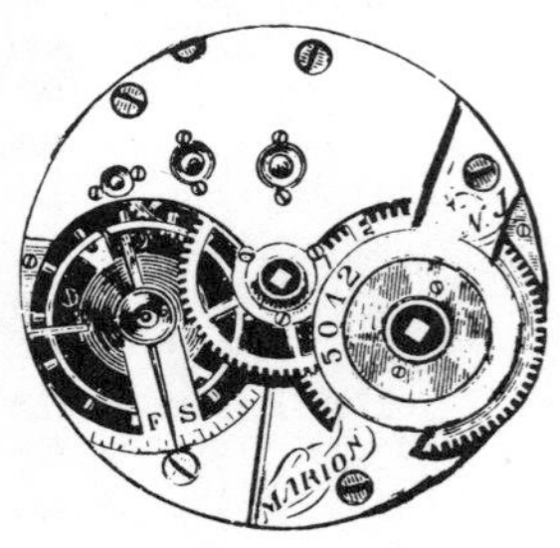

United States Watch Co., 10 size, 7-17 jewels, key wind & set from back.

12 OR 10 SIZE

Grade or Name — Description	Avg	Ex-Fn	Mint
Empire City Watch Co.	$150	$175	$250
Chas. G. Knapp, 15J, gilded	150	175	250
North Star, 7J, ¾	150	175	250
R. F. Pratt, 15J, gilded	150	175	250
United States Watch Co., 19J, GJS, KW, NI ★	500	600	775
United States Watch Co., 19J, GJS, SW, NI ★	575	675	850
A. H. Wallis, 19J, KW, KS, HC ★	400	475	650
A. H. Wallis, 19J, KW, KS, HC, Coin ★	400	475	650

Appleton Watch Co. movement and dial. Printed on dial "The Appleton Watch Co." Engraved on movement "Appleton Watch Co., Appleton Wis." 18 size, 7 jewels, serial number 93106. Note stem attached to movement making it not fit a standard 18 size case.

United States Watch Co., 18 size, 15 jewels, hunting case, patented March 8, 1870. Note balance cock has two levels.

United States Watch Co., 10-14 size, 15 jewels. Engraved on movement "Royal Gold American Watch, New York, Extra Jeweled." Note balance cock is all one level.

Rockford Watch Co., 18 size, 22 jewels, serial number 437112. Engraved on movement "Wathier Superior Railway Chromometer, Chicago."

Otay Watch Co., 18 size, 15 jewels, hunting case. Engraved on movement "Otay Watch Co., Otay, California, Adjusted." Serial number 30385.

Waterbury Watch Co., 39mm, 7 jewels. Engraved on movement "Tuxedo, Trademark U.S.A., Patented." "R" and "S." Serial number 819744. Note unusual duplex escapement.

Harwood Self Winding Watch Co. Inc. (Swiss movement). Tonneau style case, 15 jewels, two adjustments, patent number 1576120.

American Waltham Watch Co., Riverside, 21 jewels, raised gold jeweled settings, adj. to temp. & positions, serial number 28748659.

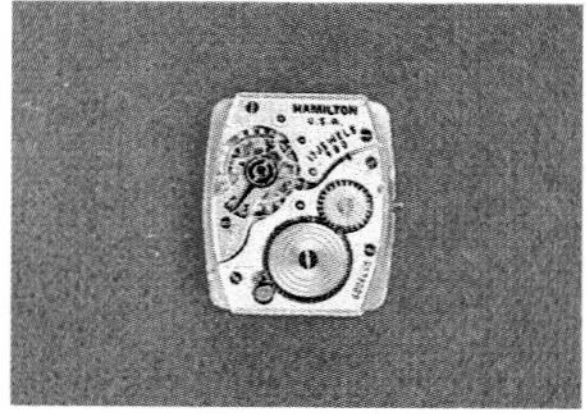

Hamilton Watch Co., Grade 980, 17 jewels, serial number G539009.

E. Howard & Co., 6 size, Model G, 15 jewels, stem wind, 18k enameled E. H. & Co. case. American made enameled cases are scarce. Note full color miniaturized bird on case. Engraved inside case ''Lizzie, from Edward, December 20, 1877.''

Albert H. Potter Watch Co., 18 size, 7 jewels, pivoted detent chronometer escapement with gold spring and lock stone. Engraved on movement ''A. H. Potter, Boston.''

George P. Reed, 18 size, fully jeweled, serial number 5, lever escapement. Note Geneva stop works, also balance wheel loaded with gold screws.

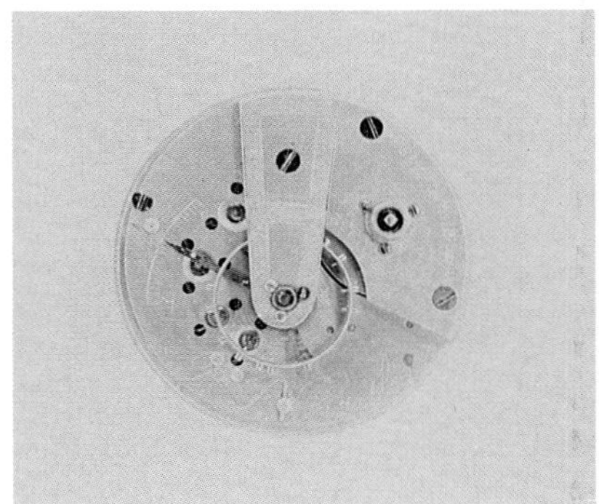

American Waltham Watch Co., 18 size, 15 jewels, hunting case, P. S. Bartlet model with pinned plate, serial number 10952.

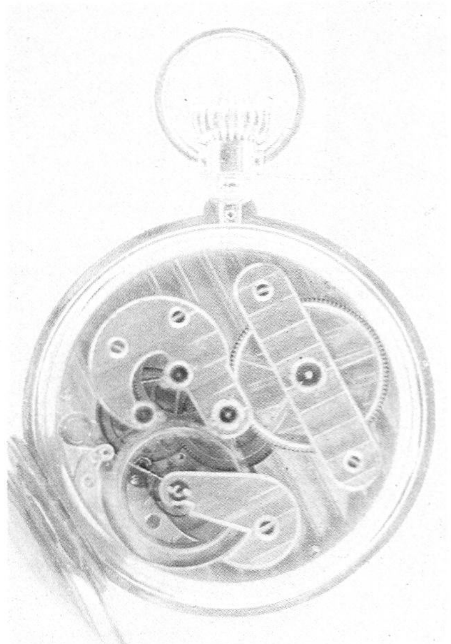

Albert H. Potter, 18 size, 22 jewels, hunting case, detent escapement, helical hairspring, swiss movement.

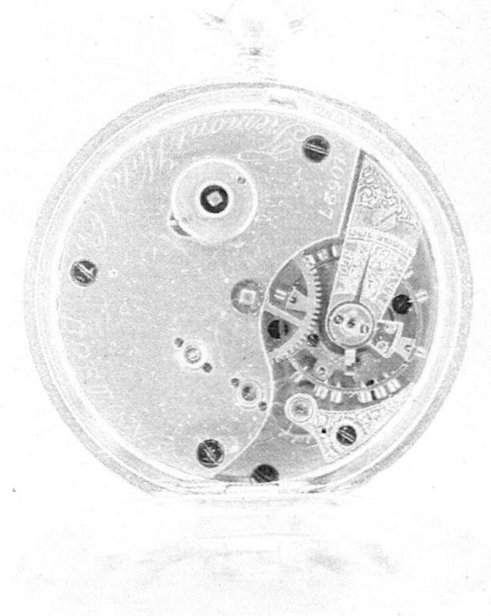

Tremont Watch Co., 18 size, 15 jewels, three-quarter plate, key wind & set from back, serial number 40627.

U. S. WATCH CO.
OF WALTHAM
Waltham, Massachusetts
1884 — 1905

The business was started as the Waltham Watch Tool Co. in 1879. It was organized as the United States Watch Co. in 1884. The first watches were 16S, ¾ plate pillar movement in three grades. They had a very wide mainspring barrel (the top was thinner than most) which was wedged up in the center to make room for the balance wheel. These watches are called dome watches and are hard to find. The fork was made of an aluminum alloy with a circular slot and a square ruby pin. The balance was gold at first as was the movement which was a slow train, but the expansion balance was changed when they went to a quick train. The movement required a special case and proved unpopular. By 1887, some 3,000 watches had been made. A new model was then produced, a 16S movement that would fit a standard case. These movements were quick train expansion balance with standard type lever and ¾ plate pillar movement. The company had a top production of ten watches a day. It was sold to the E. Howard Watch Co. in 1903. The United States Watch Co. produced some 802,000 watches total. Its top grade watch was the "President."

U. S. WATCH CO., WALTHAM
ESTIMATED SERIAL NUMBERS
AND PRODUCTION DATES

Date	Serial No.	Date	Serial No.
1887	3,000	1896	300,000
1888	6,500	1897	350,000
1889	10,000	1898	400,000
1890	30,000	1899	500,000
1891	60,000	1900	600,000
1892	90,000	1901	700,000
1893	150,000	1902	750,000
1894	200,000	1903	800,000
1895	250,000		

The President, movement and dial, 18 size, 17 jewels, nickel movement, double sunk dial, "The President" on dial and movement, serial number 150020.

U. S. WATCH CO., WALTHAM, MASS.
18 SIZE

Grade or Name — Description	Avg	Ex-Fn	Mint
Express Train, 15J, OF, ADJ	$135	$190	$295

U. S. WATCH CO., WALTHAM, 18 SIZE (continued)

Grade or Name — Description	Avg	Ex-Fn	Mint
The President, 17J, HC ★★	400	550	775
The President, 21J, GJS, HCI6P, DR, 14K ★★	700	875	1,000
The President, 17J, GJS, HCI6P, DR, NI, DMK, OF ★	375	450	675
Washington Square, 15J, HC	135	195	285
39 (HC) & 79 (OF), 17J, GJS, ADJ, NI, DMK, HCI5P, BRG	95	110	135
40 (HC) & 80 (OF), 17J, GJS	75	90	125
48 (HC) & 88 (OF), 7J, gilded, FULL	60	80	120
48 (HC) & 88 (OF), 7J, gilded, FULL, Silveroid	40	50	65
52 (HC)	65	90	150
92 (OF), 17J, Silveroid	40	50	65
52 (HC) & 92 (OF), 17J	65	90	125
53 (HC) & 93 (OF), 15J, NI, FULL, DMK	60	90	120
54 (HC) & 94 (OF), 15J	55	70	100
56 (HC) & 96 (OF), 11J	50	70	90
57 (HC) & 97 (OF), 15J	60	80	100
58 (HC) & 98 (OF), 11J, NI, FULL, DMK	50	60	75

Prices are with gold filled cases except where noted.)

NOTE: Some grades are not included. Their values can be determined by comparing with similar models or grades listed.

U.S. Watch Co., 16 size, 15 jewels, three-quarter plate.

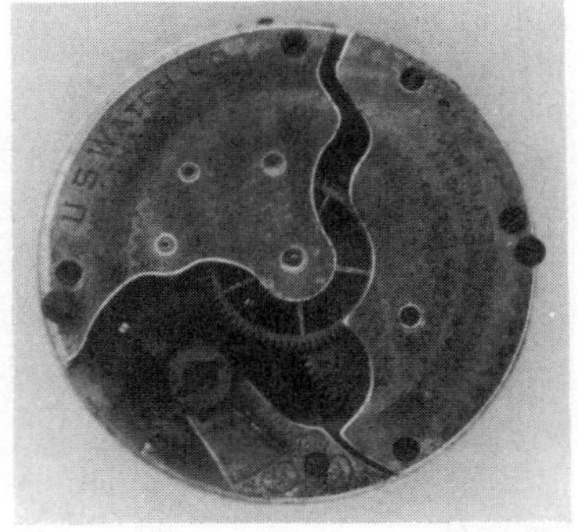

U.S. Watch Co., 16 size, 7 jewels, "A New Watch Company At Waltham, Est'd 1885" on movement, serial number 770771.

16 SIZE

Grade or Name — Description	Avg	Ex-Fn	Mint
Dome Plate Model, 7J, gilded ★★	$175	$200	$285
Early KW-KS, 7J, S# below 100	500	700	1,000
103, 17J, NI, ¾, ADJ	90	110	135
104, 17J, NI, ¾	75	85	110
104, 17J, NI, ¾, Silveroid	55	65	85
105, 15J, NI, ¾, HC	70	85	125
105, 15J, NI, ¾, OF	65	70	90
105, 15J, NI, ¾, Silveroid	50	60	70
106, 15J, gilded, ¾, Silveroid	30	40	55
106, 15J, gilded, ¾	45	60	85

U. S. WATCH CO., WALTHAM (continued)

Grade or Name — Description	Avg	Ex-Fn	Mint
108, 11J, gilded, ¾	40	60	85
109, 7J, NI, ¾	40	50	75
110, 7J, ¾, HC	40	50	75
110, 7J, ¾, OF	40	50	75

6 SIZE

Grade or Name — Description	Avg	Ex-Fn	Mint
60, 17J, GJS, NI, ¾, HCI3P	$80	$95	$135
60, 17J, GJS, NI, ¾, HCI3P, OF, 14K	225	275	345
62, 15J, NI, ¾	60	70	95
63, 15J, gilded	50	60	75
64, 11J, NI	40	50	60
65, 11J, gilded	35	40	55
66, 7J, gilded	35	40	60
66, 7-11J, NI, ¾	50	60	80
68, 16J, GJS, NI, ¾	85	100	130
69, 7J, NI, HC	45	50	75
69, 7J, NI, OF	40	50	70

Grade 64, 6 size, 11 jewels.

U.S. Watch Co., 0 size, 7 jewels, nickel plate.

0 SIZE

Grade or Name — Description	Avg	Ex-Fn	Mint
Betsy Ross, HC	$95	$125	$200
U. S. Watch Co., 15J, HC	85	100	175

THE WASHINGTON WATCH CO.
Washington, D. C.
1872 — 1874

J. P. Hopkins was better known as the inventor of the Auburndale Rotary Watch but he was also connected with the Washington Watch Co. which made about fifty watches. They were 18S, key wind, ¾ plate and had duplex escapements. Before Hopkins came to Washington Watch Co. he had made by hand about six fine watches. Most of the materials used to produce their watch movements were purchased from the Illinois

Watch Co. The company had a total production of 45 movements with duplex escapements.

Grade or Name — Description		Avg	Ex-Fn	Mint
18S, 15J, ¾, KW, KS	★★★	$2,000	$2,800	$3,800

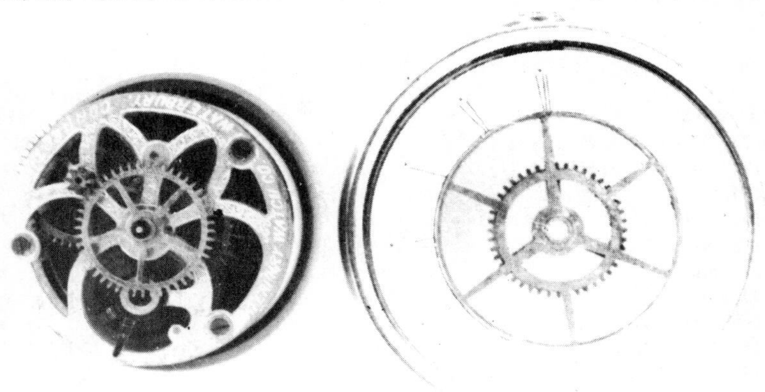

Example of a **Waterbury Long Wind** movement and dial. Note six spokes on dial.

WATERBURY WATCH CO.
Waterbury, Connecticut
1880 — 1898

The Waterbury Watch Co. was formed in 1880, and D. A. Buck made its first watch. The watches were simple and had only fifty parts. The mainspring was about nine feet long and coiled around the movement; it had a two-wheel train rather than the standard four-wheel train. The Waterbury long wind movement revolved once every hour and had a duplex escapement. The dial was made of paper, and the watch was priced at $3.50 to $4. Some of these watches were used as giveaways.

Example of basic **Waterbury Watch Co.** movement, Series C.

Series L, Waterbury W. Co. Duplex Escapement, about 18 size.

Chronology of the Development of Waterbury Watch Co.:
Waterbury Watch Co., Waterbury, Conn. — 1880-1898
New England Watch Co. — 1898-1912
Purchased Ingersoll — 1914
Became U. S. Time Corp. (maker of Timex) — 1944

18 TO 0 SIZES

Grade or Name — Description	Avg	Ex-Fn	Mint
35S, 1890-1891, back wind	$65	$75	$95
Long wind, skeletonized, 3 spokes ★	300	350	525
Long wind, skeletonized, 4 spokes ★★	500	600	800
Long wind, skeletonized, 6 spokes ★	275	350	450
Series A, long wind, skeletonized ★	275	350	450
Series C, long wind	175	200	275
Series E, long wind (discontinued 1890)	175	225	325
Series G, ¾ lever escapement	70	80	95
Series H, Columbian Duplex	65	70	85
Series I, Trump, ¾	75	80	95
Series J, Americus Duplex	75	80	95
Series K, Charles Benedict Duplex	85	90	125
Series L, Waterbury W. Co. Duplex	65	80	110
Series N, Addison Duplex	50	60	70
Series P, Rugby Duplex	75	80	110
Series R, Tuxedo Duplex	60	70	90
Series S, Elfin	50	60	70
Series T, Oxford Duplex	50	60	75
Series W, Addison	45	50	60
Series Z	45	60	75
Oxford	45	70	80
The Trump	40	65	75
Waterbury W. Co., 7J, ¾, low Serial No.	200	325	425

NOTE: Dollar watches must be in running condition to bring these prices.

Series I, The Trump, about 18 size, no jewels, pin lever escapement.

Series T, Oxford Duplex Escapement, about 18 size, no jewels.

E. N. Welch Mfg. Co., 36 size, back wind & set, made for the Chicago Exposition in 1893. Die die-bossed back depicting the landing of Columbus in America, Oct. 12th, 1492.

E. N. WELCH MFG. CO.
Bristol, Connecticut
1834 — 1897

Elisha Welch founded this company about 1834. His company failed in 1897, and the Sessions Clock Co. took over the business in 1903. E. N. Welch Mfg. Co. produced the large watch which was displayed at the Chicago Exposition in 1893. This watch depicted the landing of Columbus on the back of the case.

Grade or Name — Description	Avg	Ex-Fn	Mint
36S, Columbus exhibition watch	$75	$135	$199

WESTCLOX
United Clock Co.
Westclox & Western Clock Co.
General Time Corp.
Athens, Georgia
1899 — Present

The first Westclox pocket watch was made about 1899; however, the Westclox name did not appear on their watches until 1906. In 1903 they were making 100 watches a day, and in 1920 production was at 15,000 per day. This company is still in business today in Athens, Georgia.

Grade or Name — Description	Avg	Ex-Fn	Mint
M#1, SW, push to set, GRO	$40	$45	$55
M#2, SW, back set, GRO	30	40	50
18S, Westclox M#4, OF, GRO	35	45	55
1910 Models to 1920, GRO	30	40	50
Anniversary	25	35	50
Antique	15	20	25
Boy Proof	25	35	50

WESTCLOX (continued)

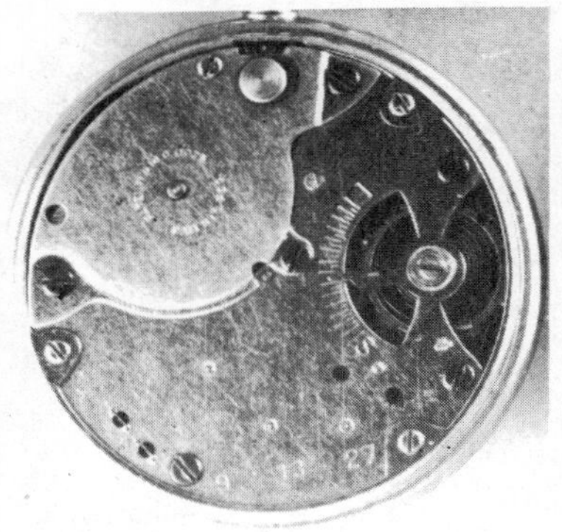

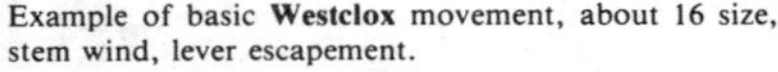

Example of basic **Westclox** movement, about 16 size, stem wind, lever escapement.

Explorer, back of case and dial, "Wings Over The Pole, The Explorer" on back of case.

Grade or Name — Description	Avg	Ex-Fn	Mint
Bingo	25	35	50
Bulls Eye (several models)	5	20	35
Country Gentleman	35	40	50
Dax (many models)	5	15	25
Elite	20	25	35
Everbrite (several models)	10	15	25
Explorer	50	60	85
Farm Bureau	25	30	35
Glo Ben	25	30	35
Ideal	25	30	35
Lighted Dial	15	20	25
Mark IV	35	40	50
Maxim	25	30	35
Mickey Mouse (1960 to Present)	25	30	35
Military Style, 24 hour	50	60	75
Mustang	35	40	50
NAWCC, ETP 1,000	25	30	35
Pocket Ben (many models)	15	30	50
Ruby	20	25	35
Scotty (several models)	5	10	20
Smile	20	25	35
Sun Mark	25	30	35
Team Mate (various major league teams)	15	20	25
Tele Time	15	20	25
Texan	25	30	35
Tiny Tim	25	30	35
Victor	75	95	120
Vote	20	25	30
Westclox	10	15	20
Zep	150	200	325

WRIST WATCHES

Style or Grade — Description	Avg	Ex-Fn	Mint
Tonneau case	$3	$4	$6
Rectangular	3	4	5
Round case	2	3	4
Round, day & date	5	7	12
Round, luminous dial	4	6	10

Zep, about 16 size with radiant numbers and hands, c. 1929.

Example of a **Western Watch Co.** movement, 18 size, 15 jewels, key wind & set.

WESTERN WATCH CO.

Chicago, Illinois
1880

Albert Trotter purchased the unfinished watches from the California Watch Co. Mr. Trotter finished and sold those watches. Later he moved to Chicago and, with Paul Cornell and others, formed the Western Watch Company. Very few watches were completed by the Western Watch Co.

Grade or Name — Description		Avg	Ex-Fn	Mint
Western Watch Co., 18S, FULL	★★★	$2,000	$2,300	$3,000

WICHITA WATCH CO.

Wichita, Kansas
July, 1887 — 1888

This company completed construction of their factory in Wichita, Kansas in June 1888, and only a half dozen watches were produced during the brief period the company was in operation. The president was J. R. Snively. These watches are 18S, half plate, adjusted, 15 jewels.

Grade or Name — Description		Avg	Ex-Fn	Mint
18S, 15J, ½ plate, ADJ	★★★	$2,500	$3,000	$4,000

EUROPEAN WATCHES

EARLY ANTIQUE WATCHES

The earlier antique watches looked quite similar to small table clocks; these drum-shaped watches were about three inches in diameter and usually over one inch thick. The drum-shaped watch lost popularity in the late 1500s. The earliest portable timepieces did not carry the maker's name, but initials were common. The cases generally had a hinged lid which covered the dial. This lid was pierced with small holes to enable ready identification of the position of the hour hand. They also usually contained a bell. The dial often had the numbers "I" to "XII" engraved in Roman numerals and the numbers "13" to "24" in Arabic numbers with the "2" engraved in the form of a "Z." Even the earliest of timepieces incorporated striking. The oldest known watch with a date engraved on the case was made in 1548. A drum-shaped watch with the initials "C. W.," it was most likely produced by Casper Werner, a protege of Henlein.

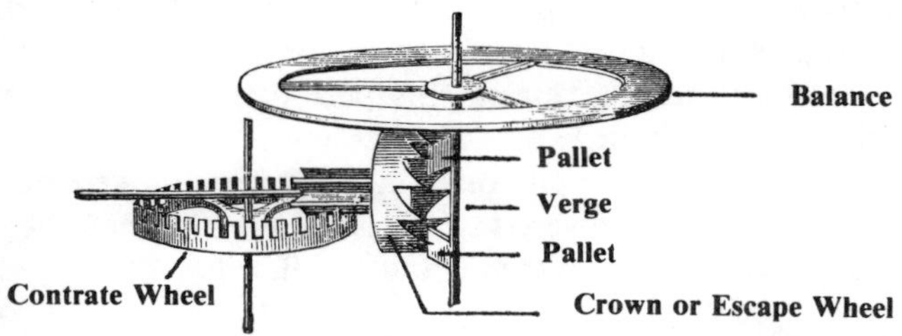

Early pocket watches were designed to run from 12 to 16 hours. The pinions usually bore five leaves, the great wheel 55 teeth, the second wheel 45 teeth, the third wheel 40 teeth, and the escape wheel 15 teeth. With one less pinion and wheel the escape wheel ran reverse to the way of a standard four-wheel watch. During the 1500s, 1600s, and much of the 1700s it was stylish to decorate not only the case and balance cock but all parts including the clicks, barrel, studs, springs, pillars, hands, and stackfreed. The plates themselves were decorated with pierced and engraved metal scrolls, and in some instances the maker's name was engraved in a style to correspond with the general decoration of the movement. During these periods the most celebrated artists, designers, and engravers were employed. The early watches were decorated by famous artists such as Jean Vauquier 1670, Daniel Marot 1700, Gillis l'Egare 1650, Michel Labon 1630, Pierre Bourdon 1750, and D. Cochin 1750. Most of the artists were employed to design and execute pierced and repouse cases.

THE MID-1700s

In the mid-1700s relatively minor changes are noticed. Decoration became less distinctive and less artistic. The newer escapements resulted in better timekeeping, and a smaller balance cock was used. The table and foot became smaller. The foot grew more narrow, and as the century and the development of the watch advanced, the decoration on the balance cock became smaller and less elaborate. About 1720 the foot was becoming solid and flat. No longer was it hand pierced; however, some of the pierced ones were produced until about 1770. Thousands of these beautiful hand pierced watch cocks have been made into necklaces and brooches or framed. Sadly, many of the old movements were destroyed in a mad haste to cater to the buyers' fancy.

THE 1800s

As the 1800s approached the balance cocks became less artistic in decoration as the decoration on movements gradually diminished. Breguet and Berthoud spent very little time on the beauty or artistic design on their balance cocks or pillars. But the cases were often magnificient in design and beauty, made with enamels in many colors and laden with precious stones. During this period the movements were plain and possessed very little artistic character.

As early as 1820 three-quarter and one-half plate designs were being used with the balance cock lowered to the same level as the other wheels. The result was a slimmer watch being produced.

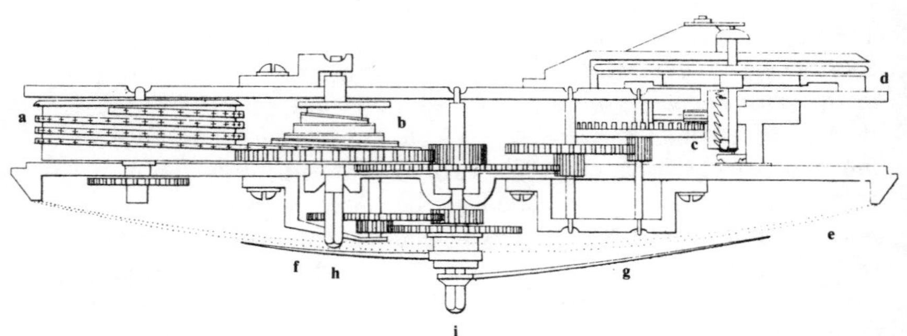

Exposed illustration of an early watch movement, c. 1800-1850. Note that movement is key wind and set from the dial side. The illustrated example is a chain driven fusee with a verge escapement: **a**-Main spring barrel and chain. **b**-Fusee. **c**-Verge escapement. **d**-Balance wheel. **e**-Dial. **f**-Hour hand. **g**-Minute hand. **h**-Winding arbor. **i**-Setting arbor.

CLUES TO DATING YOUR WATCH

To establish the age of a watch there are many points to be considered. The dial, hands, pillars, balance cock and pendant, for example, contain important clues in determining the age of your watch. However, no one part alone should be considered sufficient evidence

Example of an early pocket watch with a stackfreed design to equalize power much as a fusee does. Note dumbbell shaped foliot which served as a balance for verge escapement, and the tear shaped cam which is part of the stackfreed.

to draw a definite conclusion as to age. The watch as a whole must be considered. For example, an English-made silver-cased watch will have a hallmark inside the case. It is quite simple to refer to the London Hallmark Table for hallmarks after 1697. But this hallmark will reveal the age of the case only. This does not fix the age of the movement. Many movements are housed in cases made years before or after the movement was produced. An informed collector will note that a watch with an enamel dial, for instance, could not have been made before 1635. A pair of cases indicates it could not have been made prior to 1640. The minute hand was introduced in 1687. The presence of jewels would indicate it was made after 1700. A dust cap first appeared in 1774. Keyless winding came into being after 1820 but did not gain widespread popularity until after 1860. All of these clues and more must be considered before accurately assessing the age of a watch.

PILLARS

Pillars are of interest and should be considered as one of the elements in determining age. Through the years small watches used round pillars, and the larger watches generally used a square type engraved pillar.

(Illus. 1) This pillar is one of the earliest types and was used in the 1800s as well. This particular pillar came from a watch which dates about 1550. It is known that this type pillar was used in 1675 by Gaspard Girod of France and also by James Taylor of England in 1835.

(Illus. 2) This style pillar is called the tulip pattern. Some watchmakers preferred to omit the vertical divisions. The tulip style was popular between 1660 and 1750 but may be found on later watches. It was common practice to use ornamentation on the tulip pillar. The ornament shown *(Illus. 3)* was used by Daniel Quare of London from 1665 to 1725 and was also used by the celebrated Tompion as well as many others.

(Illus. 4) This type pillar is referred to as the Egyptian and dates from 1630 to the 1800s. The squared Egyptian pattern was introduced about 1630 and some may be found with a wider division with a head or bust inserted. This style was used by D. Bouquet of London about 1640 and by many other watchmakers.

Illus. 1

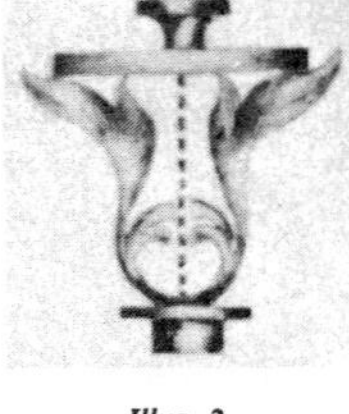

Illus. 2

Illus. 3

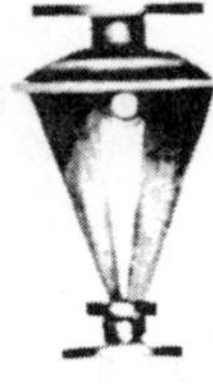

Illus. 4

(Illus. 5) This pillar was used by Thomas Earnshaw of London about 1780. The plain style was prominent for close to two hundred years—1650 to 1825.

(Illus. 6) This style was popular and was used by many craftsmen. Nathaniel Barrow of London put this in his watches about 1680.

Illus. 7) This pillar may be seen in watches made by Pierre Combet of Lyons, France, about 1720. It was also used by many others.

(Illus. 8) This style pillar and the ornament were used by John

Illus. 5

Illus. 6

Illus. 7

Illus. 8

Ellicott of England and other watchmakers from 1730 to 1770.

These illustrations represent just a few of the basic pillars that were used. Each watchmaker would design and change details to create his own individual identity. This sometimes makes it more difficult to readily determine the age of watches.

BALANCE COCKS OR BRIDGES

The first balance cocks or bridges used to support the balance staff were a plain "S" shape. The cocks used on the old three-wheel watches were very elaborate being hand-pierced and engraved. At first no screws were used to hold the cock in place. It is noteworthy that on the three-wheel watch the regulator was a ratchet and click and was used on these earlier movements to adjust the mainspring. About 1635 the balance cock was screwed to the plate and also pinned on its underside which helped steady the balance. The first cock illustrated is a beautifully decorated example and was made by Josias Jeubi of Paris about 1580. Note that it is pinned to a stud which passes through a square cut in the foot of the cock. Next is a balance cock made by Bouquet of London about 1640. The third balance cock is one made by Jean Rousseau and dates around 1650. The fourth one dates around 1655.

The next two bridges are supported on both sides of the balance cock by means of screws or pins. They are strikingly different and usually cover much of the plate of the movement. This style of balance cock was used around 1675 and was still seen as late as 1765.

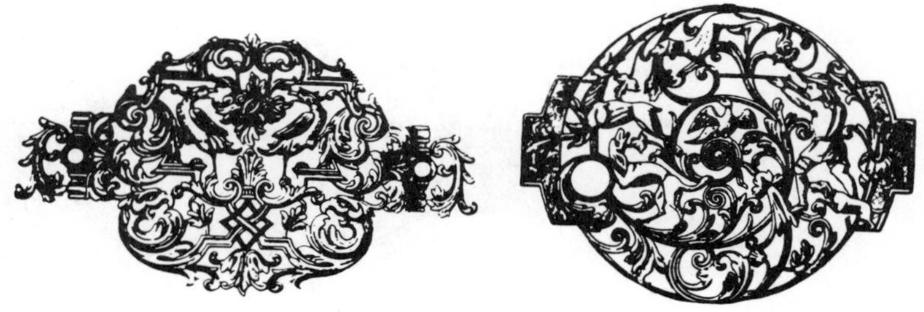

The beautiful balance cock below at left with the ornate foot dates about 1660 while the next illustrated balance cock with the immense amount of ornamentation was used from about 1700 to 1720 or longer. By 1720 a face was added to the design. The face shows up where the table terminates on most balance cocks.

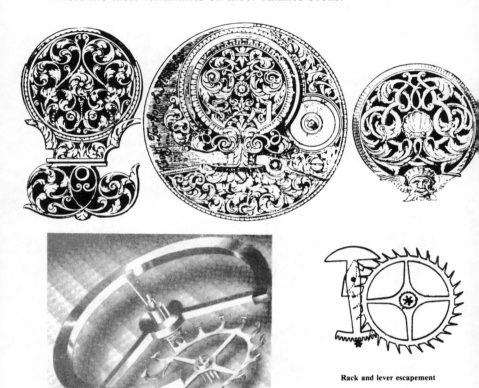

Rack and lever escapement

Invented in 1722

Cylinder escapement

Invented in 1695

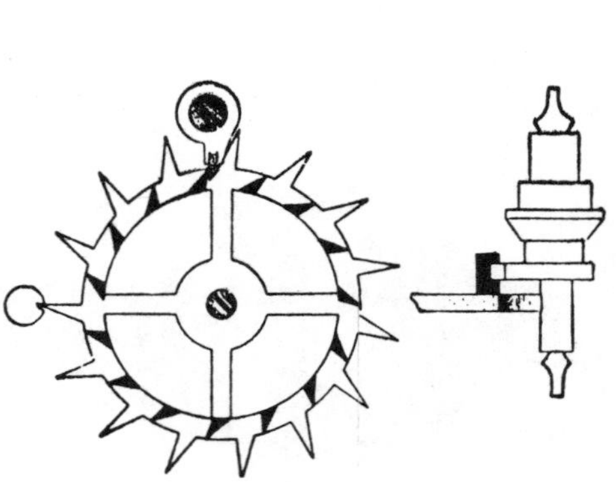

Duplex escapement

Invented in 1750

PROTECTING ANTIQUE WATCH MOVEMENTS

Many collectors of antique watches have purchased movements without cases. One cause is rooted in the Great Depression of the 1930s when watchmakers stripped the movements from pocket watches which had been traded for the increasingly popular wrist watch. The pocket watch cases were sold for their gold content. The movements, being respected as fine pieces of workmanship, were stored for use as parts. This devastating occurrence has been repeated during the last five years as the price of gold reached unprecedented levels, and many cases were once again scrapped for the gold content.

A display watch case is one excellent way to handle antique pocket watch movements. These cases hold the movements securely and protect the hands, dial, and movement from accidental damage due to moisture or dropping. This type of case, which has see-through panels on both the front and back, permits the collector to show a prospective buyer the face and back of the movement without exposing it to dirt or taking a chance of damage.

An antique watch movement can also be protected during travel with an inexpensive clear plastic shipping case which is available in both 18 size and 16 size (the 16 size will also adapt to the 12 size movement).

HALLMARKS OF LONDON

Hallmarks were used on gold and silver cases imported from England. These marks, when interpreted, will give you the age of the case and location of the assay office.

The date-marks used 20 letters of the alphabet, A-U, never using the letters W, X, Y, or Z. The letters J & I or U & V, because of their similarity in shape, were never used together within the same 20-year period. A total of four marks can be found on English cases, which are:

The Maker's Mark. 

The Standard Mark. 

The Assay Office Mark. 

1822-up

1478 to 1821

The Date Letter Mark. 

The **Maker's Mark** was used to denote the manufacturer of the case.

The **Standard Mark** was used to denote a guarantee of the quality of the metal.

The **Assay Office Mark** (also known as the town mark) was used to denote the location of the assay office.

The **Date Letter Mark** was a letter of the alphabet used to denote the year in which the article was stamped. The stamp was used on gold and silver cases by the assay office.

LONDON HALLMARKS

O 1551
P 1552
Q 1553
R 1554
S 1555
T 1556
V 1557
a 1558
b 1559
c 1560
d 1561
e 1562
f 1563
g 1564
h 1565
i 1566
k 1567
l 1568
m 1569
n 1570
o 1571
p 1572
q 1573
r 1574
s 1575
t 1576
v 1577
A 1578
B 1579
C 1580
D 1581
E 1582
F 1583
G 1584
H 1585
I 1586
K 1587
L 1588

M 1589
N 1590
O 1591
P 1592
Q 1593
R 1594
S 1595
T 1596
V 1597
A 1598
B 1599
C 1600
D 1601
E 1602
F 1603
G 1604
H 1605
I 1606
K 1607
L 1608
M 1609
N 1610
O 1611
P 1612
Q 1613
R 1614
S 1615
T 1616
V 1617
a 1618
b 1619
c 1620
d 1621
e 1622
f 1623
g 1624
h 1625
i 1626

k 1627
l 1628
m 1629
n 1630
o 1631
p 1632
q 1633
r 1634
s 1635
t 1636
v 1637
A 1638
B 1639
C 1640
D 1641
E 1642
F 1643
G 1644
H 1645
I 1646
K 1647
L 1648
M 1649
N 1650
O 1651
P 1652
Q 1653
R 1654
S 1655
T 1656
V 1657
A 1658
B 1659
C 1660
D 1661
E 1662
F 1663
G 1664
H 1665

I 1666
K 1667
L 1668
M 1669
N 1670
O 1671
P 1672
Q 1673
R 1674
S 1675
T 1676
V 1677
a 1678
b 1679
c 1680
d 1681
e 1682
f 1683
g 1684
h 1685
i 1686
k 1687
l 1688
m 1689
n 1690
o 1691
p 1692
q 1693
r 1694
s 1695
t 1696
a 1697
b 1698
c 1699
d 1700
e 1701
f 1702
g 1703
h 1704
i 1705
k 1706
l 1707
m 1708

n 1709
o 1710
p 1711
q 1712
r 1713
s 1714
t 1715
A 1716
B 1717
C 1718
D 1719
E 1720
F 1721
G 1722
H 1723
I 1724
K 1725
L 1726
M 1727
N 1728
O 1729
P 1730
Q 1731
R 1732
S 1733
T 1734
V 1735
a 1736
b 1737
c 1738
d 1739
d 1739
e 1740
f 1741
g 1742
h 1743
i 1744
k 1745
l 1746
m 1747
n 1748
o 1749
p 1750
q 1751

r 1752
s 1753
t 1754
u 1755
A 1756
B 1757
C 1758
D 1759
E 1760
F 1761
G 1762
H 1763
I 1764
K 1765
L 1766
M 1767
N 1768
O 1769
P 1770
Q 1771
R 1772
S 1773
T 1774
U 1775
a 1776
b 1777
c 1778
d 1779
e 1780
f 1781
g 1782
h 1783
i 1784
k 1785
l 1786
m 1787
n 1788
o 1789
p 1790
q 1791
r 1792
s 1793
t 1794
u 1795
A 1796

B 1797
C 1798
D 1799
E 1800
F 1801
G 1802
H 1803
I 1804
K 1805
L 1806
M 1807
N 1808
O 1809
P 1810
Q 1811
R 1812
S 1813
T 1814
U 1815
a 1816
b 1817
c 1818
d 1819
e 1820
f 1821
g 1822
h 1823
i 1824
k 1825
l 1826
m 1827
n 1828
o 1829
p 1830
q 1831
r 1832
s 1833
t 1834
u 1835
A 1836
B 1837
C 1838
D 1839
E 1840

F 1841
G 1842
H 1843
I 1844
K 1845
L 1846
M 1847
N 1848
O 1849
P 1850
Q 1851
R 1852
S 1853
T 1854
U 1855
a 1856
b 1857
c 1858
d 1859
e 1860
f 1861
g 1862
h 1863
i 1864
k 1865
l 1866
m 1867
n 1868
o 1869
p 1870
q 1871
r 1872
s 1873
t 1874
u 1875
A 1876
B 1877
C 1878
D 1879
E 1880
F 1881
G 1882
H 1883

I 1884
K 1885
L 1886
M 1887
N 1888
O 1889
P 1890
Q 1891
R 1892
S 1893
T 1894
U 1895
a 1896
b 1897
c 1898
d 1899
e 1900
f 1901
g 1902
h 1903
i 1904
k 1905
l 1906
m 1907
n 1908
o 1909
p 1910
q 1911
r 1912
s 1913
t 1914
u 1915
a 1916
b 1917
c 1918
d 1919
e 1920
f 1921
g 1922
h 1923
i 1924
k 1925
l 1926

A SHORT HISTORY OF WRIST WATCHES

In the late 1700s, Queen Elizabeth adorned her wrist with a watch heavily decorated with jewels and gold. While no one is sure who invented the wrist watch Queen Elizabeth was wearing or even the first wrist watch ever, the first few appeared around 1790. Small miniature watches had been made earlier than this, however. David Rosseau made a watch which was about 18mm in diameter (the size of a dime) in the late 1600s.

Miniaturized wrist watch by Waltham, Model number 400. Note size comparison to dime.

Miniaturization was a great challenge to many of the famous watchmakers including Louis Jaquet, Paul Ditisheim, John Arnold and Henri Capt, among others. The smallest watch in semi-mass production was 12mm by 5mm. In early 1930, the American Waltham Watch Co. made a 9mm by 20mm Model 400 watch.

Wrist watches were at first thought to be too small and delicate to be practical for men to wear. However, during World War I a German officer was said to have strapped a small pocket watch to his wrist with a leather webbed cup. This arrangement freed both hands and proved to be most useful. After the war, the wrist watch gained in popularity. Mass production of wrist watches was started around 1880 by the Swiss industry. The Swiss introduced them to the United States around 1895, but they did not prove to be very popular at first. Around 1907 the Elgin and Illinois watch companies were manufacturing wrist watches and by 1912 Hampden and Waltham had started. By 1920 the round styles were being replaced with square, rectangular and tonneau shapes and decorated with gems. By 1928 wrist watches were outselling pocket watches, and, by 1935, over 85 percent of the watches being produced were wrist watches.

Harwood self-winding wrist watch, c. 1928.

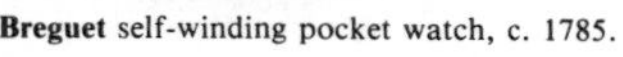

Breguet self-winding pocket watch, c. 1785.

Self-wind pocket watches were first developed by Abraham Louis Perrelet in 1770 and by Abraham Louis Breguet about 1777. Louis Recordon made improvements in 1780, but is was not until 1923 that the principle of self-winding was adapted to the wrist watch by John Harwood, an Englishman who set up factories to make his patented self-wind wrist watches in Switzerland, London, France, and the United States. His watches first reached the market about 1929. The firm A. Schild manufactured about 15,000 watches in Switzerland. Mr. Harwood's watch company removed the traditional stem or crown to wind the mainspring, but in order to set the hands it was necessary to turn the bezel. The Harwood Watch Co. failed around 1931 and the patent expired.

Early in 1930 the Rolex Watch Co. introduced the Rolex Oyster Perpetual, the first waterproof and self-winding wrist watch. By 1940 wrist watches came in all shapes and types including complicated chronographs, calendars, and repeaters; also novelties, digital jump hour and multi-dial were very popular.

A dramatic change occurred in 1957 when the Hamilton Watch Co. eliminated the mainspring and replaced it with a small battery that lasted well over one year. In 1960 the balance wheel was removed in the Accutron by Bulova and replaced by a tuning fork with miniature pawls.

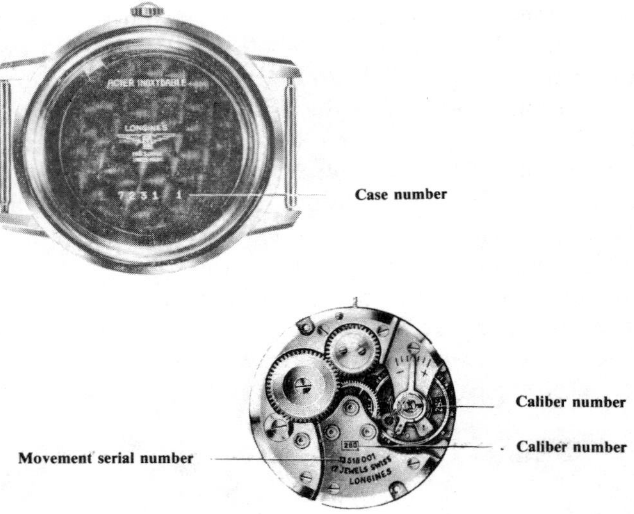

Some wrist watches have a grade or caliber number engraved on the movement. For example, Patek, Phillipe & Co. has a caliber number 27-460Q. The '27' stands for 27mm; the '460Q' is the grade; the 'Q' designates Quantieme (Perpetual calendar and moon phases).

WRIST WATCH CASE AND DIAL STYLES

Barrel

Maxine

Square

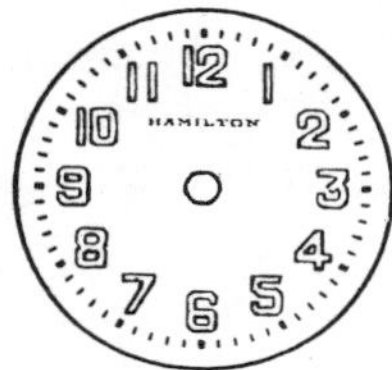

Round

Square Cut Corner

Cushion

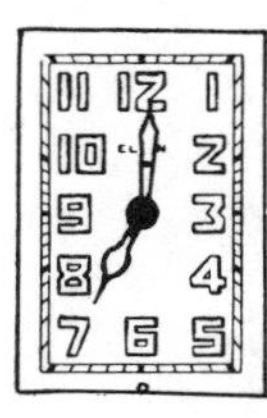

Rectangle

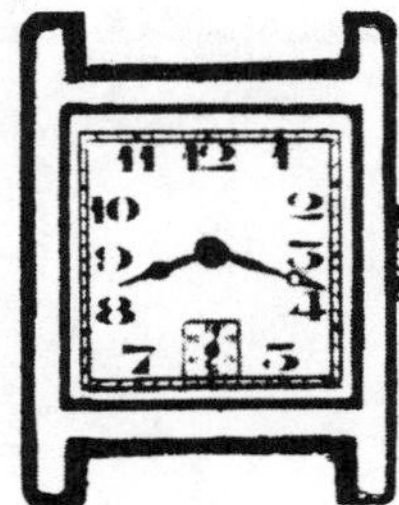

Tank

Round
(Ladies style; converts to lapel or wrist)

Curved or Curvex

Rectangle Cut Corner

Tonneau

Tonneau

Oval

CHRONOGRAPH

The term chronograph is derived from the Greek words *chronos* which means "time" and *grapho* which means "to write." The first recording of intervals of time was around 1822 by the inventor Rieussec. His chronograph made dots of ink on a dial as a measure of time. Around 1862 Adolph Nicole introduced the first chronograph with a hand that returned to zero. The split second chronograph made its appearance around 1879. Today a chronograph can be described as a timepiece that starts at will, stops at will, and can return to zero at will. A mechanical chronograph had a sweep or center second hand that will start, stop, and fly back to zero. The term chronometer should not be confused with chronograph. A chronometer is a timepiece that has superior timekeeping qualities at the time it is made.

A. Day window. **B.** Split second hand. **C.** Calendar pusher. **D.** Register for seconds. **E.** Calendar pusher. **F.** Date hand. **G.** Register for total hours. **H.** Sweep center second hand. **I.** Month window. **J.** Start/stop pusher. **K.** Register for total minutes. **L.** Return pusher. **M.** Day of month.

EUROPEAN WATCHES COLLECTED IN AMERICA

Although the primary focus of this book is American pocket watches, there is much interest in some foreign watches, especially those of early vintage and enduring quality. This section deals with some of the more noted foreign manufacturers in which pocket watch collectors have an interest.

* * *

Auguste Agassiz of Saint Imier and Geneva started manufacturing quality watches in 1832. They later became interested in making a flat style watch which proved to be very popular. Some of these movements can be fitted inside a $20 gold piece.

The company was inherited by Ernest Francillion who built a factory called Longines. The Longines factory continued the Agassiz line until the Great Depression.

Agassiz, 43mm, 17 jewels, stem wind, 14 carat case, open face, serial number 39,863.

Julius Assmann began producing watches with the help of Adolf Lange in 1852. His watches are stylistically identical to those produced by Lange, except that later on he adopted his own lever style. Assmann made highly decorative watches for the South American market which are highly regarded by German collectors.

Audemars, Piguet & Cie. was founded in 1875 by Jules Audemars and Edward Piguet, both successors to fine horological families. This company produced many fine high grade and complicated watches, predominantly in nickel and fully jeweled, with a few exceptions. Their complicated watches are more sought after than the plain timepieces. They also produced some very handsome wrist watches.

Abraham-Louis Breguet, who was born at Neuchatel in 1747 and died in 1823, was perhaps the greatest horologist of all time in terms of design, elegance, and innovation. He is responsible for the development of the tourbillion, the perpetual calendar, the shock-proof parachute suspension, the isochronal overcoil, and many other improvements. It is difficult to include him in this section because of the complexity surrounding identification of his work which was frequently forged, and the fact that so many pieces produced by his shop were unique. Suffice it to say that the vast majority of watches one encounters bearing his name were either marketed only by his firm or are outright fakes made by others for the export market. Much study is required for proper identification.

Abraham-Louis Breguet, one of the worlds most celebrated watch makers.

Henry Daniel Capt of Geneva was an associate of Isac Daniel Piguet for about 10 years from 1802 to 1812. Their firm produced quality watches and specialized in musicals, repeaters, and chronometers. By 1844 his son was director of the firm and around 1880 the firm was sold to Gallopin.

Cartier was a famous artisan from Paris who first made powder flasks. By the mid-1840s the family became known as the finest goldsmiths of Paris. Around the turn of the century the Cartier firm was designing watches and in 1904 the first wrist watches were being made. In 1917 Cartier created a watch design that was to become known as the tank-style case. The tank-style case was made to look like tank caterpillars of the U. S. This style is still popular today.

Edward John Dent worked with Vulliamy and Barraud separately before joining J. R. Arnold in 1830. After 10 successful years in that association, he established his own firm, **E. Dent & Co.**, which continued after his death in 1853. His name is associated with Big Ben, although his successor is responsible for the execution of that contract. Dent's chronometers and complicated watches are particularly desirable, whereas the later products of the company are less so.

Paul Ditisheim founded his company in 1892 at La Chaux de Fonds in Switzerland. He made extremely small watches, some as small as 6.75 millimeters. The company later became Vulcain et Volta, Ditisheim & Co.

Henry Robert Ekegren, a Swiss maker of quality watches, started in business around 1870. The firm specialized in flat watches, chronometers, and repeaters. Ekegren became associated with F. Koehn in 1891.

John Ellicott, an Englishman, made watches from 1706 to 1772. One of his most notable developments was the cylinder escapement. After Ellicott's death the company was named John Ellicott & Son.

Charles Frodsham, 55mm, jeweled through center wheel, engraved on movement "By appointment to the king, A.D. FMSZ" = 1850. Note karrusel at top of movement. Included within the Karrusel are the balance and escape wheel. The whole mechanism revolves about once every 60 minutes.

Charles Frodsham followed in the footsteps of his father William, whose father was close with Earnshaw. Charles became the most eminent of the family, producing very fine chronometers and some rare tourbillions and complicated watches. He died in 1871. The following code was used to denote the year in which the watch was made:

F	R	O	D	S	H	A	M	Z	Thus, FMHZ = 1860
1	2	3	4	5	6	7	8	0	

In 1856 the Constant Girard and Henry Perragaux families founded the firm of **Girard-Perregaux**. About 1880 the firm made a tourbillion with three golden bridges, and a replica of this watch was made in 1982. Both were a supreme expression of horological craftsmanship. In 1906 the company purchased the Hecht factory in Geneva.

E. Gubelin, 54mm, 33 jewels, minute repeater, split second chronograph.

Jacques Edouard Gubelin joined the firm of Mourice Brithschmid in Lucerne around 1854. By 1919 Edouard Gubelin was heading up the firm. In 1921 they opened an office in New York and produced fine jewelry and watches for five generations.

The firm of **Jules Jurgensen** was an extension of the earlier firm of Urban Jurgensen & Sons, which was located at various times in Copenhagen and Le Locle. Jules ultimately established his firm in Le Locle in the early 1830s, after his father's death. From that time forward the company produced, generally speaking, very fine watches of the high grade and complicated types. It appears that by 1850 the company had already established a strong market in America, which it fed with beautiful heavy 18k gold watches of exemplary quality. Most stem-winding watches until around 1885 exhibit the bow-setting

Jules Jurgensen, 17 jewels, rectangular 14k case;

feature. Almost any collectable Jurgensen watch will be fully signed on the dial and movement, with an impressively embossed "JJ" stamping on all covers of the case. Watches not so marked should be examined carefully, and untypical or inelegant stampings should be viewed suspiciously, as there has been some forgery of these fine watches. Frequently one finds the original box and papers accompanying the watch, which enhances the value. After 1885, one begins to see variations in Jurgensen watches, as the firm started to buy movements from other companies. By 1930, Jurgensen watches barely resemble the quality and aesthetics of the early period, and are not particularly desirable to the collector.

Adolf Lange, 49mm, jeweled through the center wheel, gold escape and pallet, gold jeweled settings, gold train, diamond end stones, 14k hunting case, serial number 9524.

A. Lange & Sohne was established by its founder with the aid of the German government at Glashutte, Germany in 1845. He typically produced ¾ plate lever watches in gilt finish for the domestic market, and in nickel for the export market. High grade and very practical, these watches had a banking system for the pallet that was later used briefly by E. Howard in America. Lange complicated watches are scarce and very desirable.

Le Roy et Cie. was the final product of a dynasty of great watchmakers, starting with Julien Le Roy and his son Pierre, whose credits are numerous in the development of horology in the 18th century. There is much confusion and hooplah, however, about "Le

Roy'' watches. In fact, there were several watchmakers by that name operating in Paris at most times in the family's history. And so, frequently one sees watches signed ''Le Roy'' that have nothing to do with the original family and are simply unimportant. One has to distinguish between the works of Julien, of Pierre, of Charles, and of their contemporary namesakes. The modern firm, Le Roy et Cie., established in the late 19th century, contracted and finished some very fine and, in some cases, extremely important complicated watches, using imported Swiss ebauches.

Le Coultre and Co. was founded by Antoine Le Coultre in 1833. A fine clockmaker, he created a machine to cut pinions from solid steel as well as other machines for manufacturing clocks and watches. By 1900 they were making flat or thin watches. They made parts for Patek Philippe & Co., Tissoy, Vacheron & Constantin, Omega, Paul Ditisheim, Agassiz, Longines and others.

The beautiful **Fabrique des Longines** is situated in St. Imier, Switzerland. The company was founded by Ernest Francillon in 1866. They manufacture all grades of watches.

Meylan Watch Co., founded by C. H. Meylan in 1880, manufactured fine watches with complications in Le Brassus, Switzerland.

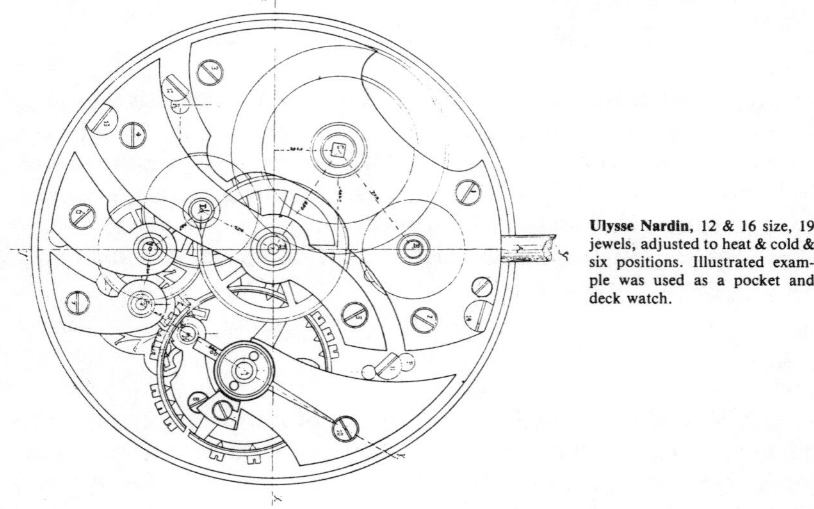

Ulysse Nardin, 12 & 16 size, 19 jewels, adjusted to heat & cold & six positions. Illustrated example was used as a pocket and deck watch.

Ulysse Nardin was born in 1823. The company started by him in 1846 produced many fine timepieces and chronometers, as well as repeaters and more complicated watches. This firm, as did Assmann, found a strong market in South America as well as other countries. Ulysse's son Paul David Nardin succeeded him, as did Paul David's sons after him. The firm also made wrist watches.

Omega Watch Co. was founded by Louis Brandt in 1848. They produced watches of different grades. By 1920 Omega had manufactured about 5,000,000 watches; by 1923, 6,000,000; and by 1931, 10,000,000.

Patek, Phillipe & Co. 39 jewels, self wind movement, 18k case.

Patek, Phillipe & Co. 18 jewels, rectangular movement and 18k case.

Patek, Philippe & Cie. has produced some of the world's most desirable factory-made watches. Antoine Norbert de Patek began contracting and selling watches in the 1830s, later became partners with Francois Czapek, and generally produced lovely decorative watches for a high class clientel. In 1845 Adrien Philippe, inventor of the modern stem-winding system, joined the firm of Patek & Cie., and in 1851 the firm established its present name. Between Philippe's talent as a watchmaker and Patek's talent as a businessman with a taste for the impeccable, the firm rapidly established an international reputation which lasts to this day.

Early Patek, Philippe & Cie. watches are generally only signed on the dust cover, but some are signed on the dial and cuvette. It was not until the 1880s that the convention began of fully signing the dial, movement and case—perhaps in response to some contemporary forgery, but more likely a necessity to conform to customs' regulations for their growing international market. Many early and totally original·Patek watches have suffered from the misconception that all products of this company are fully signed; but nevertheless, collectors find such pieces more desirable. It requires more experience, however, to determine the originality of the earlier pieces. As with Vacheron & Constantin, some watches were originally cased in America, but this lowers their value in general.

Rolex was founded by Hans Wilsdorf in 1878. In 1926 they made the first real waterproof wrist watch and called it the "oyster." In 1931, Rolex introduced a self-wind movement which they called "perpetual." In 1945 they introduced the "datejust" which showed the day of the month. The "submariner" was introduced in 1953 and in 1954 the "GMT Master" model. In 1956 a "day-date" model was released which indicates the day of the month (in numbers) and the day of the week (in letters).

Vacheron & Constantin, about 38-39mm, 21 jewels, nickel bridge movement, wolf tooth wind, 18k case, serial number 386637.

The firm of Vacheron & Constantin was officially founded by Abraham Vacheron in 1785, but the association bearing today's name did not come into being until 1819. In these early periods, different grades of watches produced by Vacheron & Constantin bore different names. The firm produced several hundred thousand watches. The association with Leschot around 1840 catapulted the firm into its position as a top quality manufacturer, whereas before that time, their watches were typical of Genevese production. Vacheron & Constantin exported many movements to the United States to firms such as Bigelow, Kennard & Co., which were cased domestically, typically in the period 1900-1935. In its early period the firm produced some lovely ladies' enameled watches, later it produced high grade timepieces and complicated watches, and to this day produces fine wrist watches.

Zenith Watch and clock factory was founded in 1865 by George Farvre Jacot. They mass produced watches of different grades in large quantities. By 1920 they had manufactured 2,000,000 watches.

---

* * *

From about 1686 to 1687 the first repeaters were made either by Edward Barlow or Daniel Quare. Each claimed to be the first. A coun-

Example of **English Clock Watch**, 20 size, jeweled through hammers, minute repeater. Note two train movement.

cil which was formed to investigate both watches decided in favor of Quare—the watch made by Quare had only one push piece while Barlow's had two.

A repeater sounds the time by means of bells or gongs. There are minute repeaters, five-minute repeaters, quarter-hour repeaters, half-hour repeaters, and hour repeaters. To operate the repeater mechanism, a small spring is wound by pushing a slide or a push piece which supplies the power for the hammers. This saves the mainspring from being spent. One or two hammers are used to strike the gongs. The minute repeater is the more elaborate of these.

A clock watch strikes the time on the hour or half hour much as a clock would but not on command as a repeater does.

PRODUCTION TOTALS

PATEK PHILIPPE

Year	Total
1845	1,500
1850	4,000
1855	9,000
1860	16,000
1865	25,000
1870	35,000
1875	45,000
1880	55,000
1885	70,000
1890	85,000
1895	100,000
1900	115,000
1905	130,000
1910	170,000
1915	178,000
1920	185,000
1925	200,000

A. LANGE

Year	Total
1870	5,000
1875	10,000
1880	20,000
1885	25,000
1890	30,000
1895	35,000
1900	40,000
1905	50,000
1910	60,000
1915	70,000
1920	75,000
1925	80,000
1930	85,000
1935	90,000
1940	100,000

LONGINES

Year	Total
1870	20,000
1880	200,000
1890	600,000
1900	1,200,000
1910	2,000,000
1920	3,000,000
1930	5,000,000
1940	6,000,000

The above list is provided for determining the approximate age of your watch. Match serial number with date.

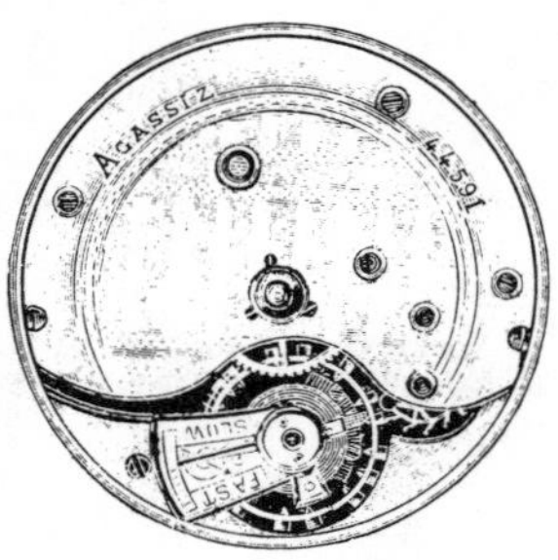

Agassiz, 43mm, 15 jewels.

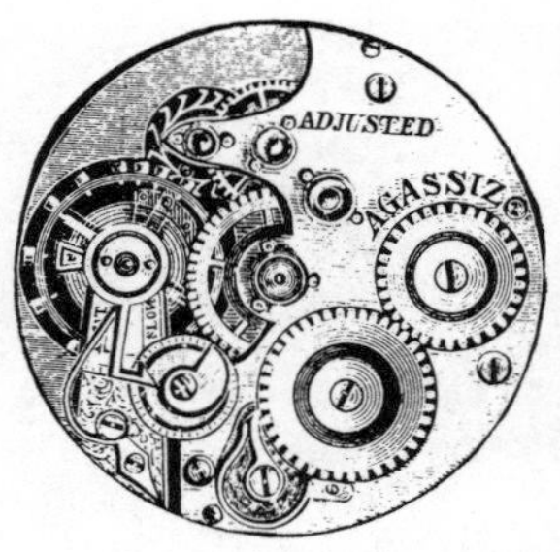

Agassiz, 43mm, 15 jewels.

AGASSIZ

Size and Description	Avg	Ex-Fn	Mint
52mm, split sec. chronograph, 14K, OF, register	$450	$550	$750
50mm, art deco, "Cartier," 1925, 19J, HCI5P	595	775	1,000
43mm, 17J, nickel mvt., 14K, OF	275	325	425
43mm, 21J, nickel mvt., 18K, OF, WI, 8 day	625	725	850
40mm, 19J, World Time, 32 Cities, 14K, OF	2,000	2,200	2,600
40mm, ladies, HC, 18K, white enamel dial	245	295	375
37mm, 8 day, wind indicator, OF, 18K	500	600	750
Wrist Watch, rectangular, 17J, 18K	350	450	600

ASSMANN
Glasshutte

Size and Description	Avg	Ex-Fn	Mint
44mm, elaborate chasing, fancy dial, for South American market, 18K, HC	$2,500	$2,900	$3,400
42mm, SW, Timepiece, OF, 18K	600	735	900

AUDEMARS, PIGUET

Size and Description	Avg	Ex-Fn	Mint
46mm, OF, min. repeater, chronograph, register, 18K	$2,400	$2,800	$3,200
46mm, OF, min. repeater, split chronograph, register, 18K	3,000	3,400	3,800
46mm, min. repeater, 18K, HC	2,500	3,000	3,800
46mm, 20J, ¼ repeater, OF, 18K	1,600	1,800	2,200
44-45mm, OF, timepiece, 18K	400	475	600
44mm, OF, min. repeater	2,200	2,500	2,800
44mm, OF, 5-min. repeater	2,000	2,200	2,500
40mm, 31J, min. repeater, 18K, OF, c. 1875	2,000	2,400	3,000

AUDEMARS, PIGUET (continued)

Audemars, Piguet, 46mm, 20 jewels, minute repeater. Note governor at right-hand side of balance bridge.

Man's Wrist Watch

Style or Grade — Description	Avg	Ex-Fn	Mint
Rectangular, 18J, 18K case	$400	$500	$650
Rectangular, 18J, day-date-month, moonphases, 4 registers, 18K case and bracelet	8,000	10,000	12,000
Square, 18J, thin model, 18K case	300	395	495
Round, 18J, day-date-month, moonphases, 4 registers, 18K case	4,000	5,000	6,000
Round, 18J, self-wind, 18K case	395	435	550
Round, 18J, 18K case	195	250	395
Round, chronograph, 3 registers, 14K case	1,800	2,000	2,500
Round, 18J, 18K bracelet & 18K case	1,200	1,400	2,000
Round, min. repeater, 18K bracelet & case	7,000	8,000	10,000

Lady's Wrist Watch

Style or Grade — Description	Avg	Ex-Fn	Mint
Rectangular, 17J, 12 small diamonds on bezel, 14K case	$600	$800	$900
Rectangular, 17J, small diamonds on case & bracelet, 14K	1,000	1,200	1,500

BAUME & MERCIER
Geneve

Wrist Watches

Style or Grade — Description	Avg	Ex-Fn	Mint
Rectangular, 18K case & bracelet	$800	$900	$1,200
Tank, 18K case	435	455	535
Round, 18K case	365	385	475
Round, moonphase, day-date-month, 18K case	850	900	1,000
Round, chronograph, 3 registers, day-date-month, 18K	295	325	450
Round, lady's, small diamonds on bezel, 18K case	645	700	800

BAUME & MERCIER (continued)

Baume & Mercier, 18 carat case and bracelet.

J. W. BENSON
London

Size and Description	Avg	Ex-Fn	Mint
58mm, Grande & Petite Sonnerie, min. repeater, perpetual calendar, moonphases	$40,000	$46,000	$55,000
40mm, KW, KS, fusee, lever, wind indicator, 18K, HC	1,200	1,400	1,700

BULOVA
Swiss and U.S.A.

Man's Wrist Watch

Style or Grade — Description	Avg	Ex-Fn	Mint
Accutron, M#214, railroad approved, GF	$70	$80	$90
Accutron, M#218, with date, GF	60	65	80
Accutron, skeletonized model, 14K case	135	195	250
Accutron, skeletonized model, GF	80	95	125
Accutron, skeletonized model, stainless	60	70	95
Rectangular, 17J, 14K case	95	125	175
Rectangular, 17J, GF	25	30	45
Square, 14K case	85	95	125
Round, 14K case	65	70	85
Round, GF	25	30	40
Round, gold plate	15	20	28
Round, 30J, sweep sec., self-wind, 14K case	125	145	180
Round, 23J, day, date, self-wind, GF case	50	60	75

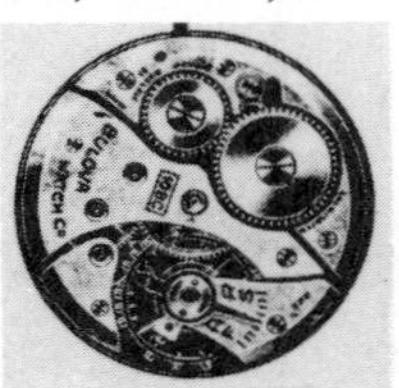

Bulova, 8/0 size, 17 jewels.

Bulova, Rectangular, 17 jewels.

Lady's Wrist Watch

Style or Grade — Description	Avg	Ex-Fn	Mint
Round, 14K case	$35	$45	$65
Round, GF	10	15	25

BULOVA (continued)

Size and Description	Avg	Ex-Fn	Mint
Rectangular, 14K case	35	45	75
Rectangular, small diamonds on 14K case	195	225	350

HENRY CAPT
Geneve

Size and Description	Avg	Ex-Fn	Mint
52mm, min. repeater, perpetual calendar, moon phases, 18K hunting case	$18,000	$20,000	$22,000

Wrist Watches

Style or Grade — Description	Avg	Ex-Fn	Mint
Round, ¼ repeater, 14K case	$2,300	$2,500	$3,000
Round, 5 min. repeater, 14K Case	2,800	3,000	3,500

CARTIER
Paris

Man's Wrist Watch

Style or Grade — Description	Avg	Ex-Fn	Mint
Round, 18K case	$600	$675	$775
Tank, 18K case	650	695	800
Rectangular or Square, 18K case, mvt. by E.W.C. Co.	2,000	2,500	3,000
Tonneau, 18K case, mvt. by E.W.C. Co.	2,500	2,800	3,100
Square, with flip up top cover, free sprung, 18K case	2,500	3,000	3,500
Min. repeater, 28J, 18K case	10,000	11,000	12,000
Round, 26J, split chronograph, by P.P. & Co., 2 registers	3,500	4,000	5,000

Lady's Wrist Watch

Style or Grade — Description	Avg	Ex-Fn	Mint
Tank, 18K case	$450	$500	$575
Rectangular or Square, 18K case, mvt. by E.W.C. Co.	1,000	1,500	1,800

H. R. EKEGREN
Geneve

Size and Description	Avg	Ex-Fn	Mint
55mm, min. repeater, jeweled to hammers, 18K case, OF	$2,200	$2,500	$3,000
43mm, min. repeater, 18K, HC, jeweled to hammers	2,500	2,800	3,200
42mm, 18K, OF, fully jeweled, SW, LS	500	600	750
39mm, min. repeater, jeweled to hammers, OF, 18K	2,200	2,400	2,800

H.R. Ekegren, 39mm, minute repeater, slide activated, jeweled through hammers, open face, serial number 78,268.

H.R. Ekegren, 43mm, minute repeater, jeweled through hammers, hunting case.

ETERNA
Swiss

Man's Wrist Watch

Style or Grade — Description	Avg	Ex-Fn	Mint
Rectangular, 17J, 14K case	$95	$110	$145
Rectangular, 17J, GF	35	40	65
Rectangular, 17J, stainless	15	20	30
Round, 17J, self wind, 14K case	95	110	145
Round, 17J, self wind, GF	35	40	55
Round, 17J, stainless	15	20	30
Round, 17J, self wind, date window, 18K case	145	155	185

Lady's Wrist Watch

Style or Grade — Description	Avg	Ex-Fn	Mint
Rectangular, 15J, 14K case	$45	$50	$65
Rectangular, 15J, GF	25	30	40
Rectangular, 15J, stainless	10	15	20
Round, 15J, 14K case	35	40	45
Round, 15J, GF	20	25	30
Round, 15J, stainless	10	12	18

Eterna, Round, 17 jewels, stem wind.

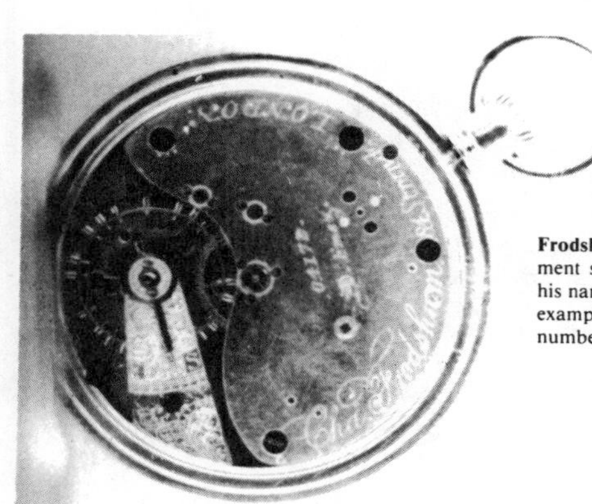

Frodsham, 44mm, jeweled through center wheel. Movement shows coded date under serial number. He used his name 'Frodsham' for numbers 1-8, and Z for 0. For example "AD. FMSZ" means the year 1850. Serial number 04172.

FRODSHAM
London

Size and Description	Avg	Ex-Fn	Mint
55mm, min. repeater, jeweled thru hammers, DES, 18K, HC	$3,500	$4,000	$4,800
44mm, detent escapement, 18K, HC	1,800	2,000	2,500
42mm, 17J, ¾ plate, GJS, DES, 18K, HC	1,000	1,200	1,475
42mm, KW, KS, wind indicator, free sprung, 18K, OF......	700	750	850
35mm, ¼ & 5 min. repeater, by Thomas Frodsham, 18K, HC	3,000	3,300	4,000

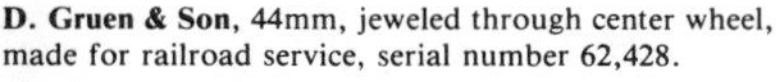

D. Gruen & Son, 44mm, jeweled through center wheel, made for railroad service, serial number 62,428.

Gruen 50th Anniversary Watch, 10 size, 21 jewels (two diamonds), placed in a five-sided pentagon case, solid gold bridges.

GRUEN
Swiss and U.S.A.

Size and Description	Avg	Ex-Fn	Mint
45mm, 14K, HC, by D. Gruen & Son, 21J, GJS, gold escape wheel, "Desden"	$800	$900	$1,200
44mm, made for R.R. Service, GF	135	195	300
40mm, 19J, "Precision," SW, LS	100	115	145
40mm, 50th Anniversary, 21J, including 2 diamonds, 18K...	2,200	2,500	3,000

GRUEN (continued)

Style or Grade — Description	Avg	Ex-Fn	Mint
40mm, "Detrich Gruen," marked Extra Precision, 31J, 18K OF	2,000	2,200	2,500
38mm, 17J, pentagon case, veri thin style, YGF	75	85	95

Man's Wrist Watch

Style or Grade — Description	Avg	Ex-Fn	Mint
Curvex, 14K case	$175	$195	$235
Curvex, GF	45	65	85
Curvex, with diamond on dial, 14K case	250	300	350
Tank, 14K case	120	135	165
Tank, GF	35	40	50
Rectangular, duo dial (doctor), GF	185	200	250
Rectangular, 15J, 14K case	120	135	165
Rectangular, 15J, GF	25	30	40
Tonneau, 14K case	125	135	150
Tonneau, GF	35	40	55
Round, GF	25	30	55
Round, chronograph, GF	30	35	65

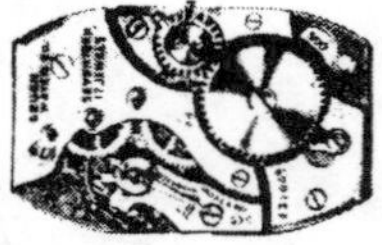

Gruen wrist watch, 17 jewels, Rectangular.

Lady's Wrist Watch

Style or Grade — Description	Avg	Ex-Fn	Mint
Round or Square, GF	$15	$20	$25
Rectangular, platinum & sapphires	150	200	225
Rectangular, platinum & small diamonds	165	210	295
Rectangular, small diamonds on case & 18K bracelet	300	450	600

E. Gubelin, 54mm, 33 jewels, minute repeater, jeweled through the hammers, split second chronograph.

E. GUBELIN
Swiss

Size and Description	Avg	Ex-Fn	Mint
54mm, min. repeater, 33J, split sec. chronograph, GT	$2,800	$3,200	$3,800
38mm, 21J, deco style, HCI5P, perpetual calendar, 18K, OF	2,200	2,400	2,800

Man's Wrist Watch

Style or Grade — Description	Avg	Ex-Fn	Mint
Square, 18K case	$295	$320	$375
Square, 25J, self wind, moon phase, day-date-month, 18K case and bracelet	2,500	2,650	3,000
Rectangular, 18K case	295	320	375
Rectangular, with horizontal shutters & crown at 3 & 9, 14K case, c. 1930	1,500	2,000	2,400
Round, GF	125	150	200
Round, self wind, center sec., date, 21J	300	325	375
Round, self wind, moon phases, day-date-month, 18K case	1,000	1,200	1,500
Round, chronograph, 3 registers, 18K case	425	445	525
Round, 18K case & bracelet	1,500	1,700	2,000
Round, min. repeater, 18K case	6,500	7,000	8,000

Lady's Wrist Watch

Style or Grade — Description	Avg	Ex-Fn	Mint
Square or Round, 18K	$125	$135	$175
Square or Round, 18K case, diamonds on case	900	1,000	1,200

HAAS, NEVEUX & CO.
Swiss

Size and Description	Avg	Ex-Fn	Mint
42mm, 18K, HC, cover wind	$2,000	$2,400	$3,000
40mm, 31J, min. repeater, 18K hunting case	2,200	2,400	3,000
34mm, $20 gold piece form watch	1,200	1,400	1,800

Haas, Neveux & Co., 40mm, 31 jewels, minute repeater, 18k open face case, serial number 11,339.

HARWOOD SELF WIND WATCH CO.

Man's Wrist Watch

Size and Description	Avg	Ex-Fn	Mint
Round, 15J, set hands by rotating bezel, self wind, 9K case ..	$300	$325	$400
Round, 15J, set hands by rotating bezel, self wind, GF......	185	200	245
Round, 15J, set hands by rotating bezel, self wind, stainless .	75	85	110

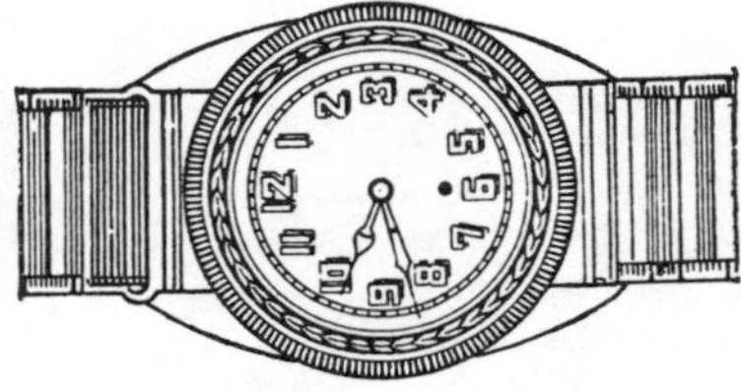

Harwood Self Wind Watch Co., 15 jewels, rim set by turning bezel clockwise.

INTERNATIONAL WATCH CO.
Swiss

Size and Description	Avg	Ex-Fn	Mint
54mm, 17J, lever escapement, GJS, 14K, HC	$400	$500	$600
42mm, early mvt., 18K, HC	450	550	750
42mm, OF, 14K case	275	325	425

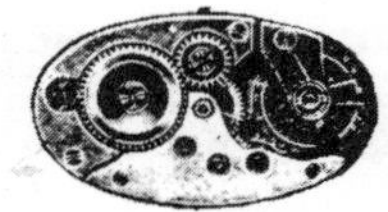

Above: International Watch Co., Oval, 7mm.

Left: International Watch Co. (New York), 42mm, about 18 size, 15 jewels, 18 carat hunting case, serial number 7,609.

Man's Wrist Watch

Style or Grade — Description	Avg	Ex-Fn	Mint
Square, 17J, 18K case	$165	$200	$300
Rectangular, 17J, 18K case	175	225	350
Round, 17J, 18K case	135	165	200

Lady's Wrist Watch

Style or Grade — Description	Avg	Ex-Fn	Mint
Round, 18K case...	$125	$145	$200
Round, small diamonds on bezel, 18K case................	450	495	595

JULES JURGENSEN
Swiss

Size and Description	Avg	Ex-Fn	Mint
55mm, OF, detent chronometer, KW, 18K	$2,800	$3,000	$3,400
55mm, OF, detent chronometer, SW, 18K	4,000	4,300	4,800
55mm, HC, detent chronometer, SW, 18K	4,500	5,000	6,000
50mm, OF, timepiece, enamel dial, 18K	1,400	1,600	2,300
49mm, ¼ repeater, c. 1880, nickel lever mvt., gold train, 18K HC	2,400	2,600	3,000
46mm, OF, min. repeater, chronograph, register, 18K	4,000	4,500	5,500
46mm, OF, min. repeater, split chrono., register, 18K	5,000	5,900	7,000
46mm, HC, min. repeater, 18K	4,800	5,500	6,000
46mm, HC, min. repeater, chronograph, 18K	5,000	5,500	6,500
46mm, HC, min. repeater, split chronograph, register, 18K	7,000	8,000	10,000
46mm, OF, chronograph, timepiece, register, 18K	1,800	2,000	2,400
46mm, OF, split chronograph, timepiece, register	2,000	2,300	2,800
46mm, HC, chronograph, timepiece, register	2,400	2,550	2,800
46mm, HC, split chronograph, timepiece, register	3,000	3,200	3,700
45mm, OF, timepiece, enamel dial	1,300	1,500	1,800
45mm, HC, timepiece, enamel dial	1,700	2,000	2,500
45mm, OF, KW, timepiece, enamel dial	650	725	950
45mm, OF, min. repeater, enamel dial	3,200	3,700	5,000
44mm, OF, 5-min. repeater	2,600	3,000	3,800
40mm, OF, timepiece, enamel dial	700	1,000	1,300
40mm, HC, timepiece, enamel dial	1,200	1,400	1,700

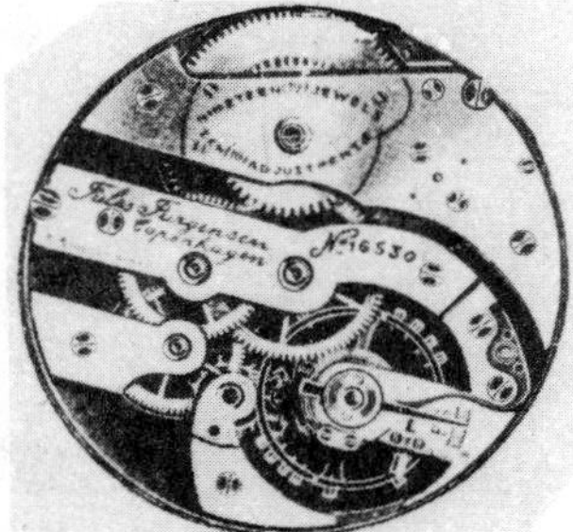

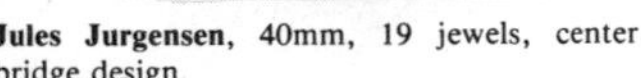

Jules Jurgensen, 40mm, 19 jewels, center bridge design.

Rectangular, 17 jewels.

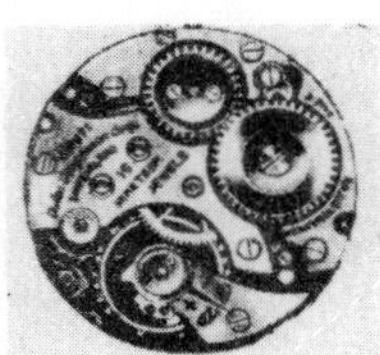

Round, 19 jewels.

Man's Wrist Watch

Style or Grade — Description	Avg	Ex-Fn	Mint
Rectangular, 18K case	$125	$155	$200
Square, 18K case	120	140	185
Round, 18K case	100	120	145
Round, 17J, self wind, sweep sec., 18K	100	130	170
Round, ¼ repeater, 18K case	3,000	3,250	4,000
Round, 17J, 4 diamonds at 12-3-6-9, 18K case	150	195	250
Tank, 17J, 18K case	135	165	215

Lady's Wrist Watch

Style or Grade — Description	Avg	Ex-Fn	Mint
Rectangular, 18K case	$75	$85	$100
Rectangular, small diamonds on case, 18K	225	265	335

A. Lange & Sohne, 52mm, wind indicator, World War II model, open face.

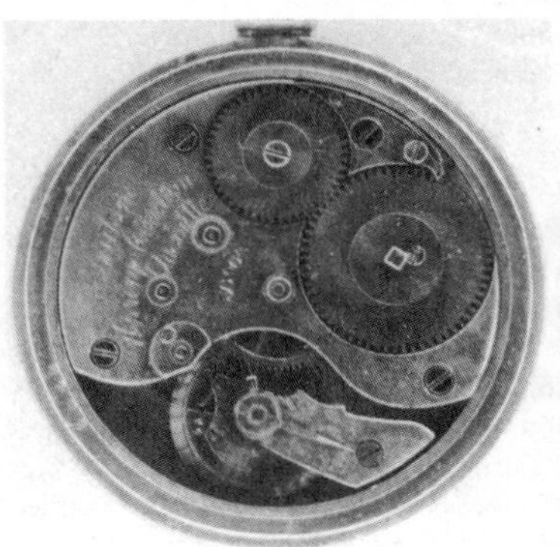

A. Lange & Sohne, 48-49mm, press jeweled through the center wheel, Deutsche Uhren Fabrikation, serial number 36464.

A. LANGE
Germany

Size and Description	Avg	Ex-Fn	Mint
55mm, min. repeater, 18K, HC, jeweled thru hammers, GJS, GT, gold escape and pallet, DES	$14,000	$17,000	$22,000
54mm, ¼ repeater, DES, jeweled thru hammers, OF	5,000	5,500	6,200
53mm, 18K case, c. 1885, GJS, GT, DES, gold pallet and escape wheel	1,200	2,000	2,400
52mm, World War II model, WI, OF	1,000	1,200	1,550
49mm, 18K case, 17J, GJS, GT, gold escape wheel & pallet, c. 1914	1,000	1,200	1,600
49mm, 18K case, HC, gild mvt., 17J, GJS, DES, gold lever and escape wheel	1,600	1,800	2,200
48mm, ¾ plate, Deutsche Uhren Fabrikation, silver	300	350	450
Wrist Watch, World War II pilot's watch, black dial	400	450	500

LE COULTRE & CO.
Swiss

Size and Description	Avg	Ex-Fn	Mint
57mm, 32J, min. repeater, slide repeat, 14K, HC	$2,000	$2,200	$2,500
55mm, 31J, min. repeater, day-date-month, moon phase, 18K, HC	3,500	4,000	5,000
54mm, min. repeater, gilt, lever escapement, 14K, HC	1,500	1,800	2,200
52mm, ¼ repeater, double dial, calendar, moon phase, 18K, HC	2,800	3,300	4,000
49mm, nickel mvt., 18K, OF	450	500	650

LE COULTRE & CO. (continued)

Le Coultre & Co., 57mm, 32 jewels, minute repeater, exposed winding gears, 14k hunting case.

Le Coultre & Co., 55mm, 31 jewels, day, date, month and moon phases, 18k hunting case, minute repeater.

Man's Wrist Watch

Style or Grade — Description	Avg	Ex-Fn	Mint
Round, 14K case	$100	$140	$200
Round, 18K case	115	150	225
Round, GF	30	35	50
Round, moon phase, day-date-month	300	350	450
Round, 17J, wind indicator, self wind, GF	95	150	225
Round, alarm, GF	65	85	125
Round, alarm, 14K case	195	225	295
Round, $20 gold piece	1,095	1,295	1,495
Rectangular, 15J, reversible case, 14K case	600	700	900

Lady's Wrist Watch

Style or Grade — Description	Avg	Ex-Fn	Mint
Rectangular, extra small mvt., 7mm, back wind, 18K case	$395	$445	$585
Rectangular, small diamonds on bezel	95	125	195
Round or Rectangular, GF	30	35	45

LONGINES

Size and Description	Avg	Ex-Fn	Mint
59mm, 18K, HC, min. repeater, chronograph, calendar & moon phases	$2,800	$3,200	$3,800
54mm, OF, 18K, split chronograph, 2 registers	1,000	1,100	1,300
50mm, chronograph with register, nickel mvt., silver	150	175	195
50mm, 8 day, wind indicator, 15J, HCI3P, silver	175	240	325
46mm, 21J, "Express Monarch," R.R. approved, HCI5P	175	195	235
46mm, rectangular case, 30 small diamonds on case, 15J	700	750	800
44mm, 15J, 3 ADJ, 8 day, WI, 14K	325	375	475

Longines, 44mm, 21 jewels, US Army AC, adjusted to temperature and 5 positions, World War II model, serial number 5939626.

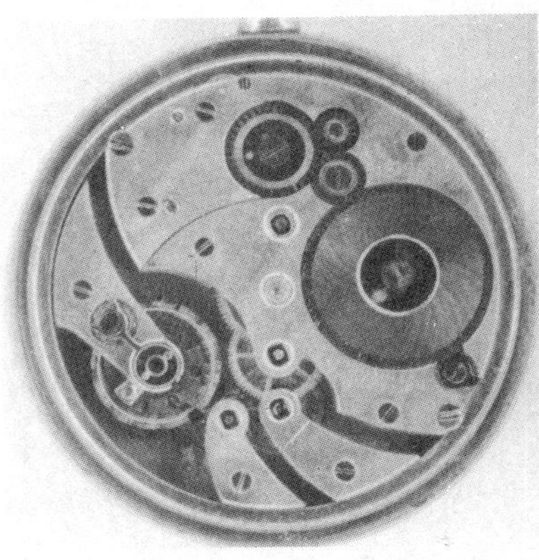

Longines, 44mm, 15 jewels, 8 day wind indicator, serial number 4,418,694.

Style or Grade — Description	Avg	Ex-Fn	Mint
44mm, "U. S. Army," sweep sec. hand, WI, HCI5P	275	325	395
26mm, ladies pendant, 18K, OF, enamel & diamonds	600	700	850

Man's Wrist Watch

Style or Grade — Description	Avg	Ex-Fn	Mint
Tonneau, 17J, 14K case	$120	$135	$155
Tonneau, 17J, GF	25	30	40
Cushion, 17J, 14K case	95	120	145
Cushion, 17J, GF	20	25	29
Rectangular, 18K case	120	135	185
Rectangular, 14K case	100	120	155
Rectangular, GF	25	30	40
Rectangular or Round, small diamonds on dial, 14K case	390	420	500
Rectangular or Round, small diamonds on bezel, 14K case	395	435	525
Rectangular, doctor style dial, 18K case	600	675	800
Round, 17J, sweep sec., date, 18K case	150	195	245
Round, 17J, 18K case	95	110	145
Round, 17J, 14K case	85	100	135
Round, 17J, GF	20	27	35
Round, 17J, "Lindberg," 45mm, large model, movable bezel & center dial, 14K	1,500	1,600	1,900
Round, 17J, "Lindberg," 45mm, large model, movable bezel & center dial, GF	1,000	1,200	1,350
Round, 17J, "Lindberg," 45mm, large model, movable bezel & center dial, stainless	895	950	1,100
Round, "Lindberg," small model, 14K case	900	1,050	1,300
Round, "Lindberg," small model, stainless	185	220	295
Round, "Nautical Miles," stainless steel	65	75	95
Round, "Weems," large model, movable center dial, GF	500	600	785
Round, "Weems," small model, movable bezel, 14K	275	300	395
Round, "Weems," small model, movable bezel, GF	155	165	195
Round, "Weems," small model, movable bezel, stainless	85	95	125

LONGINES (continued)

Style or Grade — Description	Avg	Ex-Fn	Mint
Round, 1/5 sec. chronograph, 2 registers, 18K case	300	335	395
Round, 1/5 sec. chronograph, 2 registers, 14K case	150	160	245
Round, 1/5 sec. chronograph, 2 registers, GF	65	70	85

Longines wrist watch, Round, 22mm.

Longines wrist watch, Oval, 12mm.

Lady's Wrist Watch

Style or Grade — Description	Avg	Ex-Fn	Mint
Round, small diamond on case & bezel, 14K case	$165	$250	$495
Round, plain, 18K case	80	85	95
Round, plain, 14K case	65	70	85
Round, plain, GF	15	20	28

Mathey-Tissot, 52mm, 27 jewels, quarter jump sweep second chronograph, two train, 18k hunting case.

MATHEY-TISSOT
Swiss

Size and Description	Avg	Ex-Fn	Mint
52mm, ¼ jump sec. chronograph, tandem wind, 2 train, 18K	$2,000	$2,400	$3,000

Man's Wrist Watch

Style or Grade — Description	Avg	Ex-Fn	Mint
Square, 18K case	$95	$135	$175
Round, 14K case	85	95	135
Round, $20 gold piece, hidden watch	1,000	1,150	1,400
Round, chronograph, 2 registers, 14K case	385	425	495
Round, self wind, chronograph, moon phase, day-date-month, 14K	750	800	900

MATHEY—TISSOT (continued)

Style or Grade — Description	Avg	Ex-Fn	Mint
Round, chronograph, 2 registers, moon phase, day-date-month, 18K	900	1,000	1,200

Lady's Wrist Watch

Style or Grade — Description	Avg	Ex-Fn	Mint
Round or Square, 14K case	$55	$65	$80

Mavado wrist watch, Rectangular, 10mm.

Mavado wrist watch, Rectangular, 15 jewels.

MOVADO
Swiss

Man's Wrist Watch

Style or Grade — Description	Avg	Ex-Fn	Mint
Square, art deco, black dial, 18K case	$200	$265	$335
Ermeto, purse watch, open & close cover to wind, 14K case	295	350	450
Ermeto, purse watch, open & close cover to wind, stainless	95	110	145
Calendermeto, moonphase calendar, open & close cover to wind, leather case	595	665	795
Round, GF	25	30	35
Round, day window, 14K case	95	110	140
Round, day window, GF	40	50	65
Round, day window, stainless	30	35	40
Round, moon phase, chronograph, 2 registers, day-date-month	295	350	425

ULYSSE NARDIN
Swiss

Size and Description	Avg	Ex-Fn	Mint
Deck chronometer w/mahogany box, detent mvt., silver dial	$800	$1,000	$1,200
50mm, 15J, made for Corps of Engineers, U.S.A., WWI	175	185	245
45mm, split chronograph, 2 registers, 14K, OF	700	900	1,000
45mm, detent chronometer, KW, KS	275	350	460
45mm, SW, timepiece only, 14K	300	340	475
42mm, moon phases, perpetual calendar, 18K, HC	6,500	7,500	8,500
40mm, 29J, min. repeater, HCI5P, 18K, OF	2,000	2,400	3,000

Man's Wrist Watch

Style or Grade — Description	Avg	Ex-Fn	Mint
Round, 19J, chronograph, 2 registers, 1910, 18K	$450	$535	$655

ULYSSE NARDIN (continued)

Style or Grade — Description	Avg	Ex-Fn	Mint
Round, 19J, chronograph, tachometer, 1910, 14K	400	450	500
Round, 31J, chronograph, moon phases, calendar, 18K	1,000	1,200	1,400
Round, chronograph, 1938, 18K case	295	375	500
Round, pulse meter chronograph, 2 registers, 18K case	450	550	675
Round, 21J, self wind, date, 18K case	250	275	330
Round, self wind, 14K case	175	185	225
Round, self wind, GF	40	50	65
Round, $20 gold piece, hidden watch	1,200	1,400	1,700
Tank, 14K case	150	165	195
Tonneau, 14K case	130	145	185
Rectangular, 18K case	165	175	225
Rectangular, 14K	125	135	165
Square, 14K case	120	130	160
Square, 21J, chronometer, self wind, 14K case	250	300	375
Curvex, 14K case	175	185	225

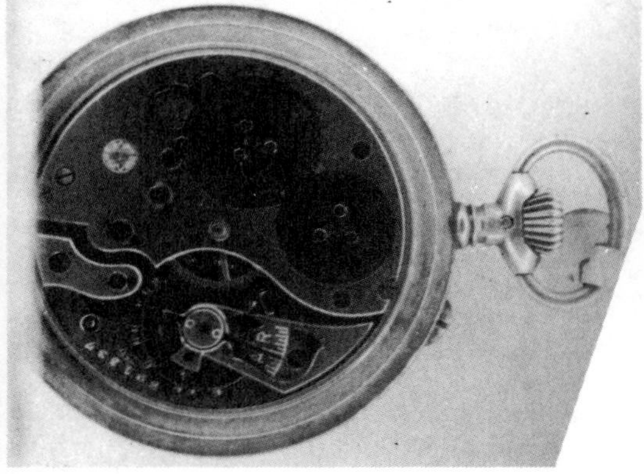

Ulysse Nardin, 50mm, 15 jewels, made for Corps. of Engineers, USA, World War I, serial number 691527-H6.

Lady's Wrist Watch

Style or Grade — Description	Avg	Ex-Fn	Mint
Tonneau, 14K case	$65	$70	$85
Rectangular, 14K case	55	60	75
Square, 14K case	60	65	70
Oval, 14K case	55	60	75
Round, 14K case	50	55	65
Round, GF	40	45	50

OMEGA
Swiss

Size and Description	Avg	Ex-Fn	Mint
45mm, 15J, lever escapement, silver	$30	$40	$55
38mm, 15J, OF	75	95	125

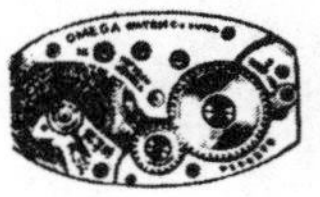

Above left: Omega wrist watch, 15 jewels, 12mm.

Above right: Omega wrist watch, 15 jewels, 10mm.

Left: Omega pocket watch, 38mm, 15 jewels, serial number 9,888,934.

Man's Wrist Watch

Style or Grade — Description	Avg	Ex-Fn	Mint
Rectangular, 15J, hidden winding crown, 14K case	$600	$685	$800
Rectangular, 14K case	95	110	175
Rectangular, GF	35	40	55
Square, 14K case	80	95	125
Square, GF	30	35	40
Tank, 14K case	120	140	175
Round, 14K case	85	100	145
Round, GF	20	25	35
Round, stainless steel	15	20	28
Round, ultra thin, 14K case	90	110	135
Round, Speed Master, Mark II, chronograph	175	185	195
Round, Speed Master, Professional, 3 registers, 18K	1,200	1,400	1,700
Round, moon phases, day-date-month, 14K	600	665	745

Lady's Wrist Watch

Style or Grade — Description	Avg	Ex-Fn	Mint
Round, GF	$20	$25	$30

PERPETUAL WATCH CO.
New York
1930

Man's Wrist Watch

Style or Grade — Description	Avg	Ex-Fn	Mint
Rectangular case & mvt., by Frey, 15J, crown at 9 o'clock, 14K	$400	$475	$600
Rectangular case & mvt., by Frey, 15J, crown at 9 o'clock, GF	125	145	195
Round, 15J, Harwood mvt., turn bezel to set hands, 14K case	250	280	325
Round, 15J, Harwood mvt., turn bezel to set hands, GF	70	95	135

PERPETUAL WATCH CO. (continued)

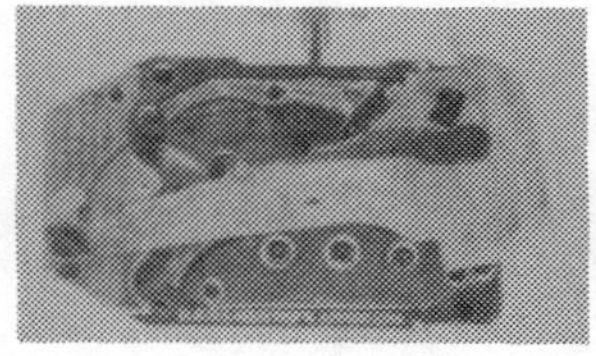

Perpetual Watch Co., 15 jewels. Note 'L' shaped weight designed to wind watch automatically.

PATEK, PHILIPPE & CO.

Size and Description	Avg	Ex-Fn	Mint
55mm, astronomic, perpetual calendar, min. repeater, 1897, white enamel dial, 3 registers, split sec. chronograph, moon phases, 38J, slide repeat, original box and papers	$45,000	$50,000	$58,000
54mm, split sec. chronograph, 14K, OF	1,100	1,300	1,600
52mm, split sec. chronograph, 18K, OF, Tiffany & Co., register	1,800	2,000	2,400
51mm, 18K, HC, gilt, lever mvt.	800	900	1,100
48mm, 18K, HC, nickel mvt.	1,100	1,200	1,400
48mm, early chronograph, fly back sec. hand, 18K, OF, wolf tooth wind	1,600	1,800	2,000
46mm, OF, timepiece, enamel dial	700	800	950
46mm, two train, min. repeater, Tiffany & Co.	6,000	8,000	10,000
46mm, "Gondolo," OF, timepiece, enamel dial	900	1,100	1,300
46mm, 18K, OF, 18J, HCI5P, cam regulator	600	700	800
46mm, HC, min. repeater, split chronograph, registers	7,500	8,500	10,000
46mm, HC, min. repeater, split chronograph, perpetual calendar	34,000	36,000	40,000
45mm, 18J, 18K, OF, Tiffany & Co.	800	900	1,100
45mm, 18K, HC, 1860, SW & set, wolf tooth wind	1,000	1,200	1,500
45mm, OF, split chronograph, timepiece, register	1,600	1,800	2,200
45mm, OF, perpetual calendar, timepiece, metal dial	4,500	5,000	5,700

Patek, Philippe & Co., 45mm, 39 jewels, open face, perpetual calendar, split second minute repeater, day, date, month and moon phases, serial number 197612.

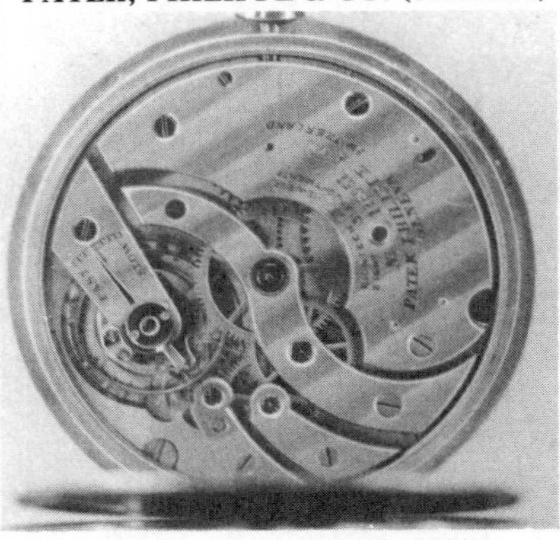

Patek Philippe & Co., 38-39mm, 18 jewels, deco bridge movement, eight adjustments, 18k open face case, serial number 196051.

Patek Philippe & Co., 38-39mm, 18 jewels, nickel bridge movement, wolf tooth wind, cam regulator, serial number 124348.

Size and Description	Avg	Ex-Fn	Mint
45mm, OF, perpetual calendar, timepiece, enamel dial	6,500	7,000	7,600
45mm, OF, timepiece, gilt dial, 14K	500	600	850
45mm, HC, min. repeater, chronograph	4,500	5,500	6,500
45mm, HC, chronograph, timepiece, register	1,500	1,800	2,200
45mm, HC, split chronograph, timepiece, register	2,000	2,200	2,400
45mm, HC, min. repeater, split chronograph, perpetual calendar, register + moon phases	35,000	38,000	42,000
44mm, OF, timepiece, gilt, dial	450	500	600
44mm, OF, timepiece, enamel dial	550	600	700
44mm, HC, min. repeater	4,500	4,800	5,500
44mm, OF, 5 min. repeater	3,000	3,200	3,600
44mm, OF, 5 min. repeater, chronograph	3,500	3,700	4,000
44mm, OF, min. repeater	4,200	4,300	4,600
44mm, OF, min. repeater, chronograph	4,500	4,900	5,500
44mm, OF, min. repeater, split chrono., register	5,800	6,200	6,800
42mm, 14K, OF, chronometer on dial, USA cased	500	600	700
39mm, 18J, wolf tooth wind, 14K, OF, BRG, nickel mvt. USA cased	500	600	750
39mm, 18J, HCI5P, enamel on bezel & back	800	900	1,050
38mm, "Gondolo," OF, timepiece, enamel dial	900	1,000	1,200
35mm, 29J, min. repeater, very thin, 18K, OF	2,800	3,200	4,000
32mm, 18K, HC, early bridge mvt., Tiffany & Co.	400	500	600
30mm, ladies, 18K, gold & enamel + diamonds, lapel watch	1,500	2,000	2,500
29mm, ladies, 18K, OF	500	550	600
26mm, ladies, 18K, OF, gold, seed pearls & enamel, lapel watch, matching pin	2,500	3,000	3,500

Man's Wrist Watch

Style or Grade — Description	Avg	Ex-Fn	Mint
Tonneau, 18K case	$1,000	$1,100	$1,350
Square, 18K case	900	1,000	1,250
Rectangular, 18K case	1,000	1,100	1,350
Tank, 18K case	1,000	1,100	1,350

PATEK, PHILIPPE & CO. (continued)

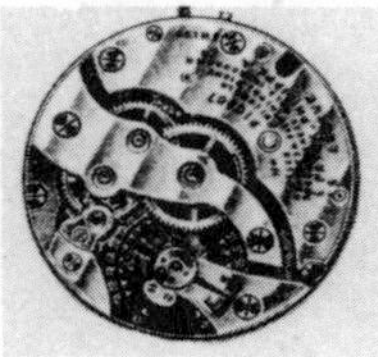

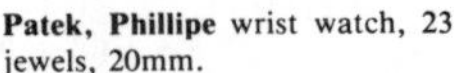

Patek, Phillipe wrist watch, 23 jewels, 20mm.

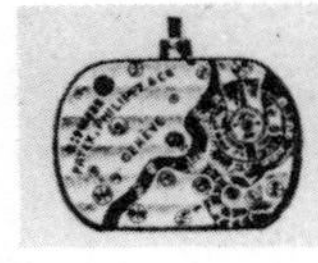

Patek, Phillipe wrist watch, Rectangular, 29 jewels.

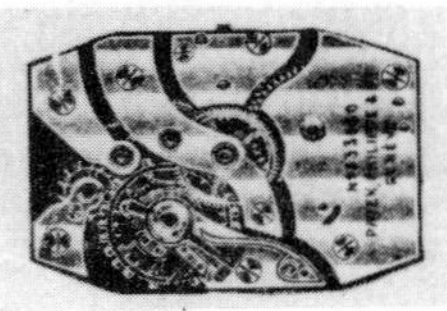

Patek, Phillipe wrist watch, Rectangular, 20mm.

Style or Grade — Description	Avg	Ex-Fn	Mint
Curvex, 18K case	1,250	1,300	1,450
Round, 18J, 18K case	600	650	725
Round, 18J, free sprung, 18K case	750	850	1,000
Round, thin mvt., 18K case	750	800	1,000
Round, 18K case and bracelet	1,200	1,300	1,500
Round, self wind with 18K rotor, 18K case	900	1,000	1,200
Round, gyromax balance, 18K case	750	800	1,000
Round, 18K rotor, date window, 18K case	1,100	1,200	1,350
Round, 23J, 18K rotor, 18K case	1,000	1,100	1,250
Round, 30J, 18K rotor, gyromax balance, 18K case and bracelet	1,800	2,000	2,400
Round, 36J, free sprung, caliber 28-255, 18K case	1,200	1,300	1,400
Round, 12 diamonds on bezel, 18K bracelet & case	2,600	3,000	3,500
Round, ¼ repeater, 18K case	6,000	6,400	7,000
Round, min. repeater, 18K case	1,200	1,300	1,400
Round, 23J, 2 registers, pulse meter, 18K case	2,200	2,600	3,000
Round, split sec. chronograph, 2 registers, 18K case	5,000	5,800	6,800
Round, skeletonized, gyromax balance, free sprung, 18K	4,500	5,000	6,000
Round, 37J, 18K rotor, perpetual calendar, moon phases, gyromax balance, free sprung, caliber 27-460Q, 1972, 18K case	7,500	8,500	9,500
Round, chronograph, 2 registers, moon phases, perpetual calendar, gyromax balance, 1965, 18K case	10,000	11,500	14,000

Lady's Wrist Watch

Style or Grade — Description	Avg	Ex-Fn	Mint
Square, 18K case	$425	$465	$600
Rectangular, 18K case	500	565	700
Round, 18K case	395	415	455
Round, 18K case & bracelet	1,000	1,200	1,500
Round, small diamond on bezel, 18K case & bracelet	1,800	2,000	2,300

PIAGET
Swiss

Man's Wrist Watch

Style or Grade — Description	Avg	Ex-Fn	Mint
Rectangular, 18K case	$500	$585	$700

PIAGET (continued)

Style or Grade — Description	Avg	Ex-Fn	Mint
Rectangular, heavy 18K gold chain link bracelet	1,800	2,000	2,500
Round, thin model, 18K case	300	350	435
Round, thin model, diamonds on bezel, 18K case	900	1,000	1,100

Lady's Wrist Watch

Style or Grade — Description	Avg	Ex-Fn	Mint
Round, small diamonds on bezel, 18K case	$785	$835	$1,000

Rolex, 42-43mm, 17 jewels, three adjustments, cam regulator, exposed winding gears.

ROLEX
Swiss

Size and Description	Avg	Ex-Fn	Mint
43mm, 14K, OF, 3 ADJ, cam regulator	$500	$600	$700

Man's Wrist Watch

Style or Grade — Description	Avg	Ex-Fn	Mint
Square, chronometer, perpetual, 18K case	$995	$1,100	$1,250
Square, precision, 14K case	895	1,000	1,100
Rectangular, 17J, 14K case	500	575	650
Rectangular, 17J, GF	125	140	195
Rectangular, "Cellini," 19J, 18K case	640	695	795
Rectangular, "Cellini," 19J, diamonds on bezel, 18K	1,400	1,700	2,300
Rectangular, jump hour in window, platinum	2,000	2,200	2,700
Rectangular, jump hour in window, 18K case	1,800	2,000	2,300
Rectangular, jump hour in window, 14K case	1,700	1,800	1,900
Rectangular, jump hour in window, GF	400	485	600
Rectangular, 17J, Prince, duo-dial, doctor style, platinum	2,000	2,200	2,600
Rectangular, 17J, Prince, duo-dial, doctor style, 18K gold	1,800	2,000	2,300
Rectangular, 17J, Prince, duo-dial, doctor style, 14K gold	1,700	1,800	1,900
Rectangular, 17J, Prince, duo-dial, doctor style, GF	400	485	700

ROLEX (continued)

Rolex wrist watch, Rectangular, 17 jewels, 7mm.

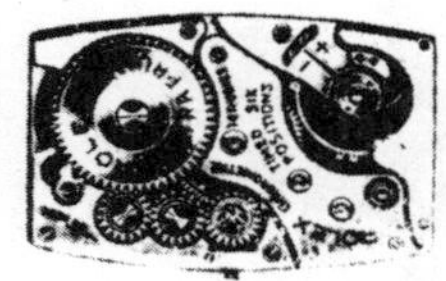

Rolex wrist watch, Rectangular, Chronometer, 18mm.

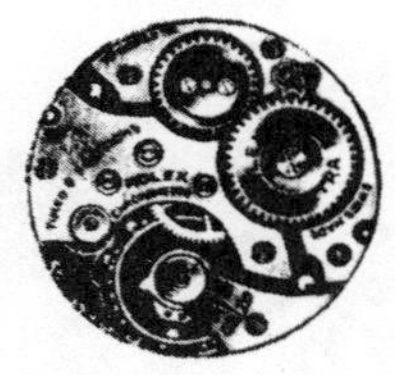

Rolex wrist watch, Round, Chronometer, 22mm.

Style or Grade — Description	Avg	Ex-Fn	Mint
Round, thin model, 18K case	200	285	325
Round, thin, chronometer, 18K case	325	375	450
Round, 18J, standard model, 14K	175	195	250
Round, 18J, gold mesh bracelet, 14K case	795	900	1,300
Round, sweep second, 18K case	325	365	425
Round, sweep second, 14K case	295	325	375
Round, sweep second, GF	75	85	135
Round, precision, 14K case	425	495	635
Round, precision, moon phases, day-date-month, 18K case	3,000	3,800	4,500
Round, precision, moon phases, day-date-month, stainless	1,250	1,300	1,400
Round, chronometer, 18K case	325	355	425
Round, chronometer, 14K case	295	325	375
Round, chronometer, GF	95	125	185
Round, oyster, manual wind, 18K case	525	555	735
Round, oyster, manual wind, 14K case	495	535	625
Round, oyster, manual wind, 10K case	395	425	485
Round, oyster, manual wind, GF	125	135	195
Round, oyster, manual wind, stainless	75	100	125
Round, oyster, perpetual (bubble back), 18K case	735	795	945
Round, oyster, perpetual (bubble back), 14K case	685	735	825
Round, oyster, perpetual (bubble back), 10K case	425	465	550
Round, oyster, perpetual (bubble back), stainless	100	135	225
Round, oyster, perpetual, date just. (date only), 18K case	995	1,100	1,250
Round, oyster, perpetual, date just. (date only), 14K case	650	720	825
Round, oyster, perpetual, date just. (date only), 10K case	495	520	595
Round, oyster, perpetual, date just. (date only), stain. & gold	295	345	450
Round, oyster, perpetual, date just. (date only), stainless	195	225	295
Round, oyster, perpetual, day, date, 18K bracelet, deployant buckle	2,000	2,500	3,000
Round, oyster, perpetual, date, president, 18K bracelet with hidden clasp, 18K case	3,800	4,500	5,400
Round, oyster, perpetual, day & date, diamond dial, president, 18K bracelet with hidden clasp, 18K case	4,200	4,900	5,800
Round, oyster, perpetual, day & date, 44 diamonds on dial & bezel, president, 18K bracelet with hidden clasp, 18K case	4,500	5,500	6,800
Round, oyster, perpetual, moon phases, day-date-month, sweep sec., 18K case	3,200	3,800	4,800
Round, oyster, chronograph, 3 registers, 18K case	1,000	1,100	1,300
Round, oyster, chronograph, pulseometer, 2 register, 18K case	1,050	1,200	1,400

Rolex, Oyster, perpetual, GMT master, 30 jewels, style 6542.

Style or Grade — Description	Avg	Ex-Fn	Mint
Round, oyster, cosmograph, 3 registers, calibrated bezel, 14K case	975	1,075	1,200
Round, oyster, cosmograph, 3 registers, calibrated bezel, stainless	295	345	455
Round, oyster, speedking, stainless steel case	75	95	135
Round, oyster, perpetual, jump sec., stainless	160	170	195
Round, oyster, milgass, anti-magnetic, perpetual, stainless	195	225	275
Round, oyster, perpetual, submariner, stainless	245	250	325
Round, oyster, perpetual, submariner, date, stainless	375	425	550
Round, oyster, perpetual, explorer, stainless	250	285	380
Round, oyster, perpetual, explorer II, 24 hour bezel, stainless	295	345	425
Round, oyster, perpetual, sea dweller	425	500	650
Round, oyster, perpetual, GMT master, 17J, stainless	350	435	450
Round, oyster, perpetual, GMT master, 30J, 18K case	3,200	3,500	4,200
Round, oyster, perpetual, GMT master, 30J, stainless	335	385	495

Lady's Wrist Watch

Style or Grade — Description	Avg	Ex-Fn	Mint
Tonneau case, 14K case	$250	$300	$400
Square, 14K case	200	235	325
Round, 14K case	135	175	250
Round, oyster, 14K case	285	350	450
Round, oyster, stainless	75	90	135
Round, oyster, perpetual, date, 14K case	350	420	550
Round, oyster, perpetual, date, stainless	95	125	195
Round, oyster, perpetual, date, diamond dial, 14K case	525	580	665
Round, oyster, perpetual, date, diamond on bezel, 14K bracelet	895	1,000	1,200
Round, oyster, perpetual, date, 40 diamonds on bezel & dial, 18K bracelet	3,000	3,500	4,000
Round, "Cellini" model, large diamonds on bezel, 18K bracelet	2,000	2,500	3,000

THOMAS RUSSEL & SONS
England

Size and Description	Avg	Ex-Fn	Mint
52mm, ½ ¼ repeater, rachet tooth escapement, 18K, OF	$2,000	$2,200	$2,400
46mm, min. repeater, ¾ plate, 18K, HC	2,800	3,200	3,600
46mm, karrusel, 52 min., free sprung, 18K, OF	4,000	4,500	5,500

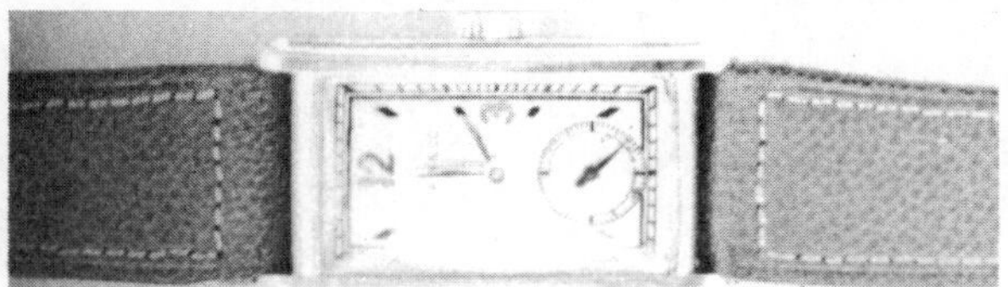

Tiffany & Co., Rectangular, 18 jewels, movement by Patek, Phillipe & Co., platinum case.

TIFFANY & CO.
U.S.A.

Size and Description	Avg	Ex-Fn	Mint
49mm, 5 min. repeater, c. 1900, 18K, HC	$2,000	$2,500	$3,200
48mm, nickel mvt., wolf's tooth wind, 18K, OF	350	425	575
47mm, 5 min. repeater, 18K, OF	1,600	1,900	2,400

Man's Wrist Watch

Style or Grade — Description	Avg	Ex-Fn	Mint
Square, 17J, 14K case	$195	$235	$300
Rectangular, 18J, P.P. & Co. mvt., platinum	1,250	1,400	1,600
Rectangular, 18J, 18K case	235	265	365
Round, chronograph, 2 registers, moon phases, calendar, 18K case	950	1,100	1,300

Lady's Wrist Watch

Style or Grade — Description	Avg	Ex-Fn	Mint
Square or Rectangular, 18K case	$225	$245	$285
Tonneau, 14K case	195	235	275

TISSOT
Swiss

Man's Wrist Watch

Style or Grade — Description	Avg	Ex-Fn	Mint
Round, 17J, world time, 24 cities, self wind, 24 hr. dial, 18K case	$300	$375	$485
Round, self wind, 14K case	95	120	155
Round, self wind, stainless	50	55	65

TISSOT (continued)

Tissot wrist watch, 17 jewels, 12mm.

Style or Grade — Description	Avg	Ex-Fn	Mint
Round, chronograph, 3 registers, 14K case	200	225	295
Round, sea star, 2 registers, 14K case	175	195	275

TOUCHON & CO.
Swiss

Size and Description	Avg	Ex-Fn	Mint
47mm, 29J, min. repeater, thin model, 1925, 18K, OF	$1,500	$1,800	$2,200
46mm, min. repeater, jeweled thru hammers, wolf tooth wind, 18K, OF	1,200	1,400	1,800
45mm, 23J, min. repeater, 14K, OF	1,000	1,300	1,600
40mm, 28J, min. repeater, 14K, OF	1,400	1,600	2,000

Touchon & Co., 47mm, 29 jewels, minute repeater, open face, jeweled through hammers.

Man's Wrist Watch

Style or Grade — Description	Avg	Ex-Fn	Mint
Round, gold & enamel, 18K case, by Cartier	$2,000	$2,200	$2,400
Rectangular, digital, jump hour, rotating minutes, 18K case	1,200	1,400	2,000
Tank, 14K case	235	275	325

UNIVERSAL
Swiss

Man's Wrist Watch

Style or Grade — Description	Avg	Ex-Fn	Mint
Round, moon phases, day & month, 2 registers, 14K case	$495	$535	$600
Round, "aero" compax, 17J, 4 registers, 18K case	895	925	1,000
Round, "aero" compax, 17J, 4 registers, 14K case	650	725	900

UNIVERSAL (continued)

Universal wrist watch, Rectangular, sweep center second hand.

Universal wrist watch, Rectangular, 15 jewels, 7mm.

Universal wrist watch, Rectangular, 17 jewels, 9mm.

Universal wrist watch, Rectangular, 15mm.

Style or Grade — Description	Avg	Ex-Fn	Mint
Round, "aero" compax, 17J, 4 registers, stainless	195	245	325
Round, duo compax, 14K case	295	325	400
Round, duo compax, stainless	45	55	85
Round, 17J, day, date, month, moon phase, 14K bracelet	800	900	1,150
Round, 17J, tri compax, tachymeter, day-date-month, 3 registers, 18K case	1,000	1,150	1,400
Round, 17J, tri compax, tachymeter, day-date-month, 3 registers, 14K case	900	1,000	1,150
Round, 17J, tri compax, tachymeter, day-date-month, 3 registers, stainless	225	270	335
Rectangular, reversible case, 14K	295	330	425

VACHERON & CONSTANTIN
Swiss

Size and Description	Avg	Ex-Fn	Mint
59mm, chronometer escapement, with silver deck case, c. 1920	$1,000	$1,200	$1,500
55mm, min. repeater, 18K, OF, ultra high grade, nickel mvt.	3,200	3,500	4,000
51mm, 14K, HC, nickel mvt., c. 1890	650	750	900
50mm, min. repeater, chronograph mvt., 18K, OF, gilt	2,800	3,200	3,800
47mm, 14K, OF, c. 1900, nickel mvt.	350	425	500
43mm, 18K, OF, c. 1920, nickel lever mvt., HCI5P	350	450	550
42mm, 14K, OF, 17J, HCI5P, c. 1915	350	400	500
41mm case size, 24mm mvt. size, skeletonized, c. 1930, 18J	1,300	1,400	1,500

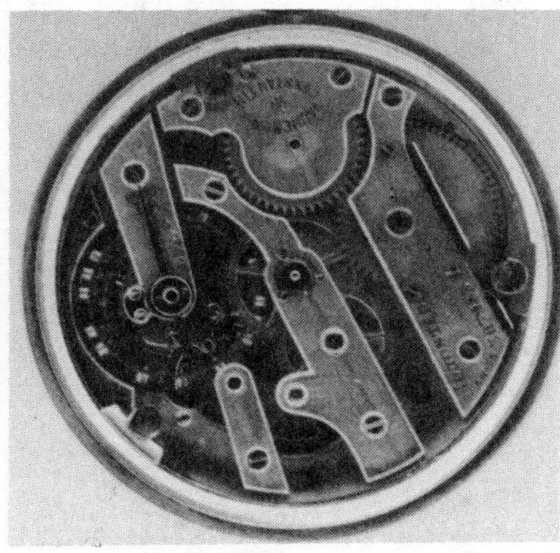

Vacheron & Constantin, 40mm, wolf tooth winding, 18k open face.

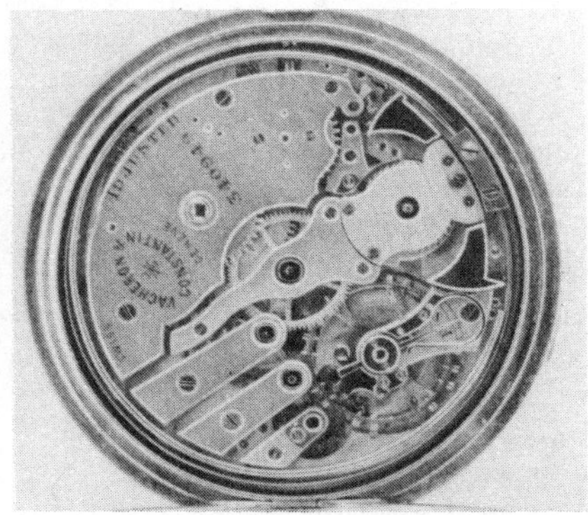

Vacheron & Constantin, 40mm, 29 jewels, minute repeater, slide repeat, wolf tooth wind, 18k open face, serial number 340,949.

VACHERON & CONSTANTIN (continued)

Style or Grade — Description	Avg	Ex-Fn	Mint
40mm, 21J, NI, BRG, wolf tooth wind, 18K, OF	400	475	550
40mm, 19J, high quality mvt., 14K, OF	350	400	475
40mm, 17J, wolf tooth wind, GF, HC	125	175	225
40mm, min. repeater, slide repeat, jeweled thru hammers, OF	1,800	2,200	2,600
40mm, 31J, min. repeater, 18K, OF, slide activated	2,800	3,200	3,800
30mm, jeweled to center wheel, 18K, OF	325	385	475

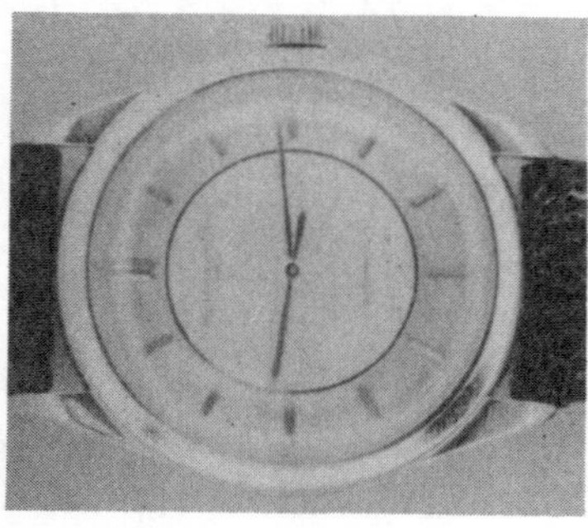

Vacheron & Constantin, Round, automatic self wind, 18k case.

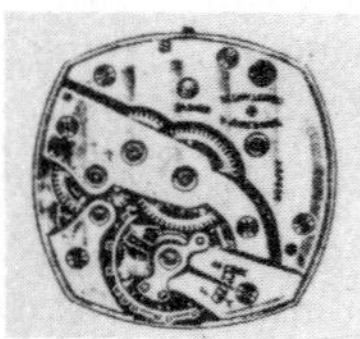

Vacheron & Constantin wrist watch, Cushion, 21 jewels, 22mm.

Man's Wrist Watch

Style or Grade — Description	Avg	Ex-Fn	Mint
Square, with shutters, crowns at 3 & 9 o'clock, 18K case	$2,000	$2,200	$2,500
Rectangular and also curvex, 18K case	600	675	850
Rectangular and also curvex, 14K case	500	565	670
Rectangular, 18K case	400	500	625
Rectangular, 14K case	300	400	535
Round, 17J, 18K case	225	300	400
Round, 17J, 14K case	200	250	300
Round, thin model, 18K bracelet & case	995	1,200	1,450
Round, "Royal," waterproof, stop/start, chronometer, 18K	550	600	695
Round, second center, self wind, 18K case	595	650	725
Round, second center, self wind, 14K case	450	485	595
Round, second center, self wind, date, gold rotor, 18K case	895	1,000	1,150
Round, second center, self wind, date, gold rotor, 14K case	695	725	800
Round, telemeter, 2 registers, 18K case	1,300	1,400	1,600
Round, calendar, day-date-month on outer ring, 18K case	1,000	1,200	1,400
Round, moon phases, day-date-month, 18K case	2,200	2,500	3,000
Round, moon phases, day-date-month, 14K case	2,000	2,300	2,700
Round, 5 min. repeater, 18K case	3,500	4,000	5,500
Round, 1 min. repeater, 18K case	7,000	8,000	9,000

Lady's Wrist Watch

Style or Grade — Description	Avg	Ex-Fn	Mint
Square, 18K case	$275	$295	$350
Square, 14K case	175	195	250
Rectangular, with 34 small diamonds, platinum	995	1,200	1,550

Size and Description	Avg	Ex-Fn	Mint
70mm, silver & horn triple cased, for Turkish market, by G. Charles, c. 1810, verge, & pierced cock, enamel dial	450	600	800
60mm, pair cased, silver c. 1800, hand painted battle scene on dial	500	550	635
60mm, ¼ repeater, pair cased, push repeat, pierced cock, 18K, repousse case	1,600	1,800	2,000
56mm, by Robert Roskell, pair cased, 18K, full plate, dust cover, rack & lever escapement	800	1,000	1,250
55mm, min. repeater, by John Barwise, jeweled thru hammers, duplex escapement, heavy 18K case	4,000	4,500	5,000
55mm, reversible case, KW, KS, cylinder escapement, 18K	1,000	1,200	1,600
55mm, fusee, lever escapement, KW, KS, by W. Chance & Sons, 18K pair cased, repousse case	900	1,000	1,200
54mm, min. repeater, by H. C. Boddington, 18K, ¾ plate	2,400	2,600	3,000
52mm, min. repeater, 18K, HC, by H. C. Boddington, c. 1877	2,000	2,300	2,650
52mm, full plate, 14K, HC, by Johnson	350	400	500
52mm, by Arnold & Dent, chronometer, fusee, KW, KS, OF, silver	1,200	1,300	1,600
52mm, demi-hunter, by Robert Roskell, resilient lever, silver case	750	800	950
52mm, gold & enamel + pearls, by John Page, c. 1800, cylinder	2,500	2,800	3,100
51mm, by Dent, OF, lever movement, 18K	350	450	550
50mm, c. 1872, WI, with resilient banking, KW, KS, 18K, HC	1,000	1,150	1,400
50mm, min. repeater, chronograph, by Dent, c. 1885, cased by Nicole Nielsen	3,500	4,000	4,800
50mm, by William Jones, pierced cock, chain driven fusee, c. 1842, pair cased	100	125	200
50mm, ¼ repeater, silver & enamel, by Weill & Harburg, c. 1886	600	700	900

John Creed, 50mm, Edinburgh, c. 1820.

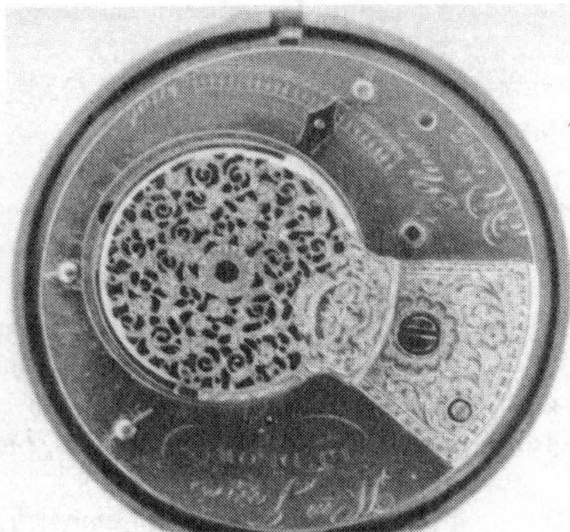

William Jones, 50mm, pierced cock, chain driven fusee, made in London, c. 1842, serial number 283.

MISC. ENGLISH (continued)

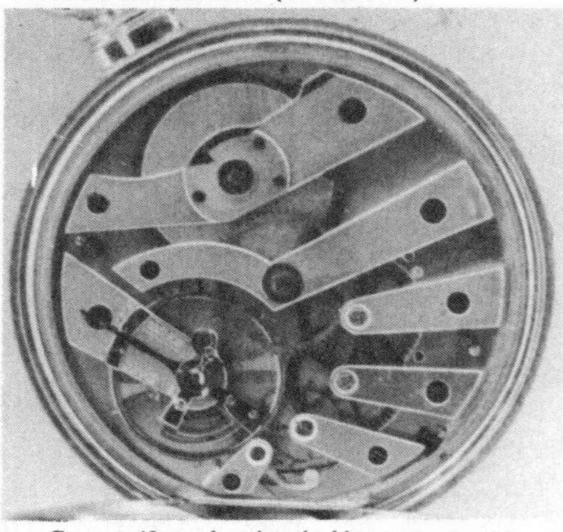

Cooper, 48mm, bar detached lever movement, key wind & set, parachute system at end stone, 18k open face, serial number 6631.

Wm. Hopetown, 48mm, chain driven fussee, verge escapement, dust cover, c. 1842, made in London, pair case, serial number 3865.

Size and Description	Avg	Ex-Fn	Mint
50mm, gold & enamel + pearls, by John Page, c. 1800, cylinder	2,000	2,400	2,800
50mm, gold & gems, set in OF watch, by James McCabe, c. 1820, cylinder, pierced cock, DES, gold dial, 18K, diamond on back	2,800	3,200	3,600
50mm, by Robert Gellatly, of Edinburgh, 18K, OF, free sprung, c. 1870	800	1,000	1,200
50mm, ¼ repeater, 18K, OF, by John Barwise, c. 1830, ¾ plate	1,200	1,400	1,800
50mm, 11J, lever escapement, fusee, gold balance, by Yates, 16K case	350	450	550
50mm, pair cased, by Creed, Edinburgh, AD1820, silver case	125	145	200
48mm, bar movement, by Cooper, KW, KS, 18K, OF, with parachute, gold dial	250	325	450
48mm, pair case, verge, fusee, pierced cock, silver	100	150	200
48mm, by M. I. Tobias & Co., Liverpool, lever, fusee, KW, KS, 18K, OF, multi-color gold dial	450	500	600
48mm, by William Hopetown, London, silver pair case, chain driven, fusee, verge	125	150	200
48mm, 18K, OF, c. 1896, ¾ plate, GJS	300	350	450
46mm, KW, KS, c. 1865, by McPherson, lever gilt mvt., silver case	55	65	75
46mm, KW, KS, fusee, dust cover, pinned plates	75	85	95
46mm, KW, KS, fusee, dust cover, Scotland	85	100	115
45mm, KW, KS, c. 1865, dust cover, lever, gilt	45	55	65
45mm, KW, KS, c. 1880, fusee, dust cover, HC	65	75	85
44mm, KW, KS, silver case, lever movement	45	55	65
44mm, fusee, lever, KW, KS, 18K, OF	350	450	550
44mm, repousse, 18K, by Williamson, pierced cock, enamel dial	1,200	1,400	1,800
23mm, small triple case, 18K & enamel, for Turkish market, by Edward Prior, c. 1815, pierced cock, translucent pink enamel	5,000	6,000	7,500

Father & Baby Time, automated minute repeater, 54mm, note animated bell striking by father and baby time, 18k hunting case.

French made movement, 50mm, chain driven fusee, verge escapement, note hand pierced two-footed cock attached on both sides.

MISC. FRENCH

Size and Description	Avg	Ex-Fn	Mint
55mm, 2 figure automaton, min. repeater, 18K, HC	$3,400	$3,700	$4,200
55mm, 3 figure automaton, ¼ repeater, 18K, c. 1830	3,600	4,000	5,000
54mm, 2 figure automaton, ¼ repeater, 18K	1,800	2,400	2,800
50mm, 1 figure automaton, ¼ repeater, silver	1,500	1,700	2,000
50mm, ¼ repeater, repeat on bell, c. 1780, 18K	850	1,250	1,750
50mm, ¼ repeater, by L'Epine, parachute, cylinder escape, gold & enamel, champleve	1,500	1,600	1,700
47mm, by La Cloche, ultra thin, 18K, OF, gilt movement	250	350	450
45mm, gold champleve enamel, by LeRoy, c. 1840, cylinder escapement	1,400	1,600	1,800
44mm, signed Breguet (by Audemars), 18K, OF, digital, 19J, c. 1925	2,200	2,400	2,600
44mm, by Robin, gold enamel portrait, parachute suspension, KW, KS	3,000	3,500	4,000
42mm, musical and ¼ repeater, KW, OF	1,600	2,000	2,400
41mm, ¼ repeater, c. 1820, cylinder escapement, KW, KS, silver	400	550	700

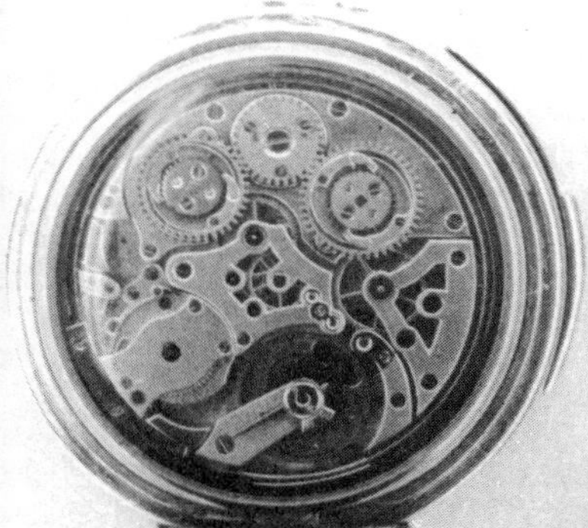

LeRoy & Co., 50mm, 49 jewels, minute repeater, jump center sweep, two train, exposed winding wheels, 18k hunting case.

MISC. FRENCH (continued)

Size and Description	Avg	Ex-Fn	Mint
38mm, gold & champleve enamel, by A. Verdiere, c. 1830, cylinder	1,000	1,200	1,500
36mm, ¼ repeater, ladies, by LeRoy et Fils, HC	1,400	1,600	2,200
32mm, gold enamel, "acorn form," by Ch. Dudin, Palais Royal, c. 1880, cylinder	1,350	1,500	2,000
32mm, ¼ repeater, 18K, lever mvt., slide to repeat, KW	1,000	1,200	1,400
29mm, gold & enamel with pearls, by Bovet Flevrier, c. 1810, verge movement	1,600	1,800	2,200

James Picard, 55mm, split second chronograph, 18k hunting case, jeweled through hammers, serial number 2,697.

Swiss minute repeater, 54mm, jeweled through hammers, 18k case.

MISC. SWISS

Size and Description	Avg	Ex-Fn	Mint
62mm, min. repeater, calendar & moon phases, split sec., chronograph, 30 min. register, GJS, 18K, HC	$4,500	$5,000	$5,800
60mm, heavy 14K HC, spring detent, by Ulysse Breting, c. 1880, nickel mvt., gold train & escape wheel	1,200	1,450	1,800
56mm, ¼ repeater, chronograph, by R. Picard, 18K, HC	1,200	1,400	1,600
55mm, min. repeater, by Paul Henri Mathey, 18K, heavy HC, gold train	2,000	2,200	2,500
55mm, detent, chronometer, by Emile Perret, KW, KS, 18K, HC, nickel mvt.	1,200	1,400	1,650
55mm, split sec. chronograph, by James Picard, fully jeweled, 18K, HC, min. repeater	2,500	2,800	3,200
54mm, min. repeater, moon phases, day-date-month, 18K, HC	2,800	3,400	4,000
54mm, min. repeater, jeweled thru hammers, 18K, HC	2,000	2,200	2,500
54mm, by Piguet & Meylan, ¼ musical repeater, c. 1815, 18K	3,200	3,600	4,400
54mm, min. repeater, 18K, HC, chronograph with calendar and moon phases	2,500	2,800	3,200
54mm, automated min. repeater, Father & Cherub, 18K, HC	3,600	4,000	4,650
53mm, 35J, min. repeater, 1900, 18K, HC, "Zenith"	1,300	1,500	1,800
52mm, Time Zone or Captain's watch, KW, KS, 18K, HC	600	650	800

MISC. SWISS (continued)

Size and Description	Avg	Ex-Fn	Mint
52mm, by L'Epine, c. 1869, cylinder escapement, KW, KS, 18K, OF	200	300	400
52mm, min. repeater, by J. Barth, 14K, HC	1,600	2,000	2,400
52mm, min. repeater, by Ernest Duval, 18K, OF	1,200	1,300	1,600
52mm, musical ¼ repeater, KW, KS	2,300	2,500	2,700
50mm, ¼ repeater, by Leresche & Fils, c. 1900, 18K, OF, slide repeat	800	900	1,100
50mm, 18K, OF, by Duchene Peyrot & Co., c. 1840, gilt, lever, parachute	400	500	650
50mm, min. repeater, Carillon chime, 18K, HC, top grade	2,800	3,000	3,500
49mm, by C. L. Guinand, split sec. chronograph, 18K, OF, 30 min. register	600	675	800
49mm, 18K, pocket chonometer, by Breting, Frers, c. 1840, spring detent, 15J	1,200	1,300	1,400
49mm, OF, c. 1820-30, by common maker, pierced cock, etc., silver case	100	135	200
45mm, 15J, OF, HCI4P	55	60	65
45mm, 21J, LS, SW, Railway Special, OF	85	95	110
44mm, Waltham Swiss mvt., 17J, "Incabloc"	55	65	75
44mm, 7J, SW, gold filled	50	55	60
44mm, multi-color, verge, pierced cock	1,000	1,200	1,300
44mm, ¼ repeater, 28J, by Bernard Reber, multi-color dial, gold train, 14K, HC	1,000	1,200	1,600
43mm, Automaton, blacksmith with hammered gun metal, pen set	400	500	695
42mm, gold & enamel, 18K, HC	650	700	950
42mm, self wind by Von Loehr, wind indicator, silver	700	800	1,050
42mm, 17J, "Dueber" chronometer, helical hairspring, OF	1,000	1,200	1,500
41mm, gold champleve enamel, floral design, 18K, c. 1830	800	1,000	1,400
40mm, self wind, by Von Loehr, gun metal	600	700	900
40mm, 15J, moon phase, day, date, month, calendar, gunmetal	165	225	385
40mm, 31J, min. repeater, split sec. chronograph, register	1,800	2,000	2,250
40mm, gilt metal & enamel, verge	275	325	350
40mm, 18K, gold & enamel + diamonds, HC, KW, KS	1,800	1,900	2,200

Dueber, 42mm, Chronometer, detent escapement, helical hairspring.

Swiss, self wind, 36mm, cylinder escapement with wind indicator, gun metal case.

MISC. SWISS (continued)

Size and Description	Avg	Ex-Fn	Mint
40mm, 18K, HC, enamel landscape scene on each side, c. 1860	1,500	1,600	1,700
40mm, ¼ repeater, gold enamel + diamonds, verge, fusee movement	2,600	2,800	3,000
38mm, 15J, ¾ plate, c. 1930, YGF	70	80	90
36mm, self wind, cylinder escapement, gun metal case	250	350	450
30mm, 18K, enamel, OF, blue & white champleve enamel, cylinder movement	600	700	800
25mm, gold & enamel watch, with matching chain of enamel	1,200	1,400	1,600
25mm, 18K gold & enamel, ladies, 17J, lever mvt.	1,000	1,100	1,200
25mm, 18K, OF, gold & 7 pearls, lapel watch	400	500	650
21mm, 5 min. repeater, by James Freres, c. 1890, 18K, HC slide repeat	1,600	1,800	2,000
Wrist Watch, "Windsor," ladies, with 6 diamonds + sapphire crown, 14K	125	155	200
Wrist Watch, auto rist, round, self wind, chronograph, 2 register, 18K	185	225	295
Wrist Watch, auto rist, tonneau, 15J, self wind, 1930, 9K	125	175	225
Wrist Watch, orator, 17J, self wind, moon phases, day-date-month, 14K	500	600	800
Wrist Watch, self wind, chronograph, 2 registers, 18K	195	225	320

German Dollar Watch, 50mm, no jewels, 3 adjustments. "Gebruder, thiel, Ruhla Germany" engraved on back plate.

Chronometer, 38mm, 44 diamonds on bezel, platinum case.

OTHER MISC. WATCHES

Size and Description	Avg	Ex-Fn	Mint
56mm, 14K, HC, min. repeater, chronograph, calendar & moon phases	$2,500	$3,000	$3,500
56mm, 18K, HC, by Union Watch Co., GJS, DES, gold pallet & escape wheel	650	750	850
53mm, 14K, ¼ repeater, chronograph, "Invicta," c. 1900, push button repeat, HC	1,000	1,150	1,300

OTHER MISC. WATCHES (continued)

Size and Description	Avg	Ex-Fn	Mint
50mm, ½ hour repeater, by J. R. Losada, c. 1870, 18K, slide repeat, HC	1,400	1,600	1,800
50mm, scarab form watch, by Goering Watch Co., enamel & diamond	2,600	3,100	3,600
50mm, German dollar watch	30	40	55
46mm, musical ¼ hour repeater, KW, KS, 18K	2,400	2,500	2,700
46mm, min. repeater, by J. Ullman & Co., 14K, slide repeat, c. 1900, OF	1,200	1,300	1,400
45mm, min. repeater, 18K, HC, case very fancy	1,650	1,750	1,850
45mm, chronometer, 15J, 14K, OF	225	250	275
45mm, lever, bar, Geneve, by Gilbert, 18K	200	250	350
44mm, ¼ repeater, 21J, recased	250	275	300
43mm, 15J, 9K, demi-hunter case	175	200	250
42mm, ¼ repeater, by Denand, 14K, OF	500	600	750
38mm, square-cut corners case, 44 diamonds on bezel, chronometer, platinum	1,000	1,200	1,400
Wrist Watch, European Watch Co., 17J, waterproof	210	250	300
Wrist Watch, 18K, min. repeater, by Van Cleef & Arpels, slide repeat	3,500	4,000	4,500
Wrist Watch, ¼ repeater, slide to repeat, enamel dial	2,000	2,200	2,400
Wrist Watch, by Benrus, 14K, chronograph, "Sky Chief," 3 registers	150	200	275

Time Zone or Captain's Watch, 58mm, key wind & set, note separate registers for two time zones, 18k hunting case.

Swiss Quarter Repeater, 50mm, cylinder escapement, note parachute shock for end stone on balance bridge.

SPECIALIZED & TECHNICAL WATCHES

Size and Description	Avg	Ex-Fn	Mint
65mm, world time, double dial in multi-color, 14K, OF	$2,000	$2,500	$3,200
58mm, 2 train, captain's watch, Courvoisier & Co., c. 1860	1,600	1,800	2,400
58mm, min. repeater, perpetual calendar, moon phases, date, date, month, chronograph, 18K, HC	9,500	11,000	14,000
55mm, 52 min. karussel, c. 1920, ¾ plat., signed T. A. Pimblett, 18K, OF	3,200	3,600	4,200

SPECIALIZED & TECHNICAL WATCHES (continued)

Size and Description	Avg	Ex-Fn	Mint
55mm, 40J, grand sonnerie clockwatch, carillion strike, 2 train, min. repeater, 18K, HC	6,500	7,000	8,200
55mm, grand & petite sonnerie clockwatch, min. repeater, 2 train, jeweled thru hammers, exposed tandem winding wheels, signed Marcks & Co., 18K, HC	8,500	9,500	11,000
54mm, one min. tourbillion, ¾ plate, signed Frodsham, 18K, OF	14,000	16,000	18,000
54mm, musical ¼ repeater, Piguet & Meylan, c. 1815, 18K	3,600	4,000	4,600
54mm, musical watch, with pinned cylinder, c. 1800, 18K	4,000	4,400	4,800
53mm, virgule escapement, by Lepine (inventor), c.1780, 18K	1,000	1,200	1,400
53mm, 2 train, clockwatch, hour repeater, signed Bourguin Le Jeune, c. 1800, 18K, OF	1,500	1,900	2,500
52mm, duplex with trapelozoidal weights, c. 1830, KW, KS, deck box, silver case	1,200	1,400	1,600
52mm, deck watch, resilient lever, free sprung, c. 1880	900	1,100	1,350
50mm, detent escapement, helical hairspring, 17J, gilt mvt., 14K, HC	800	1,000	1,250
50mm, ruby duplex, min. repeater, signed J. R. Lund, 18K OF, 4 color of gold	4,000	4,500	5,500
50mm, ¼ repeater, cylinder escapement, parachute shock, c. 1800, 18K, OF	750	850	1,000
50mm, 49J, min. repeater, 2 train, tandem wind, jump center seconds, by Le Roy, 18K, HC	4,000	4,500	5,500
50mm, carillion chimes, triple repeat gongs, ¼ repeater, chronograph, 14K, HC	1,200	1,400	1,675
48mm, gold digital repeater, parachute shock, c. 1820	1,800	2,200	2,750
45mm, detent escapement, gold escape wheel, GF case, OF	265	300	450
45mm, chronometer escapement, wind indicator, by A. P. Walsh, 18K, OF	2,800	3,200	3,600
44mm, reverse fusee, helical hairspring, detent escapement, by J. Penlinston	1,800	2,100	2,400
44mm, circuit breaker, made by Nardin	350	400	495
41mm, 2 train, min. repeater, 18K (Wittnaur)	2,700	3,000	3,500

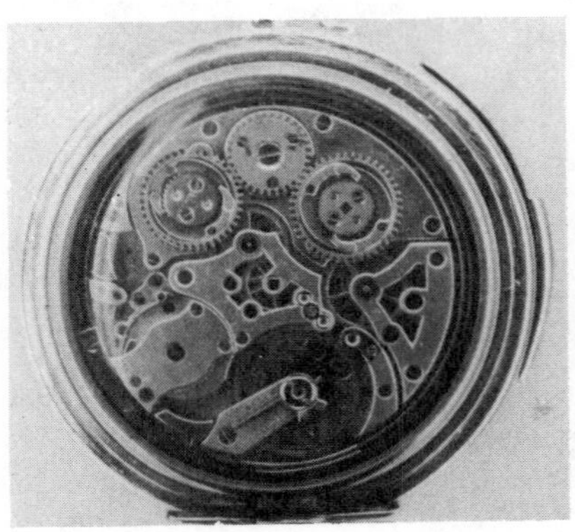

Leroy, 50mm, minute repeater, two train, tandem winding wheels, jump center seconds.

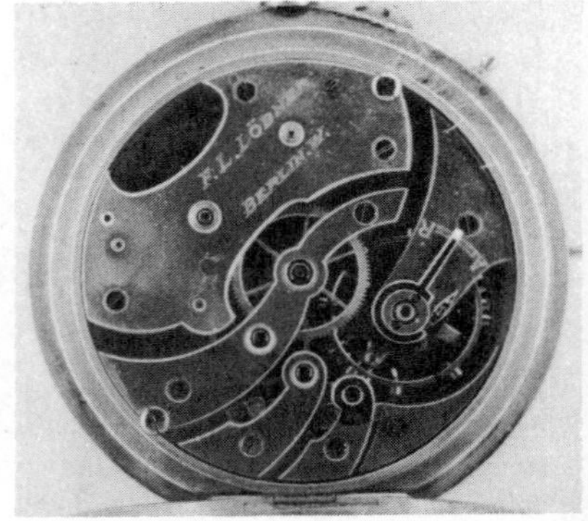

F.L. Lobner, 44mm, circuit breaker, made by Ulysse Nardin. Note two posts on right-hand side of watch.

Clayton, 50mm, pair case, verge & fusee, serial number 56,654.

Ganthony, 50mm, rack & lever escapement with fusee, key wind & set, serial number 30004.

EARLY WATCHES

Size and Description	Avg	Ex-Fn	Mint
172mm, 4 train, coach watch, grand sonnerie, alarm, repeat, repousse case, c. 1700	$12,000	$14,000	$18,000
103mm, 3 train, coach watch, with alarm, by Higgs Evans, c. 1790	3,500	4,000	4,800
60mm, pair case, by Richard Vick, champleve dial, c. 1700	1,200	1,300	1,500
50mm, pair case, verge fusee, by Clayton, silver, c. 1730	150	195	275
50mm, rack & lever, fusee, by Ganthony of London, KW, KS	250	295	350
50mm pair case, verge fusee, pierced cock, by J. A. Freeman, c. 1790, silver	125	165	200
50mm, ¼ repeater, pair case, silver repousse scene	900	1,000	1,200
50mm, detached lever, fusee, DES, compensating balance by Marshall, 18K	750	850	1,000
48mm, pair case, repousse, by Robert Allan, c. 1760, 20K	1,200	1,500	2,400
47mm, pair case, verge, pierced cock, Benjamin Lamb, silver	400	485	600
46mm, pair case, verge fusee, by Hallifax, c. 1785, 18K, repousse	1,200	1,400	1,600
45mm, repousse, fancy matchine chatelaine, pierced cock, by Grantham, c. 1750, 18K	2,000	2,800	4,000
45mm, multi-color enamel case watch, by Berthoud, c. 1780, 18K	2,000	2,200	2,500
45mm, multi-color gold, verge, KW, KS, by Louis Roch	2,300	2,400	2,600
43mm, pair cased, chatelaine, tortoise shell pique, by Cornelius Horbert, London, c. 1695, silver	1,500	2,000	2,500
41mm, multi-color gold case, verge, pierced cock, by Romilly, KW, KS	900	1,100	1,400
40mm, 3 colors gold, portrait of lady, diamonds, c. 1760	1,800	2,000	2,400
40mm, 3 colors gold & diamonds, ¼ repeater, by Mallet	2,500	2,800	3,500
40mm, pearls & enamel on gold, verge, pierced cock	2,800	3,000	3,200
39mm, pair cased, Freres Esquivillons, porcelain back	1,400	1,500	1,600
39mm, pair cased, adjustable hour dial, for Japanese market, silver	2,000	2,200	2,400

Marshall, 50mm, detached lever, compensating balance, diamond end stones, serial number 4068.

Chinese Duplex, 59mm, made for Chinese market with Chinese symbols, key wind & set.

NOVELTY WATCHES

Size and Description	Avg	Ex-Fn	Mint
67mm, barometer watch, silver case	$400	$500	$650
60mm, bar movement, day, date, month, moon phase, gun metal, pin set	75	95	125
59mm, Chinese duplex, for Chinese market, silver case	200	245	295
52mm, 8 day watch, balance seen from dial, GF OF	85	95	125
51mm, "Mysterieuse," mystery watch, min. repeater, crescent mvt., silver	900	1,100	1,450
50mm, digital jump hour & min., silver	150	225	350
49x34mm, sector watch, (fan shaped), fly back hour & min., by Record W. Co., GF	1,000	1,100	1,350
46mm, gambling devices (roulette, horse racing, & dice)	85	120	175
46mm, blinking eye, silver case	250	300	375
46mm, blinking eye, gun metal case	175	225	275
45mm, double time watch, single train, OF, silver	300	350	425
44mm, skeletonized, open numbers, open back plates, 18K	550	650	850

Mysterieuse on watch, 51mm, note hands are set with finger, silver case.

Digital, 40mm, jump hour & jump minute, silver color case.

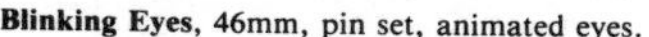

Blinking Eyes, 46mm, pin set, animated eyes.

Right: **Lock Form Watch**, cylinder escapement, 18k case.

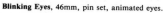

Size and Description	Avg	Ex-Fn	Mint
42mm, plates in form of bird, 22J, KW, KS	95	110	150
40mm, "Shell" watch, 7-17J, skeletonized, (Girard-Perregaux)	100	125	175
40mm, grasshopper alarm, (cricket sound), silver case	700	900	1,000
40mm, digital watch, engraved dial, silver, c. 1900	225	300	395
40mm, compass watch, KW, KS, silver case	125	175	225
30mm, ball form watch, silver & enamel, c. 1870	300	400	550
25mm, ball form watch, rim wind & set, small diamonds, 18K	700	800	1,000

Above: 8 Days, 52mm, balance seen from dial.

Right: Shell, 40mm, made for Shell Oil Co. as advertising premium.

Above: Ball Lapel Watch, rim wind & set, 18k with diamonds & sapphires.

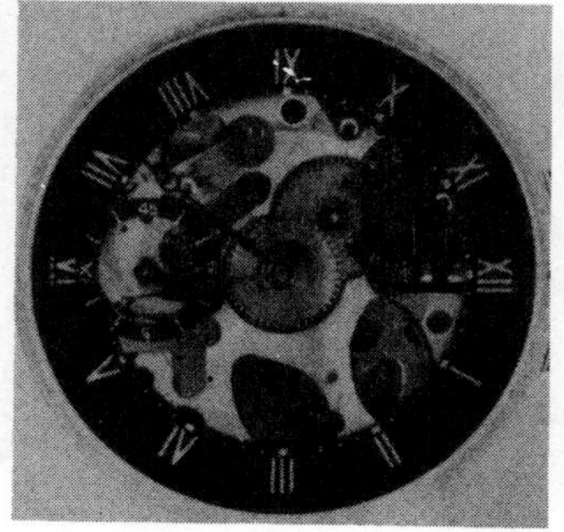

NOVELTY WATCHES (continued)

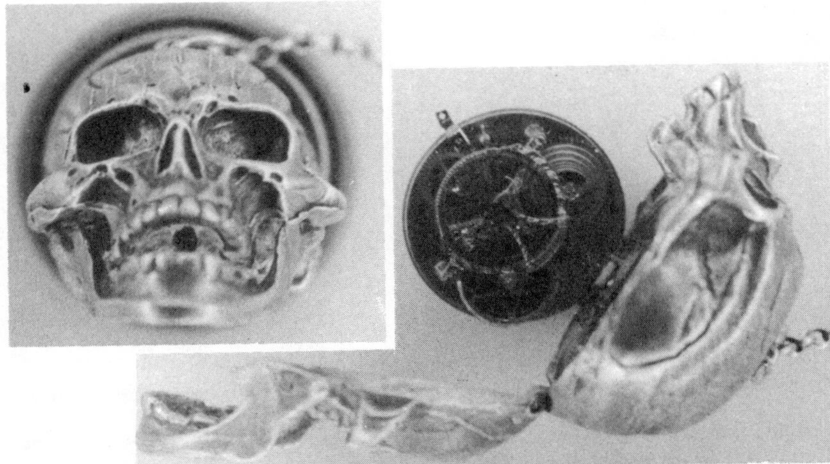

Miniature skull form watch, 30-32mm, cylinder escapement, chain driven fussee, skeletonized movement, silver skull case. Popular in the mid-nineteenth century.

Size and Description	Avg	Ex-Fn	Mint
25mm, skull form watch, miniature, cylinder escapement, silver	800	875	950
20mm, ball form watch, Juvenia W. Co., silver & enamel, c. 1900	175	195	275
Lock form watch, cylinder escapement, 18K & enamel	1,400	1,600	1,850

Novelty style watch, 40mm. Note hour and minute window. The hour jumps from hour to hour and the minute rotates.

POCKET WATCH TERMINOLOGY

ADJUSTED—Adjusted to compensate for temperature, positions, and isochronism.

ALARM WATCH—A watch that will give an audible sound at a pre-set time.

ANCHOR ESCAPEMENT—Also called the recoil escapement.

ANNEALING—Heating and cooling a metal slowly to relieve internal stress.

ANTI-MAGNETIC—Not affected by magnetic field.

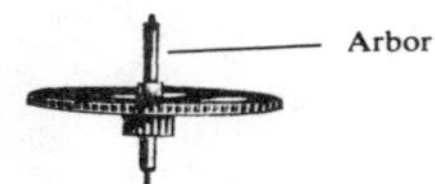

ARBOR—The mechanical axis of a moving part; on the balance it is called the "staff," on the lever it is called the arbor.

ASSAY—Analyzing a metal for its gold or silver content.

AUTOMATON—Animated mechanical objects and figures; actuated by the going, striking or repeating train.

AUXILIARY COMPENSATION—Additional temperature compensators found on marine chronometers.

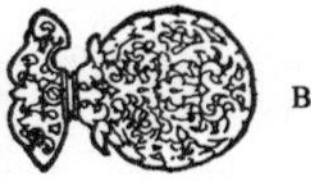

Balance Cock

BALANCE COCK—The bridge that holds the upper jewels and the balance.

Balance Spring

BALANCE SPRING—Also called the hairspring; the spring governing the balance.

Balance Staff

BALANCE STAFF—the shaft of the balance wheel.

Balance Wheel

BALANCE WHEEL—A device shaped like a wheel that does for a watch what a pendulum does for a clock.

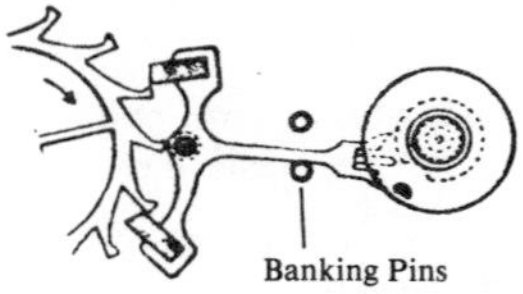

BANKING PINS—The two pins which limit the angular motion of the pallet.

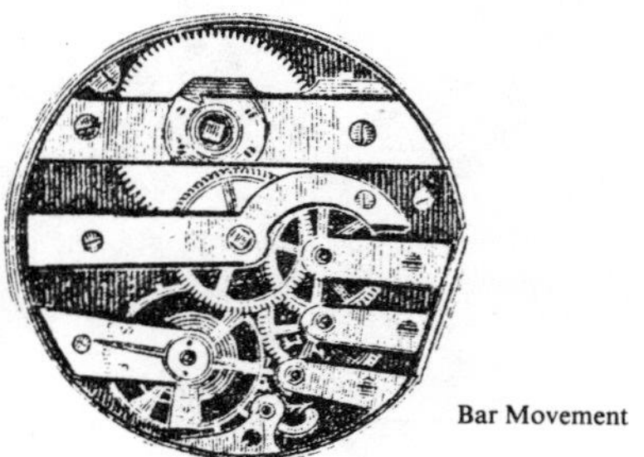

Bar Movement

BAR MOVEMENT—A type of movement employing about six bridges to hold the train.

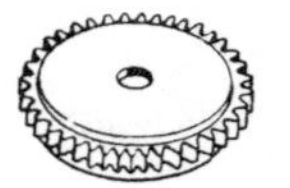

Barrel

BARREL—Drum-shaped container that houses the mainspring. A going barrel has teeth around the top or bottom and drives the gears.

BEAT—Refers to the tick or sound of a watch; about 1/5 of a second. The sound is produced by the escape wheel striking the pallets.

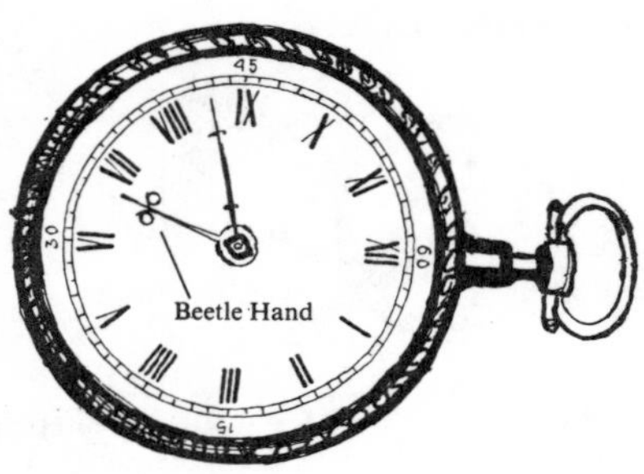

BEETLE HAND—Hour hand resembling a stag beetle; usually associated with the poker-type minute hand.

BELL METAL—Four parts copper and one part tin used for metal laps to get a high polish on steel.

BEZEL—The rim that covers the dial (face) and retains the crystal.

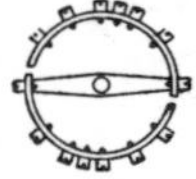

BI-METALLIC BALANCE—A balance designed to compensate for changes in temperature; made of a strip of brass and steel usually.

BISEAUTAGE—The grinding of a crystal to size it to fit a bezel.

BLIND MAN'S WATCH—A Braille watch; also known as a tact watch.

BLUING—By heating steel to about 540 degrees, the color will change to blue.

BOW—The ring that is looped at the pendant to which a chain or fob is attached.

BOX CHRONOMETER—A marine or other type chronometer in gimbals so the movement remains level.

BOX JOINTED CASE—A heavily hinged decorative case with a similated joint at the top under the pendant.

BREGUET KEY—A watch key permitting winding in one direction only.

BREGUET SPRING—A type of hairspring that improves timekeeping (see Overcoil).

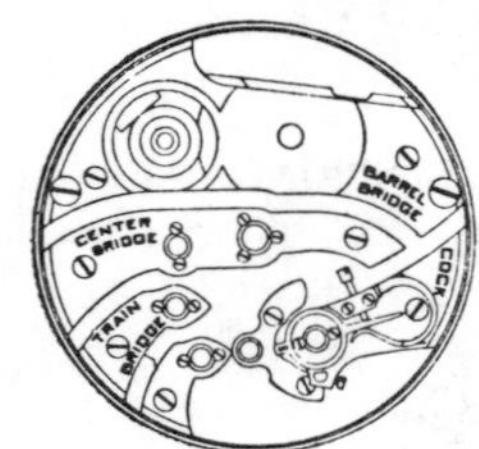

BRIDGE—A metal bar which carries the pivot for the balance or other pivot-bearing gears.

BULL'S EYE CRYSTAL—Used on old watches; the center of the crystal was polished which achieved a bull's eye effect.

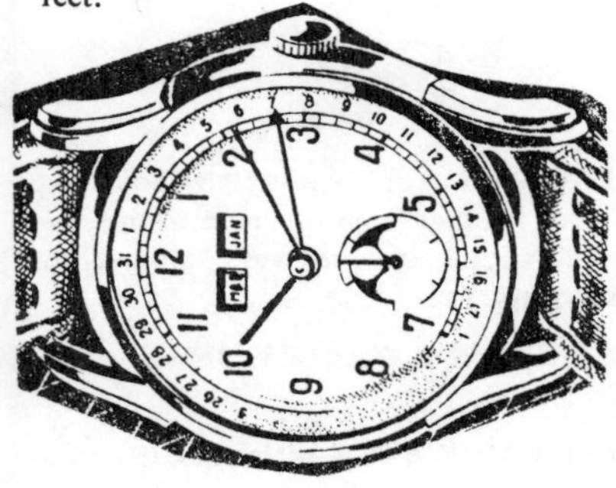

CALENDAR WATCH—A watch that shows the date, month and day.

CAP JEWEL—Also called the endstone, the flat jewel on which the staff rests.

CENTER WHEEL—The second wheel; the arbor for the minute hand; this wheel makes one revolution per hour.

CHAIN (Fusee)—Looks like a miniature bicycle chain connecting the barrel and fusee.

CHAMPLEVE—An area hollowed out and filled with enamel and then baked on.

CHRONOGRAPH—A movement that can be started and stopped to measure short time intervals and return to zero; also called a stop watch, but a stop watch does not keep the time of day.

CHRONOMETER ESCAPEMENT—A detent escapement used in marine chronometers.

CLICK—A name given to a part that permits the gear to move in one direction; a pawl and ratchet mechanism; a click can be heard as the watch is wound.

CLOCK WATCH—A watch that strikes the hour but not on demand.

CLOISONNE—Enamel set between strips of metal and baked onto the dial.

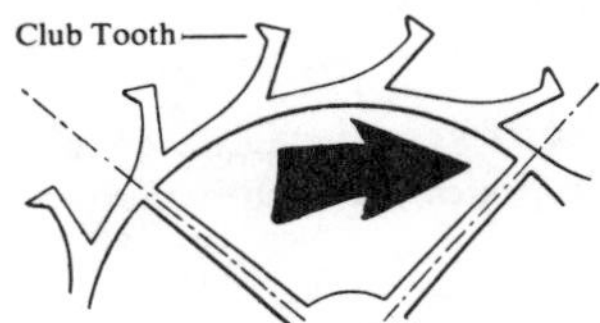

CLUB TOOTH—Some escape wheels have a special design which increases the impulse plane; located at the very tip of the tooth of the escape wheel.

COARSE TRAIN—16,000 beats per hour.

COCK—the metal bar that carries the balance wheel; a bridge.

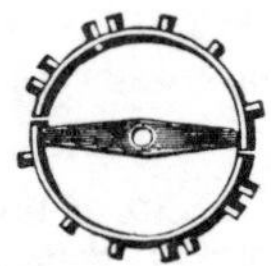

COMPENSATION BALANCE—A balance wheel designed to correct for temperature.

COMPLICATED WATCH—A watch with complicated works; other than just telling time, it may have a perpetual calendar, moon phases, equinoxes, up and down dial, repeater, musical chimes or alarms.

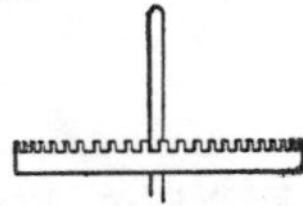

CONTRATE WHEEL—A wheel with its teeth at a right angle to plane of the wheel.

CONVERTIBLE—Made by Elgin; a means of converting from a hunting case to an open-face watch or vice-versa.

CRAZE (Crazing)—A minute crack in the glaze of enamel watch dials.

CROWN—A winding button.

CROWN WHEEL—The escape wheel of a verge escapement; looks like a crown.

CURB PINS—The two pins that change the rate of a watch; these two pins, in effect, change the length of the hairspring.

CYLINDER ESCAPEMENT—A type of escapement used on some watches.

DAMASKEENING—The art of producing a design, pattern, or wavy appearance on a metal.

DEMI-HUNTER—A hunting case with the center designed to allow the position of the hands to be seen without opening the case.

DETENT ESCAPEMENT—A detached escapement. The balance is impulsed in one direction; used on watches to provide great accuracy; found on marine chronometers.

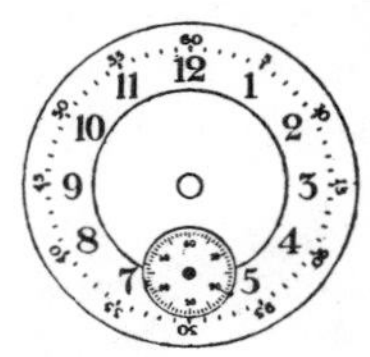

DIAL—the face of a watch. Some are enameled and hand-painted; some are made of gold or silver with diamonds for numbers, etc.

DISCHARGE PALLET JEWEL—The left jewel.

DOLLAR WATCH—Watches that sold for a dollar or close to a dollar ("the watch that made the dollar famous").

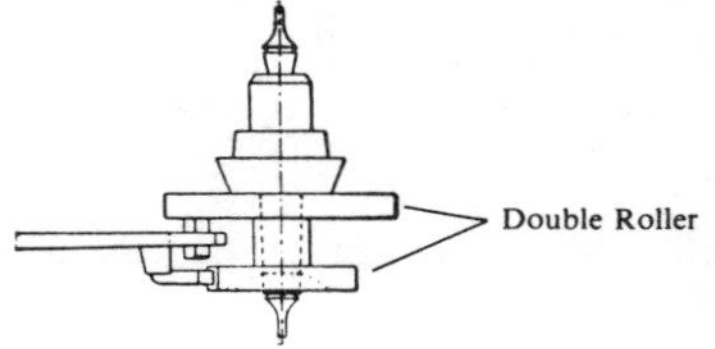

DOUBLE ROLLER—A watch with one impulse roller table and a safety roller, thus two rollers.

DRAW—The inclined position of the locking face of the pallet jewel; this causes the pallet to be drawn toward the escape wheel and the fork toward the banking pin where it is in position to receive the roller jewel.

DROP—The space between a tooth of the escape wheel and the pallet from which it has just escaped.

DUMB REPEATER—One that strikes the hour on the case or block rather than a bell or gong.

DUPLEX ESCAPEMENT—An escape wheel with two sets of teeth, one for locking and one for impulse.

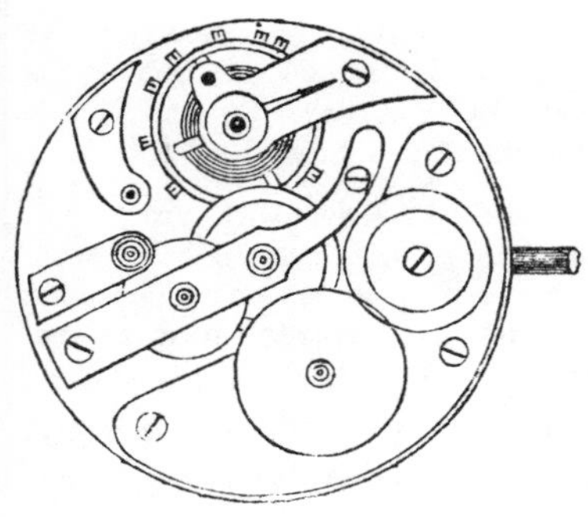

EBAUCHE (i-bo-she)—A movement not completely finished or "in the grey;" in the rough; not detailed; a movement made up of two plates or bars with pillars, barrel and train, and assembly screws. These parts were roughly filed and did not include a dial, case, or escapement.

ECCENTRIC—Non-concentric; usually a cam.

ELECTRONIC WATCH—Newer type watch using quartz and electronics to produce a high degree of accuracy; accurate within a few seconds a month and accurate to within a minute a year.

ELINVAR—A hairspring made of a special alloy that does not vary at different temperatures and is not affected by magnetism: nickel, steel, chromium, manganese and tungsten.

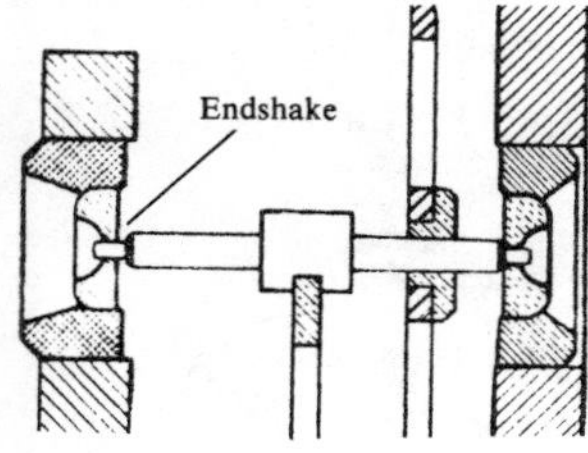

ENDSHAKE—The up and down play of an arbor between the plate and bridge or between the jewels.

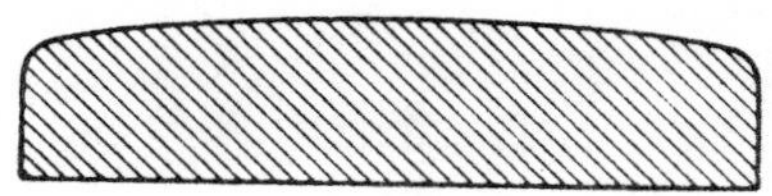

END STONE—The jewel or cap at the end of the staff.

ENGRAVING—Cutting away to form a pattern.

EPHEMERIS TIME—The time calculated for the Earth to orbit around the sun.

ESCAPE WHEEL—The last wheel in a going train; works with the fork or lever and escapes one pulse at a time.

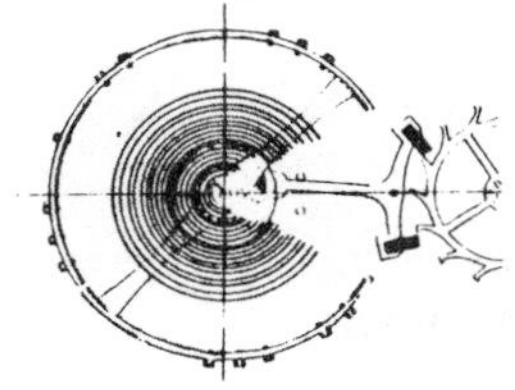

ESCAPEMENT—The device in a watch by which the motion of the train is checked and the energy of the mainspring communicated to the balance. The escapement includes the escape wheel, lever, and balance complete with hairspring.

FARMER'S WATCH—A large pocket watch with a verge escapement and a farm scene on the face or dial.

FIVE-MINUTE REPEATER—A watch that denotes the time every five minutes, and on the hour and half hour, by operating a slide.

FLINQUE—Enameling over hand engraving.

FLY BACK—The hand return back to zero on a timer.

FOB—A decorative short strap or chain.

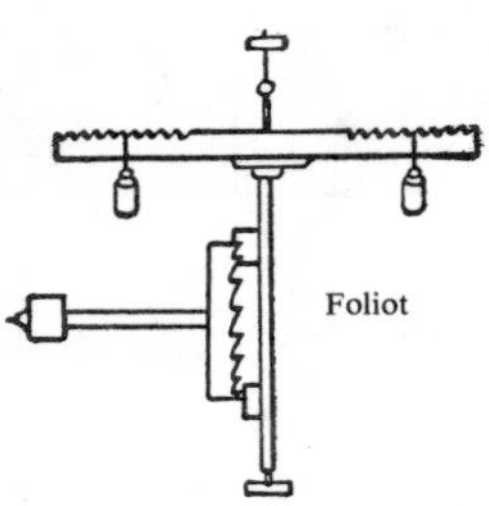

FOLIOT—A straight-armed balance with weights on each end used for regulation; found on the earliest clocks and watches.

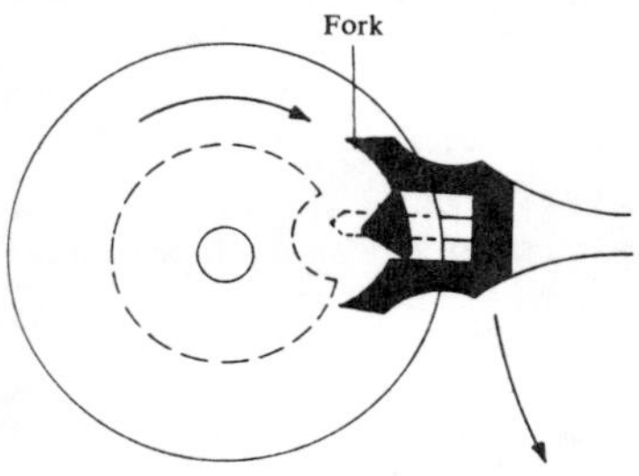

FORK—The part of the lever that engages with the roller jewel.

FREE SPRUNG—A balance spring free from the influence of curb pins. Curb pins tend to destroy isochronism.

FULL PLATE—A plate (or disc) that covers the works and supports the wheel pivots. There is a top plate, a bottom plate, half plate, and ¾ plate. The top plate has the balance resting on it.

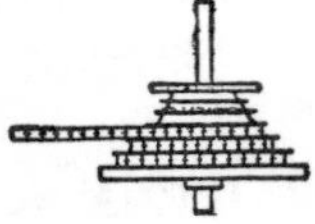

FUSEE—A spirally grooved, truncated cone used in some watches to equalize the power of the mainspring.

GENEVA STOP WORK—(See Maltese Cross)

GILT (or Gild)—To coat with gold leaf or a gold color.

GOING BARREL—The barrel houses the mainspring; as the spring uncoils, the barrel turns, and the teeth on the outside of the barrel turn the train of gears.

GOLD-FILLED—Sandwich-type metal: a layer of gold, a layer of base metal, another layer of gold—then the metals are soldered to each other to form a sandwich.

GOLD JEWEL SETTINGS—In high-grade watches the jewels were mounted in gold settings.

GREAT WHEEL—The main wheel of a fusee type watch.

HACK-WATCH—A watch with a balance that can be stopped to allow synchronization with another timepiece.

 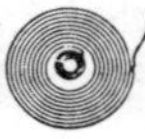 

HAIRSPRING—The spring which vibrates the balance.

HALLMARK—The British silver or gold assay marker stamp. It gave the place (town), quality marks, maker's mark, and year.

HEART-PIECE—A heart-shaped cam which causes the hand on a chronograph to fly back to zero.

HELICAL HAIRSPRING—A cylindrical spring used in marine chronometers.

HOROLOGY (pronounced Haw-RAHL-uh-jee)—The study of timekeeping or the science of time.

HUNTER CASE—A pocket watch case with a covered face that must be opened to see the watch dial.

IMPULSE—The force transmitted by the escape wheel to the pallet by gliding over the angular or impulse face of the pallet jewel.

IMPULSE PIN (Ruby pin)—A pin on the balance which keeps the balance going (roller pin).

INCABLOC—A shock absorbing device which permits the endstone of the balance to "give" when the watch is subjected to an impact or jolt.

INDEX—A regulator that can alter the length of the hairspring through means of a lever that moves two curb pins.

ISOCHRONISM—"Isos" means equal; "chronos" means time—occurring at equal intervals of time. The balance should not vary in its swing. The watch will not run any faster one hour after it is wound than it will 24 hours later.

JEWEL—A bearing made of a ruby or other type jewel; the four types of jewels include: cap jewel, hole jewel, roller jewel or ruby pin, pallet jewel or stone.

KARRUSEL (Kar-oo-zell)—A style or type similar to a tourbillion; the escapement rotates its position in an effort to solve the error of positions.

KEY SET—Older watches that had to be set with a key.

KEY WIND—A key used on earlier watches to wind the watch (crank).

LEAVES—The teeth of the pinion gears.

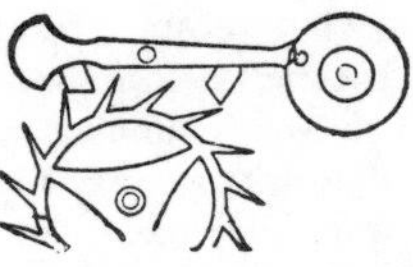

LEVER ESCAPEMENT—Invented by Thomas Mudge in 1760.

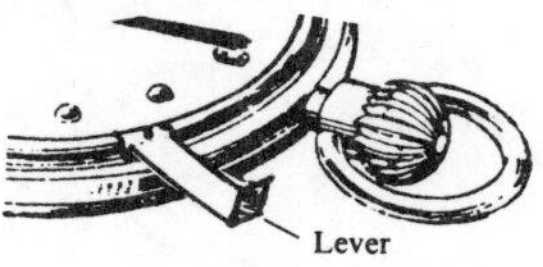

LEVER SETTING—The lever used to set some watches.

LOCKING—Holding the escape wheel (lock) while the balance swings around.

MAINSPRING—A flat spring coiled or wound to supply power to the watch. If it were not for the mainspring the watch would not be portable. The unbreakable main is made of iron, nickel, chromium, cobalt, molybdenum, manganese, and beryllium. The non-magnetic mainspring was introduced in 1947.

MAIN WHEEL—The first driving wheel, part of the barrel.

MALTESE CROSS—The part of the stop works preventing the barrel from being overwound.

MARINE CHRONOMETER—An accurate timepiece; has a dent escapement and sets in a box with gimbals which keep it in a right position; may have up and down dial.

MEAN TIME—Also equal hours; average mean solar time; the time shown by watches; hours shown by sundials vary in length. When time was averaged into equal hours, this was called mean time.

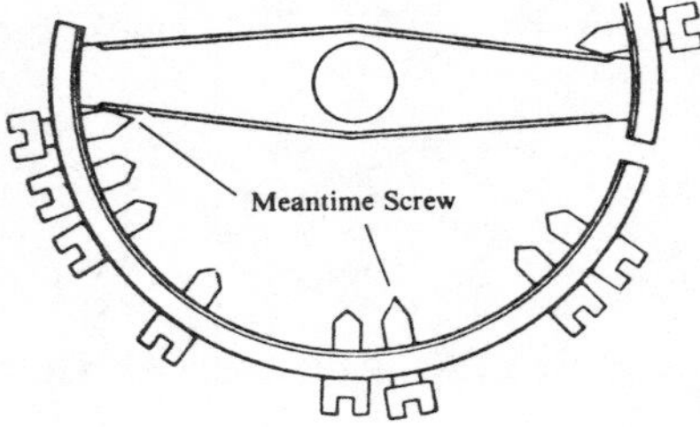

MEANTIME SCREWS—Balance screws used for timing, usually longer than other balance screws; when turned away from or toward the balance pin, they cause the balance vibrations to become faster or slower.

MICROMETRIC REGULATOR—A regulator used on railroad grade watches to adjust for gain or loss in a very precise way.

MICROSECOND—A millionth of a second.

MILLISECOND—A thousandth of a second.

MINUTE REPEATER—A watch that strikes or sounds the hours, quarter hours, and minutes on demand by moving a slide.

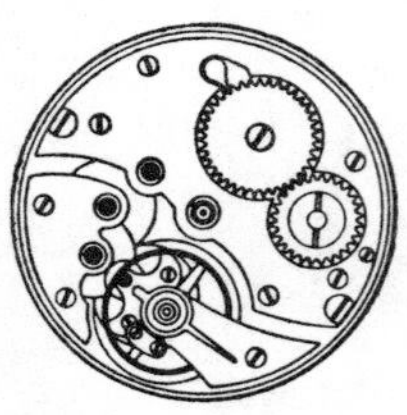

MOVEMENT—The works of a watch without the case or dial.

MUSICAL WATCH—A watch that plays a tune on demand or on the hour.

MULTI-GOLD—Different colors of gold—red, green, white, blue, pink, yellow, and purple.

NANOSECOND—One billionth of a second.

NATIONAL ASSOCIATION OF WATCH AND CLOCK COLLECTORS—Formed in 1943 to stimulate interest in the study and collecting of timepieces. Mailing address: N.A.W.C.C., P. O. Box 33, Columbia PA 17512.

NON-MAGNETIC—Resistant to magnetism; not affected by magnetic forces.

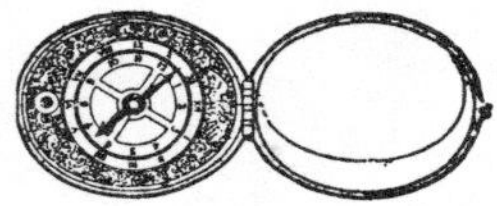

NUREMBERG EGG—Nickname for a German watch that was oval-shaped.

OIL SINK—A small well around a pivot which retains oil.

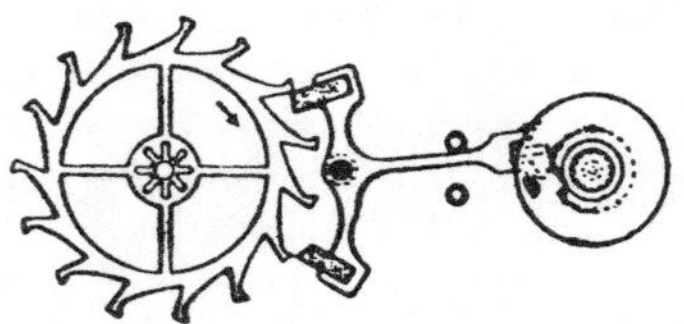

OVERBANKED—A lever escapement error; the roller jewel passes to the wrong side of the lever notch, thus causing one side of the pallet to rest against the banking pin and the roller jewel to rest against the other side, thus locking the escapement and stopping the motion of the balance.

PAIR-CASE WATCH—An extra case around a watch—two cases, thus a pair of cases. The outer case kept out the dust. The inner case could not be dustproof because it provided the access to winding the watch.

PALLET—The part of the lever that works with the escape wheel—jewelled pallet stones, entry pallet and exit pallet.

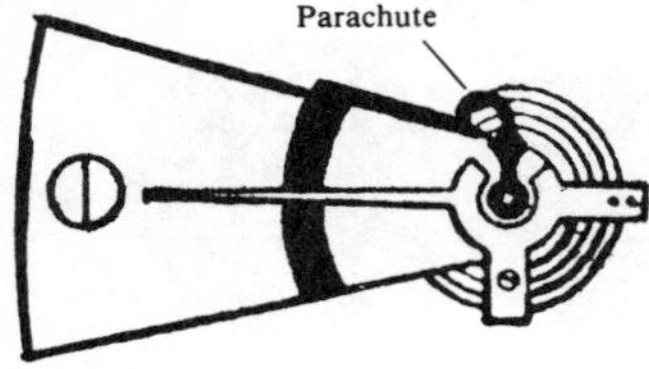

PARACHUTE—An early shockproofing system designed to fit as a spring on the endstone of balance.

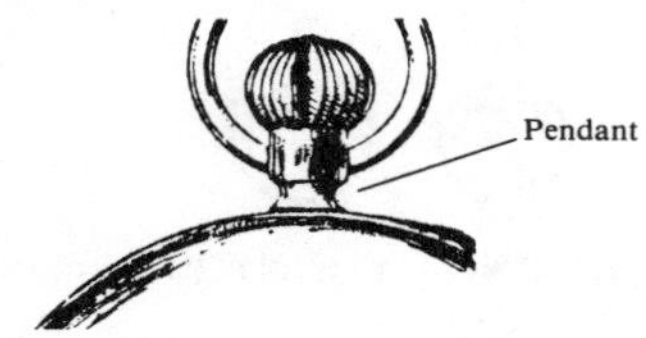

PENDANT—The neck of the watch; attached to it is the bow (swing ring) and the crown.

PILLARS—The rods that hold the plates apart. In old watches they were fancy.

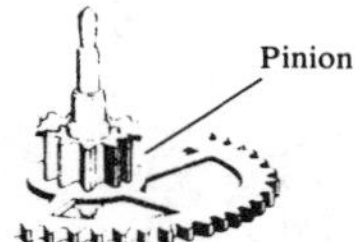

PINION—The large gear is called a wheel. The small solid gear is a pinion. The pinion is made of steel in some watches.

PLATE—A watch has a front and a back plate or top and bottom plate. The works are in between.

POISE—A term meaning "in balance;" to equalize the weight of the balance.

PONTILLAGE—The grinding of the center of a crystal to form a concave.

POSITION—As adjusted to five position; a watch may differ in its timekeeping accuracy as it lays in different positions. Due to the lack of isochronism, changes in the center of gravity, a watch can be adjusted to six positions: dial up, dial down, stem up, stem down, stem left, and stem right.

QUICK TRAIN—A watch with five beats per second or 18,000 per hour.

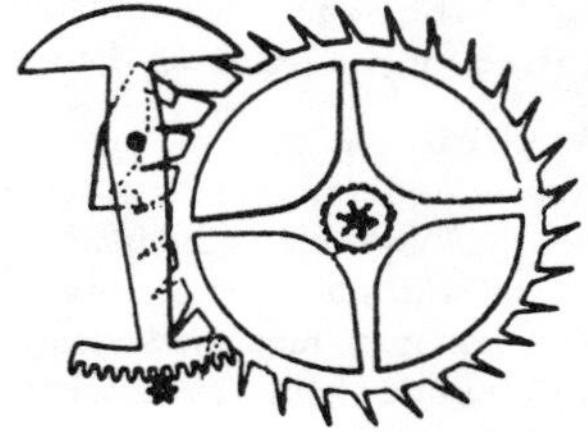

RACK LEVER ESCAPEMENT—Developed by Abbe de Hutefeuille in 1722 and by Petter Litherland in 1791; does not use a roller table, but a pinion.

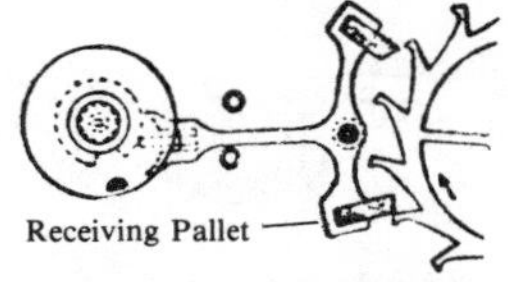

RECEIVING PALLET—Also called "R" stone; the first of two pallet jewels with which a tooth of the escape wheel comes into engagement.

REPEATER WATCH—A complicated pocket watch that repeats the time on demand with a sounding device.

REPOUSSE—A watch with a decorative design embossed on the case.

ROLLED GOLD—Thin layer of gold soldered to a base metal.

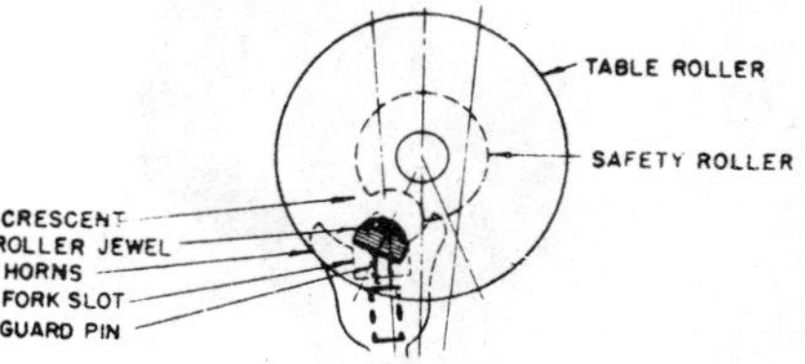

ROLLER JEWEL—The jewel seated in the roller table, which receives the impulse from the pallet fork.

ROLLER TABLE—The part of the balance in which the roller jewel is seated.

SAFETY PINION—A pinion in the center wheel designed to slip if the mainspring breaks; this protects the train from being stripped by the great force of the mainspring.

SAFETY ROLLER—The smaller of the two rollers in a double roller escapement.

SIDEREAL TIME—The time of rotation of the Earth as measured from the stars.

SIDE-WINDER—A mismatched case and movement; a term used for a hunting movement that has been placed in an open face case and winds at the 3 o'clock position. With an open face movement the pendant should be at the 12 o'clock position.

SILVEROID—A type of case composed of various metals.

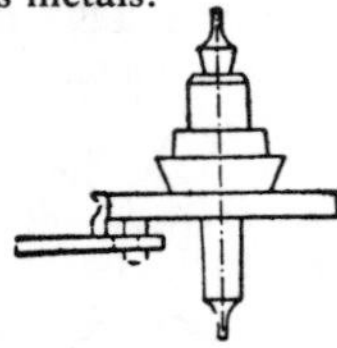

SINGLE ROLLER—The safety roller and the roller jewel are one single table or roller.

SIZE—Systems used to size the movement to the case.

SKELETON WATCH—A watch made so the viewer can see the works. Plates are pierced and very decorative.

SKULL WATCH—A pendant watch that is hinged at the jaw to reveal a watch.

SLOW TRAIN—A watch with four beats per second or 14,000 per hour.

SNAILING—Ornamentation of the surface of metals by means of a circle design; sometimes called damaskeening.

SOLAR YEAR—365 days, 5 hours, 48 minutes, 49.7 seconds.

SPOTTING—Decoration used on a watch movement and barrels of movements.

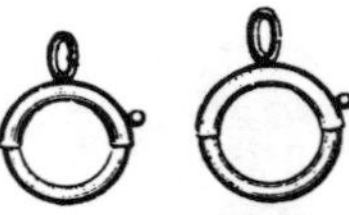

SPRING RING—A circular tube housing a coiled type spring.

STACKFREED—Curved spring and cam to equalize the uneven pull of the mainspring.

STAFF—Name for the axle of the balance.

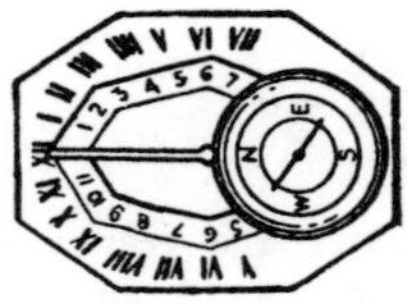

SUN DIAL—A device using a gnomon or style that casts a shadow over a graduated dial as the sun progresses, giving solar time.

SWIVEL—A hinged spring catch with a loop of metal that may be opened to insert a watch bow.

TOP PLATE—The metal plate in the back of a movement that houses the gears. This plate usually contains the name and serial number.

TORSION—A twisting force.

TOURBILLON—A watch with the escapement mounted on a platform which revolves once a minute. This is to compensate for various errors in positions. Also called a revolving carriage.

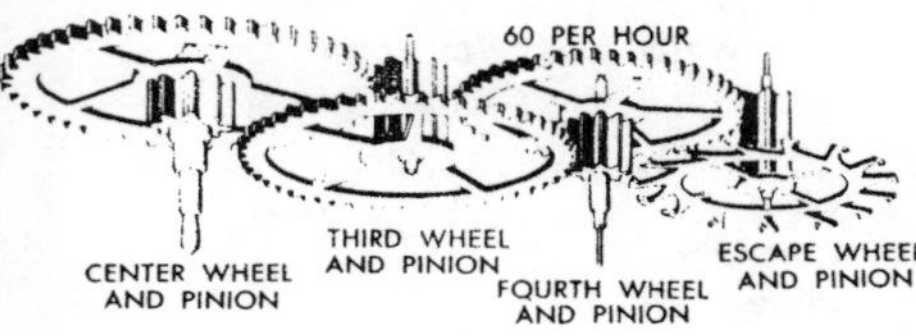

TRAIN—A series of gears that form the works of a watch. The train is used for other functions such as chiming. The time train carries the power to the escapement.

TRIPLE CASE WATCH—An early watch with three cases.

UP AND DOWN DIAL—A dial that shows how much of the mainspring is spent and how far up or down the mainspring is.

VERGE ESCAPEMENT—Early type of escapement with wheel that is shaped like a crown.

VIRGULE ESCAPEMENT—Early escapement introduced in the mid 1700s.

WATCH PAPER—A disc of paper with the name of the watchmaker or repairman printed on it; used as a form of advertising and found in pair-cased watches.

WIND INDICATOR—A dial that shows how much of the mainspring is spent.

WOLF TEETH—A winding wheel's teeth, so named because of their shape.

MOVEMENT NAME VS. TRUE MANUFACTURER

Many watch companies produced watches with names other than their own. The following list is a cross index matching these names with the true manufacturer. In most instances watches bearing these names will have to be priced in comparison to similar sizes, models and grades of the parent company.

Name on Movement	Manufacturer
Acme W. Co.	Trenton
Albany W. Co.	Trenton
Algier W. Co.	Trenton
American General	N. Y. Std.
Am. Waltham W. Co.	Am. Watch Co. (Waltham)
Appleton, Tracy & Co.	Am. Watch Co. (Waltham)
Athletic W. Co.	Trenton
Atlas Watch Co.	Elgin
Ariston Watch Co.	Illinois
Bannatyne	Ingram
Benjamin Franklin	Illinois
Burlington W. Co.	Illinois
Capitol Watch Co.	Illinois
Century USA	Seth Thomas
Club Watch Co.	South Bend
Colonial USA	Seth Thomas
Columbia USA	N. Y. Std.
Corona W. Co.	Seth Thomas
Cosmopolitan Watch Co.	Illinois
Crown W. Co.	N. Y. Std.
Des Moines W. Co.	Illinois
Delaware Watch Co.	Ingersoll
Dennison, Howard & Davis	Am. Watch Co.
Diamond Watch Co.	Illinois
Dueber-Hampden W. Co.	Hampden Watch Co.
Dundee W. Co.	Trenton
Eastern Watch Co.	Illinois
Edgemere W. Co.	Sears (several)
Elephant W. Co.	Trenton
Empire City W. Co.	U. S. W. Co. (Marion)
Empire State W. Co.	N. Y. Std.
Engle Nat. W. Co.	Illinois
Equity W. Co.	Am. W. Co. (Waltham)
Excelsior W. Co.	N. Y. Std.
Federal Watch Co.	Illinois
Frederick Atherton & Co.	U. S. W. Co. (Marion)
Garden City Watch Co.	Seth Thomas
Globe Watch Co.	Trenton
Granger W. Co.	Elgin
Grant USA	Illinois
Harvard W. Co.	N. Y. Std.
Hayward	N. Y. Std.
Hiegrade W. Co.	N. Y. Std.
Highland W. Co.	Trenton
Hollers W. Co.	Columbus & Seth Thomas

Name on Movement	Manufacturer
Home W. Co.	Waltham
Houston Watch Co.	Illinois
Imperial W. Co.	Trenton
Iowa W. Co.	Illinois
Inter Watch Co.	Seth Thomas
Keyless W. Co.	Unknown
Landis W. Co.	Illinois
LaSalle USA	N. Y. Std.
LeLand W. Co.	Rockford
Leonard W. Co.	New Haven
Liberty USA	Seth Thomas
Lincoln USA	Illinois
Marion W. Co.	U. S. Watch Co. (Marion)
Marvel W. Co.	Trenton
Massachusetts Watch Co.	Unknown
Monarch W. Co.	Illinois & Seth Thomas
National W. Co.	Elgin
New Era USA	N. Y. Std.
New York USA	Seth Thomas
Non-Magnetic W. Co.	Peoria
Paillard Non-Magnetic Watch Co.	Illinois
Pan American USA	N. Y. Std.
Peerless W. Co.	Seth Thomas
Perfection USA	N. Y. Std.
Plymouth W. Co.	Illinois, Rockford, & Seth Thomas
Railroad W. Co.	(Ball) by Hamilton
Reliance W. Co.	Trenton
Remington W. Co.	N. Y. Std.
Republic USA	Seth Thomas
Solar W. Co.	Elgin & N. Y. Std.
Springfield Ill. W. Co.	Illinois
Standard P. W. Co.	Trenton
Standard USA	N. Y. Std. & Seth Thomas
Standard Watch Co. Pa.	Illinois
J. P. Stevens	Aurora, Columbus, Hampden, Illinois & Waltham
Stewart W. Co.	Illinois
Studebaker W. Co.	South Bend
M. S. Smith	Freeport Watch Co.
Sun Dial	Elgin
Syndicate Watch Co.	Rockford
Tracy, Baker & Co.	Am. W. Co. (Waltham)
Union W. Co.	Trenton
Waltham W. Co.	Am. W. Co.
Warren Mfg. Co.	Am. W. Co. (Waltham)
Washington W. Co.	Illinois
Wyoming W. Co.	Seth Thomas & N. Y. Std.

RECOMMENDED READING

Abbott, Henry G. **Abbott's American Watchmaker and Jeweler**, 1910, Hazlitt & Wallace, publishers.

Abbott, Henry G. **The Watch Factories of America Past and Present**, 1981. Reprinted by Adams Brown Co.

Crossman, Charles S. **The Complete History of Watchmaking**. Reprinted from the "Jeweler's Circular and Horological Review" 1885-1887. Distributed by Adams, Brown Company, Exeter, New Hampshire.

Fried, Henry B. **The Watch Repairer's Manual**.

Saunier, Claudius. **Treatise on Modern Horology in Theory and Practice**. Translated by Julien Tripplin, Besancon Watch Manufacturer, and Edward Rigg, M. A., assayer in the Royal Mint. Distributed by Charles T. Branford Co., Newton Centre, Mass. 02159.

Townsend, George E. **American Railroad Watches**. 1977.

Townsend, George E. **Everything You Wanted to Know About American Watches and Didn't Know Who to Ask**. 1971.

Townsend, George E. **The Watch That Made the Dollar Famous**. 1974. Printed by Arva Printers, Inc., Arlington, Va.

"The National Association of Watch and Clock Collectors" bimonthly publication, Columbia, Pa. 17512.

Factory Catalogs by Waltham, Elgin, Hamilton, Rockford, Illinois, Howard, South Bend and others.

Advertising Sales Catalogs by several companies.

MUSEUMS WITH WATCH COLLECTIONS

National Association of Watch and Clock Collectors, 514 Poplar Street, Columbia, Pennsylvania 17512

American Clock and Watch Museum, 100 Maple Street, Bristol, Connecticut.

Time Museum, 7801 East State Street, Rockford, Illinois

Metropolitan Museum of Art, New York, New York

Smithsonian Institute, Washington, D. C.

NATIONAL TRADE ASSOCIATIONS

National Association of Watch and Clock Collectors, Box 33, Columbia Pennsylvania 17512

American Watch Association, 39 Broadway, New York, New York 10016

American Watchmaker's Institute, Box 11011, Cincinnati, Ohio 45211

CURRENT TRADE PERIODICALS PUBLISHED ON A NATIONAL SCALE

American Horologist and Jewelery, 2403 Champa Street, Denver, Colorado 80205

Bulletin, National Association of Watch and Clock Collectors, Box 33, Columbia, Pennsylvania 17512

WATCH DATA AND DESCRIPTION

DATE PURCHASED_______________ YOUR I.D. # _______________
MAKER, MFG._______________MFG. SERIAL #_______________
AGE_______ SIZE_____ # OF JEW._______ # OF ADJ. _______________
DESIGN_______________ PLATES MADE OF _______________
SETTING_______________ TYPE OF TRAIN _______________
TYPE OF ESCAPEMENT _______________
I.D. OF MOVEMENT _______________
CONDITION OF MOVEMENT _______________
____
REPAIRS TO BE MADE _______________
____
*PRICE OF REPAIRS_______________ *VALUE OF MOVEMENT _______________
CASE STYLE_______________ CASE MAKER _______________
METAL OF CASE_______________ WEIGHT OF CASE ONLY _______________
CASE CONDITION _______________
*PRICE OF REPAIRS_______________ VALUE OF METAL_______________
CASE ORIGINAL: YES, NO _______ *VALUE OF CASE _______________
NAME ON DIAL_______________ STYLE OF DIAL _______________
TYPE OF DIAL I.D. _______________
DIAL MADE OF_______________ HAND PAINTED: YES, NO _______
CONDITION _______________
*PRICE OF REPAIRS_______________ *VALUE OF DIAL _______________
PURCHASED WATCH FROM _______________
____
____

SPECIAL COMMENTS:
— _______________
— _______________
— _______________
— _______________

***COST:**
PRICE PAID_______________
REPAIRS _______________
MISC._______________

TOTAL COST _______________

***VALUE:**
VALUE OF MOVE._______________
VALUE OF CASE _______________
VALUE OF DIAL _______________

VALUE OF WATCH _______________

WATCH DATA AND DESCRIPTION

DATE PURCHASED_______________ YOUR I.D. # _______________
MAKER, MFG.___________________________MFG. SERIAL #_______________
AGE_______ SIZE_____ # OF JEW._______ # OF ADJ. _______________
DESIGN___________________________ PLATES MADE OF _______________
SETTING____________________ TYPE OF TRAIN _______________
TYPE OF ESCAPEMENT _______________________________
I.D. OF MOVEMENT _______________________________
CONDITION OF MOVEMENT _______________________________
____

REPAIRS TO BE MADE _______________________________
____

*PRICE OF REPAIRS______________ *VALUE OF MOVEMENT _______________
CASE STYLE____________________ CASE MAKER _______________
METAL OF CASE___________________ WEIGHT OF CASE ONLY _______________
CASE CONDITION _______________________________
*PRICE OF REPAIRS_________________ VALUE OF METAL_______________
CASE ORIGINAL: YES, NO ________ *VALUE OF CASE _______________
NAME ON DIAL____________________ STYLE OF DIAL _______________
TYPE OF DIAL I.D. _______________________________
DIAL MADE OF_____________________ HAND PAINTED: YES, NO _______________
CONDITION _______________________________
*PRICE OF REPAIRS_______________ *VALUE OF DIAL _______________
PURCHASED WATCH FROM _______________________________
____
____

SPECIAL COMMENTS:
__ ____
__ ____
__ ____
__ ____

***COST:**	***VALUE:**
PRICE PAID_______________	VALUE OF MOVE._______________
REPAIRS _______________	VALUE OF CASE _______________
MISC._______________	VALUE OF DIAL _______________
TOTAL COST _______________	VALUE OF WATCH _______________

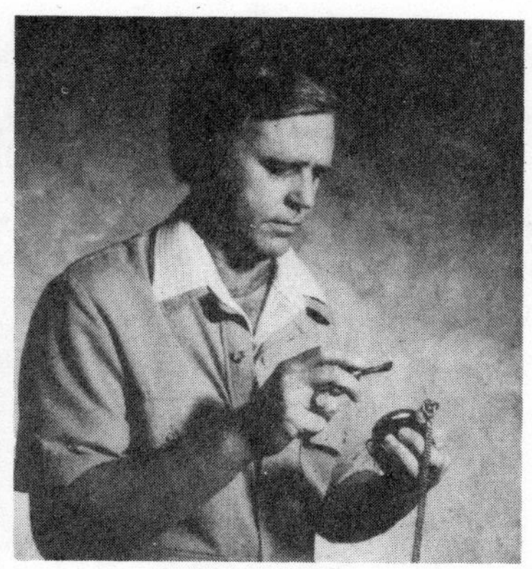
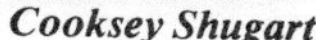
Cooksey Shugart

Tom Engle

ABOUT THE AUTHORS

Mr. Shugart, who compiled and published the highly successful first edition in 1980, has been joined with Mr. Engle, a widely known watch dealer and authority in the field. Each edition contains updated and revised information and prices, and has become the accepted standard reference work of the watch market. Both authors have been avid pocket watch collectors for the past two decades, and both have been vitally interested in seeing a reliable and accurate pocket watch guide produced. "We see this book as an extension of the information we have been gathering for years and take great pride in sharing it with other fans who have a deep and abiding interest in the American pocket watch," the authors stated.

The authors have been long-time members of the National Association of Watch and Clock Collectors and have been students of horology for many years. Both have specialized in early American and Railroad-type American pocket watches.

The co-authors travel extensively throughout the country to regional meets and shows and keep an up-to-date pulse of the pocket watch market.

Because of the unique knowledge of the market these two co-authors possess, this volume should be considered one of the most authoritative pocket watch references on the market today.

Mr. Shugart resides in Cleveland, Tennessee, and Mr. Engle lives in Louisville, Kentucky.

ADVERTISE IN THE GUIDE

ATTENTION DEALERS: This book will receive world-wide bookstore distribution, reaching thousands of people buying and selling pocket watches. It will also be sold directly to the collector's market as well. We will be offering limited advertising space in our next edition. Consider advertising with us. Since the Guide is an annual publication, your ad will pull all year long. Unlike monthly or quarterly publications, your ad will stay active for a much longer period of time at a cost savings to you.

PRINTED SIZES AND RATES

FULL PAGE—8'' long x 5'' wide.
HALF PAGE—4'' long x 5'' wide.
FOURTH PAGE—4'' long x 2½'' wide.
EIGHTH PAGE—2'' long x 2½'' wide.

Ad rates are set in the late summer prior to each edition's release. Write at that time for rates (between August and September).

NOTE: Submit your ad on white paper in a proportionate version of the actual printed size. All full—quarter page advertisers will receive a complimentary copy of the Guide. Each edition is professionally done throughout...so to reflect a consistently high quality from cover to cover, we must ask that all ads be neatly and professionally done. **Full payment must be sent with all ads**. All ads will be run as is.

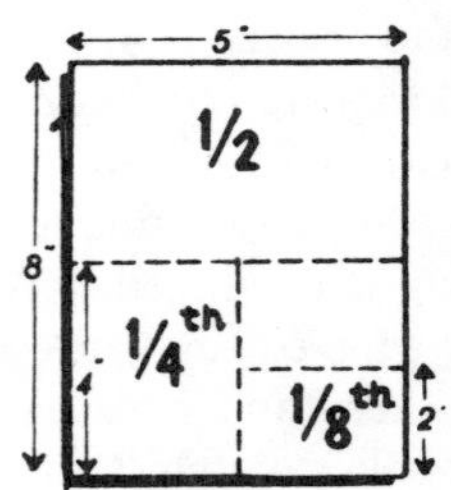

Ad deadline next edition — October 15

This comprehensive **GUIDE** is the **STANDARD REFERENCE WORK** in the field and is distributed to thousands of collectors thoughout the world. Don't miss this opportunity to advertise in the Guide.

NOTICE: All advertisements are accepted and placed in the Guide in good faith. However, we cannot be held responsible for any losses incurred in your dealings with the advertisers. If, after receiving legitimate complaints, and there is sufficient evidence to warrant such action, these advertisers will be dropped from future editions.

OVERSTREET PUBLICATIONS, INC.
780 Hunt Cliff Drive, N.W.
Cleveland, Tennessee 37311
(615) 472-4135

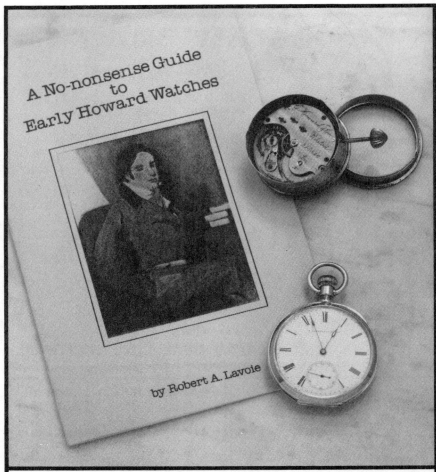